MARITIME OPERATIONS IN THE
RUSSO-JAPANESE WAR, 1904–1905

D1449426

MARITIME OPERATIONS IN THE RUSSO-JAPANESE WAR

1904 – 1905

JULIAN S. CORBETT

*With an Introduction by John B. Hattendorf
and Donald M. Schurman*

Volume II

Published jointly by
Naval Institute Press, Annapolis, Maryland
Naval War College Press, Newport, Rhode Island

This book has been brought to publication with the generous assistance of an anonymous donor through the Naval War College Foundation and Edward S. and Joyce I. Miller.

Naval Institute Press
291 Wood Road
Annapolis, MD 21402

The publisher regrets that it was impossible to reproduce the illustrations that accompanied the 1914/15 edition of this work owing to their size and condition. References to maps, charts, and plates have been left in the text in order to maintain the scholarly integrity of the work. The only known originals of these illustrations can be found in the Library of the Royal Naval College and at the Naval Historical Branch, Ministry of Defence, London.

First Naval Institute Press paperback edition published in 2015.
ISBN: 978-1-59114-198-3 (paperback)
ISBN: 978-1-61251-821-3 (eBook)

The Library of Congress has cataloged the hardcover edition as follows:
Corbett, Julian Stafford, Sir, 1854–1922.
    Maritime operations in the Russo-Japanese War, 1904–1905 / Julian S. Corbett : with an introduction by John B. Hattendorf and Donald M. Schurman.
        p. cm.
    Includes index.
    ISBN 1-55750-129-7 (set)
    1. Russo-Japanese War, 1904–1905—Naval operations, Japanese. 2. Russo-Japanese War, 1904–1905—Naval operations, Russian. I. Hattendorf, John B. II. Schurman, D. M. (Donald M.). III. Title.
    DS517.1.c67   1994
    952.03'1—dc20
                                                                94-34316
                                                                CIP

♾ Print editions meet the requirements of ANSI/NISO z39.48-1992 (Permanence of Paper).
Printed in the United States of America.

23 22 21 20 19 18 17 16 15   9 8 7 6 5 4 3 2 1
First printing

Maritime Operations in the Russo-Japanese War, 1904–1905

Confidential.

This book is the property of H.M. Government.

It is intended for the use of Officers generally, and may in certain cases be communicated to persons in H.M. Service below the rank of commissioned officer who may require to be acquainted with its contents in the course of their duties. The Officers exercising this power will be held responsible that such information is imparted with due caution and reserve.

The attention of Officers is called to the fact that much of the information on which this History is based has been obtained through the courtesy of the Japanese Government in giving facilities to our Attachés, and in placing at the disposal of the Admiralty their confidential History of the War. This was done on the understanding that the information should be kept strictly confidential, and it is therefore most desirable that the lessons to be learnt from this History should not be divulged to anyone not on the active list.

---

x (33)19215 Pk 526 750 1/16 E & S

RUSSO-JAPANESE WAR,
1904–5.

VOL II.

TABLE OF CONTENTS.

PAGE

CHAPTER XII.

CHAPTER XIII.

CHAPTER XIV.

CHAPTER XV.

CHAPTER XVI.

CHAPTER XVII.

CHAPTER XVIII.

CHAPTER XIX.

CHAPTER XX.

CHAPTER XXI.

CHAPTER XXII.

CHAPTER XXIII.

CHAPTER XXIV.

APPENDICES.

RUSSO-JAPANESE WAR.
VOL. II.

CHAPTER I.

GENESIS OF THE BALTIC FLEET.

By the middle of September 1904—at which period the previous volume concluded—the war had run half its course, and the situation to which the operations had led was one that both sides could only regard with grave disappointment and anxiety. It was one, moreover, which emphasised more strongly than ever the controlling force of the naval factor.

For the Japanese the initial stage of the war had been an entire success ; that is to say, they had obtained complete possession of Korea, the primary territorial object of the war, and had thereby secured an initiative to which Russia would be compelled to conform. The war plan of General Kuropatkin had assumed that this initiative must inevitably be secured by the Japanese, and had recognised the fact that the contest could only be brought to a successful conclusion by an unlimited counter-stroke in the form of an invasion of Japan. It was also recognised that, before adequate control of the local waters which such a counter-stroke demanded could be gained, a base must be secured in southern Korea, and till the Japanese were expelled this was impossible. The Japanese opening, then, had given them a double advantage— the positive advantage of being in possession of the object of the war, and the negative advantage of occupying a position which barred the overriding counter-stroke.

The second stage, therefore, demanded that the Japanese should perpetuate their initiative by confirming their hold upon Korea—that is, by setting up so strong a defensive situation as to convince their enemy that the cost of breaking it down was more than the effort was worth. But here the Japanese success had been far from complete. True, by the occupation of the Russian zone of concentration about Liau-yang, they had gained the necessary defensive position ; but before that position could be regarded as secure two things were needful : they must destroy the army that threatened it, .and they must render absolutely safe the oversea communications by which alone their own army occupying the position could be maintained and nourished.

There is little doubt that their original war plan contemplated doing both these things in the first six months of the war or even earlier. They believed that by a rapid concentric advance on Liau-yang they would be able to envelop and crush the main Russian army before its concentration was complete, and similarly they believed they would be able to carry Port Arthur without a siege ; then not only would the whole of their army be free for operations in Manchuria, but also by annihilating the main Russian fleet and breaking up the Russian naval position they would secure so complete a mastery of local waters that the vital sea communications would be absolutely secure to themselves and permanently denied to their enemy.

In both fields it appeared to them that they had failed. Owing mainly to the delays caused by their precarious hold on the sea communications, General Kuropatkin had been allowed time to ensure that his force could not be enveloped, and it had merely been pushed northwards a few miles with its offensive potentiality scarcely impaired. Similarly at sea, so far as they could judge the effects of the indecisive action of August 10, it had done little more than drive the Russian fleet into the arms of the Kwangtung garrison, and that garrison had exhibited its power of protecting it for a period that could not be measured. In fact, of course, as events were to prove, the enforced return of the squadron had done much more ; it had completed the demoralisation of the Russian naval spirit ; but this the Japanese could not know, and it was only what they knew that counted.

Still it was obvious they had gained much ; they had gained indeed, what is usually regarded as one of the highest strategical advantages. From their vigorous initiative they had reached a position from which they could force their enemy to take the offensive whether he liked it or not, while they themselves could remain on the defensive without suffering the moral drawbacks which usually accompany an expectant attitude. And this was true for both the land and the sea theatres. If the Japanese advantage was to be overcome not only must General Kuropatkin take the offensive and drive them from the Liau-yang zone, but their fleet that was dominating the Yellow Sea must also be attacked and destroyed. But on neither line were the Russians yet in sufficient force to assume an effective offensive, and the main problem that they had to solve was how to bring their force in both areas up to offensive strength at the end of long lines of communication which by land were inadequate and at sea insecure.

Such were the main features of the situation as it had developed ; but there was a complication that rendered the adjustment of means very difficult, and that was the situation in Kwangtung. For what has been said of the land and the sea theatres was not true of the combined theatre. There the conditions were reversed. At Port Arthur the Japanese found that they were not only forced to continue offensive operations, but also that the means they had provided were quite insufficient. Yet the task was imperative, cost what it might, and delay was inadmissible. Ever since the middle of May, when the news that a new fleet was assembling in the Baltic had brought to General Oku a sharp order to hasten his operations against the fortress, the menace of that fleet had been dominating the situation more and more strongly. The Russians were preparing for an offensive return at sea, and it was essential for the Japanese that before their enemy's reinforcements could reach the theatre of war and bring their strength up to the relative superiority which effective operations required, the Russian naval base and the fleet it contained must be destroyed. Their only chance was to prevent a concentration and beat each section of the enemy's fleet in detail. By no other means could they hope to keep control of the sea theatre, and without such control they could not maintain the position they had reached. The matter was urgent in the last degree, and naturally no one felt it so keenly as the naval commander-in-chief. Knowing how precarious was his hold on the situation, and at what cost to the fighting efficiency of his ships it was being maintained, Admiral Togo could not disguise his anxiety ; and it has been related how the moment he knew the first assault on Port Arthur had failed he had sent home a strong despatch to impress on the Imperial Staff the vital necessity of leaving no stone unturned to reduce the place without further delay

It was long before the Imperial Staff saw quite eye to eye with the Admiral, and certainly for the main army in Manchuria the urgency of the Port Arthur situation had some advantages. Probably the worst that could happen at this time for the Japanese would be that General Kuropatkin, as he had originally desired, should retire northward till he had gathered strength for an offensive return. But it was just the state of affairs at Port Arthur that made this impossible. Something must be attempted to prevent the Japanese getting possession of it before the Baltic Fleet arrived, and nothing could be done except by taking the offensive against the Japanese main army at the earliest practicable moment. For even if the Russians could not hope with the force as yet at their disposal to defeat that army decisively enough to open the way to relieving the fortress, active operations were still imperative in order to deter the Japanese from reinforcing their siege army. Thus, however correct it may have been from a purely military point of view for General Kuropatkin to delay his offensive return till he was in overwhelming force, the naval situation introduced a deflection which could not be ignored. Similarly for the Japanese in the Kwangtung area, the principle of economy of force would have dictated the masking and blockade of Port Arthur till it fell by exhaustion, but again the menace of the coming naval reinforcement forbade the correct military procedure and called for the most vigorous offensive that it was in the power of the Japanese to develop consistently with holding securely the Liau-yang position against the now inevitable Russian attack. Thus from this time onwards, till the command of the sea was definitely decided, the Baltic Fleet, for both belligerents, dominated the situation and determined absolutely the action of the respective armies.

The conception of that memorable fleet and of the operation imposed on it, which has no counterpart in the history of war, and the various developments the idea underwent, are still involved in some obscurity. One point, however, is clear, that, unlike the other naval war plans of the Russians, it originated at St. Petersburg. The organisation of the Russian Admiralty and its relations to the Far Eastern Staff were scarcely of such a character as made for the successful conduct of a war like the one in hand. When in 1898 Port Arthur was occupied the Minister of Marine, who was at the head of the Navy Department, was Admiral Tuirtov. Under him he had a " Chief of the Headquarter Staff "—the post being then held by Admiral Avelan—but this " Headquarter Staff " was hardly a staff in the sense we understand it to-day. And even before the constitution of the Far East as a separate province, it seems to have had little or no authority over the Pacific Squadron. For example, when in 1902, as a reply to the

Anglo-Japanese alliance, a diplomatic arrangement was come to with France for common action in the Far East, the Staff raised the question of a naval plan of operation in case of war with Japan. The only result was that Admiral Alexeiev, who was the local Commander in-Chief, informed the Head-quarter Staff that he had no plan, and there the matter seems to have dropped. Even when in the following year the Staff in the Far East did formulate a plan it was not communicated to the Headquarter Staff.[1]

Early in 1903 Admiral Tuirtov died and Admiral Avelan became Minister of Marine in his place, while Rear-Admiral Rozhestvenski was brought up as chief of the Headquarter Staff. His appointment was dated March 30, and he at once put his finger on the weak point of the situation. "Immediately on taking up my appointment," he has stated, "knowing the negative qualities of Port Arthur, I suggested to the Minister of Marine the selection of some other base, and pointed out the urgency of equipping it thoroughly, and of exercising the fleet in its new surroundings. The Minister of Marine at once got into communication with the Commander-in-Chief in the Far East (Admiral Alexeiev), who expressed no opinion on the essentials (that is, the question of a new base), but was only inclined to accept the proposal of sending him some ships of the Volunteer fleet to furnish supplies to the squadron and to carry out auxiliary operations. When these vessels were obtained the Commander-in-Chief refused to take up a strategically advantageous position or to carry out the necessary exercises lest he should incur the wrath of the Japanese. And he added that he had another plan, in accord-ance with which he was deploying the naval forces under his command."[2]

This was the plan indicated at a Staff conference held on April 23, 1903, when Admiral Shtakelberg reached Port Arthur with reinforcements. At this meeting Captain Ebergard, flag-captain to Admiral Stark, who then commanded the squadron, proposed basing the whole fleet at Sylvia Basin ; but the rest of the officers present rejected the idea, on the ground, apparently, that as the Japanese fleet was then held to be superior, and the proposed base was so near to the

---

[1] *Russian Naval History*, I., p. 100 *et seq.* ; for this plan *see ante*, Vol. I., pp. 42-8, and *post*, p. 399–403.

[2] *Russian Naval History*, p. 101.

enemy's headquarters and flotilla stations, the Russian squadron would run too great a risk of being blockaded.[1]

In face of this attitude on the part of the Far Eastern Staff, Admiral Rozhestvenski, like General Kuropatkin, soon came to the conclusion that in existing circumstances it was madness for Russia to go to war at all. This general view is clear from certain comments which he made upon an appreciation submitted to him by one of his Staff in October 1903. The conclusion of this officer was that only by a decisive victory over the Japanese, by which they could be deprived of the right to keep a navy, could the situation in the Far East be settled, and for this the Russians could not be ready for two years. This was also the view of General Kuropatkin, who was then Minister of War,[2] but Admiral Rozhestvenski's appreciation was not quite so pessimistic as the General's. In his opinion the Russian fleet was better prepared for war with Japan than it had ever been, and as it stood was capable of defensive action in the Far East, sufficiently strong to enable the army to settle the business. " Our object," he commented, "is not to wipe out the " Japanese, but only to annex Korea to our possessions. Until " that is done (meaning, of course, by the army) we require a fleet " equal to that of Japan in order to simplify the task of our army. " When the annexation is an accomplished fact we shall require " a fleet equal to that of the Japanese in order to live at peace " with them. . . . Victory over Japan can only be won in " Korea. . . . There is no need for us to have a crushing " preponderance at sea over the Japanese. It is sufficient to " be equal in strength and not to allow the Japanese to obtain " supremacy at sea, so that our army may be better able " to drive them out of Korea. . . . The great point is " never to have a weaker fleet than the Japanese." By this means he believed a rupture could be prevented. The preparations suggested in the Staff memorandum he approved, "but only," he added, "so that there shall be no war, for a " war with Japan can be of no possible advantage to us."[3]

A month later, on November 18, a general appreciation was drawn up by the Headquarter Staff. In summing up the situation, it laid down that the Japanese fleet was somewhat more

---

[1] See memo. by Admiral Vitgeft, second in command, May 3, 1903, post, Appendix, A. 1, p. 399.

[2] See ante, Vol. I., p. 49.

[3] Russian Naval History, Vol. I., pp. 104–6.

powerful than that of the Russian in the Pacific; that Japan from the disposition of her naval ports and the general geographical conditions had considerable advantage strategically in the theatre of the naval operations ; and that in all material resources she was overwhelmingly superior. This appreciation was followed by the despatch of a reinforcement which was calculated to go far to redress the balance. It consisted, it will be remembered, of two battleships, two armoured cruisers, one light cruiser and a flotilla, under the command of Rear-Admiral Virenius, vice-director of the Headquarter Staff. By the time, however, that the war broke out only one battleship and one armoured cruiser had reached Port Arthur, and the question had to be faced whether the rest should be allowed to go on or be recalled. In view of the recent increase of the Japanese Navy by the two Argentine cruisers and of the initial blow which the Russian squadron had suffered, the balance of the reinforcement was barely sufficient to set up the condition of equality which the Headquarter Staff's appreciation postulated. Still, though there were high authorities who were of opinion that it should proceed to its destination, the final decision of the Tsar was that it must come back, presumably with a view to increasing its strength from the reserves at Kronstadt.

Admiral Makarov was amongst those who strongly urged that Admiral Virenius should go on ; and Russian critics generally condemn the decision to recall him as one of the most fatal in the war. It was due, they say, to the influence of the maxim against dividing a fleet, to the fear of exposing the reinforcements to be beaten in detail. But it is argued that this risk must have been taken in any case. For if Port Arthur was to be saved by wresting from the Japanese the domination they had obtained in the Yellow Sea, time was the essential factor, and by no possibility could a squadron be formed in the Baltic, soon enough to acquire the necessary local superiority, which would have been capable of dealing single-handed with the Japanese fleet. At least it was a balance of risk—the risk of reinforcements getting in piece-meal by evasion, and the risk of an inferior squadron forcing its way through. Since the danger area off Shantung could be passed in the night, they considered the risk of attempt-ing the junction by evasion was certainly not serious enough to be prohibited, seeing how great was the object to be obtained. The argument in short comes to this—the whole Russian war plan hung on the ability to dispute the command

of the Yellow Sea ; without speedy reinforcements the damaged
Port Arthur squadron was unequal to the task ; therefore the
attempt to evade piecemeal was a fair risk of war which
ought to have been run.   The maxim which condemns
division of a fleet seems, however, to have shut the door to
clear thinking, and with no definite idea of what the concentrated reinforcement was to do, it was decided to adopt what
on superficial theorising seemed to be the safer course.[1]

At what time the resolution to send out a really formidable
squadron was taken is not on record, nor do we know with
any precision the steps by which its composition or its plan
of action was evolved. ˙ The first intimation we ourselves had
of the movement, was on March 17, 1904, when our Naval
Attaché at St. Petersburg announced that a Baltic squadron was
to be formed which would sail for the Far East in the summer,
and that Admiral Rozhestvenski, chief of the Headquarter
Staff, had been selected for the command.[2]   The idea, however,
had taken so little shape, that the ships that were to go were
not yet settled, and doubt was expressed not only as to
whether it could sail before the autumn, but even whether it
would sail at all.

Whatever may have been the precise intention of the
measure, we may take it that it was in substitution for that
which Admiral Makarov had proposed when he was appointed
to the Pacific command.   Not only had he been the foremost
in arguing that Admiral Virenius's detachment, whose advanced
ships had then reached Jibuti, should have orders to carry on,
but he had undertaken to solve the problem of its junction
with the Port Arthur squadron.   Admiral Rozhestvenski shared
his view, believing, as we have seen, that all that was required
to enable the army to bring the war to a successful issue
was naval equality in the theatre of operations—that is, an
equality which would enable the Russians to keep the command of the Yellow Sea in dispute—and, above all, being
convinced that on no consideration must the Russian Pacific
force be allowed to fall below that of the Japanese. So
strongly did he hold these opinions that he begged to be
allowed to take out the rest of the Virenius squadron
himself ; but this request was also refused, on the ground, it is
said that he had already been chosen to command and take

---

[1] Smirnov, *Morskoi Svornik*, April, 1913.

[2] Captain Klado says the idea was definitely formulated in the middle
of March

out the whole of the reinforcement that was available in the Baltic.[1]

The indications are, then, that higher authority at St. Petersburg did not accept the views of the Commander of the Pacific Squadron and the chief of the Headquarters Staff. Lacking their finer strategical insight, they were dominated by certain crude and elementary maxims which took no account of the possibilities of a naval situation in which no decision is immediately possible. In the most exalted quarters the prevailing view was that nothing would serve short of a decisive action against the Japanese at sea. This being so, there was reason enough for recalling the Virenius Squadron and incorporating it in a larger reinforcement. Quite apart from the probability of its being destroyed in detail if it attempted to reach Port Arthur, its force of one battleship, two cruisers and seven destroyers was not great enough to give the Pacific Squadron such a preponderance as would justify direct offensive operations to decide the command. Assuming, therefore, the correctness of the Government's view, a delay of six months was probably justified by the absolute confidence they then felt in the ability of their army, acting on the defensive, to prevent any substantial progress of the Japanese on land—provided such delay would secure such a preponderance as would place the result of a decision at sea beyond reasonable doubt.

Without attempting to pronounce which view was correct in all the circumstances, the important point to note, in considering the Baltic Fleet and its mission, is that there were two views, one based on preventive action with an equal fleet which was held by Admirals Makarov and Rozhestvenski, and the other based on obtaining a decision by offensive action, which was held by the Russian Government and War Office, and was forced on the man charged with its execution against his deliberate judgment as Chief of the Staff.

Whatever may have been the grounds of the Tsar's final decision—whether they were mainly strategical or dictated by considerations of prestige—it may safely be assumed that strong argument was found in the fact that four of the five battleships of the 1898 programme, which had been framed in view of a

[1] Beklemishev, *Lecture III.* These lectures were a series delivered on the war and its causes in 1906 by the President of the Russian Navy League. Internal evidence shows that he had a good deal of authoritative information.

war with Japan, were all but complete. The *Borodino* and *Alexandr III.* had been launched in 1901, and the *Knyaz Suvorov* and the *Orel* in 1902. They were powerful sister ships of 13,500 tons, with an armament of four 12-inch and twelve 6-inch, and a designed speed of 18 knots, and, besides, there was Admiral Virenius's flagship, the *Oslyabya*, of equal speed. Such a squadron in the Pacific would not only give the Russians a preponderance which would justify a frank offensive, but from its speed and homogeneity it would have every chance of effecting a junction with the ships already at the spot.

But, according to Captain Klado, the energies of the Admiralty were not at once concentrated on getting these ships ready for sea. They were preoccupied, he says, with other operations already in hand. This idea was to send out a squadron of six auxiliary cruisers,[1] which, from a base in the Sunda Islands, were to operate upon the Japanese lines of communication with America and Europe, and so, presumably, to loosen their hold on the main theatre by interrupting their supply of warlike stores, while Admiral Makarov was working up his shattered squadron to a state of efficiency. At any rate, the same authority asserts that it was the shock of the Admiral's death in the middle of April that awoke the Admiralty to the need of a more drastic effort, and it was not till then that the new battle squadron was taken seriously in hand.[2]

When, on April 14, after Admiral Makarov's death, Admiral Skruidlov was appointed to the command of the Pacific Squadron, the idea of aiming at a real command of the local waters became emphasised. So, at least, we gather from his first report on the situation, from which his chief of the Staff, Captain Klado, gives the following extracts[3] :—

"Our victory at sea depends mainly on the squadron which will come from the Baltic, and which consequently

---

[1] The *Smolensk* and *Peterburg*, of the Volunteer Fleet, and four ocean steamships of 10,000 tons purchased from German firms and renamed *Don*, *Terek*, *Ural*, and *Kuban*. The *Don* was the *Fürst Bismarck*; the *Terek*, the *Columbia*; and the *Kuban*, the *Augusta Victoria*, all of the Hamburg-Amerika Line; the *Ural* was the North-German Lloyd *Kaiser Wilhelm der Grosse*. All were about 15 years old. They were converted at Libau. The *Don* arrived there on March 3, the rest at various dates.

[2] *See also* Beklemishev, *Lecture III.*, and Smirnov, *Morskoi Svornik*, April 1913.

[3] "Extraits du rapport de l'Amiral Skrydlof," Klado, *La Marine Russe dans la Guerre russo-japonaise*, pp. 272 *et seq.*

ought to be *stronger* than the part of the Japanese Fleet which may be opposed to it.   What above all must be considered is not the composition of this squadron at its departure, but its condition when it reaches the theatre of war as well as the date of its arrival, which, according to whether that happens before or after the fall of Port Arthur, will have results altogether different."

" So soon as the principal engagement shall have given us the preponderance—that is to say, the command of the sea—for which we shall have made the whole of this naval campaign, we ought to devote our whole attention to reaping from it as much advantage as possible, and we shall reap the utmost advantage by assuring the army of our co-operation, which, seeing the bad state of the Manchurian roads, will afford it a priceless assistance, and will permit it to triumph over the enemy."

" The squadron which is sent from the Baltic will have for its task to assist the naval forces, which still remain to us in the Far East, to recover the command of the sea."

" In view of the divided state of our naval forces, which will find themselves separated into three groups— the squadrons of Port Arthur and Vladivostok, and that of the Baltic—the situation of the enemy, whose whole fleet is concentrated at one point, is indisputably more advantageous, since it permits him to attack our squadrons in detail before they can effect their junction.   The Port Arthur squadron and the Vladivostok division are much weaker than the Japanese Fleet ; thus they may not be able to proceed in chase of the Japanese who move out to meet the Baltic squadron.   It is for this reason that that squadron must be powerful enough to inflict *alone* a serious check upon the *kernel* of the Japanese Fleet."

" Accordingly, it must have all types of vessels necessary for a naval action, as well as fast ships capable of acting as scouts.   Its poverty in torpedo craft, for instance, may place it in a marked and dangerous inferiority, seeing how large a number of torpedo craft is at the disposal of the enemy, who, as there is reason to believe, wlll come to meet it."

He then dealt with the technical difficulties of the voyage out, recommending that, owing to the severity of neutral law, the squadron should rely on its own colliers and repair ships, and strongly urging that in case of accident, there should be several of the latter, besides those attending the flotilla, which might have to part company with the squadron. All fleet transports should proceed the whole way to Port Arthur, for they could be used as scouts and hospital ships, and, above all, as transports when the command was won "for landings in rear " of the Japanese, and perhaps even in Japan itself." "It is, he adds, "exactly to attain this result—that is to say, to invade " Japan—that we have decided to undertake upon the sea an " operation which presents difficulties without number, and " involves unheard-of cost." ˉ Here at least he is as far as possible from the idea of preventive operations with a nearly equal fleet.

He then proceeds to detail the force which he regarded as necessary and available for the execution of his scheme. The list shows six battleships, including the four *Suvorovs* of the 1898 programme, which were nearly ready for sea, and the older and slower *Sisoi Veliki* and *Navarin*. The cruisers numbered nine, of various types. Five were new ships— *Zhemchug, Izumrud, Almaz,* and *Oleg* (23 knots), and the *Svyetlana* (20 knots) ; two, the *Nakhimov* and *Vladimir Mono-makh,* were old armoured cruisers ; and the other two, the *Avrora,* a new first-class cruiser, and *Dmitri Donskoi,* another old armoured cruiser, were from the Virenius Squadron. Then follow 20 destroyers ; two repair ships ; coal, water, and provision transports ; hospital ships and parent ships for the flotilla.

This was to be the main squadron, but it was to be followed by a supporting division. For this he scheduled two battleships, the unfinished *Slava* of the 1898 programme and the *Nicolai I.,* launched in 1887, four old coast-defence ships, the old cruiser *Admiral Kornilov,* three torpedo-cruisers and the ice-breaker *Ermak.* It will thus be seen that the idea of a second division was no mere afterthought, but an essential part of Admiral Skruidlov's original scheme.

The general strategical idea as it existed at this time also comes out clearly. It was to send at once to the theatre of war a squadron powerful enough to force its way through to Port Arthur, and form a junction with the squadron already there, which it was then believed would be under the direct command of the new commander-in-chief. This being so, the strength of the squadron was also conditioned on the number of ships that could be brought forward in time to reach Port Arthur before it was too late. The junction once made it was hoped with confidence that the Russians would be able to assert a working command of the naval theatre, and that then they could at once proceed to operate in support of the army. For this stage provision was made by ships of small fighting value, and in this they were merely taking a leaf out of the Japanese book. Clearly in their original scheme this was the function and meaning of the use of those obsolescent ships, which have been the subject of so much adverse criticism. The idea, as Admiral Skruidlov conceived it, was perfectly sound, and affords testimony that he recognised clearly what his ultimate work in the war plan must be. It was to transfer to the Russian army that mobility which the Japanese army at present possessed through their fleet, and without which the tables could never be turned. To this end it was not only necessary to gain control by destroying the enemy's fleet ; he must also provide the means of effectively exercising that control when it was in his hands.

So far at least as the first division was concerned, Admiral Skruidlov's scheme seems to have been adopted in principle, and to carry it out a complete reorganisation of the commands was effected. The ships in the Far East with those destined to proceed there were formed into the " Pacific Fleet," and on May 4 were placed under Admiral Skruidlov's command with his headquarters at Port Arthur. This new fleet was to consist of two squadrons. The First Squadron included the ships already at the seat of war, and was to be commanded by Admiral Bezobrazov, who was also to hoist his flag at Port Arthur, the Vladivostok detachment being given to Admiral Iessen. The Second or Baltic Squadron was allotted to Rear-Admiral Rozhestvenski, who was appointed on May 2nd, but was still to retain his post as Chief of the Headquarter Staff, and under him as divisional commanders were Rear-Admirals Felkerzam and Enkvist, while his duties at the Admiralty were taken over by Rear-Admiral Virenius, the vice-director.

The new Commander-in-Chief had set out for the Far East immediately after his original appointment, and Admiral Bezobrazov had done the same. But since, as we have seen, before either of them could reach Port Arthur the Japanese had isolated it with their Second Army, both officers were compelled to establish themselves at Vladivostok, and the First

Squadron had to be left in the hands of the acting commander, Admiral Vitgeft, subject only to such precarious control as could be exercised in spite of the Japanese blockade.

To Admiral Rozhestvenski was left the entire charge of forming his squadron in the face of every difficulty which lack of officers, men, and material, and the apathy and disorganisation of the dockyards could present. On April 26 the reserves were called out, but the deficiency in the dockyards was less easily supplied, owing to the number of skilled hands that had been sent out to the Far East with Admiral Makarov.

In selecting ships for his squadron Admiral Rozhestvenski appears to have aimed at giving more precision to his chief's idea that the first division should be specialised for breaking through to Port Arthur, and recovering the command in concert with the First Squadron. As a battle division to deal with the kernel of the Japanese fleet, the four fast *Suvorovs* were alone commissioned from Admiral Skruidlov's list,[1] and to them was added the *Oslyabya*. From the cruiser list he only retained four of the new ships and the two that had returned with the Virenius Squadron, but he also insisted, so Captain Klado says, that the four auxiliary cruisers, which were under orders to operate on the Japanese communications from the Sunda Islands, should be added to his squadron and their proposed operations deferred till the command of the sea had been settled.

If a squadron so formidable and homogeneous could have sailed as was intended before the end of the summer, it would certainly have had a fair chance of effecting its purpose of breaking through to Port Arthur, and of inflicting "a serious check" upon the Japanese, with results that could not but have had a profound effect upon the war. The Japanese themselves were under no illusions as to the gravity of what was going on, and it was while the First Squadron was in this condition that General Oku received a peremptory order from Tokyo to drive the enemy from Nanshan and occupy Dalny without a moment's delay.[2]

But as the preparations proceeded at Kronstadt it soon became evident that in any case the squadron could not

---

[1] Captain Klado says he also selected the old and slow *Sisoi Veliki*, but according to the report of our Naval Attaché she was not commissioned till June 10.

[2] This was on May 18. *See ante*, Vol. I., p. 247.

be ready for sea till the autumn, and the clear and logical ideas which controlled its conception lost their precision. In spite of the pressure on the short-handed and ill-organised dockyards and the difficulty of finding officers, it was decided at the risk of still further delay to increase the squadron with some of the older and slower ships. Of the reason for this departure from the original idea we have no explanation, but it appears to have taken shape after the Japanese success at Nanshan, when both belligerents anticipated the early fall of Port Arthur. As Admiral Skruidlov had pointed out in his original memorandum, that event would entirely alter the results which could be expected from the Baltic Squadron, and it would have to be prepared to act single-handed without assurance of co-operation from the Far Eastern force. It is significant also that it was during June, when the extra ships were ordered to be brought forward for commission, that the strongest possible pressure was being brought to bear upon Admiral Vitgeft to induce him to take the Port Arthur squadron to sea. There is some doubt, it is true, whether the intention at that time was that he should endeavour to break through to Vladivostok. He himself did not intend to do so. We now know for certain that in the sortie of June 23 his object was to steam out to sea towards the Sir James Hall Group, pass the night in that neighbourhood, and next morning to make a raid on the Japanese base at the Elliot Islands. His general order distinctly stated the object of the movement was "to assist our land comrades to 'defend Port Arthur.'"[1] It was only the unexpected appearance of the concentrated Japanese squadron that compelled him to abandon the plan. Still it is certain that after this abortive attempt, if not before, the idea of maintaining Port Arthur as the main naval base was definitely abandoned by the Headquarter Staff at St. Petersburg and that the project of a concentration at Vladivostok held the field.

Assuming this idea could be carried out—and it was the best the Russians could hope—it was clear that the Japanese would have available at Sylvia Basin an interior position which would give them every chance of being able to deal with the Baltic Squadron in detail. For the Russians then it was no longer a question of having to meet a section of the Japanese fleet detached to intercept the coming squadron;

---

[1] *Russian Naval History*, II., 164, where the inference made in the first volume of the present work, (p. 299) is confirmed.

it would find at least the bulk of the enemy in its way, and it must consequently be given the utmost fighting strength attainable within reasonable time.   Fighting strength, in short, was now a higher consideration than manœuvring power.

Whether or not it was on these lines the Russians arrived at their decision it is certain that immediately after the battle of Nanshan there were added to the squadron the two old 16-knot battleships *Navarin* and *Sisoi Veliki* and the obsolescent armoured cruiser *Nakhimov*.[1]   Other units as good might have been brought forward, so Captain Klado says, and he expresses himself as ignorant of the reason it was not done. A possible explanation lies in the fact that about this time sanguine agents began to persuade the Russian Government that better ships might be purchased from Chili and the Argentine.   Both Powers however, when approached, were found unwilling to commit themselves openly to such un-neutral service, and consequently every artifice was exhausted to obtain the ships through some other Power that had little to fear from Japanese resentment.   Turkey, Persia, Marocco, Bolivia, Paraguay and Greece were all sounded in turn, but one and all refused to engage in the affair, and in the end not a single ship could be had.   The only result was that the expectation of securing this additional force proved a further cause of delay in getting the Second Squadron forward.

---

[1] The Nanshan position was captured on May 26. According to our Naval Attaché's Report, the *Navarin* was commissioned on May 29, the *Nakhimov* on May 30, and the *Sisoi Veliki* on June 10.   But as we do not know on what day the decision to commission these ships was taken the apparent connection with Nanshan may be only a coincidence.

CHAPTER II.

CRUISE OF THE "SMOLENSK" AND "PETERBURG."

[Chart I.]

WHILE interminable difficulties and shifting counsel prolonged month after month the preparation of the Baltic Fleet an episode developed which is of considerable interest, not only as exhibiting the friction of neutral rights and the possibilities of commerce destruction in modern naval warfare, but also as throwing a strong light in the weakness of the position of the Russian Headquarter Staff and the general confusion of the Russian organisation for war, to which the fatal delays were so largely due.

It will be remembered that when Admiral Rozhestvenski was appointed to the command he had insisted on the auxiliary cruisers of the Volunteer Fleet being attached to his flag and that their operations as commerce destroyers should be postponed till the command of the sea was won. They were, in fact, to act as transports for his squadron till after the decisive battle had been fought. Accordingly, early in May, two of them, the *Smolensk* and *Peterburg*, were brought forward for sea at Sevastopol. Both of them were loaded with coal and other contraband and both were armed, though until they cleared the Mediterranean no guns were mounted. Both also had a wireless installation, and in the first week in July both of them put to sea. From the Turkish authorities, to whom they were declared to be transports bound for Vladivostok with war material and men, they in due course received the usual firman for passing the Dardanelles, and thence they proceeded to Port Saïd.

So far there was nothing to show they were anything but what they pretended to be, nor was it till after they had left Sevastopol that their officers even were informed that their orders were not to join Admiral Rozhestvenski in the Mediterranean as they had supposed, but to pass into the Red Sea and cruise for vessels carrying contraband for Japanese ports.[1]

Whence came these orders ? They were certainly not in accordance with the Staff plan. By the naval authorities

---

[1] *New Material concerning the War*, by " B. Sc——t " ; that is, Sub-Lieut. Boris Karlovich Schubert, who served in the *Smolensk*.

the idea of operating on the Japanese lines of supply had been deliberately set aside. Our ambassador, after full inquiry, was assured and convinced that neither the Foreign Minister, the High Admiral (Grand Duke Alexis), nor the Minister of Marine knew anything about them, but that they proceeded from the Grand Duke Alexander, who, as Minister of the Commercial Marine, controlled the Volunteer Fleet and gave the orders on his own authority. That all was not regular is clear from the fact that appearances were kept up until the Canal was passed. Again the same declaration as to cargo and destination was made, but their warlike equipment, the excessive numbers of the crews, and the fact that the ships were evidently acting together, aroused suspicion, and the British consul at Port Saïd gave warning that they were probably commerce destroyers.

Once past Suez the cruisers mounted their guns, and then began overhauling all ships they met, that were on a list of those reported to be carrying contraband which had been furnished them by the Volunteer Fleet agent at Suez. The *Peterburg* was ahead, but the two ships met on July 14th at Jebel Teir, the *Peterburg* having with her a P. and O. cargo boat, the *Malacca*, with rails, armour plates, machinery and other contraband from Antwerp to Japan. So at least the Russian officers averred. This was the first actual capture, and it was especially unfortunate, for all the contraband she had was British Government stores for Hong Kong and Shanghai. Nevertheless she was sent away for Libau with a prize crew, and the two ships again parted, the *Peterburg* cruising where she was, and the *Smolensk* proceeding south for Mocha. Off Jebel Zukur, which she chose as her cruising centre, she stopped the North-German Lloyd mail steamer *Prinz Heinrich*, and took out all the mails for Japan. The mail-ship was then allowed to proceed, and the *Smolensk* went to Hodeida, where she expected to receive instructions. On her way the mail bags were broken open and the correspondence examined. "All " suspicious letters and despatches," we are told, "were set " aside and the rest sealed up again, to be forwarded by " the next mail steamer they met." For this purpose a day or two later the British ship *Persia* was stopped and the mails transferred to her.

At Hodeida no instructions were found, except something in unintelligible cypher. The *Smolensk* therefore returned to Jebel Zukur, where the *Peterburg* had already arrived with another

British ship, the *Dalmatia*, of Liverpool, which she was over-hauling. Nothing suspicious was found, and she was let go ; but during the afternoon, after a hard chase, another vessel was brought-to by the *Smolensk*. She proved to be the *Ardova*, of Glasgow, with dynamite for Japanese ports, and was consequently detained.

The difficulty of prize crews was now getting serious, and a question was raised whether she should not be sunk, but, as her cargo was very valuable, it was decided to rejoin the *Peterburg* and consult her. While she was proceeding to join her consort, she fell in with the Hamburg-Amerika liner *Scandia*, which she knew, from a bill of lading found amongst the *Prinz Heinrich's* mails, was full of contraband. No sooner was she seized than the *Peterburg* appeared. A conference was then held, and in spite of the fact that the continual draining of prize crews would soon cripple the Russian opera-tions, both of the captured ships were sent back under the Russian Naval flag for Libau.

With the limitations of commerce destroying under modern conditions thus brought home to them, the two captains decided to proceed northward to Jidda, where they had been ordered to call for instructions as to their further proceedings. Again none were found, and the officers began to feel there was something seriously wrong with the organisa-tion of their enterprise. This was probably true ; indeed, the absence of any proper arrangements for communication seems to give strong colour to our ambassador's information that up to this time neither the Russian Foreign Office nor the Admiralty knew that the two ships were in the Red Sea operating as men-of-war under the naval flag.

It was not long, however, before the two cruisers were enlightened. Proceeding south on the 24th they stopped the British steamer *City of Madras*. No contraband was found, but newspapers were obtained which forced them to reconsider their situation. The news was that the arrival of the *Malacca* at Suez as a prize had caused a violent outburst of feeling in England, and that the British Government had not only demanded her immediate release, but had protested against the whole proceedings of the cruisers as illegal. The actual words of the despatch sent on July 21st in which our ambas-sador was instructed to protest were as follows: " The " *Peterburg* left the Black Sea professing to be a vessel " engaged in peaceful avocations. In no other character

" could she leave it consistently with treaties . . . . As
" soon, however, as she got clear of Turkish waters she
" appears to have assumed the character of a vessel of war.
" She passed as a vessel of war through the Suez Canal, and
" in the Red Sea proceeded to break open mails, and to
" search and capture merchant vessels. It is evident that such
" a course of action could not be tolerated in the case of a
" cruiser which got through the Bosphorus by force, and it
" seems impossible to draw any distinction between two ships,
" both intended to carry on warlike operations, simply because
" one violates the law of Europe by force, and the other by
" something which is not force. We earnestly hope that the
" Russian Government . . . . will themselves at once give
" such orders as may prevent any further capture or search of
" British ships by vessels whose belligerent action should by
" European law be confined to the Black Sea . . . . If,
" however, the Russian Government do not see their way
" to taking this course, we have no alternative but to say that
" . . . . we shall be compelled to take whatever steps
" seem necessary." Orders were, in fact, sent for various ships
of the Mediterranean Fleet to proceed to the Canal and one
cruiser to the Dardanelles to prevent the *Malacca* being taken
to Sevastopol.

The seriousness of the situation which this despatch set up
was, of course, not actually known to the offending cruisers,
and the same evening (the 24th) they seized another P. and O.
steamship, the *Formosa*, which having some contraband on
board was made prize. While taking possession of her they
were joined by the Hamburg-Amerika ship *Holsatia*, which had
been chartered to bring them coal. Though she must have
left Suez after the situation had became acute,[1] she brought no
instructions except a telegram from St. Petersburg telling
them " to leave the Red Sea as soon as possible in order not
to fall in with a Japanese cruiser." So at least its effect was
given out to the officers, but who sent it is not stated.
Enough, however, was guessed of the actual state of affairs
for the officers to assume that the Japanese cruiser was a
myth and that it meant that British cruisers were on their
trail. A rapid decision was therefore taken to proceed
down the coast of Africa, and transfer their operations to
the Cape route to Japan. The *Formosa* was to be sent to

---

[1] Report of H.M.S. *Venus*, August 5th, *N.I.D. Diary*, p. 188.

Libau with a prize crew, and as they had still plenty of coal, the *Holsatia* was to return to Suez, and meet them in twenty days' time at Menai Bay in Zanzibar. Accordingly on the 25th and 26th they proceeded southward at normal speed, increasing to full speed, or as near it as their reduced engine-room complements allowed, on approaching Perim, where they might fall in with British cruisers. They passed it safely under French colours on the morning of the 27th, and on the 29th doubled Cape Guardafui, and were out of the danger zone.

Meanwhile with considerable tension and much misunder-standing, due to defective co-ordination between the Russian Foreign Office and Admiralty, the negotiations between London and St. Petersburg had been going on. Count Lamsdorf, the Foreign Minister, seems to have recognised from the first that the action of the two cruisers was indefensible, and that orders for them to desist and for their prizes to be released would be issued at once, as he had promised. But the Russian Admiralty was not so easy to convince, and refused to send the orders. To add to the confusion the controllers of the Volunteer Fleet were trying to get cypher instructions through by way of Suez, which were not communicated to the Russian diplomatic agent in Egypt, but this our own local agents prevented. It was not till Count Lamsdorf called to counsel Professor Martens, the great international lawyer, that he was able to make headway against the Grand Dukes and Minister of Marine. The Professor's opinion was clear and decided as to the illegality of the whole proceedings. Backed as this opinion was by the menacing despatch from the British Foreign Office, and by telegram after telegram announcing the arrival of detachments of our Mediterranean Fleet at Egyptian ports, it prevailed. Late on the 24th our ambassador received a formal assurance that the prizes would be released at once, and the cruisers ordered to make no further captures, and to withdraw. Still hitches occurred ; the *Malacca* was not stopped in the Canal, and it was not till the 28th that she was given up at Algiers. The rest were surrendered in the Canal as they arrived.

A more serious difficulty lay in the question of recalling the two cruisers. For the Russian Admiralty the release of the *Malacca* was comparatively easy to endure. She was set free officially upon the formal declaration of the British Government that all the war material she carried was their own property.

It was not on the ground that her capture was piratical. That was a view the Russian naval authorities were still unwilling to admit, and this attitude was encouraged by that of the German Government. It is true the Germans had protested against the detention of the *Prinz Heinrich*, but it was on the plea that she was an Imperial mail-ship, and not that the conversion of the Volunteer cruisers outside the Black Sea was illegal. Although, therefore, the Russian Admiralty had to submit ostensibly to the Tsar's decision, it soon appeared there was a difficulty about the conveyance of the prohibitive orders to the offending ships. On the British Foreign Office pressing in the matter our ambassador at St. Petersburg was assured on August 2nd that every precaution had been taken to deliver these instructions, but what was actually done is not clear. The earliest opportunity seems to have been the *Holsatia*, which left Suez for the Zanzibar rendezvous on August 1st, her declared destination being the German port of Dar-es-Salaam on the mainland to the south of it.

Beyond this fact and the report of coal stores at Jibuti and elsewhere all trace of the two ships was now lost. They were known by our intelligence reports to have passed Perim ; Jibuti and Mergabela in Asab Bay were searched but in vain, nor was anything more heard of them till on August 23rd Lloyd's agent at Durban reported that the British ship *Comedian* had been examined by the *Smolensk* 80 miles from East London, and that three other ships had been shadowed but not stopped.

After a barren cruise of a fortnight, she had, in fact, appeared on the Natal coast and had chased and overhauled this ship, which being found innocent had to be released. This, however, was the least disappointment, for from her captain they obtained newspapers of July 24th and 25th which announced that all their prizes were to be given up. They learnt, in fact, as one of the officers laments, that " at " the instigation of England, Europe regarded the operations " of our cruisers as acts of piracy, and to the menacing " demands of Great Britain our Government replied that they " did not know where we were, and, therefore, could not do " anything to compel us to return home. In other words, " our Government disowned us, but quietly left the omniscient " Mistress of the Seas to seek us out and bring us home."

This statement is scarcely correct. It was not till after the news of the searching of the *Comedian* came to hand—a month

after the Russian Government had promised to stop the operations—that renewed British protests led to an arrangement by
which a cyphered order was to be delivered by British cruisers
wherever the lost ships could be found. The proposal
originated with the British Admiralty the day after the news
from Durban arrived, and it was at once accepted by the
Russian Government. We had obtained intelligence that an
order actually reached the two cruisers, and that it had directed
them to continue their operations down the east coast of
Africa, and then return round the Cape. It was in that region,
therefore, they were most likely to be found, and accordingly
the South Atlantic and the Cape Squadrons were ordered to
conduct a search, but it was some days before it could begin.

The South Atlantic commodore was at the Cape Verde
Islands, and therefore in good position ; but no ship was available at the moment at Cape Town. The *Barrosa*, however, had
just left to relieve the *Partridge* at Walfisch Bay, and these two
ships were directed to search the coast north and south from
that point, and they began to do so on the 28th. The Cape
Commander-in-Chief was at the Seychelles with the *Crescent*,
Pearl and *Forte*, and about to proceed to Kilindini, where the
Odin from Zanzibar was to meet him. His orders were to
proceed south and search down the Mozambique Channel, and
he proceeded to carry them out on the 26th, sending the
Forte to Zanzibar. Of the Mediterranean Fleet the *Venus* was
at Suez, but she did not move. On the 30th, however, on a
further suggestion from the Admiralty, the Commander-in-Chief
was informed of what was going on, and directed to send two
cruisers to Gibraltar to await further instructions.[1] Consuls
throughout the whole area also received the cyphered orders,
and from Zanzibar and Tamatave they were to send agents
to Dar-es-Salaam and Diego Suarez.

In spite of all these arrangements it was nearly a fortnight
before the two cruisers were located. Since leaving the Red
Sea, so the officer of the *Smolensk* relates, the *Peterburg* had
been cruising in the neighbourhood of Zanzibar, but nothing
had been seen of her by the Cape cruisers. The *Smolensk*, in
spite of the information she had received from the *Comedian*,
continued her operations off Natal till it was time to return
to the coaling rendezvous, and on August 28th she turned

---

[1] This was done because the Cape cruisers had not range or speed
enough for the *Smolensk* and *Peterburg*.

northward.   Her farthest south had been lat. 34° 31' S.,
that is, below Algoa Bay, but although she had been cruising
for twelve days on the Cape line of communication to Japan, she
had only overhauled a single ship.   Many others were seen
and chased, but all the small ones got away inshore, and the
larger ones that were met with in the open could not be
touched.   Her engine-room staff was now too weak for high
speed, and on all but three days fog and an enormous swell
made effective operations impossible.

Proceeding up the Mozambique Channel she must have
passed the Cape cruisers while they were searching it, but
she was not seen, and on September 5th joined the *Peterburg*
at Menai Bay.   That vessel had already coaled on August 31st
and had sent the *Holsatia* to Dar-es-Salaam.   There it was
decided the *Smolensk* should proceed in hopes of being allowed
by the German authorities to coal.   As they were about to
weigh early next morning (September 6th) a white-hulled
steamship was seen to be bearing for them, which proved to
be H.M.S. *Forte*, making the signal for " Important despatches."
She had come from Zanzibar, where the previous day the
consul had heard a rumour that the missing ships were
at the south of the Island.   She had at once set off with the
cyphered orders to meet them.   The despatch was handed
to the Captain of the *Peterburg*, who appeared to have not
known of the recall, but he now informed the officer who
delivered it that he had orders to go home.   After having
delivered a protest against the use of Zanzibar waters for
taking in coal or supplies, the *Forte* then went back, leaving a
picket-boat to watch Menai Bay.[1]

On the departure of the *Forte* the Russian ships proceeded
to Dar-es-Salaam, where the order for their recall was confirmed.   Not caring to face the ignominy of re-passing the
Canal they decided to proceed to Libau round the Cape, but
a further order soon extinguished that hope, and they were
told to return the way they came.

---

[1] It is possible the *Peterburg* had already received the order.   The
decision to allow it to be delivered by a British cruiser appears to have
forced the hands of those who were obstructing the Russian Foreign
Office policy of concession.   On September 1st our ambassador heard
privately that the recall had gone to one of the cruisers' rendezvous,
and on the 31st he was officially informed from the Grand Duke
Alexander that the *Peterburg* had received the order by a boat chartered
in an East African Port (*N.I.D. Diary*, p. 192).

So under every circumstance of humiliation—derided by the natives in the Canal and kept under observation from point to point by British cruisers—their ill-advised cruise came to an end.[1] And the only purposes it had served was to give one more blow to the naval prestige of Russia and to furnish an example of what can be expected from such auxiliary commerce destroyers under modern conditions. The material points to note are that, unless such vessels are prepared to incur the moral responsibilities of sinking all their prizes, their steaming power will very quickly be reduced below operating efficiency by the drain of prize crews. In the next place it will be seen that they were powerless to act as a serious check on the flow of commerce except in narrow and fertile waters where weather conditions were exceptionally favourable. But the facility of the operations in that zone was the measure of their own danger, and at the first hint that they would not be left undisturbed they were forced to move away to more open and remoter waters. Here as their security rose their power and chances of commerce destroying diminished. This is precisely what was always found to happen in the old wars. It was in fact being demonstrated that the changed conditions of naval warfare had not affected the fundamental principle on which our traditional system of commerce defence was based.

So far, then, as any generalisation is permissible from the case in hand as to what merchant vessels equipped for this purpose can accomplish, the answer is that if fertile areas are watched by regular cruisers they are likely to make no material impression. They will be compelled to act sporadically in areas where trade is thin and widely dispersed and where the physical difficulties of overhauling passing ships are so great as to make their operations almost negligible —at least against an enemy the whole volume of whose trade is very large. In this case, of course, the ships were not true commerce destroyers—they were merely acting against the enemy's line of communication. Had they been bent on commerce destroying and not merely on the stoppage of

---

[1] The Admiralty orders were that the two cruisers were to be "observed unostentatiously," but not to be "shadowed" unless they continued to exert belligerent rights. In that case measures might be taken to release their prizes. Orders accordingly went to the Mediterranean and East Indies. The *Venus* from Suez picked the two cruisers up a little north of Suakim, but lost them very quickly for lack of speed.

contraband they might undoubtedly have done more in the Red Sea, but on the Natal coast the result would have been the same.   Moreover, even as regards the Red Sea area it is to be observed that had they been acting against the commerce of first-class naval Power they would certainly have been disturbed more quickly.   It must be remembered that even such small success as they had was due to the fact that they were operating against neutrals who had had no warning and were taking no precautions.   With all these conditions in favour of the enterprise the only effect it produced upon the war was to annoy a powerful neutral and force her to interfere in a manner that brought untimely humiliation upon the offending belligerent.   It only ended, so an officer of the *Smolensk* wrote, in "an unworthy comedy which detracted from the dignity of Russia in the eyes of the whole world." [1]

---

[1] Schubert, *New Material.*

CHAPTER III.

The Dogger Bank Incident.

[Chart II.]

During the operations of the volunteer cruisers the preparation of the Baltic Fleet had been proceeding at Kronstadt, but still under every difficulty which divided authority and ill-organised dockyards could create. It was not indeed till the middle of August that ships were sufficiently advanced for Admiral Rozhestvenski to hoist his flag. The ceremony took place on the 14th, the day of the battle of Ulsan ; but even then the force was far from complete. Two of the best battleships and two of the new cruisers were still unready for sea, besides other units ; but, on the other hand, the cruiser strength had been increased by the four ocean steamers, which had been purchased in Germany ostensibly as merchant ships and subsequently converted and armed for the purpose at Libau.[1] Of the twenty destroyers only seven were available.

Still it was not intended that the squadron should sail for another month. The interval was to be employed in exercises in the Gulf of Finland, and accordingly, on the 25th, the Admiral put to sea for a five days' cruise. On his return he filled up with four months' provisions and stores, and on September 8th the squadron was inspected by the Tsar. Three days later it sailed for Reval and everything looked as though the ships that were ready would proceed at the date appointed.

In the meantime, however, the news of the two naval defeats in the Far East had profoundly changed the situation. The attempt of Admiral Vitgeft to break through into the Sea of Japan had ended in such disaster that the prospect of his ever being able to reach Vladivostok was abandoned. The basis of the plan on which the Baltic Squadron was to operate was practically beyond recovery, and, indeed, it was soon known that at Port Arthur a resolution had been taken to devote the crews and armament of the shattered ships to the defence of the fortress. By the end of the first week in September the picture was further blackened by news of the battle of Liau-yang, which put an end to all hope of relieving the beleaguered base for an indefinite period. The position, therefore, had to

---

[1] *Don, Terek, Ural* and *Kuban. See* note, p. 10, *ante.*

be faced, not only that the Port Arthur Squadron could no longer be relied on for effective co-operation with the Baltic Fleet, but that the fortress itself would probably be in Japanese hands before Admiral Rozhestvenski could arrive upon the scene.

In these circumstances it became doubtful whether any good end could be served by despatching a relief squadron at all, and on September 15th a conference was called to reconsider the whole question. It was pointed out that the force could no longer be regarded as a relief squadron. It had an independent function which it must carry out with its own resources except for such assistance as the remaining Vladivostok cruisers could afford. If success were to be hoped for, it must go out in strength superior to the Japanese fleet. Not only was it no longer a question of dealing with the part of the enemy's navy that would be advanced to meet it; it would have to deal with the whole of it in one of the straits of Tsushima, where the enemy would have all the advantage of a full use of his flotilla.

At the conference, we are told, three postulates were accepted : (1) the improbability of keeping alive Port Arthur or the First Squadron ; (2) that the Second Squadron was inferior to the Japanese fleet; (3) that it was impossible to establish a base in Chinese territory, and that the seizure of a Japanese Island for that purpose presented difficulties that were practically insuperable.[1]

The question of cancelling the despatch of the squadron was then raised. There was no lack of opinion, we are told, against allowing it to proceed, but Admiral Rozhestvenski, according to the same authority, would listen to no such faint-hearted counsel. Insisting that the power of the Japanese was overrated, he demanded to be allowed to sail at once with the ships that were ready, and it would seem that for a time his opinion prevailed.[2] Further reflection, however, induced the Government to modify the decision of the conference. Information came to hand that the Japanese had suffered so little

---

[1] Smirnov.

[2] The authority is Captain Klado, who at this time probably had joined Admiral Rozhestvenski's Staff, a Second Flag-Captain. The Admiral had asked Admiral Skruidlov to send him a man in his confidence who could explain his views to him, and Captain Klado was sent back from Vladivostok. He joined the flagship, he says, on September 15, just after the conference was held (*La Marine Russe*, page 271).

in the two actions that there would be plenty of time for them to repair their ships before the squadron could arrive, and it would consequently find itself in decided inferiority. Admiral Rozhestvenski's idea, then, of preventive action with an equal fleet was impracticable. Accordingly it was finally resolved that the departure should be postponed for another month, not only to allow time for the backward ships to complete, but also, it is said, because at this time the hope of securing the South American cruisers had increased.[1] No definite object or plan of operations, however, was laid down, and consequently its original function remained—that is, to effect a junction with the First Squadron and take the offensive with a view to a decisive action.

Illusory as this appears in the light of later knowledge, it would seem that Admiral Rozhestvenski, at least up to the time of the postponement, had not given up all hope of Port Arthur. It is even said that in order to operate his junction with the First Squadron he intended to use Chifu as a base on the ground that its neutrality had already been violated when after the battle of the Yellow Sea the Japanese had captured the *Ryeshitelni* within the port.[2] Various other places in neutral or Japanese territory were suggested as advanced bases for effecting the junction, but all were given up before the squadron sailed.[3]

During the long delay at Reval even the Admiral had begun to take a gloomier view. "We shall complete our " voyage," he said, "and find Port Arthur fallen and the Pacific " Squadron perished."[3] Everyone, in fact, had finally turned his eyes away from the doomed fortress and was looking to Vladivostok as the centre of hope. As soon as the decision to postpone the departure of the squadron was taken, 350 more dockyard artificers were sent out to Admiral Skruidlov, and they were followed by 1,200 naval ratings from the Baltic and Black

---

[1] Captain Klado asserts that the crews for these cruisers had actually been selected and Admiral Nebogatov appointed to command them. But no confirmation of this has come to hand. It is possible that news of the failure of the assault on Port Arthur had something to do with the decision to wait another month. According to Beklemishev it was the express command of the Tsar after his inspection, that the squadron should wait for the *Orel* and *Oleg* (*Lecture III.*).

[2] The only authority for this is Semenov, *Rasplata*, p. 452 ; but it is confirmed by Smirnov's third postulate.

[3] Beklemishev, *Lecture III.*

Sea depôts.[1]   It was pointed out that the northern port, apart
from its roominess and its double entrance, was the centre of
an arc, which on a radius of less than 500 miles passed through
the whole length of the Japanese islands from Fusan to La
Pérouse Strait, and was thus excellently situated as a base for
offensive operations against the enemy's territory, by which
alone the war could be brought to a successful conclusion.[2]

These were the views both of the Viceroy and Admiral
Skruidlov, the men on the spot, and Captain Klado tells us
that when he was ordered home he was specially charged to
press them upon the Government.[3]   On this plan of prosecut-
ing the war they also urged that it would be necessary to
reinforce the Baltic Squadron as quickly as possible, and that
every torpedo craft in the Baltic or Black Sea that was fit for
service should be sent to the new base. Both the latter
recommendations, however, were ignored.

October 14 was now the date definitely fixed for Admiral
Rozhestvenski's departure, but there was still doubt in the
service as to whether he would ever sail. Endless mishaps
to the ships and the indifferent quality of the crews were daily
sapping the spirit of the force. The danger which lay in the
narrow seas through which they must pass at the outset of
the voyage became the main topic of conversation, and the
air was full of rumours that told of Japanese agents preparing in secret a coup which would repeat the opening disaster
of the war. These apprehensions originated in warnings from
the Russian consuls at Hongkong and Shanghai. As early as
the end of May they began to report that parties of Japanese
torpedo and mining officers, accompanied by cases containing
mines, were leaving secretly for Europe. To this they added
that fast steamers were being bought or hired which were to
be fitted with wireless for locating the fleet when it started.
Throughout the summer further reports followed of still larger
parties disguised as Turks, Malays or acrobats. By September
there were reports from Hongkong that some 50 Japanese had
sailed for Durban in a British ship with nine tons of dynamite
and three mysterious cases.

In Europe Russian attachés and agents were equally active.
According to the information they sent in, Japanese emissaries
had begun to appear on the south coast of Sweden and in

---

[1] Naval Attaché Report, 29th September 1904.
[2] Klado, *op. cit.*, page 58.
[3] *Ibid.*, page 285.

other suspicious places. A special department of the police was organised for the Baltic and North Sea, which hastened to justify its existence by reporting that the Japanese naval attaché in Berlin was organising a secret service on the Danish coast ; but nothing definite was discovered.[1] Still the rumours, of torpedo-boats and mines were persistent and up to the day fixed for the departure, though still of the vaguest kind, they grew more and more disturbing. Consequently when, on October 11, the squadron sailed for Libau, its last Russian port, it was in full apprehension of a torpedo attack, and arrangements were made for repelling it.[2]

Nor were the other depressing influences as yet over-come. The *Oleg* and *Izumrud* were still at Kronstadt in dock-yard hands ; the *Don*, the finest of the purchased German liners, had proved useless, and on the eve of departure the *Smolensk* and *Peterburg* arrived from their ignominious cruise. Both were at once added to the Navy, re-named the *Rion* and *Dnyepr*, and ordered to accompany the squadron as soon as they could refill with stores and coal. Finally, when on October 15 the squadron bade farewell to Libau, it consisted of the following units :—

SECOND PACIFIC SQUADRON.

Battleships : *Knyaz Suvorov* (Flag of Vice-Admiral Rozhest-venski), *Imperator Alexandr III., Borodino, Orel, Oslyabya* (Flag of Rear-Admiral Felkerzam), *Sisoi Veliki, Navarin*.

First-class Cruisers : *Admiral Nakhimov, Dmitri Donskoi* (Flag of Rear-Admiral Enkvist), *Svyetlana, Avrora*.

Third-class Cruisers : *Zhemchug, Almaz* (fitted out as despatch vessel).

Torpedo-boat Destroyers : *Blestyashchi, Bezuprechni, Bodri, Byedovi, Buistri, Buini, Bravi, Prozorlivi*.

Fleet Auxiliaries : *Kamchatka* (repair ship), *Anaduir* (for coal and provisions), *Koreya* (ammunition) *Kitai, Knyaz Gorchakov* (stores), *Rus* (ocean tug), *Meteor* (fresh water), *Malaiya*.

The cruisers *Oleg* and *Izumrud*, with the *Rion* and *Dnyepr* and five more destroyers, were to follow as a separate division when they could, but it was not for another month they were able to put to sea.

---

[1] *Documents annexed to the Russian case*, pages 3–12.
[2] *Commission Proceedings*, page 243.

From the moment Libau was left the most active precautions were taken against torpedo attack. Searchlight men and light gun crews were kept at quarters, the look-out was doubled and trebled, and at night only half the gun crews were permitted to sleep even by the guns.[1]

Till they were clear of the Belts, however, the most serious danger was from mines, but as arrangements had been made with the Danish Government for watching the narrow waters, the only precaution the Admiral took was to proceed with his fleet in four separate divisions. If we may believe Commander Semenov, who had arrived from Saigon just in time to accompany the fleet, it was not till he, on his Port Arthur experience, urged that sweepers should precede the advanced division, that anything of the kind was attempted. As the fleet, owing to a collision between a destroyer and the *Oslyabya*, had to anchor on the 17th at the entrance to the Belt, the Admiral permitted sweeps to be constructed, but owing to inexperience and the lack of suitable vessels the attempt failed. Thereupon, early on the 19th, the Admiral signalled, "The pas- " sage is to be considered as swept," and passing on he anchored on the morning of the 20th at the Skaw. Here it was he intended to stay some twenty-four hours to fill up with coal and to proceed again, probably in the evening of the 21st.[2] But it was not to be. Since leaving Libau the Admiral had received various reports of suspicious vessels in the Great Belt, the Cattagat and the North Sea. Nothing had been seen of them,[3] but now he heard something which appeared to be more certain. Strange torpedo craft, so the intelligence ran, had been seen in Langeland Fjord, and the news was quickly followed by an alarm from a transport called the *Bakan*, which had just come into the fleet. Her story was that the previous night she had seen at sea "four torpedo-boats which only " showed lights on the mizenmast-head, so that at a distance " they might be taken for fishing boats."[4] These reports the Admiral took to be true, and determined to outwit the enemy by sailing at once without completing his coal. As a further precaution he divided his fleet into six divisions, which were to sail in succession at considerable intervals. In advance he sent three destroyers with their parent transport. They left at

---

[1] *Commission Proceedings*, pp. 249, 251.
[2] *Ibid.*, p. 283.
[3] *Ibid.*, p. 44.
[4] *Ibid.*, p. 269.

4 p.m., and were presently followed by the four others with their parent ship,[1] both divisions proceeding at 12 knots, with orders to make for Cherbourg, and after coaling to carry on for Algiers and Suda Bay. Then after an interval came the light cruisers, *Svyetlana, Zhemchug,* and *Almaz* ; and at 5.0 Admiral Enkvist went off with the two heavy cruisers, *Donskoi* (flag) and *Avrora,* escorting the repair ship *Kamchatka.* These four divisions were to keep in direct touch with one another and form a screen 25 miles ahead of the battleships. To pre-serve the interval it was not till 7.30 that Admiral Felkerzam got under way with the second battle division, consisting of the *Oslyabya, Sisoi Veliki, Navarin,* and the armoured cruiser *Nakhimov* with the transports. Finally, at 10 p.m., the Com-mander-in-Chief followed with the First Division and a trans-port, leaving a second interval of 25 miles.

The night was thick, and there was difficulty in keeping touch, but in spite of their apprehensions nothing was reported and all went well, except that the *Kamchatka* had trouble in her engine-room. In the morning, as it was found she had dropped astern of the whole fleet, Admiral Enkvist reduced to half speed,[2] but the Commander-in-Chief held on. Thus the two battle divisions lost their interval and by mid-day were actually, during clear intervals, within range of vision, which was about six miles.[3]

During the day, which continued to be foggy with clearer intervals, nothing suspicious was reported by the advanced divisions ; but about 8.45 p.m the *Kamchatka* reported she was being followed by torpedo-boats. The fact was that about 8.0

---

[1] The eighth boat had been obliged to be sent back with engine trouble.

[2] *Commission Proceedings*, p. 328e.

[3] At 1.30 on the 21st the Wilson Liner *Zero,* being then in lat. 56° 8′ N. and long. 6° 19′, heading N. 66° E. at 11 to 12 knots, sighted and passed the 2nd destroyer division ; at 2.0 she sighted *Donskoi* and *Avrora,* and between that and 3.15 she passed both battle divisions (*Commission Proceedings,* p. 61), but her captain, in his evidence, says nothing of the 1st destroyer division or the light cruisers. The Commissioners, in their report, say he saw all the divisions, but this is not borne out by the evidence, which points to the order having become confused. Admiral Enkvist, in reply to a telegram from the Commission, said he was in sight of the First Division at 11 a.m. ; but the *Zero's* report and other indications suggest that this was an error for 11 p.m., particularly as the *Suvorov* had not seen these two cruisers up to the time of the incident and believed them to be 15 miles ahead (*ibid.,* p. 245). The light cruisers and flotillas were supposed to be 50 miles ahead.

she had sighted a German steamer, and mistaking her for a destroyer had opened fire. Then she sighted the *Aldebaran*, a Swedish steamer, fired on her twice, and believed she was surrounded by torpedo craft. According to the official evidence the wireless message by which she gave the alarm was not taken very seriously on board the flagship, but when after the *Kamchatka* got a reply from the Admiral she asked him to indicate his position a suspicion arose that the affair was a trick of some hostile craft to locate their objective, and the required information was not sent.[1] The Commander-in-Chief contented himself with warning her to keep clear of the coast, and about 10.0 p.m. sent an order to Admiral Enkvist, who was then supposed to be some 25 miles ahead, to close on her. The order was acknowledged, and an hour later the Commander-in-Chief called up the *Kamchatka* again to know if she still could see torpedo-boats, and the reply was that she could not.

In the course of the next hour Admiral Felkerzam came across a Hull fishing fleet of about 30 or 40 sail on the Dogger Bank, and having ascertained their character with his searchlight altered course so as to pass to the northward of them and held on, without, however, making any communication to the First Division.[2] Shortly before 1.0 a.m., as the *Suvorov* approached the same spot, she saw ahead a green rocket, which was the fishing "Admiral's" signal for throwing the trawls. Immediately afterwards the officers of the watch thought they could make out on the starboard beam "the " shape of a small vessel very low " going at high speed about 20 cables away. The searchlights, which were now unmasked, having confirmed the impression, the Admiral gave the order to commence firing, and the other ships rapidly took it up. In the flagship almost immediately a quartermaster reported he could see another torpedo-boat to port, and the port guns opened. But by this time it was clear to the officers on the. bridge that they were in the midst of a fishing fleet; the course was altered to avoid them,[3] and the Admiral gave orders they were not to be fired on. Still the firing went on for about eight or ten minutes, till suddenly it was seen

---

[1] Semenov, *Rasplata*, p. 286.

[2] *Commission Proceedings*, p. 340.

[3] Captain Klado in his deposition says this was done for fear a trawler right ahead of them was dropping mines, as they supposed the Japanese had done on August 10.

that close by in the direction where the firing had been heaviest Admiral Enkvist's flagship, the *Donskoi*, was making her number. The discovery was startling, for three hours earlier his division had been ordered to fall back from its advanced position and close on the *Kamchatka* which was far in the rear. Orders were immediately repeated with all energy to cease fire, but it was not before the *Avrora*, the other cruiser of the Enkvist division, had been hit five times and her chaplain had been mortally wounded. In the fishing fleet two men were killed and six wounded, one trawler was sunk and five more or less damaged.

On board the Russian flagship opinion at the time was strongly divided upon the incident. Some thought they had seen torpedo-boats disguised as trawlers ; others that they had seen them undisguised making off when they were detected ; others again said openly that the whole affair was a fatal blunder. Whatever else had happened two things were now clear—one that they had been attacking a British fishing fleet, and the other that they had been firing on their own advanced cruisers. Still so confident were the men who had reported seeing torpedo-boats amongst the trawlers that the Admiral was convinced there were some at least in his neighbourhood. On this assumption he protested he could do nothing but hold on, without stopping to render assistance to the damaged fisher craft.

When subsequently the whole affair was investigated before an International Commission of Inquiry at Paris, the explanation at which the British representatives arrived after hearing all the evidence was the one which the Commission practically adopted so far as the incomplete evidence permitted. Ever since leaving the Skaw the Russians had obviously been under a strong apprehension of torpedo attack, and these apprehensions can only have been increased by the *Kamchatka's* mistake and the fact that the Admiral's arrangements for a flotilla and cruiser screen in front of him had broken down. The result of the failure was that Admiral Enkvist's two cruisers, instead of being where he expected, were within gunshot of the flagship. The first " shape " seen was probably, therefore, the *Avrora*. As she was too far away to be lit up by the searchlights when they were turned on, their only effect would be to make her invisible ; but as they partially lit up some of the trawlers these vessels were mistaken by the excited gun crews and others for torpedo-boats and fired on. This explanation gained special colour from the fact that the damage to the *Avrora* was concealed for a long time and only discovered by the deciphering of a wireless message intercepted at our Felixstowe station. It was also considered highly significant that no officer from that ship appeared before the Commission, nor were her logs produced.

At the time, of course, a far more serious view of the incident was taken. That it should have occurred on a well-known fishing ground out of the true course of the fleet gave it in the eyes of an uninstructed public the appearance of a wanton outrage. A violent outburst of national resentment, as yet barely cold from the irritation of the volunteer cruisers, could be the only result. The knowledge that the Russians had proceeded on their voyage without offering any assistance inflamed the feeling to a very dangerous point, and the British Government at once took steps to see that the offending fleet did not leave European waters till satisfaction had been received.

For this purpose our naval disposition was at the moment far from favourable. The Home Fleet was at Cromarty, the Channel Fleet was at Gibraltar, and the bulk of the Mediterranean at Venice about to proceed to Pola. On the 24th, as soon as the situation was realised, the Home Fleet was warned to be in readiness to proceed to the Forth, the Channel Fleet to stand fast at Gibraltar, and the Admiral at Venice was to be prepared for orders to send six battleships and an armoured cruiser to join it there. A cruiser squadron was also warned for service at Sheerness. By that time it was known that Admiral Felkerzam's division, after coaling off Brighton, had proceeded down Channel without communicating with the shore. Admiral Rozhestvenski did not put into Brest to coal, according to his programme ; but assigning as a reason that fog made the approach dangerous, he carried on for Vigo. The flotilla had coaled at Cherbourg and gone on, so that by the 25th the whole fleet was clear of the Channel.

On that day operation orders went off to all British Commanders-in-Chief. Six battleships and the *Bacchante* left Venice for Gibraltar and the Admiral was ordered to follow with his flagship and another battleship, and two more were to be ready to go if required. The Home Fleet moved to the Forth, and at Gibraltar all was made ready for coaling six battleships, two amoured cruisers, and 18 destroyers which had also been ordered there. In the evening it was known that Admiral Rozhestvenski had put into Vigo. His light cruiser division, owing to a breakdown, had had to stop at Arosa Bay, and although the rest of the fleet was unlocated it was assumed that all units would join the Commander-in-Chief.

Next day formal warning was issued that relations with Russia were seriously strained, and that the attitude of France and Germany being unknown, all concerned must be on their guard, although there was no reason to expect unfriendly action. The Commander-in-Chief at Gibraltar was told that an apology had been demanded and that till matters were settled the Russians must be detained at Vigo by force if necessary. He was further specially informed that the reinforcement from the Mediterranean was designed to place him in such superiority that the Russians could submit without dishonour. The same day the Home Fleet proceeded to Portland, where three flotillas were concentrating, and the rest of the Mediterranean Fleet was ordered to Malta, with special instructions to watch for volunteer cruisers which were under orders to join the Baltic Fleet from the Black Sea.

On the 28th the Russian Foreign Office proposed an International Court of Inquiry, and the situation eased a little, but a cruiser watch at Vigo was to be maintained, as well as at Tangier, at which port the 1st destroyer division had arrived. Next day the strain was further relaxed by the Russian Government accepting in principle our conditions and all offensive demonstrations were directed to be avoided. This day all the missing Russian divisions reached the general rendezvous at Tangier, and that place as well as Vigo was watched discreetly.

On the 30th it was understood that the Russians had consented to detain the fleet pending the inquiry, though, in fact, it would seem that in their view they had only agreed to detain it till the terms of the inquiry were settled. Admiral Rozhestvenski was still at Vigo, having been waiting there till the Spanish authorities decided whether he might remain to coal. The Russian Government had thus been able to get into communication with him and eventually to inform him that he must send home officers to give evidence. The chief of them was Captain Klado, his second flag-captain, with one officer from each of the other ships in his division and one from the *Kamchatka*. None, however, were sent from Admiral

Enkvist's division.   In the meantime permission had come
from Madrid that each ship might take in 400 tons of coal,
and the Admiral at once proceeded to get it aboard preparatory to sailing.   It was thus under a misapprehension that on
the 30th all British Commanders-in-Chief were informed that
the crisis was less acute.   By the evening of the 31st, however, it became clear that there was a misunderstanding
between the two Foreign Offices, and the Admirals had
to be warned that the situation was still dangerous, since
the Russians seemed to be trying to minimise the effect of
their concessions.   There must therefore be no relaxation of
vigilance.

It would seem clear that as the Russians had consented
to the inquiry and ordered officers home to attend it, Admiral
Rozhestvenski considered that our demands had been met and
that he was free to sail.   Thus it was that while the question was
in its gravest state of suspicion and disagreement he left Vigo.
To British eyes the movement had all the appearance of a
defiance and a breach of faith, and a conflict seemed inevitable.   At Gibraltar the British Admiral had 11 battleships,
two more were close at hand, and he was ready to act at
a moment's notice.   Fortunately our Foreign Office clung to
the hope that there had been a real misunderstanding ; in fact,
orders for the Russian Admiral to remain where he was three
days longer had only just missed him.   Word accordingly
went to Gibraltar that the move did not necessarily mean that
the engagement was being broken and that nothing was to
be done that would make war inevitable till it was certain
redress was not to be had without it.

This was on November 1, and for the next three days it
looked as though a conflict could scarcely be avoided.   A convention to settle the affair was being actively negotiated, but
in the inflamed state of public opinion on both sides the
difficulty of finding a formula which would satisfy what Great
Britain was bound to demand, without too deeply wounding
Russian *amour propre*, seemed still insuperable.   On the 3rd,
while the *impasse* was at its height, the Gibraltar cruisers
reported Admiral Rozhestvenski's division making for Tangier.
Both divisions of his flotilla had already proceeded eastward,
and it looked as though the concentrated fleet intended to
enter the Mediterranean.   The possible meaning of such a
move had to be faced, and the British Government had to
prepare a redistribution of the fleet to meet the new outlook.

It rapidly increased in gravity. As soon as the Russian Admiral reached Tangier he gave his force its final organisation for the voyage. It was divided into two squadrons ; one under Admiral Felkerzam, consisting of the *Sisoi Veliki* and *Navarin,* with the light cruisers *Svyetlana, Zhemchug,* and *Almaz,* was to proceed to Suda Bay, where it would be joined by the seven destroyers and by five volunteer ships and five transports from the Black Sea, and it was then to proceed through the Canal. With the other squadron comprising all the rest of the fleet the Commander-in-Chief would go by the Cape, since, it is said, that the designed draft of the new battle-ships had been so much exceeded that it was doubtful whether they could pass the Canal. This was unknown to our Admiralty, and Admiral Felkerzam's move gave so much colour to the worst that was feared, that it became necessary to carry out the redistribution of the British fleet immediately. On the 4th the admiral at Gibraltar was told that if the rest of the Russians went up the Straits he was not to follow. His orders were at once to send two battleships to Malta and four more under false orders and at full speed to reinforce the Home Fleet at Portland. In the evening, however, our ambassador at St. Petersburg was able to report that a draft convention was practically accepted. Next day, the 5th, it was formally agreed and Admiral Rozhestvenski put to sea for the Atlantic. The British Admiral did not move, but, being without orders, he telegraphed next day to ask that he might be informed of the political situation. In reply he was told that the crisis was over, but that he was to stand by where he was till further orders. Four more days passed before the sky was quite clear, but on the 11th Admirals on all stations were told that the incident was at an end and they might resume ordinary duties.

So ended an affair which while it lasted might have been turned to disaster by the slightest false step. It remains now as an example of how under modern conditions naval warfare is more than ever liable to unforeseen complications with neutral Powers. The increased importance of night operations which the torpedo has introduced, the exhausting vigilance and sudden resolutions which it calls for must inevitably increase the risks of committing acts of hostility on peaceful shipping. So quick is its action and so vulnerable a fleet in darkness or fog, that often there can be no time to think. At all costs immediate action must be taken, and nothing but a frank recognition of the new danger to international relations and cool heads in the Governments concerned can prevent such inevitable incidents generating unnecessary conflict.   Fortunately in this case it was naval opinion that from the first grasped the situation and, realising in a manner that was not to be expected from landsmen how promptly and boldly an admiral at sea must come to a decision in such eventualities as had occurred on the Dogger Bank, it was able to view the incident with a sympathetic inclination to wait for explanations.

CHAPTER IV.

THE SITUATION AT PORT ARTHUR TO THE FIRST ATTACK ON 203-METRE HILL, SEPTEMBER 19TH TO 23RD.

[Map IIIA, Charts IV, V, VI.]

AT the actual seat of war these events were naturally exercising a profound influence. The situation there, indeed, was such that for both belligerents the Baltic Fleet and its movements were the controlling factor, and for the Japanese this was so in the highest degree.

Owing to their successive failures to secure decisive results, not only at sea, but also at Port Arthur and in Manchuria, their whole scheme had been reduced for the time to a condition which is always fraught with anxiety—a state of arrested offence. True, the great battle of Liau-yang, in which their elaborate combination had culminated, had given them the strategical key they sought ; they had driven their enemy from his chosen zone of concentration, and by so doing had obtained a position at which by use of the central mass they could cover both their occupation of Korea and the siege of Port Arthur. But it had done no more. The protracted efforts of the week-long battle had so completely exhausted the army that no pursuit had been possible. The Russians were necessarily permitted to retire to a fresh position a few miles to the northward, where their losses could quickly be made good, and where they could rapidly and undisturbed prepare for an offensive return.

For this was now obviously inevitable. The Japanese, having seized the Liau-yang area, had fully secured the initiative. So long as they held it the limited object of the war must remain in their hands and the beleagured naval base could not be relieved. If, therefore, the Russians were to succeed in the war they must attack, and break down their enemy's position. Had it been, therefore, a question of land operations alone the Japanese could have been well content; for it must be recalled that in spite of their arrested offensive their general position was one of the most favouable war can give. As a broad principle it is now universally recognised that, other things being equal, the greatest military advantages are to be sought in offensive strategy and defensive tactics. And this was the situation which the Japanese had reached.

With all the moral advantage of having taken the strategical offensive they were forcing the tactical offensive on their enemy.

Regarded, however, in the light of new developments which were threatening to modify the whole balance of the war, the picture was by no means so bright. There was another side to it, darkened by the deepening shadow of the Baltic Fleet, which made the factor of time all-important. To the Japanese it was obvious that sooner or later the Russians would be forced to attack ; every week of inaction, therefore, meant that the enemy's concentration which they had interrupted would be proceeding to ever-increasing strength, and they were powerless to prevent it. Till their severe losses were made good from Japan and their lengthened supply lines reorganised they were unable to advance ; all they could do was to stand fast hoping to have gathered sufficient power of resistance by the time the attack was delivered.

Had all the resources of the country been at Marshal Oyama's disposal in Manchuria, as the original war plan contemplated, the situation need not have caused grave anxiety. But this was not so. For the Third Army, which it had been calculated would at this crisis be at the Marshal's service, was still held fast in Kwang-tung and with no measurable prospect of release. For the unexpected failure of its first assault on the fortress demonstrated that before anything further could be done it must be reorganised as a siege army and supplied with a siege train which as yet did not exist. Nor was this all. In the abortive assault it had suffered relatively even more severely than the massed armies in the north, and its losses could only be made good from the reserves which should have been devoted to securing the situation in Manchuria.

It was a situation in fact which brings out with unusual emphasis how in wars of this nature neither service can ever be entirely free to work for its own special ends. Each theatre of operations was crying out for reinforcement with equal cogency. Before the Manchurian army lay the main force of the enemy, and there all military principle demanded the utmost concentration ; but into the scale of the Kwang-tung army was thrown the whole weight of the paramount demands of the navy upon which the security of the concentration ultimately depended. And here it was that the shadow of the Baltic Fleet disturbed the normal lines of the military situation. But for that no immediate renewal of effort against

Port Arthur would have been needed ; a mere masking force would have met the case, and the northern armies would have clearly had the first call on all the country could give ; but now that Admiral Rozhestvenski's flag was flying in the Baltic the navy could not wait. The fleet in Port Arthur must not only be reached, it must be reached quickly in order to give Admiral Togo time to recuperate his force before the Russian naval attack could fall.

It is clear that from now onward this was the controlling anxiety both of the Naval Staff and of the Commander-in-Chief. Over and above the need of docking and a general overhaul, it must be remembered that in the battle of the Yellow Sea the flagship had lost two of her 12-inch guns,[1] the *Asahi* two of hers, and the *Shikishima* one, besides numerous casualties to the secondary armament. All these defects cried aloud for remedy before the second crisis came. For with his battle strength reduced by one-third and three of his cruisers, besides minor units, totally lost, Admiral Togo felt unequal to the trial before him without everything that remained being in perfect condition. The Imperial Staff were of opinion that the work might begin at once, and it has been related how after the 10th of August they had given Admiral Kamimura permission to begin docking his squadron, and how on the Commander-in-Chief's protest the order had been revoked. After the failure of the first assault at the end of the month, the Staff had repeated the suggestion, but though he assented to Admiral Kamimura sending in the ships of the Straits squadron two at the time to Sasebo, he refused to part with a single unit of his own command. His last word was : " The " case is such that all the ships and vessels on the station must " as far as possible be retained here till Port Arthur falls."[2]

The truth was that being on the spot he saw the situation in a different and less rosy light than that which shone in the Staff Bureau at Tokyo. To a man in his directly responsible position it was only what he knew for certain that could afford a justifiable basis of action, and as yet he had no assurance as to the real effect of his late battle on the Russian squadron. Moreover, being in close contact with the Army, he could realise more vividly than his superiors at Headquarters how much the pure considerations of naval strategy were restricted

---

[1] By September 10 it was found that one of them, the injured after 12-inch, could be used.

[2] Vol. I., 465–6.

by the practical need of adjusting it to the plans and needs
of the Army.   In his eyes, therefore, his task in the Yellow Sea
was far from done, and as he was able to appreciate the situation
he had work enough and more than enough for everything
he could lay hands on.   It was not only that he believed
he had inflicted a merely temporary check on the Port Arthur
squadron and that sooner or later it must make another dash
for Vladivostok, but it is clear that a loyal anxiety to assist
his military colleague in doing for the fleet what it could not
do for itself had taken possession of him.   We have already
seen how his keenness to assist the recent abortive assault with
his best ships, even at great hazard, had brought him from
headquarters a caution that was almost a reprimand.   But the
sense of his duty to General Nogi and the decimated Third
Army was unshaken.   The day the assault failed he had
telegraphed to the Imperial Staff that the Third Army should
be strengthened by fresh and good reinforcements and that
the Naval Heavy Gun Brigade should receive four more
12-centimetre guns and an increase of ammunition "as an
" emergency measure at this pressing juncture."   At the same
time in informing General Nogi what he had done and conveying to him the sympathy of the Fleet for his losses, he
begged him to fire occasionally on the dockyard and harbour
to obstruct the work of repair on the Russian ships.   A
week later (September 3rd), at the General's request, he sent
ashore twelve 47-millimetre quick-firing field-guns.   Not content
with this he gave orders for landing and making carriages for
two 6-inch guns taken from the *Fuso*, which was still acting
as guardship at Dalny.   In an explanation to the Imperial
Staff he telegraphed on September 5th : "It is absolutely
" necessary that the next assault on Port Arthur should achieve
" its object.   The enemy may make their last stand on the
" Tiger's Tail Peninsula, and thinking it most advantageous
" for the Army to have powerful quick-firing guns I am
" landing two of the *Fuso's* 6-inch Armstrong guns and pro-
" viding them with a Naval Brigade."   But this only brought
him another rebuff, for Admiral Ijuin, Vice-director of the
Naval Staff, telegraphed to Admiral Shimamura, Chief of the
Combined Fleet Staff, that the Imperial Staff should be con-
sulted before the landing of ships' guns or field guns for the
use of the Army.   There is, however, nothing to show that
the orders the Commander-in-Chief had already given were
cancelled.

On the following day (September 6th) General Nogi's appreciation of his colleague's efforts was marked by a message which gave fresh hope that a solution of the situation might be reached sooner than was expected. The purport of the message was that the Russians had established a new battery of 12-centimetre guns at the point of Lao-lui-chui, which by a vigorous shell fire was seriously hindering the operations of the Army. The General, therefore, begged that it might be silenced from the sea and at the same time intimated that he did not intend to wait till his approaches against the front of attack were complete before making another attempt on 203-metre hill, which, so far as the Navy was concerned, was the key of the position. For by this time it was fairly clear that if the Japanese could seize it as an observing station the Russian squadron could be destroyed by shell fire whether the place was taken or not.

" It has been secretly decided by the Army," so the telegram ran, "to send the 1st Army Division to make a sudden " seizure of 203-metre hill. In that district as the engineers' " work on the North Hill of Lung-yen is nearly completed, it " is arranged that an attack shall be carried out there as " well, at the same time as that on 203-metre hill or a day " or two after it . . .²

" Although a bombardment of the shore by the Tamba " detachment³ at the time of the above attacks is hardly " expected by the Army on account of the dangerous condition " of that part of the sea from which the shelling would take " place, it is thought it would be a great advantage to the " military advance if the ships would come as close inshore as " they can and give assistance. If we succeed in capturing " the hill a few howitzers will be mounted on it, which will

---

¹ The 1st Division with the 1st Kobi or Reserve Brigade formed the Japanese right from Pigeon Bay to the river which flowed into the harbour. In the centre facing the front of attack was the IXth Division. Then came the XIth prolonging the left to the shores of Ta-ho Bay.

² Lung-yen was just beyond the left of the Ist Division in front of the northern salient of the fortress formed by Forts Shung-shu and Erh-lung.

³ The Tamba detachment was a section of the Seventh or Coast Defence Division under Captain Tamba in the *Saiyen* (3rd class coast defence ship). Besides that vessel there were the gunboats *Maya* and *Chokai* with some auxiliary gunboats. Sent originally to Louisa Bay to support the last general attack, the detachment had been continued there for blockade purposes.

" enable us to command the interior of the harbour and should
" put the enemy's fleet in a very unpleasant position." [1]   The
Admiral's reply was to order the *Heiyen* [2] to Louisa Bay to
reinforce the Tamba detachment, and Captain Tamba was
informed that this was done to increase his power of assisting
the military operations.   She was to be sent back as soon as
convenient.

To the strain of maintaining the general blockade was thus
added the immediate prospect of the Port Arthur Squadron
being forced to make another attempt to break away.   On
September 9th came news which rendered another action little
less than a certainty.   On that day it was known that Prince
Ukhtumski had been superseded and that Captain Viren had
been promoted over the heads of the captains of the Russian
battleships to the command of the squadron.   As Captain of
the *Bayan* he had proved himself one of the most efficient
officers the Russians had, and though having fouled a mine
on July 27, while operating against the Japanese left, he
had had no share in the recent battle, his sensational
elevation could have but one interpretation.   " Since this
officer," says the Confidential History, " had been appointed
" Commander-in-Chief over the heads of so many others,
" Admiral Togo, thinking it probable that the enemy's subse-
" quent operations might show some unexpected development,
" warned the blockading squadron to be very strictly on their
" guard."

Accordingly on the same day Rear-Admiral Togo, who
commanded the observation squadron, summoned all his
captains on board his flag-ship to explain the situation.   They
were told, amongst other things, " that while drifting or tem-
" porarily anchored they were to scrape off weed and shells
" as far as possible below water-line and that extra efforts must
" be made by all in view of the fact that the Army's pre-
" parations for the assault on the rear of the fortress were now
" complete and the fall of Port Arthur was approaching."
Every night two or three picket-boats were sent to lay fresh
mines in the entrance, and the same evening the new device
was tried of letting go a junk to induce the enemy to waste
their ammunition.   But the event only increased the impression

---

[1] *Japanese Confidential History*, Vol. II., p. 344.

[2] *Heiyen*, armoured gun-vessel, 2150 tons, with one 10-inch and four
4.7's.

of their new alertness, for they left the junk alone and shelled the picket-boats, though with little or no effect.

Now if we recall that this day, September 11th, was the same on which the Baltic Fleet sailed from Kronstadt to Reval, it is easy to feel the tension of the situation before Port Arthur. At what time the news that the long-delayed reinforcement was really coming reached the Japanese we do not know, but Admiral Togo now completed his final arrangements for another battle. His general disposition of the fleet was much the same as before, with the important exception that the First or Battle Division no longer waited at the Elliot Islands. After the action of August 10th it had returned there for emergency repairs and coaling, but it had left again when, on the 16th, there was a false alarm that the Russians were making another sortie. It then took up a permanent position ten miles south of Round Island, where it had remained ever since, drifting in open order during the day, taking in all its coal and stores at sea, and retiring at dusk to a night position off Shantung Promontory. In the middle of September its strength was increased by calling up the *Iwate* and *Tokiwa* from Admiral Kamimura, the *Yakumo* being eventually sent to Takeshiki in their place.[1]

The Third Division, under Admiral Dewa, kept its station off Liau-ti-shan to assist in the general blockade and to cover the small detachments which were operating from Louisa Bay, against blockade runners, and in the Liau river to open up that line of supply for the army.[2] On the arrival of the *Iwate* he shifted his flag to her, and had now under his command the *Chitose* and *Tatsuta*, which had just joined from Sasebo after docking. He also had the *Takasago*, but the *Kasagi* was sent to Admiral Kamimura. On September 16 he received the new 3rd-class cruiser *Otowa*, which had just been

---

[1] By "Daily Order" of September 18th the battle division was organised as follows :—

> 1st Sub-division, *Mikasa* and *Fuji*; 2nd Sub-division, *Shikishima* and *Asahi*; 3rd Sub-division, *Asama* and *Iwate*; 4th Sub-division, *Kasuga* and *Nisshin*. Repeating ship *Tatsuta*. She relieved the *Yaeyama*, who went home for boiler repairs.

[2] His day position was 1251, lat. 38° 30′, long. 121° 10′, 15 miles south of the top of Liau-ti-shan. The night position was *Ni*, or 1110, lat. 37° 50′, long. 121° 50′ (Order of August 18). By an order of September 9 the division was to remain stopped during the day, with one "watch-ship" with steam for 12 knots always to the northward. The rest would repair boilers and machinery, but any work that would take more than half an hour must receive the Admiral's permission.

completed at Yokoska, the only new ship added to the Japanese
Navy during the war.

Admiral Yamada's section of the Fifth Division was occupied, as before, on the left of the Japanese Army, and in
guarding the army bases at Dalny and Talien, and the new one
which had been established for the XIth Division at Ho-kou, just
inside Ping-tu-tau [1] ; but on September 12 he was deprived of
the *Matsushima*, which, at the suggestion of the Imperial Staff,
was detached to keep guard at Chemulpho and protect the
Varyag, which was then being raised.[2]

At night Admiral Yamada's orders were to have one ship
in Ping-tu-tau, East Bay, and with the rest to patrol the neighbourhood of Round Island, while the First Division was away
at its night station.   In the morning they returned to Ping-
tu-tau.

The day position of the Sixth Division was west of Encounter
Rock, but after the failure of the first assault Rear-Admiral
Togo received orders to keep one ship anchored three miles
east of the Rock all night.   His function was to maintain the
blockade, observe the enemy, and pass on to the Commander-
in-Chief all reports as they were received from the duty flotillas
inshore.[3]

The Seventh Division, with its attached flotilla of auxiliary
gunboats, or so much of it as was not detached to co-operate
with the Army on the further side of Kwangtung, was handled
by Admiral Hosoya from the *Fuso*, permanently moored at
Dalny.   This command was known as "the Talien-hwan

---

[1] See *post*, p. 58.

[2] Admiral Kataoka's subdivision *Nisshin* and *Kasuga* was still
officially in the Fifth Division although attached by the battle-plan
to the First Division.   Admiral Yamada's was *Hashidate, Itsukushima,
Matsushima,* and *Chinyen*.   The reason for devoting so powerful a
unit as the *Matsushima* to guarding a wreck is nowhere clearly
explained.   But she was incidentally used as an intelligence ship.   Besides
assisting in the salvage operations, she was to arrange for reports from
all Korean look-out stations to be telegraphed directly to her.   All
"urgent intelligence" was to be telegraphed by her to the Commander-in-
Chief and the Imperial Staff.   She also had authority to telegraph to
Takeshiki and Admiral Kamimura—orders which look as though arrangements had been made to restrict indiscriminate telegraphing in order to
prevent the choking of the wires, which had occurred in the week of the
battle.   On news of a sortie from Port Arthur, she was to go at once to
Position 180 (25 miles N.W. of Clifford Island).   *Japanese Confidential
History*, Vol. II., p. 425.

[3] His division was composed of the 3rd class cruisers *Akashi* (flag),
Suma, Akitsushima, and *Idzumi*.

Permanent Defence Force." Besides fleet picket-boats and other extemporised torpedo-craft, it included a flotilla consisting of four to five divisions of second and third class torpedo-boats, and this flotilla was quite distinct from the destroyers and larger boats which formed the blockade flotilla. Their regular duty was to guard the swept areas as far as Patrol Section A, off Lung-wang-tang, and to perform communication duties, though from time to time they were drawn upon for special service, such as to supply temporary vacancies in the blockade flotilla.

The blockade flotilla consisted of all the destroyers—nominally five divisions—two divisions of first-class torpedo-boats and two or three divisions of the second-class, but, owing to wear and tear, particularly to hulls and boilers, scarcely any of them were up to their full strength of four boats. On September 1st two destroyers were ordered to Sasebo for boiler repairs. On September 3rd the destroyer *Hayatori* had been lost with 17 hands on a mine off Ping-tu-tao while proceeding to her patrol station, and immediately afterwards the sweeping flotilla had found five mines in the locality. This compelled Admiral Togo to complicate his watching system by an order that each division must change its watch station from day to day as a precaution against similar misfortunes. Already his destroyer force was so much reduced that the original organisation of the flotilla would no longer work, and he made up his mind it must be entirely reorganised. But this apparently he had no power to do of his own authority, for he telegraphed to Tokyo for permission. Several divisions he said were reduced to three boats, and some to one only, and as each division had its commanding officer, the "unity of purpose in the operations" was continually disturbed. He therefore urged the suppression of the 3rd and 5th divisions, and the incorporation of their effective units in the 1st, 2nd, and 4th. The Staff, without at once giving permission, replied that they were awaiting an opportunity of carrying out such a reorganisation, and that meanwhile they hoped he would temporarily combine the destroyers as convenient. This apparently he proceeded to do, but, in order to carry out the new arrangements, he had to call upon Admiral Kamimura to replace his most defective torpedo divisions with some that were refitting at Takeshiki as fast as their repairs were complete.

A further change in the handling of the flotillas was that on September 2nd they were organised into three watches instead

of two, and took successive spells of 24 hours' duty at the three
patrol sections, by groups.[1]   The idea was to relax the rigour
of their watch when the failure of the assault on Port Arthur
eased the intensity of the immediate strain ; but, at the same
time, they had received from Headquarters a serious admonition
which their successive failures had earned them.   It came
from the Director of the Naval Staff, to be communicated to
all flotilla officers.   " In the battles of June 23rd, July 1st,[2] and
" August 10th," he telegraphed, " our whole armed forces
" anticipated that great results would come from the activity
" of the destroyers and torpedo-boat flotillas, and the com-
" paratively small effects of the numerous torpedo attacks is a
" matter of deep regret.   Now, when the situation of the
" enemy's fleet is becoming more and more like that of a rat
" in a hole, and the probability of its coming out is increasing,
" it is greatly on the officers of the destroyers and torpedo-
" boats that we rely for a satisfactory issue of the Combined
" Fleet's arduous operations, which have now lasted more than
" six months.   I earnestly hope that each of you will do his
" utmost, and that when the opportunity comes you will
" make up your minds to run close in and give a *coup de*
" *grâce.*" [3]

The message reveals how bitter was the disappointment at
the failure of an arm on which so much trust had been placed ;
and by men so proud of their special branch of the Japanese
torpedo officers it was felt as a severe rebuke.   Seeing how
much they had gone through, it must have been considered
sorely needed to have been given at all, and, in communicating
it, Admiral Kataoka added a sympathetic memorandum, indicating certain points where improvement might restore their
reputation.   " It is a matter of deep regret to me," he wrote,
" as well as to you, that we should have received such a tele-
" gram from the Director of the Staff.   It appears that many
" of the torpedoes fired by us on August 10th did not sink,

---

[1] The patrol sections were B. south-east of Port Arthur, D. south-east
of Liau-ti-shan, and E. south-west of Liau-ti-shan.   Section A. off Lung-
wang-tang was watched by the Taiien-hwan Defence Force.   Section C.
was west of Position X, and was left vacant because that position was
full of Russian and Japanese mines.   Section E. was very difficult to
maintain owing to the strength of tides round Liau-ti-shan Point.
(*Japanese communication.*)

[2] It is not known what this refers to.   Nothing of importance occurred
on this day.

[3] Instructions of August 18.   *Confidential History*, II., 387.

" but floated up to the surface. The reason for this is not
" known, but it is thought probable they were set to run such
" a distance that the sinking valve was unable to work.   I
" consider that torpedo attacks, especially those made at night,
" have no hope of success unless the attacking boats run close
" up to fire. You must fully realise this, and I hope that in
" the future great results will be obtained."[1]

For the fleet as a whole Admiral Togo was preparing
new battle instructions, in view of the expected effect of the
coming assault.   As it had been found necessary to postpone the attempt for a few days, owing to a sortie from
203-metre Hill having destroyed a Japanese trench, there was
plenty of time, and the memorandum was eventually issued on
September 14.

In its general lines it followed the tactical ideas of that he
had previously issued, particularly in the point of command.
During the approach up to 10,000 metres the established order
was to be preserved, but after that separate divisions were to
"adopt suitable movements." The formation was based on
two lines :—*Starboard line :* Third Division with the duty
blockade flotilla, and the Fifth Division with the flotilla of the
Talien-hwan Defence Force. *Port line :* First Division with
Nisshin and *Kasuga,* and the next watch flotilla and the Sixth
Division with the third watch flotilla. The objective of the
First Division was the enemy's battleships, and that of the
Third Division the cruisers *Bayan* and *Pallada,* which were
to be chased "to the end" if they tried to escape.   If they
remained in the line, the Japanese line was to be reinforced
by Admiral Dewa's two armoured cruisers, which constituted
the third sub-division in the full organisation of the Battle
Squadron.[2] The Sixth Division would devote itself to protecting the Japanese destroyers, and bringing them up to attack
as convenient, and to dealing with the enemy's destroyers.
The Fifth Division would take station as convenient, and act
as a Reserve, with the special duty of dealing with the
enemy's crippled ships, and destroying any that should try to
get back to Port Arthur.

A new feature in the flotilla's duties was that every boat
was to carry dummy mines (an obvious lesson from the last
action), in order, by dropping them in front of the enemy, to

---

[1] *Japanese Confidential History,* II., 413.
[2] See *supra,* p. 47, note.

disturb their formation and retard their escape in a chase, but
this was only to be done by signal from Divisional admirals.
On taking in the signal the units indicated would proceed at
full speed 10,000 to 12,000 metres ahead of the enemy, cut
across their course, and rapidly throw the mines overboard.
In case of a night sortie, the flotilla would attack till dawn,
while the ships proceeded southwards to an indicated guard-
line. In case of need Admiral Kamimura would be called up
as before to Ross Island.[1]

A few days later he added an order dealing with fire-control.
" The objective," it laid down, "for the fire of each ship of
" the First Division in battle should generally be the nearest
" ship of the enemy. Sights should be laid on the ship's
" foremast, and efforts should be made to destroy the forepart
" of the ship as much as possible," an order which seemed a
natural deduction from the shot that had saved him from failure
on August 10.[2]

It was the day after the general instructions were issued
that the *Iwate* and *Tokiwa* were called up from Admiral Kamimura, their orders were to come by Ross Island to Shantung
Promontory and thence towards Yentoa Bay as they might have
to be used for maintaining communications. As Admiral
Kamimura had just sent his flagship, the *Idzumo*, into Sasebo
to dock, this left him very weak, and he was told that as soon
as the two ships arrived he would be reinforced with one of
the older armoured cruisers, *Yakumo* or *Asama*. At the same
time he was warned that if the enemy came out again and he
got word to join the Combined Fleet he was to proceed to
Position 127 (27 miles south-east of Ross Island) and there
await orders.[3]

It was not till four days later, the 19th, that the Army was
able to deliver its promised attack, and then the impossibility
of the Navy's rendering any material assistance was once more
brought home by a disheartening catastrophe. On the morning of the 18th the *Heiyen*, which had been specially sent for
the purpose of supporting the attack, had gone out on patrol
duty, and on the 19th she failed to appear. Wreckage indicated that she had struck a mine, but nothing could be heard
of her fate, and the Army had to proceed without her while

---

[1] For the text of these orders *see post*, Appendix B. 1, *post*, p. 411.
[2] Daily Order, September 18.
[3] *Japanese Confidential History*, Vol. II., p. 125.

the fleet watched in acute expectation of the rat being bolted from its hole.

All that day and the next the battle raged, and though the Russian sweeping flotilla was working hard in the entrance there was not a sign of movement in the harbour. On the Japanese right the *Saiyen* and *Akagi*, in the absence of the *Heiyen*, did their best to support the attack by shelling the Russian left from the north shore of Pigeon Bay, but their guns were too weak to produce material effect. Their difficulties were fully realised to General Nogi's Staff and "an instruction" reached them from the naval officers attached to it, which presumably reflected the feeling at the Army Headquarters, "Though you must do your utmost," these special instructions ran, "to assist the Army you need not face bad weather or " pass over dangerous parts of the sea in your endeavour to " secure efficiency for your firing . . . and I trust that braving " so many difficulties you will ride triumphant over accidents, " and finally bring about some decisive result."

The hope was not realised. By the evening of the 20th, the *Fuso* was able to report that the Waterworks and Temple Redoubts had been captured by the IXth Division, but the Ist Division, although it had captured Namako - yama had failed to make any definite impression on 203-Metre Hill. Still the message stated that the fight was being energetically carried on. At the same time, the loss of the *Heiyen* was confirmed by the discovery of four survivors of her crew on Reef Island. All day on the 18th she had been on blockade patrol between that point and Iron Island. It so happened that the previous night the Russian destroyer *Skori* had succeeded in stealing out and laying 14 mines close to the island unobserved.[1] Consequently, as the *Heiyen* making to the northward was passing to the west of it, she struck one of them which had apparently broken adrift. It took her amidships, and in five minutes she was gone. In all 196 hands were lost, including her captain and ten officers.

This disaster seems to have sealed the fate of the attack on 203-Metre Hill. All day on the 21st and 22nd it was renewed with such tenacity that a lodgment was actually made near its summit. But the defence was equally heroic, and as the *Saiyen* had to be sent away to search for her lost consort and any survivors there might be, the attack received no further

---

[1] *See* Chart of Russian minefields.

support from the sea. The result was that a Russian battery
was able to come into action on the very ground the *Saiyen's*
shells had been searching, and from that position it was able to
deny the Japanese any possibility of maintaining their lodgment. By the evening of the 22nd the truth was realised,
and a message came from the naval officer on General
Nogi's Staff to say the attack had failed. " As the hill
" is so difficult to take," the message continued, " the Ist
" Army Division has decided to commence anew an attack
" by regular siege operations, but the date of this is not quite
" settled. The Army will have no objection to the withdrawal
" of the *Saiyen* detachment, except such vessels as are needed
" for dealing with blockade runners."

Here, then, Admiral Togo had to face the fact that the now
almost unendurable strain on the fleet must continue for a
further period of indefinite length, in waters where the insidious
mine danger seemed to be increasing every week, and with
a diminishing fleet crying out for repairs. A meeting was at
once arranged at Dalny between Admiral Shimamura, Chief of
Staff to the Combined Fleet, and General Kodama, Chief of
Staff to Marshal Oyama. What passed we do not know ;
Admiral Shimamura spent the next day ashore and did not
return to the fleet till the 24th ; but it seems to be fairly clear
that one result of the conference was that General Kodama persuaded his chief that the Third Army ought to be reinforced
with another division.

There were still two in reserve—the VIIth and VIIIth—
which it will be remembered had been held back in northern
Japan on either side of the Tsugaru Strait, at the time when
Admiral Togo's plan of campaign was accepted—a plan which
provided no naval defence against raids from Vladivostok against
the coasts of Yezo and the north of the main island. We are
told that " Marshal Oyama requested the Imperial Staff to send
" the VIIIth Army Division as a reinforcement for the Third
" Army at the time of the second general assault."[1] His request,
however, was not granted, the Imperial Staff being of opinion
that the Marshal must take that Division himself to increase his

---

[1] *Japanese Confidential History*, Vol. I., p. 239, under date November 15.
The VIIIth Division was stationed on the extreme north of Nippon, south of
the Tsugaru Strait. It was brought down by rail to Osaka on the Inland
Sea, and embarked there for Talien-whan about October 12 (*N.I.D.
Diary*, p. 126). One regiment seems to have been held back and given as
a reserve to General Nogi (*C.I.D.*, II., p. 620).

own force. The reason for overruling Marshal Oyama in this case was probably that at this time the Japanese information indicated that General Kuropatkin was about to return to the offensive for the relief of Port Arthur.

To Admiral Togo the decision must have been all the more unwelcome in that while the conference was going on there was a new claim which had to be met. On the 28th a telegram came in from Commander Prince Ichijo, who was then in France, to say that the Vladivostok Squadron had completed its repairs; and this was confirmed next day by the Military Attaché in London, who reported that the *Rossiya* and *Gromoboi* with three torpedo-boats had put to sea on the 21st. Admiral Togo at once sent off the *Yakumo* at high speed to reinforce the weakened Straits Squadron. Admiral Kamimura was in fact at the moment in no condition to deal with a bold raid. His flagship had returned to him from dock, but Admiral Uriu's squadron was widely dispersed. Since the battle he had been occupied in guarding a cable ship which had been laying new lines between Takeshiki and Okinoshima, Okinoshima and Tsunoshima, and between Tsunoshima and Mishima. This work was completed on September 7, and on the 9th orders came for a new cable to be laid between Matsushima and the Korean mainland at Chukupen Bay.[1] This was completed on the 16th, and the cable ship was then directed to find and repair a break in the cable between Chukupen Bay and Hondo. The *Niitaka* was guarding her and was now promptly ordered to stop the work and close. Another ship was engaged with the Railway Staff inspecting the new line from Fusan to Seoul, and a third was patrolling in the Okinoshima area. Far to the north were the two auxiliary cruisers *Hongkong Maru* and *Nippon Maru*, which had been sent up at the end of August to stop vessels which were said to be running contraband into Vladivostok through the Tsugaru and La Pérouse Straits. After stripping the wreck of the *Novik* of all removable guns and gear they had begun to operate with Hakodate as their base on September 7, devoting their chief attention to the Kunoshiri Channel and Yetorup Strait. The alarm, however, proved false, and by the 28th, as the Russian cruisers had not appeared, orders were given for the cable ship to carry on and the

---

[1] The time-table of the order was :—(a) Search for Vladivostok cable near Chukupen Bay, three days; (b) Landing at Chukupen Bay, two days; (c) Repairing cable south of Chukupen Bay, about two or three days; (d) Laying Matsushima-Chukupen cable, three to four days.

Yakumo, by Admiral Togo's directions, was sent into dock the day after she arrived.

Meanwhile, in the Port Arthur area, a further concentration had been rendered necessary by the recent losses. The *Saiyen* was recalled from Louisa Bay and the *Atago* from the Liau River, where she had been operating with the *Tsukushi*. So till the improvised siege train should arrive to complete the business, the fleet settled down once more to the weary blockade, which by this time had become a problem of great complexity, and to which we must now turn.

CHAPTER V.

THE BLOCKADE OF KWANGTUNG.

[Map IIIA, VII.   Charts IV, V, VI.]

THE blockade for which Admiral Togo had to provide, in addition to all his other arduous duties, extended by the proclamation of· May 26—the day of the battle of Nanshan—to the coasts of the Liau-tung peninsula from Pi-tsu-wo to Port Adams.   The difficulty of the operation, as it had now developed, was not merely the ordinary one of dealing with a peninsular rich in landing places and, as it were, encircled by neutral mainland.   There was also a feature about it which is perhaps without exact precedent.   This peculiar feature was that the Japanese had to blockade an area which contained the bases of their own Army.   Had the oversea supply of the Army been entirely in the hands of the Navy this complication need not have caused great difficulty ; but, as under the Japanese system the Army made its own arrangements, the possibilities of confusion are obvious. To complete the picture it must be borne in mind that the blockade-runners were of two classes.   In the first place there were sea-going steamers acting under direction of various Russian consuls as well as private adventurers, and in the second there were native junks which could steal over from the Chinese coast and creep along the Liau-ti-shan shore into Port Arthur or make any of the numerous creeks in Kwangtung immune by their shallow draft from mines.   Finally, we have to note the fact that vessels of both these classes were used not only by the blockade runners, but also by the Japanese Army Transport Department.

So long as all transports had to make for the Elliot Islands and wait there till they could be passed on to Talien-hwan by the naval transport guard little or no confusion arose and the blockade worked well.   In the first four weeks over a hundred junks and a dozen neutral vessels were examined.   But when after the battle of August 10th transports were permitted to go direct to Dalny the confusion began.   As the Army oversea supply lines lengthened and became more complex this confusion was more marked.   At the same time, as the increasing pressure on Port Arthur proclaimed its need for supplies from outside, there was a continual rise in the number and activity of

the blockade runners, and this in its turn brought more and
more urgent requests from the Army that they should be stopped
effectively. General Nogi was, in fact, realising more clearly
the difficulties of his task, and Admiral Togo on his part,
feeling acutely how little he could do directly to assist the
Army in performing what was the first duty of the Navy, was
straining every nerve to satisfy his colleague's demands, while
at every point he was being hampered by obstacles placed in
his way by defective joint staff work.

To realise the situation a general view of the Army supply
system is necessary.[1] The First Army may be eliminated, for
it was supplied by the light railway, which had been constructed from its sea base at Antung on the Yalu. All
the three other armies, however, were being served from or
through the Kwangtung area. The base of the Third Army was
Dalny, but, in order to ease the strain on the land line, a
subsidiary base for the left wing had been opened at Ho-kou in
Ping-tu-tau east creek, which was fed by junks from the main
depôt at Dalny. The base of the Second Army, which now
formed the left wing of the Manchurian Army, was Talien,
whence it was served by the main railway line and the Man-
darin road, and this line was now also used by the Fourth Army,
which after it joined hands with the Second at Haicheng,
formed the centre of the Main Army.

The arrangement would scarcely have sufficed but for
the alternative sea line in the Gulf of Liau-tung. This, it will
be remembered, had been set going from Kinchau with a junk
service by the Army Staff after the sortie of June 23rd had
made it impossible for the Navy to do it for them. Since
that time the line had greatly developed. The original landing-
place, which had been established at Gobo for filling the
Hsiung-yao-cheng depôt, had been moved on to the mouth of
the Kaiping river in July and at the end of the month to Newchwang when the battle of Ta-shih-chiao had given the Japanese
possession of the mouth of Liau-ho. Since that time, as
we have seen, a small detachment of the Seventh Division
had been developing the river line and clearing the estuary
of mines. In August steamers began to arrive direct from
Japan, and the junks then carried on up the Liau-ho and its
tributaries, as the naval party cleared away the obstacles. By
the end of August a hundred of them were arriving daily

---

[1] For the excellent account of it, see *C.I.D.*, Vol. II., p, 211 *et seq.*

at the main depôt placed at the junction of the Haicheng and Taitzu rivers. During the first week in September this line had been extended by the naval surveying party as high up the Taitzu as Hsiau-pei-ho, that is abreast of Liau-yang, and thenceforth this was the most capacious of the lines on which the combined Manchurian armies depended. It will be seen, therefore, that the Navy had to deal with two steamer lines—those to Talien-hwan and to Newchwang—and with one junk line—that between Dalny and Ho-kou—all three of which passed into or through the blockaded area. In the absence, therefore, of very careful staff arrangements the naval blockade and the army line of communication service could hardly work without friction.

The first sign of trouble was at the beginning of September. In the last days of August twenty-six suspicious junks were captured between Cap and Round Islands. They had papers from Wei-hai-wei to Dalny with provisions, but on some evidence that they were really making for Port Arthur they were all confiscated. On September 1, however, it was reported that junks were still going in and out of Louisa Bay, and on the 5th word came, apparently from the Army, that three junks with ammunition had got into Port Arthur. A few days later intelligence arrived that a large number of junks were running contraband from Kyau-chau and that by some means they were able to obtain forged certificates of the Army Transport Department. The Commander-in-Chief promptly issued orders that when these vessels were caught both hull and cargo were to be confiscated and that they were to be dealt with "in such " a way as to be a warning to others." He also instructed Admiral Hosoya to form a special Preventive Squadron composed of auxiliary gunboats and torpedo-boats and base it at North Hwang-ching-tau, the outermost of the Miau-tau Islands, with the special duty of watching for junks operating from that group. Though small at first it was gradually increased as the complaints of the Army continued. At this time also a further step seems to have been taken, for on September 11 Rear-Admiral Togo, presumably on a general fleet order, instructed his captains that no neutral vessel was to be allowed within twenty miles of Port Arthur.

This prohibition, indispensable as it was regarded by the Fleet Staff, very soon brought them into conflict with the Army. On September 16 Admiral Dewa telegraphed from the *Yakumo* : "Last night the 14th torpedo-boat division stopped

" the *Yamaye Maru the Second*, an Army transport which was
" passing six miles from the top of Liau-ti-shan. This is the
" second time this particular ship has broken into our blockade
" zone and has caused us a great amount of trouble. I beg
" you will write to the Army about this." The message was
directed to Admiral Hosoya in the *Fuso* at Dalny, who had
general charge of the inshore blockade and the regulation of
the approaches to the Army bases in Talien-hwan.[1] He promptly
addressed a letter of remonstrance to the Lia-shu-tun Line of
Communication Staff—that is, the line northward from the base
at Talien—to which the vessel was attached, and at the same
time begged the attention of all the directors of Army departments
at Dalny. "In order," he said, "to maintain the blockade
" of the Liautung peninsula as proclaimed by our fleet and
" to prevent the running of contraband into Port Arthur, as
" requested by the Third Army, it has been decided to pro-
" hibit the passage of any vessels, even those of our own
" country, along the shore between the entrance of Talien-
" hwan and the west coast of Liau-ti-shan, especially the
" strait called Liau-ti-shan Channel between the Promontory
" and North Hwang-ching-tau (the nearest of the Miau-tau
" islands). I beg you will take note of this. Moreover, for
" some time past vessels of the Akita Company and others
" claiming to be employed by the Army frequently break
" through our blockade line and give a great deal of trouble."
At the same time he informed the Naval Staff at Tokyo of
what he had done and begged that after consultation with the
Army Headquarters strict orders in the desired sense should
be issued by the Imperial Staff.

Three days later (the 19th) this remonstrance brought a
communication from the Chief of the Third Army Staff to
Admiral Togo's Chief of Staff, pointing out the difficulties
the new order would raise. "Although," he said, "it is very
" difficult for the fleet to distinguish between junks bound
" for Port Arthur and those for Dalny, materials must be
" brought into Dalny for the Third Army. We should like
" to arrange some system by which communications between
" Chifu and Dalny could be carried on by regular steamers
" flying some signal considered suitable by the fleet." What,
if anything, was done we do not know. Admiral Togo this

---

[1] On August 28, he had also been put in direct command of the
Liau-ho and Newchwang area.

same day ordered Admiral Dewa from time to time to detach
from his station off Liau-ti-shan a small cruiser to patrol
inside the Gulf of Pe-chi-li to stop Chinese vessels running into
Port Arthur, but on the 22nd he repeated the twenty-mile
prohibition more strictly than ever. "It would be advisable,"
he said, "occasionally to sink any Chinese vessel which may
" come within twenty miles of the top of Liau-ti-shan." Next
day he captured, with his own division off Round Island, 18
junks, all of which were confiscated for breach of blockade.

It would seem that this incident, coupled with the Army
Staff's insistence on the need of their junks going to Dalny,
caused the Admiral to telegraph to Tokyo for definite information as to what junk lines the Army was using : for on the
25th he received a telegram from the Naval Staff explaining
the actual state of affairs. "The junks," it said, "at present
" in use for Army Transport Service only ply between
" Dalny and Ping-tu-tau East Bay (that is, Ho-kou), or up
" and down the Liau River, and no others are being employed
" by us. Some junks employed to carry clothing from Dalny
" and Newchwang for the Second Army have not yet been
" reported as arrived, but there is no reason to suppose them
" to be still near Port Arthur. I hope, therefore, you will
" adopt the plan of letting none of the junks sailing about
" round Port Arthur go free, even though they should have
" flags given them by our Army."

There must obviously have been confusion somewhere,
for the information from Headquarters was not in accordance
with the belief of the Third Army Staff that supplies were
being brought in junks to Dalny. The drastic treatment
recommended for junks ostensibly under Army protection
could therefore easily lead to serious unpleasantness, particularly as it was just now the Army was smarting under the
losses it had sustained in failing to capture 203 Metre Hill
in the interests of the Navy.

But this was not all. On the previous day (September 24)
the trouble between the Services was further aggravated
by a new source of difficulty. At daylight there appeared
in the entrance of Talien-hwan the German steamer *Holstein*.
She was laden with rice, which she protested was for
the Manchurian Army, but as she was not a regular Army
transport Admiral Hosoya seized her and ordered her to be
detained till he could enquire of the Army whether her story
was true.

No sooner was this incident known than news came in from Admiral Yamada of a still more irritating affair of a similar character.   About 2.30 that morning, while on his night patrol station west of Round Island, he had seen a strange steamer proceeding westward.   The *Itsukushima* was ordered to examine her and gave chase, firing blank as a signal for her to stop.   As she took no notice it was assumed she was a Russian ship breaking out.   Till 3 a.m. the cruiser chased, and as three practice projectiles failed to have any serious effect, she turned on her searchlight and gave the chase three live shells, two of which hit and finally brought her to.   On examination she proved to be the *Nanyetsu Maru*, a Japanese Army transport bound from Ujina to Newchwang with 400 troops on board, and it was found that one domestic had been killed and eight of the crew injured.   The captain explained that he had taken the *Itsukushima* to be a Russian cruiser in chase of him and had felt it his duty to try to get away ; whereupon he was allowed to proceed.

Here, then, was another case of faulty Staff work between the two Services.   Admiral Togo, so the *Confidential History* explains, had repeatedly asked the military authorities that the route of Army transports and junks bound for Newchwang should not approach the blockade line.   Yet, in spite of all he could say, some of them would persist in entering the prohibited zone off Liau-ti-shan in order to make a short cut.   He now, therefore, formally requested the Admiralty that a conference should be held with the General Staff at Tokyo to fix definitely the transport route.   Coming as the incident did on the top of the *Holstein* affair, it was not likely to smooth the irritation which the Dalny Admiral's action in that matter must necessarily cause.   It so happened that when Admiral Hosoya made his representation to the Third Army, General Kodama, who was Marshal Oyama's chief of staff, was in the neighbourhood and was able quickly to explain.   But the explanation only made matters worse.   He had to say that without informing the Navy he had requested the Governor of Formosa to arrange with a local company for the supply of 40,000 bushels of rice in a series of neutral vessels which were to deliver it at Dalny or Newchwang during September, October and November, and that the *Holstein* was only the first of them.   She would, of course, have been directed to Newchwang had there been time to communicate, and it was now urged that she should be permitted

to sail at once for that port, with orders to divert the other vessels, which were on their way to Dalny. But Admiral Hosoya saw difficulties. The omission of the Army Staff to inform the Fleet of the arrangement that had been made was too serious to pass over lightly, nor, in view of the last instructions from the Naval Staff, did the explanation afford ground for releasing the ship. He therefore telegraphed to Tokyo to explain his attitude to the Army's request and to ask for instructions. " I expressed my intention," he said, " of assisting
" in any future arrangements, but as our regulations would
" not allow me to let go unreservedly a ship which had
" broken the blockade and even forced her way into this
" port, I replied I had no course but to detain the ship for
" the present. The ship's entrance into this port was pre-
" ceded by no sort of notification to us ; she came without
" warning straight over the centre of the unswept area in
" the middle of the entrance. As it was early dawn signals
" could not be exchanged and we were unable to stop her
" till she was just outside the boom off the mole." He then pointed out the danger of permitting neutrals to get familiar with the approaches in this way, and added, " I have never
" seen the necessity of employing these foreign vessels, and
" to use them in a manner which gives trouble to the Fleet
" and to send them without permission into ports captured
" by us seems to me most irresponsible and thoughtless
" behaviour."

Before Tokyo answered, the Manchurian Army Staff sent a formal request to the Fleet Staff that the *Holstein* should be allowed to proceed to Newchwang, and Admiral Togo, in his usual broadminded way of avoiding difficulties with the Army, ordered her to be released. By that time Admiral Hosoya had seized the second of the series, the British steamer *Haitung*, and he telegraphed to the Army Staff begging that as they had both found out the safety channel the crews should be sworn to secrecy before they were let go. General Kodama at once replied that the required secrecy would be guaranteed by the Army, and on the 28th both ships were set free.

The Chief of the Army Staff handsomely recognised the justice of the naval attitude, but foreseeing further difficulties he did not let the matter drop till he had come to a satisfactory arrangement with the Fleet. On October 2 he explained in a letter to Admiral Hosoya that some of the Formosa rice could not reach Newchwang before the river froze. He requested, therefore, that one or two of the foreign ships, "which had been chartered for economy," should be allowed into Dalny "if it was not too disadvantageous for naval reasons." The request was, of course, referred to Admiral Togo, who, still anxious to meet the Army Staff as far as possible, telegraphed his views to the Imperial Staff. The Fleet, he said, were anxious that foreign steamers with military stores should not ply to Dalny, but in view of General Kodama's representations he was prepared to permit it on the following conditions :—(1) He must be informed in advance of the name and nationality of the vessels ; (2) no foreigners besides the crew must be allowed on board ; (3) the crew must take an oath to divulge nothing they had seen ; (4) the vessels must not go in or out of Dalny except between 11 a.m. and sunset, and in approaching the port must stop five miles east of North San-shan-tau (off Talien-hwan), make their number and await orders ; (5) they must not be allowed on their return voyage to put into Shanghai, Kyau-chau, or Chifu.

The result was remarkable, for in spite of the Admiral's readiness to make the best of arrangements which General Kodama had made behind his back, the Imperial Staff evidently decided that at all events in the present juncture the naval requirements must take precedence of those of the Army. We know at least that a reply came through from Admiral Ijuin at Tokyo to say that the Imperial Staff had decided that so long as Port Arthur remained in the present condition they would send no foreign ships to Dalny, even after the freezing of Newchwang.

In appreciating this decision and the incidents which led up to it, it must be remembered that we have only the naval view. Still, considering that on September 19, the Third Army Staff had expressed a wish to have a line of foreign transports arranged, it is certainly curious that no one informed Admiral Togo that it had already been set on foot. In any case it is clear that the joint Staff work left much to be desired. Had there been any real co-ordination in these details between the two Services the Formosa transports could easily have been met and diverted as soon as it was known that Newchwang was open, and the troop transport would never have approached the blockade line at night. It can only be said that, however well the two Headquarter Staffs were working individually, they did not in practice operate as a joint Staff, and we may conclude that the mere official union

of the Naval and the General Staff for war purposes into a combined Imperial Staff will not provide trustworthy machinery
for effective co-ordination of the detail of combined operations
on a large scale.

That the trouble was due entirely to lack of system is evident from the fact that after the defects had so glaringly declared
themselves they were removed.   Henceforth, though occasional
night chases of Japanese ships took place, no further complaint is
recorded.   Having been granted its twenty-mile limit the Navy
seems to have considered that all it could reasonably demand
had been conceded and the work went forward smoothly.
On the other part the Army must have been permitted to use
a direct junk-line to Dalny ; for, on October 28, one of these
vessels was found near Encounter Rock derelict and capsized,
and on examination she was found to have a cargo of winter
clothing for the XIth Division and to be under the flag of the
Dalny Line of Communication Staff.

Nevertheless the Admiralty continued to insist on the most
drastic treatment of offending junks.   They had received an
impression from the Fleet reports that the Commander-in-
Chief was dealing with them too leniently in confiscating their
cargoes only and letting the vessels go free with their crews.
Accordingly, on October 5, he received a telegraphic " request "
that he should burn or sink all such vessels captured whether
carrying contraband or not, whenever it was inconvenient to
bring them into port.   But Admiral Togo could promptly
re-assure them.   " The Fleet," he replied, " has dealt unhesi-
" tatingly with ships that have broken the blockade, as well
" as with suspicious vessels and fishing-craft, in hope of
" enforcing the blockade and putting a stop to all contraband
" running.   To this end the vessels and cargoes have been
" confiscated, sunk or burnt.   Only to save life and to avoid
" exiling the crews have we given them a suitable junk, and
" then we have as far as possible sent them to the Army,
" who are employing them as coolies."[1]

Later on this rigorous dealing must have produced a
diplomatic protest, for in the following month the Minister

---

[1] The instructions as to how offending junks were to be dealt with
were apparently not put in writing. In Admiral Hosoya's orders for
the Miau-tau Preventive Squadron issued on September 12, the officer
in command was informed " Your treatment of the cargoes, hulls, and
" crews must be in accordance with the verbal instructions given you."
See *post*, p. 68 note.

of Marine found himself obliged to send out instructions which to some extent overrode the "request" of the Admiralty Staff. These instructions as issued by Admiral Yamada to the Seventh Division on November 18 were as follows : " The treatment " of junks under Admiral Togo's instructions for dealing with " contraband-running junks after capture is by order of the " Minister of Marine to be reported in detail. Those concerned " are to note this, but are to take, as before, active measures " for the prevention of running and the enforcement of the " blockade." Then followed the words of the Minister's in-structions : " The treatment after capture of junks trying to " run contraband into Port Arthur is to be carried out as " follows : (1) Junks which on examination are judged to have " been employed by the enemy's military forces for transporting " provisions into Port Arthur are, as before, to be confiscated " hull and cargo, and the crews to be released as convenient. " (2) In cases of junks which cannot be considered as used " by the enemy for war purposes the ship's name and country, " owner's and captain's name, place where captured, and all " such details as will be necessary for charging her with having " broken the blockade are to be noted and sent with the " captain or one of the crew, if possible, to the Prize Court " for examination. All dealings with junks in either category, " since they are connected with diplomacy, must be reported " in detail at once."[1]

From the time the arrangement was come to about the Army transports the only disturbance of the routine of the blockade was that produced by information which continually reached the Fleet from consuls and others concerning the movements of ocean blockade runners. As the situation of

---

[1] Seventh Division, Confidential Order No. 334. This was one of the few communications mentioned in the Japanese History as made by the Minister of Marine to a Commander-in-Chief at sea. They seem generally to have dealt with a point of International Law, and not with war direction ; and, further, they were " instructions " and not " requests." The Minister did, however, send instructions that had to do with supply, and these sometimes distinctly affected operations. For instance, on August 31 he instructed Admiral Togo that 12-inch and 8-inch guns should be served for the present with common shell only, Mark I. and II. armour-piercing shell being employed only when absolutely necessary. On September 26, we are told, " the Commander-in-Chief gave the Minister " his views on the subject." This was when it was found that a spotting station could be erected at Namako-yama as a result of the recent assault, and presumably it means that Admiral Togo suggested a modification of the order (*see post*, p. 69).

the beleaguered fortress became more and more desperate, vessels of this class became more numerous and venturesome, and they began to work from ports both within and without the Gulf of Pe-chi-li. The first instance is typical. On September 26 information came in that the Chinese steamer *Fu-Ping* had been purchased by Russia and would leave Taku under the German flag in the course of a few days for Port Arthur and would pass through the Gulf by night. Thereupon Admiral Dewa was directed to detach a light cruiser to Position 104 (lat. 38° 40', long. 119° 30')—that is, midway between Taku and Liau-ti-shan—to intercept her. The cruiser returned on the 30th, having seen nothing ; but she was immediately replaced, and on October 4 another cruiser was detached to assist her with permission to go as far as Taku if necessary. For a week the sailing of the *Fu-ping* was delayed, during which time the Japanese Consul-General tried to induce her captain to let her fall into the hands of the blockading squadron. When she finally got away she appears to have eluded the two advanced cruisers successfully. But there was still the Miau-tau Preventive Squadron to evade.[1] This detachment by successive increases now consisted of one gunboat, the *Atago*, which had just been recalled from Newchwang, one auxiliary gunboat, and two divisions of torpedo-boats. The result was, when she had got safely ten miles north of North Hwang-ching-tau, where the detachment was based, she was suddenly boarded and captured by a patrolling torpedo-boat. She proved to be full of arms, ammunition and stores, and on board was General Kuropatkin's private secretary Captain Eggard. When examined he said his orders were if captured to throw his documents overboard, which he had done. He was also to have fired the ship, but so smart had been the capture that he had had no time to do so.

Information of the same kind now came in rapidly. A number of vessels were working from Chifu and elsewhere through the Miau-tau group, and it was found necessary to keep two cruisers to watch the channels through those islands and to the west of them for ships carrying contraband. These channels were not within the blockade zone and could not be declared closed like the Liau-ti-shan channel, for something must be left open for legitimate trade in and out of

---

[1] The inshore blockade flotilla also had orders to sink her at sight, if she was seen in a position where the fire of the batteries protected her from capture.

the Pe-chi-li Gulf.[1] Eventually two cruisers from the Sixth Division were permanently told off for this work and were based at the island of North Hwang-ching-tau, while for runners trying to get in from the direction of Shanghai a cruiser patrol area was established off Shantung Promontory, and the watch was kept up continuously by regular reliefs.

The system proved very effective. A few junks continued to steal in from time to time with Russian telegrams and mails from Chifu, but the Miau-tau Preventive Squadron practically killed the junk blockade-running from that direction, and though few avowed blockade-runners of the ocean type were captured, not one succeeded in getting through. Still the maintenance of the system occupied practically the whole of the Japanese light cruisers.

This was the more annoying, since towards the end of October Admiral Togo was informed that a number of neutral ships were preparing to run contraband from Shanghai and Kyau-chau into Vladivostok before it was closed by ice. In informing Admiral Kamimura of this he told him he must carefully watch the Tsushima Straits for them, but the Northern Straits must still depend on the *Hongkong Maru*, the *Nippon Maru* and the Tsugaru guard. " I should like," he added, " to " send from here some ships to keep watch before Kyau-chau " Bay, but at present I have not enough cruisers for observing

---

[1] A nice point arises here as to whether the offending vessels were regarded as guilty for running contraband or for attempted breach of blockade. Strictly speaking, the waters west of the Miau-tau group, to which the officers concerned were instructed to pay special attention, were not within the blockade area, being a fairway into the Pe-chi-li gulf which must be left open. But as all vessels attempting to reach Port Arthur this way carried provisions, which were of course contraband, they could be seized without pressing blockade rights. The text of the Japanese orders appears to dwell on contraband rather than breach of blockade. These orders are set out in the *Confidential History*, Vol. II., pp. 378–382. It is there stated that Chinese junks were found to be constantly endeavouring "to smuggle provisions," but it is also added that by taking advantage of the night wind "they would cunningly slip past our blockade line." Admiral Togo therefore gave Admiral Hosoya an order to station certain vessels at Hwang-ching-tau "to patrol the west side of the Miau-tau Group to prevent junks from running contraband into Port Arthur." Admiral Hosoya thereupon issued orders accordingly, referring to "the smuggling by junks of contraband into Port Arthur." Subsequently the officer in command sent in a report entitled "The First Preventive Squadron's report on contraband-running junks." It would seem, therefore, that so far as the written orders went the Japanese preferred to base their seizure of vessels outside the blockade area on the plea of contraband.

" Taku, Chifu and Shanghai as well as for carrying on the
" all-important watch over Port Arthur."

In the last words he is, of course, distinguishing between
the naval and the commercial blockades. The two had never
been quite reconcilable, and from now onward the diver-
gence between their respective requirements became wider and
a source of ever-increasing anxiety.

By the end of September " the all-important watch over
Port Arthur" to which the Commander-in-Chief referred had
acquired a fresh significance, which was communicated to the
fleet by a general signal on October 2nd. "The Port Arthur
" fleet," it ran, " are reported to have been repainted and to
" have taken down their topmasts. This may be a prepara-
" tion for a night sortie, so you must be on your guard."
Next day the warning was emphasised by a further signal
that the military bombardment of the rear of the fortress was
becoming so effective that the enemy might seek to escape
from their difficulties by a night sortie.

The meaning of this was that the recent assault on 203-
Metre Hill had not been so great a failure as at first was
thought. The hold that had been gained on the adjacent
heights of Namako-yama permitted an observing station to be
established there on September 28th, and it was found that it
commanded a great part of the harbour. Next day a hit
below the waterline was recorded on the *Sevastopol* : on
October 1st the Naval 6-inch and 4·7 guns opened on the
Peresvyet, which could be clearly seen from the new station,
and nine hits were recorded. The other ships, however, had
moved out of sight. On the same day, moreover, twelve
11-inch howitzers, which had been brought from various
Japanese coast defence works to form a siege train, were able
to test their mountings and emplacements against the forts of
the East Face, and the results were excellent. Captain Bubnov
describes the bursting of these shells as terrific. On the 2nd
more hits by the smaller guns were made on the *Peresvyet*
and some 11-inch shells were dropped close to her. So
promising indeed was the outlook that, on the 6th, Admiral
Hosoya was able to report that the Third Army had decided
to bombard the enemy's ships every day with the Naval guns
and all the 11-inch howitzers until their fate was settled.
On that day, however, it was found that the fall of the
shells of the smaller guns could not be marked while the
howitzers were firing. The 4·7 batteries were therefore trained

on the enemy's sweeping craft and the 6-inch on the dock-yard. This difficulty was the less serious, for next day, the 7th, six more 11-inch howitzers arrived, making eighteen in all, and there was consequently every reason to expect that the Russian ships would soon find the harbour too hot to hold them.[1]

Next morning, October 8th, this view received sudden con-firmation. At 9 a.m. the *Fuso*, on the report of the observation station, signalled " The *Retvizan* has come out and is under Manju-yama."[2] Admiral Togo immediately cleared for action and moved his division to the battle rendezvous south-east of Encounter Rock and there remained stopped. But nothing could be seen of the *Retvizan*, nor was there any report of further movements which would indicate a sortie. The natural inference was that a scheme was on foot for getting the ships away one by one. It was an eventuality which at least had to be considered, and one with which Admiral Togo would have great difficulty in dealing effectually. For it so happened that it was a moment when he was very short of cruisers. The same morning a large blockade-runner with a full cargo of arms, ammunition and oil was reported to have left Shanghai. She was too important to be disregarded, and just as he was reaching his rendezvous he had to send Rear-Admiral Togo with two of his division down to Shantung Promontory with orders to remain there till the following morning and do his best to stop her. Consequently his blockade system was dislocated, and when the morning passed without the *Retvizan* moving he found it necessary to make fresh arrangements for the night. At 2.30 he told Admiral Yamada that with two of his ships he would have to take the Sixth Division's night station and leave one at Ping-tu-tau to keep up communications with the *Fuso* and the flotilla. He was also told that if the *Retvizan* did not go back into harbour a torpedo attack was to be made on her after dark by the 15th torpedo-boat division, which had recently returned from a refit at Takeshiki and was on guard off the entrance that day. Admiral Yamada sent on the order, but added that he had already arranged for such an attack by the four divisions of

---

[1] Captain Bubnov records hits on the *Peresvyet*, *Pobyeda*, *Angara*, and *Poltava* on different occasions during these days, but none on the *Sevastopol*, which had moved into the inner basin.

[2] No. 5, Map E. No explanation of this movement has come to hand but the suggestion is she was seeking shelter from the bombardment.

the Dalny Defence Force, and his plan was at once confirmed
by the Commander-in-Chief.

What followed is mainly interesting in view of the recent
reprimand to the flotilla. The Dalny Defence Flotilla consisted at this time of the 2nd division (two boats only)
which was on its way back from acting with the Louisa Bay
detachment ; the 6th (four boats) ; the 12th (three boats), and
the 16th (two boats). Admiral Yamada's instructions to the
commanding officers were that they were to meet in conference and make their own arrangements, and were also to make
a thorough reconnaisance before sunset. The 2nd division had
not yet arrived, but the commanding officers of the other
three went off in a torpedo-boat to the entrance. At 4.0 they
returned, having decided to attack by divisions in succession
between 10.30 and 11.30, with a report that the *Retvizan* was
anchored only five cables S.E. ½ S. of Man-tse-ying Fort.[1]

It is evident that Admiral Yamada now became uneasy,
fearing lest the reprimand under which the flotilla was smarting
might lead to some reckless sacrifice that could be ill afforded.
At all events after hearing what the commanding officers had to
say he gave them a serious caution against making foolhardy
attempts and told them to confine themselves to a demonstration of attack. To Admiral Togo he went further, and, after
explaining by telegraph what had been done, he added, "To
" set a lot of divisions to attack at the same moment leads
" only to confusion. No more than two divisions should
" attack, while the others make a diversion, and if the
" enemy's position is too far inside the harbour, no reckless
" behaviour should be indulged in." The only explanation of
the modification of his own plan is, that he was apprehensive
of the effect which the last general order to the flotilla might
have on officers determined at all cost to restore the reputation of their special arm. The Commander-in-Chief must have
agreed, for the order was passed to all divisions, and at 6.30
Admiral Yamada moved off for his night position.

At 7.30, when the sun set, the 15th division went in, and, as
the night turned very dark and few searchlights were burning, its
commander decided to attempt an attack with half his division.
The *Retvizan*, however, was nowhere to be found and while

---

[1] This fort was No. 9, Map E, one of those on the Tiger peninsula.
The Man-tse-ying light, however, appears to have been the Japanese
name for the lighthouse on west side of the entrance. *Confidential
History*, Vol. II., p. 437.

he was searching for her he was picked up by the Russian lights and subjected to so heavy a fire that he had to run out again. By that time the 12th division had come up, and after speaking his second subdivision had gone in. The second subdivision of the 15th soon followed, and then the two boats of the 16th; but the 6th division, just as it was starting at 8.0 o'clock, had received a shore signal to say that the battleship had returned to port. It therefore went back, but all the rest carried out a close search and came in for a heavy fire, but all got away without casualty, and so the affair ended.

Some doubt, however, was felt about the truth of the shore report. In the morning it was found that the *Retvizan* had certainly disappeared; there was no trace of her outside the port, but neither was there inside, and an impression prevailed that possibly she had escaped to sea. In fact she had returned into the harbour in the evening to a point where she could not be seen, and in Admiral Togo's belief this was the explanation of her disappearance. Nevertheless, he felt it necessary to re-arrange his night dispositions to forestall a still possible intention of the Russians to get their ships away piecemeal. To this end he determined to divide his battle squadron, being assured he could safely do so, since on the reports from the Namako-yama observing station he felt sure too many of the ships had been injured by the past week's bombardment for a sortie to be possible *en masse*.

By the new order the squadron as before was to remain stopped all day in open order at Position O, 10 miles due south of Round Island. At dusk the four battleships would proceed to Position H, 22 miles north-east of Shantung Promontory, turning back at dawn for Position O. For the armoured cruisers, which were committed to Admiral Kataoka, the night routine was to steam through Position 1032, 30 miles north of Wei-hai-wei, to Position 861, halfway between the battleships' night position and Shantung Promontory. Between 1.0 and 2.0 a.m. the armoured cruisers were to turn back N.W. ½ W. towards Position 1032 till dawn, when they would head back for the day Position O.[1]

It is uncertain whether this arrangement was kept to exactly. Our attaché, who this day joined the *Fuji*, reports the routine differently. Under date October 14 he says that generally about 6.0 the armoured cruisers parted company to the westward,

[1] First Division Daily Orders No. 10, Oct. 10th.

and at 6.30 the battleships moved away, forming line-ahead half an hour later and steering S.S.E. $\frac{1}{2}$ E. at 7 knots, which would take them towards Position H. At 2.0 a.m., when at 7 knots they would be some 20 miles short of it, they turned back N.W. or N.W. $\frac{1}{2}$ N., a course which would bring them to the battle rendezvous at Encounter Rock. About daylight a further alteration was made for Position O, which was reached between 9.0. and 10.0 a.m., the armoured cruisers rejoining a little later.

A comparison with the normal situation before Brest during the Great War is not without interest. Ushant was the same distance (25 miles) from the *goulet* of Brest as Encounter Rock was from the gullet of Port Arthur. The distant rendezvous "O" near Round Island was 45 miles from Port Arthur. The distant rendezvous from Brest varied with the wind and weather, but the central position may be set at 20 miles west of Ushant, the established rendezvous of the Signal Book being "3 to 7 leagues due south-west of Ushant," which gives an extreme limit of nearly 40 miles west of the *goulet*. The Shantung rendezvous was 110 miles from Port Arthur about the exact distance of the corresponding Lizard rendezvous from Brest. The mid-sea rendezvous between Shantung and Ross Island which Admiral Togo fixed for his junction with Admiral Kamimura was about the same distance from Port Arthur as the Cape Clear rendezvous was from Brest (250 miles). Thus the actual rendezvous distances of the two blockades were the same; yet, if account be taken of the higher certainty of movement and rapidity of intelligence which steam and wireless have since introduced, it will be seen that the Japanese blockade was in effect much closer than that of the British prototype—a conclusion of no little interest in view of the opinion, which was then held universally in European navies, that the torpedo had rendered a blockade of the Brest type no longer a possible operation of war. The explanation would seem to be that in practice the torpedo danger proved to be no greater under steam than the weather obstacle under sail.

CHAPTER VI.

FIRST EFFECTS OF THE BALTIC FLEET—THE JAPANESE DILEMMA.

[Maps IIIA, VII.   Charts I, V, VI.]

THE day on which this new routine for the naval blockade was established marks the beginning of a fresh period in the war and of an aggravation of the tension between the two Services which was destined to continue with increasing force till the end.   Both by land and sea the Russians had returned to the offensive.   On October 9th General Kuropatkin began to attack the Japanese position on the Sha-ho, and on the 11th the Baltic Fleet sailed from Reval.   The need, therefore, of a rapid end of things at Port Arthur was more pressing than ever, and the Army at this time reported that, owing to the ships in the harbour having shifted their berths, they could no longer be hit by the howitzers and that their 11-inch shell would be devoted to the forts.   To increase the strain, on the afternoon of the 11th nine Russian destroyers came out as far as Liau-ti-shan and began to fire on the rear of the Japanese army.   They retired after a short action with the Japanese patrol destroyers, but the attempt was evidence that the Port Arthur Squadron was still alive ; and next day, to make matters worse, another destroyer was lost on a mine.[1]

In testimony of the prevailing anxiety a step which Admiral Togo took on this day is noteworthy.   It will be remembered that some time before, without consulting the Naval Staff, he lent two of the *Fuso's* 6-inch guns to reinforce the Heavy Gun Brigade ashore.   Two more had been sent out to replace them, but these also the Army asked for.   The request was granted, and he told General Nogi they would be sent, but whether or not he obtained Staff permission is not stated. Next day (the 12th) things improved, for the naval officer attached to General Nogi's staff ashore was able to report that the howitzers were again on the *Pobyeda*, and that out of 35 rounds they had hit her 10 times.   It was also known that the Baltic Fleet had stopped at Libau.

---

[1] The *Harusame* of the 4th division ; her stern was blown off and her doctor and eight men were wounded ; but she did not sink and was towed into Ping-tu-tau by the last survivor of her division.   This division was now suppressed in the flotilla organisation.

All this time the battle on the Sha-ho was raging and no one as yet could tell the issue. If Marshal Oyama were defeated the situation at Port Arthur would assume a very grave aspect. Actual relief, it is true, must be a matter of considerable time, but a Russian success in front of Liau-yang would mean that all the additional forces that were now being mobilised in Japan would have to go there and little or nothing would be left with which to reinforce the siege army and hasten the fall of the fortress. During this period of stress the Port Arthur Squadron continued to show signs of activity. On the morning of the 16th the *Bayan* came out into the roadstead. The *Iwate* and *Asama* were immediately sent to Hwang-ching-tau to prevent her escaping that way or attacking the blockade detachments ; but the Japanese batteries quickly found her and she had to go back. Then came news from the Sha-ho. It had arrived in the form of a special telegram to the Fleet from Marshal Oyama's Chief of the Staff and it told how after a six days' battle the Japanese had won a complete victory. At all points the attack had been repulsed and the enemy were now in full retreat up the Mukden road, leaving 10,000 dead on the field, 500 prisoners, 34 guns and quantities of ammunition, arms, stores and clothing, while the Japanese loss, he said, had not exceeded 10,000 all told. How fully the Army Staff realised the extent to which the naval situation depended on their efforts is evidenced by the fact that they announced the victory as "a defeat of the Russian attempt to relieve Port Arthur." Its main significance indeed was that there now seemed to be an end for a long time of all danger of the siege being interrupted from the north. But there was a reverse to the picture ; for next day in the midst of the rejoicing over the Army's success came a telegram from Tokyo to say that just at the time General Kuropatkin had abandoned his offensive movement the Baltic Fleet had sailed from Libau.

Nor was this all, for it must soon have been known to the Fleet Staff that General Kodama's telegram gave far too sanguine an estimate of the battle. The pursuit which he spoke of amounted to very little. It was soon checked, the Russians merely retired behind the Sha-ho and had even re-covered two positions which the Japanese had seized close to its south bank. The two armies were brought to a stand-still in actual contact over the greater part of their fronts with nothing but the insignificant stream between them. The Japanese had lost nearly 4,000 killed and over 16,000 wounded as well as 14 guns, their tactical counterstroke had failed, and they could do no more than entrench themselves on the ground they had occupied in expectation of a renewal of the Russian attack.

This indeed General Kuropatkin at first contemplated, but having lost in killed, wounded and missing over 40,000 men besides much material, ammunition and stores, he was forced to stand fast. Yet he did not retire even as far as the lines he had prepared in front of Mukden. The position he occupied was some twelve miles south of it with his Eastern Force out-flanking the Japanese right. For all they could tell, therefore, he might renew his offensive movement at any moment, and there was grave doubt whether with their inferior force they could again repel a resolute attack. Of what was passing at Marshal Oyama's headquarters we have no record, but what-ever was in his mind it is evident that the fleet in Port Arthur was the paramount consideration, to which his plans had to be adjusted.

We have but one glimpse into Staff deliberations at this time, but that is significant enough. On October 19th a tele-gram came from General Kodama with a question for Admiral Togo's appreciation : "According to the situation at present," it said, "the enemy's Port Arthur Squadron should be nearly " destroyed after the combined attack by land and sea. Do " you think their final plan will be to come out into the " roadstead ? As this question has now the greatest influence " on our plans in this district I beg the favour of your " answer." From these words we may take it that what he wished to know was whether Admiral Togo thought he would shortly have a chance of settling the Port Arthur Squadron with his ships or whether the work must be carried through to the end by the Army. What prospect, in fact, was there of the Third Army being liberated for action in the main military theatre and of its ceasing to be a drain on the available reinforcements ?

Admiral Togo in reply telegraphed to both General Kodama and Tokyo the following appreciation : "It is very difficult to " come to any conclusion as to the future plans of the enemy's " fleet at present, since we are not sure of the amount of " damage done to the ships by our bombardment. If their " damages are confined to the parts above the lower deck,

" and the machinery has not been injured in vital parts, the
" temporary repairs of a score of hits would not take long,
" and we must conclude that they will come out when they
" see an opportunity. Even if only one or two of the battle-
" ships come out and join the Baltic Fleet, which, according to
" a telegram of the naval attaché at our French legation, started
" for certain on the 17th ; or if the whole squadron remain
" in Port Arthur, continue their repairs, turn their whole
" energy to the defence of the land front of the fortress and
" wait for the arrival of the Baltic Fleet—either of these
" alternatives must have great influence on every part of our
" strategy ; and I consider that now, when the Baltic Fleet is
" on its way out here, the urgent necessity is to capture Port
" Arthur as quickly as possible and to dispose of the ships
" there. The above I beg to offer as my answer."[1]

It would look as though he took this appreciation as
settling the matter—as indeed it probably did—for next day
(the 20th) we are told that he wrote to the Naval Staff
concerning the re-organisation of the Combined Fleet after Port
Arthur should have been disposed of. Four days later,
moreover—that is, on the 24th—his Staff officer ashore informed him that that day a conference of all the divisional
Staffs had been held to consider a second general assault. The
decision had been that it should begin on the 26th with a
preparative bombardment by all the 11-inch howitzers. The
following morning the rest of the guns would join in, and
in the afternoon all sections of the Army would advance to
the assault.

At the same time the Army sent in information obtained
from a Russian seaman prisoner as to the state of the squadron.
The *Retvizan* had been hit six times, the *Peresvyet* twenty-seven,
and the *Pobyeda* eight, but all were capable of fighting except
the *Bayan* and *Sevastopol*. The former had her machinery
entirely disabled and the latter was in dock with only three
12-inch guns left. The *Pobyeda* had no 6-inch, and 70 guns
in all of various calibres had been landed for the defence of
the fortress and two-thirds of the crews were employed ashore.
Of the flotilla the *Bobr* and 17 destroyers and torpedo-boats
were left.[2]

---

[1] *Japanese Confidential History*, Vol. II., p. 230.

[2] According to an official report of Admiral Viren to the Viceroy
dated October 23rd, the damage to the ships since the howitzers began
to find them on September 27th was as follows : Number of hits, 33

On this information Admiral Togo made his disposition for intercepting a sortie. The whole of the blockade flotilla were o take up their emergency patrol stations, half to be on duty every day, and the off duty group to remain at Ping-tu-tau " strictly on guard and with everything ready for proceeding " at short notice," except for one division, which was to go to the patrol station 10 miles west of Liau-ti-shan.[1]

For the battle squadron the routine he had established in view of the enemy's squadron being driven to sea, either singly or in force, remained unaltered. There was nothing else to be done although the prescribed movements involved risks which were growing more and more hazardous every day. By this time it was clear that the number of floating mines which had always been a danger inshore had become much more numerous and were drifting in all directions. During the long spell of heavy weather which had been prevailing numbers of them had broken adrift, not only those of the Russians but many of those which almost every night had been laid by the Japanese themselves. Vessels were constantly cruising to look out for them, and up to October 20th over 200 had been destroyed. Latterly they had begun to appear as far away as the Shantung patrol area and consequently the night cruising became highly dangerous. Still Admiral Togo, reduced as his battle squadron was, continued to take the risk, and in doing so came near to a disaster which might have changed the face of the war.

It was at the critical moment when on the 26th, according to programme, the new general attack on the fortress had begun. Towards sunset as usual Admiral Togo, after parting company with Admiral Kataoka and the armoured cruisers, proceeded on his night patrol. The howitzers had been firing since the early hours of the morning and obviously with good result. A great fire had been seen in Port Arthur and some

---

11-inch and 55 others. *Peresvyet* had suffered most, having three holes below the water-line. The *Retvizan* had one hole 12 feet below the water-line. *Bayan*, starboard engine disabled. Casualties: 15 men killed, 3 officers and 34 men wounded. The holes in the *Sevastopol* had been repaired. (*Russian Military History*, Vol. VIII., part ii., p. 507.)

[1] His blockade flotilla was now composed as follows:—

> Group A. 1st and 3rd destroyer divisions with 9th, 10th and 14th torpedo-boat divisions.
> Group B. 2nd and 5th destroyer divisions with 15th and 20th torpedo-boat divisions.

In all, four divisions of destroyers and five of torpedo-boats.

sweeping vessels escorted by torpedo craft were observed to be at work in the entrance. With every expectation of the possibility of a sortie, therefore, the *Mikasa* was leading the battleships in line-ahead towards the Shantung rendezvous when at 10.15 p.m., about 45 miles from the Promontory, she saw a mine floating close by her port side. There was no time to give helm to avoid it and she held on passing within five metres and giving the warning to her next astern, the *Fuji*. This ship having already seen the danger had stopped her engines to let the wash of her bow waves take it clear and thus managed to miss by about three feet. The *Shikishima* also cleared it, but the *Asahi* was less fortunate. She happened to be slightly to port of the line and was using port helm to recover her station when she took in the *Shikishima's* warning. She immediately put her helm over to starboard, but the mine caught her under the ladder on her port quarter and exploded. In a short time her captain was able to report that the injiury was slight and the Admiral ordered her away to the Elliot Islands, signalling to Admiral Hosoya to send the Dalny repair ship to join her there.

It was a narrow escape of a great disaster, and as it was the incident was serious enough, for the damage to the *Asahi* meant that at a highly critical juncture Admiral Togo had only half the battleship force with which he had started the war. It must have been, then, with a considerable sense of relief that he heard next day of the Dogger Bank affair. For it was this day, the 25th, the British fleet was warned that relations with Russia was strained.[1]

He was further relieved on the 27th by the re-appearance of the *Asahi* with her emergency repairs complete.[2] Thus before the day appointed for the development of the Third Army's attack his battle squadron was once more complete.

On the 30th at the hour appointed the general assault began. As the front of attack upon which it concentrated was only the northern section of the *enceinte* from the Chikuan Battery westward to Fort Sung-shu, the Fleet was unable to assist on either flank. For two days the devoted Japanese infantry hurled themselves against the Russian works and for a time it was believed in the Fleet that they were on the brink

---

[1] There is no reference to the Anglo-Russian episode in the Japanese *Confidential History.*

[2] The damage had proved to be very slight ; some rivets were started and plates bent, but her steaming powers remained unaffected.

of success.   On November 1st Admiral Togo gathered that
the two forts in front of the Japanese left were taken and
that the two which formed the northern salient were so much
shattered that both were expected to fall in two or three days.

These sanguine anticipations, however, were soon at an
end.   In the morning it was announced that another destroyer, the *Oboro*, had been disabled by a drifting mine, and
scarcely was the news received when it became known that the
assault had failed.   With a loss of 124 officers and 3,611 men
the Army had merely obtained possession of a few outworks
that brought them little nearer to their end.   This meant that
the losses since the siege began, not including loss by disease,
amounted to nearly 30,000 men, of whom some 8,500 were
killed, and the back of the work was still to be broken.

It was then with a gloomy prospect that November opened.
The one ray of light was the plight into which the Baltic
Fleet had got itself.   It was during the first three days of the
month, it must be remembered, that relations between Great
Britain and Russia were most acutely strained.   Admiral
Rozhestvenski had left Vigo before the negotiations were complete and a collision appeared inevitable.   If that occurred it
meant for certain that the Baltic Fleet would never complete
its voyage and the situation in the Yellow Sea would be
eased of all its anxiety.   The pressure on Port Arthur could
be relaxed and that on Mukden increased and the balance
would turn distinctly in favour of Japan.   To give reality to
the picture, this same day, November 2nd, the British destroyer
Hart came into the fleet and on board her was the flag-captain
of the China Squadron who had come from Wei-hai-wei to
confer with the Japanese Admiral.   For some time he was
with him in the *Mikasa*, and then, after visiting the *Asahi*, he
returned to his own Commander-in-Chief.   What passed is
not recorded.   For one day longer the situation in Europe
remained in a state of intense strain.   Then it began to relax ;
on the 5th Admiral Rozhestvenski sailed from Tangier and
once more the shadow of the Baltic Fleet was upon the
Yellow Sea.

Nor was this the only indication that Russia was in-
augurating a new period of effort to recover the situation.
From first to last her evil genius had been Admiral Alexeiev,
into whose inadequate hands the whole conduct of the war
had fallen, and now at last the truth seems to have been
realised.   By what means the eyes of the Tsar were opened

we do not know, but this much is certain that, on October 27th, the day after the British Government had given to all stations the warning "strained relations," the Viceroy was recalled by telegram. On the 25th the command of all the forces in the Far East, both Naval and Military, had been given to General Kuropatkin.

This significant change was made known in Port Arthur by a junk that stole in on November 3rd. When the Japanese were aware of it is not clear ; but quite apart from the drastic change in the Russian higher command, the situation was now one under which Admiral Togo could not rest quiet. It was obvious that things could not go on indefinitely as they were, and he determined to make a serious representation to the Imperial Staff. Accordingly, on November 6th, the day after Admiral Rozhestvenski left Tangier, he instructed his Chief of Staff to send to Admiral Ijuin, Vice-director of the Naval Headquarter Staff, the following telegram : " Please inform me " of the movements of the Baltic Fleet, as the Combined Fleet " must make arrangements to meet them. These will depend " on their progress, since we cannot forecast at what date Port " Arthur with fall. Cannot the numbers of guns and men in " the Naval Brigade and the howitzer batteries be increased " from home ? At any rate I beg that you will promote a " discussion in the Imperial Staff as to how the fall of Port " Arthur may be brought about more quickly." This same day, either before or after sending this telegram, he received another request from General Kodama for his appreciation of the situation at Port Arthur, and particularly, it would seem, as to what indications there were of the Russians breaking out. He replied that the enemy's destroyers and sweeping boats were carrying on as before (that is, merely coming out every day and apparently doing nothing definite). Most of the squadron, he said, were under Quail Hill, out of sight from the observation stations, so that nothing could be learnt about them, and his estimate of the enemy's intentions was the same as he had given when the Army Headquarters last inquired.

Next day (November 7th) Admiral Ijuin telegraphed what was known of the Baltic Fleet's movements, together with his own views about the capture of Port Arthur. At this time it was certain that Admiral Rozhestvenski had left Tangier, but the course he meant to take was still undetermined. If he held on for the seat of war Admiral Ijuin was of opinion that he must be expected in the Straits of Formosa early in January

1905, but whether or not he would seek a decisive action would depend mainly on the fate of Port Arthur and on the relative strength of the two fleets at the moment. Still it might be taken for certain that, seeing how great were the efforts which Russia was making to continue the struggle, she would contend to the last for the command of the sea, and in any event the presence or absence of her fleet in Pacific waters must have a material influence on the issue of the War.[1] It was even doubtful whether the crisis might not arise before the New Year. There was at least a possibility that the Baltic Fleet might appear at the end of 1904.

It was in view of this contingency that Admiral Ito, as Director of the Naval Staff, made an official suggestion as to what should be done. It was in effect a renewal of his earlier proposal that the Combined Fleet should commence its refit at once. It is clear that after the succession of disappointments in the operations against Port Arthur the Naval Staff regarded the capture of the fortress as too remote a contingency to be relied on in their calculations. " Since " the reduction of Port Arthur," he said, " may still take a " long time and it is impossible to fix any date for a successful " seizure of even the heights and positions in rear of the " fortress ; and, moreover, as the enemy's reinforcing fleet is " coming quickly in this direction, how would it be to take " this opportunity of preparing our fleet for them by sending " in your battleships and other ships one at a time for a rapid " overhaul ? "

To Admiral Togo it did not seem by any means a happy moment for reducing the strength of the blockade. He had just lost another gunboat, the *Atago* of the Miau-tau Preventive Detachment, which had gone ashore and become a total loss, and the bombardment of the harbour was showing no decisive result.[2] Moreover, the Russian destroyers and sweepers were as busy as ever in the entrance. In the morning of the 8th no less than eleven destroyers and four sweepers emerged and remained out all day. Nevertheless Admiral Togo decided to fall in with the Staff suggestion, and this day informed Admiral

---

[1] *Japanese Published History*, Part IV., ch. i., sec. 1. The date of this appreciation is fixed by the *Confidential History*, Vol. II., p. 236, under date November 7th.

[2] According to the Russian official report for the week since the last return (October 27th to November 5th) there had been only five 11-inch hits and 12 others, "with no extensive damage."

Ito he was sending to Sasebo the *Asahi*, which, after the loss of two of her barbette guns in the action of August 10th and her trouble with the mine, stood in greatest need of repair. The *Takasago* would also go there and the *Akitsushima* to Kuré. The departure of these ships, however, would so much weaken his blockade that he felt compelled to call up the two merchant cruisers, *Hongkong Maru* and *Nippon Maru*, from their duties in the Sea of Japan. These vessels had already been recalled from the northern area, where they had been cruising for contraband, and were at the moment forming part of the patrol of the Tsushima Straits. An order accordingly went to Admiral Kamimura that he was to send them to Round Island at once. At the same time the Commander-in-Chief directed the complete dismantling of the Elliot Island base. Henceforth everything was to be concentrated at Dalny, where all fleet transports would proceed direct and where he intended to carry out a thorough refit of his seven remaining divisions of torpedo-boats in turn.

For the rest, he devoted much attention to strategical preparation against the coming of the Baltic Fleet. It will be recalled that in Russia there was a widely held view that the reinforcing fleet could do little good unless it could secure a convenient base within the theatre of war. It was with this obvious possibility that Admiral Togo was now concerned. He was specially anxious about Matsuda Bay in Ikishima (which lies between Tsushima and the Japanese mainland) as well as the South Korean harbours and such places as Amami-o-shima in the Liu-kiu group, the nearest large island in the chain that connects Japan with Formosa. He had already suggested that coastal torpedo-boats should be prepared to defend them, but he now wished to have mine-layers instead, as mine-fields could easily be laid and were in his opinion more effective. The Staff, however, saw objections. As they had at present no means of rendering mines innocuous when they broke adrift, they regarded them as too dangerous to their own side, and they wished to use them as little as possible. They were therefore fitting coast-defence torpedo tubes to 16 temporary gunboats so as to complete the defensive arrangements as quickly as possible. Nevertheless, they informed him they were fitting 10 vessels with mine-dropping gear, which could also be used as convenient.[1]

---

[1] *Confidential History*, II., 237, Nov. 13, and *see post* App., p. 419.

At the same time Admiral Togo was making preparations
for the action which he now saw clearly before him, a special
feature of them being that he asked the Imperial Staff to
prepare 1,000 dummy mines—half at Sasebo and half at Takeshiki—a device which we know from his last instructions he
intended to employ in battle.[1]

A more serious consideration were the reports which were
reaching him of the Russians buying cruisers from South
America and Holland. We have seen already how they had
been making every effort to do so, since the lack of good
cruisers was the weak point of Admiral Rozhestvenski's command. On this Admiral Togo had been calculating in his
plans and he felt he must know the truth. "Since any increase,"
he telegraphed to the Staff on the 9th, " or alteration in the
" number of their cruisers will make a considerable difference
" in our plan of operations, I beg you will make certain,
" either in South America or when these ships arrive, what
" the facts are and what are the names of the ships." Admiral
Ijuin replied that they as yet had no certain information. They
were officially informed, however, that no such sale would
take place. Still, as it was quite conceivable something of the
kind was on foot, they were approaching the governments
concerned to induce them not to sell off their men-of-war.

It was next day, the 10th, that Admiral Togo came to a
conclusion which considerably hardened the situation. Four
days before, when General Kodama had pressed him for an
appreciation of the probable intention of the Russians, he had
felt unable to give a certain answer. Now he had made up
his mind, and it was in the sense least agreeable to the Army.
Reports of the daily emergence and movements of the Russian
destroyers and mine-sweepers convinced him that no preparations were being made by them for a sortie of the fleet.
They seemed to do nothing outside, and he was sure their
restlessness meant no more than a search for comparative
shelter from the Japanese batteries ashore. It was clear, then,
that the squadron meant to abide the fate of the fortress and
its speedy fall was therefore the paramount necessity of the
stage which the war had reached. This view he once more
urged upon the Imperial Staff and at the same time sent a
special officer from his own Staff to express the same desire
to General Nogi. The text of his message is not available,

---

[1] See *post*, *Appendix* B. 1., p. 413.

but from the reply he eventually received from General Nogi it is evident he must have urged him to change his plan of attacking the main works by making 203-Metre Hill his primary objective.[1]

In Port Arthur they were by this time fully alive to the mistake that had been made in neglecting to fortify that position. It was realised as the weak point which seriously reduced the prospects of a prolonged resistance, and they saw that the salvation of the place depended on what was being done to raise the siege. But here they were absolutely in the dark, except for persistent native rumours that General Kuropatkin's attempt to move southward had been defeated at the Sha-ho. Clearly it was now imperative to ascertain the truth, but that was by no means easy. For some time communication with head-quarters had been cut off by the closeness of the blockade, and on November 4th it had been decided that an effort must be made to find out how they stood and to inform the new Commander-in-Chief of the desperate position of the squadron. The movements of the destroyers which the Japanese had noticed had at first been directed to getting one of them through to Chifu. For four successive nights she tried, and each time found Japanese destroyers barring the way. Then as moon-light nights set in the attempt had to be abandoned, and the destroyers kept guard off the entrance. While thus engaged on November 11th and 13th three were disabled, and a fourth lost by mines,[2] and the defence of the roadstead had to be recon-sidered. A conference was accordingly held on the 15th. It so happened that on the 8th the gunboat *Otvazhni* which was the flagship of Admiral Loshchinski, the officer commanding the flotilla defence, had been disabled by an 11-inch shell, and, amongst other matters, it had to be decided what was to be done with her. Admiral Loshchinski earnestly begged to be allowed to take her out, and after two days' discussion his request was granted. He was to be permitted to anchor his ship under the shelter of Jo-to-san in the north of White Wolf Bay, and to take nets from the *Retvizan* to protect her from torpedo attack.

As to a sortie, the general view was that " the half-sunken " ships were unfit for active operations, and the thing to con- " sider, therefore, was not putting out to sea, but what to do in

---

[1] See *post*, pages 87 and 91.

[2] *Bditelni, Serditi, Silni, Stroini* (sunk).

" case of the fall of the fortress," and it was decided to grant
the Army's request for armour-piercing shell for the land front.
Against this decision Captain von Essen of the *Sevastopol* and
one other captain vehemently protested, arguing that the ammunition should be kept for combined action with the Baltic
Squadron. "The function of a fleet," he urged, "is to be at
" sea, and our duty at the first opportunity is to put to sea."
To his spirited counsel there was no response. So hopeless
indeed were the majority that a proposal had actually been
made for definitely blocking the gullet, but in deference to
his protest it was decided not to do so for the present, but
to close it with a torpedo-net boom. A pious opinion was also
expressed that the *Bayan* should be made ready to break out,
but for the rest of the ships the only thought was how best
to make an end of them. "In case of urgency," it was
formally resolved "—that is, should the capitulation of the
fortress be close at hand—the vessels which are in a state
" to move are to proceed to the gullet and be sunk near the
" blockships. In other cases everything possible is to be
' blown up." Finally, on a demand from General Stessel, it
was agreed that the destroyer *Rastoropni* should attempt to
break through to Chifu with mails, and ascertain the truth
about General Kuropatkin.[1]

Scarcely were these dispiriting resolutions arrived at when
they were disturbed by a demand from General Stessel that
at the next assault, which was seen to be close at hand, the
ships should go out to Cross Hill to keep down the fire of
the Japanese batteries at the other end of Ta-ho Bay, and
endeavour to prevent their ships firing on the defences of the
extreme Russian right as they had done before. On the 17th,
therefore, a second naval conference was called to consider the
demand. The reply was another *non possumus*. The *Sevastopol*,
Pobyeda and *Pallada* were the only ships that could move,
and all of them, from the nature of their gun-mountings, were
outranged by the enemy. They could only go out at high
water, and must return at night for fear of torpedo attack,
nor in any case could they take the position required without
elaborate sweeping or retain it in bad weather. They further
objected that it would require 300 ratings from the reserve
to man each battleship, and the men could be employed much
more effectively as they were, defending the land front. The

---

[1] *Russian Military History*, VIII., ii., 631 *et seq.*

considered decision, therefore, was that it was better for the defence of the fortress, that the ships should not go out, but that their crews should continue to assist the troops ashore [1] This opinion for devoting the fleet to the defence of the fortress " to the last projectile " was embodied in a memorandum by Admiral Viren, with a proviso that when the place was *in extremis*, the surviving destroyers would make a dash for Chifu and Kyau-chau and would be available for taking out the last reports and such documents as it was desired to preserve.

To this attitude of Admiral Viren, waiting in hopeless inactivity for the end, the feverish anxiety of the Japanese Admiral forms a curious contrast. By this time his impatience with the slow progress of the Army was intensified by the fact that he had now in sight the means by which the end he sought might be expedited. A week earlier (November 11th) a group of transports appeared which were carrying the first regiments of the VIIth Division to Dalny. Like the VIIIth it had been called up from its headquarters in the far north of Japan, but as yet it would seem that its destination had not been settled— at any rate it had not yet been allotted to General Nogi, and there was no reason to suppose it would not go north like the VIIIth Division. While it was in process of landing the General sent back a reply to the message which the Admiral had sent urging the extreme necessity of the rapid capture of Port Arthur.[2] It was to say that a conference of the Divisional Staffs had been held to consider his request, and the decision was that 203-Metre Hill could not be attacked at present since the engineers' work was not yet completed, but that the next general assault would be directed chiefly to the point desired.[3] Next day, as an indication of the time when the next general assault would take place, the General sent a further message to say that he expected to be able to blow up the counterscarp of both the forts of the northern salient, Sung-shu-shan and Erh-lung-shan before a week was out.

Such an answer could only be regarded as unsatisfactory. It meant that the fall of the fortress was still in the indefinite

---

[1] *Russian Military History*, VIII., ii., p. 634 *et seq.*

[2] The advance guard landed on the 12th at Dalny, the other groups arriving in succession, till by the 21st the whole fighting line was ashore. The General's reply came on the 13th.

[3] The assurance that 203-Metre Hill would be the main objective in the next assault is from the *Published History*, I., 233. The *Confidential History* does not mention it.

future ; but the Imperial Staff had already taken the question in hand. A decision must have been difficult in the extreme, and a most delicate matter to handle. On the 13th the Minister of Marine summoned to Tokyo Admiral Hosoya, who all along had been the point of contact between the two Services in the Port Arthur area, and was the man best able to inform them of the situation from the combined point of view. He left and Admiral Yamada took his place. But before he could arrive the Imperial Staff had come to a very serious decision, on the points at issue between General Nogi and the Fleet Staff. On the 15th, while in Port Arthur the Russian naval conference was deciding that all further action of the squadron was impossible, a telegram from Headquarters reached Admiral Togo to say that on the previous day a council had been held at Tokyo in the presence of the Emperor on the subject of naval and military strategy. The outcome of it was that the Chief of the General Staff had informed Marshal Oyama, "that if the situation at Port Arthur had not " progressed when the enemy's Second Pacific Squadron was " within a month's steaming of Japan, the Imperial Fleet must " raise the blockade, and most of it must be withdrawn to " the home country to prepare for the enemy, whether Port " Arthur had fallen or not." This, the message concluded, would have a very great influence upon the whole of the Japanese strategy. So serious indeed was the outlook that it outweighed all anxiety for Marshal Oyama's position on the Sha-ho, and at the same council it was decided that the VIIth Division must be added to the siege army.[1]

So far as is known this addition of force made no change in General Nogi's plans—at least not in the sense of a more direct and vigorous effort against 203-Metre Hill—and the situation remained as it was. It is true that on the 16th there was a ray of hope that the position had been misjudged. The Russian destroyer *Rastoropni* had managed to steal out and get into Chifu with what seemed to be highly urgent information. The inference was that an attempt was about to be made to break out. As we know, part of her message was that such an attempt was no longer possible ; but, as usual in war, the Japanese interpreted the intelligence by the light of their gravest anxiety, and immediate orders went forth for the utmost vigilance during the night. A torpedo-

---

[1] *Confidential History*, II., 239.

boat division was sent to Chifu to deal with the escaped destroyer, but with strict orders from Tokyo that no warlike steps were to be taken against her in the harbour as on the last occasion. The same evening (the 16th), probably anticipating a repetition of the last high-handed dealing, the *Rastoropni* blew herself up. In Port Arthur all remained quiet; there was no sign of movement, and in fact, as we know, the dash of the destroyer had only been made at General Stessel's demand, mainly with the view of seeking the truth about the incredible rumours that had reached the garrison of the defeat of General Kuropatkin's attempt to relieve them.

This incident, however, served to deepen the anxieties of the situation and to bring out in clear relief the precariousness of the Japanese prospects so long as a squadron existed in Port Arthur. From this time forward the need for its speedy destruction began definitely to override the needs of the Manchurian theatre; and if any doubt remained it was now removed by a clearing of the situation, which brought to a crisis the issue between the Naval and the General Staff.

CHAPTER VII.

203-METRE HILL.

[Maps IIIA, VII. Charts I, V.]

EVER since the Baltic Fleet in two divisions had left Tangier—one eastward up the Mediterranean and the other out into the Atlantic—its object had been wrapped in mystery. Admiral Rozhestvenski's course and whereabouts were entirely unknown, and the purpose of his dividing his fleet could not be fathomed. It raised a doubt as to whether his force was intended for the Far East at all, and for some time there were no indications on which the Japanese could act. It was not indeed till November 17th that the fog began to lift. On that day it was known that Admiral Rozhestvenski was coaling at Dakar in the French colony of Senegambia and the Imperial Staff was able to clear the points which hitherto had been uncertain and to arrive at a firm appreciation of what lay before them. The effect of the news is thus recorded : " A consideration of the " arrangements made by the Baltic Squadron leaves no doubt " that it is making for the Pacific. Calculating its voyage " from the distance it has covered up to to-day we can antici- " pate its arrival in the Straits of Formosa in the early part " of January. Now since working as fast as possible we " must allow two months to carry out the necessary refit " of the Fleet, if the operations at Port Arthur are prolonged " over the end of November our squadron will be obliged to " raise the blockade."[1]

This drastic decision was at once telegraphed to Admiral Togo by the Naval Staff with an explanation that two months would be required for a refit because the dockyards were not of a capacity to handle the whole fleet at once. Presumably it was also communicated to Marshal Oyama. At any rate Admiral Togo sent a staff officer to General Nogi to inform him of the new situation, improving the occasion with another effort to wean him away from his preoccupation with the formidable forts on his front of attack and to persuade him to devote himself to the points from which the fleet inside could be reached more directly. The gist of his message was, we

---

[1] *Japanese Published History*, I., 233-4.

are told, that the actual condition of the Combined Fleet
made it impossible for them to stay much longer in the Port
Arthur area and to reiterate the hope—from the Fleet's point of
view—that in the next assault 203-Metre Hill would be the
primary objective.

Startling as is the decision at which Headquarters had
arrived, there can be no doubt that it was taken deliberately,
and that the Imperial Staff were fully prepared to face the
possible consequences of not maintaining the fleet at sea
beyond the end of November. This is clear from a letter
which Admiral Ijuin wrote to Admiral Togo next day (the 18th),
which shows that they were contemplating having to leave the
all-important military base at Dalny to torpedo and mine
defence. "If by the end of the month," wrote Admiral Ijuin
on the 18th, "we have to recall the main force of the fleet
" must we not get ready two or three more coastal torpedo-
" boats in addition to the two at present in the Dalny district?"
In reply Admiral Togo asked for the necessary gear to be sent
out to him.

All this time the VIIth Division had been arriving at Dalny;
by the 21st its landing was complete; and General Nogi was
in a position to make his last great effort against the fortress
before the fleet had to leave. A Staff conference was held
this day at which it was decided that another attack should
be made at once. It would begin with a bombardment on
the 25th and a general assault was to follow next day; but
still General Nogi could not see his way to adopting the
objective which Admiral Togo desired. On the 22nd the
Admiral received from his emissary a telegram giving the
General's reply: "With regard," it said, "to the removal of
" the cause of anxiety which the Fleet has endured up to the
" present, the Army, although they have sworn to achieve
" success, find to their great regret that it would be impossible
" to seize 203-Metre Hill before all the other points." This
was followed on the 24th by an official intimation from the
Army Staff that the attack would begin next day on the
principal points of the northern defences from Sung-shu-shan
eastward to Chi-kuan-shan. They would then advance within
the *enceinte* to the chain of hills near Wang-tai—that is, the
heights behind Chi-kuan-shan which commanded the harbour—
and finally, if possible, would do their best to attack 203-Metre
Hill. A general signal to this effect was then made to the
Fleet with the usual warning to be ready for a sortie, the *Saiyen*

detachment at Louisa Bay being specially ordered to assist the Army on that side as its attack developed.

The fear that the Russian squadron would make an attempt to break away can hardly have been very serious. On the 21st a spy, who was employed in a ferry boat at Port Arthur, was able to report that the *Poltava, Peresvyet, Pobyeda, Pallada* and *Retvizan* were still crowded under Quail Hill. The holes in their sides had been stopped with iron plates and each kept a crew of about 100 men, except when they were called ashore to resist assaults. All seemed able to steam, except the *Sevastopol*, which was still in dock. Since that time, however, the Naval Heavy Gun Brigade had been doing effective work. On the 23rd they had got the range of the machine shops and had scored at least one hit on the *Peresvyet*. Next day they had established an observing station on 93-Metre Hill (south-west of the village of Shui-shih-ling), a point from which the ships could be seen, and so many hits were marked that there was little doubt, so the Naval Brigade reported, that they must have lost their power of steaming.

It was not till the 26th, a day late, that the bombardment began, and then, says the *Confidential History*, " the voices of " the guns in one long roll reverberated through ·heaven and " earth. The bursting of the shells of both armies near East " Chi-kuan-shan was a most inspiring spectacle." Next day the assault was delivered and the Fleet waited eagerly for the result without any possibility of assisting, or even of discerning what was going on. Such scraps of news as reached the ships were not inspiriting. " There was a mist over Port " Arthur," says the same authority, " and nothing could be " seen of the enemy's movements. Many telegrams about " the battle on shore came in from the morning onwards. " The Third Army, with its reinforcements of fresh troops, " made bold attacks and surprises, but our losses were so " great that we were unable to attain our object." In the afternoon, in fact, it was known that General Nogi's plan had failed.

Three successive assaults on the forts had been repulsed with enormous slaughter, and very little ground had been gained. Still, we are told, he was for persevering ·and bringing up the whole of the VIIth Division, which hitherto had been in reserve in rear of his centre. But to the westward certain demonstrations had been going on in the direction of 203-Metre Hill, and the result of reports from that quarter and elsewhere finally convinced him that its capture was the easier task.[1] He therefore decided, while keeping up a demonstration on his chosen front of attack, to move the whole of the VIIth Division to his right and deliver on the position the Navy coveted a full-power attack with all he could combine by land and sea. Of this resolution he informed the Admiral early on the 27th, saying that the attack would open at 6.0 that evening. Orders were promptly sent to the *Saiyen* detachment to assist from the swept area, and the *Akagi* was despatched to Louisa Bay to reinforce it, with orders to go as close inshore as was safe and to carry on till her assistance was no longer required.

Then for four days that famous struggle for the point on which hung the fate of the Russian Squadron raged almost without intermission. The heroism of the defence was only equalled by the desperation of the attack, and for long its end hung in the balance. Early on the 28th Admiral Togo got a message to say that one of the enemy's trenches near the summit had been captured during the night after two assaults, and the Army was resolved not to stop till they had gained their object. Next morning he heard they had established themselves the night before on the summit, but in the early hours of the morning they had been dislodged. Still they had sworn to capture the hill; the whole VIIth Division and all the reserves were now in position and the attack would be renewed.

On the 30th the effort was made, but again it was the same story. In spite of appalling losses and almost superhuman endurance the splendid resistance of the devoted Russian band that still clung to the shell-swept summit could not be broken, and to complete the depression word came in that another invaluable coast-defence ship had shared the fate of the *Heiyen* in her efforts to assist the attack. In the early afternoon the *Saiyen* had closed in to about a mile from shore between Pigeon and Louisa Bays and there at 2.40 had fouled a mine. It took her under her forward boiler room which was smashed open eight feet below the water line, and in three minutes she had disappeared, carrying with her Captain Tamba, who had so long commanded the detachment on its desperate service, three of his officers, and 34 other ratings.

This double check, by sea as well as by land, was not a little disturbing. It was the last day of November, the day

---

[1] *Japanese Published History*, II., 131.

on which the General had to expect that the Fleet might be
withdrawn. What was to be done ? How was he to face
the completion of the siege if the blockade was raised ?
What he did was to hasten to assure the Admiral that he
was not yet beaten, and that he meant now to proceed in
accordance with the naval view. The hill, he said, had no
permanent works, it was exposed to severe artillery punishment, and he therefore meant to bombard it heavily and try
again ; and he ended with a frank appeal to the Admiral not
to desert him. "The loss of the *Saiyen* at this juncture," he
said, "is very much to be regretted. The assistance rendered
" by the Fleet to the Army up to now is a cause of deep
" gratitude, and we are much grieved that this great mis-
" fortune should have occurred at this moment. We are
" bitterly disappointed that my Army's object in seizing
" 203-Metre Hill has not yet been fully attained, but we are
" putting forward our full force and doing our utmost to
" achieve it. Once we have occupied it, we shall be able
" to settle the fate of the ships in the harbour. This being
" the situation I must earnestly ask the assistance of part
" of your Fleet, though they must risk their existence in
" giving it."[1]

The message is curious, for the same day the Naval Staff
officer who was attached to the Third Army's headquarters
reported to Admiral Yamada that as the Army did not
urgently require the assistance of the detachment he thought
it would be advisable to recall the *Akagi* as soon as her
rescue work was done. The explanation is that General
Nogi seems to have been thinking of the blockade rather than
tactical assistance from the ships. "We have always hoped,"
he said in concluding his appeal, "that the prevention of
" blockade running might be complete, and I must now beg
" that you will make arrangements to that end so far as you
" can without risking the safety of our all-important men-of-
" war. On learning of the disaster to the *Saiyen* I hurriedly
" bring this to your notice."

To this appeal the Admiral did not turn a deaf ear. Some
advance had certainly been made and no order came from
Tokyo to withdraw. The fleet remained where it was and
next day, though the remainder of the *Saiyen* detachment was
recalled, the Hwang-ching-tau Preventive Squadron was ordered
to take its place and maintain the blockade of that part of

---

[1] *Confidential History*, II., 244.

the coast. Nor was it without good cause that the departure of the Fleet was delayed; for it so happened that the gloomy situation on 203-Metre Hill had unexpectedly improved. The previous evening the advanced troops had succeeded in re-establishing themselves on part of the summit, and were still holding it in spite of the most desperate efforts of the enemy to dislodge them. What had made it impossible for them to maintain a complete hold on 203-Metre Hill was the enfilading fire from the summit of the adjoining hill Akasaka-yama; this position they had now captured, and a sanguine message came in that they were ready to go any lengths to make good their occupation of the whole of the hill.

Admiral Togo replied with a cordial message that showed how deeply he felt the sacrifices the Army was compelled to make, and left no doubt he meant to stand by his colleague. "The Combined Fleet," he telegraphed, "offer from warm " hearts their congratulations on the great victory achieved " by your Army in seizing, with your invincible spirit and " after a protracted struggle, a position from which you " may pronounce sentence of death upon the Port Arthur " Squadron. We wish to express our deep sympathy for the " loss of so many officers and men."

This was confirmed next day (December 2nd) by a message from the Naval Staff at Tokyo showing they regarded the position as practically won. Although at this time it was known that Admiral Rozhestvenski had reached the Gaboon in the French Congo, and that Admiral Felkerzam's Division had passed down the Red Sea from Suez, there was no suggestion of raising the blockade. They had heard that an observing station had been erected on the south-west shoulder of the hill which the Japanese had occupied and were expecting the destruction of the fleet to begin at once. All they had to ask was that when the bombardment opened the General would "fire a large number of shells in the shortest " possible time to give the enemy no leisure to extricate " themselves from their difficulties."

This sanguine view did not last long. The report that an observing station had been established was itself premature. The belief that the point in question commanded the harbour had, however, been confirmed and the place reported fit for a station. Ten ships at least could be clearly located and the Naval Officer commanding the observation party was sent up to get the work done.

He arrived to find the chosen spot the centre of a furious hand grenade fight between the two sides. The fact was, that at 1.0 oclock that morning the Russians with heroic persever- ance had begun a desperate counter-attack to recover the position. All night assault after assault was delivered, which as reinforcements came up reached a culmination at 7.0 a.m. Nothing could withstand the energy and determination of the Russian effort, and at last the Japanese were driven back not only from the south-west shoulder, but also from the adjoining height of Akasaka-yama.

It was a terrible set-back, for so costly had been the fights to the Japanese that there was no immediate prospect of their being able even to attempt to recover the lost ground. In communicating the melancholy news to the Admiral, the General explained that they still held the north-east shoulder o. 203 and as soon as possible would renew the struggle ; but at present the men were exhausted with hunger and fatigue, the regiments were all mixed up together and some time must be taken to rest and reorganise the troops. Up to date he had lost in killed and wounded some 23,000 men, but he de- clared he meant to increase the attacking force as much as he possibly could and drive back the enemy to the limit of his power. The Naval Officer in charge of the observing party stated in his report that the Army expected to enable him to establish a sufficiently secure observing station on the following day, but in his opinion it was impossible to forecast the time at which the whole summit could finally be occupied. In reply, the Admiral sent another warm message of sympathy and added to it an offer of practical assistance. On receipt of a request from the General he was ready to organise another Naval Brigade and send it to attack the enemy before they could recover from their difficulties.

No request came, nor was the attack renewed on the 3rd. On the other hand, no recall came for the Fleet, nor did Admiral Togo suggest it. All he did was to telegraph to the ships of his command that were under refit in the home ports, that they must hurry on the work to the utmost and that the crews must assist, since there was no telling when the situation at Port Arthur would alter.[1] It is clear that the idea of raising the blockade was abandoned for the present, but the risk that

---

[1] The *A'sahi* returned from Sasebo on November 29th ; Admiral Nashiba shifted his flag to her, and the *Shikishima* was sent home. The *Yakumo*

was run in still maintaining it must have been patent ; for on December 1st Admiral Rozhestvenski sailed from the Gaboon to the southward, and next day the Felkerzam Division was sighted from Perim passing out of the Red Sea.[1] It was also known that a third division was leaving the Baltic.[2]

The line the reinforcing fleet would take was, of course, still obscure. That the two advanced squadrons would unite might now be assumed, but where the junction would take place and how the combined fleet would proceed there was as yet nothing to determine. The appreciation of the Imperial Staff at this time was that they had to face three hypotheses : (1) The enemy, in spite of all the difficulties, might proceed direct to Vladivostok and make it their base of operations ; (2) they might proceed through northern Chinese waters into the Yellow Sea and there endeavour to re-establish their beaten forces ; or (3) they might seize a harbour in the vicinity of Formosa or on the south coast of China and there await an opportunity of carrying out one or other of the aforesaid operations. On this appreciation their conclusion was as follows : " In order to " enable our Fleet to manœuvre as circumstances may require " it was necessary to profit by our geographical position, that " our forces in all quarters could call on each other and " respond, and that in every direction they should be rapidly " informed of the enemy's movements."[3] The key of the problem was, in fact, intelligence and rapid communication.

So long as Port Arthur held out it was impossible to say whether that port or Vladivostok would be the Russian destination ; but, as regards the third hypothesis, something could be done at once to fix the probabilities. The region by which the new force would approach the theatre of war must be reconnoitred

---

arrived refitted on the 15th and became Admiral Dewa's flagship, while the *Tokiwa* was sent to refit at Kuré. On the 18th the gunboat *Tsukushi* arrived at Chemulpho to relieve the *Matsushima*, which then went to Yokosha to refit.

[1] It is not quite certain that the Japanese Staff knew this. Lloyd's agent reported it on December 2nd, but on December 5th the staff orders to the cruisers detailed for reconnaissance (*see* next page) only mentioned that on November 21 the main force had coaled in Namaqualand and that the Felkerzam Division had left Suez.

[2] This was known officially as the "Overtaking Division." It consisted of the two belated cruisers *Oleg* and *Izumrud*, with the *Smolensk* and *Peterburg* (now on the Navy List as *Rion* and *Dnyepr*), the armed transport *Okean* and five destroyers one of which was left at Algiers. The *Okean* went back from Tangier.

[3] *Japanese Published History*, Part IV., ch. i., sec. 1.

even at the cost of weakening the blockade, and accordingly, a few days after the *Hongkong Maru* and the *Nippon Maru* had joined Admiral Togo's flag to replace the cruisers he was sending home, he received a telegram asking if they were in a fit state for a voyage as far as Singapore. This was followed on November 29th by a definite order that he must part with them. "We consider it most advantageous," so the Staff telegram ran, "that before the arrival of the Baltic Fleet we " should reconnoitre such straits and bays on the coasts of " Cochin-China and among the islands of the Malay Archi- " pelago as might be passed or visited by them, and accord- " ingly we desire you to send these two ships back to Japan" to refit for this service. They were at once recalled from their blockade stations in the Pe-chi-li Gulf and next day left for Sasebo.

Their special mission, it will be seen, was to go forward quite outside the theatre of war in search of intelligence which would throw light on the line of the enemy's approach. For examining the area in which an advanced base might be formed and the concentration of the Baltic squadrons completed a further call was made on Admiral Togo's blockading force, and the *Niitaka*, then under refit at Yokoska, was put in orders for a reconnaissance of the Formosa zone and the coasts of Southern China.

There still remained the question of refitting the fleet, seeing that it was felt impossible to recall it at the moment. Much, however, could be done by speeding up the work on the ships as they could be spared in succession, and to this end, on December 10th, all commandants of dockyards and naval ports were summoned to Tokyo and there impressed with the vital necessity of carrying out the refit with utmost possible energy.

Meanwhile, General Nogi had been hard at work perfecting his arrangements, but so severe had been the punishment that it was not till December 4th, that he was able to announce that he was in a position to renew the fight for 203-Metre Hill. He intended to begin next day and hoped also at the same time to open on the ships which they had been able to locate. It seems clear that feeling in the Fleet was depressed and that there was little expectation of success, for we are told that when during the afternoon there came news of an improvement in the situation it was quite unexpected. But the fact was, that the splendid endurance of the Russian defence was at last exhausted. The bombardment of the past few days had reduced their works to a heap of ruins, their heroic chief, Colonel Tretyakov, who at 203-Metre Hill had surpassed all he had done even at Nan-shan, had been carried to the rear wounded ; his splendid regiment was a mere wreck ; his two successors had been quickly struck down ; scarcely any officers were left, and no reinforcement could face the storm of shrapnel that desolated the rear slopes of the hill. On the other hand, the Japanese were able continually to send up comparatively fresh troops and their attack was overwhelming. In three hours they had retaken the south-west shoulder, and while an observing station was rapidly improvised they pressed on to the summit. By five o'clock the whole top was in their possession and the Naval observation party had established telephonic communication. As it was late, and at 6.30 the Russians made a desperate counter-attack, little good could be done in the way of fire direction that evening, but the *Poltava* was certainly hit badly. For two or three hours the efforts of the Russians to recover their loss continued, but by midnight all was over, and the line of heights of which 203-Metre Hill was the centre was abandoned to the exhausted Japanese. " Now," said General Kondratenko as he gave the order to retire, " now begins the death agony of Port " Arthur."[1]

---

[1] Schwarz and Romanovski, *Défense de Port Arthur* (trans. Lepoivre), Vol. II., p. 442.

CHAPTER VIII.

Destruction of the Ships in Port Arthur and the Torpedo Attacks on the "Sevastopol."
[Map IIIB, Charts, I, V, VIII.]

So ended an affair which is perhaps the most striking feature of the war, as it certainly was its turning point. Seldom has there been a case when the fortunes of a struggle for interests so great and in so vast an area turned so conspicuously on the possession of a few rods of barren rock.

It marked, in fact, one of those advances in the art of war which occur as the power of weapons develops, but which do not always declare themselves till some special experience forces them to the light. The reaction of the continually increasing range and destructive effect of artillery on the attack and defence of fortresses had of course been abundantly studied, but continental artillerists and engineers had naturally concentrated their attention on land fortresses, where the protected objective was an army only. The modification of the conditions for a sea fortress where the protected objective is a fleet had escaped notice. But here was a case in point which had not been taken into adequate consideration. It was a case of dealing not merely with a fortress and its garrison, but of dealing with a fleet that refuses to hazard fortune in the open. Rich as is British experience of such operations, they were almost a sealed book on the Continent, and no sooner was the unfamiliar problem confronted than certain well-known features were found to have assumed a new character.

The importance of 203-Metre Hill had long been recognised by the Russians, but in common with Liau-ti-shan it was looked upon as an outpost which commanded the fortress. Up to the outbreak of the war current military doctrine had regarded such points as vital only when they were liable to be turned into artillery positions by the enemy, and as in both cases the ground was extremely difficult for effecting such a purpose, all suggestions for regularly fortifying them had been laid aside. The danger they menaced was not sufficiently serious, as military science then stood, to outweigh the economic need of reducing expenditure on the fortress, and of not extending its defence beyond the manning capacity of the garrison. It is, of course, not to be asserted that the progress of high-angle fire had not already called attention to the new importance of such points as fire-control stations, but the new element in the art of war had not yet obtained so general a recognition as would avail to override the older views. For this reason, it is said, both points had been neglected.[1]

It was not till May, after the final Japanese bombardments had emphasised the real dangers, that work for the defence of 203-Metre Hill had been begun, and as the Japanese efforts seemed to be more and more directed to it as an objective, so the works had been continually improved and extended. But it was nothing more than a field work in the end and quite incapable of withstanding the heavy guns which eventually the Japanese were able to bring against it. Had anything in the nature of the permanent forts of the east and north fronts been found there it seems undeniable that the course of the war must have been profoundly affected. So far as can be seen the Japanese would have been compelled to raise the naval blockade before the Russian Squadron had been destroyed and before they had secured a death grip on the fortress. Had that happened the Baltic Fleet would have had quite another significance, and, as the Russians themselves put it, " a check at sea might have deprived the Japanese of all " they had gained on land."

---

[1] Schwarz and Romanovski, II., 66. The views of these two distinguished officers are confirmed by the *Russian Naval History*. It relates that after the Japanese bombardment of March 22nd Admiral Makarov telegraphed to ' St. Petersburg for H.E. and A.P. shell to reply to the enemy's ships, saying he had secured hits at 14 versts (16,300 yards) with high-angle fire. On this telegram Admiral Rozhestvenski, as Chief of the Staff, made a sarcastic and incredulous comment. The Minister of Marine referred it to the Central Artillery Department, who expressed the view that A.P. shell was only effective at decisive ranges (say 3 versts or 3,500 yards) and dismissed somewhat contemptuously the idea of bombardment at ranges "which would only give a few accidental hits." Thereupon Admiral Makarov called for a Joint Conference at Port Arthur, and in accordance with its resolutions telegraphed home that the Artillery Department clearly did not understand the question. He repeated his claim that by hits at $13\frac{1}{2}$ versts he had stopped the last Japanese bombardment, and he finished by claiming to have the matter referred to the Tsar. The result was that the Artillery Department had to order 1,000 A.P. shell from Krupp (*Russian Naval History*, I., 440-4).

Engineer Byelov, of the *Sevastopol*, describes the effect of one indirect hit from the *Nisshin's* 9-inch guns in March as much more serious than any of the direct 12-inch hits she received on August 10th (*Morsko: Sbornik*, January 1906).

Why General Nogi did not make these heights his first objective has never been clearly explained. So destitute was the whole area of adequate defences against an attack in force that the neglect of the Japanese remained to the Russians a mystery to the end. But it is quite conceivable that the Japanese Army were as little alive to the new development as the Russians; that in their eyes the western heights were merely commanding positions in the old sense and were therefore excluded as objectives by their German-taught theories of direct action. Loyal as was the co-operation between the two Japanese Services, the Imperial Staff seems to have failed to fathom the whole of the special consequences that an amphibious war entails, with the result that the mutual deflections of purely naval and military methods were never thought out to a logical conclusion. From first to last the idea of making 203-Metre Hill the primary objective was a naval idea. It is true a general belief has prevailed that the Imperial Staff had given an order for the position to be taken at all costs, but of this there is no endorsement in the *Confidential History*. According to that, the highest authority we have, the naval view was not forced upon the Army. Categorically, Marshal Oyama was merely given a limit beyond which he was not to expect the co-operation of the Fleet in the siege of Port Arthur. At the end of that period the blockade would have to be raised, and this would mean not only that General Nogi's army would be faced with the disheartening task of besieging a fortress open to the sea, but the communications of the army in Manchuria would be liable to interruption by the Russian squadron. Such a warning, it would have been thought, should have been enough to indicate the necessity of modifying purely military methods, so far at least as to a frank recognition of the squadron as the main objective demanded such modification. But yet nothing was done till, at the eleventh hour, the eyes of the Army Staff were opened by hard facts they could not longer blink. In spite of the Imperial Staff's warning, till the specified period had actually expired General Nogi persisted in making his main attack on the permanent works of the fortress, and only when he was at last face to face with the threatened withdrawal of the Fleet did he turn his strength against the Naval objective.

On the naval side it must be said there appears to have been a deeper appreciation of the deflections which the nature of the war entailed, at least in the view of the Commander-in-

Chief. For we have seen how ready Admiral Togo was, even in despite of his superiors at Tokyo, and at great risk, to modify orthodox naval methods in conformity with the needs of his colleague ashore. His efforts to give tactical assistance to the Army were, indeed, of little avail, but failure and loss did nothing to change his view of what a naval Commander-in-Chief owes to a General in the same theatre of operations as himself.

The apparent failure of the Japanese to rise to the full height of combined service may not, however, be so marked as it seems, for in judging their plan of operation there remains at least one other point to take into consideration. The height known as Wang-tai or " Eagle's Nest " lay immediately behind General Nogi's front of attack, and it was believed to command a clear view of the whole of the harbour, whereas there seems to have been some doubt as to whether 203-Metre Hill did so entirely. So much at least we must conclude from the fact that in the Fleet the full extent of the success that had been gained by the occupation of 203-Metre Hill was scarcely realised. By nightfall on the day of the capture (December 5th) the shore-observing stations reported that an 11-inch shell had exploded the *Poltava's* magazines and sunk her, while the *Retvizan* was seen to be heeling 10 degrees and the *Pobyeda* seriously damaged. But in the fleet the news was received with incredulity. Having no experience of indirect fire they could not believe it could sink a well-protected ship. All they expected was to see them rendered incapable of fighting by the destruction of their top sides.[1]

But the truth was soon evident. From the new observing station there were found to be clearly in view in the western basin four battleships, *Peresvyet*, *Poltava*, *Retvizan* and *Pobyeda*, and the cruiser *Pallada*. Partly hidden in the eastern basin were the *Bayan* and *Amur*, while only the masts of the *Sevastopol* could be seen as she lay in the eastern basin. On the 6th as the morning mist lifted the 11-inch howitzers opened, using the new observation station, while naval guns were directed from the old one on 93-Metre Hill east of Division Hill.[2] The main battery of howitzers was near the village of Tien-han-kou, behind Headquarter Hill with a range of about 8,000 yards, while four other pieces joined in from the north-

---

[1] *Attaché Reports*, II., 66.   [2] Hill 305, Map IIIB.

east near Chu-chia-tun beyond the Ta-ho.[1] That day 280 rounds of 11-inch were fired and all the ships in the western basin were seen to be hit many times. Next day (the 7th) the bombardment continued with even more satisfactory results, and by the end of it the *Retvizan* was also sinking. For two days longer the hail of shells continued and by the evening of the 8th the *Pobyeda*, *Pallada* and *Gilyak* had been sunk, the *Peresvyet*, reduced to a wreck, had been scuttled, and the *Bayan* was in flames.

Of all the fine squadron on which the Russian war plan had been founded only the *Sevastopol* remained. Up till now she had been left alone, but she was to be taken in hand next day, and till she was settled Admiral Togo remained as he was. Still he felt justified in reducing the blockading force at once and this day the *Iwate* and *Asama* were sent home to refit, leaving him with three battleships and two armoured cruisers. The new arrangements which, as we have seen, had been made for refitting the fleet in batches were probably now regarded as all that the circumstances required. Admiral Rozhestvenski had been almost five months out and had been last reported at Great Fish Bay in the extreme south of the Portuguese West African territory where he had coaled, and Admiral Felkerzam was off Jibuti.[2] By its rate of progress, therefore, the Baltic Fleet was not yet within another two months steaming of the seat of war, while the "overtaking" cruiser division was only just entering the Mediterranean.

The relief felt by the Japanese at the destruction of the Port Arthur Squadron is only to be measured by the depression it caused in the spirit of the garrison. Coming as it did after the disastrous end of their nine days' defence of 203-Metre Hill, the sight of the ships perishing one by one with no power of saving them is described as plunging the Russians into something like despair. Still the *Sevastopol* was afloat. Hitherto she had been struck only five times by 11-inch shell and the slight damage done had been repaired, but it was

---

[1] *Japanese Published History*, II., 143. The 11-inch howitzers with a muzzle velocity of 1,020 feet had at 45° elevation a range of 12,242 yards, charge 16½ lbs. smokeless powder; weight of projectile, 480 lbs. (*Attaché Report*, II., 108).

[2] The arrival of the Felkerzam Division at Jibuti was reported in the Press on December 5th. On the 9th the main division was known to our N.I.D. to have reached Great Fish Bay on the 6th and to have sailed next day after coaling.

clear her turn was coming, and that the Japanese, having disposed of the rest, would now devote their attention to her.
She was still commanded by Captain von Essen, who as
captain of the *Novik* had won in Japanese estimation the
highest reputation in the war, and it was a situation under which
such a man could not rest inactive.[1]

For some time he had been bent on breaking out, and ever
since his repairs had been completed he had been doing the
best he could to coal with the slender remains of his crew.
In a month he had managed to get 700 tons aboard, and by
refusing to obey orders to send ammunition ashore had
succeeded in retaining about 25 rounds per gun. But part
of his secondary armament and all his quick-firers were in
position on the land front. In such a condition he could not
expect to go far or to fight a serious action, but when after
the capture of 203-Metre Hill the bombardment began, he
begged to be allowed to go outside, protesting he was ready
for sea. His request was made at a Conference of Flag-
officers and Captains which was held on the evening of the
6th to consider the new situation. At first Admiral Viren
consented, and the question was raised as to whether the net-
boom that closed the entrance should be given him to protect
his ship outside and the gullet be blocked by sinking in it
all ships that could still move. The result of the discussion
was that the Admiral changed his mind and refused Captain
von Essen's request. However, on the night of the 8th–9th,
after the destruction of the other ships, he returned to the
charge, and after "long and vehement entreaties" he was
allowed to put to sea. The Admiral said, " Very well : do what
" you think best," but his request for more men was still
refused.[2]

For Captain von Essen that was enough. He had only
40 men on board, but somehow he managed to scrape together

---

[1] He had been one of Admiral Makarov's special appointments, like
Captain Vasilev to the *Tzesarevich* and Schulz to the *Novik*, which almost
led to a rupture with Admiral Alexeiev. The Viceroy had candidates of
his own whom he pressed upon the Minister of Marine. Admiral Makarov,
however, insisted on the necessity of appointing his own commanding
officers if he was to carry on, and five days before his death he telegraphed
that if these appointments were overridden the Admiralty must find
someone else to take his place as Commander-in-Chief. Upon this threat
the Viceroy had to give way. (*Russian Naval History*, I., 450–1.)

[2] *Russian Military History*, Vol. VIII., Part ii., page 636; and *Proceedings of the Port Arthur Court Martial*, pages 692–4 (Rear-Admiral von
Essen's evidence).

about 60 more, and then under his own steam began to make
his way out. It was no easy matter. There had been no time
to remove the boom, but he managed to ram his way through
it and came to anchor outside near some of the sunken
blockships. The spot was in clear view of 203-Metre Hill,
but about two miles further out on the northern extremity of
White Wolf Bay there was a berth completely protected by
the heights on which stood the Jo-to-san Forts. Here ever
since the first week in November the *Otvazhni* had been lying
in comparative security, and Captain von Essen decided to join
her till he was in a condition to put to sea.[1]

The roadstead was full of Japanese mines, but as the tide
fell they came to the surface and were easily avoided, and he
succeeded in anchoring safely close to the shore and in line with
the *Otvazhni*. As originally arranged certain measures had been
taken to protect the gunboat. A little to the southward and
seaward, where the cliffs of Tiger Peninsula fall away to the low-
lying isthmus, she had installed her searchlight and two of
her 3-pounder guns, and in addition had constructed a boom
defence to protect her bows. Captain von Essen took steps to
do likewise. The necessary guns with some more ammunition
were coming out in lighters as well as 200 men whom Admiral
Viren sent off to him. As soon as they arrived the nets were
got out and work commenced to extend them round the
unprotected bows. The extra men would only bring his
crew up to half his complement, but ill-found and ill-manned
as he was, he says it was still his intention to take advantage
of the first dark night to break the blockade and put to sea,
and there is little doubt he would have made the attempt had
not the Admiral sent him a categorical order forbidding it.[2]

Compelled to remain inactive where he was, he set to work
to get in position the boom which was towed out to him and
from day to day the work went on under fire. To complete the
position, the two duty destroyers were at his request instructed
to anchor inshore of him to stop attacks from that side. The
weakest point of the arrangement was that, besides the

---

[1] She must have been in the north of White Wolf Bay and not in the
south as shown on the chart in *Attaché Reports*, III., 38. Captain von
Essen says he anchored off the White Wolf Hill (*ibid.*, page 232), and on
December 18th (after he had moved nearer in) the Japanese observing
station fixed the position as " S. 10° E., 5½ cables from the top of 416
hill of Jo-to-san." *Confidential History*, Vol. II., p. 253).

[2] Captain von Essen's evidence, *ubi supra*.

Otvazhni's 3-pounders, there was no anti-torpedo-boat armament available. The battleship had only her two forward 12-inch and four 6-inch left and the gunboat one old 9-inch and two badly-mounted 12-pounders. The destroyers that were available could bring to bear no more than seven 12-pounders and ten 47-mm. Still the various batteries commanding the anchorage could give a good deal of support and develop a considerable fire on attacking flotillas.[1]

The movement was made none too soon, for on the morning of the 9th 11-inch shells began to rain upon the spot where the *Sevastopol* had been lying. This led the Russians to believe that her exit had not been detected. But, in fact, it had been seen at daylight, and by 7.30 both the *Chinyen* and *Fuso* reported to Admiral Togo, as he was coming in from his night position, that she was moving in the roadstead. He immediately sent ahead the two remaining armoured cruisers of his division to watch her closely, and suspecting an attempt to get to Chifu or Kyau-chau, directed the *Chiyoda* to watch that line, doubled the destroyer patrol, and took the battleships up to the Encounter Rock position. Shortly after 11.0 he was there, and by that time knew the *Sevastopol* had anchored under Jo-to-san. As the hours passed and she made no move, he proceeded with arrangements for the night for preventing her escape or torpedoing her where she lay. With the battle division he would fall back to the "First Watch Line," that is off Shantung Promontory, while the cruiser divisions and destroyers maintained the usual night patrols.[2] For the torpedo attack the destroyers were not to be used; their blockade duties absorbed all their remaining power and they were probably

---

[1] The batteries in question, according to the official plan, were—

White Wolf—Four 3-pounder Q.F. and four field guns.

No. 1.—Two field guns.

No. 2.—Five 6-inch Canet and searchlight.

No. 3.—Two field guns, two 6-pounder Q.F. and searchlight.

No. 4.—Four 9-inch howitzers and two 6-pounder Q.F.

Lieut. Dudorov, however, only mentions as immediately bearing two 6-inch at White Wolf and two 47 mm. in the Signal Battery (*Japanese Pub. History*, I. 261, *Russian note*).

[2] Detailed orders for the battle division were—3.0 p.m., proceed S.E. ½ E. (magnetic) at 10 knots. 6.0, reduce to 7 knots. 2.0 a.m. (off Shantung), alter to S., except *Nisshin* and *Kasuga*, who were to hold on. At 7.0 a.m. all turn 16 points. *Tatsuta* between squadron and mainland from 2.0 till 7.0; *Yaeyama* to stop two-thirds of distance between Port Arthur and Shantung to keep up wireless connection (*Attaché Reports*, II., 95).

regarded as in themselves too valuable to be risked.   Even the
torpedo-boat flotilla was to be husbanded, for the Commander-
in-Chief's orders to Admiral Yamada were to arm the minelayers
of the Dalny Defence Flotilla and two picket-boats (*Mikasa's*
and *Fuso's*) for the attack.   He was also to endeavour to lay
mines that night and the next to cut off the *Sevastopol's* retreat
into harbour.   One torpedo-boat division only, the 14th, was
ordered to attack if the weather was favourable.   But here there
seems to have been some confusion.   For Captain Imai of the
Chinyen, who was at the observation point off Ping-tu-tau, says
that he got orders for the 9th and 15th divisions to attack.   All
these divisions were first-class boats belonging to the blockade
patrols.   Admiral Yamada had also ordered all his divisions to
prepare for attack and assemble at Ping-tu-tau, but the idea
of their attacking was subsequently abandoned either by superior
order or on account of the weather.[1]

Winter had now set in with unusual severity.   There were
continual gales with heavy seas and snow squalls and very
low temperatures.   On this night, it is said, "there was a strong
" northerly gale and the sky was full of yellow dust which
" came right over the sea and covered even the ships.   With
" it there was hail and snow and intense cold, which froze
" the spray as it fell on the decks."   Nevertheless the 9th and
15th divisions went in.   The three boats of the 9th reported
they had found the enemy and had fired between them eight
long-range torpedoes at from 1,000 to 2,000 metres, but that
they were rolling so heavily that accurate laying was impossible and they had been unable to see what the effect had
been.   The four boats of the 15th division had also gone in
in two subdivisions; but all of them were so blinded by the
glare of the enemy's searchlights on the snow that they could
find nothing to fire at.   As for the Russians, they were not
even aware that an attack had been made.

---

[1] The various Japanese official accounts of the *Sevastopol* episode are
not easy to reconcile.   Chapter XVI. of the *Confidential History* is devoted
to it, and for the actual attacks this account has been followed.   But
the orders under which the boats acted are given or referred to in
various sections of Chapter XV., especially Section 1, "Summary";
Section VI., "Movements of the Seventh Division," and Section VIII.,
"Movements of the Torpedo-Boat Flotillas," and these do not always
agree with the statements in Chapter XVI.   There is also a condensed
account in the *Published Naval History*, Part I., Chapter XVII., Section 2.
There seems certainly to have been some confusion owing to the
delegation of command, for, as will be seen, the direction of the
operation was twice changed.

All day the gale continued with such severity that communication with the shore broke down, and it was very difficult to pass orders to the flotilla. But as the *Sevastopol* was reported still in the same position, and Admiral Togo on his return to Round Island had received an urgent telegram from the Staff at Tokyo that he must not permit her the glory of escaping, he had to make the best arrangements he could. The plan he formed was to keep the *Mikasa* permanently at Round Island where he could control everything, and to send the rest of his division under Admiral Kataoka to hold the First Watch Line till further orders. His chief fear was that in the weather that prevailed the *Sevastopol* might get away to Chifu, and then steal down the coast to Kyauchau. Admiral Dewa was therefore told off to watch the Chifu line with his division, which now consisted of the *Yakumo*, *Takasago*, *Otowa*, and the Korean gun-vessel *Yobu*. Rear-Admiral Togo was patrolling alone in the *Akashi* between Encounter Rock and the Miau-tau Islands.[1]

The orders for the torpedo attack contemplated something more drastic than the night before. All the patrol torpedo-boats and everything attached to the Dalny force, except boats employed in despatch running and those under repair, were to be used, and the senior divisional commander was given entire charge. It seems doubtful, however, whether the order ever got through correctly, but in any case the gale, which was blowing harder than ever, rendered all flotilla operations impossible. Not a boat could even reach the rendezvous at Ping-tu-tau, and the *Sevastopol* had another·day's respite to complete her defences.

But this was by no means the worst. About 8.0 that night (the 10th), when the gale was at its worst, the *Mikasa* at Round Island took in a signal from the *Akashi* to say she had struck a mine. Admiral Togo immediately ordered Admiral Dewa, who was nearest, to go to her assistance, but soon after cancelled the order and told the *Hashidate* and *Itsukushima* to go instead with all the Ping-tu-tau flotilla. The two ships started at once, but the weather was too bad for the order to be passed to the flotilla, and it did not move.

It was eleven miles south of Encounter Rock that the *Akashi's* accident had occurred. The mine took her abaft the

---

[1] The *Suma* was going home to refit, *Chiyoda* was at Hwang-ching-au, and *Idzumi* had gone for water, etc., to Dalny.

starboard anchor davit, and ripped a hole that opened six feet or more upwards from her armoured deck. Three compartments flooded at once, and she was down by the bows with a list to starboard. Seeing what the weather was, she was thus in a really desperate condition. "There was a strong " north wind," says her report, "with a force up to six ; the " sea was high so that she rolled a great deal : it was a very " dark night and bitterly cold ; the upper deck was covered " with ice, and the frozen ropes were almost impossible to " handle." Still by closing the flooded compartments and shoring up the bulkheads, she was able to clear most of the water, and by shifting coal and stores to correct the list. Emergency repairs were then taken in hand, and by 11.30 when the two cruisers of the Fifth Division reached her she was out of immediate danger. By dawn she was able to proceed with them very slowly under her own steam towards Dalny, which she reached by midday on the 12th, a feat of seamanship of which the Japanese Navy might well feel proud.

All day on the 11th the gale and the cold continued undiminished—the thermometer reading 17° below freezing point, and the whole surface of the sea being white with spray. Consequently no orders were issued by the Commander-in-Chief for the flotilla. Owing to the *Akashi's* disaster, however, the watch had to be re-arranged, and Admiral Dewa was told to do his best to occupy the Pe-chi-li and Miau-tau Channels.[1] As for the remnants of the Sixth Division the old gun-vessel *Yobu* was to relieve the *Chiyoda* at Hwang-ching-tau, and the *Chiyoda* and *Idzumi* were to occupy the patrol section whose centre was Position K, 40 miles due south of the entrance to Talien-hwan.[2]

---

[1] His orders were with one or both of his light cruisers to keep guard between Position 1217 (29 miles due east of Toki Island) and Position "L" (13 miles due east of Toki Island); *Yakumo* to carry on as before, that is—night position Position 1110 (25 miles N.E. of Chifu), moving at dawn to Position "Ro" (20 miles south of Liau-ti-shan). He ordered *Takasago* and *Otowa* to "Ro" for the day. At night *Takasago* was to patrol 5 miles east and west of Position 1217 ; *Otowa* was to patrol 8 miles west of and back to Position "Ha" (5 miles north of Position 1249).

[2] Position "K" was in lat. 38° 10′, long. 121° 50′—that is, 40 miles east of "L," and about 20 miles north of *Yakumo's* night position. These positions covered Chifu, while Admiral Kataoka with the armoured division barred the way to Kyau-chau.

Towards evening the weather abated a little, and all the Dalny flotilla came out in succession to Ping-tu-tau, but there was no order for an attack. Captain Imai of the *Chinyen*, however, sent in the 15th division which was on duty, and two mining launches of the Talien Defence Force armed with coast-defence torpedoes ; and feeling sure that since the last attack the *Sevastopol* would be fully protected by nets, he gave special orders that no long-range torpedoes were to be used, and that net-cutters must be fixed.   The Russians describe them as coming up after midnight from the southward, then turning eastward across the bows of the *Sevastopol* to deliver their attack and making off uninjured.[1]   According to the Japanese they approached from the south-east, and, creeping in at half speed, the first two boats of the 15th division got within 1,000 metres, turned to port, and discharged three shots before they were discovered.   The third boat crept on to within 400 metres and then, turning to port like the others, fired three torpedoes.   Then she was discovered and fired on, but got away untouched.   By this time the last boat had been picked up by the searchlights and was so heavily fired on, that the glare on the shot splashes prevented her seeing anything, and she made off without firing at all.   The two mining launches followed, coming in more from the southward full in the searchlight beams.   A storm of fire greeted them, but everything passed over their heads. Both launches reported getting in two torpedoes at about 1,200 metres, with the beams full on them, and they also got off scot free.   Thus ten torpedoes in all were fired, but none took effect.   Three of them struck the *Otvazhni's* net-boom and did not explode, and two were found unexploded on the shore.[2]   It is, in fact, fairly clear that the *Sevastopol* cannot have been seen or attacked at all, and though the torpedo-boats claimed to have fired at not above 1,000 metres, the Russians say the attack was delivered at a long range.   The launches reported feeling the vibrations of two explosions, but that they could not hear anything for the shells exploding round them.   Nevertheless it was obvious the attack had miscarried, and Admiral Togo so reported to the Army in the morning.

---

[1] Lieut. Dudorov, *Morskoi Sbornik*, June 1908.

[2] Lieut. Dudorov says the first three were 19-inch [really 18-inch] with net-cutters.   The safety-pin of the one examined was sheered, and the needle short of the detonator by 2 mm.

The gist of his communication to General Nogi was, however, something with which the Army was much more closely concerned. Owing to the disturbance of his blockade arrangements a British blockade runner, the *King Arthur*, had got through the cruiser line, and at daybreak was sighted under Liau-ti-shan making for Port Arthur. One of the patrol torpedo-boats made a dash to cut her off but was too late, and the Admiral had to report that she had anchored safely inshore of the *Sevastopol* and the gunboat. Being laden with flour, vegetables and other stores she would be a godsend to the garrison, and he determined to attack the exposed anchorage again that night. Captain Imai telegraphed that he had told off the 20th torpedo-boat division and the picket-boats of the *Mikasa* and *Fuso* for the purpose, under escort of the 10th division, but the Commander-in-Chief ordered the 10th, 14th and 15th to attack as well.

It is clear there was no thought of the Fleet leaving till the business was complete, but the exigencies of the refit compelled the Admiral to take a delicate step. None of the total losses during the blockade had been made public. The crews of the lost ships had been distributed in various special service vessels, auxiliary cruisers, gunboats and the like, and some of these ships were now in serious need of a refit. He therefore proposed that the loss of the cruiser *Yoshino*, the gunboat *Oshima* and the two destroyers *Akatsuki* and *Hayatori* should be announced, and the vessels their crews were manning sent home.

Scarcely had his telegram gone off when there was another cruiser to add to the list. Just after midnight on the 13th he took in a signal from the *Takasago*: " I have struck a " mine; come quickly." She had proceeded according to the last orders to her night station, Position 1217, 29 miles due east of Toki Island, and instead of patrolling as directed was drifting, because, as her report says, " although no floating " mines had been sighted in the neighbourhood a strong " northerly wind had been blowing for some days past and " she anticipated danger." About midnight, in spite of her care, a huge explosion took place under her port bow. She immediately called up her consort the *Otowa*, who was also drifting 12 miles W. by N. of her, and got out a collision mat ; but it was still blowing hard with blinding snow, and all efforts to correct the list she had taken were unavailing. In twenty minutes she was heeling 25°. By that time three boats had been lowered, but the list prevented the steamboat and pinnace being got out. It was now found possible to start the engines and after turning her to windward and slipping the port anchor the list began to lessen. By a quarter to one, however, it was 30°, the engines had stopped again, her search-light failed so that she could no longer indicate her position, and, helpless to hold up to the wind, she began to take the seas badly on her starboard side. The list now grew rapidly worse and the captain called up all hands on deck. Then " with three *banzais* for the Emperor and singing war songs " the crew waited calmly for their ship to sink. At 1.10 the " port side toppled over ; in two or three minutes the whole " ship had disappeared beneath the surface and all the crew " except 25 men in the boats were in the sea. There was " a strong north-easterly gale ; snow-flakes were whirling " round and the cold pierced to the marrow ; the sky was so " black that a man could not see his own hand. With only " the *Otowa's* searchlight flickering through the snow-flakes to " guide them, most of the crew clung to the floating spars " and hammocks cheering each other as they drifted in the " breaking waves, till the cold gradually benumbed their bodies " and most of them slipped unconscious away."

By that time the *Otowa* had succeeded in finding her and was close up just in time to see her go down. In spite of the sea that was running all boats were lowered, but they could do little in the weather that prevailed. " The snowflakes " absorbed the rays of the searchlight and the rescue parties " could only be guided in their hunt for the drowning men by " their cries." Yet for three hours the work went on, and in the end they saved the captain, ten officers (of whom three died later) and 151 petty officers and men (of whom three died). The commander, 21 officers and 210 men were lost and were returned officially as killed in action.[1]

While this tragedy was proceeding the third torpedo attack was being delivered on the *Sevastopol*, but for some reason, possibly owing to the difficulty of communicating, it was not made in the force Admiral Togo had ordered. Besides the 20th division and the two picket-boats which Captain Imai had originally detailed for the operation, only the 14th division took part in it. At a conference of the divisional commanders

---

[1] The *Yakumo* also arrived on the scene at 2.50 and took part in the search, but her boats were too late to find anyone alive.

it was arranged that the 20th division should lead S.W. by S. from Ping-tu-tau till the Jo-to-san searchlight bore N.W. ¾ W., and would then alter for it and attack. The picket-boats coming next would carry on for the top of Liau-ti-shan till Jo-to-san bore due north and wait till the leading division had attacked. The 14th division came last.[1]

This programme was duly carried out, but the Russians were now thoroughly on the alert, and before the leading boat (No. 26) of the 20th division located the enemy she was picked up by the Golden Hill light and then by all the others and subjected to a storm of fire from the Jo-to-san and other batteries. A shot went right through her on the waterline, but getting a clear view of the *Sevastopol* she held on, and stopping the holes with blankets, fired two torpedoes at an estimated range of 300 metres and made away south-east. The second (No. 64), keeping in the leader's wake, was able to get in three shots at the same distance without being touched. But seeing her leader in trouble she went to her assistance and immediately was hit below the water line by a shell which burst in the ward-room and stopped the engines. They were hastily re-paired and she began to make off. In the interval the third boat (No. 63) had attacked, getting in only one shot at a range of 500 metres, and not being able to find her consorts went back to the rendezvous. No. 65 fired two torpedoes at the same range, but having seen the two injured boats as she went in was able to pick up No. 64 after her attack and take her in tow as soon as they were out of the fire zone. No. 62 was able to take care of herself, and thus all four got back; but not one of the eight shots had taken effect.

As soon as the injured boats were clear the 14th division went in. Its senior officer, Commander Seki, had strong ideas as to the folly of attacking unless it was possible to make fairly sure of hitting, and he had strictly charged his officers not to fire unless they got a clear sight of the ship.[2] He was not even sure of the wisdom of attacking the *Sevastopol* at all since he doubted whether 14-inch torpedoes were any good against a battleship's nets. He had therefore directed that the blockade-runner should be regarded as the first objective and

---

[1] The 20th division were second-class boats of 110 tons and 27 knots. The Japanese say they headed N.W. ½ W. and then W.N.W. Lieutenant Dudorov says they attacked from the southward. Probably, therefore, the attack was made the same way as the last.

[2] *See post*, p. 416.

that short-range torpedoes with net cutters were to be used. On approaching he was at once picked up by the searchlights and, true to his principles, retired, knowing that in their beams he would never get a clear sight ; but it was only to await a better chance.   Four times they tried, but always with the same result.   With the beams on the snow it was quite impossible to make certain of laying correctly, and finally at 6.0 a.m., as it was now nearly low-tide and the enemy's mines would be dangerously near the surface, they retired without attacking at all.

But this was not the end.   The two picket-boats were still inside.   According to programme they had proceeded, after parting company with the 20th division, till the Jo-to-san search-light bore due north and then at 2.45 a.m., had stopped to await their turn.   In half-an-hour they could see the opening attack was over and began to steal slowly northward.   They passed the rocks of Kai-yang-chau very close but soon after were aware of a destroyer moving about ahead of them, and seeing it was useless to proceed ran back again to their original station to await a better chance.   In White Wolf Bay all was quiet till nearly daybreak, and the Russians believed the affair was over, when they were suddenly aware of the two picket-boats.   So close did they come that Captain von Essen says he could hear the words of command.   Both of them discharged two torpedoes before they were seen at a range which the Japanese put at 200 metres, and Captain von Essen at 60 fathoms (120 yards), and then made away.   The picket-boats reported that all four torpedoes exploded ; but Captain von Essen speaks only of two.   One, he says, struck the nets and sank, but the other forced in the bow net and exploded so close to the ship's side that a crack opened and the large submerged torpedo-flat filled.[1]   As soon as possible he opened fire on the retiring enemy and with some effect.   The *Fuso's* boat was hit astern and the *Mikasa's* more seriously in the engine-room and stoke-hold, but not badly enough to prevent her from getting away with only three men wounded.   Both she and her consort reached Ping-tu-tau in safety.

In spite of this small success the morning report was that all three ships were in the same state, except that four destroyers were guarding them.   Admiral Togo, therefore, took steps to give more energy to the attack.   Informing the Army that he

---

[1] *Attaché Reports*, III., 233.

meant to stay where he was and persevere till he had succeeded, he requested them to fire on the *Sevastopol* from time to time to give her as much trouble as possible. He also decided, with a view probably of avoiding the confusion that had occurred, to modify the system of command. On December 13th, after receiving the report of the last attack, he had sent instructions that three or more divisions (excluding the 15th and 20th) were to attack that night, and that instead of operating independently they were to attack together. For the *Sevastopol* torpedoes were to be adjusted to run at a depth of 6 metres, but that the most important thing was to destroy the blockade-runner. Therefore, Captain Imai of the *Chinyen*, who, as commanding the guardship in the Ping-tu-tau area, was senior officer on the spot, directed the attack to be made by the 10th division and a composite division composed of two boats of the 12th and one of the 6th. Up to this time the control of the torpedo operations had been divided in an indeterminate way between him, Admiral Yamada, and the senior flotilla officer, Commander Kasama of the 15th division. But a little later in the day, with a view probably of remedying the confusion of orders that had occurred, Admiral Togo definitely placed Captain Imai in provisional command of all the destroyers and torpedo-boats which were based at Ping-tu-tau—that is, the base of the blockade patrols—with authority to decide which of these should maintain the blockade and which attack the ships in White Wolf Bay. But still there was no unity in the command, for the order did not extend to the Dalny Defence Flotilla, which was still under Admiral Yamada, nor was the position of Commander Kasama of the 15th division modified as director of the actual arrangements of the attacks.[1]

For the attack that night (13th–14th) Captain Imai's original orders stood and it was arranged that the 10th division should

---

[1] So many changes had been made in the flotilla organisation that the distribution is uncertain. By an order of December 9 Admiral Togo had relieved from blockade duty all boats of the second class and under, The four remaining destroyer divisions (1st, 3rd, 4th, and 5th) and the three first-class torpedo divisions (9th, 14th, and 15th) now constituted the three patrol groups. What remained of the other patrol torpedo divisions (1st, 10th, 14th, and 20th) seem to have remained at Ping-tu-tau under Captain Imai. The 6th and 12th seem also to have been under him. All the rest that were fit for service, together with 10 auxiliary gunboats and the two picket-boats, were stationed at Dalny under Almiral Yamada.

attack at high water (3.30 a.m.) and then retire south-eastward, trying to divert the enemy's searchlights to itself, so as to give the composite division a good chance of getting in. But owing to the weather the plan miscarried. With nightfall came a driving snowstorm, so thick that although the 10th division burnt lights they lost touch in the approach. The enemy's searchlights could not be seen and though they remained inside till dawn not one of them succeeded in finding the ships.

The composite division, which were all three third-class boats, did better. They kept together till, by dead reckoning, they judged they were due south of Jo-to-san. Then they slowed down to feel their way, but the snow came thicker than ever, and they quickly lost touch with one another and sought the enemy independently. The leading boat, No. 52, found them shortly after 4.0, but could not get a clear enough sight to lay. She therefore held off again, and as she did so was aware that another boat was attacking. This was the third boat, No. 58, which suddenly came on the enemy at 200 metres distance, discharged two short-range torpedoes and then made off to the rendezvous. As she cleared, No. 52 went in again and discharged both her tubes at 400 metres. But by this time the floating net boom was complete and all four torpedoes were stopped. As for the third boat she was never seen again. The Russians believed she had struck a mine, but it seems that her commander had an idea of turning the fixed defences by stealing in between the shore and the ships and, if possible, destroying the *Sevastopol's* cable with dynamite. Possibly in attempting this daring scheme he ran on a reef. The Russians say cries of help were heard on a rock, but when the spot was examined next morning nothing could be found. Both the other boats reached Ping-tu-tau in safety.

For the fourth time a complete failure had to be registered. Over 30 torpedoes had been spent and things were getting desperate. Although towards evening the shore stations believed the *Sevastopol* was settling down by the head the *Fuso's* report was that the position was unchanged. The Commander-in-Chief, therefore, instructed Admiral Yamada and Captain Imai that two of the blockade divisions, the 9th and 14th, all first-class boats, were to be added to those previously detailed for another attack that night. Later information, however, or further consideration, convinced him that more drastic measures were necessary.

The flotilla officers had come to the conclusion that the enemy's defences were really formidable and would require special treatment if they were to be penetrated. Some were for setting their torpedoes deep enough to pass under everything, others for setting the depth at zero for destroying the boom and then testing the effects of 14-inch torpedoes on the ship's nets. Admiral Togo, himself, had evidently come to the conclusion that the obstacles were now so perfect that nothing but a massed attack could break them down. The weather was also improving and he sent an order to Captain Imai that that night the whole of the flotillas must go in. He also directed that a destroyer's 18-inch torpedo should be mounted in a first class torpedo-boat. His order to Admiral Yamada and Captain Imai was as follows : " You " are to send all the torpedo-boats out to attack the " *Sevastopol* to-night. They are all to use short range " torpedoes and are to make their attacks at under 600 " metres. You must leave to Commander Kasama's dis- " cretion whether the attacks are to be delivered simultaneously " or in succession. A certain number of divisions may make " a diversion without attacking. The patrol will be maintained " by destroyers only."

In compliance with this order everything available was sent to Ping-tu-tau, but owing to various casualties there were found fit for present service only 24 torpedo-boats belonging to nine divisions and one picket-boat, the *Fuji's*. The other two picket-boats and the 20th division had all been put out of action in their last attack.[1]

By this time Captain von Essen had completed his arrangements for their reception. The booms protecting the two ships were finished and to the southward was stationed the destroyer *Serditi* to pick up with her searchlights anything coming from that direction. She would follow them with her beam till they came into the arc of White Wolf Hill which in turn would pass them on to the gunboat. Finally, another destroyer, the *Storozhevoi*, would keep them in view till they retired. If, on the other hand, they approached from the east the *Storozhevoi* would pick them up and the process would be reversed as they made their attack to the southward, The other three destroyers were

---

[1] The *Fuji* had been called up from Shantung to Round Island on the 13th on purpose to furnish her picket-boat for this attack.—*Attaché Reports*, II., 99.

anchored in-shore.[1] The system was completed by the search-lights of the more distant forts, which the Japanese describe as being used very skilfully. To them it appeared that those on Golden Hill and Man-tse-ying were kept on the waters near the *Sevastopol* and never moved, so that no boat could get within effective range without passing through the illuminated zone. Jo-to-san light, which at first had served to guide the attack, was now not used except to light up the attacking boats when they were quite close. The Lao-lui-chui light was the only one that revolved, and it was used to search the water outside the anchorage.

The Japanese had thus to face a situation more difficult than ever, and a special plan of the grand attack was drawn up by Commander Kasama.[2] It was arranged on the basis of two groups, the first being merely an advanced guard composed of three second-class boats (Nos. 52, 56 and 58), which were all that was left of the 6th and 12th divisions, with the *Fuji's* picket-boat attached. Their object was to break down the defences for the main attack by the second group, which comprised all the rest of the flotilla.

It was a fine moonlight night when, at nine, the first group started off. As they approached from the eastward at 11.30 clouds obscured the sky and it began to snow again, so without waiting for the moon to set they attacked at once. They were discovered, but all discharged their torpedoes within the prescribed range under a heavy fire and made off. No. 56 was hit several times, but not seriously. No. 58 received a score of projectiles, and had three men wounded, a blade of her propeller broken, and one of her tubes damaged, while No. 52 was untouched. The *Fuji's* picket-boat followed close, meaning to attack in rear, but finding something wrong with her tube, she waited for the second group. It was made up of 21 boats and organised in five divisions, two of which were composite and comprised the second-class units.[3]

---

[1] Lieut. Dudorov's Journal ; *Japanese Published History* (note), I., 260 ; and *Morskoi Sbornik*, June 1908.

[2] *See post*, Appendix B., II. (a), p. 414.

[3] A. 15th division, *Hibari, Udzura, Sagi, Hashitaka.*
    B. 37, 45, 46 (2nd division), 49 (21st division) Second Class.
    C. 40, 41, 42, 43 (10th division), 39 (16th division), Second Class.
        110 tons and 27 knots (Yarrow).
    D. 14th division, *Hayabusa, Kasasagi, Manadzuru, Chidori.*
    E. 9th division, *Kari, Aotaka, Hato, Tsubame.*

They approached as before from the eastward, and the Russian accounts describe them as coming on at full speed in single line ahead. They were duly picked up by the *Storozhevoi's* searchlight, but held on till they were close to the *Otvazhni*, and then at a range of about 1,200 metres they turned to the southward and ran along the Russian line discharging their torpedoes at her, the *Sevastopol* and the destroyer *Smyeli*, and then turned again to the eastward. The night was clear and during the whole attack they were fair in the Russian field of fire. It was more severe than on the previous occasions, and observers ashore believed that two boats were sunk and that another was torpedoed by a launch. One was certainly lying motionless when the attack was over; and an effort to rescue her was frustrated by the severity of the Russian fire. A destroyer went out to capture her, but the batteries, mistaking their own boat for an enemy, opened on her and she was compelled to torpedo the disabled Japanese boat and retire.[1] The same impression is conveyed by another Russian officer, who adds that the whole affair went off like a review, the searchlights taking up the enemy as in an ordinary night exercise, and the Japanese coming up from the east at regular intervals of about two cables, then turning to the south, and after firing their torpedoes at from 400 to 1,000 yards, going off again whence they came.[2]

What really happened according to the reports of the various Japanese commanding officers was as follows. The 15th division led in from the eastward, and as they came up at 1.15 they were discovered and fired on, but all succeeded in firing one to three torpedoes at ranges of 600 to 800 metres; in all nine torpedoes were fired. This division according to the programme had had the further duty of creating a diversion in favour of the rest by stopping $2\frac{1}{2}$ miles south of Golden Hill to attract the enemy's attention; accordingly, after the attack, the senior-boat led off to the diversion point, and the others followed.

The four boats of the first composite division (2nd and 21st) were already coming on full in the beams of the search-lights. Nevertheless, they managed to fire ten torpedoes at 400 to 500 metres, and all got away untouched except No. 49, which was badly hit under the conning tower, but not disabled.

---

[1] Captain von Essen's Report. *Attaché Reports*, III., 233.
[2] Lieutenant Dudorov. *Japanese Published History*, I., 260, note.

Then came the 10th division (four boats with No. 39 of the 16th division attached). No. 43, the senior officer's boat, fired at the *Sevastopol*, No. 41 at her and the gunboat successively. Though the second boat was hit several times, she was not disabled ; but No. 42, as she turned away after firing, received a shot through a boiler, which brought her to a standstill about 1,000 yards from the enemy, where shell continued to hail round her. One hit the conning tower and her commander entirely disappeared. The second officer took command and signalled for assistance. The boat was still being struck continuously, seven men were already killed and it was clear she must sink, when No. 40 came up after delivering her attack and took off the crew. She then, under a heavy fire, tried to take the disabled boat in tow, but four wires in succession were cut by shells. She then tried to lash herself alongside, but the lashings were quickly severed. Both boats were suffering badly under the concentrated fire of all the ships and batteries, and finally the disabled boat had to be abandoned. The effort to save her did, however, allow the last boat, No. 39, to attack without being noticed, and to get away scot free. So far it was the best attack that had been made, each of the five boats having got in three torpedoes at under 500 metres.

The next to follow were the four first-class boats of the 14th division, which had not fired in the previous attack at all. In the morning its senior officer, Commander Seki, had issued instructions insisting on his rule that no torpedo must be fired unless a clear sight was obtained. There must be no trusting to a momentary gleam of a searchlight. "People," he said, "who do that sort of thing think it is enough to run " up and fire a torpedo, which can hardly be called attacking " a ship." Others held that a torpedo should be fired in any event, but as he did not believe this was the view of the Admiral or Staff he enjoined them to adhere to his rule, promising to lead them up in what experience had shown was the best way.[1] This he did, and with so much skill that, assisted also possibly by the enemy's attention being concentrated on the disabled No. 42, all his four boats were able to fire three shots at under 500 metres, and the only damage was a shot through the conning tower of the *Hayabusa*.

Last came the 9th division, and they were not so fortunate. The Russian fire was now becoming heavier than ever, and

---

[1] See *post*, Appendix B., II. (*b*), p. 416.

better directed. All four got off three torpedoes at from 400 to 600 metres, but the *Aotaka*, who led, had a shell burst in the stokehold, which killed two men and wounded two others and an officer. The *Tsubame*, who was next, had her starboard engine disabled and one man killed and seven seriously wounded. For a while with the *Hato* standing by she managed to hold on with one engine only, but the water soon rose so high in her stokehold that the other engine also stopped. The *Hato* then found her own injuries were too severe to allow of her giving assistance, and finally the *Tsubame* was only saved from destruction by one of the 15th division, which had been waiting all this time south of the Golden Hill, taking her in tow. The only boat that escaped unhit was the *Kari*, and she in making off at 25 knots crashed into the *Aotaka* as she was painfully retiring, with the result that the *Kari*, although she just escaped sinking, was completely disabled. Last of all the *Fuji's* picket-boat, which had been waiting for a chance, ran up and fired her torpedo, and, although she became engaged with the Russian destroyers, got clear off without damage.

So the attack ended. Captain von Essen estimated that as many as 60 torpedoes were fired—the Japanese actually record 57—and he claims that not one of them took effect. According to one of his officers, Lieutenant Dudorov, 4 burst in the net ahead of the *Sevastopol*, 8 exploded on the rocks, and 16 were found on the beach next day. In some cases net cutters were used, but it is clear they proved ineffective. The Japanese observation station, it is true, reported that the *Sevastopol* seemed to be more down by the head, and it is possible the shock of the explosions had opened the crack in the bows which had been the result of the previous night's attack.[1] Otherwise the situation in White Wolf Bay seemed unaltered by all that had been done. The grand attack had cost the Japanese one boat sunk, three first-class boats permanently disabled, and many others more or less damaged. The casualties were one officer and nine ratings killed, and two officers and thirteen ratings wounded, not a heavy list for what they had gone through.

To the torpedo officers it was incredible that nothing vital had been done, and even Admiral Togo was inclined to believe the last reports from the look-out stations that the *Sevastopol*

---

[1] There is some doubt on the point, but Lieutenant Dudorov says a crack in the battleship's bows was caused in this way during the grand attack, but he places it on the night of the 13th and 14th.

seemed to be aground and immovable. He did not feel sure, but his report to the Imperial Staff was as follows : " The " *Sevastopol* has been more or less damaged in the successive " night attacks by our torpedo craft. This morning she is " down by the bow, and seems to have lost her steaming " power. Further attacks will be made to-night."

The result of this message, coming as it did upon the news of what had happened to the *Takasago* and *Akashi*, seems to have been that Admiral Togo received from the Imperial Staff something in the nature of a recall, or at least a suggestion that their old plan should be resumed of abandoning a close blockade and keeping the battleships in a place of safety.[1] In any case what the Commander-in-Chief did was to remodel his blockade arrangements with a view to the withdrawal of the battleships and the larger cruisers that remained to the Elliot Islands or Japan. That afternoon he telegraphed instructions to Admiral Kataoka at Shantung to send the *Kasuga* home for a refit, and to bring the rest of his division to Round Island. This was followed by an order to Admiral Dewa to take the *Yakumo* next day direct to the Elliot Islands, where the Commander-in-Chief intended to meet him, and to leave his blockade section to the *Otowa* and *Yaeyama*. The Encounter Rock section was to be held by Rear-Admiral Togo with the *Chiyoda* (to which he had just shifted his flag at Dalny) and the *Idzumi*, his night station being Takin-tau in the Miau-tau group or Ping-tu-tau as convenient. The watch against contraband runners was, therefore, now reduced to four cruisers and four divisions of destroyers, which were on guard half at the time. Finally, Admiral Yamada was told to stop mining the entrance till further orders.

Before leaving for the Elliot Islands with the battleships Admiral Togo waited where he was till after the attack which he intended to make that night in order to complete the *Sevastopol's* destruction. On receiving the instructions Captain Imai told off two divisions, the still uninjured 14th and the composite one, which was made up of three boats of the 2nd (Nos. 45, 37 and 46) and two of the 21st (Nos. 47 and 49). This division was under Commander Ezoe, the senior officer of the 21st division, but his boat, No. 47, was not in a fit state

---

[1] It is incidentally stated in the *Confidential History*, Vol. II., p. 461, that his three remaining battleships had been ordered home, but the recall is not mentioned elsewhere.

to proceed. At Dalny, however, was another boat of the division, No. 44, just completing her repairs. Commander Ezoe, not to be denied, hurriedly got her clear and made off in her with all speed to the rendezvous at Ping-tu-tau just in time to find his consorts gone, but he followed on at once. As before, the composite division of second-class boats led. They started at 12.45 a.m. on the 16th, but before they were within distance it began to snow again heavily. Thus the leading boat, No. 45, was able to fire two torpedoes at about 500 metres undetected. The second, No. 37, following in her wake, at first could see nothing for the blinding snow, but presently getting glimpses of a searchlight, crept slowly up to it and discharged all three tubes at 200 metres. She was immediately attacked by a destroyer but got away. Till now the Russians had not opened fire, and the third boat, No. 46, also got within 300 metres, putting in three shots, but just as she turned to make away the Russian guns began and a shell burst in her forward boiler-room, killing three men. No. 49 was so entirely blinded by the snow that she failed to find anything and drew off to the south-eastward to determine her position. Then she went in again and succeeded in getting two shots at the *Sevastopol* at 500 metres without being seen. No. 44 was not so fortunate. Unable to overtake his division, Commander Ezoe had decided to attack alone. Sighting the *Sevastopol* at about 500 metres he ran straight for her according to the usual practice and fired his bow fixed tube. He then gave her his two revolving tubes, but at the first shot he was seen and fired at. A shell burst in the conning tower and blew him to pieces, but only one other man was hurt and the boat got away without serious injury.

It was now 4 o'clock, and as yet no harm had been done to any of the Russian ships. All the torpedoes had exploded in the nets of the boom, which by this time had been considerably extended so that those of the gunboat and the battleship were joined in one. Still the 14th division was yet to attack. Commander Seki, its senior officer, was now bringing it up, but the snowstorm was thicker than ever, and for a time nothing could be seen. But again the Russian searchlights afforded the desired direction. They were, in fact, the lights of the destroyers, but the leading boat *Chidori*, believing them to be shore lights led in for them much closer than she intended, so that when she turned for her attack she found she had left the *Sevastopol* quite close on her starboard quarter and was too late to hit her. She therefore gave a torpedo at 100 metres to the next ship which was taken to be the *King Arthur*. Then under a storm of fire she turned away to avoid a search-light ahead which her commander still believed to be ashore. Suddenly, however, he found it was in a destroyer, whose stern he almost fouled as he turned. She was, in fact, the *Serditi* watching for an attack from the southward and he saw his chance for a smart piece of service. It so happened that as his object was to break the boom for his following boats he had a torpedo set to run near the surface and the moment he had turned enough for the tube to bear he fired. The torpedo exploded almost directly it took the water, and so severe was the shock to the *Chidori* that for a moment it was thought she was torpedoed, but she steadied and got away.[1]

Her second, the *Hayabusa*, had realised the situation in time to give two torpedoes to the *Sevastopol* very close. The other two boats fired three as they came up from astern. Thus, ten torpedoes were fired in all by the division and six explosions were heard.[2] As they held away they became engaged with the Russian destroyers, but nothing worse happened than a hit on the *Kasasagi* that holed her, but did no harm.

But this time on board the *Sevastopol* there was a different tale to tell. Two torpedoes had got through the gaps that had been blown in the boom, and bursting in the ship's nets had damaged her side ; a third got fairly home in her unprotected stern, and blew a huge hole. Everything aft was quickly flooded even to the ward-room and she took a list of 10° to starboard. As for the torpedoed destroyer she was a wreck and had to save herself by running on the rocks.

Such was the end of Captain von Essen's gallant defence. Though he managed to right his ship, her stern now touched the bottom every tide, and she could no longer be counted as an active unit. Still it had taken the Japanese six successive attacks in which, according to the official return, no less than 124 torpedoes had been fired. In all, 30 torpedo-boats had been used, besides two mine-launches and three picket-boats. Of these, two torpedo-boats had been lost and five commissioned and warrant officers and 30 men killed and " a large number

---

[1] For Commander Seki's own account *see Attaché Reports*, III., 38, where there is a track-chart given to our Attaché. But it curiously places the Russian ships in the wrong place, close to the Kai-yang-chau rocks.

[2] Lieut. Dudorov says one burst in the nets of the boom, three on the rocks, and two on the *Sevastopol ;* two others were found on the beach unexploded.

wounded"; and besides other casualties to material, three whole divisions, the 9th, 10th and 20th, and two picket-boats were rendered unfit for service without a dockyard refit.[1]

But Admiral Togo was not yet content. Being, as we are told, "determined to sink the *Sevastopol* by torpedoes, however long the attack might last," he ordered Captain Imai to select three divisions for a seventh attack that night (17th–18th), and as the parent-ship was running out of torpedoes he directed his three battleships before leaving to supply her from their 14-inch stores. Later on, however, the order to attack was counter-manded. The reason is unknown, but it was presumed to be that on further information as to the *Sevastopol's* condition the Admiral decided to suspend operations till he could get a more certain report. Thus this remarkable episode closed. " I wish," the Admiral's order ran, " to express my satisfaction " at the attacks made by the torpedo-boats so courageously " and often. Cease attacking till further orders."

So the shattered *Sevastopol* was left with her flag flying to the last, in spite of all that the Japanese could do—as though to proclaim to the world that the spirit was still alive, which half a century before had month after month preserved from the combined efforts of four great Powers the famous Black Sea Fortress whose name she honoured in bearing.

---

[1] For the official return *see Confidential History*, Vol. II., p. 463–5.

CHAPTER IX.

THE FALL OF PORT ARTHUR.

[Map IIIB. Charts I, IV, V, VIII.]

WITH the cessation of the attacks on the *Sevastopol* another stage in the development of the naval situation had been reached. So far as the bulk of the Japanese Fleet was concerned the Port Arthur operations were at an end. During the day (December 16th) Admiral Togo received a friendly message from General Nogi by one of his staff, conveying the condolences of the Army for the loss of the *Takasago*, and in earnest of his sincerity he begged that to prevent further disasters to the blockading force, now that the enemy's squadron was practically destroyed, the Admiral, after making suitable arrangements for preventing blockade running, would withdraw the bulk of his fleet and not trouble further about the Third Army.

It was a handsome request, typical of the cordial and sympathetic relations that appear to have existed between the two commanders-in-chief through all the long period of friction. The suggestion, which removed any scruples the Admiral had in withdrawing to a place of rest, must have been very welcome. For four harassing months he had not dropped anchor. Since, on August 16th, the battle division had left the Elliot Islands on a false alarm of a sortie, it had remained steaming or drifting at sea, day and night and in all kinds of weather, and some relief to the strain upon officers and men must have been by this time an urgent necessity. Accordingly, having made the necessary dispositions for the blockade as detailed above, he held away for the Elliot Islands, and that night, with the *Mikasa*, *Fuji*, *Asahi* and *Nisshin* and his despatch-vessel *Tatsuta*, he came to rest in the deserted anchorage.

At this time he must have been expecting to go home at once, for the previous day (December 15th), when the Imperial Staff re-call was apparently to hand, he took a significant step, which shows how confident the Japanese were that the end of the fortress was near and how religiously the honours were to be shared between the two services. In view of the expected surrender at the next attack he appointed a naval plenipotentiary to represent him at the capitulation. His credential which was obviously for presentation to the Russian delegates together with a similar one from the General, was as follows :—

"I join with the Plenipotentiary of the Siege Army Captain "Iwamura Danjiro of the Staff of the First Squadron. For all "that concerns the surrender of the Russian army and fleet at "Port Arthur, I give him full powers to confer with the "Plenipotentiaries of that army and fleet and to sign any "convention taking immediate effect without waiting for my "assent." And he signed it as "Commandant of the Block-"ade Squadron of the Liautung Peninsula."

Still no peremptory order for his return can have come. Possibly the Imperial Staff felt no immediate anxiety; but two or three days later some intelligence of the Baltic Fleet seems to have reached Tokyo, which once more forced to the front the question of a complete refit of the Fleet. On the 14th Admiral Felkerzam left Jibuti and after coaling near Alula on the 17th proceeded to the north of Madagascar. On the same day Admiral Rozhestvenski completed his coal at Angra Pequeña and started for the same rendezvous. At what date precisely these movements were known to the Japanese Staff is uncertain, but on the 18th they sent a telegram to the Commander-in-Chief asking for "his conclusions "on the extent of the damage and losses of the Port Arthur "Squadron." [1] He made a preliminary reply that he could answer for all the Russian ships except the *Sevastopol*. About her he still could not speak decisively although she seemed to have lost all power of movement, but it was certain that six destroyers were still in being. Then in order to clear up the situation as far as possible he shifted his flag to the *Tatsuta* and proceeded to Dalny for a round of inspection; but before leaving the Elliot Islands he broke up the Third Division, sending the *Yakumo* home to Sasebo, and incorporating the *Otowa* and *Yaeyama* in Rear-Admiral Togo's Sixth Division to carry on the blockade.

The first thing he learnt on reaching Dalny was that the *King Arthur* had gone into Port Arthur. He also found that at 2.0 that afternoon the Army had blown up East Chikuan-shan North Fort and was to assault it that night. The breach was successfully stormed and by midnight this important work was in General Nogi's hands. Next day

---

[1] H.M.S. *Fox* reported to the Admiralty on the 17th that the Russians had left Jibuti; on the 19th the British consul at St. Vincent (Cape Verde) reported colliers leaving for North Madagascar.

the Admiral landed to visit the observation stations, and shortly after 5.0 p.m., while he was thus engaged, the *King Arthur* was seen to be making off. Though the *Otowa* and *Yaeyama* were despatched in chase—one to Chifu, the other to the Gulf of Pe-chi-li—she succeeded in eluding both, but at midnight was captured by the destroyer *Asagiri* when only 12 miles N.N.E. of Chifu. She had been able to discharge her cargo, and it proved a great relief to the garrison, but she was only the second steamer which had succeeded in breaking the blockade since its declaration in May.

This same day, the 20th, the Admiral for the first time had a conference with General Nogi and next day he returned to the Elliot Islands and made his report to Tokyo. After summarising the results of the capture of 203-Metre Hill and the recent torpedo attacks, he says : " The Port Arthur squadron " is completely destroyed for all practical purposes." He has therefore relaxed the blockade and withdrawn the battle division to the Elliot Islands. "Throughout this long blockade," he concludes, "under war conditions, with ever-present danger " from mines either placed or drifting, and in frequent stress of " weather and fog, we have lost two battleships, two cruisers, " one despatch-vessel, four of the Seventh Division and two " destroyers. Moreover, a large number of officers and men " have laid down their lives for the country. But we have " succeeded in maintaining the blockade and have crushed " the enemy's schemes every time he made a sortie, till with " the very great help of the besieging Army, we at last see " the almost total destruction of the enemy's fleet in this part " of the world."

Thus he seems to enunciate the success of the defensive method on which he had acted throughout with the Fleet. It had succeeded in time, but only just in time. It was known that on the 19th Admiral Rozhestvenski had passed the Cape on his way to join Admiral Felkerzam at the north of Madagascar, and the final struggle seemed now within measurable distance and the preparations for it could no longer be delayed. This was clearly the view of the Imperial Staff, for that evening (the 20th) the Admiral received from the Vice-director of the Naval Section private information that it had been decided to transfer part of his command to the Korean Strait, leaving at Port Arthur the remains of the Third Squadron, which had originally formed the Straits Guard, with a small flotilla and a proportion of the Naval

Brigade. All ships in need of repair would be taken in hand in the home yards without delay and he himself would be summoned to the capital.

Admiral Togo replied by ordering home the *Fuji* and *Idzumi* at once, but added that he could not feel sure of the *Sevastopol* at any rate till some of the 11-inch howitzers had been mounted on 203-Metre Hill. If, therefore, an order came for him to go home he should leave the *Asahi* behind and attach her to the Third Squadron. The howitzers were expected to be in position before the end of the year. This suggestion was approved and shortly afterwards the official order for his recall was received. Accordingly on Christmas Day he sailed for Sasebo, leaving Admiral Kataoka in his place with the Third Squadron, which had been that Admiral's original command as the Fleet was organised at the outbreak of the war.[1]

The orders he received from Admiral Togo were to carry on with the blockade and the support of the Third Army. In case of a sortie from the port he had authority to call to his assistance the Second Squadron, "now temporarily in the Korean Straits." Should any Russian ships escape into a neutral port he was to try by threatening demonstrations to get them to destroy themselves. His most powerful ships he was to keep at the Elliot Island base and generally to do his utmost not to hazard the safety of the ships and vessels under his command.

Admiral Kataoka at once took up his station at Dalny and issued the usual careful instructions for maintaining the blockade. His divisional Admirals did the same. These orders announced that for the complete destruction of the remains of the enemy's fleet he trusted to the guns that were being mounted on 203-Metre Hill, but that as fog or snow gave opportunity he would attack the *Sevastopol* with the few picket-boats that he had. In case of a sortie he would engage with the *Asahi* and the Fifth Division, and the rest were to co-operate as convenient.

---

[1] The Third Squadron was now as follows, besides the *Asahi* (temporarily attached):—

FIFTH DIVISION. *Itsukushima* (flag), *Hashidate*, *Chinyen*.

SIXTH DIVISION. *Chiyoda* (flag of Rear-Admiral Togo), *Akitsushima* (just refitted), *Otowa*, *Yaeyama*.

SEVENTH DIVISION. *Fuso* (flag of Rear-Admiral Yamada) and five gunboats.

Three AUXILIARY CRUISERS.

FLOTILLA ATTACHED. Five destroyers, six divisions of torpedo-boats (about a dozen units at this time) and nine auxiliary gunboats.

Otherwise these orders do not call for detailed notice ; for the end was too near to test them.

On the 28th, the day after he arrived at Dalny, the Army blew up the face of Fort Erh-lung and stormed it, and on the last day of the year the same fate befell Sung-shu. Only the Chinese wall now lay between the besiegers and the Wangtai heights, and before New Year's Day was at an end that coveted position was also in their hands. With that all thought of further resistance was gone. General Kondratenko, the soul of the defence, had been killed on the 15th and there was no one left with power to inspire the garrison or to dominate the faint-heartedness of its commandant. Even before the fall of Wangtai General Stessel had given up hope, and on the afternoon of January 1st a flag of truce was sent into the Japanese lines to invite the appointment of delegates to arrange a capitulation.

There was, however, no intention of allowing any part of the shattered squadron to fall into Japanese hands. Ever since the fall of 203-Metre Hill it had been determined that when the fortress was in the last throes they were to be destroyed where they lay. At a conference of experts held under Admiral Viren's presidency it was agreed to use for the purpose six or eight torpedo-heads placed in pairs under the stem, at the thrust-blocks and as much as possible under the turrets, as well as in the engine and boiler rooms, and to complete the destruction two torpedo-boats were kept ready in case the other measures failed. As soon as the flag of truce was on its way General Stessel ordered the Admiral to carry out the work and blow up the ships during the night.[1] The order was sent on by Admiral Viren to Captain von Essen, and in the harbour the work began at once.

The two or three harbour service vessels which remained afloat were taken out into the gullet and sunk there with a view of rendering the port useless to the Japanese. The rest were dealt with where they lay on the bottom ; but in many cases, it is said, the connections with the torpedo-heads proved defective. The two torpedo-boats were inadequate to do the work instead, and in the end the destruction was carried out very imperfectly.

Thus, so far as the ships in the harbour were concerned, ignominious failure was their portion to the last ; but for those

---

[1] Schwarz and Romanovski, II., 539. *Russian Military History*, VIII., ii., p. 714.

in White Wolf Bay the end was better—worthy, indeed, of the fine spirit they had shown throughout.   During the night, in accordance with the decision of the last naval conference, the remaining six destroyers and three picket-boats, which had been standing by the *Sevastopol*, stole out.   Such a dash for liberty was fully expected by the Japanese.   On December 30th, in fact, there had been a false alarm that they were breaking out and they were being carefully watched.   On the 31st, moreover, the *Sevastopol* was reported by the observation station to have decreased her list, and this was confirmed by the 5th destroyer division, which, being on guard, was sent in to observe her more closely.   Captain von Essen had, in fact, with the assistance of some of the hands from the Baltic yards, succeeded in rectifying the list and stopping the cracks caused by the last torpedo attack.[1]   In his evidence he even stated that he still hoped with a month's respite to get her fit for sea again.   At nightfall the Russian destroyers could be seen smoking heavily and a general signal was made for a strict look out.   As soon as Wangtai had fallen Admiral Kataoka added a special caution for exceptional vigilance, but in spite of the utmost alertness, when the morning mist cleared on January 2nd, nothing could be seen in White Wolf Bay except the *Sevastopol* and *Otvazhni*.

At 9.0 o'clock the shore stations reported that the destroyers seemed to have escaped and that inside the harbour the *Peresvyet*, *Pobyeda* and *Poltava* were in flames.   As yet it was not known that the Russians had sent out a flag of truce ; in the fleet, therefore, they could only conclude " that something " strange was happening in Port Arthur."   Admiral Yamada, on his own initiative, sent off two of his gunboats to search for the destroyers, but as yet Admiral Kataoka did nothing. At 9.30, however, the destroyers on guard saw a terrific explosion behind the *Sevastopol*, and when the smoke cleared the *Otvazhni* was seen to have gone down.   Half-an-hour later they could see the battleship being towed out, and by 10.15 this was reported by the shore stations.   Then Admiral Kataoka took action.   Calling up the *Asahi* from the Elliot Islands he told her to join him at Round Island, and at 10.30 telegraphed to Rear-Admiral Togo to send a cruiser of his division and the 1st destroyer division to Chifu.   Half-an-hour later, however, before the orders could be executed word came in that

[1] Engineer Byelov. *Morskoi Sbornik*, January 1906.

the *Sevastopol* had gone down a mile-and-a-half south-east of Jo-to-san, and the Port Arthur Squadron had finally ceased to exist.

The explanation was that Captain von Essen had acted up to the last in the high spirit which had marked him throughout the war. What happened is best told in his own simple words : " On the night of January 1–2," he says, " to " my great astonishment—for I was ignorant of all that had " been taking place in the fortress—I received an order to " destroy my ship in view of the capitulation of Port Arthur. " The *Otvazhni* was soon blown up. Not wishing to destroy " my ship in shallow water I decided to attempt to take her " out. The majority of the crew and all the gear possible were " sent ashore during the night, and at daybreak I had raised " steam and was ready to get under way. Being unable to " get the boom clear we towed it astern and moved out sea- " wards with the assistance of the tug *Silach,* as my rudder " was disabled and useless owing to the damage related above. " When in 30 fathoms of water I landed the officers and " crew, of which there were 40 remaining in the boats, and " opened the Kingstons and water-tight doors. The battle- " ship heeled over to starboard and commenced to sink. I " then went on board the *Silach* and waited for the *Sevastopol* " to go down, which she did stern foremost. She was 10 to " 15 minutes in sinking." [1]

As for the six destroyers and the picket-boats of the *Retvizan, Pobyeda* and *Tzesarevich,* as early as December 11 they had been directed to hold themselves in readiness to break through to a neutral port at any moment, and they had now received the word. A small steamer, the *Bintang,* with troops and seamen on board accompanied them. In the destroyer *Statni,* by General Stessel's orders, were embarked all the regimental colours, and with this precious freight she and three others made for Chifu. Here they were found on the evening of

---

[1] *Attaché Rep.,* III., 235. According to Engineer Byelov, Captain von Essen intended to blow his ship up in deep water, but on his way out he received an order from the Port Commandant not to do so, since " an " explosion would contravene the conditions of the capitulation." No capitulation had yet been signed, but Captain von Essen directed her to be laid over on her side or capsized to prevent any possibility of her being raised. The compartments on one side were kept closed and those on the other opened. The Kingston valves on that side were then opened and she eventually sank on her beam ends with her bilge keel showing. These measures were so far successful that she was never raised.

January 2nd by the three boats of the 1st destroyer division which had arrived ahead of the *Akitsushima*, their escorting cruiser. The other two with the *Bintang* got into Kyau-chau, and nothing was known of their whereabouts till in the afternoon of January 3rd Rear-Admiral Togo, who had been ordered there after the *Sevastopol* sank, arrived off the port with the *Chiyoda*, *Tatsuta*, and the 5th destroyer division. The picket-boats also made for Chifu, but being belated did not arrive before the Japanese destroyers. During the night, however, they managed to slip in unobserved. All were at once disarmed and interned by the German and Chinese authorities and the chasing detachments returned to resume their blockade duties.

But their labours were now at an end. On the 5th they found Admiral Kataoka assembling his whole command at Dalny and the Japanese flag flying over Port Arthur. At 4.30, on the 2nd, after terms of capitulation were agreed an armistice had been signed by General Ijichi, Chief of Staff to the Third Army, and Captain Iwamura, on behalf of the Fleet, the Russians being represented by the chief of the Garrison Staff and the captain of the *Retvizan*. By the second article of capitulation the warships and other craft in Port Arthur, including torpedo craft, were to be handed over to the Japanese Army " in the condition they then were " ; but they were actually taken over by the Naval Heavy Gun Brigade, and as soon as the capitulation was signed Admiral Kataoka sent ashore a number of engineer officers and ratings to assist them " in receiving and dealing with the Russian " ships and buildings, &c., connected with the Navy." So after eight months effort the combined operations against Port Arthur and its squadron came to an end, and during the week all units of the Japanese fleet were called home except Admiral Kataoka's flagship, the *Akitsushima*, the despatch-vessel *Yaeyama*, the *Fuso*, and a few other units of the Seventh Division. Of the flotillas nothing remained except two divisions of second-class torpedo-boats. With the exception of a gunboat as guard at Chemulpho, everything else was at home, either in dockyard hands, patrolling the Straits of Korea, or engaged in the reconnaisance work of feeling for the Baltic Fleet.

For all preparations for meeting that squadron upon which the last hopes of Russia depended there was now plenty of time. In other words, the policy of devoting the Port Arthur squadron to the defence of its base had failed to secure its object. At one time it is true, when in the first week in November the Baltic Fleet had proceeded on its voyage without a rupture with Great Britain, it looked as though it were going to succeed. By the unanimous opinion of the Port Arthur garrison the assistance of the ship guns ashore and the devotion and heroism of the officers and seamen serving on the land front prolonged the life of the fortress by many weeks. Delay was of the utmost importance to the Russians ; for the Japanese in opening the war as they did had taken the initiative at their selected moment, and time was essential for redressing the advantage they had thus obtained. With all the events of the war before us we can now see that the devotion of the Fleet to the fortress could not have secured the delay required. But this was not so clear to the authorities in Port Arthur. The interminable hesitation in despatching the Baltic Fleet and the persistent interruptions of its voyage were beyond anything on which they could be expected to count.

Still whatever the plausibility of the course that was taken the result was to add one more failure to the list of analogous cases. The most conspicuous of these are Louisbourg and Sevastopol. In both the squadron was devoted to the passive defence of the base instead of operating at sea, and in both the object was delay. In the case of Louisbourg it was believed that if the passage into the St. Lawrence were barred for a year the position of France in Europe would be sufficiently improved to make a British conquest of Canada impossible. In the Crimean case a successful issue of the war was anticipated if Sevastopol could hold out till the winter. But in both cases, as at Port Arthur, though the anticipated delay was secured it proved insufficient to affect the issue of the war. Passive defence as usual gave way before patient and persistent attack.

So constant has been the experience of this method of defending a naval base that we cannot but suspect a fallacy underlying the idea. And that fallacy probably is that the devotion of the squadron to land defence is not the best way of securing delay—at least it is not the most certain, or the one that promises in any event to give the best chances of success in a war. If it fails the squadron is lost with the base without having inflicted any material damage to the enemy's fleet. The whole object, it must be remembered, of a belligerent's keeping a naval base in being is to enable his fleet to act from it so as to prevent the enemy's fleet accomplishing something in the area of that base ; and all experience shows that with anything like equal force the best way of thwarting the enemy's fleet is to attack it, especially for a Power having reserves against an enemy that has none. If the Russians had attacked, as was Admiral Makarov's intention, their squadron might still have been annihilated, but it would not have been beaten without so far .crippling the Japanese that the siege must have been greatly delayed and the effective value of the Baltic Fleet materially enhanced. This was the worst that could be counted on. If, on the other hand, the action did not result in annihilation and some of the Port Arthur Squadron remained undestroyed, the advantage derived even from defeat would have been so much the greater. The survival of ships in the port would have still further delayed the fall of the fortress, and, what was even of more importance, the hope of combining with the Baltic Fleet would have materially increased the relative power of the Russian Reserves.

Why, then, did they not fight ? In spite of all that has been hastily written on the point, it is certain that Russian naval thought thoroughly understood what was the sound strategy to pursue. Of that there is abundant evidence in the appreciations and minutes of their Staff conferences. To dwell on their error is therefore both ungenerous and unprofitable. The only point that merits inquiry is how it was they were led into a false position to which their eyes were wide open.

The germ of the malady under which their strategy succumbed was undoubtedly the choice of Port Arthur as their main Pacific base. Fairly well placed as it was for dominating China and as an emporium for the Pacific trade, it was not well placed for a struggle with Japan for Korea, which its occupation immediately precipitated. Its defects—particularly its liability to blockade both by land and sea—were fully realised by naval opinion. That this was so has been shown in the previous volume, and more recent information confirms the impression that it was forced upon the Russian navy by the political, commercial and military situation.

In 1901 Admiral Skruidlov, who was then in command of the Russian Squadron in the Far East, drew up a plan under which the fleet was to be based at Vladivostok, but Admiral Alexeiev, his Commander-in-Chief, rejected it on the military ground that the primary function of the fleet was to prevent a Japanese landing at Chemulpho or the Yalu.[1] In the following year an elaborate war game set by the Minister of Marine was played in the Naval Academy at St. Petersburg, the general idea being " War with Japan in 1905." Admiral Rozhestvenski took a prominent part, and the result was to condemn the Kwang-tung base. "The main body of our " fleet," the decision ran, "must not be confined in Port " Arthur, since the entrance is narrow and could easily be " blocked. A still worse position is Dalny, since it has no " fortifications. Incomparably the best anchorage for the " fleet is Vladivostok, and it ought to be established there " in time of peace. The most convenient position would " be somewhere in South Korea. . . . The issue of " a general action would then have to be decided before " the Japanese could transport any troops."[2] On this the final conclusions of the Staff were that Sylvia Basin was necessary as an intermediate base and that the only possible place for the main base was Vladivostok. Even when it was fully understood that military considerations forbad the transference of the main base to the northern port, the need of a subsidiary base in South Korea, as a means of minimising the defects of Port Arthur, was not lost sight of. At a naval conference held at Port Arthur in April 1903 under Admiral Alexeiev, when Admiral Stark was in command of the squadron, his flag-captain urged that the whole fleet should be based in Sylvia Basin, but his idea was rejected by all the flag-officers. The reasons, which were embodied by Admiral Vitgeft in a closely-argued memorandum, were, shortly, that the key of the problem was to command the Yellow Sea, and for this object Port Arthur was the only possible base. Sylvia Basin, he pointed out, was practically within the Japanese zone of highest control, and Vladivostok was not only too eccentrically placed, but was on the far side the barrier-line—Fusan-Tsushima-Sasebo—where Japanese control was at its zenith. But it was further laid down as an essential of the selection of Port Arthur that it must be used as the base of active and untiring offensive against the lines of passage of the Japanese Army and against their Fleet, and that the parrying of the enemy's operations in Korea and Manchuria would amply justify substantial losses to the Russian Fleet. In his eyes,

---

[1] *Russian Naval Hist.*, I., page 62.
[2] *Ibid.*, I., pages 107-121.

seeing what the relative force of the opposed fleets was likely to be—the primary objective was the enemy's line of transit and not the enemy's battle fleet, and it was with the same end in view that he supported the idea of a cruiser detachment at Vladivostok.[1]

It is abundantly clear, then, that the error of devoting the Port Arthur Squadron to the defence of its base was not due to any lack of strategical insight. It was the inherent defects of the port as a base that doomed the squadron to share its fate. The trap-like nature of the place, with its liability to successful isolation and attack on the land side, was fully recognised, but there was no other point which satisfied the geographical and political conditions of the case. It was also recognised that the only chance of using it with effect was that the operations based on it must be of the most active character. But the first blow of the Japanese rendered such operations extremely difficult, and so great were the technical defects of the place as a base that the Japanese by an unceasing expenditure of energy were just able to maintain the domination they had gained.

Had Admiral Makarov lived there is little doubt the squadron would have recovered its offensive temper. He at least believed that as a defensive weapon it must be used at sea and was determined that the Japanese should not land in Liautung without dispute. But this was not his main object. He brought with him the conceptions of the Headquarter Staff, which saw in Vladivostok the correct base. Now that the Japanese had landed high up on the west coast of Korea the basis of the Far Eastern plan had broken down. By the unfulfilled postulates of that plan the continued existence of Port Arthur as a base was too precarious to rely on, and he came out with the intention of massing the whole Pacific Fleet at the northern port.

But here friction at once arose. The new plan meant the abandonment of Port Arthur to its fate, and in the eyes

---

[1] *See post*, Appendix A., p. 399, "Russian preparatory strategy." At p. 407 will be found an account of the staff war-games and the resulting appreciation of the lines on which the war plan should be framed.

The memorandum which Admiral Makarov wrote on the dangers of Port Arthur as a base the day before the war broke out and his remarkable prophecy of what would happen has been referred to in Volume I., p. 92. The text and the reason his warning was not acted on are now available and are given in full. Appendix A. IX, *post*, p. 409.

of the garrison such a move was nothing less than desertion on the part of the Fleet. Their opposition consequently was strenuous, even to acrimonious reflections on the honour of the sister service. It is possible that a man of Admiral Makarov's character might have overcome the difficulty, but it was quite beyond the power of his successor. The moral objection to a Fleet abandoning an Army that has been devoted to the defence of a naval base must always be very great. In the case of an Imperial outpost so remote and so completely isolated the objections were peculiarly strong; and as the ever increasing pressure upon the place from the land side emphasised the propriety of the Fleet's escape, so it also made heavier the moral difficulty of desertion. Thus it was that the actual physical disadvantages of Port Arthur as a fleet base—its remoteness, and its liability to isolation— almost inevitably involved the squadron in its doom. Only a man of the strongest personality and the highest warlike spirit could have broken the spell. But Admiral Vitgeft was not of that stamp; moreover, he was subordinate to the military commandant of the place; and, owing to the ease with which it could be invested, neither man could be replaced by officers whose grasp of the general situation might have steeled them to consummate the sacrifice.

It was not, then, that the men who were guiding the war did not see right, nor that the right spirit was lacking in the Fleet as a whole. It was that the premature seizure of Port Arthur involved the Russians in a strategical situation so vicious that the comparatively small initial success of the Japanese was enough to entangle them in it inextricably. The only possible means of recovering strategical freedom was a decisive victory at sea and for that the naval strength of Russia was unprepared.

Whether the plan of the Headquarter Staff which Admiral Makarov was charged to carry out could have retrieved the situation is another question; in any case it must have involved a radical change in the Russian war plan. The concentration of the Fleet at the northern base would have meant abandoning the actual objects of the war to the Japanese, and if this had been done it is difficult to see how eventual success could have been won, unless indeed the Russians were prepared to give the war an unlimited character and launch from Vladivostok an overwhelming counterstroke against Japan itself. A comparatively late development of naval strength in the theatre of war might conceivably have made such a method feasible, but no trace of such a change of plan has been found.   All we know is that from the moment the Baltic Fleet was set on foot the intention was to make Vladivostok the main naval base ; everything possible was to be concentrated there ; and from now onward the interest of the war centred on the effort to realise the new idea which the fall of Port Arthur had left without any rival.

CHAPTER X.

PROGRESS AND ALTERED FUNCTION OF THE BALTIC FLEET.

[Charts I, VI.]

EVEN before the fall of Port Arthur the practical destruction of the squadron had cleared the board for a fresh plan of campaign, and it was mainly for the purpose of framing one to meet the new outlook that Admirals Togo and Kamimura had been summoned to Tokyo. The Chief of the Naval Staff, we are told, " was anxious to come to an understanding " with them on the question of operations against the Russian " re-inforcing squadron." [1] On December 30th they made a public entry into the capital, where an ovation awaited them. As soon as the ceremonies and rejoicings were over serious work began and from that day forward the two Admirals with their staffs were installed at the Imperial Headquarters.

The arrangement is remarkable if only in contrast with the method under which the original plan had been prepared. In that case, so far as we know, it had not been thrashed out in conference; everything had been done by a somewhat meagre and perfunctory correspondence at the last moment between the Naval Staff and the Admiral at sea.[2] The change seems to indicate a more experienced grasp of the conditions under which naval staff work may be expected to give the best results. It at least finds a parallel in our own war experience and conforms to our early practice of summoning Admirals at sea, when opportunity offered, to assist at the deliberations of the Secret Committee of the Council which was then the equivalent of the Committee of Imperial Defence, such conferences being usually held on the eve of the spring campaigning season.

In order to grasp the problem which the conference had to solve we must recall what the actual situation was in the first week of the new year when the deliberations took place. By that time the two main divisions of the Baltic Fleet had concentrated in the north of Madagascar, but the belated cruiser division, or the "Overtaking Squadron" as it was officially called, was still in the Mediterranean.[3] Under Captain

---

[1] *Japanese Published History; Revue Maritime,* Vol. 188, p. 399.

[2] *See ante,* Vol. 1, pp. 72 *et seq.,* and for Admiral Togo's summary of what took place *see post,* p. 383.

[3] Cruisers *Oleg* and *Izumrud,* three destroyers, and two auxiliary cruisers, *Dnyepr* and *Rion.* Two destroyers and the *Okean* had fallen out.

Dobrotvorski of the *Oleg* it had left Libau on November 16th, but, owing to various breakdowns, it was a month before the leading ships reached Suda Bay. There a long delay ensued while the various units gathered from the French ports to which they had gone for repairs, and, finally, it was not till January 8th that the bulk of the squadron was able to sail for the Canal—more than a week, that is, after the main concentration had taken place at Madagascar.

With the main portion of the fleet things were equally unsatisfactory. When the two divisions parted at Tangier it was on the understanding that they were to meet at Diego Suarez, where they would be able to complete in comfort their final preparations for the critical part of the voyage. Their impression was that they would be able to make as free with the colonial ports of their ally as they had hitherto done with those in European waters. On this supposition both divisions acted as they proceeded, to the serious annoyance of the French Government,[1] and hitherto neither neutral protests nor those of the Japanese had produced any effect. But in the case of Diego Suarez it was no mere question of coaling and ordinary repairs, but of using a neutral port as a rendezvous and point of concentration. Such use came near to making the neutral port a base of operations, especially as extensive arrangements had been made for the purpose. Moorings had been laid down, quantities of provisions (including 1,000 bullocks) had been collected, and the staff of the " Messageries Maritimes " workshops had been increased. It is not surprising, therefore, that the Russian Staff in this case felt compelled to take seriously the remonstrances which the French were obliged to make, and to telegraph to both admirals that they must not enter Diego Suarez. The Russians, however, had been given to understand that no objection would be raised to their using Nossi Bé, an open roadstead amongst the islands on the north-west coast, about 130 miles from the prohibited port. There Admiral Felkerzam was ordered to proceed, and there he arrived on December 28th.[2]

Next day the main division, after ten days' steaming from Angra Pequeña, anchored on the east coast of Madagascar

---

[1] After leaving Tangier the Felkerzam Division coaled at Suda Bay, Suez, Jibuti, and Alula, near Cape Guardafui. The main division used Dakar and Gaboon (French), Great Fish Bay (Portuguese), and Angra Pequeña (German).

[2] Semenov, *Rasplata*, 333, 342.

between St. Mary Island and the mainland. Somewhere on his way down the west coast of Africa Admiral Rozhestvenski had received the instructions from home that he must not go to Diego Suarez ; but the alternative which the French government was ready to permit was not to his liking ; he was eager to get on as soon as possible, and Nossi Bé was 600 miles out of his course. Furthermore, he knew that the waters in that part of the Mozambique Channel had been very imperfectly surveyed ; they were full of uncharted coral reefs, and were consequently highly dangerous as the rendezvous of a large fleet. He had, therefore, telegraphed in reply that he intended to use St. Mary Channel, and requested that the Second Division might be ordered there. Clearly he expected to find Admiral Felkerzam at this spot, and, as he had not arrived, he did not know where to look for him.[1] This, however, was a small matter compared with the news he received a few hours after anchoring. It was brought during the afternoon by the hospital ship *Orel*, which had put into Cape Town for supplies, and it was to say that the Port Arthur Squadron had been destroyed in the harbour.

Here, then, was a complete breakdown of the plan of operations that had been imposed upon him. The idea of concentrating a superior fleet by a combination with the Port Arthur Squadron and then fighting a decisive action for the control of the theatre of war was now definitely abandoned. The effect upon his mind seems to have been to revive the hope of being allowed to act defensively on his original plan ; and eager to be gone at the earliest moment he sent his ocean-tug the *Rus* down to Tamatave to get confirmation of the news and to find out where his colleague was.

On the morning of December 31st the *Rus* returned with news that Admiral Felkerzam was at Nossi Bé. She also brought telegrams with intelligence that ten days previously two Japanese armoured cruisers and six light ones had passed Singapore steering to the southward, and that two auxiliary cruisers had left for Mozambique. Admiral Rozhestvenski immediately despatched one of his Staff in a transport to Diego Suarez with orders to send him the colliers which were waiting there, and

---

[1] Semenov, on the authority of the Flag-Lieutenant Sventorzhetski, *Rasplata*, 333. The lieutenant said that the Admiral was very much incensed at this autocratic decision of our " armchair strategists." *See post*, p. 144, note.

to get off a telegram to Admiral Felkerzam bidding him to join the flag at St. Mary at once. The impression formed by his Staff was that it was then his intention to carry out his original scheme. They believed that his idea was to proceed with all speed to the seat of war in order to break into it before the Japanese had time to refit their ships and replace their worn guns. Could he do this he would endeavour with his seven battleships and his two best cruisers to force his way through to Vladivostok, leaving behind all damaged or otherwise useless units, and then from the northern base he would commence active operations against the enemy's lines of communication.[1] In this idea he was probably encouraged by a telegram he received from Admiral Skruidlov asking for a rendezvous at which he could join the Baltic Fleet, presumably with the two remaining armoured cruisers, which, thanks to the reinforcement of the Vladivostok yard, were being rapidly repaired. Admiral Rozhestvenski's reply was, " February 2 in " the Sunda Archipelago."[2]

While awaiting news of his colleague Admiral Rozhestvenski proceeded to coal, but the weather proved too bad, and on January 4, by the advice of the local French officials, he moved to a new sheltered anchorage of which they told him, known as Tang-tang Roads.[3] The *Rus* had been sent again to Tamatave to get into communication with Admiral Felkerzam and find out what he was doing, but she had not returned nor was there any sign of the colliers from Diego Suarez. The reports that had been received of Japanese cruiser movements led to the belief that both the tug and the colliers were afraid to move, and three cruisers of Admiral Enkvist's division were sent to Diego Suarez to fetch them and also to repeat the order for the Second Division to join the flag.

On the 5th, after they were gone, a collier came in, bringing news at last from Admiral Felkerzam. It was far from good. Of the five purchased merchant cruisers only one, the *Kuban*, had arrived; of the rest and Captain Dobrotvorski's " Overtaking Division " there was no news whatever; and, worst of

---

[1] Semenov, *Rasplata*, pp. 335, 348.

[2] Letter of Lieutenant Sventorzhetski, dated "Nossi Bé, February 3, 1905." *Dvadtzati Vyek*, 14 June 1906. The writer, as flag-lieutenant on Admiral Rozhestvenski's staff, had the duty of cyphering and decyphering correspondence, and was therefore entirely in his confidence. *See* Semenov, *Rasplata*, pp. 337-8.

[3] Antongil Bay seems to be the place, as marked on our maps.

all, the Admiral reported that, in obedience to orders from the Naval Staff at home, he had begun overhauling machinery where he was. Everything had been opened up, and he could not possibly move for a fortnight. In his exasperation at the interference from headquarters, Admiral Rozhestvenski now decided to take his whole division round to Nossi Bé in order, as he said, "to dig his colleague out."

He had fixed the departure for the next morning, but before he weighed the *Rus* returned with nothing from Admiral Felkerzam, but with news that Port Arthur had fallen. It was a catastrophe which had been already discounted so that it made no great impression in the squadron, and at the appointed hour they weighed for Nossi Bé. On the way they met a cruiser which Admiral Felkerzam had sent round with his only two serviceable destroyers, one of which had broken down. From them they learnt in detail the condition of the Second Division, and the events of its voyage, which were one long list of every conceivable breakdown. It was in these depressing circumstances they spent the Russian Christmas Day (January 7th), but the Admiral was still undaunted. After mass and parade he assembled the hands and made them a stirring speech, bidding them remember that, hard as their work was, he and they were serving a grateful country, and an Emperor who would not forget them. "Our task," he said in conclusion, in a voice of deep emotion yet ringing with confidence, "our task is heavy, our goal far " distant, and our enemy strong. But always remember the " eyes of all Russia are upon you in confidence and firm " hope. May God help us to serve her honourably and " justify her trust." The effect was to rouse the men to the highest enthusiasm, and with renewed spirit they proceeded on their course. Cleared for action and with the crews sleeping at their guns they felt their way through the perilous waters, and on January 9th anchored at Nossi Bé without mishap.

In the Second Division the Admiral found a very different spirit from that which he had roused in his own. They were doing repairs leisurely in sure expectation of a recall home, but the presence of the Commander-in-Chief quickly stirred everyone into activity. At St. Mary, on hearing the condition of the Second Division, he had fixed January 14th for the start on the last stage of the voyage. He now saw that that was impossible, and decided to move in any event on the

18th, no matter what ships had failed to arrive. But in this resolution he again counted without headquarters.

Since November Captain Klado had been employing the enforced leisure of his attendance on the Dogger Bank arbitration in writing a series of vigorous articles to the Russian Press inculcating with much plausible and well-informed argument an entirely new plan of campaign.[1] His general line was that the war plan then in operation could not possibly result in success. For the final triumph of the Russian arms everyone was looking to the Army—to General Kuropatkin's expected offensive return which was to relieve or recover Port Arthur and drive the Japanese from Korea. Fortified as he was with local knowledge and the plain strategical condition of the theatre of war he could point out that such a hope without command of the sea was chimerical. It was a simple question of communications. Owing to the extreme difficulty of the inland lines they were quite inadequate for the advance of a large army without being supplemented by coastwise and riverine lines. This fact, as he pointed out with perfect truth, the Japanese had proved by experience, and it was solely because their armies had had the assistance of the fleet working along the coast and in inland waters that their troops had been able to advance as they had done. Similarly the Russians, so soon as they began to push forward in an offensive return, would find themselves in the same predicament. Unless their fleet was able to acquire such a predominance that it would be able to establish coastal bases, as the Japanese had done, in time with the army's advance, there would be no possibility of subsistence at any distance from the railway and the army must be more or less tightly tied to the metals.

But this was only half the problem. Assuming that by superhuman efforts adequate lines of supply could be established for an advance into Liau-tung and Korea it was unavoidable that there would be many points at which they must run within striking distance of the sea and these points would become more numerous and more costly to guard the further the advance was pushed; at all such points the lines of supply would be open to constant interruption by comparatively small combined expeditions at the hands of a Power in control of

---

[1] These articles appeared daily in the *Novoe Vremya*, November 24–29. They were republished with additions, in book form, at the end of December, and were translated into French under the title: *La Marine Russe dans la guerre russo-japonaise.*

adjacent waters. To attempt to preserve them from such attacks by a lavish use of line of communication troops could only end in exhausting the mobility and offensive power of the operating force; by no means, in short, could adequate protection be found except upon the sea. Unless such protection could be established it was obvious that in Korea at least the lines of communication would be so weak that an army depending on them could not possibly hope to dislodge a determined enemy securely supplied by the new Fusan–Seoul railway. Their own experience had already proved the truth of his view, for it was for these very reasons, he urged, that the idea of forming an army under General Linevich to operate in Korea from the Ussuri district had been abandoned. The plan of thus striking in rear of the Japanese, inviting as it was, had been found quite unworkable without control of the Sea of Japan.

His case, in fact, came to this. Having been in touch with the Staff on the spot he realised that Russia, for all her vast military power, was caught in the toils of a war based on limited territorial objects, which the enemy had practically isolated by sea and occupied in strength, and that only in breaking down that isolation by naval effort lay the way to getting possession of the objects. No matter what military strength Russia might eventually develop in Manchuria, it would avail her nothing unless she could wrest from Japan the control of the sea on which depended the security of her own communications and her power of paralysing those of her enemy, and that could only be done by a decisive fleet action.

This appreciation being admitted there arose at once the question — was Admiral Rozhestvenski's squadron powerful enough to win such a victory? Clearly it could not be relied on for such an achievement; and the only way was to reinforce him before he reached the theatre of war with every ship that could be found of any fighting value. Unless this was done the war must continue for an indefinite time, or else be brought to a conclusion with a peace that would be nothing less than a humiliation of the name of Russia. So to his solid strategical reasoning he added a stirring appeal to national pride to save the face of their country; and the appeal took hold and spread like fire.

Within a week the Government had decided to take action, and at the eleventh hour they gave orders to form that third squadron which Admiral Skruidlov had urged as early as

April, and for which Admirals Dubassov and Birilev had been pressing during the autumn. The instructions issued on December 16th were to prepare for service the old battleship *Imperator Nikolai I.*, the three "Admiral" coast-defence ships *Senyavin*, *Ushakov* and *Apraxin*, and the obsolescent armoured frigate *Vladimir Monomakh*. It was at best a sorry squadron which by no means could render Admiral Rozhestvenski strong enough to play the new part that was assigned to him. No one knew this better than Captain Klado himself, and he was soon busy with another impassioned appeal to the Government to tread all diplomatic difficulties under foot and send out the whole Black Sea fleet. It was a counsel of despair to which no Government could listen for a moment, and they were forced to be content with the available ships in the Baltic—with a squadron in fact in whose efficacy no one could possibly have believed, except as a device for satisfying a forlorn and dangerous popular outcry.

Tidings of the new departure reached Admiral Rozhestvenski while he was still at St. Mary, and it struck him with consternation. To hang such a dead weight round his neck was to doom him to destruction. He was still of opinion that a rapid appearance in the theatre of war was his only chance ; if only he might start on his appointed day he could be there by the end of February, and he earnestly begged to be allowed to go without waiting for the Third Squadron, or even for the "Overtaking Division." His insistence seems to have had the effect of bringing about a compromise, for we are told that on Christmas Day (January 7th), he received categorical orders that he was to await the arrival of the "Overtaking Division."[1] At this time there was no prospect of the Third Squadron being able even to leave Libau for at least a month, and when Admiral Rozhestvenski reached Nossi Bé it must have been in confidence that he was to proceed without it. As for the "Overtaking Division," since he had fixed January 18th for his departure after he had received the order to wait for it, it is to be presumed that he intended to meet it at some other rendezvous than Nossi Bé.

Such being the actual situation at sea when the Japanese Staff conference began to sit, it remains to see how far its deliberations were able to penetrate it and what course was adopted as a consequence of the appreciation arrived at.

---

[1] Smirnov.

CHAPTER XI.

JAPANESE PREPARATIONS FOR THE BALTIC FLEET.

[Map IX. Charts I, IV, VI, XA.]

IT is clear there can have been no real certainty about the condition of the Baltic Fleet and its intentions when the Japanese Naval Headquarter Staff and the Fleet Staff sat down in conference to consider the plan of operations to deal with it We have already seen how towards the end of November, when it was obvious that the two divisions were making for the Pacific, the Japanese Staff calculated that they might unite and reach the Formosa Channel—that is, the entrance to the theatre of war—in the early days of January. It was still doubtful whether their object was to proceed direct to Vladivostok or whether they would seek to operate in the Yellow Sea with a view of recalling into being the remnants of their defeated First Squadron. Knowing as we do now how completely paralysed that squadron was, it seems strange after the event that the Japanese could still regard it as an element of danger. These apprehensions are to be explained by their entire ignorance of the internal condition of Port Arthur and the deep moral impression its obstinate defence had created. Nothing is more disturbing to naval plans than that an enemy should possess a base within the zone of operations. This source of disturbance the Japanese had calculated confidently on eliminating long before, and so galling was its continued existence to the appreciations of the Staff, that it set up a fresh apprehension; and this was the prospect of having to face a new disturbance of the same kind. Their dominant anxiety, in fact, at this time was that, whichever of the two possible intentions the Russians might have in mind, their primary object might be to establish a temporary base of operation at some point near Formosa or on the southern coast of China.[1]

In order to clear up the situation as far as possible it was desirable to ascertain whether any gathering of colliers or transports was taking place which would indicate the time and point of concentration, and also whether there were any signs of the formation of a temporary base in the suspected area. To this end a thorough reconnaissance had been decided upon, and it will be remembered that Admiral Togo on the eve of the final

---

[1] *See ante*, p. 97.

attack on 203-Metre Hill had been called on to provide three cruisers for the purpose, viz., the *Hongkong Maru* and *Nippon Maru*, which had just been added to his force for the crisis of the blockade, and the *Niitaka*, which was completing her refit at Yokoska.

The orders to these ships reveal to some extent what the information of the Staff was at the time. The two merchant cruisers which were to act in company received their instructions on December 5th. The latest intelligence, they were informed, was that on November 27th the main Baltic Division had coaled at Angra Pequeña ; that the Second Division had left Suez ; and that the "Overtaking Division" had passed the Skaw. "The " object of your cruise," so their instructions ran, " is, after " making movements near Singapore, and if time permits near " the Sunda Strait, to reconnoitre such harbours on the Cochin " China coast as might be used by the Baltic Fleet and to " observe the condition of the China Seas before the enemy " arrives at Singapore or Java." They were warned, however, that should the arrival of the Baltic Fleet be more rapid than was expected, so that no time would be left for the movements off Singapore, "they were to confine their work to the Sunda Strait and the coasts of Cochin China."

With these instructions they left Sasebo on December 13th and ran down to Makung, the advanced Japanese station in the Pescadores, where they were to call for intelligence and orders. As on arriving there they found no fresh news they carried on for Singapore and anchored ten miles off the port on December 22nd. Here their consul came off with telegrams stating exactly what the Headquarter Staff knew the previous day. Admiral Rozhestvenski had passed the Cape of Good Hope on December 19th ; the Second Division left Jibuti on the 14th, and the "Overtaking Division" was apparently still at Crete. A later telegram gave the first suggestion of what the concentration point was to be. There was a report, it stated, that the Second Division was proceeding to Madagascar to join the Main Division, but it added that this information was not absolutely certain. A final telegram informed them that the enemy were hurriedly organising a Third Squadron at Libau which Admiral Birilev was to command. They were further instructed that as the Dutch neutrality seemed not too rigid they must examine Telok Betung and Padang, two little-known harbours in Sumatra.

Passing through the Sunda Strait they reached Telok Betung on the 25th. Nothing suspicious was found, and a staff telegram reached them to say there was no further news, and that, instead of Padang, they were to examine Tjilatjap on the south coast of Java. This they did on the 28th, but finding it useless as an anchorage, they returned through the Sunda Strait to carry on with their original programme. After appearing before Batavia they passed northward through the Gaspar Strait and then up the west coast of Borneo as far as Labuan, where they anchored on January 3rd. Having thus completed their reconnaissance of the Malay Archipelago without finding any sign of Russian preparations, they ran across the China Sea to Cambodia, where they separated to search the islands and inlets at the entrance of the Gulf of Siam. But it was still without seeing any indication of a base being prepared, or indeed any spot really suitable for the purpose.[1] Their task being now ended they returned to Makung on January 14th and there found orders recalling them to Sasebo.

Meanwhile the *Niitaka*, having left Sasebo on December 20th, had been carrying out a similar examination of the Chinese coast southward from the mouth of the Yangtse. Having examined all the likely inlets southward as far as Formosa, she was able on December 26th to report to Tokyo, through the Taiko Wireless Station in the north of the island, that she had found nothing. Thence she went off Amoy, and after communicating with the consul, pushed on as far as Hongkong, whence she stood across to the north point of Luzon. Making the Bojodor light early on 29th, she ran south along the coast and turned back at nightfall. So making her way past the south end of Formosa, she reached Makung on the 31st. Here, after waiting a day, she received a staff order to go back to Luzon and examine it as far as Manila Bay. This she did, passing that port on January 5th, and then, holding on till nightfall, she extinguished her lights and turned back northward. By January 11th she was home again, having to report no trace of a base being found nor any sign of Russian colliers or other transports.

With the board so far cleared it would seem that the Combined Staff had little difficulty in coming to a conclusion. The negative evidence of the reconnaissance, combined with the fall of Port Arthur, had greatly simplified the problem.

---

[1] The points visited were Kamput Koh-Tron, and Alpha Island (6 miles south of it), Water Island and Pulo Condore.

So long as Port Arthur continued in being the destination of the Baltic Fleet had been in some doubt, and the probability had to be faced of having to deal with Admiral Rozhestvenski operating from a base in the China Sea with a view to effecting a junction with the Port Arthur Squadron and relieving the blockaded fortress. In these conditions the proper distribution of the Japanese Fleet was an open question. It could be argued that to ensure contact it might be necessary to abandon a defensive concentration in their zone of highest control and operate offensively, advancing to a concentration point possibly as far south as Formosa. An advance of this kind was the Russian anticipation of what was likely to happen, but if any such idea had ever existed in the Japanese Staff, the grounds for it had been removed. There was now only one line of operation open to the Russians and that was to proceed direct to Vladivostok either by the Straits of Korea or by one of the northern straits. What, therefore, was required was an interior position at which could be formed what the French call the *masse centrale ;* or, in other words, a position where the fleet could be massed in certainty of getting contact whichever route their enemy adopted.

Such a position was to be found at Sylvia Basin, the old strategical centre which had played so prominent a part in the diplomatic manœuvres before the war. Not only was it interior as regards Vladivostok either for the direct or the north-about routes, but from its extent and natural features it was an ideal field for tuning up an expectant fleet to fighting pitch. As soon, therefore, as the fleet admirals with their staffs were installed at headquarters, it was decided apparently without any hesitation that the fleet should be concentrated in the Straits of Korea. For this purpose the old organisation in three squadrons was retained, the First and Second Squadrons which formed the old "Combined Fleet" being based at Masampho in Sylvia Basin, while the Third Squadron, consisting of the Fifth, Sixth and Seventh Divisions under Admiral Kataoka, was, as before, based at Takeshiki, as a guard for the Straits.

An absolute concentration was, in fact, not possible, and this was due to the failure of Admiral Kamimura to deal decisively with the Vladivostok cruisers. They were by this time again in being and were having their old disturbing effect. And apart from this consideration, when once it was clear that Vladivostok was to be the new Russian base of operation, it became necessary to see that so far as possible its efficiency for that purpose should not be increased by the inflow of coal and other naval stores from the sea. Since the recall of the *Hongkong Maru* and *Nippon Maru* for their reconnaissance to the south, the Tsugaru Strait, the only approach to Vladivostok that was not ice-bound, had been left unwatched except by the slender Tsugaru guard, consisting of two gun boats and a division of torpedo-boats.[1] But already, on December 30th, Admiral Misu, then at Kuré, was ordered by the Staff to proceed to Takeshiki, take under his command the two armoured cruisers *Adzuma* and *Asama* and form the guard of that area.[2] From this time forward the watch on the approaches to Vladivostok was strictly maintained, and as the season advanced and the navigation became more open the blockading squadron was gradually increased. On January 22nd the command was taken over by Rear-Admiral Shimamura, hitherto chief of the staff to Admiral Togo and now promoted to flag rank, Admiral Misu on the reorganisation of the fleet being made second-in-command in the First Division.

The reorganisation was issued on January 12th, after the joint staff had been at work ten days. By this time the Japanese Government knew that the two main divisions of the Baltic Fleet were concentrating at Madagascar and a formal protest had been handed to the French Government, but the only reply was that there was no official knowledge of the alleged violation of their neutrality. It was also known at Tokyo that the " Overtaking Division " was passing through the Canal. It was none too soon, therefore, to have everything in order.

Under the new organisation[3] the two Argentine cruisers were definitely allotted to the First Division in place of the two lost battleships, and, as before, Admiral Dewa with the Third Division was attached to it. This formed the First Squadron. The Second Squadron, still under Admiral Kamimura, included his own, the

---

[1] One of the gunboats, *Takao*, was recalled on January 12th to reinforce the Seventh Division in the Third Squadron at Takeshiki.

[2] Captain Fuji, the former commander of the *Adzuma*, had been made chief of the staff to Admiral Kamimura of the Second Squadron. Her new commander was Captain Murakami from the *Chiyoda*. The change was brought about by the promotion of Captain Shimamura to flag-rank and his being replaced as chief of the staff to the First Squadron by Captain Kato from the Second Squadron.

[3] For details of the organisation in its fully developed form, *see* *post*, p. 217, note.

Second Division, now comprising six armoured cruisers, and, as before, Admiral Uriu's Fourth Division. Attached to the First Squadron was a flotilla, consisting of three destroyer divisions and one of first-class torpedo-boats. The Second Squadron's flotilla was made up of the other two destroyer divisions and two divisions of first-class torpedo-boats. All these were stationed at Sylvia Basin.[1] The Third Squadron at Takeshiki was unchanged, except for the lost units, and it had attached to it a flotilla of five divisions of torpedo-boats. Besides these, as a permanent guard for the Straits zone, there were distributed between Moji and Takeshiki four divisions of torpedo-boats (14 boats), and in addition there were twenty-five auxiliary gunboats for harbour defence and special service.[2]

The weak point in view of the strategical conditions was the dearth of light cruisers for scouting purposes. To meet this, five more merchant steamers were shortly afterwards converted into auxiliary cruisers, bringing the total number of them under the naval flag to a round dozen.[3]

The concentration zone may be taken as extending as far as what was known as the Fourth Guard Line—that is, a line some 50 miles south-west of Tsushima, which started from an outlying skerry of the Goto group, called Shirose—50 miles due west of Sasebo, and ran about north-west to the Castle Group, a little east of Port Hamilton. This line was eventually occupied by regular light cruisers, and in advance of it were a series of four patrol sections, to the guard of which as the crisis approached the new merchant cruisers were detailed.[4]

---

[1] The losses in the destroyer flotilla had been more than made good by three new ones—*Fubuki, Ariake, Arare,* and the Russian prize *Ryeshitelni,* renamed *Akatsuki.* All these, with the *Harusame,* were in the 1st division, making five units instead of the usual four.

[2] The names of 25 are traceable from various sources. They were rated in three classes. Most of them had been armed in April and May 1904. When the crisis came 11 of these boats were at Sylvia Basin, two at Gensan, and one at Hakko. Admiral Togo had left nine at Port Arthur, and probably they were still in that district. *See post,* App. D., p. 418.

[3] From the Japanese Confidential Machinery Reports it appears that the following four ships were armed at various ports during March 1905 :— *Shinano, Bingo, Sado,* and *Manshu,* while the *America,* having been armed in February 1904, and injured by fire, was repaired and commissioned in February 1905. *See post,* App. D., p. 418.

[4] Details of these Patrol sections are not to hand. The *Confidential History* speaks of the First Patrol Section as "west of the Goto Group," and also says the four auxiliary cruisers "were stationed in the westerly Patrol Sections and arranged from east to west." Our Attaché was.

General instructions in this sense were issued on January 21st by Admiral Togo from Tokyo, but although it was known that the "Overtaking Division" had reached Jibuti the concentration did not take place at once. The whole of the ships were not yet out of dockyard hands, and besides the increasing call of the northern blockade there were other special services demanded of the Navy which forbade its being left free for training, rest and preparation for the coming trial of strength. The fact was that military considerations once more asserted themselves, and the fleet was called upon for important combined work.

During the winter the two hostile armies had remained facing each other in their positions on the Sha-ho, each on its guard against an offensive movement by the other. For the present, however, the Japanese had no intention of pushing forward. Having foiled the attempt of the Russians to break down the dominating defensive attitude the Japanese enjoyed, they were content to maintain it, while every effort was exhausted to increase their force from home and repair the ravages of the recent battles. Even General Nogi did not move from Port Arthur, and it was not till January 13th that he made his formal entry into the captured fortress. The reason for the delay does not appear to have been entirely the desire to rest and recruit the exhausted troops. A contributory cause was that since Newchwang was closed by the ice, the Dalny railway was the only line of supply for the Japanese left and centre, and it was scarcely equal to transporting the Third Army to the front and to supplying the other armies that were already there.

The Russians, however, were bent on resuming at the earliest possible moment the offensive movement which was so evidently necessary. The capture of Port Arthur and the destruction of the squadron, so far from relieving them of the

---

informed that they "extended approximately from Quelpart to the south " of the Goto Islands and usually steamed to the south-west at slow " speed during the daylight and returned during the night " (*Attaché Reports*, III., 91). The normal Japanese Patrol Section had a radius of 15 miles from a given point. The distance between Quelpart and the south Goto island is about 130 miles. Four normal patrol sections would cover 120 miles. As to the "guard lines," the position of the Fourth is the only one known. Another seems to have run between Osaki and Sentinel Island across the Western Channel, and a third between Ski and Tsushima for the Eastern Channel. For other cases of "guard lines," *see ante*, p. 107, and *post*, pp. 358 and 368.

necessity, rather accentuated it ; for now if success were to be
won it must be by the Army sweeping the Japanese from the
territory they had occupied.   Though it had been General
Kuropatkin's wish to renew his advance directly after the
battle of the Sha-ho, it had been found necessary to postpone
action till further reinforcements arrived.   Thanks to the
improvement of the Siberian railway fresh troops had been
pouring in fast and in the second week of January it was
decided to commence operations.   They were to begin by a
great cavalry raid on the Japanese communications with a view
of breaking the railway in their rear so as to prevent General
Nogi's army being brought up in time and also with the object
of destroying their main depôt at Newchwang.

Accordingly on January 8th a vast body of cavalry—over
80 squadrons—under General Mishchenko began a move round
the Japanese left.   On the 10th and 11th they struck the
railway in the rear, but owing to defective arrangements and
indifferent topographical knowledge they failed to do any
permanent harm.   They then moved against Newchwang and
on the 13th while General Nogi was making his state entry
into Port Arthur they attacked it, and the Japanese Staff were
able to realise how formidable was the danger to which they
had been exposed.   Fortunately, owing to the slowness and
lack of precision in the Russian movements, the Japanese had
been able to throw in reinforcements.   The attack failed,
and on the 14th General Mishchenko ordered a retirement
as the enemy's line of communication troops began to press
him.

Beyond the capture of some convoys and the destruction
of a certain amount of stores little harm had been done, but
so great was the shock to the Japanese Staff that they immediately ordered General Nogi to set out for the Sha-ho.
He was to take three of his four divisions, the XIth being
left for the time as a guard at Port Arthur.   But the troubling
of the waters which followed the raid did not cease here.
Whether or not it was the sudden demonstration of the
insecurity of the Japanese left flank we cannot tell, or whether
the idea was part of a long-prepared war plan, but certain it
is they now inaugurated an extensive scheme for protecting
their right flank and it was in this work that the Navy was
called upon to co-operate.

The idea was to form a new army for Northern Korea—
to be called the Fifth Army or the Army of the Yalu.   A

nucleus already existed in certain brigades of the First Kobi
or Reserve Division which had been landed at Antung, and
to these were added the XIth Division from Port Arthur and
another Reserve Division which was to be landed on the east
coast.　The XIth Division would start first, since, owing to
the impossibility of landing it in the Yalu on account of the
ice, it was to march round the head of the Bay of Korea.
The arrangement had an additional advantage in that the
Russian renewal of the offensive which General Mishchenko's
raid had heralded was just beginning and the division could
be used as a reserve for the main Japanese army if necessary.
On January 24th the battle of San-de-pu began by General
Kuropatkin attacking the Japanese position and next day the
XIth Division started on its long winter march.

It was with bringing the other Reserve Division into position
that the Navy was directly concerned, but for this there was
still plenty of time.　The movement may be regarded in a two-
fold aspect.　Primarily it was part of the defensive arrangement of the Japanese for retaining their dominating position.
But as such it was also a step to the inauguration of a new
strategical phase.　In fact the time for the third stage of
the war was at hand.　In the first stage they had seized the
territorial objects; in the second they had perfected their
hold upon them so far as the general situation permitted;
but the second stage, well established as it was from the
military point of view, could not be regarded as complete
in its combined aspect until the Baltic Fleet had been met
and fought.　Without definite command of the sea the
Japanese could not regard their territorial hold as absolute,
and until the Baltic Fleet was decisively defeated their command was still in the balance.　Such, however, was their
confidence on the result of the coming battle that there was
reason enough to prepare the opening of the third stage
to which the expected naval victory would directly lead.

The war was, in fact, now on the borderland of the
two stages and the operations contemplated may be regarded
as having a dual end—they would further strengthen the
territorial hold and at the same time operate as a means
of general pressure in order to persuade the enemy that they
had more to lose than to gain by refusing to recognise the
Japanese conquest.　That is to say, there were two objects in
view—the one defensive, to make secure their conquest of the
objective territory, the other offensive, to force a speedy peace.

Later on when the naval crisis developed there is reason to
believe that the object of the new movement was primarily
defensive. What the Imperial Staff had to provide against was
that while their attention was concentrated upon the sea by
the coming of the Baltic Fleet, the Ussuri army might seize
the opportunity to advance from the Tumen and restore their
lost hold on northern Korea.[1] But in its inception at any
rate the new development is probably to be regarded as a
preparatory or precautionary step in line with the general
advance which the Japanese were now about to set on foot
for at once improving their position in the conquered territory
and increasing the pressure on their enemy. The plan of the
new campaign involved a forward movement of the whole of
Marshal Oyama's army with the object of capturing Mukden,
the capital of Manchuria, and the proposed landing on the
north-east coast of Korea may well have been conceived primarily as part of this essential idea. Such at any rate would
seem to be the interpretation of the official declaration as to
the object of the new expedition. Hitherto it is said the troops
which from time to time had been allotted to Gensan were
intended to make head against a possible irruption of the
Russians into northern Korea. The actual situation was that
the Russian advanced post held Mieng-tsien, about 40 miles
north of the little port of Song-chin, in Pallada Bay. The
port itself was menaced by the Japanese, who having advanced
to the north of Broughton Bay had pushed their outposts
as far as Ham-heng, some 30 miles south-west of the Russian
outpost. Song-chin was therefore occupied by two squadrons
while two other regiments of Cossacks were deployed to the
northward as far as the Tumen estuary to keep up communication with Posiette Bay.

Broadly stated, then, this was the general military position when the new Japanese movement was inaugurated, "At
" the beginning of 1905," the official account continues, "the
" Imperial Staff, desiring to attack the Russians north of the
" Tumen estuary (that is across the Korean frontier), were
" only waiting till the troops at Ham-heng had seized Song-chin
" where they wished to land the Second Reserve Division."[2]
A somewhat different statement is also given of the object of
the Imperial Staff, viz., that it was " to extend their domina-

---

[1] See post, p. 178.

[2] Japanese Published History, Revue Maritime, Vol. 188, p. 411

" tion in the north of province of Ham-kyeng."[1]   But in
whichever aspect it is regarded, the intended operation was
clearly part of the general offensive movement.   Regarded
either as aimed at the complete occupation of Korea or as a
menace to Vladivostok that would hold a substantial part of
the enemy's forces in the Ussuri district, it was an operation
important enough to justify any reasonable interference with
the purely naval work of the Fleet.

Apart from its strategical interest, the affair is remarkable for
the extreme care with which it was conducted, affording, as it
does, a notable example of the moral effect of the loss of troops
at sea.   It was in this region that at the end of April 1904,
during Admiral Iessen's raid from Vladivostok on Gensan, a
Japanese transport had been sunk, and the elaborate care that—
in spite of the critical naval situation—was now taken to prevent
a recurrence of the disaster testifies how deep and lasting an
impression had been made.[2]   The blow which Admiral Kamimura had inflicted on the northern cruisers could not be trusted
to keep them quiet, and in any case the Vladivostok flotilla was
still intact.

So serious was the menace in the eyes of the Japanese Staff
that the conduct of the naval part of the affair was committed
to Admiral Kamimura in person, and on January 26th he hoisted
his flag again at Sasebo in the *Idzumo*.   As a preliminary
operation in view of a possible repetition of the earlier raids
from Vladivostok, it was intended to fortify Gensan, which
was to be the base of the new force.   His general instructions
from Admiral Togo, issued on February 1st, were " to protect
" the passage of troops in the Straits of Korea and as high
" as Gensan."   At the same time besides the squadron required
for this purpose the advancing season called for a reinforcement
of the Vladivostok blockade and the *Matsushima*, *Hongkong
Maru* and *Yakumo* were added to Admiral Shimamura's force,
bringing it up to three armoured cruisers, besides minor
units.   For the actual defence of Gensan, the Navy had to
provide one or two gunboats[3]; the fortification of the place
was undertaken by the Army, and Admiral Kamimura's first
duty was to escort there the Engineer Officer in command and

---

[1] *Japanese Published History, Revue Maritime*, Vol. 188, p. 401.   Ham-
kyeng is the Korean province, which stretches along the coast northward
from Gensan.

[2] *See* Vol. I., pp. 193–5.

[3] *Revue Maritime*, Vol. 188, p. 410.

the necessary material. Leaving Sasebo on February 2nd for
Sylvia Basin, he formed an escort squadron of his armoured
cruisers *Idzumo, Tokiwa* and *Kasuga*, with the light cruiser
Suma and two destroyers.

That so large a force was deemed necessary is specially
significant in contrast with the actual state of affairs at
Vladivostok. The squadron there was absolutely inert and
hopeless. At this time the whole energies of the Ussuri Staff,
as will appear later, were absorbed in preparing for an attack
in force which they regarded as practically certain to follow
the fall of Port Arthur,[1] and no better use could be found for
the *Rossiya*, the only ship fit for action, than to keep her out
in Amur Bay to prevent the Japanese seizing Russki Island
across the ice from the mainland.

Equally remarkable is the extreme caution with which
Admiral Kamimura proceeded. Leaving Sylvia Basin on
February 6th, he was off Gensan next morning. There he
stopped off Nikolskogo Island and sent in a destroyer to search
for mines, but it was blowing too hard for the reconnaissance
to be made. Next day the search was renewed in company
with the *Suma*, who was charged with taking the transport in
while the three armoured cruisers took a covering position off
the Nakhimov Peninsula to the northward. All being found
clear the *Suma* led the transport in that evening, and next day
the disembarkation began. By February 12th it was complete
and Admiral Kamimura returned to Sylvia Basin, sending the
Tokiwa to Sasebo presumably for a refit.

Meanwhile the general situation had developed considerably.
The battle of San-de-pu was at an end, and once more the Russians
had failed to make any impression on the Japanese position.
All was therefore ripe for the contemplated offensive return.
Nor was there much difficulty about the Navy affording the
further assistance that was required. So far as was known
Admiral Rozhestvenski had not moved from Nossi Bé, and
the " Overtaking Division " was still at Jibuti. On February 11th
there was further news that the Baltic Fleet had received a
serious and quite unexpected check. For the supply of his
own coal transports Admiral Rozhestvenski was relying on a
squadron of German colliers hired from the Hamburg-Amerika
Company. It was understood that they were to accompany
him to his destination, but now that Port Arthur had fallen
their owners gave them positive orders that they were to proceed

---

[1] *See post*, p. 345, *et seq.*

no nearer than they were to the seat of war.[1] The " Overtaking Division" was leaving Jibuti, and Admiral Rozhestvenski had intended to start as soon as it joined, but until something was settled with the German company this was now impossible, and it was reported that he was not likely to get away till the end of February.

On the Japanese side everything was ready for the campaign to begin in earnest. On February 6th, the day Admiral Kamimura had started for Gensan from Sylvia Basin, Admiral Togo had left Tokyo for Kuré to rehoist his flag in the *Mikasa*. Two days later Admiral Kataoka received a summons to Tokyo from Port .Arthur preparatory to taking up the command of the Straits with the Third Squadron. The Ham-heng troops had seized Song-chin, the Cossacks retiring before them to Kengsheng with their advanced guard at Mieng-tsien, and on February 13th, the day after Admiral Kamimura returned to Sylvia Basin, the Commander-in-Chief received orders to assemble in the Straits the transports for the expeditionary force, and tell off a detachment for their escort. The force he detailed was extraordinarily strong, consisting as it did of the battleship *Fuji*, three of the latest armoured cruisers, *Idzumo*, *Nisshin* and *Kasuga*, the Sixth Division of light cruisers, one despatch-vessel, and seven destroyers. The whole was again placed under Admiral Kamimura's personal command.

The detachment of such strength meant, while it lasted, a serious loosening of the Japanese concentration, but it was by no means the whole of the dispersal that now prevailed. The northern blockade had been still further strengthened, and extended as high as Yetorup Strait.[2] The northern approaches to Vladivostok were held by three merchant cruisers, *Hongkong*, *Nippon* and *Kumano*, and in spite of almost continuous blinding snow, ice floes and the terrible cold, it proved very effective. By the end of February, nine neutral contraband runners had been captured, averaging about 3,000 tons, and five more were taken later. With two armoured and two light cruisers, Admiral

---

[1] This was reported by Reuter on February 11th. The position of the company is not quite clear. Semenov, *Rasplata*, 347, says they would not undertake to deliver coal anywhere outside neutral waters, and in neutral waters delivering was forbidden. This appears to mean that they objected to deliver their coal at an open sea rendezvous.

[2] This was not strictly speaking a blockade in the legal sense. No blockade had been declared, presumably because formal declaration was regarded as superfluous in view of the fact that everything likely to seek Vladivostok at this time would be contraband.

Shimamura in person was watching the Tsugaru Strait, mainly with the idea of preventing the enemy's cruisers breaking through.[1]

Besides this blockading force there was yet a third detachment, which is of special interest. Its purpose was a strong and bold reconnaissance in the direction of the Baltic Fleet. The mystery of that fleet's inactivity was growing for the Japanese deeper every day. They could assume that the "Overtaking Division" had reached Nossi Bé, as indeed it did on February 15 after sending back from Jibuti the destroyers which had so much delayed its voyage. It was therefore to be expected that Admiral Rozhestvenski would be moving very shortly if he meant to come at all. Next day, the 16th, the Third Pacific Squadron at last started from Libau, under the command of Admiral Nebogatov. The natural inference was that the main division would make no serious movement till it arrived. But the Japanese were not yet aware of its departure when the Staff decided on another attempt to clear up the situation. For it was on the same day, the 16th, that the instructions were issued, and they contain no reference to it. The text of the instructions, as delivered by the Staff to Admiral Togo, reveals the situation as it was seen at Tokyo :—

(1) "From reports recently received," they ran, "we judge that of the Vladivostok Squadron the *Gromoboi* and *Bogatuir* have not yet finished their repairs. The *Rossiya* comes out from time to time. The enemy's Second Pacific Squadron is still on the north-west of Madagascar diligently practising drills and evolutions.

(2) "The enemy have engaged five pilots and are keeping them under orders at Batavia. They are also preparing large quantities of war stores at Saigon, Shanghai, and other places, and apparently intend to embark these somewhere east of the Dutch Indies.

(3) "We intend to send one regular cruiser and the temporary cruisers *America Maru* and *Yawata Maru* from Sasebo by way of the Pescadores to operate in the Singapore area in order to examine the important points in the Southern China Seas, for the benefit of the future strategy of our fleet, and also, if possible, to

---

[1] He had now *Iwate* and *Asama*. The *Adzuma* and *Yakumo* had been recalled to Yokoska and Kuré for a final overhaul.

threaten and hinder the transport of war stores to the
Batavia area before the arrival of the enemy's, main
fleet in Eastern waters."

It is clear, however, that this was not the whole function
of the "Southern Detached Division" as it was called officially.
The officer in command was to receive his instructions from
the Imperial Staff and not from Admiral Togo, and after he
had received them, in issuing detailed orders to his captains,
he explained the object of the cruise in these words : "The
" Southern Detached Division will operate with the intention
" of causing the enemy to hesitate in their appreciation of the
" future movements of our fleet, and of gathering materials for
" our subsequent strategy by reconnoitring the important
" positions in the southern parts of the China Sea." From
this it would appear that in the eyes of the Imperial Staff
the chief object of the cruise was to confuse the enemy, and
leave him in doubt as to where he might expect to meet the
Japanese main fleet.   It was from the Imperial Staff that the
scheme emanated.   Admiral Togo was definitely informed that
the actual movements of the detachment would be laid down
by them and all that was left to him was the selection of the
officer to command and of a cruiser to serve as a flagship.[1]

The officer he selected was Admiral Dewa, who hitherto
had had charge of the Straits.   The cruiser selected was the
Kasagi, but Admiral Togo begged to be allowed to add the
Chitose to the detachment, and this request was granted by
the Staff.   The orders he communicated to Admiral Dewa on
February 21st, the day he arrived in Sylvia Basin to resume
his active command at sea.   To supply his place in the straits
Admiral Misu in the *Nisshin* was withdrawn from the expeditionary escort and put in command of the Takeshiki area.

On the 23rd Admiral Dewa went over to Sasebo with his
flag in the *Chitose* to take up his command and next day
received from the Imperial Staff the programme he was to
follow.   He would leave on February 27th and after calling
at Makung would visit the neighbourhood of Hongkong and
the eastern edge of Hainan Island (off the Gulf of Tonkin).
Thence he would proceed off Saigon and Singapore, where
he would turn back along the north-west coast of Borneo
to Labuan, then through the Palawan Channel up the coast
of Luzon and so back to Makung, whence he was to make

---

[1] *Confidential History*, Part II., Book I., ch. ii.

Sasebo again on the 37th day—that is, April 5th. From this it is to be concluded that in the opinion of Headquarters the battle, as Admiral Dewa told his captains, was still a long time ahead. Hence the confidence with which the Staff were opening out their concentration ; and in any case should the approach of the Baltic Fleet be quicker than they anticipated, a fast cruiser squadron pushed so far forward could be relied on to give ample notice for reforming their central mass at Sylvia Basin.

On February 24th, the day after Admiral Dewa received his final orders, Admiral Kamimura left Sylvia Basin with eight transports, six military and two naval. Early on the second day the whole expedition was off the Nakhimov Peninsula, and the same careful search for mines was conducted as before. A severe snowstorm greatly impeded the work, but, nevertheless, three transports with men and stores for Gensan got in that night. Next day the snow was still so bad that the Admiral decided to postpone the movement to Song-chin. But on the 28th, the weather having cleared up, he carried on, leaving behind him the battleship *Fuji*, one cruiser, and a division of torpedo-boats to guard the two store-transports which had not yet been cleared. Next morning (March 1st), as the Manchurian army was making its opening movements for the great advance on Mukden he was off Song-chin. Here he dropped the transports with the flotilla to guard them and search for mines while he himself with the strength of the escort took up a position five miles south of Kil-tsiou Point, Kil-tsiou being the village which the Russians had been occupying from their advanced post at Mieng-tsien.[1] Two light cruisers were thrown out to keep observation immediately south and east of the point, while the boats of the squadron went back to Song-chin to assist in the landing.

By midday the flotilla was able to report that the bay was clear of mines, whereupon all the transports went in and anchored and the army landed a reconnoitring force. In about an hour's time it was able to pass the word that the Russian patrols were retiring on Kil-tsiou, and shortly before 2.0 o'clock the disembarkation began in earnest. Half-an-hour later there was landed, under command of a " Frigate-captain," a beach party drawn from what was called " The Administration of Naval Ports." It consisted of eight officers or principal

---

[1] By Kil-tsiou Point is probably meant Blagovyeschenski Point, just below Cape Bruat.

assistants, an interpreter, 42 naval ratings and 68 dockyard hands, and their main duty was to construct jetties and landing-stages, the necessary material being furnished from one of the naval transports.

In this case it would seem at first sight that there was a very wide departure from the orthodox Japanese practice and a close approximation to that of our own services. Instead of the Navy securing the *pied-à-terre* and occupying a covering position, as had been done in former landings, the work was carried out by the Army, while the beach arrangements which had been normally the province of the Army disembarkation staff were carried out entirely by the Navy. But the explanation is that Song-chin was a port already in the possession of Japanese troops and for that reason a naval landing party was not required. The naval contingent was, in fact, an administrative force charged with establishing the little port as a sea base for the Army.

By the evening the whole of the troops were ashore and for the next three days the landing of stores and material proceeded. The Cossack patrols were driven in, and on March 7th they fell back to report that the Japanese had occupied Kil-tsiou and were advancing up the coast. So slight indeed had been the opposition that on the 4th Admiral Kamimura had felt able to regard his work as completed, and calling out the *Fuji* detachment from Gensan to meet him off Cape Duroch next morning, he made for Sylvia Basin. But still with unabated caution he sent the transports and flotilla ahead while he covered their retirement with the squadron a considerable distance astern.

On the 6th he had rejoined the Commander-in-Chief's flag, to find that ever since the 2nd the battle of Mukden had been raging and was still not decided. Next day there arrived in the fleet the Emperor's principal aide-de-camp bearing the Imperial instructions to Admiral Togo. This meant the solemn inauguration of the new naval campaign ; and warlike ardour, we are officially told, now rose to its height.

CHAPTER XII.

FLEET MOVEMENTS IN MARCH AND APRIL.

[Charts I, VI, XB.]

AT Nossi Bé by this time the tone of the Russian fleet, no less than its outlook, presented a marked contrast with the elation and confidence in the Sea of Japan. As early as the first week in February an officer on Admiral Rozhestvenski's Staff had written : " The personnel of the expedition, after " hearing of the fate of Port Arthur and the destruction of " our fleet had no longer any faith in the success of our " enterprise. . . . We shall never in this war gain the " command of the sea ; that is, we shall never accomplish " the task imposed upon us. . . . What ought to be " done ? It is shameful to acknowledge it, but I say, quite " impartially, it is necessary to put an end to the naval " operations."[1]

Since that time things had been going steadily from bad to worse. Of all the errors that were committed by the Russian Headquarters in handling this forlorn hope none was greater than that they should have condemned it to wait so long in a climate known to be one of the most enervating in the world. Its evils for Europeans are only intensified by hard work, and of this there was plenty in drill, coaling and repairs. The labours of the Japanese were no less severe, but carried on, as they were, in inspiring operations amidst ice and snow and all the rigours of a North Pacific winter they were hardening the men for the crisis day by day, while in Madagascar waters the spirit and endurance of their enemy were being sapped as surely and persistently. Admiral Felkerzam, the second-in-command, was already struck down by the sickness of which he was soon to die, while harassing and incessant activity had reduced the Commander-in-Chief to a state of feverish irritability that was ill calculated to weld the crude fleet into a weapon fit for the work before it.

The constant practice in drill and evolutions of which the Japanese had heard had proved little better than a farce and had only increased the depression of all ranks. The attempts at tactical exercises had but brought out the incapacity of the

---

[1] Letter of Lieut. Sventorzhetski, 2 February, 1905, in *Dvadtzati Vyek*, 14 June 1906.

captains to handle their ships even in the most elementary
evolutions, and the target practice was even more depressing.
The Commander-in-Chief could only condemn it as a mere
waste of ammunition and it had to be stopped altogether till
an expected ordnance transport should arrive to increase the
supply.   And to all the Admiral's difficulties with the training
of the fleet was added the strain of an exhausting correspondence with headquarters, especially in regard to the recal-
citrant German colliers and the plan of operation.

In the middle of January, that is about a week after he had
received categorical orders to wait for the " Overtaking Division,"
a telegram—notorious in the fleet as No. 244—was received
from St. Petersburg, which completely knocked the heart out
of the Admiral.   It pointed out—echoing the Klado articles—
that in view of the fall of Port Arthur and the destruction of its
squadron, the function of his fleet was altered.   A task of higher
importance had devolved upon it.   It was no longer a reinforcing or relief squadron ; it was the main fleet, and its
function must be by its own efforts to secure the command of
the sea and cut off the active Japanese cruisers from their home
base.   If, therefore, in the opinion of the Admiral the squadron
as then constituted was not of sufficient strength to accomplish
the task, it must be reinforced as soon as circumstances permitted
by all available ships in the Baltic.

This appears to have been the first definite information
which Admiral Rozhestvenski had that the Government had
formally adopted the Klado policy, and it filled him with
something like despair.   The telegram had asked for his plans
and views in the light of the new situation and he hastened to
reply in a manner which he seems to have expected would open
the eyes of his superiors to the stern realities of the case.

Here is the gist of his answer : (1) With the forces at his
disposal he had no prospect of obtaining the command of the
sea ; (2) the old ships in need of a refit, which it was intended
should be sent out to him as a reinforcement, had for the most
part been failures from the first and would only serve to hamper
the fleet and not to strengthen it ; (3) the only feasible plan was
his original one of attempting to get through to Vladivostok
with the best ships and thence to operate on the enemy's communications.[1]   But to any such view it was impossible for the
Government to listen with public feeling inflamed as it was,

---

[1] Semenov, *Rasplata*, 379.

and the Admiral's clear opinion was disregarded. In the belief
of his Staff his real view was that the situation was now so
hopeless that the squadron ought to be recalled, and that he
expected his report would have that result. The Government,
however, dared do nothing but cling stubbornly to their impossible plan, and the Admiral, it is said, to whose failing health
the new scheme was insupportable, begged to be relieved.[1]

Nor was the demoralising effect of the new Staff orders
confined to the Admiral. The fleet as a whole was, of course,
ignorant of what was passing over the wires, and the cause of
the protracted inaction was unknown to both officers and men.
The inexplicable waiting became more unendurable than ever.
All the auxiliary cruisers which came by way of the Cape had
arrived by this time, and on February 15th the " Overtaking
Division " joined. Still no move was made, for the trouble
with the German colliers had still to be settled.

But this in itself was no absolute bar to a move. Their own
coal transports could carry enough fuel to take all the battleships
and the two best cruisers to Vladivostok. The Admiral, indeed,
seems for a time to have hoped that the attitude of the German
Company might prove a compelling reason for allowing him to
carry out his own plan of a dash through with his best ships.
But all hope was abandoned when on February 16th, the day
after the " Overtaking Division " joined, it was known that
Admiral Nebogatov with the Third Squadron had left Libau.

The effect in the fleet was disastrous. A spirit of insub-
ordination which the procrastination was fostering day by day
now declared itself seriously in mutiny and desertion. The
wireless experts and other civilian ratings, not bound by their
contracts to proceed, began to leave the fleet ; courts-martial
were of daily occurrence, and the Admiral in person had
constantly to deal with more or less serious outbreaks amongst
the crews. The spirit even amongst the officers was so bad
that at last to set it at rest the Admiral had to summon the
flag-officers and senior captains, and explain to them the fatal
telegram No. 244, and how his reply to it had been received.
Russian loyalty then asserted itself. The delay had been ordered
by the Tsar, and that was enough.

By the last day of the month the atmosphere was further
cleared by the completion of an arrangement with the German
colliers. The Company agreed to let them go as far as one

---

[1] Semenov, *Rasplata*, p. 380, *note*.

of the neutral ports in the South China Sea, but not higher
than the 12th degree north latitude, that is the latitude of
Kamranh Bay in French Cochin-China, over a thousand miles
short of the Pescadores. It was now possible to make a start,
except for the ordnance transport with the expected supply of
ammunition, which had not yet arrived.   But, on the other
hand, the Admiral was more deeply impressed than ever with
the hopelessness of his task. While his own fleet had not
improved in any appreciable degree, that of the Japanese must
have had time to make good all defects, and he would have
to deal with the whole of it in the highest state of efficiency.
Not only would the Russians be numerically inferior to the
Japanese, but while they themselves were without training or
experience of active service, their enemy would fight with a
ripe knowledge, as veterans well versed in the last word of naval
warfare.   In such conditions his Staff were convinced not
only that success was impossible, but that disaster could be
the only end. They held, indeed, more strongly than ever
that the one sane policy was to recall the fleet to Russia ;
persistence in its voyage could only add another victory to
the Japanese prestige, and make an endurable peace more
difficult than ever.

The Admiral, so they had reason to believe, fully shared
these views, but although on the ground of broken health he
had asked to be relieved he was no man to request or advise
a recall of the fleet.   The most he would do was to make
one more effort to open the eyes of the men who were sending the fleet to its doom.   Already Captain Klado, possibly
with the same intention, had demanded that, in spite of all
treaty obligations, the Black Sea Fleet should be thrown into
the scale, and now Admiral Rozhestvenski, as his last word,
endorsed the demand.   On March 2nd he formally reported
to the Tsar that in view of the new task imposed upon him
of obtaining command of the sea, it was desirable to strengthen
Admiral Nebogatov's squadron by adding to it the Black Sea
ships.[1]

To act on his suggestion was, of course, impossible—as
impossible as to adopt the implied alternative of recalling the
fleet.   Still the Admiral's representations seem to have been
so far effective that he received no categorical order to wait
for the Third Squadron. By this time it had passed Cher-

---

[1] *Russian Official Chronological Abstract*, Vol. III., p. 98.

bourg, and was expected to enter the Canal on March 15th.[1] Admiral Rozhestvenski's staff believed that it was now his intention to run away from his reinforcement, but till the ordnance transport arrived he could not move ; and while he waited through the first week in March the battle of Mukden was raging, Admiral Kamimura was completing the Fifth Army by his landing at Song-chin, and Admiral Dewa was well away on his reconnaissance of the South China Sea.

At the last moment the programme of this reconnaissance had been significantly modified by the Imperial Staff, for on February 24th Admiral Dewa had been instructed to include in the places to be visited Kamranh Bay. The reason given was that it was " the most suitable harbour north of Singa- " pore' large enough to take a Russian fleet of some score or " so of ships " ; but it is, of course, possible that the terms on which the Hamburg-Amerika Company were prepared to allow their vessels to proceed had leaked out, and indicated Kam- ranh Bay as a place to be attended to. Leaving Sasebo on Febuary 27th, Admiral Dewa reached Makung on March 2nd, the day Admiral Rozhestvenski was asking for the Black Sea Fleet. The news which the Japanese Admiral received from Headquarters next day (the 3rd) was that the Russian Third Squadron had coaled at Cherbourg and passed on its voyage, that a Fourth Squadron was being organised in the Baltic, and that there was no further intelligence from Vladivostok or Madagascar. He was also informed that the revolu- tionary disturbances which had broken out in the interior of Russia were unabated, and that the Siberian Railway was believed to be blocked. The last item is significant, baldly as it was communicated. The most alarming manifestation of the unrest was a widespread strike on the railways in the east of Russia, which made it more impracticable than ever to supply the port of Vladivostok by land, and one reason why the Government could not permit Admiral Rozhestvenski to make his dash was that it would be useless for the squadron to go through unless it could carry its own flying base with it. How far the Japanese Staff saw into this difficulty we do not know, but it may well have afforded them an additional reason for believing the Russians would try to act from some southern base, such as Kamranh Bay.

All we know is that on this intelligence Admiral Dewa

---

[1] The Russian Consul-General at Cairo so informed Lord Cromer on February 25th.

started on the 4th and passing Hongkong and Hainan made the French Annam coast about Touran Bay on the 7th. Here next day he divided his squadron to search Kamranh Bay and Van Fong. Both places were found suitable for harbouring a fleet, but there was no trace of preparation for receiving the Russians. He therefore carried on down the coast, clearing his collier at False Obi near Cambodia Point, and thence made Singapore on the 15th. Here he was met with the glorious news of the great victory at Mukden, but there was no word or sign of the Baltic Fleet. It was still apparently quite inert as though waiting for the Third Squadron. To this satisfactory situation he could add evidence that his cruise was achieving the desired object of clouding the movements of the Japanese Fleet. The local papers had a report that twenty-two Japanese men-of-war had been sighted in the neighbourhood, and that the cruisers which were off the port were part of a squadron which was probably commanded by Admiral Togo. Having thus shown himself with some effect Admiral Dewa turned back east the same night and made for Labuan to carry out the rest of the search programme in the Dutch sphere.

In fact the inertness at Nossi Bé was not what he supposed. On March 11th the long-expected ordnance transport had arrived, but to everyone's dismay it was found that she brought no ammunition. The disappointment was followed next day by intelligence that the Russian Army had been completely defeated before Mukden with the loss of 50,000 prisoners, 23 colours, and 500 guns. On March 10th Marshal Oyama occupied Mukden itself, affording fresh demonstration of the inability of the Russian Army to dislodge the Japanese without the aid of a fleet to operate on their communications. For without such aid they could neither check the impetus of the Japanese advance nor when the time came for an offensive return would they be able to dominate the coastal operations on which the possibility of an advance into Korea depended. It is even possible, in view of the representations which Admiral Skruidlov had made on this latter point when he first took over the Far Eastern command, that this further set-back may have hardened the determination of the Russian Government to proceed with their forlorn hope.[1] In any case Admiral Rozhestvenski's representations remained without effect ; he and his fleet were clearly to be made a sacrifice to the

[1] See his appreciation of April 4, 1904, ante, p. 13.

honour of the Russian name, and the only relief was that he was still without actual orders to await the coming of the Third Squadron. Admiral Nebogatov had only got as far as Crete and there was still time to get away from him ; but whether or not the idea was in the Admiral's mind we have no direct information. What his Staff relate is that on the morning of March 15th (the day Admiral Dewa appeared at Singapore) a Havas telegram was handed to him saying that Admiral Nebogatov had been hurriedly coaling in Suda Bay and was expected at Port Said next day. He retired with it to his cabin and presently came out to startle the fleet with an order that he meant to sail within twenty-four hours. His Staff asked if there was a rendezvous—his reply was : " No ! Nothing—to no one " and they were simply given orders to telegraph home that he was proceeding to the East. So, at 1.0 o'clock in the afternoon of the 16th he weighed—the same night that Admiral Dewa was turning back for Labuan.

The peculiar circumstances of the move left the whole fleet convinced of what was meant. The words of the telegram—the hurried clearing of a newly-arrived transport—the silence about a rendezvous—it all could only mean, even to the most intimate of his Staff, that he had finally decided to run away from his reinforcements—to leave them far behind in a last hope of forcing his superiors' hands and compelling them to recall Admiral Nebogatov's impotent squadron, and allow him at the last moment to carry out his own plan.

For the rest of the world the suddenness and secrecy of the Russian Admiral's move left his intentions a complete mystery. The Japanese Published History states that on March 18th their Staff heard from "a sure source" that he had left on the 16th, but as he had begun by steering north it was uncertain whether he had actually commenced his approach and whether he was merely moving to meet the Third Squadron at Jibuti. After that there was complete darkness until March 30th, when the Japanese Staff learnt from a steamship that the Russians had been sighted about 300 miles north-east of the northern point of Madagascar steering north-east.[1] This

---

[1] The position of the 19th was given as lat. 9° South, long. 53° East. The source of the Japanese information is unknown. Politovski (*From Libau to Tsushima*) says a German steamer overtook the fleet on the 19th and that a light was seen on the night of the 18th–19th. On March 18th our Commander-in-Chief on the Cape Station sent home a report that the Russians had left on the 12th, which as we know was

indicated a course for the Malacca Straits and not Jibuti, but after that nothing was heard of them.

Admiral Dewa failed to get any light. On March 25th he was again at Makung, having visited Labuan on the way. Neither from the British authorities there nor from his own at Makung is he stated to have received intelligence of the lost fleet. From Tokyo apparently he got nothing but a telegram bidding him carry on home and by April 1st he was back in Sylvia Basin. Here he found the whole combined Fleet was now gathered, and with the exception of the five additional auxiliary cruisers which must have been taken up during this period of anxious uncertainty, and that Admiral Togo was keeping his command incessantly engaged in tactical exercises and target practice. His return enabled the Commander-in-Chief to complete his organisation, and this was done on April 5th by placing Admiral Kataoka in command of the Third or Straits Squadron.

During all this period of uncertainty the Press of every country was filled with the most various conjectures as to the route the Baltic Fleet would take and as to what the Japanese would do to meet it. There was a general impression that Admiral Togo would make a move "to seek it out" and that the Russian Admiral would move by some indirect and improbable course in order to elude him. By no principles of strategy could either idea be justified. Never—except, as we shall see, in a moment of special provocation—did the Japanese think of quitting their commanding interior position in the Straits of Korea, which gave them every advantage of the strategical defensive combined with tactical offensive in their zone of highest control. But in those days the American exaggeration of the principles of "seeking out the enemy's fleet" so dominated naval thought in Europe that even Admiral Rozhestvenski expected that his adversary would advance to meet him, at least as far as the South China Sea. Scarcely anywhere was the nature of the war grasped with sufficient clearness to reveal how purely defensive was the strategical function of the Japanese fleet. Seeing how definitely the object of the war was a piece of sea-girt territory, the dominating object of Admiral Togo was to

---

untrue. On March 27th in response to an inquiry from the Foreign Office (dated March 25th), as to when they left Nossi Bé, our Consul at Tamatave reported that the Baltic Fleet was still there waiting for the Third Squadron. Not till the 31st was he able to report their departure.

isolate it—to keep a firm hold on the adjacent waters so that
they should be free for the passage of his own men and
stores, and denied to those of the enemy. Nothing could
justify or even suggest moving forward out of the zone he was
charged to defend, except the prospect either of definite
tactical advantage against an enemy bent on breaking his hold
or of making contact more certain for his ultimate tactical
offensive. But in this case a forward movement could serve
neither purpose. From every point of view the position at
Sylvia Basin could not be bettered. If it was the Russian
intention to hazard a decision directly, they must seek out
the Japanese fleet, since it stood there between them and the
control of the essential lines of passage and communication ;
and for the Japanese the greatest of all advantages was that
their fleet should be found in its zone of highest control. If,
on the other hand, Admiral Rozhestvenski meant first to secure
a base of operation at Vladivostok, he must either force the
Japanese position or endeavour to turn it by one of the northern
straits. Sylvia Basin was interior to all possible routes—thence
Admiral Togo could enjoy the utmost attainable certainty of
contact before his adversary could reach Vladivostok by whichever route he came. Any forward movement would detract
from that certainty and at the same time would involve an
abandonment of the area to be defended and a sacrifice of the
tactical advantages of the zone of highest control.

Had Port Arthur still been in being the problem would
not have been quite so simple. Two destinations would then
have been open to the Baltic Fleet and it is possible that the
Japanese, for whom a decisive action was essential, would
have had to seek it by advancing to a position interior to the
enemy's alternative lines of operation. But it was one of
the great results of the sacrifice which General Nogi's army
had been called on to make that Port Arthur was eliminated.
The Russians were reduced to a single practical line, and the
true position for the Japanese, the position which best
served every strategical and tactical purpose, was consequently
defined with a precision that has seldom been surpassed.
The wonder is that everyone could not see it as clearly
as did the Japanese. The general failure to appreciate the
situation correctly is only to be explained by the darkening
effects which are caused by the abuse of maxims, by the
endemic tendency to use them crudely as solutions, instead
of reasoning by the principles they purport to condense. In

this case the maxim does not adequately condense the principle. The principle is to get contact with the enemy in the most advantageous attainable conditions and this is not always best arrived at by seeking out the enemy's fleet. If the advantage of strategical defence is not on our side it is usually the only way—we must seek out our enemy and fight him where he chooses to be found, or where by a rare chance we may succeed in surprising him. If, on the other hand, the advantage of strategical defence is with us, then to seek out the enemy's fleet is to waive that advantage and make a present of it to the other side.

It was a general misapprehension of these fundamental principles combined with a misapprehension of the Japanese strategical tendencies that led to the widespread belief that they would probably make an offensive strategical movement with their main fleet to meet the Baltic Squadron. This idea the Japanese Staff seems to have done its best to encourage, and it was an idea which seems certainly to have been in Admiral Rozhestvenski's mind. If such a movement were made it would open the door to evasion and hence the gratuitous advice that was showered upon him in the Press as to the route he should take. But he himself never, so far as we know, wavered between more than two alternatives, the Straits of Malacca and the Sunda Straits. Before he left Nossi Bé he had chosen the former. It had many advantages. It was the usual commercial route, and to take it boldly was just what was wanted to rehabilitate the fallen prestige of the Russian Navy and to raise the broken spirit of his fleet. Moreover, the earlier reconnaissance of the Japanese, combined with the reports of the inadequate intelligence agents on whom the Russian Staff depended for information, had led to a belief that the Sunda Archipelago was being watched. On the whole, therefore, besides the moral advantage of the natural route, it was the one most likely to lend itself to evasion. It was for the Straits of Malacca, then, that Admiral Rozhestvenski was making.

It was not, however, till April the 8th that the veil was lifted. On that day a British India ship reported at Singapore that the previous day she had passed the lost fleet off One Fathom Bank. Admiral Rozhestvenski had, in fact, reached the Straits on the 5th but had not been reported. In spite of continual breakdowns of all kinds, of having to coal three times in the open and to tow the destroyers in order to save their machinery, he had accomplished the distance in twenty days.

The news of his appearance reached Sylvia Basin on the 8th, and Admiral Togo, presumably by previous arrangement, assumed direction of the whole fleet.   Hitherto, as we have seen, the movements of the Northern Division had been directed by the Imperial Staff, but now the Commander-in-Chief took control.   His first step, in fact, was to telegraph the news to Admiral Shimamura, who was then to the northward, upon the approaches to Vladivostok, with an order to leave an auxiliary cruiser at Yetorup Strait to stop contraband, and to concentrate the rest of his command in readiness to oppose any movement of the Vladivostok Division southwards.   The instructions which the Commander-in-Chief gave to Admiral Shimamura were, that the watch on the Russian cruisers was henceforth to be his primary object and the stoppage of contraband secondary.   The division now consisted of the *Asama, Iwate, Takachiho* and *Akitsushima*, with three auxiliary cruisers (*Hongkong Maru, Nippon Maru, Kumano Maru*), while two more, *Bingo Maru* and *Sado Maru*, were at the same time sent up to reinforce the surveillance of the Kurile Channels.   On these orders Admiral Shimamura proceeded to station his two armoured cruisers in the western entrance of the Tsugaru Strait with his light cruisers in the narrows to the eastward, the torpedo-boats keeping night-guard between the two western capes.

Next day came intelligence that the Baltic Fleet was passing Singapore.   It was also known that the Nebogatov Division had reached Jibuti and left again on the 7th after coaling.[1] On this intelligence Admiral Togo proceeded at once to operate the measure which had been long arranged to keep the Vladivostok cruisers quiet, since two of them as well as the flotilla were reported to be active again.   It will be remembered that some months before, in view of the crisis which now seemed at hand, he had asked for a very large number of mines, and he now ordered Admiral Kamimura to prepare those intended for Vladivostok with all possible despatch, and to proceed to lay them so as to blockade the port.   So urgent did the situation appear that he was directed to be back at Sylvia Basin by the 22nd at latest, that is within a fortnight.

To some extent the appearance of the Baltic Fleet was a

---

[1] Reported by Reuter on the 8th.

surprise, so that the mines were not ready. Admiral Kami-mura took three days to complete his preparations, and it was not till April 13th he was able to leave Sylvia Basin with the squadron detailed for the work. It consisted of three armoured cruisers *Idzumo* (flag), *Tokiwa* and *Kasuga*, the Third Division of light cruisers, *Kasagi*, *Chitose*, *Niitaka* and *Otowa*, the Admiral's despatch-vessel *Chihaya*, two divisions of destroyers, four mining vessels, and three other auxiliaries.[1] Meanwhile, before he left, intelligence had come in that Admiral Rozhest-venski the two previous days had been sighted going north as though he did not intend to wait for the Nebogatov Division.[2] The inference was that the crisis would mature more rapidly than had been expected, and it was found necessary to hurry on the final concentration. Admiral Shimamura was in-formed that Vladivostok would be mined on the 15th. He was therefore to send away the *Takachiho* at once to the main fleet and follow with the rest of his force in time to reach Sylvia Basin not later than the 17th. He sailed accordingly on the 14th. At the same time the *Bingo Maru* and *Sado Maru*, which had just arrived, were immediately recalled to Takeshiki as they were required for the advanced patrol sections. The *Kumano Maru* was also recalled a few days later. Captain Inoue of the *Hongkong Maru* was left alone with his own ship and the *Nippon Maru*, together with the gunboat *Musashi* and the 4th torpedo-boat division of the Hakodate guard to do his best to watch the Tsugaru Strait. His instructions were to regard observation of the enemy's movements as his first care, but not to neglect opportunities of capturing vessels bound for Vladivostok.

As Admiral Shimamura's Division cleared away, the Second Squadron appeared before Vladivostok, and on April 15th laid 715 mines between Askold and Korsakov Islands, that is, right across the mouth of Peter the Great Bay on a line about 35 miles long and 25 miles to seaward of the port. He was thus able to start back next day well within the limit of his programme.

But, according to information furnished by our representa-tives in Korea, the Japanese preparations for the coming of

---

[1] *Japanese Official Service List.* The detachment cut through all the organisation of the Fleet. *Kasuga* belonged to the Battle Division, and the Third Division to the First Squadron. The *Idzumo* and *Tokiwa* alone belonged to the Second Squadron, Admiral Kamimura's command.

[2] Reported by Reuter on the 11th and 12th.

M

the Baltic Fleet by no means ended with the naval concentration. At Yung-hing Bay, within which Gensan lies, the new base was in course of active preparation. On April 26th the British Minister reported, on information from the Gensan Consul, that the harbour had been mined, that the fortifications at the entrance were being pushed forward with all speed, that gun emplacements were being prepared and roads and cable connections constructed. The torpedo craft which had been there had left, but a large number of transports were in the neighbourhood, and quantities of compressed coal had been landed for a depôt which was being prepared at Port Lazarev in the extremity of the bay. Gensan was being connected by cable with Nakhimov Point and all the adjacent islands, and Yung-hing Bay was a scene of great activity. The Japanese had also definitely re-established their settlement at Song-chin 120 miles up the coast, and had 4,000 troops at Kil-tsiou watching the Russians at Kengsheng. Our Minister further said that he had been officially informed that it was expected that while the Japanese attention was occupied with the Baltic Fleet the Russians would probably make an effort to recover North-Eastern Korea ; but that the Japanese had no intention of again withdrawing from it and the preparations were intended to meet the anticipated Russian advance. Three days later the consul reported that on April 27th four Japanese transports had arrived and were landing troops, who were to proceed north towards Vladivostok by land. All arms were represented and the intention was to bring the total force landed up to 10,000 men. In forwarding this intelligence on May 9th our Minister said, in confirmation of the Consul's report, that from the Japanese legation he had learnt that 15,000 men had been landed and that the object in view was to forestall a Russian movement across the Tumen which was expected to synchronise with the approach of the Baltic Fleet.[1]

It would look, therefore, as though the Japanese Staff were contemplating the possibility of the Russians seizing Gensan by a combined operation of the Baltic Fleet and the Ussuri Army either as a temporary base or a harbour of refuge. Seeing that in addition to this the success of such a design would have the effect of extending to the sea the Russian Army of the Yalu which formed their left wing and of bringing it into touch with their fleet, a situation of great irritation, to say the least,

---

[1] Sir J. N. Jordan's despatches, April 26th and May 9th.

would be set up ; and it is not unreasonable to suppose on the evidence, that the Japanese with their characteristic care in making every foot of ground good were taking urgent measures to prevent so disturbing an eventuality.

As events turned out the whole of these hurried preparations proved to be premature ; but it so happened that, although there is nothing to show the Russians had any designs on Gensan, the Japanese appreciation of the other possibilities of the situation were at the time by no means unjustified. Admiral Rozhestvenski, so far as our information goes, was within an ace of coming on as they expected, and his reason for wishing to do so was closely connected with the intended "confusing" effect of Admiral Dewa's reconnaissance. As the Baltic Fleet was passing Singapore the Russian Consul came out with such intelligence as he had been able to gather. From newspapers which he brought off they learnt that the Manchurian Army had been decisively defeated at Mukden (a fact which had hitherto been concealed from the fleet), and that General Linevich, who had superseded General Kuropatkin, was in full retreat on Tieh-ling. The chief naval item was that about three weeks previously the Japanese Fleet had steamed towards Singapore and had then proceeded to Borneo, where they had formed a temporary base connected by cable with Singapore. The other important item was that on April 7th, Admiral Nebogatov had left Jibuti.[1] The general effect of the news in the fleet was not bad. Their fine achievement of bringing so large a force across the Indian Ocean intact, culminating, as it did, in their defiant passage of the Straits of Malacca, had raised a spirit of elation that even the Army's misfortunes could not damp. But with the Admiral and his staff it was different. The last piece of information, that Admiral Nebogatov was still coming on and had already passed out of the Red Sea, produced a feeling of something like exasperation in their minds. They had contemplated with some confidence that their sudden stealing away from Nossi Bé without giving a rendezvous would lead to the recall of the obsolete squadron. But it was clear the scheme had failed and that the Government had ordered Admiral Nebogatov to carry on.

---

[1] Politovski, p. 202. Semenov, 406, 410. The *Orel's* log records the information thus : " The main Japanese force is' on the north coast of " Borneo. There are five submarines in the Straits of Malacca intending " to attack us. Nebogatov was at Jibuti on the 4th of April. Our Army " has retreated to Tieh-ling. Linevich is Commander-in-Chief. Kuropatkin " commands the First Army." (*Attaché Reports*, IV., 231.)

What had actually happened was this. Admiral Nebogatov had reached Jibuti on April 3rd—that is, more than a fortnight after the main squadron was clear of Madagascar. There he had telegraphed home for its position, and the reply was that nothing was known to the Staff of its whereabouts, but that he was to hurry up to the Sunda Strait where accurate intelligence might be obtained from the Russian intelligence agents.[1] After coaling he proceeded accordingly, on the 7th, in entire ignorance of his chief's intended movements. He had still, however, a chance of getting the information he required, for it seems that arrangements had been made for getting into touch with him from Colombo. Accordingly after passing Cape Guardafui he sent away the transport *Kuronia* to that port, and to give her time to fulfil her mission he took the squadron into Mir Bat on the Arabian coast, about 500 miles east of Aden, on the 12th. Then he waited two days and then sailed again, setting his course for the Sunda Strait.[2]

By this time Admiral Rozhestvenski, such at least was the impression of his Staff, had formed a remarkable resolution in a last effort to throw off the unwelcome reinforcement. It was founded on the prevailing false appreciation of the probable strategy of the Japanese, which Admiral Dewa's cruise had been intended to emphasise. His confusing movement did indeed give so much colour to the categorical information of the Russian Consul as to the supposed forward movement of the Japanese Fleet, that it could admit of only one interpretation. Admiral Togo had made an attempt to "seek them out" in the neighbourhood of Singapore and, having missed them there, had gone off to Borneo in order to intercept them in their passage northward from the Sunda Strait. Admiral Rozhestvenski could therefore believe that by his sudden and secret move he had eluded his adversary. By carrying on at once he might possibly pass Formosa ahead of him, and this idea took firmer shape as, in readiness for meeting the enemy at any moment, he proceeded onward through the China Sea without finding any trace of them.

---

[1] Smirnov, citing *Chronological Abstract*, p. 170. There is some doubt as to this. For the account of an officer of the *Nikolai* says a conference of Captains was held at Jibuti at which it was decided to make for the Strait of Malacca. But as he was a junior officer he may have been mistaken, and in any case the Russian official abstract is the higher authority.

[2] So says Smirnov, but the officer of the *Nikolai* says "shaped his course for Ceylon." The two statements are, of course, not incompatible.

He was actually bound for Kamranh Bay, and a few days before reaching the Straits of Malacca he had issued to the fleet a chart of the place with anchoring billets laid down. But by the second day (April 10th) the new idea of pushing straight on had so far taken hold of his imagination that he called his Staff to conference. There were present besides the Chief, the Flag-Lieutenant Sventorzhetski, who had charge of the secret correspondence, and Commander Semenov, presumably on account of his local knowledge.[1] Opinions differed widely. The Chief of the Staff was inclined to the view that the fleet must " take up its strategical position " and then act according to the latest information of the enemy's distribution. By this he seems to have contemplated holding on, in accordance with the existing plan, for Kamranh Bay, which would mean contact with the telegraph, and almost certainly an order to wait for Admiral Nebogatov. Commander Semenov was for pushing on at all costs, while the fleet was in high spirits over their supposed evasion of the enemy and their bold and successful passage of the Malacca Strait. He believed the Admiral approved his words, but Lieutenant Sventorzhetzki took a more sober view, which as Commander Semenov believed was based on the secret correspondence with Headquarters. Shortly it came to this—that all further naval effort was useless. It was idle to suppose they would get through to Vladivostok without a battle, or that a battle could result in anything but a more or less decisive defeat. Even if by luck of weather they managed to get through without serious damage they would still be impotent, since at Vladivostok there was only one dock, and as they knew the railway was strained to the utmost in supplying the army they could not hope that it would be able to supply the naval base as well. Without hesitation, therefore, he pronounced that the right course was " to make all use of the effect which our appear-
" ance in full strength in the South China Seas has undoubtedly
" produced and hasten to conclude an honourable peace. To
" count on the success of further operations at sea was to
" count on miracles."

It is not difficult to divine the nature of the secret correspondence which was only known to him and the Admiral. Even before the Battle of Mukden the question of making peace

---

[1] Semenov, *Rasplata*, p. 407 *et seq.* The authority is not absolutely to be depended on, but in this case it is so circumstantial that it may be assumed that something of the kind took place.

had been raised, but only to be quenched by the military party on the ground that with 400,000 invincible troops deployed in face of the Japanese it was impossible not to fight. After the defeat the discussion burst out with renewed vigour ; even in military circles and high society to speak of peace was no longer treason. Almost the whole Press was in favour of opening negotiations, and reports were rife that the President of the United States had offered his mediation. Only in the highest quarters was there a stubborn determination to continue the war, which no naval, military or political argument had yet been able to overcome.[1] The opinion that our ambassador at St. Petersburg had formed was that the presence of the Baltic Fleet in the theatre of war was as insuperable a bar to giving way as the 400,000 invincible troops had been before the battle of Mukden. It was blindly believed that Admiral Rozhestvenski had succeeded in bringing his fleet to a high state of efficiency, while the Japanese ships were persistently represented as having leaky boilers, damaged turrets, worn-out guns, and diminished speed. " The question whether such a victory as may be " achieved," he wrote, " would give the remains of the Russian " fleet more than temporary command of the sea is studiously " ignored. It seems as though the Emperor and his advisers " refuse to recognise the situation as it really is, and regardless " of the consequences are now about to stake their last card " on the chance of Admiral Rozhestvenski's obtaining a naval " success. It is argued that even if Admiral Rozhestvenski is " decisively beaten the army will be in no worse position than " before, and it is hoped that a few ships may be able to escape " either to Vladivostok or to some neutral port, where they " would be disarmed, but would still form the nucleus of a " fleet after the conclusion of peace."

This view of the situation, as gathered by our ambassador, seems to have coincided very closely with that of the Admiral. His intimate knowledge of affairs at Headquarters forbade him to hope seriously that peace would be contemplated before the last card had been played, and he was the last card. He knew he would have to go, and if he had to go his only wish was to go at once while there was still a hope he might have outwitted the Japanese and before contact with the telegraph would force him to wait for the Nebogatov Squadron. The facts which give us an insight into his mind are hardly mistakable. On April

---

[1] Sir Charles Hardinge's despatch, St. Petersburg, April 11th.

11th, the day after the conference, he sent the hospital ship *Orel* into Saigon to replenish her stores, giving her Kamranh Bay as a rendezvous, but if he was not found there she was to endeavour to find him elsewhere or ask for orders from Head-quarters. Next day the fleet, although only 60 miles from Kamranh, was stopped for coaling and it was obvious to every-one that the Admiral was labouring under some great excitement. He had long conferences with the master of the fleet over the chart " Hongkong to Vladivostok " as well as with the fleet engineer, and then came general signals for a special coal report and to know whether boilers and machinery were in good order for a long passage. The replies were generally satisfactory, but to the Admiral's mortification one battleship reported she was 400 tons short. As she was reputed to be the smartest in the squadron the signal was at first believed to be a mistake, but it was confirmed. To take in that quantity at sea would mean a delay of two or three days and it was not to be thought of, and the Admiral reluctantly and in deep disappointment gave the word for Kamranh Bay. Next day they were off the rendezvous, and on the 14th, after making dispositions against a surprise attack, they entered the bay and anchored in the positions which had been assigned on April 3rd.[1]

So at last, after steaming 4,560 miles from Nossi Bé without touching anywhere and with no unit missing except the hospital ship *Orel*, they reached the "strategical position" so often referred to in the communications from Headquarters. The German colliers arrived with equal punctuality and next morning the ships began coaling in haste, and the *Orel* came in from Saigon. It was no small feat and one of which all concerned were justly proud that so great a fleet had been brought so far. Nor was it only the fleet, for in effect it carried its flying base on its back, and the Admiral believing, as it would seem, that all arrangements must have been made with the French Govern-ment proceeded to establish it by closing the mouth of the bay with a temporary boom.

As we know now, the accident of one battleship being short of coal which forced him into Kamranh Bay lost him little beyond what the tone of the fleet suffered by the further weary delay that was entailed. His idea of evading the Japanese

---

[1] The above episode rests solely on the authority of Commander Semenov (*Rasplata*, 413–7), but it is told with too much circumstantial detail to be ignored. At the same time it should be regarded as awaiting confirmation.

fleet by a rapid and direct movement to his destination was chimerical, for, as we have seen, Admiral Togo had his whole force already concentrated in his interior position. All that Admiral Rozhestvenski's frustrated plan would have gained him was that by running away from the Nebogatov Squadron his force would have gained something in compactness and mobility. To that extent his chances of evasion in thick weather would have been increased, and, as events proved, such chances were not entirely imaginary, narrow as were the waters where the danger lay. On the other hand, by waiting for the reinforcement, poor as it was, his actual fighting power was certainly increased, and with the increase of that power there was also an increase in the probability of at least a substantial part of his fleet being able to force its way through. On the whole, then, it cannot be said that the result was materially affected by the default of the offending battleship, but none the less the case affords a remarkable instance of how the negligence of one officer in a matter so small as an error miscalculating the amount of coal on board, and so misleading his Admiral by a false return, may change the whole strategical outlook of a war.

CHAPTER XIII.

CONCENTRATION OF THE BALTIC FLEET IN THE THEATRE OF WAR.

[Charts I, VI, XB.]

THE presence of the Baltic Fleet in the well-known Annam anchorage was quickly reported to Tokyo. It so happened that the Japanese Admiral Prince Arisugawa with a naval aide-de-camp was going to attend the wedding of the German Crown Prince in the North German Lloyd mail steamer *Prinz Heinrich*, and in the course of April 14th the ship passed so close to Kamranh Bay that the Russian fleet could be distinctly seen lying inside. How the German liner came to be there has never been satisfactorily explained. She was making for Singapore and her true course would have taken her nowhere nearly in sight of the suspected bay. When for this reason the correctness of the information was doubted in diplomatic quarters, the Japanese foreign minister suggested that as the vessel had a Japanese Admiral on board she had probably made a deviation to avoid meeting the Russian fleet. The irony of the suggestion is evident when we recall how piratically this very ship had been treated in the previous July when the *Smolensk* had stopped her in the Red Sea and robbed her of her mails. Whether or not this was the real reason nothing could have been more convenient to the Japanese Staff at the moment than that a Japanese officer should have had an opportunity of observing the Annam coast. On the 16th the news was telegraphed all over the world by Reuter's agent at Singapore, and the Japanese at once proceeded to make a firm but courteous protest to the French Government.

The line they took was that Kamranh Bay raised a very different question from that of Madagascar and the other French ports which the Russians had used. It was much nearer to the seat of war, being actually within striking distance of Formosa and the Japanese naval station at Makung in the Pescadores. It was no longer, therefore, a mere question of necessary coaling and repairs, but of using a neutral port as a concentration point and base of operations. It meant, in fact, that if the Russians were allowed to establish themselves there and make use of the place as a base, which was their apparent intention, they would gain a strategical position which to a great extent undermined the Japanese war plan. It was impossible to permit them to establish themselves indefinitely on the trade route with Europe, upon the freedom of which the progress of Japanese arms so much depended. It was a position, moreover, which would give the enemy the power of continually harassing the Japanese coasts and communications, and possibly of seizing some part of their territory. To this extent it transferred the initiative to the Russians, and sooner or later the Japanese would be forced to abandon their defensive attitude and seek out the enemy's fleet in order to obtain a decision. If this became necessary and if the Russians, as it now seemed, were bent upon wearing out the Japanese by an indefinite prolongation of the war, they would probably decline an action in the open and then there would be nothing for it but to attack them where they lay.

Such were the objections from a purely Japanese point of view ; but, as they argued, there were others which had a much wider horizon. Public opinion in Japan was already demanding that drastic action should be taken in view of the unneutral service which France was rendering to her ally.[1] If, therefore, the Russian use of French ports was persisted in, there was every prospect that the Japanese Government would be forced to give their fleet orders which could only end in a violation of French territorial waters. Obviously such orders, if they proved to be unavoidable, would in all probability enlarge the area of war, and this it was the interest of the other Great Powers concerned to prevent. This presentation of the danger they knew was one to which it would be difficult for any of the neutral Powers to shut its eyes, and with confidence it was laid before the British Government with a request that they would support the Japanese protest to Paris. The seed fell on good ground ; for these were the days which saw the birth of the *entente cordiale*, and nothing could be more unwelcome either at Paris or London than an incident which would cloud the promising dawn of the new era. The two Governments therefore set to work at once in the most cordial and loyal spirit to give effect to the Japanese protest.

Meanwhile it became known in Japan that Admiral de Jonquières, second-in-command of the French Indo-China

---

[1] Sir C. Macdonald's despatch, April 24. *N.I.D. Diary*, p. 238.

Squadron, had appeared at Kamranh in a small cruiser the day after the Russian arrival ; but he had left again, apparently after merely exchanging compliments, and the situation rapidly became acute. The *rapprochement* between France and England had not yet been made public, and under the belief that French policy was wholly subservient to Russian interests there was an outburst of indignation in the Japanese Press which rapidly set up a highly dangerous state of opinion. Day by day news came in that Admiral Rozhestvenski did not move and was defiantly using the French waters as a base. An immediate attack upon him where he lay was openly and even angrily called for. So tense grew the situation and so violent the pressure of public opinion that according to our information the Naval Staff had actually under consideration the prospects of such an attack succeeding.[1]

But whether or not this serious step was really contemplated, there was an aspect of the situation which was grave enough without it. The Japanese Government had been officially informed from Paris that on the 18th categorical orders had been sent to the Governor-General of Indo-China that he was to request the Russians to leave at once ; but still nothing happened, and even the more responsible Japanese papers began to claim that a *casus fœderis* under the British treaty of alliance had arisen. It was argued, that in permitting Russia to use Kamranh as a base, France was rendering active assistance to her as a belligerent within the meaning of the treaty, and that England, therefore, could be called upon to give effect to the terms of the alliance. For some time, indeed, it appeared that we were on the brink of being dragged into the war, but in fact it was not so. Although it was impossible for the Japanese to believe that the French Government were in earnest, the first approaches which our Foreign Office made at the instigation of our ally revealed that they were even indignant at the selfish and inconsiderate manner in which the Russians all along had been compromising their neutrality. An energetic protest was made against the persistent use of French territorial waters with a categorical objection to operations against the Japanese communications being carried on from a base on the Annam coast.[2] To those then, with whom the decision rested, it was known that the

---

[1] Sir Claude Macdonald's despatch, Tokyo, April 24th. He stated that his information was from "a very reliable source."

[2] Smirnov.

disturbing delay was due, not to any lack of correctness on the part of the French Government, but to the natural sympathy which their local officials both civil and naval felt for an ally and to the impossible position in which the Russian Admiral had been placed by his superiors.

The real explanation of Admiral Rozhestvenski's remaining so long as he did in French waters is still wrapped in some obscurity. According to the best authority we know that he completed his coaling from the German transports on April 18th.[1] But although, as we have seen, all other evidence points to his anxiety to proceed at once, he did not move. The same authority professes to be ignorant of his motive. We are told the Admiral himself, after the battle, gave as his reason that he was short of coal. At that time, owing to his wounds, he was certainly not responsible for what he said, and the explanation has to be dismissed. The idea of making a demonstration with a view to a good peace has also to be set aside, since, owing to the attitude of France, no base in the China Sea could be obtained. "It must be supposed, therefore," this authority concludes, "that the cause of the delay was the " desire of the Admiral that the squadron should be recalled " to Russia, at which he hinted in his reports from Kamranh, " though he did not express his opinion openly." We have every reason to believe by the testimony of men on his Staff that this was, in fact, his opinion ; but other indications suggest that it was not the real reason for his long wait, although it was officially adopted in Russia as affording a plausible ground for laying the whole responsibility of the breach of French neutrality on the shoulders of an Admiral who had failed.

The reason, according to the only authority we have, was a direct order from St. Petersburg.[2] We know, at any rate, that by the 18th Admiral Rozhestvenski was in communication with Headquarters through Saigon, and possibly also by a land telegraph office that existed not far from Kamranh. We know also that Admiral Nebogatov was within about a fortnight's steaming of the position. Further, it must be remembered that Admiral Rozhestvenski believed that the main Japanese fleet was somewhere in the South China Sea, and reports that Makung had been mined and fortified indicated that his adversary was based on that port. On the prevailing appre-

---

[1] Smirnov, citing the *Chronological Abstract*, and "Documents in the Archives."

[2] Semenov, *Rasplata*, p. 431. See *post*, p. 190.

ciations, therefore, a rapid attempt by the Japanese Admiral to strike at him where he lay before the Nebogatov Division arrived was highly probable and he could wish for nothing better. It was obviously to his advantage to accept battle far from the enemy's zone of highest control, and in an area where numerous ports of a friendly neutral were available as harbours of refuge.

On April 16th he made every preparation for this eventuality The casemates, which up till now had been used for storing extra coal, were cleared, and the officers' quarters were used instead. At the same time he issued battle instructions, based on the idea of leaving his transports under cruiser and flotilla protection in the bay, and keeping his best fighting ships free to engage the enemy without preoccupation.[1] These orders, indeed, make it quite clear that the Admiral was not only anticipating an action where he was, but being fully determined not to await it at anchor, he meant to offer battle in the open, where he would be able to manœuvre free of the incumbrance of his transports.

This idea, then, is quite sufficient to explain his delay on strategical grounds which had much to justify them. But that it was not the sole reason seems clear from the following facts. After his first visit Admiral de Jonquières had gone on to Nhatrang, the capital of the district, twenty miles to the north-ward. Four days later he reappeared, and going on board the *Suvorov*, informed the Russian Admiral that instructions had arrived from Paris by which he was to request him to leave French waters at once, and that twenty-four hours' respite was the utmost that could be granted. The communication appears to have been received with something of a shock, for till this moment the Russians seem to have believed that Admiral de Jonquières' benevolent attitude represented that of the French Government, and that so long as they kept away from regular ports their ally would shut her eyes to their proceedings. To the bitterness of what they regarded as desertion there was added a practical difficulty of the most serious kind which the Admiral had now to lay before his officers. Next morning, the 22nd, he summoned his flag officers and captains on board the flagship, and communicated to them the notice to quit. But he also had to add that he had received orders not to proceed till the Third Squadron

---

[1] For these orders see *post*, p. 197.

arrived. " My orders," he is reported as saying, " are to wait
for Nebogatov."[1] His intention, therefore, he added, was to
put to sea and remain outside territorial waters off Kamranh
Bay where the supply ships and fleet auxiliaries would be left.
From this position he would endeavour to keep up communication with Headquarters through Saigon, and would
remain till he had only just enough coal left to reach
Vladivostok. If Admiral Nebogatov had not arrived by that
time there was no help for it, and he would go on. The
conference was then dismissed, and at 1.0 in the afternoon,
exactly 24 hours after the notice to quit had been received,
he put to sea.[2]

As Admiral Rozhestvenski had also agreed, so long as he
was using French waters, not to operate with his cruisers
either for intelligence or in search of contraband, he now
thought he had done all that was necessary to regularise his
position and rid himself of the charge of using a neutral port
as a base. Nothing but noncombatant vessels being left in
the bay he assumed that the claims of French neutrality were
satisfied. The French Government, however, took a different
view. For them he was obeying the mere letter and not the
fair spirit of the law. They had hoped that their declaration
that orders had gone to Indo-China to request the departure
of the Baltic Fleet would have quieted Japanese resentment, but as the Russians were still reported to be clinging
to the place, and as they had sent their half-emptied transports into Saigon, the well-meant declaration only inflamed
the popular outcry. France was openly accused of bad faith
and the cry of a *casus fœderis* under the British Treaty grew
more violent than ever. Both in French and in Japanese eyes
the mere putting to sea of the fighting ships was a quibble
so long as the colliers and other fleet auxiliaries remained
within territorial waters. True these vessels were not tech-

---

[1] Semenov, *Rasplata*, 431.

[2] Commander Semenov's statement that an order had been received
to await the Third Squadron is corroborated by the log of the *Orel*.
Though no order is actually mentioned, it says, " It was evident that
" there was no plan of waiting for Nebogatov's Squadron, and we
" cannot tell when we may expect to meet it." The natural meaning
of this from the context is that they had been told to wait for the
squadron, but no arrangement for the junction had been communicated.
All, however, that Smirnov says is that Admiral Rozhestvenski received
from St. Petersburg an intimation of the reinforcement of his squadron
by that of Admiral Nebogatov.

nically men-of-war, although some of them were actually armed, but they were under the direct control of the Admiral and formed an organic part of his force ; they constituted, in fact, the flying base of the Russian fleet, and to permit such a base to be established in French territorial waters was unneutral service of a flagrant nature. It was impossible for any self-respecting Power to sit down under such an inconsiderate trespass upon its territorial waters, and on April 25th Admiral de Jonquières reappeared in Kamranh Bay with a still stronger message. Its terms are unknown, but the result of it was that next morning the whole of the Russian ships put to sea, while the French flagship stood by till they had disappeared to the eastward.

Admiral Rozhestvenski's position was now quite impossible. Seeing that the Japanese Fleet, as he believed, was in his neighbourhood with its formidable flotilla in company, it was out of the question to cruise about in those waters for an indefinite time till the Third Squadron should appear. Something must be done to meet the danger, and the only course he could think of was to conceal his fleet in some deserted part of the coast. Some 20 miles north of Nhatrang was the little-known bay of Van Fong which might serve his turn. He knew the French Admiral was going back to Saigon, and accordingly as soon as he and the Kamranh coast were well out of sight, the whole fleet went into Van Fong and anchored. In this remote place, inhabited only by a few fishermen, he might well hope to be lost for a considerable time, but luck was still against him. Once a month a small coasting steamer visited the bay to buy the fishermen's catches, and it so happened she came in that very day. On April 27th she left again for Saigon, and three days later the position of the Baltic Fleet was known all over the world.[1]

The situation was now very serious. The Japanese Government had only just succeeded in quieting popular indignation by an official announcement that France had formally requested the Russian Government to issue orders for the Baltic Fleet to leave, that such orders had been sent from St. Petersburg, and that France had given assurances that she would take all necessary steps to see her neutrality respected. Naturally then, when it was known that the Russian fleet had

---

[1] On May 1st Reuter's Saigon agent reported, "Baltic Fleet lying off " Port Dayot in Bingkoi Bay, 40 miles north of Kamranh outside " territorial waters," meaning, of course, outside the three-mile limit.

merely moved a few miles, a new and more violent outburst in the Japanese press threatened to ruin all that diplomacy was striving to achieve. From Paris instructions were immediately telegraphed to the French Administrateur at Nhatrang and to the Admiral at Saigon to proceed at once to Van Fong and insist upon the departure of the unwelcome guests. On May 3rd Admiral de Jonquières reappeared, this time in his flagship the *Guichen*, but it was to find that the Russian Admiral, who had been warned of his approach, had taken his squadron to sea for tactical exercises, and that there was nothing in the bay except destroyers and transports.[1] What happened is not quite clear. Admiral de Jonquières signalled that he had a telegram to deliver, and apparently waited all next day while the rest of the Russian fleet were called out. Then having intimated that his orders were to cruise along the coast for 24 hours to see that no other French anchorage was violated, he departed. An auxiliary cruiser had been left to watch his movements and as soon as she signalled that he was gone, Admiral Rozhestvenski quietly headed back for Van Fong, and anchored there early next morning.

Such behaviour was, of course, inexcusable, but what was the Admiral to do ? His orders condemned him to wait and he could not wait at sea. As yet there was no news whatever of the Third Squadron ; and seeing that until there was he had no course but to carry on his game of hide-and-seek in neutral waters, he sent away his Master of the Fleet to find another shelter not open to passing ships like Van Fong, and as far removed as possible from a telegraph. Vung Ro and Port Dayot were visited and the latter was found to be just what he desired, but it was unsurveyed and dangerous. For the present, then, the Admiral made no move, his excuse being that he had word from Nhatrang that a typhoon was approaching, and stress of weather gave him good ground for remaining where he was. The excuse seems to have been accepted by Admiral de Jonquières, who again put in an appearance on May 7th. But what made it unnecessary to press matters further was that he brought news which promised to end the dangerous situation in a few days. On May 4th Admiral Nebogatov had been sighted entering the Straits of Malacca, and the end of the long and exasperating delay was in sight.

---

[1] Schubert, *New Material*, and Semenov, *Rasplata*, 433.

Only the day before, when Admiral Rozhestvenski received full information of the diplomatic tension his proceedings were causing, he began to despair of hearing of the lagging squadron. Timed from its leaving Jibuti, it was long overdue and the delay could not be accounted for. What had happened was this. As we have seen, Admiral Nebogatov, on leaving Jibuti, had made for Mir Bat on the Arabian coast. Thence, on April 13th, he had proceeded for the Strait of Sunda, but had stopped at a rendezvous south of Ceylon, to wait for the transport *Kuronia*, which he had sent to Colombo for news of the main fleet. For two days (April 29th and 30th), he waited, and so fine was the weather that he was able to use the delay for coaling with the colliers alongside. When the *Kuronia* returned, she brought nothing apparently, except the false intelligence that Admiral Togo was somewhere in the Sunda Archipelago with a flotilla of destroyers and submarines. Of his chief's whereabouts and intention there was no information, and he therefore decided to adopt a line of his own. Convinced of the practicability of coaling at sea, his idea was to take an independent course for Vladivostok by way of one of the Kurile Channels, and since the Japanese were in waiting near the Sunda Strait. he would boldly take the direct route through the Straits of Malacca.[1] In pursuance of this enterprising resolution he passed Singapore on May 5th, and there he received information from the Russian Consul as to where Admiral Rozhestvenski had last been heard of. Accordingly, he abandoned his independent plan and headed at once for Saigon, where he could hope to get the last word as to how and where the concentration was to be effected.

It was, as we have seen, two days after he had passed the Straits that Admiral Rozhestvenski heard of him, apparently from the French Admiral, who left again the same evening. Early next morning (the 8th) four cruisers were sent out to find the approaching squadron, but their wireless gear was so defective that they had much difficulty in getting touch. In the meantime, at dawn on the 9th, the *Guichen* had come back and anchored close to the Russian flagship, and Admiral Rozhestvenski had been forced again to put to sea. Two of

---

[1] This is Smirnov's account from official sources. In another account, written by an officer of the *Nikolai*, it is stated that the resolution to go by the Malacca Strait was taken at the conference held at Jibuti. But they may be reconciled with Smirnov's version on the supposition that it was a contingent resolution depending on later information.

the cruisers, however, had by this time managed to get into communication with the Nebogatov Squadron, and shortly before noon its signals began to be felt. Off Saigon it had been met by a scout who brought word of the Commander-in-Chief's position, and that the junction could not be permitted in neutral waters. They therefore held on, and by 3.0 p.m. the concentration was at last effected in the open.

Admiral Rozhestvenski had now assembled under his flag a fleet that in appearance at least was really formidable. Its composition and organisation were as follows :—

BATTLE SQUADRON.

First Division—Vice-Admiral Rozhestvenski.

Knyaz Suvorov (Flag).
Imperator Alexandr III.
Borodino.
Orel.

Second Division—Rear-Admiral von Felkerzam.

Oslyabya (Flag).
Sisoi Veliki.
Navarin.
Admiral Nakhimov.

Third Division—Rear-Admiral Nebogatov.

Imperator Nikolai I. (Flag).
General-Admiral Apraxin.
Admiral Senyavin.
Admiral Ushakov.

Attached cruisers *Izumrud, Zhemchug.*

CRUISER SQUADRON.

First Cruiser Division—Rear Admiral Enkvist.

Oleg (Flag).	*Dmitri Donskoi.*	*Rion.*
Avrora.	*Vladimir Monomakh.*	*Dnyepr.*

Second Scouting Division—Commodore Shein.

Svyetlana (Broad Pennant)	*Kuban.*
Terek.	*Ural.*

DESTROYER FLOTILLA.

1st Division.	2nd Division.
Byedovi.	*Blestyashchi.*
Buini.	*Bezuprechni.*
Bravi.	*Bodri.*
Buistri.	*Gromki.*
	Grozni.

TRANSPORT SQUADRON.—Captain Radlov.

Almaz[1] (Broad Pennant).   *Vladimir.*
Kamchatka (Repair ship.   *Livonia.*
       Armed).   *Kuronia.*
Irtuish (Armed).   *Meteor* (Tank vessel).
Anaduir (Armed).   *Koreya* (Ammunition).
Merkuri.   *Rus* }
Tambov.   *Svir* } Ocean tugs.
Voronezh.   *Orel* }
Yaroslavl.   *Kostroma* } Hospital ships.

The completion of the concentration appears to have done something to raise the failing spirit of the fleet. There was a general feeling that the Japanese had been again outwitted, and that another strategical success had been won. It was further noted, with agreeable surprise, that alterations which had been made in the structure and armament of the old ships had greatly improved their appearance and fighting value.[2] The Admiral seized the moment to issue a stirring order, in which, while dwelling on the fair chance of success with the increased force he did not disguise the fact that the utmost effort would be required to compete with so formidable an enemy as the Japanese had proved themselves to be. Search, practice and tactical exercises had recently been so faultily carried out that he had been compelled to issue order after order calling attention to the fatal results of not keeping station and of inefficient cruiser work. But now that all that was possible had been done for tuning up the fleet his note was one of patient encouragement. " To-day, the 9th of May," so the order ran, " at 2 p.m., the squadron of Rear-Admiral Nebogatov, which " left Libau on February 15, four months later than our

---

[1] The cruiser *Almaz* also formed part of the Scouting Division and when she was serving with it the Transport Squadron was. led by the *Anaduir.*

[2] *Attaché Reports*, IV., 247.

" squadron, joined up. While giving credit to this fine
" squadron which has accomplished such a brilliant passage
" without the use of convenient ports and with *hindrances*
" well known to you all at the stoppages in desert localities,
" I am not belittling the value of the labours of the other
" detachments of the squadron which have had to await their
" comrades in circumstances which have made the necessary
" halts as arduous as the passage itself. With the junction
" of this squadron the strength of the Fleet has not only been
" placed on an equality with that of the enemy, but has
" obtained some advantage in ships of the line. The Japanese
" have a greater number of fast ships than we have, but we
" are not going to run away from them, and we shall get
" through our business if our worthy engine-room crews work in
" action as quietly, zealously, and conscientiously as they have
" done hitherto. The Japanese possess far more torpedo craft,
" they have submarines, and floating mines which they have
" had experience in dropping. But such weapons must be
" met by keeping a strict look-out ; we must not sleep through
" a torpedo attack ; we must not fail to see floating bodies or
" a periscope sticking out of the water ; we must not lose our
" heads in working searchlights ; we must not make such heavy
" weather at the guns, and we must take better aim. The
" Japanese have a great advantage in their prolonged fighting
" experience and their great practice in firing under war condi-
" tions. This must be remembered, and without being carried
" away by the example of their rapid firing, we must not hurl
" projectiles into space, but correct the laying of the guns for
" every round by the results obtained. . . . The devotion of
" the Japanese to Throne and Country is boundless ; they do
" not tolerate dishonour, and they die like heroes. But we also
" have taken a vow before the Most High Throne. God has
" fortified our hearts and has helped us to overcome the burdens
" of a voyage without precedent. God will also strengthen our
" right hand, and will give us his blessing to carry out the will
" of our Sovereign and with our blood to wash out the bitter
" shame of our Fatherland." [2]

Such an order was all that was required to confirm the
reawakened spirit of the fleet, and the Admiral's idea had
been to proceed at once before a moral reaction could take
place ; but Admiral Nebogatov was not ready. He begged

---

[2] Schubert, *New Material concerning the War. See post*, p. 241, note.

for time to coal and to study the numerous fleet orders that had been issued. It had to be granted, but as the weather made it impossible to coal at sea the Third Squadron had to be sent into the hidden harbour of Kua Bé, while the rest of the fleet returned to Van Fong, and a further delay and a fresh violation of French territorial waters were entailed.[1]

Amongst the most important of the orders which Admiral Nebogatov had to study was one which had been issued on April 16th in anticipation of having to fight an action in the neighbourhood of Kamranh. It ran as follows :—" If the " enemy's main fleet comes within range of vision from " the anchorage, I intend to go out and fight them. The " strength of my command will be the main force of " the fleet : that is to say, the two battleship divisions " and the division composed of the *Zhemchug, Izumrud,* the " 1st destroyer division, and the *Oleg, Avrora,* and *Donskoi.* " The position of the *Zhemchug, Izumrud,* and the destroyers, " when we meet the enemy, has been already detailed : " their duty is to protect the battleship line and keep off " attacks from the enemy's destroyers. The cruiser divi- " sions will keep on the disengaged side of the battleships, " taking care to keep out of range of the enemy's shells. " Should the enemy's cruisers attempt to come round the rear " of our line to put us between two fires, our cruisers will " engage them. The *Oleg* and *Avrora* will also protect the " battleships and assist any ship injured by the enemy's guns, " and should they see an opportunity they may engage the " enemy. The *Donskoi,* since she has not the speed for such " action, must avoid being drawn into the battle ; she must " remain in a position from which she can assist the battle- " ship line, and must not get separated from them." Then follow directions for the remainder of his force *Almaz, Rion* and *Dnyepr,* with the 2nd destroyer division and the ship-borne torpedo-boats, explaining how they were to protect the transports in harbour from an attack in the absence of the main body. The three armed transports *Kamchatka, Anaduir, Irtuish* were not to engage unless the enemy entered the harbour, and the torpedo craft were to be hidden behind the islands in the entrance of the bay. To the picket-boats was

---

[1] Kua Bé is really part of Van Fong, forming its eastern entrance, the two anchorages being separated by a long island, which lies about north and south in the mouth of the bay.

assigned the special duty of endeavouring to ram and sink the submarines.[1]

These orders, it will be seen, were obviously intended to meet a repetition of the tactics which the Japanese had attempted at the Battle of the Yellow Sea, and the day before Admiral Nebogatov actually joined they were supplemented by a set of tactical instructions designed to meet the new condition of the Baltic Fleet having to force the Japanese position with all its transports in company. Their text dated May 8th was as follows[2] :—

Commander-in-Chief's Order No. 227.

From now onwards, whatever may be the formation of the battle fleet, the transport squadron, in the absence of special orders, is to act as follows :—

(1) If the enemy appear on our starboard bow the signal O Q 0557 will be hoisted and the Main Division will advance to battle. The Third Division, the Cruiser Division and the Scouting Division will act independently according to circumstances in support of the Main Division.

The transports will follow the Transport Commodore's pennant flying in the *Almaz* which will alter to a course 8 points to port of the enemy's bearing. Thus if the enemy is sighted 3 points on the starboard bow, the transports will turn 5 points to port.

When they are 5 or 6 miles from the fleet, following the motions of the *Almaz* they will adjust their course and speed so as to keep at a distance of 5 or 6 miles on the disengaged side of our fleet.

(2) If the enemy appears on our port bow, the signal O Q 0558 will be hoisted and corresponding movements to those of Article 1, will be made.

(3) If the enemy appears on our beam, the transports will at first continue their course, and then will adjust course and speed in conformity with the last part of Article 1.

---

[1] For the full text of this order, No. 182, see *Attaché Reports*, IV, 236-7.

[2] *Attaché Reports*, IV, 245. The above translation is made from the Japanese version of the original. Smirnov gives it only in an abbreviated form.

(4) If the enemy appears astern (port or starboard) the
signal O Q 0556 will be hoisted and the transport
squadron without altering course will withdraw from
the fleet's tactical area, and so long as the enemy
are visible astern, will proceed to a distance of 5 to
6 miles from the fleet, and maintain that position.

(5) If the enemy appears right ahead the transports will
reduce speed and move in conformity with Article 4.

If in the course of the action, I find it necessary to make
any transport take up a special station or position (for example
to open out or close up more or less than 6 miles) or to proceed
to a certain rendezvous, appropriate signals will be made. The
signal code used will be that of the Commander-in-Chief's
Order of November 19th, 1904, and Order No. 24 of January
21st, 1905.[1]—ROZHESTVENSKI.

On May 10th, while Admiral Nebogatov was coaling
and studying these orders another was issued with special
reference to what was expected from his division in action,
and its wording gives it the appearance of a reply by the
Commander-in-Chief to a request from his subordinate for
some general battle directions. "The Third Battle Division,"
it said, "acting on the signals of its own admiral, will in all
" cases hasten to join the main body."[2] He was thus given
complete liberty of action to support his chief as best he could
without any line to guide him; for, in Admiral Rozhestvenski's
opinion, as will appear later, it was impossible in the circumstances to lay down such a line.[3]

It was under these instructions, without anything further
as to the actual tactics of the battle division, that the fleet
sailed on the last stage of its remarkable voyage. It had made
its last halt, and it was not a long one. By dint of the most

---

[1] From the log of the *Orel*. (*Attaché Reports*, IV., 245.) The text
above is a translation from the Japanese version, which was distributed
to the fleet after the *Orel's* capture.

[2] Smirnov, Order No. 230.

[3] There existed two other minor orders relating to battle—one of
January 23rd at Nossi Bé, and the other of March 27th. The first dealt
with fire control, enjoining deliberate firing and concentration of the
whole fleet on one indicated ship of the enemy. There was no provision
for distributing a defensive fire against other ships. The extreme range
was to be 30 cables (*Attaché Reports*, IV, pp. 215-6). The second dealt
with succouring ships in distress during an action, with general directions
as to which ships in each division were to perform this service (*ibid.*,
page 225).

strenuous exertions they were able to get clear of French waters on May 14th, just as the French Admiral came in sight to observe them for the last time. Their information at this juncture was, that a certain number of Japanese destroyers had been in southern waters, as well as the *Hongkong Maru* and *Nippon Maru* carrying submarines. On these points their "information was such as not to admit of any doubt." They also had learnt that their approach had bewildered the Japanese, and that, after Admiral Nebogatov's appearance in the Straits of Malacca had caused them to show themselves hurriedly at the Pescadores, they had concentrated in Sylvia Basin.[1]

The rumour about the Pescadores was probably intimately connected with the wavering plans of the Russian Headquarter Staff. When, on the reports which Admiral Rozhestvenski sent from Kamranh, they realised how improbable was the success of their plan of winning command of the sea by a decisive fleet action, the idea of establishing a base on the fringe of the theatre of war seems to have been vaguely revived as an escape from the *impasse* they had created. But the responsibility was left with the Admiral subject to restrictions which practically left him no choice. There was no longer a question of using French waters ; so much was quite plain. The Admiral's own idea of a position suitable for the plan under consideration was the Chusan Archipelago, near the mouth of the Yangtse, but here again he was given to understand that a violation of Chinese neutrality would bring Great Britain into the field, even more surely than would a violation of French neutrality. Chinese waters were therefore also barred, and there remained nothing but the seizure of some Japanese harbour. But in the whole range of their southern islands there was no place fit for the purpose except Makung, in the Pescadores, and as to that it was clear the Japanese were on the alert. It would seem, indeed, that as soon as the correctness of the French attitude on the question of the neutrality of their ports was understood, the Japanese Imperial Staff realised what was the only alternative for the Russians, if the plan of seizing an advanced base and operating from it was that on which they

---

[1] Semenov, *Rasplata*, page 443. The source of this information is not known. But in February a Russian secret agent had reported that the Japanese fleet was concentrated at Sasebo and that their intention was to entice the Baltic fleet over mine fields which had been prepared in the Korean Straits. *See post*, p. 346.

were bent.   About this time the fleet auxiliary *Bingo Maru* was sent down to Makung,[1] probably with mines ; for on May 8th a general warning was issued to mariners that the Pescadores were unsafe to approach, and we were informed that this was done "for a large strategical purpose."   As the warning specified a six-mile limit of safety, our Minister at Tokyo was instructed to inquire whether mines had been laid outside territorial waters.   The reply of the Japanese Admiralty was that the six-mile limit was only intended as a precaution for the safety of neutral ships ; but in sending home this information our Minister added, "They do not deny that it was one of " the inducements to tempt the Russian Commander-in-Chief " to the Tsushima Straits."[2]   How far this device influenced the Russian Admiral's decision we cannot tell, but, in addition to the warning to mariners, the Formosa area on the 13th was declared a prohibited area within the war zone, and in a state of siege, and Admiral Rozhestvenski also had information that Makung had been fortified with heavy guns and garrisoned.[3]   He came, therefore, to the conclusion that its seizure would demand a regular operation, which must mean some damage and considerable expenditure of his slender store of ammunition.   Even when taken it would require holding, and to this the Third Squadron would have to be devoted. At the last moment, in response to his representations of the uselessness of that squadron, he had been given liberty to leave it behind, but his relations with Headquarters were now so strained and mistrustful that he regarded the permission as a snare.   We are given at least to understand that he saw in it a device for shifting to his shoulders the odium of defeat.   The disaster which he felt to be inevitable would be attributed to his having divided his fleet and basely deserted his comrades. He determined, therefore, to avoid the trap, and carry out to the bitter end the plan of the Headquarters Staff of forcing his whole fleet through to Vladivostok in a mass.

In the unhappy circumstances of his position his decision can hardly be blamed, but as a pure question of war policy it is doubtful whether the seizure of Makung was not the best move at this time open to Russia, and we have seen that there is reason to believe that this was what the Japanese least

---

[1] *Japanese Published History : Revue Maritime*, Vol. 188, page 408, note.

[2] *N.I.D. Diary*, pages 164, 166–7.

[3] Semenov, *Rasplata*, p. 442.   As to these " Prohibited " or " Defended " Areas, *see* Vol. I, p. 133.

wished to see. For the general naval position of Japan the
command of the Pescadores Channel, constituting as it did a
defile in the main line of communication with Europe, was
only second in importance to that of the Tsushima Straits,
and the occupation of Makung by the Baltic Fleet would
have given the Russians that command so long as they could
maintain themselves there. The difficulty of coal and supplies
would have been serious, but not so much so as at Vladivostok,
seeing that the line to Europe would be open, and seeing how
eager adventurous neutrals were to accommodate them. The
inflow of supplies could only have been stopped by blockade,
and, situated as the port was on the southern limit of the
theatre of operations, in which was the Baltic Fleet, it could
not have been blockaded unless the Japanese had moved down
their whole fleet—a movement which would lay open their own
lines of communication with Manchuria, as well as the route
to Vladivostok. Yet it is difficult to see how the move
could have been avoided. It is probable, at least, that the
Japanese could not have remained where they were till the
enemy's hold was loosened by exhaustion. Peace was looming
up on the horizon ; the Japanese Government, now at the
end of their tether for all serious offensive action in Manchuria, were anxious for negotiations to begin. At such a
moment in our old maritime wars the question of what used
to be called "eggs in the basket" always forced itself to
the front, and now for the Japanese to permit Russia to come
to market with such an egg as Makung in her basket was
not to be thought of. It is difficult, therefore, to see how
its seizure could have failed to break down the practically
impregnable position Japan had taken up. It would surely
have given Russia the initiative and Admiral Togo would have
been compelled to conform by leaving his zone of highest
control, and seeking the enemy where he lay. The best the
Russians could hope was to avoid a decisive defeat at sea,
the worst they had to fear was a resounding naval victory
for the Japanese ; and what plan in the circumstances could
promise an easier end ? Seeing how strongly the peace
movement was growing in Russia, it is a source of wonder
that it was not seen how the lines of pure strategy were
deflected by the political needs of the case and that this
device was not at least put seriously before the Admiral. But
it is only too clear that by this time the voice of strategy and
policy had been drowned in personal recriminations, and that

the paramount idea of every one responsible was to find a scapegoat on whom to lay his sins. So it happened that, so far as is known, the policy which was so familiar to and so adroitly handled by the experienced statesmen of the old Anglo-French wars was never attempted, and Admiral Rozhestvenski was forced to go on upon his hopeless mission.[1]

There was however another way in which it would appear that he might have used the Third Division, so as not only to rid himself of the millstone about his neck, but also to provide himself with an instrument for breaking the Japanese concentration. And that was by employing it for diversion. As will be seen directly, he had made up his mind that his best chance of success was to rush the Korean Straits. All along he had believed that it was at least a practicable scheme with a fairly fast and homogeneous squadron, and events went to show that he was not far wrong. It is equally clear that he regarded the addition of Admiral Nebogatov's division to his fleet as reducing the chances of his plan succeeding. It would seem natural then that he would seize any chance of detaching it and particularly if by so doing he could facilitate the execution of his original scheme. Why then did he not throw off the incumbrance and direct it to make a diversion off Tokyo and to threaten an attempt to pass one of the Northern Straits? In view of what had happened during Admiral Iessen's raid on the east coast in the previous July it is certain that such a demonstration in force could not have been ignored by the Japanese Imperial Staff. Even if Admiral Togo had not been ordered to move part of his fleet, as had been done before, to the protection of the capital, he must at least have detached a considerable force to the entrance of the Tsugaru Strait. If then the diversion were well-timed Admiral Rozhestvenski might have made his attempt with all the chances that were to be extracted from the situation. With

---

[1] Admiral Rozhestvenski's remarks on the subject make it clear that the political aspect of the problem was not before him. In his first report he says : "The enormous preponderance of the Japanese cruisers, " regular and auxiliary, capable, with the benevolent co-operation and " guidance of the English, of destroying any vessels bringing supplies to " our squadron as it moved northwards . . . all this taken together " compelled us to refrain from any places for making a temporary base " on Japanese territory, more or less isolated from their main islands " . . . and to strive to attain our immediate object—to break through " to Vladivostok." As to this report see post, p. 240, note.

a compact and fast squadron he would have found the
guard of the Straits dislocated and its cruiser screen weakened,
and seeing how inadequate it proved to be even at its full
strength there seems no reason why he might · not well have
hoped to get through.

It is true that such a scheme would have involved dividing
his fleet, and theoretically each section of it would have been
exposed to defeat in detail, but since his own argument all
along had been that the Nebogatov Division really reduced
the potential strength of his fleet it followed that to use it to
break the enemy's concentration overrode the normal rule
against division.   But even if the plan failed in its intention
and each part was taken in detail, yet the event would have
been no worse than it actually turned out and this should
have been fairly evident.   He himself realised,—at least such
is our information—that what best suited the Japanese hand
was that they should have the chance of dealing with his
whole fleet in the Straits of Korea.   It was to their distinct
advantage—since they had the better fleet—that their enemy
should keep himself concentrated.   If it came to a battle in
full force within the Japanese zone of highest control it was
a foregone conclusion that the Russians could not defeat the
Japanese.   The best they could hope was to give them such
a check as would enable a large part of the Baltic Fleet
to get . through to Vladivostok.   As the balance of the war
then stood this was the one development by which the
Russians would expect to turn it in their favour.   To bring
the war to a victorious issue was recognised as impossible ;
peace was already in the air and what they had to aim at
was setting the board to the utmost advantage for the
coming negotiations.   For this purpose the best they could
do was to establish a squadron at Vladivostok, for there
another siege like that of Port Arthur would be forced on
the Japanese before they could claim that their position was
impregnable.   This being so it was bad policy to give the
Japanese a chance of a decisive action at sea.   The true
Russian policy was to get as many ships as possible through
to Vladivostok and so far as possible to avoid an action.
The worst way to attain these ends was to take the fleet in
a mass through the enemy's zone of highest control : the
best way was to divide into two portions each formidable
enough to demand serious attention.   If one section were
defeated by superior force it would mean such a disposition

of the enemy's fleet as would give the other the greater
chance of evading. We know that the Japanese up to the
last were seriously anxious on the point of evasion and that
anxiety was due to the fact that there was more than one
approach to Vladivostok. This was the real weakness of their
naval position, and the one way to take advantage of it was
for the Russians to divide their fleet and avoid simplifying
their enemy's problem to keeping to one approach only.

If we try to picture what the effect of such a division
would have been upon the Japanese we see them confronted
with a strategical dilemma of the greatest difficulty. Since
their whole position in regard to an advantageous and speedy
peace turned, as it did, on their preventing anything substantial getting through to Vladivostok, only two courses
were open to them ; they must either divide their fleet
between the Korean Strait and the Northern Straits, or else
they must move the whole of it northward to a position that
was interior to all the lines of approach to Vladivostok.
Either alternative was highly objectionable. Assuming they
adopted the first there was the difficulty of settling how
to divide their fleet. Their information could not have been
sufficiently accurate or trustworthy to leave them in no doubt
as to the strength and composition of the two sections of
the Russian force, and yet they would have had to decide on
the moment what force they should allot to each section of
their own. If in the face of this difficulty they adopted the
plan of defending one of the straits with the flotilla and the
other with the fleet the position would have been scarcely
less difficult. The necessary support of the flotilla would have
seriously reduced the cruiser strength of the fleet and by
so much would have increased the difficulty of locating the
enemy. In addition to this, the separation of the flotilla
from the fleet would have deprived the Japanese of the means
on which they counted most strongly of making their battle
decisive by following it up with a night torpedo attack.

Under the pressure of these considerations the Japanese
might well have been forced to seek an interior position to
the northward and this would at once have given Admiral
Rozhestvenski all he could hope for. Not only would the
elaborate arrangements of the Japanese for locating his approach
have been upset at the last moment, but the battle would
have been deferred till he reached the fog-infested waters
close to his destination and to the Russian zone of highest

control. Under such conditions, even if a battle had been forced on him, he could scarcely have failed to get a substantial part of his fleet through to Vladivostok.

Why then did he not adopt this apparently obvious plan ? It was not that superior orders compelled him to keep his whole force together ; for he had just received authority to leave the Nebogatov Division behind. It would seem rather that he allowed himself to be dominated by the rule of con- centration without having duly considered its underlying principles or its application to the problem in hand. Sound, almost sacred, as it is, where the attainment of the strategical object depends on inflicting the utmost possible damage on the enemy's fleet, it does not necessarily apply when the immediate strategical object is best to be attained by evading that fleet. It would indeed seem that this aspect of the problem was not in his mind, for his last order to the fleet, as we shall see, was to impress upon his Divisional flag-officers that the one object was to get through to Vladivostok and that the only way to do this was to keep the fleet concentrated.

There is however another conceivable explanation, which had nothing to do with strategy. It may have been that knowing he was to be made a scapegoat he was unwilling to give his unscrupulous critics a hold upon him by sinning against the dogma of concentration. Placed as he was, a man must have moral courage of almost superhuman strength to depart from the " correct" course, and it is possible that his only idea was, like that of Admiral Cervera at Santiago, that as his fleet by his superiors' bad manage- ment was doomed to failure, he would do his best to gild the failure with all the honour he could win from defeat. If the Russian flag was to go down in the Far Eastern Seas, it should fall with everything he could muster fighting to the last. It was magnificent but it was not war.

But of all this we know nothing for certain. Whatever the motive, the fleet for good reason or bad was kept in one body and the only question that remained was by what route should he go. The Pescadores Channel was, of course, eliminated. In his approach it must be turned by passing out into the Pacific by the channel between Formosa and Luzon ; and what then ? There were three possible routes to his destination, one by La Pérouse Strait, another by the Tsugaru Strait, and the third by one or other of the two channels of the Korean Straits. Of the three Tsugaru was strategically the best. It was recognised that the Sylvia Basin position was interior to it, but it was calculated that if the approach of the Baltic Fleet could be concealed until the Strait was reached, Admiral Togo would only have time to bar the line to Vladivostok with his fastest divisions, and in all probability he would find himself at the crisis deprived of the slow Fifth and Seventh Divisions, and all his torpedo-boats.[1] The Russians could therefore hope to fight in no distinct inferiority, and in an open sea close to their base, where the prevalent fogs would give a fair chance of breaking through.

On these grounds Admiral Rozhestvenski has been severely criticised by his own countrymen for not taking this route. The reasoning of his critics after the event was practically the same as that above indicated in considering what he would have gained in forcing the Japanese to meet him as close as possible to Vladivostok. Similar advantages, though in a minor degree, were of course offered by La Pérouse Strait, but that route had to be rejected on account of the distance and the extreme difficulties of the navigation.

Clearly, then, on strategical grounds, it could be rightly contended that the Tsugaru route was the one the Admiral ought to have chosen. But what his critics omitted to observe was that the decision was not so much a question of strategy as of the navigational possibilities of a fleet such as that the Admiral commanded. With a numerous and heterogeneous force, in which even the best units showed themselves unable to keep station, with inexperienced and nervous officers, and with half-trained crews, the problem presented itself to him in quite a different aspect from what it did to the men with chart, dividers, and speed-tables in the serenity of the Staff Bureau at St. Petersburg. From bitter experience, and above all from his recent attempts to handle the fleet as a whole, the Admiral knew it could be called on for nothing but the simplest evolutions and the plainest sailing. "It only managed with difficulty," says one of his Staff, "to " maintain something of a formation even in clear weather and " in the most favourable navigational conditions."[2] In addition

---

[1] The calculation was as follows :—Sylvia Basin to Vladivostok, 550 miles ; Tsugaru Strait to Vladivostok, 430. Japanese units capable of maintaining 15 knots would be off the port in 37 hours, and the Russians doing 10 knots (the assigned speed of their slowest ships) could arrive in 43 hours.

[2] Semenov, *Rasplata*, 463.

to these objections the Russian secret agents were reporting that the Tsugaru Strait was thickly mined and strongly fortified ; but whether the Admiral had this information is not known.[1] Be that as it may, in his opinion to attempt to take it through so narrow and foggy a strait, with its dangerous current, its tortuous channel, and its torpedo guard, could only spell disaster. For the small, compact, and efficient squadron that was his ideal it might have been done, but with the amorphous collection of ships that had been thrust upon him it was impossible, and for all its advantages the Tsugaru route had to be rejected as impracticable.[2]

Such at least, we are informed, was his line of argument, and if, indeed, these were his reasons it is almost impossible to believe that he did not deliberately reject the solution which they clearly indicate of dividing his fleet in the manner above suggested.

There remained, then, the choice between the two channels of the direct route through the Korean Straits. The Western channel had little to recommend it. Not only did it pass between the two Japanese bases, Sylvia Basin and Takeshiki, but it was the narrower of the two, and contracted towards its northern end. The Eastern channel, on the other hand, was furthest from the enemy's base, and when once the line between Ikishima and the south of Tsushima was passed it rapidly opened out into the Sea of Japan. The wide fairway was absolutely clear from shore to shore, it presented no navigational difficulties, and if therefore by luck of heavy or thick weather he could run the narrows without serious damage, he would have sea room enough to give him some chance of getting away. For these reasons the Eastern channel was chosen. For the rest he would trust to the surprise of a sudden appearance by covering his tracks till the last moment and by doing what he could to lay a false scent.

With this plan in his mind he set his course to pass to the northward of Luzon, keeping his fleet in compact steaming order. Ahead was what was known as the "Scouting Division"— the *Svyetlana* and the three auxiliary cruisers *Kuban*, *Terek*, and *Ural* ; but as his design involved covering as small an

---

[1] See *post*, p. 346.

[2] The only authority for this is Semenov (*Rasplata*, 161 *et seq.*). He was on the Admiral's Staff, but does not make it clear whether the reasoning was the Admiral's or his own. He says, however, that for the reasons given "the Tsugaru Strait could not be considered at all."

area with his fleet as possible these ships were not thrown out
to true scouting distance, but were kept only four or five cables
in advance.   Then came the First and Second Battle Divisions
in two lines ahead disposed abeam.   Close astern of them were
the transports also in two columns with the rest of the cruisers
on their flanks, while the rear was brought up by the Third
Battle Division in line-abreast.   This was the day formation,
and at night the only variation of the order was that the two
leading battle divisions opened out to allow the transport
columns to close up and take station between them.

The special feature of this steaming order was of course that
there was no provision for long-distance scouting, either ahead
or on the flanks.   For this omission the Admiral has been
criticised, on the ground that if the enemy had appeared there
would have been no time to form battle order.   But it seems
clear that by this time he was quite satisfied that the Japanese
did not mean to commit the error of leaving their perfect
position and advancing in force to meet him.   All he had to
fear was a cruiser or destroyer attack and against this he must
protect the transports.   He now saw clearly that everything
turned on his being able to rush the Japanese position.   For
this his chance was surprise, and if his approach was to be
concealed the less sea he covered the better.   Even apart from
these considerations there was the fact he could rely on nothing
but visual signalling ; for the Slaby-Arco system of wireless
which the Russian Admiralty had adopted was proving quite
untrustworthy.   It was only, therefore, twenty-four hours
before he intended filling up with coal that he sent cruisers
thirty miles ahead to see all clear.

As he proceeded the customary breakdowns caused frequent
delays ; but by the 19th he was passing the north of Luzon,
having captured the previous evening the British steamer
Oldhamia, which on suspicion of contraband was eventually
sent on to Vladivostok with a prize crew by way of La Pérouse
Strait, part of her own crew being transferred to the hospital
ship *Orel*.   This was the first event of the kind since Admiral
Rozhestvenski's undertaking with the French Government not
to operate with his cruisers from French waters, but again he
had used a Red Cross ship for a naval purpose.   The prize
never reached her destination.   She ran on a rock in trying to
pass the Yetorup Channel, and was burnt by her Russian crew.

On the 21st, while they were still out in the Pacific, she
parted company and next morning the fleet turned N. 20° W.

to pass back into the China Sea between Miyako and Liu-kiu. Two days earlier, being now on the point of entering the war zone, the Admiral had issued a special order to provide against a danger which his information led him to expect.   It was as follows :—

COMMANDER-IN-CHIEF'S ORDER No. 240.

At night when passing through the chain of islands which run down from Japan, the destroyers will form single line abreast (1st division to starboard ; 2nd division to port ; *Blestyashchi* in the centre).   They will be $1\frac{1}{2}$ miles in front of the line of scouts, and will have lights showing on both beams (lights of low power).   But the ships on the outside of the line will not light up lights on their outer sides.

In command of all destroyers will be the Commanding Officer of *Blestyashchi*.

If a ship is sighted ahead a destroyer on the side nearest her is to be despatched to determine who she is.   Thus if on the starboard hand a destroyer from the starboard wing ; if on the port hand a destroyer from the port wing; if right ahead the Commanding Officer of *Blestyashchi* will send from either starboard or port wing as he thinks fit.   The signal for this will be made by three consecutive flashes from a lamp shown in the direction of destroyer which is to be detached.

If there is any reason to suppose that the vessel encountered is laying floating mines, unless it is an occasion on which the burning of searchlights is forbidden, they are to be switched on at once, and search made for any floating bodies.

If a floating mine should be sighted one of the destroyers is to throw up the beam of her searchlight at an angle of 45° and thereby signal to the Fleet to stop.   The destroyer nearest the mine should take steps to sink it by firing at it. The others observing this all of them should sweep the sea elsewhere with their searchlights.

On seeing the above warning signal (searchlight beam elevated at 45°), all ships and transports should stop engines and await orders.

If the signal " 5 " starboard, or port, is made from the flag-ship, the scouting squadron first and then all ships of the Main Fleet are to alter course in succession and change the direction of the Fleet 8 points to starboard or port as indi-cated.   All Commanding Officers are to take the greatest care and to proceed so as not to interfere with the motions of the ships astern of them. Also while turning they are to do their best to avoid entering the lines of destroyers engaged in searching for mines.

When all ships of the battle fleet have finished turning they will reduce speed, and the destroyers will alter course 8 points together in the same direction as the Fleet and proceed at full speed.,

After this, when the *Blestyashchi* comes abreast of the leading ship of the line of scouts she will make a signal, and the whole of the destroyers will alter course 8 points together so as to get on to the original course. When the destroyers are seen to have proceeded 15 cables on their original course, the scouting squadron, and then the Main Fleet will change direction to the original course, and proceed with the centre of the Fleet right astern of the centre destroyer. If a destroyer should engage in destroying another mine before the Fleet has altered course, the destroyer next her will throw the beam of her searchlight on the horizon and with it describe the arc of a circle.

Destroyers are on no account to close on the Main Fleet, except in cases of absolute necessity. In the event of unavoidable necessity the destroyer closing should illuminate her ensign and the distinguishing marks on her funnels with her own searchlights, and also make the signal which has been agreed upon for the night in question.

19.5.05.
China Sea.
(Signed)   ROZHESTVENSKI.[1]

There was nothing further about tactics, but for this omission he had at least a plausible reason. He had made up his mind that his own motions must necessarily depend on the form of the Japanese attack, and for repelling it he must trust to leadership at the moment. It is natural then that his last battle instruction was one to provide, as far as possible, that leadership should not fail, and this was issued on May 23, the day they entered the China Sea. " During an " action," it ran, " the ships in the line of battle will steam " past their own damaged ships, or any ships that cannot

---

[1] This is from the Japanese version of the original captured in the hospital ship *Orel*.

" keep station. If the *Suvorov* is damaged and out of
" control, the fleet will keep station on the *Alexandr*, and
" should the *Alexandr* be disabled, they should follow
" the *Borodino*, and then the *Orel*. At the same time the
" *Alexandr*, *Borodino* and *Orel* will act on the signals of the
" *Suvorov* until the flag of the Commander-in-Chief has been
" transferred, or until a junior flag-officer has assumed com-
" mand." Then follows a provision for the 1st destroyer
division to stand-by to come up to disabled flagships and take
off the Admiral and his staff. " The *Byedovi* and *Buistri* will
" be always ready to steam up to the *Suvorov* with this object,
" and the *Buini* and *Bravi* to the other flagships." The destroyers of the 2nd division were to perform the same service
for the cruiser flagships. " The flags of the commanding
" officers," it concluded, " will be transferred to the corre-
" sponding destroyers until it is found possible to transfer them
" to a battleship or cruiser." [1]

The last order of all, issued the same day, was devoted to
emphasing what the real object of the fleet was, and what
was the best means of obtaining it—and it shows how the
Admiral's one hope was to evade by the help of thick weather
and close concentration. " In the event of falling in with
" fog," it said, " Divisional Admirals should endeavour to
" prevent their divisions losing company. The leading trans-
" ports should endeavour to prevent other transports losing
" company. All destroyers are to keep close to the ships to
" which they are attached, and to assist the two battle
" squadrons in keeping touch. Each Divisional Admiral
" should act in accordance with the idea that the primary
" object of the Fleet is to reach Vladivostok, and I would
" impress upon them that their object can only be attained
" by the whole force of the fleet acting in combination."[2]

It was now that while frankly facing what was likely to
happen, he took the inadequate steps already referred to for
lightening the task before him. Although, as we have seen,
he did not adopt the best and most obvious means for the

---

[1] Smirnov, Order No. 243, May 23rd.

[2] Order 244, from the Japanese version. Smirnov does not give the
whole text, but in summarizing it says it terminated with the words—-
" Every officer in command of a division, in view of the fact that the
" object of the squadron is to close Vladivostok, must remember that
" the attainment of this object is only possible with the combined
" force of the squadron."

surprise and confusion of his enemy, he was not content
with merely hurling his fleet against the Japanese position.
He had still a faint hope of loosening their concentration by
diversionary movements, and now, if ever, these must be set
on foot. The first device he had in his mind was to attempt
a repetition of Admiral Iessen's effective raid. Two auxiliary
cruisers, the *Kuban* and *Terek*, were told off for the purpose
and were now detached with instructions to pass up the east
coast of Japan and operate off Tokyo Bay. It was little
enough to rely on for the effect he desired, but the far-reaching
effects of Admiral Iessen's appearance in the same quarter (if
indeed they were known to the Admiral) offered some justification for an operation which has been widely ridiculed.

His next step was to lead the fleet for the Saddle Islands·
off the Yangtse, straight across the thronged trade route, where
he must infallibly reveal himself. This is the deepest mystery
of his campaign. The meaning and intention of the movement have never been explained. It is usually assumed that
his passage outside Formosa was dictated purely by a desire
to conceal his approach, and on this hypothesis his showing
himself on the great Far Eastern highway becomes inexplicable.
But if we conjecture that his detour into the Pacific was made
mainly to avoid the danger area of Makung, a reason for the
other move will at once suggest itself. His object was not
so much to conceal his approach as to raise a false impression
of his purpose. We know—and possibly the Japanese knew,
so open had been discussion in Russia—that he had once
wished to prepare in the islands off the Yangtse an advanced
base for further operations of a less ambitious kind than those
which had been forced upon his inadequate fleet. It is conceivable, therefore, that his object was to revive this impression
in a faint hope of drawing the Japanese from their formidable
position.

But here it must be admitted he went counter to well established principles which condemn double diversions of the kind.
In the first place a diversion, if made at all, should be in such
strength as to force the enemy to attend to it ; and in the
second all possible means should be taken to conceal the fact
that it is only a diversion. Both considerations should have
shown him the error of the double effort. For by dividing his
diversionary force he rendered each section too weak to do serious
harm, and told his enemy plainly that he had nothing but
diversion in his mind. The only explanation of his mistake is

the temptation offered by the chance of threatening the establishment of a base within the war zone, and the measures he took on reaching the selected point give some colour to the supposition that this was actually his idea.

On May 23rd he had stopped to fill up with coal for the last time, the orders being that enough was to be taken in to have the bunkers full on May 26th. While the coaling was going on he issued a general order that they were to be ready for action at any hour. Next day he proceeded across the fairway, and on May 25th he was off the Saddle Islands. Here he detached the two notorious cruisers *Dnyepr* and *Rion* to escort all but six of his best transports into Shanghai, which was some 90 miles away. This service done they were to proceed to make a demonstration in the Yellow Sea, apparently with the intention of threatening from the supposed new base the most sensitive nerves of the Japanese system—the main lines of supply to the Manchurian army.

It was under depressing conditions that Admiral Rozhestvenski made these last arrangements ; Admiral Felkerzam, his energetic right hand, had been growing worse day by day ever since leaving Nossi Bé, and on May 24th he died. The loss was peculiarly serious, since for fear of the moral effect on the fleet his death had to be concealed. His flag was kept flying in the *Oslyabya* and her captain was given command of the division. Seeing how much the faint chances of success depended on manœuvring so as to seize any happy chance that occurred, nothing, perhaps, could have hit the Commander-in-Chief harder than the loss of his capable second-in-command and the leader of his Second Battle Division.

It was then with every omen of failure that he led his fleet, freed from some of its incumbrances, direct for the channel he had chosen. His formation had been somewhat modified. Ahead, but still only three or four cables in advance, was the *Svyetlana* with the *Almaz* and *Ural* on either quarter. The double quarter line thus formed was prolonged by the *Zhemchug* and *Izumrud* round the head of the squadron and in the wake of each of these two cruisers were two destroyers of the 1st division. The squadron thus covered was in two lines ahead. In the starboard line were the First and Second Divisions, and in the port line the Third Division and the First Cruiser Division. Between the rear divisions were the six transports that remained, and in rear of the port line was the 2nd destroyer division in line-ahead. In rear of all were the two hospital ships. The fleet was thus more compact then ever—there was still no distant scouting—and so far the Admiral's preoccupation was still concealment and

Svyetlana

Almaz   Ural

Nikolai I.   Suvorov

Izumrud   Zhemchug

Apraxin   Alexandr

D. 1   Borodino   D. 1

Senyavin

D. 1   Ushakov   Orel   D. 1

Oleg   Oslyabya

Avrora   Sisoi

Donskoi   *Transports*   Navarin

Monomakh   Nakhimov

D. 2

D. 2

D. 2

D. 2

D. 2   Orel (Hospital)

Kostroma (Hospital)

D. 1 = 1st Destroyer Division.
D. 2 = 2nd   ,,   ,,

STEAMING ORDER OF THE BALTIC FLEET.

surprise. Even when towards evening Japanese wireless messages began to be felt he would not permit his own wireless to
be worked for interference. Scouting could do no good. He
was sure enough of Admiral Togo's position to be certain that
if the weather was anything like clear the Japanese must get
contact sooner or later, and the only thing to do was to
reduce the chance of being located till the last moment and
then to try to rush his fleet through in a mass.

The weather, which was growing thick, promised to assist
him, and it only remained how best to time his approach to
the narrows. In waters swarming with hostile torpedo craft
it was scarcely advisable to attempt the passage at night, in
spite of the small results the Japanese flotilla attacks had hitherto
produced. By making the attempt in open day this danger
at least would be avoided, and if the narrows were reached
about noon it would ensure that by nightfall he would, with
luck, have reached the open sea, where his chances were
greatest. It was in this manner, therefore, that he decided his
approach should culminate.

Since there was plenty of time for appearing at the designed
hour, the fleet was practised on the 26th in the various movements he had laid down for forming battle order according
to the direction in which the enemy was sighted. Many
hours were spent in these exercises, and as they proceeded the
wireless messages of the Japanese grew clearer and clearer in
the Russian receivers. All that was possible had now been
done, and at the conclusion of the evolutions, after " Prepare
for action," he signalled, " To-morrow at the hoisting of the
" colours battle flags will be sent up."

For not interfering with these wireless conversations, the
Admiral was as sharply taken to task as for not scouting. His
explanation was convincing. He did not choose to interfere
because the distant Japanese cruisers were telling him all he
wanted to know. He gradually made out there were at least
seven of them in his front. So large a number could mean but
one thing—it could only confirm what he was counting on,
and " he did not," he says, "send his scouts away because he
" knew quite well that he was about to meet the whole force
" of the Japanese Fleet in the Korean Straits." [1]

---

[1] See his official letter sent with the sanction of the Admiralty to
the *Novoe Vremya*, 3rd January 1906 (*Attaché Reports*, IV., 135).

CHAPTER XIV.

FINAL APPROACH OF THE BALTIC FLEET AND MOVEMENTS UP TO CONTACT.

[Charts XB, XI.]

UPON the Japanese Staff Admiral Rozhestvenski's attempts at diversion produced no effect. They were not even aware that any such attempt had been made when the crisis came, and the position in the straits was confidently maintained. Still they had not been without their moments of anxiety.

As early as May 18th they must have known that Admiral Nebogatov's Squadron had joined and that the concentrated Baltic Fleet had sailed from Van Fong on the 14th to the eastward.[1] The Vladivostok cruisers and torpedo craft were known to be active, occasionally putting to sea, and on May 21st a report reached Admiral Togo at Sylvia Basin that six vessels, apparently destroyers, had been seen off Okinoshima in the Eastern Channel that morning. This was just the area in which the Vladivostok cruisers had made their successful raid on the Japanese transports in June the previous year, and as it was possible that another attempt of the kind might be in hand Admiral Kamimura with three of his division was sent away in search at 4.0 p.m. Shortly afterwards there was a general signal for the whole fleet to prepare for sea and all steamboats were sent away to the transports that were to look after them in the absence of the fleet.[2]

---

[1] This was reported by Reuter on May 18th.

[2] The organisation of the Japanese fleet available for the battle will be useful for reference.

FIRST SQUADRON.

First Division.—*Mikasa* (flag of Adm. Togo), *Shikishima, Fuji, Asahi, Kasuga, Nisshin* (flag of Vice-Adm. Misu), *Tatsuta* (despatch-vessel).

Third Division.—*Kasagi* (flag of Vice-Adm. Dewa), *Chitose, Otowa, Niitaka.*

SECOND SQUADRON.

Second Division.—*Idzumo* (flag of Vice-Adm. Kamimura), *Adzuma, Tokiwa, Yakumo, Asama, Iwate* (flag of Rear-Adm. Shimamura), *Chihaya* (despatch-vessel).

Fourth Division.—*Naniwa* (flag of Rear-Adm. Uriu), *Takachiho, Akashi, Tsushima.*

THIRD SQUADRON.

Fifth Division.—*Itsukushima* (flag of Vice-Adm. Kataoka), *Chinyen, Matsushima, Hashidate* (flag of Rear-Adm. Taketomi), *Yaeyama* (despatch-vessel). [OVER

Next day, however, Admiral Kamimura returned to report that he had found no trace of the enemy, and, indeed, the fact was that all chance of effective interference from Vladivostok had just been brought to an abrupt end.   Rear-Admiral Iessen was now in command of the squadron ; for after the fall of Port Arthur and the final destruction of the First Squadron in its harbour, Vice-Admiral Skruidlov, who was officially in command of it, had been recalled with the solace of a seat on the Admiralty Council.   In his stead Vice-Admiral Birilev had been appointed and was now on his way out to take up the post of Commander-in-Chief of the Pacific Fleet, of which, of course, the Second and Third Squadrons under Admirals Rozhestvenski and Nebogatov formed practically the whole.   Of the Vladivostok Division there was little left.

It so happened that on May 21st a floating mine had been discovered off the port, and a general order had been issued that no ship was to go out unless accompanied by sweepers for not less than 35 miles to seaward.   With this precaution Admiral Iessen himself went out on the 23rd (the day after Admiral Kamimura returned) in the *Gromoboi* to test his wireless installation, but for some unknown reason he dismissed his sweepers only 12 miles out.   The result was she struck a mine which tore a hole in her side 33 feet long by 16 feet

---

Sixth Division.—*Suma* (flag of Rear-Adm. Togo Masaji), *Chiyoda, Akitsushima, Idzumi.*

Seventh Division.—*Fuso* (flag of Rear-Adm. Yamada), *Takao, Tsukushi, Chokai, Maya, Uji.*

AUXILIARY SQUADRON.

Merchant Cruisers.—*America Maru, Sado Maru, Shinano Maru, Manshu Maru, Yawata Maru, Dainan Maru, Daichu Maru.*

Torpedo Parent Ships.—*Kumano Maru, Nikko Maru, Kasuga Maru.*

FLOTILLA.

(a) Destroyers :—

1st *division.*—*Harusame* (Capt. Fujimoto), *Fubuki, Ariake, Arare, Akatsuki II.*

2nd *division.*—*Oboro* (Capt. Yashima), *Inadzuma, Ikadzuchi, Akebono.*

3rd *division.*—*Shinonome* (Commander Yoshijima), *Usugumo, Kasumi, Sazanami.*

4th *division.*—*Asagiri* (Commander Suzuki), *Murasame, Shirakumo, Asashiwo.*

5th *division.* — *Shiranui* (Commander Hirose), *Murakamo, Yugiri, Kagero.*

(b) Torpedo-boats :—

1st, 10th, 11th, 9th, 14th, 15th, and 20th divisions attached to the Fleet (27 boats).

5th, 16th, 17th, and 18th attached to Straits ports (15 boats).

high. As the bulkheads were not seriously damaged she managed to regain the port but was put entirely out of action for
a long time to come.

While this catastrophe was taking place all was in hurried
movement at Sylvia Basin. At 9.0. a.m. an alarm had been received by wireless that the Baltic Fleet had been sighted 120
miles from the Japanese coast heading for the Straits. It must
have come from one of the auxiliary cruisers, which it will
be remembered were occupying the advanced or western line of
patrol sections between Quelpart and the Goto Islands. It was
quickly followed by a message that possibly as the weather
was thick in the Quelpart area a mistake had been made,
due to a Japanese merchant vessel burning native coal. Still as
the matter was in doubt Admiral Togo decided to take the
fleet to sea. The ships were cleared for action and battle
order was taken up, but by noon it was certain that the alarm
was false and the fleet returned and came to anchor in
Douglas Inlet, at the entrance of the bay.

The fog of war which shrouded the enemy's movements
was as deep as ever. Not a word had been heard of them since
they left Van Fong, and the 24th passed without any news.
Their non-appearance was incomprehensible, and it began to
cause no little anxiety as to what their plan could be. It
was not till the 25th that any light was obtained and then
it was such that only added to the uncertainty. On that day a
Norwegian vessel reported that on the 19th she had seen and
been visited by the fleet off Batan or Grafton Island in the
Bashi Group, which lies between Luzon and Formosa. The
inference of the Staff, as communicated to our Ambassador, was
that unless the Russians were sighted by the advance patrols
within 36 hours they must be making for Vladivostok by La
Pérouse Strait. Accordingly Admiral Togo that evening began
to prepare for an order to operate at a distance from his
base. The steamboats which had been sent away were recalled
and hoisted in ; all units, even the torpedo craft, took in heavy
deck cargoes of coal, and the Admiral himself brought his flagship right up the bay into Sylvia Basin.

The reason of this curious movement at a crisis when the
Russians might be reported at any moment is nowhere
explained. It is obvious, however, that the non-appearance of
the Baltic Fleet must have raised a serious doubt as to whether
Admiral Rozhestvenski meant to face the Korean Straits. It
was possible he was already on his way to turn the Japanese

position by passing through one of the northern straits. If so, Admiral Togo was wrongly placed, and he ought to lose no time in taking up an interior position in the north of the Japan Sea. It was afterwards whispered indeed that the Imperial Staff had been on the brink of ordering him to shift his ground, but of this we know nothing officially. All we can tell is that in the acute anxiety of the strategic fog there was reason enough for the Commander-in-chief being brought into the closest possible communication with the Staff at Tokyo.

Next morning, the 26th, however, the fleet did not move, nor did the Admiral return. During the night news had come in that a Russian merchant cruiser with three transports had arrived at Wusung, and that another similar cruiser had been sighted off the Yangtse.[1] The general impression was that these ships were intended to operate as a diversion to conceal the real movement, and the Japanese Fleet stood fast in Douglas Inlet. Of the enemy's main body there was still no news, but later in the day information came in that it had been seen to anchor the previous night off the Saddle Islands less than 400 miles away from the Japanese screen. The Russians, therefore, might be heard of at any moment, and that night, for the first time for many days, nets were not got out, in spite of the exposed position of the squadron.

It is possible this was done in readiness for an order to hurry northwards at a moment's notice. For the strain of doubt was as great as ever. Owing to the radical defect of the Japanese dispositions it could not be otherwise since, short as they were of fast cruisers, they had not been able to push their outposts far enough forward or ascertain in proper time by what route the Russians would come. They had indeed nothing but a close cruiser screen covering the concentration. On the critical night of May 26th–27th it was composed and distributed in the following manner :— The "Fourth Guard Line," which ran from Shirose due north-west to the Castle Group, had this day been occupied by the Third Division under Admiral Dewa,[2] and his practice seems to have been to gather it somewhat closely during the night about the centre of the line (Position 246 : lat. 33° 40′ N., long. 128° 10′ E.). On either flank was a cruiser of the Sixth Division, the

---

[1] These ships were, of course, the *Dnyepr* and *Rion* escorting the transports which had been ordered into the Yangtse on the 25th. There were six of them in all. *See ante*, p. 214.

[2] *Kasagi* (flag), *Chitose*, *Otowa*, *Niitaka*.

Akitsushima towards the Castle Group, and the *Idzumi* towards Shirose. The function of these two cruisers is stated to have been to act as supports to the auxiliary cruisers in the western Patrol Sections between the Goto Islands and Quelpart, and to assist them in guarding the Straits ; but at night they were in the wing sections of the Fourth Guard Line.[1] The four auxiliary cruisers *America Maru*, *Sado Maru*, *Shinano Maru*, and *Manshu Maru*, which held the westerly Patrol Sections, were deployed from the south end of Goto Islands in the direction of Quelpart, the *America Maru* being the most westerly, and the *Manshu Maru* nearest the Goto Islands.[2] From their recorded movements it is to be deduced that the routine was to steam seawards during the day, and at sunset to return so as to reach certain assigned positions about 10 miles in advance of the Fourth Guard Line at dawn, when they turned and stood to the west again. To complete the screen a division of destroyers should also have been on the Guard Line. The 4th division had actually come out with Admiral Dewa on the 26th, but the weather had proved so bad that they had turned back and taken refuge in Osaki Bay. In rear of the Guard Line there was very little. During the night a division of torpedo-boats belonging to Admiral Yamada's Third Squadron kept guard in the Iki district at the entrance to the Eastern Channel, but at dawn on the 27th, according to routine, they left for their base at Takeshiki. Admiral Yamada himself in his flagship, the *Fuso*, was cruising to and fro some 15 miles south of Tsushima, presumably in order to keep up wireless connection between the screen and the Commander-in-Chief at Sylvia Basin, a duty this same ship had discharged so long during the blockade of Port Arthur.

What the actual scheme was for ensuring contact in the best manner is only to be inferred by similar deductions. The stations for all units were laid down in a definite plan, but its text is unknown. From what took place, however, the general idea of the dispositions is clear, but obviously they were based on the assumption that the enemy would chose one or other

---

[1] *Akitsushima's* station is given as Position JE (20 miles S.E. of the Castle Group), and that of *Idzumi* as Position JU (20 miles N.W. of Shirose). At dawn on the 27th *Akitsushima* was in Position 270 (16 miles S.E. of Castle Group), while *Idzumi* was in Position 205 (18 miles N.W. of Shirose). The guard line ran through all these positions. JE lay within the area of Position 270, and JU within that of Position 205.

[2] These were all four British-built vessels, averaging 6,000 tons, and of recent date.

channel of the Korean Straits. As we have seen, one division
of cruisers and half another were on the Fourth Guard Line.
A precisely similar force, as soon as the enemy was reported,
was to proceed to the south of Tsushima, and thence act
according to circumstances so as to feed the Commander-in-
Chief with the most accurate information as to the course,
speed, numbers and formation of the enemy. In this work
the Fifth Division was to share, instead of being held in
reserve as in the tactical scheme for the battle of the Yellow Sea.
This function was assigned to the Seventh Division, which it
would seem was to guard whichever of the two channels
the main Russian force did not take. To clear up this point
as soon as possible was the first duty of the cruisers detailed
for observation, for it was Admiral Togo's intention apparently
to take his battle squadron, which was formed of the two
armoured divisions and the remaining light cruiser division, to
the north end of Tsushima, and thence to act in accordance
with the cruisers' reports.

Such being broadly the plan, the position in the early hours
of the 27th was as follows. At 2.45, in accordance with the
advanced patrol routine, the *Shinano Maru*, the second ship from
the Goto Islands was falling back with the others on the
Fourth Guard Line. She was then standing north-east and
was in Position 186, about 40 miles west of Shirose, when
she saw a strange ship two points abaft her port beam. As her
lights were suspicious and the moon was rising in the east in
a bad position for observing her the *Shinano* increased speed,
and steaming round her stern came up close on her port side
at 4.30. The Japanese commander, Captain Morikawa, could
then see the stranger was unarmed and apparently a hospital
ship. She was, in fact, the *Orel*, whose station was in the
extreme rear of the fleet on the starboard side, and, from this it
is evident that the main force had passed the auxiliary cruiser
line unobserved.[1] As at the moment she was sighted the *Orel*
began making private signals, it was concluded she must have
consorts, but dawn had not yet broken and there was too much
haze for anything to be seen clearly in the moonlight. Captain
Morikawa therefore determined to overhaul the solitary ship and

---

[1] By dead reckoning from noon positions on the 26th and 27th the
leading Russian ship would be just entering the area of Position 203,
which is immediately north-east of Position 186, where the *Orel* was seen.
The Russian speed is given at nine knots, but the current may have given
them a knot more.

search her, when suddenly he was aware of half-a-dozen other ships less than a mile away on his port hand, besides smoke streaks indicating the presence of many more. Believing himself to be in the midst of the enemy he at once turned 16 points and at 4.45 gave the wireless cypher " Enemy's smoke in sight." He followed this at 4.50 with " Enemy's Second Squadron sighted in Position 203 " (lat. 33° 20' N. ; long. 128° 10' E.).

Now the centre of this position was about 15 miles short of the guard line at the point where there was a gap between the *Idzumi* and the Third Division. This probably should have been filled by the absent destroyers ; but as it was it was wide open for the Russians to pass. They were, indeed, actually doing so and the position which the *Shinano* had given was wrong. It would seem that owing to the continued thick weather, she was out in her reckoning, and was further to the eastward than she thought ; or else that the *Orel* was a considerable way astern of her station and the *Shinano* believed the main force was nearer to her than it really was. Probably both reasons had something to do with an error which came near to having serious consequences. For by this time the bulk of the Russian fleet must have been between 10 and 20 miles ahead of Position 203, and were actually about to cross the guard line through the unwatched gap.

Such a gap there certainly was, but what the precise position of the Third Division was at the time is nowhere given. All references to it, however, point to its being concentrated about the centre of the line, as though held ready to support the auxiliary cruiser which first got touch. The gap was all the more serious because the *Idzumi*, which is stated to have been the "guardship of the day," was, for reasons that are unexplained, not on the guard line, but between eight and nine miles north-east of it at a point 13 miles W.N.W. of Ukushima, the northernmost island of the Goto Group. Taking in the *Shinano's* signal in two minutes, she promptly turned W.N.W., a course which would take her to the Third Division, and right across the line the Russians were actually steaming. Still, for an hour she got no further intimation of their whereabouts, for by this time the *Shinano* had lost them in the mist. Presently the *Idzumi* altered course to north, but still could see nothing. At 6.5, however, the *Shinano* recovered touch, but had to give the enemy a wide berth to avoid a destroyer. Then seeing more smoke astern she altered course and followed the fleet at a distance of four or five miles continually reporting

their numbers and course, so far as she could ascertain them.
In this work she was not interrupted. Though requested by
some of his officers for permission to interfere, Admiral
Rozhestvenski refused, still insisting on his policy of keeping
his own wireless quiet in order to conceal his course and
position as much as possible.

The movements of the other auxiliary cruisers are also of
interest, since every captain had to act on his own initiative.
The *Sado Maru*, which was next the *Shinano* westward, and
was also closing in accordance with the night routine, had
reached Position 221 (12 miles short of the Third Division's
position at the centre of the guard line) about 4.30. Here,
according to programme, she turned back seawards, but
on taking in the *Shinano's* signals that the enemy were in
Position 203, she turned N.E. by E. to try to close the
Third Division. The Third Division, however, was not to be
found, for, misled by the *Shinano's* erroneous report, Admiral
Dewa had hurried off south-eastwards down the guard line
to try to get contact as the enemy passed across it.

The *America Maru*, which was the next ship and furthest
to the westward, did better. When she took in the warning
signal she was just approaching her dawn turning point, but
instead of going back as usual she held on, and "kept watch
for signs of the enemy." Later on, as further signals indicated
the Russians were heading for the Eastern Channel, her captain
judged it possible that while the main fleet attempted to pass
that way the transports and weaker ships might try to slip
through the Western Channel. He therefore decided to make
direct for Sentinel Island and remain there on guard. The
Manshu Maru, whose station was nearest the Goto Islands,
was still more enterprising. She was to be relieved that
morning by the *Yawata Maru* from Takeshiki, and was not
turning back like the others, so that by the time she got the
warning she had reached as far as the guard line (10 miles
N.W. of Shirose). Getting no further intelligence she presently
steamed N.W., that is, along the guard line, to close the
enemy, and kept this course till she sighted the Third Division
coming down from the northward. Concluding from this that
the enemy could not be in that direction the *Manshu* turned to
search south-west.

In fact, Admiral Dewa at 5.50, being then in Position 223
and still on the guard line, had sighted a hospital ship in
Position 224, the next to the eastward. Had he followed her

he must soon have found the Russian fleet, but at the moment seeing smoke to the southward he decided to chase in that direction. Presumably, it was the smoke of the *Manshu* he saw (or that of her relief ship *Yawata*), but in any case the effect of his change of course was that he must have passed across the wake of the Russians 12 or 14 miles astern of them. It was not long, however, before he was aware of the mistake he was making, for a signal came in at 6.50 to say that the enemy had been sighted in Position 225, about 25 miles N.W. of Ukushima, the northernmost island of the Goto Group, and over 10 miles beyond the guard line. Thereupon he increased to 16 knots, and went off north-eastwards in chase. Whether or not the *Manshu* also took in the signal, her captain, seeing the Third Division's movement, thought it was his duty to search in the opposite direction, and went away to the westward. In an hour's time, having found nothing, he turned back for Tsushima. His relief ship *Yawata Maru* did much the same thing. She had already reached her section when she got the original warning, but her captain argued that possibly the ships that had been seen were not the main Russian force, but merely a detachment which the rest might be following. He therefore thought it right to carry on with the appointed routine, and held away to the south-west to see if he could find anything more to seaward.

During all this time, while the Russians were lost in the mist, the rest of the Japanese Fleet had been in hasty preparation for action. Admiral Kataoka, at Osaki, having taken in the *Shinano's* warning, had passed it on about 5.0, and had ordered the whole Third Squadron to get to sea "for their appointed stations."[1] Rear-Admiral Togo, with the section of the Sixth Division which was not out on the guard line, that is, *Suma* (Flag) and *Chiyoda*, and two torpedo-boat divisions (10th and 16th), got away at 5.44, calling up the *Akitsushima* and *Idzumi* to meet him off Kosaki at the south end of Tsushima. Admiral Kataoka was off a quarter of an hour later (6.0 a.m.) with the Fifth Division and five divisions of torpedo-boats, and he, too, made for the south of Tsushima, with Tsutsu Misaki for his rendezvous.

It was from him that the main battle force in Douglas Inlet (the First, Second and Fourth Divisions) received the

---

[1] No details of these stations are to hand, but they are to be inferred from the positions taken up. *See post*, pp. 229 and 230 *note*.

warning a few minutes after 5.0. Admiral Togo was still up
in Sylvia Basin at the end of the telegraph wires, and it must
have been with intense relief that he received the news which
justified his determined faith in the position of his choice.
His absence caused little delay, for Admiral Kamimura, on
getting the cruiser report, at once gave orders for all units to
prepare for sea, and by 6.0 they were ready to weigh.

At that time the precise position and course of the
Russians were still uncertain, but almost immediately afterwards the situation began to clear. The *Shinano Maru* had
recovered touch, and at 6.5 was able to report that the
Russians were keeping the same course as when first seen
and were obviously making for the Eastern Channel. But
for half-an-hour more she was the only ship in direct contact, and was still reporting the enemy some 15 miles
astern of their actual position. Two destroyers, she says,
made a show of driving her off, but she merely gave
them a wide berth and kept observation astern. At 6.40
she began to have help from the *Idzumi*. This ship, having
started her search from within the arc of the Shirose light at
the end of the guard line, could determine her position exactly.
At 6.10 she had turned from her original course W.N.W. to
north and was now some 26 miles N. by W. of Shirose and
just upon the line dividing the Positions 225 and 226.[1] Here
she got sight of the smoke of the enemy's van on her starboard bow, and that of their rear on her port bow.[2] Being
thus able to determine their course and position with sufficient
accuracy, she shortly afterwards took over the watch from
the *Shinano*, and steaming parallel to the enemy about 4 to 5
miles on their starboard hand began sending in reports of
their numbers and movements. Thus it was, as we have
seen, that Admiral Dewa first ascertained the error with which
he had been led by the *Shinano's* mistaking her position.
How far the failure of the Third Division was due to faulty
dispositions we cannot be quite certain, for the details of
Admiral Dewa's movements are too scanty. It seems clear,

---

[1] In the *Confidential History* the Summary gives her position at 6.40
as 226. Her own report at 6.45 gives 225.

[2] This accords precisely with the position of the Russians calculated
from their position given for noon on the 26th, and that observed by the
Japanese at the opening of the action. By dead reckoning from these
two positions, their van at 6.40 must have been in 226 and their rear
in 225.

however, that he had not spread his division but had come down the guard line from his central position with his ships all together in line-ahead.[1]

In any case, the fact remains that this division, which formed the main strength of the screen, entirely failed to get contact with the enemy, and, by what appears to be a very serious miscalculation, passed across the enemy's course some 10 or 12 miles astern of them in spite of having fallen in with one of their rear ships. The unusual vagueness of the Confidential History on the whole episode would indicate that it was not contemplated by the Japanese with satisfaction. The guard line was certainly ill covered and Admiral Rozhestvenski, thanks to his close concentration, must have got his fleet clear across it, had not the hospital ship *Orel* wandered from her station. It was apparently nothing but this that led to the *Shinano Maru's* stumbling upon her and making a movement which led her unexpectedly to the main body of the enemy. Otherwise, so far as can be seen, the Russians would have been quite undetected, and once across the guard line they would have found nothing between them and the Eastern Channel. The channel itself was wholly unguarded. The *Fuso* in the course of her patrol was steaming to the westward out of the Russian course and the Iki flotilla patrol was well on the way to Takeshiki. It was rather, then, by luck than judgment that Admiral Togo got contact in time to engage his enemy in the waters of his choice; it was even but an accident that the Baltic Fleet was not in a fair way of getting through in the mist entirely undetected. Whether or not the cruiser force at his disposal admitted of a better arrangement of his observation screen he was undoubtedly taken by surprise, and it is no wonder that when all was over the *Shinano Maru*, who saved the situation, received a letter of honour for her timely service. It may at least be argued with confidence that Admiral Rozhestvenski's plan of keeping his fleet closely concentrated in steaming order was thoroughly justified by events.

As it was, all was well for the Japanese. Shortly after 6.30 the *Mikasa* came down from Sylvia Basin and joined the fleet

---

[1] This is to be inferred from the machinery report, which says that the Division at 5 a.m. was steaming at 6 knots, implying that the ships were in company. At 5.10 after the *Shinano's* warning there was an increase to 10 knots, then to 12 and then at 6.0 to 14 and upwards till at 11.46 it was 16. It is from this report that Admiral Dewa's movements have been plotted on the chart.

in Douglas Inlet.   A few minutes later the *Idzumi's* signal came
in to say that the enemy were in Position 225 keeping their
course steadily for the Eastern Channel, and, placing himself at
the head of the line, Admiral Togo led to pass round the north
of Tsushima, having made up his mind to engage off Okinoshima as the spot where, nearly a year before, the tragedy of
the military transports had so profoundly stirred the nation.
It was the place of his deliberate choice where the spirits of
the unburied Japanese dead would inspire the determination of
his men with the fire of revenge.

It was not till a quarter to eight that he was clear of Craigie
Island[1] and was able to head for the north of Tsushima.
By that time the *Idzumi*, which was still the only ship that
had hold of the enemy, received Rear-Admiral Togo's recall.
Instead of obeying she telegraphed she was in touch with the
Russians, and in reply received an order from Admiral Kataoka,
as commander of the Third Squadron, to carry on.   Observation
was none too easy.   It was still misty and the range of vision
only five to six miles.   Moreover, it was blowing from west-
south-west with a force of five to seven, and there was a
high sea.   So bad indeed was it found in the open that an
hour later (8.50) the Commander-in-Chief had to make a signal
for all torpedo-boats to take refuge at Miura Bay, the eastern
outlet from Takeshiki, and to rejoin the fleet when they saw a
chance.

This necessity was the more regrettable, for at the moment
the situation was in much uncertainty, and the Commander-in-
Chief apparently was getting anxious as to where to lead the
battle squadron.   He had just reached about mid-channel, and
as was only natural, owing to the conflict in the *Idzumi's* and
Shinano's information he seems still to have felt that his
intelligence was not sufficiently trustworthy for him to judge
finally by which channel the enemy meant to pass.   At 8.40 he
called up Admiral Dewa, who was the officer responsible for the
screen, asking him for the enemy's course and position ; but
Admiral Dewa could only reply he was not yet in touch.   At
8.47 he called him up again, but still he could tell him nothing.
At 9.0, however, came a message from the *Idzumi* which seemed
to have satisfied him, for he held on as he was at full speed.[2]

---

[1] Craigie Island is the outermost of the Korean rocks at this point,
about 10 miles from the entrance of Douglas Inlet.

[2] The Machinery Reports give his speed as 15 knots from 7.15 till noon.
The message from the *Idzumi* is unfortunately uncertain.   The translation

By this time the other cruisers that had been assigned observation duties were doing their best to get on the line. Admiral Kataoka with the Fifth Division and Rear-Admiral Togo with the *Suma* and *Chiyoda* of the Sixth had reached the south end of Tsushima where they had slowed down to wait for the enemy. The *Idzumi*, keeping to the south of the Russian Fleet and on a parallel course, was still reporting their position, and Admiral Kataoka appears to have inclined to the view that the Russians meant to pass by the Eastern Channel. Though by no means certain, he decided to proceed to search in that direction, taking the precaution to telegraph to Admiral Yamada to guard the Western Channel with the Seventh Division. Then having sent his flotilla in charge of the *Yaeyama* into Tsutsu Bay for refuge from the weather, he led away south-east.

From Admiral Yamada's account of his movements it seems clear that now and for some time longer there was considerable doubt as to whether the ships that had been seen were the enemy's main body. At 6.10, he says, he learnt for certain that the Russian Fleet had been seen, and proceeded to patrol the Strait on guard. At 8.10 however, he took in the signal, " Two " ships of the *Zhemchug* class, which are considered to be the " enemy's advance guard, are in Position 251 (27 miles S. by " W. of Tsushima) steaming northward by themselves." The main force of the Russians must have actually passed across this area between 7.30 and 8.30, and a northerly course would take them up the Western Channel. Wishing to attack these two cruisers, Admiral Yamada says he proceeded rapidly towards Position 280, which was the section immediately west of Ikishima. Though he does not say where he was at the moment, the course must have taken him across the entrance of the Eastern Channel, but, after proceeding for half an hour, at 9.0 he took in a signal from Admiral Kataoka to the *Takao*

---

of the *Adzuma's* wireless log (*Attaché Reports*, III., 101) gives it thus : " 9.0 " *Idzumi* to *Mikasa*.   Enemy's position is S.E. of 33° 50' N., 128° 50' E. " Course E.N.E."   This would mean the S.E. quarter of Position 276, but by dead reckoning the Russians at 9.0 had just crossed the southern limit of Position 278.   The *Fuso* was then in Position 276 and did not see them.   There must, therefore, be an error of transcription or translation, which is emphasized by the fact that in the same log *Idzumi* is made to give her position at 7.55 as 276, although it is certain she was then some 15 miles S.W. of it.   The *Idzumi's* message was probably : " Enemy's " position, S.E. quarter of 278.   Course, E.N.E.," which would leave no doubt they were making for the Eastern Channel.

and *Tsukushi* that the Seventh Division was to keep watch in
the Western Channel between Sentinel Island and Osaki.[1]
He then turned back, and at 9.30, meeting Admiral Kataoka,
received from him the order " to keep watch between Sentinel
" Island and Osaki Bay and endeavour to find the enemy's
main force."

From this order, then, it is clear that Admiral Kataoka was
still by no means certain as to either the course or the position
of the Russian battle squadron. Nevertheless, from this time
forward the Western Channel was left to the Seventh Division
On reaching the line assigned to him, Admiral Yamada found
upon it his 2nd subdivision, which had been ordered to watch
it in his absence. He now sent them to Oguchi Bay while he
patrolled the line between Sentinel Island and Gosaki, with
the *America Maru* in company, and these positions they
maintained for the rest of the day.

Meanwhile the Commander-in-Chief had been keeping his
original course, apparently in no uncertainty, till at 9.39
Mitsu Sima lighthouse at the north extremity of Tsushima
bore S.S.W. $\frac{1}{4}$ W. 10 miles. So far as is recorded he had
received no further information from any of his cruisers, yet
in all probability he had. Everything indicates at any rate
that he had by this time made up his mind for the Eastern
Channel, for he now turned to starboard direct for Okinoshima. Possibly what decided him was an inference that if
the enemy were making for the Western Channel they must
before this have been sighted by the cruisers that were south
of Tsushima. In any case he cannot have been long in
doubt, for at 9.50 Admiral Kataoka could see dimly through
the mist what seemed to be over a score of ships in two lines
ahead.[2] Thereupon " desiring to lead the enemy to the main

---

[1] This was the old Patrol Section D of the Straits Squadron, but it may
now have been the First Guard Line. The *Takao* is stated to have been
near Osaki Bay returning from guard and the *Tsukushi* was in the bay.
These ships with the *Fuso* formed the 1st subdivision of the Seventh Division,
and it is stated that on taking in the alarm at dawn both of them proceeded " in accordance with the battle plan towards Tsutsu Misaki to
" join the *Fuso*." The 2nd subdivision *Chokai* and *Maya* were ordered to
keep guard at Oguchi Bay. The remaining gunboat of the division, *Uji*,
was stationed at Ukushima to keep touch with a provisional look-out
station which had been established on that island, but it was too thick for
anything to be seen from it.

[2] By D.R. the Russians would thus have been about 8 miles south-
east of him.

squadron" he hoisted his battle flags and turned N.E. by N.
Gradually closing to five or six miles he kept on a parallel
course on their port bow, followed by Rear-Admiral Togo,
who shortly afterwards was joined by the *Akitshushima*.   By
10.15 Admiral Kataoka had apparently realised that he was
in presence of the enemy's main body and that there was no
longer any danger in the Western Channel, for at that hour
he hauled down his battle flags and called the *Yaeyama* to
bring back his flotilla. At that hour, also, he got a message
through to the *Mikasa* to say "the enemy's intention appears
" to be to pass the Eastern Channel."[1]

By this time, therefore, it was fairly clear when and where
the action would take place, but owing to the mist the cruisers
had great difficulty in observing accurately, and as yet little
was known of the Russian strength or formation. Admiral
Rozhestvenski was, in fact, still preserving his original steaming
order, except that when he found from the Japanese wireless
signals that he was discovered he ordered his Second Cruiser
or "Scouting" Division (*Almaz*, *Svyetlana* and *Ural*), which
was ahead, to fall back and protect the transports in rear,
and in their place at 6.50 the *Izumrud* and *Zhemchug* were
ordered to take station ahead of the squadron, four points
before the beam of the flagship on either hand,[2] and it must
have been this arrangement which led to the *Fuso's* movements
to engage them.

Admiral Rozhestvenski, of course, had no choice but to
maintain his steaming formation, for as he was still entirely
ignorant of the whereabouts of the Japanese battle fleet he
could not tell which of his five alternative fighting formations
to take up. When towards ten o'clock the shadowy forms
of Admiral Kataoka's division began to be reported coming
up on his port quarter he made a signal to stand by for an
attack from astern, directing, on the lines of his general plan,
that if the enemy's battleships appeared on that quarter his own
battleships were to form line-abreast to starboard and port
of him, and the cruisers and transports to proceed ahead.[2]
But as the hostile cruisers could presently be clearly made out
steaming on his port beam upon a parallel course, he seems
to have regarded an attack as being about to develop from
that direction. He would appear, indeed, to have been so much
assured of this that he considered it unsafe to maintain his

---

[1] *Attaché Reports*, III., 101.   [2] *Ibid.*, 213.

steaming order any longer, and decided to prepare to take up battle formation, so far at least as to form single line-ahead. He did not, however, make the established signal to the transports for an attack from to port, but merely issued the following preparatory order :—" First and Second Battle Divi- " sions to steam 11 knots ; the port column and transports at " 9 knots."[1]

As the movement began the Japanese cruisers to port almost disappeared again, but the *Idzumi* was still in sight to starboard, and so pressing in her attentions that the Admiral signalled he was going to fire a 12-inch shell at her. This, however, he did not do, probably because just then more cruisers could be seen on the port quarter which were soon recognised to be "the greyhounds" as they called Admiral Dewa's cruisers. It was, therefore, useless to try to conceal his evolution, and at 11.30 he signalled for its completion by the starboard column turning two points together.[2]

The menace of the Japanese Third Division also caused him to withdraw the *Izumrud* from his port hand and order her to take station astern of the *Zhemchug* on the disengaged side, while at the same time the two old ships of the First Cruiser Division (*Donskoi* and *Monomakh*) were directed to fall out and reinforce the transport guard. In this way he pre- pared to meet an attack from to port by the main Japanese force, and to protect his weak rear-guard from their cruisers.[3]

This, in the circumstances, he believed was the best he could do. As we have seen, he had issued no definite battle

---

[1] As Admiral Rozhestvenski was mercilessly criticised for not forming battle order soon enough, the time of this preliminary signal is import- ant, but it is also very difficult to fix. Local time, which the Russians were using, was 34 minutes behind Japanese at noon on the 27th, and 20 minutes behind on the 28th, but it is not known when the altera- tion was made in the fleet ; nor do the Russian authorities agree. Semenov says it was "after 10.0." Schubert gives 10.30, and the author of *The Last Days*, 9.45. So that we have to deal with a difference of an hour, viz., 10.5 to a possible 11.4 Japanese time.

[2] *Last Days of the Pacific Squadron.* The Russian authorities differ slightly, but 11.30 coincides with the time at which the Third Division sighted the enemy. *Adzuma's* wireless log has " 11.14 *Kasagi* to *Mikasa* " through *Itsukushima*. My position is 34° N. ; 129° 30′ E. I see enemy " to S.E. 7 miles." (*Attaché Reports*, III., 102.)

[3] This was in accordance with order No. 182, April 16th ("Cruiser Battle Instructions," *see ante*, p. 197). They had provided specially for the *Donskoi* as a slow ship, and her newly joined companion *Monomakh* was now associated with her.

plan on which he intended to handle his three battleship
divisions, nor had he explained his intentions to his commanding officers, but from time to time he had issued orders
indicating his general ideas as to the management of the
fleet as a whole. It will be recalled that the general tenor
of these was that when the enemy appeared the main body
(that is, the first two Battle Divisions) would steam towards
them by signal in order to engage them, supported by the
Third Division and by the Cruiser and Scout Divisions (First
and Second) which were to act independently according to
the conditions prevailing at the time.[1] The Third Battle
Division, acting on the signals of Admiral Nebogatov in the
Nikolai I. was in all cases to hasten to join the main body.
As for the cruisers, the *Izumrud* and *Zhemchug* with the
destroyers had the special duty of protecting the flanks of
the battle squadron from torpedo attacks. The Scouting
Division were to act independently for the protection and
direction of the transports. The First Cruiser Division had
been given its battle station in rear of the centre of the line
of battle on the disengaged side, with the duty of operating
against the enemy's cruisers which might attempt to turn
the flanks and also to cover and assist battleships in distress.
But this arrangement, as we have seen, had been modified
by adding the slow cruisers *Donskoi* and *Monomakh* to the
transport guard. The general orders of the transports were
to turn eight points in succession away from the enemy and,
when at a distance of five or six miles, to conform to the
movements of the battle divisions.

The scheme may be regarded as crude and vague, and the
Admiral was blamed for not having worked out something
more enterprising and definite. It was, in fact, nothing but
a defensive plan ; but the explanation he gave in justification
is certainly not without weight, when we consider the position
in which the nature of his force and the strategical situation
placed him. Its nature has already been indicated, but to
judge it fairly his own words must be given. " It was
" known," he said, " that the enemy could oppose to our
" main body an equal number of armoured ships, having an
" advantage of speed and armament ; to our cruisers, double
" the number ; and to our destroyers, a greatly superior
" flotilla. It was known that, owing to the relatively
" high speed of the Japanese battleships, the initiative in

---

[1] *See ante*, p. 198.

" choosing the relative disposition of the main forces would
" rest with the enemy, both before the commencement of the
" action and during its various phases, as well as the choice
" of range. It was expected that the enemy would manœuvre
" in line-ahead. It was thought that he would use his
" advantage in speed to attempt a concentration of fire on
" our flanks. It remained, therefore, for our squadron to
" recognise that the initiative in action would be with the
" Japanese, and that not only could there be no question of
" previously working out the details of a battle plan for various
" periods of the action, but even the deployment for striking
" the first blow could not be pre-arranged."[1]   He might well
have strengthened his argument by the consideration that the
incapacity of his captains for smart manœuvre condemned him
as it did Villeneuve just a hundred years before, to adopt a
defensive plan.   His argument, in short, was that however
clever an Admiral's tactical design may be, it is impossible for
him to force it on an enemy who has a distinct advantage
in speed and mobility. All that is left to him is to conform
to the enemy's movements, keeping ever on the alert to seize
any opportunity that the chances of the action may afford.
It was a depressing conclusion with which to enter upon an
action, but when we consider how seldom even the greatest
naval tacticians, with all the advantage of highly mobile and
efficient fleets and without the preoccupation of a convoy,
have been able to carry out more than approximately their
prearranged plan, the severe judgments that have been
passed on Admiral Rozhestvenski seem certainly lacking in
just appreciation of the adverse factors which cramped his
initiative.   Right or wrong he held to his deliberate plan,
and pursued his course up the Eastern Channel, ready to
accept action on his port hand.

As a matter of fact his chances of getting through without
a decisive defeat were at this time not unfavourable, for unknown to him his change of formation had not been observed
by the Japanese cruisers. Their messages, indeed, during this
period must have been not a little confusing for the Commander-in-Chief. At 10.55 the *Idzumi* reported the enemy to
be in two columns, the First and Second Divisions to starboard,
and the Third to port.[2] But five minutes later Admiral Dewa
gave them as 28 ships in single line-ahead.   Thereupon the

---

[1] Smirnov, ch. ii.
[2] *Adzuma's* wireless log (*Attaché Reports*, III., 101).

Commander-in-Chief called up Admiral Kataoka to ask him
" Which side is the enemy's main body ? " The reply was,
" Starboard side apparently," and at 11.30 this was confirmed
by the *Idzumi*.[1] At this time she must have been fairly close
in owing to an incident which gives a vivid impression of
the extent to which the Japanese were surprised by the sudden
appearance of the Russians. About 11.10 it appeared to her
that the *Zhemchug* was making for a Japanese merchant vessel
which had appeared in the offing, and the only way of protecting her was to run in between her and her pursuer, so as
to cover her while she made off to the southward. The fact
was that the Russian fleet was now passing across the main line
of communication with the Manchurian army, and no warning
had reached the Japanese transports. During the next two
hours the *Idzumi* was able to save two more vessels, one an
army hospital ship which was heading straight into the enemy's
fleet, and the other a transport full of troops that was running
into serious danger. With some difficulty she was able to warn
them both to make off to the southward, but except for the
fact that this cruiser chanced to be on that side of the enemy
the Japanese could scarcely have avoided a dispiriting loss.[2]

Meanwhile, Admiral Dewa had been coming up fast on
his way to take the station which the battle plan had assigned
him with the battle squadron, and he was doing his best to
get exact information as he passed. By 11.40, while the *Idzumi*
was busy saving the hospital ship, he had closed to within
8,000 metres on the enemy's port beam and judged them to
be in two lines, as they actually were ; for the evolution of
forming single line was not then completed. Still he was
not satisfied, and on this occasion did not repeat the error of
his first reconnaissance at Port Arthur, but pressed in till about
11.45 he drew the enemy's fire. It was very good, he says ;
all the shots fell close to him, and turning four points together
to port, and increasing speed to 18 knots, he hurried out of
range without, however, having been able to see what the actual
formation of the Russians was. As it happened the firing was
accidental and not by Admiral Rozhestvenski's orders. The
range was too great to warrant expenditure of his slender store of
ammunition, and he stopped the firing at once. Still Admiral

---

[1] *Adzuma's* log has " 11.29. *Idzumi to Itsukushima.* Enemy's main
" body is leading starboard column." (*Ibid.*)

[2] *Japanese Published History. Revue Maritime*, Vol. 189, p. 352.

Dewa was apparently content, and held on as he was at high speed to join the battle squadron.

The result of this and a sudden thickening of the mist was, that by noon there was not a single Japanese cruiser in sight from the Russian flagship. Believing he had been thoroughly observed, Admiral Rozhestvenski determined to seize the opportunity to change his formation in order to thwart whatever design his enemy might have formed. He was just through the narrows and had reached a point 12 miles north of Ikishima where, by previous arrangement, the fleet was to alter course direct for Vladivostok. This, and the fact that Admiral Dewa, when last seen, had appeared to be heading to pass across his course, seems to have led him to believe that the attack might come from that direction instead of from port. Whatever his precise idea he decided to form line-abreast and signalled for eight points in succession to starboard. But scarcely had he commenced to lead the movement, when a slight clearing of the mist revealed the Fifth and Sixth Japanese Divisions still standing with him on his port bow. Not wishing to disclose his new idea to the enemy, he promptly made the annulling signal to his Second Division, and with his own turned back eight points to port, the effect being that the fleet was brought into two lines, his own division forming a starboard line, ahead of the cruisers and transports, and the Second and Third Divisions forming a port line. This formation he held, hoping perhaps for another thickening of the mist to give him a fresh opportunity.

Owing to the state of the weather these movements were not reported to Admiral Togo with accuracy. By noon he had reached his chosen battle ground, being then according to his reckoning 12 miles N. by W. $\frac{1}{2}$ W. of Okinoshima; but he still kept his south-easterly course, merely reducing speed from 15 to 12 knots. He had just received from Admiral Kataoka a precise statement of the enemy's force and formation. It was a final confirmation of the previous reports that the Russians were in two lines with their two most powerful divisions to starboard. Yet during the whole hour that these reports had been coming in Admiral Rozhestvenski had been forming single line, and not a single Japanese cruiser had noticed it. Nor was it till 12.25 that Admiral Togo received from the *Idzumi* the enemy's noon position. It was given as 18 miles north of Wakamiya-jima, the north-west point of Iki,[1] and their course was stated

---

[1] By Russian reckoning it would be nearer 10 miles North.

to be N.E. by E. For nearly a quarter of an hour Admiral Togo held on as he was, but at 12.38 he turned S.W. ½ W. His reason is not stated, but the point he reached before altering course was precisely on the line of the Russian fleet if, as he believed, it was proceeding N.E. by E. from its alleged noon position, and Admiral Togo's new course being half a point west of the contrary course would bring him where he wanted to be on the port side of his enemy.

But his information was not correct. Not only was the noon position given too far to the north, but at 12.20, five minutes before *Mikasa* got the misleading signal, Admiral Rozhestvenski had altered to port on the direct course to Vladivostok, that is N. 23 E. (true). Of this, however, Admiral Togo was informed almost immediately ; for two minutes later, Admiral Kataoka got through a signal to say the enemy had altered course to N.E., and five minutes later again he corrected this to E.N.E.,[1] the actual course being N.N.E. ½ E. Thereupon, at 12.47, Admiral Togo, having reached a point whence Okino-shima bore S. by W. ½ W. about 10 miles, turned west.[2] In his official despatch he says that his object was to engage the weaker port column of the enemy. He also says that he was fully informed about the enemy by the "accurate and "frequent reports of his scouts." But accurate they certainly were not. Of the enemy's forming battle order in single line he was never informed at all. His main tactical idea was based on false intelligence, and, as we have seen, it was purely owing to the accident of an arrested manœuvre in the Russian fleet that when the crisis came he found his appreciation of the situation was even approximately true.

It is possible that he may have received some later information as to the Russian formation which is not recorded. At 1.06 Admiral Kataoka telegraphed his position and the exact bearing and distance of the enemy, but nothing further.[3] At 1.15, however, the range of vision having by that time increased to 7 or 8 miles, the Third Division was sighted bearing S.W. by W., and within a quarter of an hour the Fifth

---

[1] *Adzuma's* wireless log (*Attaché Reports*, III., 102). It is probable that "E.N.E." is an error of transcription for "N.N.E.," for had the signal been E.N.E. Admiral Togo would scarcely have made the movement he did.

[2] Courses and speeds as logged would make it nearer 9 miles from Okinoshima.

[3] *Adzuma's* wireless log. Unfortunately, here again there is an obvious clerical error. For the position given is 30° 20' N. 130° E. and that of the enemy S.S.W. ½ W. about 5 miles—which is all quite impossible.

Division also came into view with the Sixth following it.[1] And now a curious movement took place which it is difficult to account for.   Our information is that Admiral Dewa, who believed he had his Third Division right ahead of the enemy, reported that they were about 5 miles astern of him, though only occasionally visible.[2] The actual distance according to the official track chart must have been nearer 8 miles, and the effect of the information was apparently to cause the Commander-in-Chief to believe he was already passing across their course.[3] At any rate, at 1.31 Admiral Togo altered to S.S.W., and Admiral Dewa had to turn his division eight points together to get out of his way. Presumably Admiral Togo thought this course would bring him out on the port side of the enemy, but apparently Admiral Dewa knew it would not do so. He must have believed that his Chief intended to engage the enemy on their starboard side ; for in clearing out of his way he turned to starboard as though he expected the port side of the Japanese battle squadron to be the disengaged side. There certainly seems to have been a misapprehension, for in a few minutes (1.39) the enemy became fairly discernible from the *Mikasa* bearing south-west, that is on her starboard bow, and not as Admiral Togo must have expected on his port bow. The moment this was realised (1.40) he swung round in succession to N.W. by N., and at 1.50 increased to 15 knots. The inference is that he now realised that he had miscalculated the tactical situation so far as to convince him that he could not at once carry out the attack he intended, and that he must break away to secure a more favourable position.

As for the cruiser divisions, having brought the two opposed battle squadrons into practical contact, they could regard their observation work as complete and could attend to their battle functions. What these were is not quite certain, since no tactical instructions are recorded for the whole fleet acting in one body. By the original instructions issued for the Combined Squadron before the outbreak of war, on which we are told the tactics of the battle of Tsushima were founded, the battle squadron was composed

---

[1] So says the First Division report and the official plan, but Rear-Admiral Togo says at 12.10 he had been ordered by Admiral Kataoka to go ahead of the enemy and keep in touch with them. This order he obeyed by taking his ships out on the starboard side of the Fifth Division and closing the enemy's van.

[2] *Attaché Reports*, IV., 3.

[3] *Ibid.*

of the First and Second Divisions, while the Third and Fourth Divisions were to form a detached squadron " to engage the " enemy's weaker ships and destroyers, and also to destroy and " capture damaged or isolated ships." They were also to protect the Japanese destroyers from fast cruisers. For the other three divisions no instructions were issued at the time since they then formed a Third Squadron not under Admiral Togo's command.[1] By the later instructions, however, issued in July 1904, the Fifth Division was to act as a General Reserve, while the Sixth was charged with operating against the enemy's flotilla and isolated ships and bringing up its own flotilla to attack when it saw a chance.[2] If any further instructions had been issued it is clear they were only a modification of these two sets in order to adapt them to an action by the whole fleet. For what happened was that the Third Division, circling widely to starboard, stood to the northward across the wake of the Battle Squadron, and then steamed a parallel course about a mile-and-a-half on its starboard hand. At the same time the Fourth Division, which hitherto had been following the Battle Squadron, circled to port and "parted company" in accordance "with the battle plan," finally turning in a north-westerly course "to co-operate " with the Third Division."[3] The Fifth Division, on the other hand, with the Sixth in company, after getting well to the northward, turned eastward and headed for the disengaged side of the Battle Squadron.

None of these movements, however, were completed when in testimony that all preliminary manœuvring was over an order came according to Japanese practice, for all private ships to disconnect wireless, and at 1.55 Admiral Togo, hoisting his battle flag, made his Nelsonian signal to the fleet : " The existence of our Imperial country rests on this " one action, and every man of you must do his utmost."[4]

---

[1] Vol. I., App. B., p. 474.

[2] *Ibid.*, pp. 315–6.

[3] *Confidential History*, Sec. V., Fourth Division Report.

[4] Admiral Kataoka, commanding the Third Squadron, made a similar signal as he turned for the Battle Squadron: "The mist has lightened " and the sea is once more quiet. Our trust in the gods is boundless. " Victory or defeat rests on this one battle; all of you do your " utmost."

CHAPTER XV.

THE BATTLE OF THE SEA OF JAPAN.

First Phase.

[Charts XI, XII. Diagrams 1 to 5.]

No great naval battle since the prolonged and loosely handled actions of our own Dutch wars is probably so difficult to reconstruct as that of Tsushima, or the Sea of Japan, as it was officially named by the Japanese. After the first hour it degenerated into a game of blind man's buff, in which independent divisions of the Japanese hunted the shattered fragments of the enemy through bewildering mists, and fired upon everything they met so long as it remained in view. To attempt, therefore, to reconstruct it in detail is wasted labour, for not only would the picture be untrustworthy, but it could serve no useful purpose. The tactical interest ended after the first few moves, and from the indiscriminate chase that consumed the rest of the day there is little professional profit to be gained. The following account, therefore, is aimed at elucidating from the facts, so far as they are ascertainable, what was Admiral Togo's battle plan, what his tactical idea, and how far the tactics were carried out for the achievement of the plan.[1]

---

[1] The main Japanese authorities for the battle are:—

(1) The Official Confidential History, Book II., Part ii., Section 2. It consists of (a) summaries of the action of each division, which are quoted as "Staff Reports" of the respective Divisional Admirals, and (b) detailed accounts of each ship's action quoted thus: "*Mikasa's* Report."

(2) The Official Published History, the references to which are from the *Revue Maritime* in which a French version of the original Japanese is appearing.

(3) The reports of British officers who were present. (*Reports from Naval Attachés*, III. and IV.)

(4) Admiral Togo's official despatch. (*Attaché Reports*, III., 185.)

(5) The Japanese official track chart and PZ diagrams. These do not in all cases coincide with the various Reports, but as no evidence exists on which more correct versions can be framed they have been adopted for this work as the best obtainable.

The chief Russian authorities are:—

(1) Two reports by Admiral Rozhestvenski read in a lecture given by Mons. Beklemishev, President of the Russian Navy League, in 1906. The first was sent in while the Admiral was a prisoner in Japan still suffering

On none of these matters have we any direct and authoritative statement. Probably the best summary is that given by Admiral Enkvist, the Russian cruiser commander. "The "Japanese tactics," he telegraphed from Manila a week after the battle, "were directed to preventing us from getting through "to Vladivostok. With this object, every time our fleet altered "its course and stood to the north, they profited by their "superiority in speed to draw across our battleship line and "place the leading ship *hors de combat.*" [1]

Though this is doubtless correct, the actual Japanese tactical instructions, as we have seen, are only to be inferred from previous instructions which we are told governed this action, and here we certainly stand on firm ground. Read in the light of the ascertained facts of the action these instructions reveal to us, in the first place, that the scheme of command was still divisional but without precise definition. We can trace, for instance, a grouping of divisions in pairs over which the senior Admiral of the group had some degree of control. Thus we see the Fourth (Uriu) Division supporting the Third (Dewa), and the Sixth Division (Rear-Admiral Togo) following the Fifth by Admiral Kataoka's express order. Similarly the battle

---

from the effects of his wounds; the second was a supplementary report sent in later and is stated to be compiled from the reminiscences of officers, collated with what had then appeared from Japanese sources in the foreign Press. These reports are cited as "*Rozhestvenski 1 and 2.*"

(2) An anonymous book entitled *The Last Days of the Second Pacific Squadron*, by one who took part in the action of Tsushima. The details of what took place in the battle on board various ships, he says he gathered during the six months he was a prisoner in Japan from other officers and seamen who were his fellow prisoners.

(3) *The Battle of Tsushima* by Commander Semenov, translation by Captain A. B. Lindsay, Murray, 1912; but this version should be compared with the technically more accurate one by Captain C. J. Eyres, R.N. (*R. N. War College*, No. 5).

(4) *Naval Action in the Strait of Korea* by M. Smirnov, who had access to official archives. *Morskoi Sbornik*, April 1913.

(5) *New Material concerning the War*, by Sub-Lieutenant Boris Karlovich Schubert, an officer in the *Oleg*, to which ship he had been transferred from the *Rion* (formerly *Smolensk*).

(6) Telegraphic Report by Rear-Admiral Enkvist, sent from Manila, June 5, 1905. (*Attaché Reports*, III., 200.)

(7) Evidence given at the Court Martial of Admiral Nebogatov, an incomplete abstract of which is given in *Attaché Reports*, IV., App. 5.

(8) Various reports on the individual ships communicated by their officers to the Russian Press.

[1] *Attaché Reports*, III., 200.

squadron or "main force" was composed of the First and Second Divisions receiving tactical signals from the *Mikasa*.[1]

The general tactical idea underlying this grouping, seems at least for the Battle Squadron to have been based on the single line more definitely than were the original instructions; and this, no doubt, was mainly owing to the larger number of battle units in the Russian Fleet which led to a revival of the old principle of equalising the line. Under the original instructions which contemplated concentrating on a part of the enemy's fleet, Admiral Kamimura's division was to break away and attack the rear when the First Division attempted to cross the van. But how far this was the understanding on the present occasion is doubtful. Still it would seem that Admiral Kamimura was left considerable discretion as to whether he operated in the Commander-in-Chief's wake or formed a distinct line of his own. Generally it may be said that the junior divisional commander in each group was entitled to act independently in the absence of a definite order from the senior Admiral, and that similarly the Commander-in-Chief retained the right to control all the groups and all the divisions.

So much may be accepted without hesitation on the evidence available, but with regard to the general plan of the battle we have no information at all. Still here, also, inferences are possible with some degree of certainty. In its broad lines, as Admiral Enkvist stated, it closely resembled that of August 10th. The primary strategical object was the same—to prevent the Russians getting through to Vladivostok. The means of obtaining that object were also fundamentally the same—an overwhelming concentration on the enemy's van. But behind these resemblances there were wide differences. In the first action it was not absolutely necessary for Admiral Togo to look beyond the purely strategical object; by the plan of the war, as it then stood, he could perform his function by forcing his adversary back into the death-trap of Port Arthur, and it was therefore a question of the balance of risk whether he adopted this slow and possibly surer solution of the problem or played for the direct solution which involved staking everything on the result of a decisive battle. But in the second action there

---

[1] The battle order was as follows :—

First Division—*Mikasa* (flag), *Shikishima*, *Fuji*, *Asahi*, *Kasuga*, *Nisshin* (flag of Vice-Admiral Misu).

Second Division—*Idzumo* (flag of Vice-Admiral Kamimura), *Adzuma*, *Tokiwa*, *Yakumo*, *Asama*, *Iwate* (flag of Rear-Admiral Shimamura).

was something beyond the strategical object to be considered. The state of the war, the failing of the Japanese resources, and the exhaustion of their offensive energy on land demanded a crushing victory at sea to force an acceptable peace. All risks must be run to secure such a decision and there was no longer any reason why the risks should not be run ; and herein lay the second great difference. There was now nothing in the background for which the Japanese fleet need be husbanded. The Russians had put on the table practically every card they had available and the time had come for the Japanese to stake their last ship against them. It must, therefore, be a fight to a finish at such ranges as Admiral Togo regarded as most likely to lead to a decisive issue.

If the end could not be attained in one day the fight must be resumed on the next ; but as to what the precise scheme was we again have no clear information. As we have seen, the enemy was first to be engaged in the neighbourhood of Okinoshima, a battle-field which, apart from the moral grounds on which it was selected, would commit the Russians irrevocably to the Japanese zone of highest control. There are indications that the effort was not to be confined to the ships, but that during the day flotilla operations of some kind and in considerable strength were to be combined with the squadron attack. The whole of the torpedo craft put to sea with the fleet, and it would seem that a special detachment was formed under the protection of the *Asama* for dropping mechanical and dummy mines in the enemy's path.[1]

---

[1] The matter, however, remains very obscure. The evidence we have is as follows. In speaking of the fleet putting to sea on the alarm of May 23, our Attaché with the Second Division wrote : "On the way out " of the harbour the *Asama* left the line and took station astern of the " First Division. Having been assigned certain particular duties in case " of an action, the performance of which necessitated her operating " independently of the battle division, she was temporarily attached to " the First Division." (*Attaché Reports*, III., 54.)

Speaking of the *Asama* on the 27th our Attaché with the First Division says, "She had been originally detailed to conduct a similar force (one of " two divisions of destroyers), whose duty it would be to hamper the " movements of the enemy by strewing in his way dummy and explosive " mines, but weather and other conditions not having been propitious it is believed the scheme was not executed. (*Ibid.*, IV., 11.)

This view is confirmed by the following entry in the *Adzuma's* signal log :—" 10.8, *Mikasa* to *Asama* and special duty destroyers and torpedo-" boats. Part company and rejoin your proper divisions." (*Ibid.*, III., 100.) Also, by a statement in the *Confidential History* (Sec. 1), that the *Asama* did not put to sea with the battle divisions as her " departure was delayed

This part of the design, however, whatever it was, the bad weather prevented from developing. The second stage would be a night attack with the massed flotillas ; and the third, another fleet action. This would develop from their now fully equipped intelligence centre Matsushima, which was to be the fleet rendezvous for the second day, corresponding to the rendezvous which Admiral Togo had given in the south of Yellow Sea for his August battle. What further was to follow we cannot tell, for at this point the victory was complete and no further operations were needed ; but such in broad outline so far as can be gathered were the conceptions in Admiral Togo's mind when the leading Russian ships loomed up out of the mist. It remains to see how his tactics were adjusted to the ends in view.

At the moment of contact, as we have seen, he found himself in a position of some difficulty which called for instant decision. Believing that the enemy were still in steaming order in two columns with the most powerful ships to starboard, he had been manœuvring to engage them on the port side before they could deploy. This was all in accordance with the idea expressed in his instructions for concentrating on a part of the enemy's fleet ; and it had the further advantage that it would force on the action at a moment when if the fire of the most powerful Russian ships was not to be masked they must involve themselves in a hazardous change of formation. But owing to the shortness of the range of vision his cruisers had not reported their approach quite accurately and he found them still on his starboard bow and that he was out of position for his intended attack. He could not yet see that their formation was not the order of steaming, nor does he seem to have been aware that Admiral Rozhestvenski was already altering course with his division and increasing speed to place himself at the head of his fleet and so restore his temporarily dislocated battle line. Still it is, of course, possible that he had observed the movement, and that he took it to indicate that the Russian fleet as a whole

---

" by her having to embark the men and officers who had been transferred
" to the hospital ship *Saikyo Maru*" which suggests she had to wait for a special service **party.** The 4th destroyer division also left separately and moved so as to **join** the Third Division with which it will be remembered it ought to have operated on the Fourth Guard Line. For evidence that these destroyers carried mines *see post*, pp. 295 and 304, but it would seem that they did not form part of the *Asama's* special detachment.

was inclining to port. If so, this may be the real reason why he found it necessary to break off in so pronounced a manner to starboard. In any case he believed the chance on which he had been counting was still within his grasp and to seize it, as we have seen, he promptly turned to starboard to cross their course at 15 knots, his "battle speed." He did not of course stand directly across them, but inclined to N.W. by N. whereby he crossed them obliquely and by increasing the distance gave himself time to secure the commanding position on their van which his intended attack required. This course he held for a quarter of an hour and it was not till 1.55 when the last ship of the Second Division was about clear of the Russian line of advance that he turned west, and hoisted his battle flag.

By that time the Russians bore from his flagship S. by W. about 7 miles, so far as could be judged in the mist, that is, he had brought them just abaft his beam. He could then see that their starboard column was ahead of their port column and that it was composed of the four *Suvorovs* only, but still he does not seem to have realised what was happening. The fact was that at 1.50, five minutes before the Japanese turned west, Admiral Rozhestvenski had signalled to his own division to increase to 11 knots, and to the Second Division to edge into his wake and this movement for re-forming single line had been in progress for over 10 minutes, when at 2.2 Admiral Togo made his next movement.

It was a manœuvre of the most hazardous kind, for which no satisfactory explanation is given. For instead of turning at once to press their van, he simply altered to S.W. by S., "which looked," says the *Confidential History*, "as if he " intended to pass the enemy on opposite courses." In his own official despatch he says he made the move "so as to " make the enemy believe that he meant to pass him in the " opposite direction." There can be no doubt, then, that it was intended as a feint, but what advantage he thought it would give him is not clear. Nothing at any rate is apparent of sufficient moment to justify the risk, for it was obvious the movement would involve a turn of about 14 points under fire not only from the port column, but also from the Russian First Division, which was drawing clear of the Second.

It was only for about three minutes that he kept his new course and then at 2.5 he put his helm over to lead round E.N.E. in order "to press the enemy's van obliquely." The effect of the remarkable manœuvre in the Russian fleet was a thrill of exhilaration.   It seemed that their enemy had been surprised into making a false move which beyond all expectation must deliver him into their hands.   Admiral Rozhestvenski seized the chance with cool deliberation.   Waiting till the *Mikasa* was well round and the Japanese were committed to the turn, the *Suvorov* at 2.8 opened fire on her at 7,000 metres.   All the leading ships took it up at once, except the *Orel*, which, being rearmost of the First Division, was still masked by the leading ship of the Second.   A terrific concentration took place on the *Mikasa* and on each successive Japanese ship as she reached the turning point.   At first there was no reply, but at 2.10, when the range was down to 6,000 metres, the maximum of the Japanese battle instructions, the *Mikasa* began, and as ship after ship steadied on the new course a counter-concentration was developed on the *Suvorov* and *Oslyabya*, the leaders of the two Russian lines.

It was an attack as risky as that of Nelson at Trafalgar, but, like Nelson, Admiral Togo probably counted with confidence on the ineffectiveness of the enemy's long range fire. If so, he counted well, for by something like a miracle, although "the heavy shell fell like rain about them" and the turn took 20 minutes for the 12 ships to complete, both Japanese divisions accomplished it without serious injury.   In the case of the armoured cruisers this immunity was no doubt partly due to the protective fire which the First Division was developing, but probably also to no small extent to Admiral Kamimura having moved independently, but what he did is not quite clear.   His own Staff Report says that at 2.9, that is just as his next ahead, the *Nisshin*, was completing her turn and laying her guns on the *Oslyabya*, he altered a point or so to starboard, that is, away from the enemy, so that he "opened out from the First Division."   The effect, according to the official track chart, was that as he made his turn he led his division much wider than his chief had done.   His turning point is shown some 1,500 metres further from the enemy than that of the First Division, and at 2.15, when he had completed his turn, he says, his range to the *Oslyabya* was 8,000 metres, while that of the *Mikasa* to the *Suvorov* when she opened is stated to have been only 6,400.   But, on the other hand, our Attaché with the Second Division records that the range passed when the *Adzuma* opened fire was 4,800 metres. (Her own report gives at 2.17 4,600 metres.)   He also noted at the time that, owing to a bad turn by *Nisshin* and *Kasuga* (the rear ships of the First Division), the Second Division came up inside the First, that is, nearer the enemy. He further states in corroboration that Admiral Kamimura had directed a signal to be made for a 4-point turn together with the intention of re-forming in Admiral Togo's wake ; but as he found that the enemy's shell were going over him and that he was over-powering his immediate opponents the flags were unbent and he led his ships on until the circling of the First Division to starboard enabled him to form astern of it. The truth, then, seems to be that although Admiral Kamimura, when his time came to turn, was forced to edge to starboard, he did, in fact, by moving in a larger circle than his chief, come up into action inside him.[1]

The whole episode is a curious repetition of Admiral Togo's experience during his first action off Port Arthur in February 1904. There, too, he was forced to make a similar turn under fire of forts and ships, and there, too, he escaped with scarcely any damage. From two instances only it would be rash to assume that such a turn is not in actual war so dangerous as it is deemed to be in manœuvres, but at the same time it is just possible in such cases there is a personal factor which may not be without its weight : for it may be that where a fleet exposes itself in this way, the keenness of the hostile gunners, and even of fire-control officers, to make the most of the chance while it lasts will tempt them to fire too rapidly and to trust to the large target rather than to careful and accurate laying on individual ships.[2]

Daring, even reckless, as was the manœuvre, its reward was great. From the very outset of the action it enabled Admiral Togo to enjoy at decisive ranges his favourite device of an oblique concentration on the enemy's van, and its effect was almost immediate. When he saw what the enemy's actual

---

[1] See *Attaché Reports*, III., 93. In the first 10 minutes the *Mikasa* was hit 10 times and the *Idzumo* not at all. One reason for her immunity may well have been that, as the Attaché observed, the *Oslyabya* was using a good deal of helm. "As the action began," his note says, " I saw " the *Oslyabya* turn to starboard to get into line with his First Division, " almost presenting her stern." (Copied from the original note-book.)

[2] Our own reports state that, in contrast with the deliberate fire of the Japanese at this time, that of the Russians was rapid (*Attaché Reports*, III., 104). The Japanese did not begin "rapid firing" till 2.20 when the range was down to 4,600 (*Mikasa's* report), and the 12-pounder crews were called up to take their stations.

formation was—that is, that they were just forming single line
with the Admiral leading—he attacked the *Suvorov*. The *Asahi*,
the third ship, did the same ; but all the rest of the division, as
well as most of the cruisers, concentrated as originally intended
on the *Oslyabya*, while the *Iwate*, the last Japanese ship, after
firing on her with her port guns changed after the turn to
Admiral Nebogatov's flagship, the *Nikolai*, at 6,800 metres.

The Japanese were slow in picking up the range—ten
minutes, says Admiral Rozhestvenski—and at first their fire
was deliberate ; but as the range lessened " overs" and " shorts"
became fewer and it grew quicker and more and more accurate.
By 2.12 the range from *Mikasa* to *Suvorov* was down to 5,500,
which appears to have been that which Admiral Togo regarded
as most effective.   But just then the enemy edged to starboard
upon a parallel course,[1] and Admiral Togo, owing to his
superior speed, found the range opening out. At 2.15, therefore, just as his rear ship was completing her turn, he also
altered to starboard and led E. by S. for three minutes till it
was down again to 5,400 metres, when he turned back N.E.
by E. $\frac{1}{2}$ E. The two lines must thus have become about
parallel, although, as we have seen, the Japanese track chart
shows Admiral Kamimura making his turn further out on the
port quarter of the First Division and not in her wake.[2]

The Japanese were now beginning to use their 12-pounders
while their large shell were hitting almost incessantly, and as a
result the Russians' fire, which at first had been surprisingly
good, began to degenerate.   The *Oslyabya* was the first to
suffer under the tremendous concentration.   By the time the
Japanese turn was complete and before the Russian line was
perfectly formed, a terrific explosion had been seen on board
her.   A heavy shell had holed her below the water line forward,
which immediately gave her a list and made her settle down
by the head.   Already her decks were covered with killed and
wounded, both she and her next astern were on fire, and a
few minutes later her fore turret was disabled.

---

[1] As to this movement, *see post*, p. 250 note.

[2] An additional reason for doubting the correctness of the track chart is
that at this point it cannot be reconciled with the Second Division reports.
Idzumo gives her range to *Oslyabya* at 2.20 as 6,500 metres. *Adzuma* (2.15
after her turn was completed) gives her range to *Suvorov* as 6,000, and at
2.17 to the ship she was engaging 4,600 metres. *Tokiwa* (No. 3) at 2.17
opened on *Oslyabya* at 5,000. The track chart shows their ranges to be
about 8,000 metres, which must be incorrect.

The *Suvorov*, though terribly punished, had suffered no such dangerous wound, but, says a Russian account, after two or three "overs" and some "shorts" almost every shot hit. Everything that was not protected was literally swept away by the shell, and even in the conning-tower it was impossible to stand owing to shell-splinters flying through the apertures.[1]

The Russians were, in fact, encountering a new element in naval warfare that was simply astounding. Amongst all the sources of inferiority upon which they reckoned, the new Japanese explosive had never been taken into account. They saw with horror that the new shell burst at the slightest contact even with a rope and as they touched the water. It was no longer a matter of armour-piercing shell; it seemed that they were being bombarded with mines that shattered everything in their path. Nor was it only the unprecedented force of the blast and the small splinters into which the shell broke up, penetrating every aperture; the deadly fumes and above all the devastating heat were worst of all. "The paint," wrote Admiral Rozhestvenski, "burnt with a clear flame on the steel "surfaces; boats, ropes, hammocks and woodwork caught fire; "cartridges in the ready racks ignited; upper works and light "guns were swept away; turrets jammed." One of his Staff who had been present at the battle of the Yellow Sea found it was child's play to what he was now experiencing and could scarcely understand it. "The steel plates and superstructure "of the upper deck," he says, "was torn to pieces and the "splinters caused many casualties. Iron ladders were crumpled "up into rings, and guns were literally hurled from their "mountings. Such havoc could never be caused by the simple "impact of a shell, still less by the splinters. It could only "be caused by the force of the explosion . . . In addition "to this there was the unusual high temperature and liquid "flame of the explosion which seemed to spread over every- "thing. I actually watched a steel plate catch fire from a "burst. Of course the steel did not burn but the paint on it did. "Such practically incombustible materials as hammocks and "rows of boxes drenched with water flared up in a moment. "At times it was impossible to see anything with glasses "owing to everything being so disturbed with the quivering, "of the heated air. No! it was different from the 10th of "August."[2]

---

[1] *Last Days.*   [2] Semenov, *Battle of Tsushima*, p. 63.

Eager as Admiral Rozhestvenski was not to be forced off his course altogether, and firmly as he believed his ill-trained fleet would develop its highest striking power at short range, it was impossible to stand up to such punishment. For a quarter of an hour—too long as many thought—he held on doggedly in face of the ever-closing concentration, and then about 2.25 edged away two points to starboard.[1] It was high time for such a move, for the *Mikasa*, steaming 15 knots to the Russian 9 or 10, had reached ahead and was beginning to circle to starboard to envelop their van, and this she continued to do so as to keep the range between 5,000 and 6,000

---

[1] This at least seems to be what happened on the balance of evidence, but there is some uncertainty as to what Admiral Rozhestvenski actually did. In his first report he says: "For 10 minutes the Japanese were " getting the range . . . but at 2.0 (= 2.20) they began to hit " continuously . . . Wishing to change the range, I altered course " 2 points to port but did not continue on this course more than 5 " minutes because the *Mikasa* and the five battleships with her were " fast forging ahead and were concentrating their fire on the *Suvorov* " and *Alexandr*, whilst the *Mikasa* herself was not sufficiently subject to " the fire of our ships. At 2.5 (= 2.25) I gave orders to alter course " 4 points to starboard." For the first turn to port he has been severely criticised (Admiral Sir R. Custance, *The Ship of the Line in Battle*, p. 175). But it is more than doubtful if it was ever made. No other authority, Russian or Japanese, mentions it, nor is it shown in any authoritative chart. Semenov says: "The enemy drawing ahead began quickly to " edge to starboard, endeavouring to cross our T, but we also turned " to starboard and brought them again nearly on our beam. It was " now 2.5 p.m." (= 2.25). Shortly before that, being then in the conning tower, he says a conversation took place on the question of changing the range between the Admiral and his flag-captain. In the original it stands thus: "We must alter the range," said the captain, "they " have already got the range very well—they are giving us h—ll." "Wait " a bit," replied the Admiral, "we also have got the range." Here is a distinct statement that the Admiral refused to turn at all. Yet in the chart at the end of the book both turns are shown. But the chart is not by Semenov; its provenance is unknown; it is very inaccurate and con-tradicts Semenov's narrative, nor is there anything to show it was not constructed purely upon Admiral Rozhestvenski's first report. In the latest Russian chart, that annexed to Smirnov's semi-official narrative, the turn to port is not shown. The author of the *Last Days* has: "At " 2.5 the *Suvorov* turned two points to starboard . . . . At 2.10 " the *Suvorov* turned two points to port." In revising his account after consulting his fellow prisoners in Japan he gives the 2.5 turn as 2½ points to starboard and omits the 2.10 turn to port. Schubert has: "In order " to prevent being turned (or headed) our battleships began to edge to " starboard to the east." Smirnov—a very hostile critic—does not mention the turn to port. It would look, therefore, as though, when writing his first report, Admiral Rozhestvenski's memory had played him false owing to the severity of his wounds.

metres. As the range had opened out again the Japanese had stopped rapid firing (2·28), but the *Suvorov* found no relief.[1] Shell splinters kept entering even the conning-tower; the shelves that had been fitted to the aperture proved of no avail against the small fragments; casualties came fast, till by 2.35 the Admiral himself and his flag-captain as well as others were wounded. Realising it was impossible to continue their effort to break through directly, the flag-captain begged to turn away four points to starboard and at 2.40 the Admiral consented.[2]

The action was now at its height. Using "ordinary firing" the whole Japanese line was concentrating mainly on the *Suvorov* and *Oslyabya*, but with a certain amount of defensive fire on other ships at the discretion of individual captains. So appalling was the scene that the most war-hardened spirits were awed. "The shells," says the First Division report, "burst on " the water or the sides of the ships, the fumes from them " covering the sea with a black curtain pierced by glittering " violet flashes; the thundering voices of the guns answered to " the roar of the angry waves and the spectacle stirred to the " depth the feelings of those who saw it." By 2.40—in fact, when the *Suvorov* had turned away—the laden mist had become impenetrable. The smoke from the fires that were raging in the Russian flagship and some of her consorts, added to that of the bursting shells, so says the same report, "hid the " Russian ships up to the mast-heads till we could see nothing " but their battle-flags fluttering at the trucks." Range-finders had been useless for some time; now it was no longer possible to lay a gun at all, and apparently by common consent the First Division ceased fire, while the Second Division transferred their aim to other ships. Then for some minutes the Russian flagship had respite.

In the Japanese line, although there had been many hits, and some of them severe, and casualties were mounting up, every ship had kept her station except the *Asama*. She was No. 5 in the Second Division, and at 2.28, within ten minutes

---

[1] The changes to "rapid" and "ordinary" firing are taken from the *Mikasa's* report Other ships do not give so much detail, but they appear to have followed her lead, as they successively brought the range well below 5,000. Admiral Kamimura began with his 12-pounders when at 2·43 his range was 4,300 metres.

[2] The Admiral in his first account possibly confused this turn with that which he put at 2.25.

after beginning her turn she was hit by a 12-inch shell which disabled her steering gear and forced her to turn away to port. The damage took only ten minutes to repair, but by that time her division had disappeared in the fog and she found herself alone and exposed to a concentration from the Russian rear. For three-quarters of an hour she remained thus isolated and although she received no vital hit, her upper works were cut to pieces mainly by the enemy's 12-pounders. Next to her Admiral Kamimura's flagship had suffered most. One 6-inch gun-crew was entirely wiped out by a 6-inch shell, but as she received no 12-inch hits her striking and manœuvring power was practically unaffected. The only serious hit by a 12-inch shell was on the *Nisshin*. It burst at 2.40 on her fore barbette, "smashed it," and caused 19 casualties, including an officer and two men killed; and these were her only losses during this part of the action.

Three minutes later, as the smoke cleared a little and the *Suvorov's* movement to starboard was revealed, Admiral Togo led still further round to S.E. $\frac{1}{2}$ E. "right across the enemy's " path, practically crossing the T. . . ." and re-opening action " raked them with a terrific fire in which the Second Division " joined."[1] It was more than the shattered enemy could endure, and the Japanese harvest began. About 2.50 the *Oslyabya* was seen to leave the line to starboard. She had received almost simultaneously two more heavy shells on the water-line, one of which tore another huge rent close to her first bad hit, and caused her list to increase so rapidly that the water poured in through every hole and swept away everything with which attempts were made to patch them. A few minutes later the *Suvorov* was forced to do the same. The Admiral had been wounded again in the head and legs. With the change of course, moreover, the gun's crews in the turrets were suffocated with the fumes of the conflagration that was raging and the flames drove into the conning tower and made it untenable. The Admiral and all who remained alive were forced to descend into the lower fighting position, the decks being impassable with the wrecked and distorted upper works—and then it was found the helm had jammed to port, so that the 4-point turn could not be stopped and she continued to go round to starboard.

The *Alexandr III.*, her next astern, at first followed, but quickly seeing something was wrong took the lead according

---

[1] *First Division Report* (2, 43), subsection 1.

to the standing order and led the fleet on the intended new course to the eastward. The two opposing lines were now about parallel again, and she, in her turn, became the objective of the Japanese concentration, which was specially severe; for just then the *Borodino*, her next astern, also had to fall out, so that she, the *Oslyabya* and the *Orel* were masking each other's fire and giving a splendid target to the Japanese rear. However, the *Borodino* was quickly able to repair her damages, and by 2.50 was in her station again astern of the *Alexandr*.[1] But the effect of the punishment which the Russian Second Division had been receiving was that it had lost station and a large gap was opening between it and the First Division, so that the line was seriously broken.[2] The *Suvorov* was circling apart helpless and clearly out of control. It was the moment when one of her two attached destroyers should, by the Admiral's standing order, have run up to transfer the flag. But nothing came near her, and as, owing to broken connections, she could not steer with the engines, she continued to yaw about in the same spot in a vain effort to proceed.

The destroyers were, in fact, fully employed elsewhere. Close by, where the disordered Russian rear was passing, lay the *Oslyabya* in an even worse plight than the *Suvorov*. She had stopped, entirely disabled, though still firing occasionally; but her list was increasing so fast that it was clear her last moments had come. The crew were crowding to the starboard side under a hail of shell that continued to fall upon her. "When we got abreast of her," says a Russian eye-witness, " the whole of the starboard side as far as the keel was laid " bare, her bright plating looked like the wet scales of some " sea monster; and suddenly, as if by command, all the men " who had crowded to the starboard side jumped down upon " these scales . . . Most of them were dashed against " the bilge keel and fell crippled into the sea. In the water " they formed an unimaginable mass . . . and the enemy's " shell never ceased the whole time from bursting over them. " A few more seconds and the *Oslyabya* disappeared beneath " the water."[1] The effect of such a catastrophe in full view of an already half-defeated fleet can well be imagined. As for the Japanese, the First Division were unaware of what had happened, but the armoured cruisers saw it all as they gave

---

[1] *Last Days.*
[2] Admiral Nebogatov's evidence.

the ship her *coup de grâce*, although so dense was the smoke that the rear ship *Iwate* believed it was a cruiser of the *Zhemchug* class that had sunk.   Three Russian destroyers then ran in in spite of the Japanese fire to rescue all they could, and so well was the work done that they were soon too crowded to do any further effective service.   And thus it was the Admiral was left helpless in his flaming flagship.[1]

Indeed, he was soon entirely deserted ; for the action was now taking on a new phase.   Up till this time the Russians had attempted no manœuvre beyond turning on the inner circle, and at first, as we have seen, the ships in the wake of the *Suvorov* thought her prolonged circling to starboard was a continuation of the movement.[2]   But when Captain Bukhvostov of the *Alexandr* realised that the flagship was out of control and felt the concentration increasing upon him, as the Japanese First Division again worked up on his port bow, he decided to submit no longer to being pushed to the southward and away from his disabled chief.[3]   The last of Admiral Rozhestvenski's battle instructions could leave him in no doubt what to do.   Order No. 243 of May 23rd provided as follows :—
" During an action ships in the line of battle will steam past
" their own damaged vessels or any vessels that cannot keep
" station.   If the *Suvorov* is damaged and out of control the
" fleet will keep station on the *Alexandr*, and should the
" *Alexandr* be damaged they should follow the *Borodino* and
" then the *Orel*.   At the same time the *Alexandr*, *Borodino*,
" and *Orel* will act on the signals of the *Suvorov* until the
" flag of the Commander-in-Chief has been transferred or
" until a junior flag-officer has assumed command."[4]   As no
signals were to be seen the Captain of the *Alexandr* was therefore not only entitled, but bound to take the lead and without further hesitation, a few minutes before 3.0, that is

---

[1] Out of the *Oslyabya's* crew of 35 officers and 865 men, 23 officers and 491 men were killed or drowned, 5 officers and 188 men were taken prisoners to Japan, and 6 officers and 186 men escaped to Vladivostok and Shanghai in the destroyers *Bravi* and *Bodri* respectively.

[2] *Rozhestvenski No. 2.*

[3] There is some doubt as to how long the *Alexandr* kept the lead.   *The Last Days* says she gave it up to the *Borodino* at 2.40 (= 3.0), and that the *Borodino* led the next manœuvre.   The *Japanese Confidential History*, however, says the Russian leader turned at 2.50 and *Rozhestvenski No. 2* says distinctly that the *Borodino* did not take the lead till 3.20 (= 3.40).   Semenov also gives the credit to the *Alexandr*, p. 113.   It is assumed, therefore, in what follows, that the leading ship was the *Alexandr*.

[4] Smirnov, p. 78.

five or ten minutes before the *Oslyabya* sank so suddenly he
turned 8 points to port and began leading to the northward
or, as the *Mikasa's* report puts it, "charged for the middle of
" our squadron."

The effect of this bold move was to throw the action into
a confusion that is difficult to penetrate.   Whatever Captain
Bukhvostov's precise intention was, the move showed a masterly
grasp of the situation.   As the Japanese were now to leeward
the manœuvre was partially at least concealed by the smoke.
It also enabled him to lead back to his disabled chief, and
might give him a chance of crossing the enemy's rear.[1]   The
danger of such a counter-attack seems quickly to have been
realised by Admiral Togo.   So pressing, indeed, was it, that it
was too late to parry it with a turn in succession.   As soon,
therefore, as he was aware of what had happened he turned
his division promptly together 8 points to port (2.58), "partly,"
so his Staff report says, "to give the enemy no chance of firing
" torpedoes, and partly owing to the possibility of his going
" round astern of us and escaping northward."   His idea,
then, presumably was that, after turning away together to avoid
torpedoes, he would complete his 16 points by another 8 points
together into reverse order, so as to head off the enemy as
quickly as was compatible with getting out of torpedo range.
It is fairly certain that the Second Division was intended to
do the same.   At this time they were very hotly engaged, and
receiving a good deal of punishment at ranges which, by the
Iwate's report, fell as low as 3,100 metres to her nearest ship.
A cruiser of the *Zhemchug* class was even seen to run up as
though to torpedo her, till she was beaten off with a concentrated fire.   All of them were hit more or less severely—there
were many casualties, and the *Adzuma* lost one of her after
turret-guns.   But at these close ranges they could see their fire
was telling heavily on the Russians.   "Our firing," says the
Divisional Staff report, "improved every minute, and large shell
" hit and burst on the target, presenting a splendid spectacle.
" The enemy also were fighting very well, and a good many
" shell of various sizes flew all round us, the columns of spray
" standing like a forest of fir-trees round our ships."   There were
still only five of the armoured cruisers in line, but the *Asama*

---

[1] Semenov (p. 113) states, or rather suggests, this was his idea.   Admiral
Rozhestvenski (*Report* No. 2) says, "intending probably to return to the
spot where the *Suvorov* had been left."

could just be seen a mile astern, engaging the rearmost Russian battleships alone, and trying to rejoin. But so severely was she punished that she could gain no ground, and began to fall astern once more.[1]

In this situation Admiral Kamimura, being engaged at close quarters with armoured cruisers against battleships, might well have followed his chief's lead, and for a time he contemplated doing so. "The Second Division," says the same Staff report, " was about to follow their (the First Division's) motions ; but " at this time the leading ships of the Russian Fleet were " greatly disorganised, and seemed as if they were going to " turn to starboard. Accordingly, the Second Division, to " prevent the enemy from escaping southward, did not alter " course, but increased speed to 17 knots, and kept straight " on, passing under the stern of our First Division, which was " in line abreast." On this movement the corresponding report of Admiral Togo remarks : " Just at this moment the Second " Division, which was coming up without change of course to " the rear of the First Division's line, masked the First Divi- " sion's fire, and forced them to cease action."

There is nothing, therefore, to show whether Admiral Togo approved of the movement or regarded it as spoiling his own, but it raises a nice point as to the limit of a divisional com- mander's initiative. Is a flag-officer in Admiral Kamimura's position justified in breaking the concentration of the battle squadron on a mere impression ? For this is what he did. " So difficult was it," we are informed by our Attaché in his division, " to make out their (the enemy's) movements that " observers at first differed as to whether they were turning " to port or to starboard."[2] What was actually seen from the *Idzumo* was that a ship, supposed to be the second in the Russian line, lost a funnel, and began to turn to starboard. It was not much to go by, and with so little certainty it might have been better to conform to the movement of the Com- mander-in-Chief, who was also group-leader. But, on the other hand, it was clear the enemy's line was broken ; there was no time to think, and Admiral Kamimura boldly elected to incur a risk which his chief had declined, and to rush across the bows of the advancing enemy. Like his chief he may thought they were intent on getting into position for using

[1] *Asama's Report* and *Attaché Reports*, III., 106.
[2] *Attaché Reports*, III., 106.

their torpedoes, and he was probably trusting to his increased
speed to carry him safely out of the danger arc.   Passing at a
range of about 3,000 metres, he seems to have developed a
very effective fire.   "The enemy," he says, "repeatedly caught
" fire, and, smothered in the smoke from the conflagrations and
" bursting shells, gradually swerved off to starboard.   The
" Second Division also moved round to starboard to a south-
" easterly course, and, circling round the enemy's van, com-
" menced an enveloping attack on him."   So close did he pass
that his despatch-vessel *Chihaya*—which, finding her station on
the off side very unsafe from "overs," had boldly fallen astern
of the rear ship, and was blazing away with everything she
had—ran in to 2,500 metres, and fired two 14-inch torpedoes
at the *Borodino*.

In the light of Admiral Togo's report all this is difficult
to visualise.   For according to that report at the time Admiral
Kamimura asserts he was encircling the enemy's van, the First
Division was also pressing the van while steaming in the
opposite direction to the Second Division.   At 3.5, when
Admiral Togo saw the Second Division was clear, he had
turned his second eight points together into single line in
reverse order with the *Nisshin* leading W.N.W. and "began to
" press the enemy's van."   "At 3.7," the *Mikasa's* report proceeds, "we engaged the disorganised Russian fleet with our
" port batteries and poured in a heavy fire on all the ships
" at ranges between 3,000 and 5,000 metres."

It is clear, then, that what with the mist and the smoke of
the guns and the burning ships the Japanese were at a loss to
know what the Russians were doing from the moment the
Alexandr assumed the lead.   Their bewilderment must have
been completed by another cause which was adding to the confusion in the enemy's ranks.

From Admiral Nebogatov's evidence at his court-martial,
it appears that a radical change in the Russian order of battle
was proceeding.   The check given to their Second Division
by the disabling of the *Oslyabya*, as has been said, caused it
to lose station and the tragic end of the flagship for a time
demoralised it.   "This catastrophe to the *Oslyabya*," said the
Admiral, "perceptibly disconcerted the Second Battleship
" Division. . . . It was falling behind the First, and a great
" interval was formed there.   Noticing this I immediately put
" on the fullest speed of which the *Nikolai* was capable in order
" to take station in this gap.   My captains followed me and

" we occupied it. . . . We steamed past on the side nearest
" the enemy."

This movement, which was, of course, in accordance with
the Russian battle instructions,[1] may have had a good deal to
do with Admiral Kamimura's misconception, and possibly what
he took for a general alteration of course to starboard was the
falling away of the Russian Second Division, before he could
realise that the Third Division was coming up to take station
ahead of it.

The manner in which Admiral Kamimura realised his mistake is very obscure. At 3.5, when in circling he was going
about south-east, clear away from Admiral Togo's division, a
12-inch Russian shell coming from aft hit the *Idzumo* obliquely
on the starboard quarter about $7\frac{1}{2}$ feet above the waterline.
Exploding on a beam in the lower deck it wrecked the officers'
sick bay and wounded four men. Two minutes later, at 3.7,
the *Adzuma*, her next astern, says the enemy had entirely disappeared in the smoke, and she ceased fire. At the time the
Russians seem to have been thus lost, and the direction of the hit
on the *Idzumo* must have suggested to the Admiral that they were
passing astern of him, that is, that he had overrun them. The
Oslyabya was the only ship within effective range of the
Idzumo, and when she went down, believing the rest were
running off to the northward, he says, at 3.10, he " followed
the motions of his next ahead," and altered course to north-
east.[2] Seven minutes later (3.17), finding this led to nothing,
he turned north-west, completing a 16-point turn, and then
settled on a west-north-west course to return to the point where
he had parted with the First Division, which was now quite
out of sight.

Whatever the Commander-in-Chief may have thought of
Admiral Kamimura's move, it affords an example of how
cautious a divisional commander should be in using his discretion for independent movements in thick weather. At the
critical hour of the action, when the enemy were so far beaten
as to be exposed to annihilation, he broke the main concentration. As a consequence, Admiral Togo lost the dominating
control of the battle, which he had exercised up to this moment,

---

[1] Order No. 243. *See ante*, pp. 211-2.

[2] There is nothing to show he could see the First Division at this
time. The expression is a technical one, and seems to mean merely that
he was conforming to the movement which he had last seen the First
Division make—that is, the turn to N.E.

and a new phase began in which all that was done was mainly a matter of chance.

It would also suggest that for an inferior fleet—inferior in speed and hitting power—almost anything is better, at least in thick weather, than merely conforming to the enemy's movement when once his fire had began to assert a domination. So far as can be seen, it was nothing but Captain Bukhvostov's bold manœuvre that by threatening a counter-attack saved the Russians from complete destruction then and there. As it was they had won a valuable respite.

———————————

CHAPTER XVI.

THE BATTLE OF THE SEA OF JAPAN.

Second Phase.

[Charts XII. Diagrams 4 to 8.]

THE first stage of the action, in which the Japanese had practically defeated their enemy, had lasted for about an hour. The second phase occupied about two hours, that is roughly from 3.0 till past 5.0. But as it took place over nearly the same ground as the hottest of the previous fighting in the reverse direction and a little to the north and to leeward, the whole field was obscured by smoke-laden mist. The Russian formation, moreover, was broken up, and none of the leading ships survived to tell what they did. A clear picture of what happened is consequently impossible to reconstruct, and we have to be content with a vague impression of the general lines on which the action proceeded.

For some minutes after Admiral Togo had turned away together nothing could be seen of the enemy clearly enough to make out what they were doing. Even when he had turned his second eight points and reformed his division in reverse order their presence was only known by shells that came flying out of the mist from the port side. But scarcely had he settled on his new north-westerly course to cut across that which the Russians were believed to be taking for Vladivostok, when their leading ships came dimly into view and his division was able to reopen fire on its port side at ranges varying from 3,000 to 5,000 metres.

What the Russians were doing at the moment is quite obscure. It would appear that as the *Alexandr* led the fleet to the northward she had been headed off to starboard by Admiral Kamimura's movement, and was forced to complete the circle before she could head to the northward again. But this she did, we gather, not so much with the idea of breaking through to Vladivostok as to cover the *Suvorov*, which, not far from where she had first fallen out, was burning furiously, but still firing gamely with some of her secondary guns. Indeed, she was already recovering some control over her movements. After she was forced out of the line to starboard she had

continued to turn in that direction till she had almost completed the circle, and was now heading to the northward to
cross the wake of both the fleets. The consequence was that
by the time Admiral Togo's port batteries came into action with
the leading Russian ships, their 16-point turn had brought
them again into the flagship's vicinity.

It was at 3.7 that the Japanese First Division reopened fire
on the leading Russians, while Admiral Kamimura was still
racing on at 17 knots almost in the opposite direction. As the
Nisshin led on, in accordance with the Japanese practice, without reducing the "battle speed," Admiral Togo's division soon
ran past the enemy, but not before, so far as can be seen, he
had headed them back again to the southward. Such, at
least, seems to have been what happened, judging from what
our Attaché with the First Division saw at this time. One of
the three ships of the Russian First Division, which he took
to be probably the *Alexandr*, came up gallantly into the
lead, and then for a moment all three headed straight for the
Japanese. "The range," he continues, "having been reduced
" by 3.18 to 2,500 metres (2,734 yards) [1] the Russian leader,
" being then about a point abaft the beam of the Japanese
" was subjected to a terrific gun attack that must have
" aggravated a situation which a fire on board had already
" rendered uncomfortable. For a brief space those in the
" Japanese fleet who had witnessed the somewhat similar rash
" effort of the *Retvisan* [on August 10th] [2] thought they saw
" repeated an attempt to ram." The result was the same. The
storm of fire that greeted her, though it headed her off, did no
vital injury, and she continued to turn to starboard. Not so
the others. "Less resolute," the same report continues, " or
" more prudent, the companions of the *Alexandr* (in one of
" whom a severe explosion had occurred) swung to port and
" gained the same course though west and south." [3]

The whole episode of the attempt and failure of the
Alexandr and her consorts to save the Flagship is graphi-
cally described by an officer on Admiral Rozhestvenski's staff.
Speaking of Captain Bukhvostov's bold lead he says, "From

---

[1] This range seems underestimated. *Mikasa*, says at 3.12 it was
3,000 metres and that she then reopened with her 12-pounders. At 3.15
she was on the *Nakhimov*, the rear-ship of the Nebogatov Division, at
3.300. After 3.21 the range increased from 3,900 to 4,200.

[2] *See* Vol. I., p. 395.

[3] *Attaché Reports*, IV., 9–10.

" the ports of the starboard battery we were now able
" plainly to see the *Alexandr*, which was almost on the
" beam and steering straight for the *Suvorov*, the rest were
" following her. The distance rapidly diminished and with
" binoculars I could distinctly see her battered sides, broken
" bridges, burning chart-houses and booms, but her funnels
" and masts were still standing. After her came the *Boro-*
" *dino* burning furiously. The enemy had already suc-
" ceeded in forging ahead and had begun to incline to cross
" the course. Our ships approached from starboard ; the
" enemy, however, could be seen from the port side of the
" *Suvorov*.[1] They fired into us and across us. Our fore turret
" (the only one remaining in action at this time) took an active
" part in the fight. . . . All waited, holding their breath.
" Apparently the whole fire of the Japanese was concentrated
" on the *Alexandr*. At times she appeared wrapped in flame
" and billowy clouds of smoke, and around her the sea boiled
" and rose in gigantic columns of water. Closer and closer—
" the distance is not more than 2,000 yards. Now see, one
" after another, a whole string of shells, distinctly visible,
" strike on her forebridge and port 6-inch turret. The
" *Alexandr* abruptly turns to starboard almost on the opposite
" course and goes off. After her the *Borodino*, *Orel*, and the
" rest turn hastily, hardly keeping in line-ahead—it was not
" ' in succession ' nor yet ' together.' A dull murmur ran through
" the battery. ' They have given it up. They are off ! ' "[2] Their
punishment had been more than they could bear. Indeed so
severely had the *Alexandr* suffered that for a time she was
unable to keep her speed, and, according to the instructions,
the *Borodino* assumed the lead.[3]

The *Suvorov* was now left exposed and began to make an
attempt to pass astern of the Japanese as the whole of the
division began to concentrate upon her. She was still wrapped
in smoke and flame and scarcely able to move, and one more
effort to protect her had failed. Both the *Nisshin* and *Kasuga*
report that a cruiser of the *Zhemchug* type who, according to
instructions, may well have been trying to get to the flagship's relief, " came charging up at full speed as though to
fire a torpedo." But both of them turned their light guns

---

[1] This probably refers to the leading Japanese ships.
[2] Semenov, pp. 116–8. The War College translation by Captain C. J.
Eyres, R.N., is here followed.
[3] *Rozhestvenski No.* 2.

upon her, and when the *Alexandr* and her consorts gave up she too made off.

About the same time (3.15) the Japanese line was reinforced by the *Asama*. It will be remembered that for the last half hour, in trying to rejoin her flag, she had been engaged alone with Admiral Nebogatov's division. Although she had managed temporarily to repair her first injuries, she was suffering again heavily in the unequal contest, and as soon, therefore, as she saw the First Division coming up from the eastward, she seized the occasion to escape from her peril and took station ahead of the *Nisshin*. She thus got free from Admiral Nebogatov who appears to have led the Second and Third Russian Divisions after the three remaining *Suvorovs*. Some of his command were under fire as the seven Japanese ships were concentrating on the burning flagship at ranges from 2,000 to 3,000 metres.[1] At 3.21 as the *Mikasa* came up she passed one of the *Suvorov's* sisters close enough to give her a torpedo, but apparently without effect. Still "battle speed" was not reduced, and the division rushed by without completing the *Suvorov's* destruction. The result was that by 3.28 the Russians were disappearing in the mist, and the *Mikasa* ceased fire.

In vain the armoured cruisers were looked for to complete the work of destruction, for it seemed precisely an opportunity for making themselves felt.[2] But Admiral Kamimura was, of course, far away, though he was doing his best to resume his station.

By 3.15, when the *Asama* joined the First Division, it will be remembered that he had completely lost the ships he had been engaging, and was turning to the north-westward to recover touch with the Commander-in-Chief. The move quickly brought him in sight of what he took to be the enemy's main body "steaming northwards in a confused line"; and if, as is supposed, Admiral Togo had forced them off their course some ten minutes earlier, his conjecture was probably correct, although from the ship reports it seems that only two or at most three units were clearly made out. They were slightly before his port beam about 6,000 metres away. He at once opened fire—that is, at 3.20, in the

---

[1] *Nakhimov* and *Sisoi Veliki* are mentioned by various battleships to have been under their fire at this time at ranges varying from 3,300 metres to 6,400.

Attaché Reports, IV., 10.

height of the First Division's concentration on the *Suvorov*—
and the battle, he says, was again very hot, the range falling
as low as 3,000 metres by 3.26, so that the *Idzumo* fired a
torpedo. But he could not keep it up for long, for it was
now his turn to feel the embarrassment of his independent
action. The range rapidly increased again and in the dense
mist, somewhere on his port bow, he must have heard the
guns of the First Division, but not being able to tell how
near they were he was compelled practically to cease action, for
fear of injuring his own friends. "At intervals," his report
says, "the fog suddenly thickened. Owing to this and the
" smoke we were prevented from making certain of the enemy's
" movements, and finding it difficult to distinguish our own
" ships from the Russians, we slackened our fire for a while,
" continuing to engage only such ships as could be recognised
" from their mast-head flags." The result was that another
chance of dealing a decisive blow was lost. The enemy must
have turned to starboard to meet his attack on the opposite
course, for, he says, "the enemy's main squadron which had
" disappeared in the fog and smoke went past the rear of the
" Second Division apparently intending to escape northward."
Probably he did not arrive at this conclusion at once, for he
still held on as he was, till, as we shall see, he had cause to
abandon independent action.

By half-past three, when Admiral Togo had ceased fire,
the bulk of the Russians were scarcely visible on the *Mikasa's*
port quarter, making apparently in a north-easterly direction
as though to pass astern of him. But for some reason he did
not go about at once. It would seem as though he did not
know where the rest of the Russian battleships were, for he now
(3.30) signalled to the *Nisshin* to lead four points to port which
made the course about S.W. For about ten minutes he kept
to this, but nothing could be seen of the enemy he was seeking.
It was believed they had gone south, but as it was obvious
they might again turn northward across his wake, Admiral
Togo decided it was time to hark back. By two successive
turns together to port, therefore (at 3.42 and 3.49), he reformed
his line in right order, and reassuming the lead held away to
the north-east.

Meanwhile, Admiral Kamimura, whether or not by this time
he knew where his chief was, was doing what had been expected
of him. During the desultory action which he had been afraid
to press he had gradually edged to port till he was going W. by

N.—a course which soon brought him close to the abandoned *Suvorov*. Passing her at a range of less than 2,000 metres he gave her the fire of his whole line.[1] The effect must have been terrible. "The enemy," he says, "who was already greatly " damaged, had her mast, funnels, bridges, and upper deck " structures nearly all smashed to pieces by our fire at such " close quarters." Then he could see his despatch-vessel *Chihaya* bringing up his attached destroyer division (the 5th) to finish her. "As she was no longer under control," his report continues, "and seemed to have lost all her fighting " power, except for some small calibre guns aft which she " occasionally fired, we ceased firing at her."

The moment (3.39) was seized by the *Chihaya* to deliver her attack. Closing in to 1600 metres she reduced to half speed, and discharged two 14-inch torpedoes from her port side. A burst of smoke and columns of water seemed to proclaim one of the shots a hit. Still as the *Suvorov's* condition seemed unchanged she turned to fire her bow torpedo, but, as the report says, the shock of the gun fire and pounding of the heavy seas caused it to jam half-way out of the tube. By that time some other Russian ships, probably some of those which Admiral Nebogatov was leading, came up to the rescue ; for it would seem that mindful of his chief's last injunction that all depended on keeping the fleet together, he was once more trying to get back to the *Suvorov*. The movement quickly brought the *Chihaya* under a heavy fire, and after two hits in the rigging she was so badly holed on the water-line that the courageous little ship was put out of action for over two hours while emergency repairs were executed. She was suc-ceeded immediately by the 5th destroyer division, who had been only waiting for their chance. At the first call they had passed from the disengaged side of the armoured cruisers and at 20 knots had crossed their bows. They now "charged down on the " *Suvorov* through a very heavy sea," and delivered their attack by running along her port side. At ranges of from 400 to 800 metres they fired between the four of them five torpedoes, two of which they claimed to have got home, though no hit is recorded by the *Suvorov*.[2] They themselves, on the other

---

[1] *Idzumo* gives her range as 1,700 metres ; *Adzuma* as 1,400 ; *Tokiwa* gives 2,000, and so does *Yakumo* who fired a torpedo. *Iwate* gives 1,500.

[2] Semenov says he did not even know an attack had been made till he learnt it from Japanese sources.

hand, did not come off scatheless.   For so well did the burning wreck defend herself that the senior officer's boat was twice badly hit by 12-pounder shell, and, besides having a boiler smashed, lost four men killed and six wounded.   It had been a well-delivered attack at close range and under just such circumstances as were believed to promise torpedo craft their best and most telling effect in a fleet action.   And yet it was a complete failure.   The heroic resistance of the Russian flagship was not crushed and out of the pall of flames and smoke that smothered her there still came shots which forced the destroyers to run off out of range.

While the attack was being delivered Admiral Kamimura was still holding on ; for, before it was over, away through the driving mist on his port bow he could dimly see Admiral Togo making his first 8 point turn.   In a few minutes more he was aware that the scond turn had been made and that the First Division was coming back towards him.   With the intention of taking station on their port bow he carried on across their course till his rear ship was clear and then swung round until he was approximately upon the same course as his chief.   The movement brought him in view of the *Asama*, who, after Admiral Togo's simultaneous turn, had become rear ship.   She at once increased to full speed to pass on the disengaged side and rejoin her proper flag ; but again the luck was against her.   Before she could get into station the Japanese, as will be seen directly, were again under fire, and at 4.10 a 6-inch shell coming from no one knows where crashed through the base of her aftermost funnel.   Her speed at once dropped to 10 knots and a second time she had to fall behind for repairs.

It was in this way that the misfortune had come upon her so unexpectedly.   For some minutes after the last Japanese turn was completed, the enemy had been out of sight.   It was only, we are told, from a blurr here and there in the mist and from the fall of the shot, that Admiral Togo could judge where the Russians were,[1] but at 3.55 he had sight of their main body about 7,000 metres E. by S. of him.   In the van could be made out the *Alexandr*, *Borodino*, and *Orel*, and astern of them was Admiral Nebogatov's division with the three remaining ships of the Second Division in rear of all.   So thick was the fog at this time that only

---

[1] *Attaché Reports*, IV., 12.

the leading ships could be clearly seen from the *Mikasa* and they were apparently heading about N.N.E. as though to get back to the *Suvorov* and cover her. For she also had come into sight of the Japanese Second Division and could be seen on their starboard bow. At 4.0 both divisions opened on the Russian main force, the First Division at about 6,500 metres and the Second at 5,000. As the Japanese were going about east the two courses were rapidly converging, but since the Russian leaders were before the Japanese beam, Admiral Togo found it necessary in three or four minutes to lead more to port about N.E., so as to get a position from which he could head them off from the northward. About the same time the Russians, as they felt the Japanese fire, swerved off to starboard and thus instead of passing to the northward of the *Suvorov* went by on her disengaged side. In this way the flagship found herself in a similar position to that of the *Rurik* at the battle of Ulsan ; that is, she was in the line of fire from the Japanese to her own friends. Admiral Kamimura says that seeing how badly damaged she was he would not waste ammunition upon her, but merely gave her a few shots in passing and then began to edge round to starboard, so as to co-operate more closely with the First Division in pressing the main body. At this time the Russians seemed to him to be again losing their formation and to be turning in confusion to starboard as though intending to run off to the southward.

But for some reason Admiral Togo did not at once press the advantage he had gained. At 4.8 he, too, was aware of the *Suvorov* and turning his fire from the leading ship which he had been engaging he began to concentrate on her at a range of 5,600 which continually decreased. At 4.15 to close the range faster he began turning to starboard and soon brought it down to under 3,000. He then fired his second torpedo and ten minutes later at 2,000 metres he fired his third, but neither took effect. The *Shikishima* his next astern fired another, but how far the rest of his division devoted themselves to the disabled ship is not clear ; the rear ships at any rate seem to have been engaged principally with the enemy's rear, for the *Asahi* (No. 4) says she was at first on the *Nakhimov* and then on the *Suvorov* ; and the *Nisshin* (No. 5) that she was on the *Nakhimov* and the *Navarin*, and none of them mention close action with the *Suvorov*. The Admiral, however, was clearly absorbed with her. " She

now," says the First Division's report, "came under the
" concentrated fire of our ships till her funnels, bridges,
" masts and upper works were practically all blown
" away. A conflagration was spreading over her deck and
" even her gun-ports · emitted tongues of flame. The
" spectacle she presented was awe-inspiring—it was like an
" eruption of Iwashima." And still she moved and fired, a
never-surpassed example of the length to which the loyalty
and fortitude of a devoted crew can carry the defence of a
beaten ship. "Her after turret,"[1] says one British report, "still
" kept up the hopeless struggle and fired occasionally, but the
" gallant effort was unrewarded and the shell all fell short,
" which may have been due to her heavy list. . . . She was a
" striking and most awful sight. Still covered with dense
" smoke, through which her one remaining mast was still
" visible, she struggled slowly ahead, the list to port still
" continuing, though she was less down by the head. From
" time to time shell-bursts were seen, the flashes of the de-
" tonations seeming immense and looking as if it were impos-
" sible for any living thing to exist in her superstructure."[2]
Regardless of the Russian main force both Japanese divisions
were circling round her, but at a gradually increasing range.
"At about 4.30," another British officer reports, "when she
" was being struck repeatedly, a 12-inch shell burst in between
" the decks close to the after turret for 6-inch guns. The
" explosion was accompanied by a back-rush of flame that
" must have projected 50 feet from her side and then through
" the enormous rent thus made could be seen the glow of a
" newly-ignited interior. . . . The foremast had long been
" down. Now fell the main topmast and at the same time
" a terrible explosion occurred. . . . It was thought the
" end must at last have come. . . . but still the *Suvorov*
" maintained the unequal contest."[3] It seemed incredible
that any ship could endure such punishment and still remain
afloat.

Yet float she did and the tremendous effort to sink her
was worse than wasted. For by this time, as Admiral Kamimura had continued to edge to starboard, the Russians were
fairly enveloped ; their fire had almost ceased and so far as

---

[1] According to Semenov her main after turret was already out of
action. Possibly a 6-inch turret is meant.

[2] *Attaché Reports*, III., 108.

[3] *Ibid.*, IV., 14.

could be seen through the fog, they had lost all semblance of formation. The *Alexandr* in fact had been so severely punished that she could no longer keep the lead, the *Borodino* had not had time to take her place, and the whole squadron was running off to the southward in a broken and confused mob incapable of manœuvre or deployment. It was the moment, so far as can be judged after the event, when the utmost effort should have been made by the Japanese to complete the decision. Yet it was the moment when Admiral Togo in his pre-occupation with the *Suvorov* completely lost his hold. Possibly the peculiar faith of the Japanese in their cherished principle of alternating high and low pressure as the secret of success in war may not have been without its influence on men exhausted with two hours of almost incessant fighting, but the more probable explanation is that he simply lost the enemy in the mist and smoke. Owing to the weather conditions, it was almost impossible to see any movement the enemy was making until it was completed ; no one could even tell whether an individual ship was turning to port or to starboard,[1] and the Second Division's report says that for this reason they were completely thrown out. " The enemy," says the *Idzumo*, "apparently altered course and disappeared in " the fog."

The actual situation at 4.30 when the Russians escaped was as follows :—Admiral Kamimura was steaming about S.E. with his ships practically in line with the First Division but some distance ahead ; the Commander-in-Chief was still heading east, not yet having followed the Second Division round. From the *Mikasa* the main force of the enemy was hardly visible, but it appeared to Admiral Togo that they were still turning to starboard as though intent on another attempt to get round his rear. He therefore promptly signalled for 8 points together to port in order to get more to the northward and repeat the movement by which he had previously headed them off.[2] The Second Division, on the other hand,

---

[1] *Attaché Reports*, III., 106.

[2] Such at least is the official explanation of this remarkable manœuvre, which, of course, could only result in his losing touch with the enemy altogether. The Divisional Staff Report has : " The enemy sheered " off more and more to starboard till they were eventually steaming " southward, whereupon we at 4.35 turned 8 points together to *star-* " *board*." So it stands in the MS. copy which has been furnished, but *starboard* must be an error for *port*, since a *port* turn is given in the

which had quite lost sight of the Russians, continued to edge
to starboard till it was going due south in chase. In ten
minutes, however, Admiral Kamimura became aware that the
First Division was disappearing to the northward, and at 4.47,
finding he had lost touch, turned sharply to starboard and ran
back about N.W. to try to rejoin. The disappearance of the
First Division in the opposite direction from the enemy was
to some extent an accident. Very quickly after making his
turn together to the northward, Admiral Togo had realised
that the enemy were, in fact, still running off south. He
therefore signalled for another 8 points together to starboard
to get back into line ahead on his previous course, and
follow the Second Division. But for some reason the ships
were so long in hoisting the answering pennants that it
was 4.43 before he could make the turn. Simultaneously,
seeing he was obliged to leave the *Suvorov*, he threw out
blindly into the mist the signal, " Destroyer divisions attack
the enemy." He had no idea where the boats were, for owing
to his constant changes of course they had quite lost touch with
him, but it was all he could do, and at 4.51 he altered to
south and hurried away after Admiral Kamimura.

The *Chihaya*, however, whose special charge the destroyers
were, was not far away. At 4.0, after her attack on the *Suvorov*,
she had stopped to clear the torpedo which had jammed in
her forward tube, and to repair damages. After three-quarters
of an hour's work she had just recovered the torpedo, but
still had over an hour to spend on the shell damages she had
received, before she would be fit for service again. Still she
was able to transmit the signal, and the 4th destroyer division at once took it in. These four destroyers, which were
amongst those which carried mines, were properly attached to
Admiral Dewa's group, but during his operations against the
Russian cruisers, to be related directly, his speed had been so
great in the heavy seas that they had been unable to keep
company and had recently attached themselves to the Second
Division. On receiving the order they increased to 18 knots,
and ran up "to press the enemy's bow." The *Suvorov*, they
say, though "all ablaze and wrapped in rolling smoke," was
maintaining a speed of about 10 knots, and as they came up

Official Track Chart and by *Mikasa*. The report then proceeds to state
that the object was " to forestall any movement on their part, which
should have for " its intention an escape northward round the rear
of our line." (*Confidential History*, II., 227.)

she turned her head quickly to starboard to avoid them.
But at 5.5 the *Asagiri* and *Murasame* ran by her on a parallel
course, and each discharged a torpedo at 800 metres. Then
finding " the force of the sea striking the sides of the torpedoes
rendered them ineffective" they turned round to try again to
starboard on the reverse course. The *Asashiwo*, following
closely, had time to get off two shots, both without result.
The fourth boat, *Shirakumo*, failed to attack at all. She had
come up with the others; "but," says her report, "seeing
" that the enemy had no further power of steaming, she did
" not discharge her torpedoes." From this it is to be assumed
she must have had to wait till the second attack from the two
leading boats was over, and that in the interval the *Suvorov*
had stopped. As her two consorts came back to starboard on
the course opposite to the enemy, they each fired one torpedo at 300 metres. That of the *Asagiri* was a miss-fire,
owing to the breakdown of the electric circuit, but that of the
Murasame was believed to have scored a hit, for a burst was
seen under the *Suvorov's* port quarter, and she heeled over
about 10 degrees.

The 3rd destroyer division which was one of the three
specially attached to Admiral Togo, had also come up and
was waiting for its chance, but before the 4th division was
clear a quite unexpected development forced it to sheer
off. The impression on board the *Suvorov* was that she had
driven off the Japanese with her two or three remaining guns;
but, in fact, they had suddenly to deal with something much
more formidable. Already during the latter part of the 4th division's attack it had been under fire from other ships besides
the *Suvorov*, and the senior officer's boat *Asagiri* had been
hit twice. But when in spite of the dropping shells the 3rd
division was about to go in, they caught sight of part of the
Russian fleet emerging out of the mist to the south-eastward
and pressing on to their flagship's rescue. They were only
3,000 metres away and firing briskly, and there was nothing for
the destroyers but to run off at high speed out of their
perilous position, leaving the *Suvorov* still afloat and defiant.

To explain this startling reappearance of the mass of the
Russian fleet where it was least expected it will be necessary
to see what had been happening in that part of the field of
action for which Admiral Togo had been making. After
throwing out his signal for the destroyers, he had run on
south till he recovered touch with the Second Division and

he then took measures to ensure that a second separation should not occur. For now he made a signal by which, " as Commander-in-Chief of the Combined Fleet," he definitely ordered Admiral Kamimura to take station ahead of him ; and as in this formation they held on to the southward in chase the second phase of the battle may be said to have ended. Making all allowances for the difficulty of vision, it certainly seems to have lacked decision and concentrated energy in its final stages. The enemy were permitted what appears to have been a needless respite, and, as has now to be told, the consequences narrowly escaped being very serious.

CHAPTER XVII.

The Battle of the Sea of Japan.

Third Phase with the Cruiser Operations.

[Chart XII.   Diagram 9.]

THE danger of the situation which arose out of Admiral Togo's halting pursuit lay with the Japanese cruisers. At the outset of the action, it will be remembered, they had been detached in two groups to attack the enemy's rear. Since that time practically the whole of the movements of the opposed battle divisions had been taking place in the northern half of a circle, having a radius of about 10 miles, and its centre about the spot where the *Oslyabya* went down and where Admiral Togo, at the end of the first bout, had begun definitely to assert his superiority. In the southern half of this imaginary circle the cruiser operations had been taking place ; or, as Admiral Enkvist summarised the position in his despatch, " the Japanese " forced our fleet to manœuvre so as to describe the circumference of a circle, in the centre of which were our transports and destroyers. The Japanese operated on the circumference of a circle of greater diameter."[1]

At 1.50, when Admiral Rozhestvenski first sighted the Japanese Battle Squadron, he had signalled to the cruisers and transports to haul out of the line to starboard, as provided by his battle instructions. The resulting formation which Admiral Enkvist carried out was, that the four transports *Anaduir, Irtuish, Kamchatka* (repair ship) and *Koreya*, with the fleet tugs *Rus* and *Svir*, were in line-ahead on the starboard quarter of the battle line with the old armoured cruiser *Monomakh* on their starboard beam. To port of them was Admiral Enkvist in the *Oleg* leading the *Avrora* and *Donskoi*, while the "Scouting detachment" (*Svyetlana, Almaz* and *Ural*) under Commodore Shein, brought up the rear of the transport line.[2] Ten minutes, however, before the action began, the *Idzumi* was seen approaching on the starboard hand. The *Monomakh* opened fire on her at long range and Admiral Enkvist, to guard against an attack in force from that side, pushed his division

---

[1] *Attaché Reports*, III., 200.
[2] *New Material* and *Attaché Reports*, III., 212.

on ahead of the transports in order to pass over to their
starboard side and cover them. The "Scouting detachment"
conformed by also forming up to starboard.[1] The *Idzumi*
then came under a heavy fire, and, finding it too hot for her,
ran off to the southward, and in doing so managed to cut off
the two Russian hospital ships, which, in pursuance of their
general instructions, were three or four miles astern.[2] But
neither distance nor their pose as non-combatants availed to
save them : for the persistent use of them for intelligence
purposes was regarded by the Japanese as having annulled
their immunity under the Red Cross.

It was at 2.25, just as the *Idzumi* had run off and the
main attack on the Russian van was developing its full intensity, that Admiral Dewa, having got well clear of the battle
squadron, began to lead his group[3] to the southward, according
to the Tactical Instructions, to attack the enemy's rear. Admiral
Uriu followed on his port quarter with the Fourth Division and
near enough to the rear half of the Russian battle line to fire
upon it as he ran down on the opposite course. By 2.45 they
had outreached the enemy's last ship, and Admiral Dewa, seeing
that their cruisers had passed over to the starboard side turned
S.W. to cross their rear, and opened fire at 7,800 metres upon
the *Oleg, Avrora, Donskoi* and *Monomakh.* Admiral Uriu,
possibly because the range was very great for his lighter armament, or possibly because the weakly-armed "Scouting detachment" was his objective, turned shorter, so that he engaged
well inside his leader at a range of 6,500 to 6,000 metres.
But the Russian fire proved surprisingly good, and the weather
conditions were not favourable for effective reply. "The wind
" and sea were very high," says the Third Division Staff report.
"The ships rolled heavily ; many seas came inboard ; and when
" the ships were steaming against wind and sea the forward guns
" could not be fired, and all the time the guns' crews were
" working in overalls." The Fourth Division must have felt the
weather even more severely. Probably, therefore, because he
found things too hot for him, Admiral Uriu quickly turned
his division four points to starboard together and steered away
more into the Third Division's wake, still, however, keeping

---

[1] Smirnov ; the *Idzumi's* report ; *New Material* ; *Attaché Reports,* III., 214.

[2] " Hospital ships will act as convenient, keeping out of range and
not interfering with the conduct of the action." Commander-in-Chief's
order, No. 239, Art. *d.,* May 17th.—Smirnov.

[3] Third and Fourth Divisions, that is, his own and Admiral Uriu's.

well on the inside course.   Since by this time the Russian cruisers, conforming to their battle squadron's motions, had altered to starboard, the two Japanese divisions soon found themselves steaming parallel to them, and on this course a regular action developed at a mean range of about 5,000 metres.

Admiral Kataoka with his group did not do so well.[1]   When at 2.10 he got the Commander-in-Chief's order to attack the rear, he and Rear-Admiral Togo were so far to the westward that the Russians were out of sight in the mist, and all he could do was to fix his course by the sound of the guns.   Up till 2.20 he was steering nearly east, but five minutes later, thinking he could see enemy's transports to the southward, he ordered Rear-Admiral Togo to chase while he himself turned south-east.   The Sixth Division went off at once at increased speed, but only to find the strange sail were the two auxiliary cruisers *Sado Maru* and *Manshu Maru*, which during the period of watching the Russian approach had been following Admiral Kataoka's group northward and trying to join.   Thereupon Rear-Admiral Togo turned to port to regain touch with the Fifth Division, and as Admiral Kataoka in his search for the enemy had altered to starboard, S. by W., he soon came in sight. Admiral Kataoka then signalled, "Sixth Division is to act as convenient."   Having thus been given liberty of action, Rear-Admiral Togo began an independent search for the enemy's rear, with the two auxiliary cruisers and his attached torpedo-boats in company.   A ship was sighted almost immediately, but as she proved to be the *Orel*, one of the two Russian hospital ships which the *Idzumi* had isolated, he left her to the auxiliary cruisers and carried on, and as his flotilla could not keep up in the heavy seas, he sent it away to join that of the Fifth Division.   As for the two auxiliary cruisers, in obedience to his orders they ran down for the stranger and quickly came upon her consort the *Kostroma*.   As there was too much sea running for a boat to be lowered they were signalled to follow, and were eventually taken into Miura Bay, where their belligerent character was confirmed by finding the British prisoners from the *Oldhamia* on board the *Orel*.

While the Kataoka group was thus engaged the action of the Third and Fourth Divisions had been proceeding with

---

[1] The Fifth and Sixth Divisions, that is, his own and Rear-Admiral Togo's.

great spirit. The Russian rear, where the transports had fallen astern of the cruisers, was already in disorder, and on the Japanese side the *Kasagi*, Admiral Dewa's flagship, at 3.10 had been badly holed on the water-line. Still encouraged by his success, he continued to close and in about ten minutes forced the *Oleg* and *Avrora* to turn back to save the transports, so that the opposed cruisers were soon engaged on opposite courses.[1] This southerly movement of Admiral Enkvist brought him in sight of Admiral Kataoka who was coming down on a south-easterly course and now turned to port towards the Russian cruisers, opening fire with his heavy guns at 10,000 metres.

It was some time apparently before Admiral Dewa realised what was happening. He notes the Russians' turn at 3.30, and then says, "The Third Division, to conform to this move- " ment and to avoid hindering the operations of our main " force now bearing about north, made an 18 point turn to " starboard at 3.35 and threatened the forward progress of " the enemy."[2] The Fourth Division did the same, and on the turn the *Takachiho* was hit by a large shell below the water-line, on her starboard quarter, which, though it made no hole, shook her so severely that her steering gear broke down and she had to leave the line and stop for repairs.

The movement, however, combining as it did, with Admiral Kataoka's attack, was so far successful that it headed back the two Russian ships who began to swing round with a wide turn to starboard while at the same time it brought together all four of the Japanese cruiser divisions. Incidentally they also repelled a destroyer attack from Admiral Enkvist's attached flotilla and some of the ships were able to fire on the deserted *Suvorov*. By 3.45 the Sixth Division, which had just picked up the *Idzumi* and was now complete, sighted the Fourth (Uriu) Division and steered to take station in its wake. At the same time the Russian cruisers also became concentrated by

---

[1] Admiral Dewa's report says the *Donskoi* also turned back. Schubert (*New Material*) says she was in rear, and it was on a signal from her to the effect that the transports were in danger that *Oleg* and *Avrora* turned back.

[2] What he means about hindering the main force is not clear. By the Japanese Official Chart the First Division was then 12 miles N.W., and the Second Division about 9 miles N.N.W. Probably, therefore, he could only hear the sound of their guns, and not knowing they had turned back to the westward feared he was steering to cross their course.

the *Zhemchug* and *Izumrud* joining up with Admiral Enkvist's line.[1]

As the Russians on their wide turn edged more and more to starboard, Admiral Dewa conformed till shortly after 4.0 all three of the Japanese light divisions, that is, the Third, Fourth, and Sixth were heading nearly north. Admiral Kataoka with the Fifth, being still on his easterly course, could not yet see them, and had just passed across their wake about three miles to the southward ; but at 4.10 he got sight of them to the north-west, that is, on his port quarter, and at once turned to join them. At the same moment Admiral Dewa made a new movement which facilitated the junction. Finding that by his great superiority of speed he had steamed completely round the enemy till he was south-westward of them, he now turned to the eastward and began engaging with his port guns. The Fourth and Sixth Divisions conformed by independent turns to starboard, while the Fifth Division held on to meet them.

During this period Admiral Enkvist's picture of the Russian cruisers and transports being the centre of a ring of fire was fully realized. They seem to have been getting shell not only from the enemy's cruisers but also either direct shots or "overs" from the Japanese Battle Squadron to the northward. "Passing by the transports," says an officer of the *Oleg*, "which "had been driven into a heap on the starboard side of our "course we noticed the *Ural* was signalling : 'I have a hole "'below the water-line which I cannot stop.'"[2] In the confusion she had been rammed by one of her consorts—either the *Monomakh* or else the *Izumrud* which was then apparently trying to get through the throng to join Admiral Enkvist.[3] The two tugs hurried up under a heavy fire to the *Ural's* assistance and in the confusion the *Anaduir* collided with the *Rus*, but with no fatal result. The two tugs took off the crew of the *Ural*, but in trying to get her in tow the *Rus* was sunk by a 12-inch shell.[4] The Russian cruisers could only reply with 6-inch and

---

[1] About 3.15, it will be remembered, one of these ships had attempted to torpedo the *Nisshin* and *Kasuga* and had then run off to the southward. (*See ante*, p. 262.)

[2] *New Material.*

[3] *Rozhestvenski No.* 2 and Smirnov.

[4] So the Russian account. Both the Japanese Sixth Division and also the Fourth were firing on a two-masted, two-funnelled steamer, thought to be the *Rus*, from 4.20 to 4.35, when the Sixth Division claimed to have sunk her. Their heaviest guns were 6-inch. The Fifth Division, which had 12·5-inch, did not claim her.

that with no degree of effectiveness. The light and sea were against them, for though the sea was stormy and covered with mist the sky was brilliantly clear. "The sun was in our eyes," says the *Oleg's* officer, "and as we were to leeward the surf " splashed up through the gun-ports and poured over the " lenses rendering them useless for some time. Besides this " the transmission of ranges from the after bridge ceased and " the automatic apparatus for firing failed to work, and so " did the gear for the supply of ammunition to the casemates. " The guns' crews were thinning down." . . . . "The " Japanese," the same authority adds, "were hardly visible. " There somewhere in the distance, out of an impenetrable wall " of fog and smoke incessantly burst forth the flashes of the " enemy's shell and immediately afterwards the water boiled " round our column." The repair ship *Kamchatka* was also entirely disabled : and the *Svyetlana* was making water fast from a hole forward. In the confusion that reigned the concentrated fire of the Japanese was in fact overwhelming, but the tables were soon to be turned.

The E. by S. course which the Russians were maintaining and which the Japanese divisions—steaming parallel—were turning to so much advantage was, in fact, forced upon them by the necessity of avoiding their own battleships. That these ships were coming south had been unknown to the Japanese, but now one after the other they became aware of the Russian main force looming out of the mist to the northward and bearing down straight for them. The Japanese cruisers were thus in a very precarious situation, especially the slow Fifth Division, which was some five miles astern of the others, Admiral Kataoka having only just got into their wake. Their own battle squadron was quite 10 miles away, and it was only at 4.50 that Admiral Togo turned south in chase of the broken divisions which had escaped him.

The precise development of the situation is not easy to trace. It would appear that as the leading Russian ships reached abreast of their own cruisers they began to turn to starboard in order to get between them and the Japanese cruisers ; and also probably with the intention of making another attempt to get to the northward. Admiral Dewa responded by leading the Third Division to port about N.E.; the other two light divisions followed his lead, while with the Fifth Division Admiral Kataoka held on to rejoin his friends. Thus they all became involved in an action with the Russian main force on opposite courses at less than 5,000 metres. It was a position far too hot to be held. Admiral Dewa's flagship, the *Kasagi,* was still making water fast from her former hit, her pumps were choked with coal dust, and he could neither stop the leak nor clear the water. He therefore turned frankly to the eastward to run off out of range. Admiral Uriu followed his example with a turn together, but not before his flagship the *Naniwa* was badly holed on the water line. The *Akashi,* his next astern in the absence of the *Takachiho,* received shell after shell and was only saved from serious injury by most of them going through her without bursting. As for the Sixth Division, its escape was miraculous. Heavy shell kept falling all round it, but only the *Idzumi* and *Akitsushima* had been hit, when, not a moment too soon, Admiral Kamimura came up at high speed and with his full division, for the *Asama* having repaired her funnel had just succeeded in rejoining, rushed in between the two opposed lines to cover the light cruisers. As he turned south-west he could see Admiral Kataoka hotly engaged. He therefore held on to cover him, and thus the Fifth Division also was able to get away with no material damage except for the *Matsushima,* who was forced to leave the line with her steering gear disabled.

The narrowest escape of all was that of the isolated *Takachiho.* She had just repaired her damages and was putting on full speed to overtake her division, when she found herself in danger of being cut off by the leading Russian ships. At 5.11 she says she saw, about 5 miles on her port bow, three of their battleships and several cruisers coming straight for her. Though she promptly broke away to the southward she came under fire, and was only saved, as it seemed, by Admiral Kamimura carrying on to cover her escape.

In the end the only important damage was that done to the *Kasagi.* All efforts to master the leak had proved unavailing. The engine room was soon flooded ; one section of the fires had to be drawn, and Admiral Dewa decided he must shift his flag. He selected the *Chitose,* ordering his other two ships to carry on and attach themselves to the Fourth Division. His intention was to follow as soon as his flag was rehoisted, but as by this time the *Kasagi* was in so critical a state that she could not be left alone, and moreover, as the intended transfer was highly hazardous from the state of the sea, he decided to take her to the nearest land himself, with the *Chitose* standing by. This was accomplished safely, and before 9.0 that night both ships put into Aburatani Bay near Tsuno-shima.

In this particular phase of the action the First Division took no part, being too far astern of the armoured cruisers to get up before it was over. It was, however, to some extent engaged. At 5.5, that is five minutes after Admiral Kamimura had gone ahead, two battleships of the *Borodino* class were seen coming up from the south-west. Neither Admiral Togo's Staff report nor that of the *Mikasa* mentions having seen them, but all the other ships of the division, except *Nisshin*, the rearmost, fired on them for about ten minutes at ranges that fell below 5,000 metres as they passed on opposite courses. The Russians must have replied, for at 5.20 the *Nisshin* was hit on the after barbette by a 12-inch shell, which broke off the gun. It is possible they were not seen from the flagship, for Admiral Togo, in spite of their having disappeared to the northward, held on south. Soon after 5.15, however, a confused mass of ships of all classes came into view going north-west. Amongst them they recognised the *Ural* and *Nakhimov*, and though the former, having been abandoned, can hardly have been moving, both received a heavy fire. Still it was not till ten minutes later, about 5.25, that Admiral Togo realised that he must change his tactics. Obviously it would not do for his whole fleet to chase further to the southward, nor could he feel safe in turning the whole of it back in chase of the ships he had passed. In spite, therefore, of his last strict order to the Second Division he decided he must divide his force once more if the scattered enemy was to be dealt with decisively. From his Staff report it appears that he himself was still unaware that any battleships had gone to the northward but only that he thought it the best direction in which to look for them. "As " the First Division," says his report, "failed in the course of " half an hour to discover the enemy's battleships on account " of the denseness of the fog and smoke, he concluded that " the chase must be to the northward, and, detaching the " Second Division, altered course at 5.28 to N.N.W. with the " object of barring the enemy's escape up the Japan Sea."

Why he did not come to this conclusion twenty minutes earlier, when the *Shikishima* and the rest distinctly saw battle-ships going north, is nowhere explained. The observation of his captains was quite accurate and coincides precisely with the Russian accounts of how their fleet managed at this time to steal away. Shortly before 5.0, apparently when they in running south lost sight of the Japanese, they had turned S.W., by which movement, as we have seen, they covered their cruisers. Then continuing the turn in no regular order as Admiral Kamimura appeared on their port quarter, they proceeded N.W., and finally at 5.5 steadied to N. 23° E. (true) thus tracing a loop till they were on the true course again for Vladivostok.[1]

This accords with what the *Takachiho* saw and took for an attempt to cut her off. The ships that threatened her must have been the rear of the Russian mass making their wide turn to the northward, those which Admiral Togo's captains saw a little earlier must have been the leading battleships which had completed the turn.

This, then, was the movement which brought the Japanese destroyers under fire during their attack on the *Suvorov*. Admiral Kamimura's dash had headed the Russian fleet back and brought them up just in time to save the flagship from destruction.[2]

Which ships they actually were which came to the *Suvorov's* rescue it is impossible to say. Cruisers, transports, and battleships were now all mingled together. By this time " about 5.30 " says the Second Division report " the enemy's formation had been " completely destroyed. Some ships were running northward, " some westward, and some were making off to the south-west ; " and the Russian fleet, like a flock of ravens, made no attempt " at co-operation." Admiral Kamimura says nothing of having received a signal giving him liberty of action, as the First Division report implies, but what he did was to hold on as he was to head off the ships which seemed to be making to the south-west.

His prompt dash had without doubt saved the light cruisers and completed the confusion of the enemy, but its continuation whether authorised or not, again completely separated him from the First Division. When at 5.27 Admiral Togo decided to double back the enemy were disappearing into the mist and smoke on his starboard quarter. The turn he made was

---

[1] *Last Days* and *Rozhestvenski No.* 2. The latter's times are followed. Those of the *Last Days* are too late to agree with the Japanese accounts.

[2] The *Last Days* suggests Admiral Togo turned back on receipt of a wireless message from Okinoshima. The island was visible to the Russians about the time of his turn, but the Japanese History says nothing of any such message.

about 14 points in succession, so that he was now running back about N.N.W.

As for the cruisers, the Fifth Division continued to run on its south-easterly course till 5.30, when, finding no trace of the fleet it turned north-east. The Third, Fourth and Sixth Divisions, which were more or less together, went back south-west with the idea of repeating their attack on the enemy's rear, which was then actually to the westward of them. Thus the third phase of the action came to an end with the Japanese fleet scattered into four portions and the main force of the enemy ahead of them somewhere to the northward on its true course for Vladivostok.

CHAPTER XVIII.

The Battle of the Sea of Japan.

Fourth Phase—The Chase.

[Chart XII. Diagrams 8 to 12.]

For the Japanese, when Admiral Togo turned northward in chase of the lost enemy, the situation was far from favourable. That they had broken up the enemy's formation was clear. It was also evident they had done them considerable damage, but the actual extent of it was unknown. Two battleships were certainly missing, but so far as they could tell the main Russian force was still formidable, and that force, as on August 10th and at Ulsan, had succeeded at last in getting past them. The position was even worse than on the two previous occasions, for the enemy's battle squadron was now unlocated, and with failing daylight deepening the obscurity of the mist the chances of recovering touch before nightfall were precarious.

To add to the anxiety, although the Japanese claim that their "battle speed" of 15 knots was being maintained, yet, owing to the shell damage which they had received, it can only have been done at the cost of great strain on the engine-room staff. At this time, too, the seas, which were breaking heavily on the port bow, were also causing trouble, especially to the *Nisshin* and *Kasuga*.[1] Nor was the fighting efficiency of the battle squadron unimpaired. The *Mikasa* had been hit 29 times, and though her armament had been but little hurt, her funnels and ventilators were much damaged, her armour had been pierced several times, and her casualties were little short of a hundred, including five officers wounded. The other flagship of the division, *Nisshin*, being the rear ship had also suffered a good deal. Her casualties numbered nearly 50, including Admiral Misu and two of his staff, and she had lost both guns in her fore barbette, and one in the other. The *Fuji* and *Shikishima* had each lost a 12-inch gun (the latter from a burst), but in the other ships there was no very serious injury.

Under these conditions, with nothing between the enemy and their destination except the flotilla which had failed so

---

[1] *Attaché Reports*, IV., 16. The course at this time was about N.N.W. and the wind presumably was still a little south of west.

often before, a stern chase could give little hope of turning
the success they had gained into the decisive victory that was
wanted. And as for annihilation, it seemed out of the question,
even if the action could be resumed next day, since all ships
had expended from a third to half their ammunition.[1]

The first thing that Admiral Togo came across as he chased
N.N.W. was the *Ural*, and not being able to see she was
abandoned, he altered course to run by her at a distance of
2,000 metres, and for about 10 minutes wasted more ammunition on her. The *Mikasa* even gave her a torpedo (her fourth),
and so did the *Shikishima*, the latter claiming a hit. The 47
millimetre guns (3-pounders) were used and "made such
" excellent practice," the report says, "that the shell-bursts
" dazzled the eyes, and a huge conflagration was started." It
was now nearly a quarter to six, and Rear-Admiral Togo could
be seen coming up with his Sixth Division. At 5.25, when the
Russian main force had disappeared, he had turned back from
his north-easterly course about 16 points to close the enemy's
rear, and on his way had sighted the *Ural*, when he at once
turned north to deal with her. The abandoned cruiser was
therefore left to him, but at 5.51, before he could fire a shot,
she sank.

To continue the chase Admiral Togo was heading N.N.W.
and firing again on the helpless *Kamchatka*, but not seeing the
Suvorov, which must have been close by. About half a mile
away from where the repair ship was drifting the destroyer
Buini had found the burning flagship, and by a very fine display
of seamanship had succeeded in taking off the wounded admiral.
Scarcely conscious from his fractured skull, he had been carried
to the destroyer in spite of his protests, murmuring in a scarcely
audible voice, "Command to Nebogatov—Vladivostok—course
" N. 23° E."; and by 5.50 the *Buini* was away flying the signal,
" Admiral transfers the command to Nebogatov." The rest of
the Russian fleet has just passed by the flagship northward, and

---

[1] *Attaché Reports*, III., 115. The Japanese regarded the expenditure as
small compared with that of August 10 and 14. They claimed it as
evidence of the perfection of their fire discipline. "The Japanese fire,"
says the report, "was sometimes irritatingly slow, not because they could
" not fire faster, but that it seems to have been generally known that they
" were in for two days' fighting at least, and that the ammunition had
" got to last. They were therefore most deliberate. . . . The dis-
" cipline in this respect was marvellous. . . . At long ranges there
" was no necessity to steady the men, though this was sometimes done;
" they did so obvious a thing as to slow down of themselves."

by this time the courses of the opposed forces had converged sufficiently for each to have sight of the other.

At 5.52 Admiral Togo had altered to W.N.W. in his search for the enemy, but in a minute or two, seeing indications of destroyers threatening an attack, he was forced to turn away to N.E. and opened fire to drive them off. While thus engaged at 5.57 he made out two battleships of the *Borodino* class some 6,300 metres W.N.W. of him. As they appeared to be heading north he turned back at 6.0 to his previous course N.N.W. and opened fire ; " but," says the *Mikasa's* report, " as they were " steaming on the same course we experienced considerable " difficulty in reducing the range." It was, in fact, the old story of August 10 and 14 over again, as Admiral Togo quickly discovered.

In a few minutes it began to appear that all the other Russian battleships that were still effective, were following the two he had first seen, and he realised what the long respite had meant for the enemy. They had, in fact, been able to re-form. The *Borodino* was now leading and had just made the signal " Transports' course N. 23° E. out of the Korean " Strait. Speed 8 knots." [1] Following her was the *Orel*. Then some way astern came Admiral Nebogatov in the *Nikolai* leading his division, *Apraxin*, *Senyavin* and *Ushakov*, while the shattered *Alexandr* being unable to keep station had fallen out and was struggling on abreast of the *Senyavin* to starboard. Then followed the three remaining ships of the Second Division, *Sisoi*, *Navarin* and *Nakhimov*. The cruisers and transports which, presumably in consequence of the *Borodino's* last signal, had been trying to get to the eastward of the battleships, altered as the Japanese battle squadron appeared in the S.E. so as to get to the disengaged side. There they formed two lines—the three transports, *Anaduir*, *Irtuish* and *Koreya* with the *Almaz* and *Svyetlana* to starboard, while to port and a little in advance Admiral Enkvist led a line composed of the rest of the cruisers in the following order : *Oleg*, *Avrora*, *Donskoi*, *Monomakh*, *Zhemchug* and *Izumrud*. The destroyers were partly with the *Oleg* and partly with the transports.[2] Except, therefore, for the fact that the Japanese were slightly astern the position at the beginning of the action was reconstituted and a new engagement began.

---

[1] Schubert, *New Material*.
[2] *Last Days* and *Rozhestvenski No. 2.*

At first the Japanese fire was ineffective, while the shells of the Russians began to fall very close. They had, in fact, the great advantage that the setting sun was behind them, and it was impossible at the great range for the Japanese with the glare in their eyes to lay accurately or mark the fall of their shot. They were concentrating as usual on the leading ships, but it was not till 6.12 that even the *Mikasa's* range was down to 6,000 metres. A few minutes later the *Borodino*, which had hitherto been leading north, altered two points to port, presumably to avoid the increasing pressure from the Japanese fire which followed the turn they had made N.N.W. at 6.0.[1] The Russian movement seems to have exposed the *Alexandr* to a heavy concentration. Being in difficulties from her previous punishment, she was, as we have seen, out of line to starboard, and she now began to fall still more astern flying a signal of distress and showing a heavy list to port. "An enormous fire," says an eye witness, "was raging on her boat deck, her stem was " quite distorted, and on the port side forward could be seen " a hole 20 feet across. I thought that in a few seconds she " would share the fate of the *Oslyabya*, but apparently she " began to recover, and slowly she joined the line astern of " the *Senyavin* and continued the action."[2]

The Japanese fire was improving in spite of the bad light. By 6.25 the range was down to 5,500 metres, the enemy being still before the beam of the *Mikasa*; but the Russian fire was scarcely less good. "They straightened out the lines of their " formation," says the Report of the Japanese First Division, " and gave us a well-aimed bombardment. The action again " became very hot. All our ships first of all concentrated their " fire on the Russian leader; numerous hits were made and she " was soon completely hidden in smoke, which made aiming " difficult. Moreover, the second Russian ship, said to have " been the *Orel*, fought very well; her projectiles fell together " and close to our ships, the spray they dashed up frequently " drenching the bridges. We therefore changed our aim to the " second ship "—a clear case of the danger of concentration without a proportion of defensive fire. Still, by good luck the

---

[1] At 6.0 ($=$ 6.20) according to *Rozhestvenski No. 2*, when the range did not exceed 7,000 yards. The report says the Japanese conformed five minutes later, but nothing is said of any such alteration in their own reports. The Japanese Chart does not show a Russian turn till about 6.30.

[2] *Last Days.*

Japanese suffered no serious hit. A 12-pounder shell burst on the *Shikishima's* foremast killing an officer and one man and wounding two officers and three men. The *Mikasa* had a 6-inch shell (her 30th hit) through No. 10 casemate, which, bursting inside against the barrel of the gun, wrecked it, killed a first-class petty officer and wounded an officer and six of the gun's crew. None of the rear ships were touched.

Although it must have been before 6.30 that the Russians began to turn away [1] it was not till 6.42 that Admiral Togo was aware of the movement. By that time the range was found to have increased to 7,000 metres, and three minutes later he began to lead round to port on a north-westerly course. "But," his Staff report adds, "the Russians then went "further round to port and made it difficult for us to close "on them." No further effort, in fact, was made to do so, and this may partly be explained by the fact that just as the *Mikasa* turned, a 12-inch shell burst on the skylight of the dispensary abaft the fore barbette, smashing up the contents of the room and the surrounding structures, and wounding a petty officer. The next entry in her report is: "After this "the range opened out again, till at 6.59 the enemy's leader "was 7,200 metres away; but we continued firing our main "armament."

The range continued to increase, for Admiral Togo, by keeping the course he was on for his rendezvous north of Matsushima, was now forging ahead of the Russians. For about five minutes more he could see he was still making hits, but so were the enemy; for at 7.0 the *Nisshin* received a 12-inch shell on her fore barbette, which broke her last 8-inch gun, besides two smaller shells which together killed two men and wounded two officers and six men. But at 7.10, as the sun was close down on the fog bank, the *Mikasa* ceased fire, and ship by ship the rest of the division did the same.

It would seem that Admiral Togo was content to have headed off the enemy once more. At that late hour he may well have considered it useless to close, and have made up his mind to trust to the flotilla attack and a second action next day. As to his ability to recover contact next morning further to the north he can have had little doubt, for his light cruiser divisions were now all coming up upon the

---

[1] The time marked on the chart published by Smirnov is 6.30.

enemy's rear, and he knew his armoured cruiser division must be pressing them from the southward.

About 6.0—that is, just when Admiral Togo was beginning to engage the enemy's main force—Admiral Kamimura had, in fact, abandoned his chase of the Russian cruisers. His reasons are interesting. " Their speed," he says, "was greater " than ours, and the range gradually increased ; " but, in truth, it would seem that, although it is evident his division was no longer getting its full speed, the cause of the range increasing was not loss of speed, but that the Russians had turned north again after their main force, and he was chasing in the wrong direction. "There was no hope of overtaking " them," the report continues, "and, moreover, it was near " the time of sunset, and the Second Division was out " of sight of the First. This last fact had the greatest " weight with Admiral Kamimura, since it would be dis- " advantageous in the subsequent operations should the First " and Second Divisions become widely separated during the " night. Accordingly at 6.3 he abandoned the chase, turned " to port, and proceeded for a spot where he judged he " would find the First Division and the enemy's main force."[1]

As to what this spot was he was quite at fault. Instead of turning to starboard and going north he had turned to port and, at 6.7 steamed on a course E.S.E., "wishing," he says, " to rejoin the First Division." It is clear, then, he can have had no idea that Admiral Togo had turned north, and he was on quite a wrong scent. Nothing was to be seen but the *débris* of the first action. As the course he was pursuing led him over the waters where the fight had culminated, he reported that he passed through "drifting masses of broken boats and " half-burnt ship's fittings ; and a large number of men, " thought to belong to the *Oslyabya* were seen struggling " amongst the breaking waves, and supported merely by " broken spars and wreckage. They waved their hands and " shouted to us with piteous cries for help, which wrung " the hearts of all those that heard and saw."[2]

But there could be no thought of giving assistance, for as he was then hunting blindly for his chief he caught sight of the Sixth Division away on his port bow, firing into the

---

[1] *Second Division Staff Report* ("Second engagement"). See also *Attaché Reports*, III., 110.

[2] *Ibid.*

Kamchatka and *Suvorov*. Accordingly, to quote his Staff report, "Admiral Kamimura at 6.15 turned to port on a northerly "course in order not to obstruct the operations of our small "cruisers." But there can be little doubt that his main object was to find out where the First Division was and by good luck he had stumbled on the only people that could tell him, for it was Rear-Admiral Togo alone of all the cruiser admirals who had seen the Commander-in-Chief disappear to the northward. There can, in fact, be little doubt that it was the Sixth Division that put him on the right scent again, and but for the information he thus chanced to obtain it is difficult to see how he could have been in position to take part in what was to prove the decisive episode of the day.[1] As it was he was now in a fair way to rejoin his group, and seeing as he came abreast of the two Russian ships that they were little better than wrecks, he contented himself with giving them a few shots as he passed and carried on to the northward.

Rear-Admiral Togo's presence on the spot was due to the fact that of all the cruiser divisions he had been first to get away north, and, having seen the *Ural* sink, by 6.0 he was firing into the two isolated ships. In half-an-hour he was joined by Admiral Uriu, who had picked up the *Takachiho* again, and with the *Otowa* and *Niitaka* of the Third Division, which Admiral Dewa had attached to him after the mishap to the *Kasagi*, he had six ships in line. A quarter of an hour later Admiral Kataoka came up with the three ships he had left, and joined in with his heavy guns. Thereupon Admiral Uriu, seeing the flashes of the guns of the enemy's battleships, ahead, ceased fire at 6.30, and going off in chase of them left the *Suvorov*, as Admiral Kamimura had done, to the Kataoka group, whose special function it was to deal with the enemy's disabled ships.

Soon after Admiral Kamimura had passed the *Suvorov* and carried on northward he had been rewarded with the sight of a number of Russian ships about 11,000 metres on his port bow. He could make out that the *Nakhimov* was rearmost of them, and that they appeared to be "coming southward."[2] From

---

[1] His flagship's report has these words : " Meeting the First (sic) Division at 6.11 the *Idzumo* turned round to the north." But it is clear that the flag-captain must have written "Sixth," not " First" Division.

[2] *Tokiwa's* report says she could make out a battleship of the *Borodino* class, as well as the *Sisoi Veliki*, *Navarin*, and *Nakhimov*.

their apparent course, and possibly also from the sound of
firing, he concluded they were being pressed by the First
Division.   It was just at this time that the *Borodino* had begun
to lead away to port under Admiral Togo's fire, and there are
indications that some of the ships at least may have been going
actually south of west.   "Fighting on the starboard side," says
a Russsian account, "the squadron edged more and more to
" port, so that at the moment the *Alexandr* went down (about
" 6.55) our course was again towards the Island of Tsushima." [1]
Some movement there clearly was which went far to justify
Admiral Kamimura's appreciation, and, having formed it, he
altered course to north-west.[2]   His intention, he says, was "to
" close the Russians," though it is evident his move would
also have the effect of heading them back to his chief.   But
in a few minutes he could see away on his starboard bow
the flashes of the First Division guns showing clearly out of
the fog in the gathering darkness, and, in accordance with his
resolution that his duty was to rejoin if possible, at 6.40 he
altered towards them N. $\frac{1}{2}$ E.   He then became aware that
more Russian ships were directly ahead of him, which at 6.46
began to fire on him.   He therefore inclined half a point to
starboard to bring his guns to bear, and engaged four big ships
that were now to the N.N.W., but not nearer than 7,000 metres.
For a few minutes the Russian shell fell very close, but it was
growing dark so rapidly that it was soon impossible to see
accurately at so great a range.   The fire consequently died
away, and at 7.4 Admiral Kamimura turned his Division
4 points together to port, in order to close the scarcely visible
enemy.

During all this time the Fifth and Sixth Divisions had been
pounding the ill-fated *Suvorov* at close range, but without
either sinking her or silencing her fitful fire.   Yet it is difficult to
imagine what the Russian Flagship's condition must have been,
as Admiral Kataoka's 12·5-inch shell kept bursting upon her.
" She scarcely looked like a man-of-war at all," he says.   " Her
" interior was ablaze, and the holes in her side and gunports
" shot out tongues of flame.   Thick volumes of black smoke
" rolled low on her deck, and her whole appearance was in-
" describably pathetic.   She turned to starboard and port, as
" if seeking to escape, while the two or three stern guns, which

---

[1] *Last Days.*
[2] At 6.29, *Attaché Reports*, III., III.

" were all that remained to her, kept up an heroic defence."
At 7.0 the *Kamchatka* turned over and went down, and then
Rear-Admiral Togo was for finishing the flagship with his torpedo-boats. But the Fifth Division kept up a deliberate fire,
and he could get no chance. "Thereupon, fearing," he says,
" to lose touch with the enemy's main force in the approaching
" darkness, he called his attached flotilla up to him, and
" proceeded rapidly in the direction of the Russian battle
" squadron."

No sooner was he gone than Admiral Kataoka ceased fire,
and, " on account of the approaching darkness and desiring to
" save his ammunition, ordered the 11th torpedo-boat division
" to attack."[1] Running in at 20 knots over water dotted with
the drowning crew of the *Kamchatka*, they swept round the bow
of the forlorn flagship, and at 7.20 delivered their attack at 300
metres. Seven torpedoes were fired, and "three of them," says
the flotilla account, "exploded with tremendous reports, and the
" target ship began to take a list to port. The third apparently
" exploded the magazines, for black and yellow fumes poured
" out of the *Suvorov*, and, wrapped in these and in spurting
" tongues of flame, she finally turned over. For a short time
" she floated bottom upwards, and then at 7.30 lifted her bow
" high in the air and slid rapidly out of sight." While she had
a gun above water she fired, and not a man survived her of all
that crew, to whose stubborn gallantry no words can do justice. If there is immortality in naval memory it is hers and
theirs.[2]

Meanwhile, tragedies as terrible had been occurring in the
main force. One of them had been seen by Admiral Kamimura
as, in quarter line, he began to close the enemy. About 6.50
the *Alexandr*, which had been struggling on astern of the
Senyavin, listed heavily to port, and with a signal of distress
flying sheered out of the line to port. Then, before anything
could be done to assist her, she suddenly turned turtle and sank,
carrying with her every man of her company except four.[3]

After the catastrophe there was a lull in the firing for about
five minutes. Admiral Togo was just losing sight of the enemy,
and the Second Division was still in quarter line trying to

---

[1] The 11th division (Commander Fujimoto Uruijiro) were 2nd class
Japanese-built boats of 88 tons and 24 knots. This division was one of
five attached to the Third (Admiral Kataoka's) Squadron.

[2] There perished with her 40 officers and 888 men.

[3] The loss with her was 30 officers and 806 men.

close the range. In the respite the *Zhemchug* ran in to try to save the crew of the lost ship, but the whole scene had been visible to Admiral Kamimura, and at 7.10 he turned into line ahead N.N.W., and, seeing there were two destroyers with the *Zhemchug*, opened fire. The cruiser was quickly hidden in the smoke of bursting shells, and when she could be seen again she was hurrying away after the main force.

But even this was not the end. At 7.20 the *Borodino*, on whom and the *Orel* the First Division was concentrating its last shots, was seen to be badly hit, and all her after-part was quickly wrapped in flames.[1] A few minutes later the *Fuji* fired her parting shot, and with startling results. It struck the *Borodino* forward, and as it burst an immense column of smoke shot up, and in two or three minutes the whole ship was a mass of smoke and fire.[2] In this condition she kept firing her 6-inch guns, and then quite suddenly turned over and floated bottom upwards. From the nearest Russian ships a few men were seen for a time waving their arms on her keel, but nothing could be done for them. They soon disappeared in the wash of the other ships as they passed, and the *Borodino*, hanging for a while on the surface like the back of some monstrous fish, gradually went down no one knew when.[3] So at the eleventh hour the battle was turned beyond question into a decisive victory for the Japanese, and the heart of the Russian fleet was broken. " The loss of the *Borodino*," says an officer of the *Oleg*, "which happened before our eyes, was so unex-" pected that we were stupefied, and, uncovering our heads, " we gazed on the foaming grave of this heroic ship. . . . " The sun had set, and in its golden rays on the horizon from " south-west through west to north appeared the black specks " of the Japanese torpedo craft barring our passage." There was no going on, and the *Orel* rounding the spot where the *Borodino* had disappeared led away to the south-west, forcing the cruisers and transports, which had been on the port quarter, to conform to the movement.

By that time even the Japanese Second Division had ceased fire, and as the enemy, turning to port, disappeared to the westward Admiral Kamimura was holding on to join his chief. For a while Admiral Togo steamed to the north, and then

---

[1] The *Shikishima* claims these hits.

[2] *Attaché Reports*, IV., 19.

[3] *Last Days* and Admiral Nebogatov's evidence. Only one man was saved. The loss was 32 officers and 822 men.

about half-past seven, having sent away his despatch-vessel with orders for all divisions to make for the north side of Matsushima, he turned due east till at 8.0 the Second Division had come up, and then together they headed for the rendezvous. As the four cruiser divisions got the order they all threw off their attached flotillas and did the same. So in the gathering darkness the great battle came to an end, with the torpedo craft creeping up to play their part on all that was left of the Baltic Fleet.

CHAPTER XIX.

The Battle of the Sea of Japan.

The Flotilla Attack.

[Chart XII.   Diagram 12.]

WHEN at sunset Admiral Togo broke off the action he was about abreast of the extreme northern point of Tsushima and his rendezvous at Matsushima lay nearly 200 miles to the northward.   Ahead of him were three of his attached flotilla divisions (the 1st and 2nd of destroyers, the 9th of torpedo-boats), which for some time past in anticipation of the order to attack at nightfall had been pushing forward so as to get into position for running in on the reverse course to the enemy.   The two destroyer divisions had been attending the battle squadron all day in spite of the heavy seas, but the performance of the 9th torpedo division was specially creditable.[1] When in the morning the signal was made for the flotillas to take refuge this division with others had run into Miura Bay, but at 2.52, shortly after getting word that an action was proceeding, its commander had taken it to sea to rejoin. Though the weather had mended a little it was all they could do to proceed.   Still they persevered, till shortly before 7.0 p.m. they got sight of the battle squadron and were thus just in time to get into correct position.

Further to the southward were three other destroyer divisions the 3rd, 4th, and 5th, which had been held back by their attempts to torpedo the *Suvorov*.   Since that time the 4th, after running from the Russian battleships that surprised them, had been acting independently while the other two had been keeping company with the Second Division.[2]

---

[1] *Aotaka, Kari, Tsubame, Hato* (Commander Kawase), all first-class boats (137 tons, 29 knots) built at Kuré, apparently on the design of the Normand boats.

[2] By the organisation of the fleet Admiral Togo's attached flotilla consisted of the 1st, 2nd, and 3rd divisions of destroyers and the 14th of torpedo-boats; Admiral Kamimura's of the 4th and 5th of destroyers and the 9th and 19th of torpedo-boats; but apparently as the 4th division of destroyers had subsequently been given special duties it would seem that the 3rd division had been attached to Admiral Kamimura in its stead and the 9th torpedo division transferred to Admiral Togo.

The case of the 4th destroyer division which had not actually attacked the *Suvorov* also calls for notice. It will be recalled that on the 26th it had been attached to Admiral Dewa's division to assist in the watch on the Fourth Guard Line, but had been forced back by the weather to Osaki. In the morning of the 27th it had rejoined him and during the action had remained under his orders till 2.35, when he went off at high speed, and as it could no longer keep up Admiral Dewa then gave it liberty of action, but the signal was not taken in and it eventually joined Admiral Kamimura. This, however, cannot have been with a mere view of acting with his other attached divisions, for according to the Published History it had been given special functions which were not to come into operation till after the mass of the flotillas had attacked. Of these special functions the Confidential History says nothing. But from information supplied to our Naval Attaché it appears they were to be used for offensive mining. "The 4th destroyer division," he was told, "was ordered to " take on board each unit eight 100 lb. mines previous to " the battle, and these mines were to be used if occasion offered " to lay across the path of the enemy." Whether or not it was intended to lay them on the Fourth Guard Line we do not know, but in any case the weather rendered such an operation impossible. But it is clear they still had them on board, a fact which renders their attack on the *Suvorov* under fire a venture of extraordinary daring, for primarily they were entitled to regard themselves as mine-laying vessels rather than as torpedo-craft. Their actual position at sunset was about abreast of the Russians, so that while the 3rd and 5th divisions ran in from the eastward, the 4th division moved round the stern of the armoured cruisers as though to get into a favourable position for mining if the enemy were headed back.

The rest of the torpedo-boat divisions were not so well placed. Most of them had taken refuge at Miura or Kosaki according to orders, while two, the 10th and 15th, being part of those attached to the Third Squadron, had followed the Sixth Division ; but all had found the greatest difficulty in steaming and were well to the southward of the enemy with no very clear idea of where their objective was, or what the rest of the flotilla was doing. The whole of the crews, moreover, must have been greatly exhausted, and in no trim to do themselves justice. Starting from Miura with a gale at S.S.W. they had had it abeam as they made for the scene of action and from four to ten hours the various divisions had been struggling with a sea which the Commander-in-Chief considered unsafe at least for torpedo-boats. The Staff Report gives a graphic picture of what they had gone through when the time came to attack. " The wind," it says, " which had " been blowing a gale all day, now relented a little, but there " was still a high sea sufficient to roll the boats as much " as 50° or 60°. The racing of the propellers and the shock " of the heavy seas seemed enough to snap the hulls in " two. The compass-needles spun round and rendered the " binnacles quite useless for steering. Telescopes and glasses " were so drenched with spray that nothing could be seen " through them, and the men in the torpedo craft had been " blinded all day with spray and spume till their eyes were " suffused with blood and their sight much impaired."[1] Other reports confirm the disastrous effects of the day-long exposure upon the all-important factor of vision. As for the torpedo-boats they had been in constant danger of foundering. The 10th division, which with the 15th had clung to Rear-Admiral Togo's Division, report that from time to time they were swamped by following seas and even took them in over the beam " so that they had the utmost difficulty in steaming."[2]

On the other hand, if the Japanese flotilla was in no condition to develop its highest power of attack, the Russian fleet was in no condition to receive one. Of the four ships of the First Division all were gone except the *Orel* and she was severely damaged. Most of her guns were out of action and her funnels so knocked about that she could get no speed. In the Second Division the flagship *Oslyabya* had been sunk, the *Sisoi* was so badly holed below the water-line that she could scarcely steam and the *Navarin* was in an even worse condition. In Admiral Nebogatov's Division the *Ushakov* had also very severe underwater injuries, but the other two, *Apraxin* and *Senyavin*, though a good deal knocked about, were in fair fighting trim. Of the cruisers, the only one that had been seriously crippled was the *Svyetlana*, which was down by the head with some holes below the water-line forward. All the rest were still capable of high speed and had suffered little or nothing to their armament.

With eight or nine hours of darkness before them and an open sea there was some hope of the bulk of them getting

---

[1] *Confidential History*, Bk. II., Ch. ii., Sec. 1, " General Summary."
[2] *Ibid*, Sec. 9.

through to their destination. But for the moment their way was barred, and as they saw the destroyers coming in from both the northward and eastward they turned away, through south-west to about south, to throw them off. Although it was generally known that the command had been transferred to Admiral Nebogatov he had not yet got a hold on the demoralised squadron and the movement he had made to avoid the flotilla attack was executed in no order and a good deal of confusion. Ships turned together or in succession as they pleased, while the cruisers, instead of endeavouring to cover the battleships from the threatening attack, scrambled away to keep on their disengaged side.

To some extent this confusion served them well, for, blinded as the leading Japanese boats were by the head seas as they came down from the northward, they could not make out what the enemy's formation was and so were unable to decide how to attack. Shortly before 8.0, when it became quite dark, the enemy was entirely lost sight of, but as they then began to burn their searchlights their general position was easily located. The 2nd destroyer division, which was amongst those which had been coming down from the north, then decided to rush in on the van of the enemy's main body. By this time the Russians had restored something like order. Admiral Nebogatov was leading the battleships, the *Orel* had taken station astern of him and the *Apraxin* and *Senyavin* were in her wake. The *Ushakov*, owing to her injuries, was falling behind, but she was closely supported by the *Sisoi* and *Navarin*. The *Izumrud* had just joined up, and the injured *Svyetlana*, with the slow armoured cruisers *Monomakh* and *Donskoi* were in sight, but Admiral Enkvist, with the fast cruisers *Oleg*, *Avrora*, and *Zhemchug*, was nowhere to be seen.

Having thus got fair control, Admiral Nebogatov had begun to turn to starboard in order to get north again, and as the Japanese destroyers reappeared to make their attack he was heading west.[1] According to the Japanese, Admiral Enkvist was ahead of him, and Admiral Enkvist himself says he, too, was trying to get north when the first destroyer attack headed him back. The result was that as the Japanese rushed in they came under a heavy cross fire from the battleships and the fast cruisers, but without flinching they turned to port and delivered their attack on the battleships upon the opposite course.

---

[1] *Last Days.* "The squadron at 7.50 (= 8.10) was steering westward."

Keeping a correct line they fired their torpedoes in succession, at from 400 to 500 metres, but not with impunity. The Russian light armament was well served, and though the leading boat got off both her torpedoes, she was hit many times on the deck and funnels, and lost one man killed and five wounded. The second boat had her main steam pipe cut by a shell before she could fire, and for about ten minutes was exposed almost at a standstill to the enemy's fire. Before she could get clear she had lost an officer killed and 12 men wounded, and was so badly damaged that she had to crawl back to Takeshiki. The other two boats each got in two torpedoes, with the loss of only four men wounded, and were not put out of action. Still, not a single hit had been made, and having spent their ready torpedoes they had to make off to the Matsushima rendezvous getting up their spare ones on the way, an operation which they describe as very difficult and dangerous in the high sea and without lights.

This attack was all over at 8.20 and by that time the Russians seem to have turned again south-west, so at least they are described by the next group to attack. This was the 5th destroyer division, one of those to the eastward which had been engaged with the *Suvorov ;* but having the wind on the port bow, it was making heavy weather of it and was already broken up. " The waves," they say, " drenched the bridges and " the spray lashed the faces of those on deck, blinding them so " much that soon after sunset all the boats became separated " and were forced to decide upon attacking separately."[1] No. 1 failed to find anything till 10.30, when she fired her last torpedo at an isolated ship and had to go back to Miura for a fresh supply. No. 2 got suddenly into the rays of a searchlight, when her tubes were still lashed up for fear of the rolling, and was forced to run out of range with a shell in her bunkers, that started a fire. No. 4 managed to get in both her torpedoes at 500 metres, without visible effect, and then went off to Fusan to get more. No. 3, *Yugiri,* was the most unfortunate of all. Having fired one shot, she missed the chance of a second, and was retiring to seek a fresh opportunity when she saw another destroyer, which she took for one of her lost consorts and made to join her.

In fact, it was the *Harusame,* leading boat of the 1st division, which had come down from the northward. This division

---

[1] *Confidential History,* Bk. II., Ch. ii, Sec. 6.

consisted of five boats, and for the attack had been divided by its senior officer, Commander Fujimoto, into three sub-divisions.[1]   At 8.40 the first subdivision was in full career to attack when, according to Commander Fujimoto's report, he suddenly saw another division (which was the 5th) rushing upon him two points on his starboard bow.   By putting his helm hard over he just managed to clear the leader, but her next astern, the *Yugiri*, crashed into him and rammed a hole nearly a yard wide below the water-line forward.   Her consort had to stand by, so that neither could attack.   Still, the damage was made good with blankets, and not only was the *Harusame* kept afloat, but she and her consort continued searching for the enemy in constant danger, he says, of a fresh collision from other divisions, " which were running in all directions at great speed through " the high seas."[2]   As for the *Yugiri*, her bow was bent over to starboard, and with great difficulty she was kept from sinking.   Still, in an hour, the danger was over, and at three knots she was able to make her way back to Sasebo.

The failure of this attempt was the more serious for the general success of the flotilla attack, because just before it was made Admiral Nebogatov, in accordance with his chief's last-mentioned order, had begun to head N. 23° E. for Vladivostok.   Immediately after the attack he also extinguished his searchlights, with the result that the main force was scarcely troubled again.   "The Japanese torpedo craft," says a Russian authority, "steaming ahead at full speed usually did not notice " them at first and rushed past them, whilst those that did " fire their torpedoes only made misses."[3]   This is corroborated by the Japanese authorities, who say that it was only the enemy's searchlights which enabled the flotilla to find them, and the searchlights were burning only in the second-class battleships and the old cruisers which had been falling astern.

Guided by their lights the 3rd destroyer division, another of those from the eastward, got in between the battleships and the cruisers between 9.0 and 9.15, and found itself in no little danger.   One of the boats was very nearly run down, and owing to the irregularity of the Russian lines all found difficulty in selecting a favourable target.   Still under

---

[1] Commander Fujimoto Hideshiro to be distinguished from Commander Fujimoto Uruijiro of the 11th torpedo division.

[2] *Ibid.*, sec. 2.

[3] *Last Days.*

a hot fire, both from guns and rifles, they fired between them seven shots and only one had to retire to Fusan for repairs.

During this period there was considerable confusion in the attack, for at least six other groups were also trying to get in —namely, the two remaining sub-divisions of the 1st destroyer division, and the 1st, 17th and 18th torpedo-boat divisions, the earliest to come up from the south-west, as well as the 9th from the north. The second section of the Fujimoto division carried out a clean attack in the full glare of the searchlights about 9.10. Both boats fired two torpedoes very close and both got away unscathed ; but with the third section, which consisted of the *Akatsuki* alone, it was very different. As the 1st torpedo-boat division was running up at high speed they saw her cutting athwart their course, and to avoid a collision the leading boat No. 69 had to wrench her helm over so violently that her hull was badly strained. Water came in fast, she could no longer steer, and two hours later she sank, her crew being saved by a boat of the 9th division that was standing by. As the *Akatsuki* charged through the line, the rest of the division was broken up, and only two boats succeeded in attacking. One of them was so much cut up that she lost three killed and five wounded, and only just succeeded in reaching Takeshiki ; while the other only got off one shot.

The 17th division which was attacking at the same time fared no better. The leading boat before she could fire a shot received a shell through her starboard boiler, and her forward tube and rudder chains were smashed. Thus helpless she found herself close to what seemed a disabled Russian ship. It must have been either the *Nakhimov*, which was torpedoed in one of the first attacks, or more probably the *Navarin*, which about 9.0 was so much down by the stern, owing to injuries received in the battle, that she had to slow down and fall out of the line.[1] Whichever ship it was she was able to defend herself and the helpless torpedo-boat

---

[1] She had been holed four times on the water-line, twice by 12-inch shell. Her captain was severely wounded and had given up the command. "Up to 9.0 p.m.," says the author of *The Last Days*, "she had managed to keep up with the squadron, whilst successfully repelling all the torpedo attacks, but by that time she had settled so much by the stern that the water was on the upper deck aft and had reached the 12-inch turret." This account was obtained from a seaman who was her sole survivor. For his account of how she was torpedoed, *see post*, p. 302.

before drifting clear had lost seven men killed and one officer and several men wounded. All efforts to save her failed, and soon after 10.0 she suddenly went down stem foremost, all the crew but seven being picked up by another boat. The other three boats managed to attack, but the last was badly cut up and all had to go back to Takeshiki.

The attack of the 18th division was similarly spoilt by something else crossing their bows, so that they had to turn away to avoid a collision, and they also got separated. When at last they were able to come in again the heavy sea rendered the boats so unmanageable that accurate work was impossible. Still each got off one or two torpedoes, but they were all severely handled, and the rear boat, after losing two killed and nine wounded, had to be abandoned in a sinking condition.

It is possible that what spoilt their attack was one of the 9th division. They were then coming down from the north in two sections, and being first-class boats did better in the heavy seas. Between them they fired on the rear ships two torpedoes, rescued the crew of No. 69 of the 1st division, and, although heavily fired on, got away with nothing but a few traces of shell marks on their hulls and fittings.

Up to this time, then, the work of the flotillas had been anything but effective. The three best Russian battleships had got clear away on their course to the northward and were completely lost. So also had Admiral Enkvist with three of the best cruisers. His actual movements are very uncertain. He himself says he made several attempts to follow Admiral Nebogatov to the north, but every time was headed off by torpedo attacks, till finally he gave it up and headed south in hopes of meeting the fleet in the morning, and getting coal from the colliers that had been left behind.[1] According to an officer in his flagship, who gives a more detailed report, he first ran S.S.W. till nearly 9.30, and then turned through west to the northward again.[2] Then he says they were again attacked, and seeing the enemy's lights ahead they turned back S.W. According to this authority, these attempts to get to the north were repeated several times and were always frustrated by torpedo attacks, of which seventeen in all took place, and it was not till 1.0 a.m., he says, that they finally held away to pass the Korean Strait. The Japanese, however,

---

[1] Admiral Enkvist's despatch in *Attaché Reports*, III., 201.
[2] Lieut. Schubert, *New Material*.

assert that no such attacks took place. Not a single boat
reported having found any ship of the class that composed
his following. They were easily distinguishable in the clear
starlight by their three funnels, and they suggest he must
have been headed off by his own destroyers. In any case he
had escaped, and his whereabouts was quite unknown.
Moreover, in spite of the large number of torpedoes that had
been fired very few hits had been made, and all of them
were on ships of little or no fighting value.

Quite at the beginning — about 8.30 — the old cruiser
Nakhimov was holed forward by a destroyer which she mistook
for one of her own, but although she had to leave the line
and get out collision mats she was not touched again, in spite
of repeated attacks. The *Monomakh* was also hit about an
hour later owing to a similar mistake. The destroyer *Gromki*
had come up to her making the private recognition signal.
This signal was repeated by another destroyer which was
consequently allowed to approach. She too came up quite
close and then fired a torpedo. It got home and so violent
was the explosion that it is said the crew of a 6-inch gun above
were blown into the sea through the gun port. The *Monomakh* was attacked again and again as she got out her collision
mats but was not hit a second time. The only other ship to
be touched was the already disabled *Navarin*. According to the
confused narrative of her sole survivor, she was unscathed
until after she was forced to stop. While thus isolated she
was attacked, he says, on all sides by a swarm of boats one
of which at last crept up unseen right under her stern and
torpedoed her. In the panic that ensued another boat hit her
amidships, but that one she claimed, and probably as we have
seen with justice, to have sunk as it made away.[1]

On the other hand, the Japanese had lost three torpedo-
boats sunk, and several other units completely disabled by
collisions and shell-fire. The scene is thus described by the
10th torpedo-boat division, which, with the 15th division, had
been keeping company all day with Rear-Admiral Togo. At
9.20 they sighted "a group of five or more Russian ships
steaming north-eastward," and turned to approach them. " At
" this period," the report says, " the attack from our torpedo
" craft was at its height. Numerous destroyers and torpedo-
" boats had surrounded the enemy on all sides, and some

---

[1] All these details are from *The Last Days*.

" could be seen running close up through the glare of the
" moving searchlights. Some vomiting white smoke were
" enduring a hail of shell from the enemy's converging guns ;
" some had lost all power of movement, and were rolling
" about in the trough of the angry sea. With numberless
" boats rushing like the wind through the darkness, scraping
" past each other's bows and sides, the danger of collision
" was very great indeed."[1]   It was a danger they themselves
found real enough. As the leading boat, about 9.30, led in
and was just about to make her attack, another boat was seen
crossing her bows. Her helm was forced over, but it was
too late, and she crashed into the crossing boat, damaging
her own bows so severely that she was quite disabled. The
vessel she rammed was the *Sagi*, a first-class boat belonging
to the 15th division which had come up at the same time.
Though very badly holed she managed by throwing her coal
overboard to keep afloat, and with her starboard engine under
water and "the engine-room staff up to their necks," she
managed to get back to Tsushima next morning. The other
three boats of the 10th division, owing to the high seas and
mutual interference, failed to get off more than two torpedoes
between them, while in the 15th division the leading boat
about half an hour later fired three shots, but the other two,
owing to the enemy's searchlights being extinguished, failed
to find a target at all.

The same fate awaited the other four torpedo divisions,
the 14th, 19th, 16th and 20th, all of which came up from
Tsushima. None of these succeeded in attacking, either because,
owing to taking a wrong course, they never located the enemy
at all, or because they did not get up till the Russian searchlights had been extinguished. The remaining destroyer
division, the 4th, was equally unfortunate. As we have seen,
their orders as mine-layers were to wait till the main attack
was over, and it was not till 9.40 that they began to make
attacking movements ; but just then all the enemy's lights
went out, and though they steamed east and west in growing
desperation they could find nothing. By 11.30 one of their
number, which had been hit by a ricochet during the action,
was taking in so much water that she was obliged to make
for Takeshiki for repairs, while the other three headed north-
west for Fusan to get replenished with coal and water.

---

[1] *Confidential History*, Bk. II., Ch. ii., Sec. 9.

But now their luck turned. About 2.0 a.m., when they were 27 miles N.E. by E. from Karasaki Point, the northernmost extremity of Tsushima, and "all hands were nearly in a frenzy of despair," for all chance of meeting with the enemy seemed gone, they were aware of what was evidently a Russian battleship about 600 metres away on their starboard bow. As their recognition signals were unanswered they steamed past her and each boat dropped her mines, 24 in all, about 300 yards ahead of her, and hurried on. In a minute or two, so they reported, "there was a dull thud, followed immediately " by a loud explosion and the air was rent with cries of con- " fusion and panic on board their victim. As firing was going " on in the distance at the time and as the destroyers were " racing at full speed against a strong wind and sea, it was " impossible to hear or notice all that went on, but it was " felt certain that the Russian had gone to the bottom."[1] They were not mistaken. It was the *Navarin*, which, owing to her injuries, had been obliged to slow down to keep herself afloat and by this time was completely isolated. The few survivors believed she had been torpedoed. What they describe is a terrific explosion which seemed to heave up her whole stern, and then another amidships to starboard which caused her to heel so far over that she began to capsize. As she went down keel uppermost everyone leaped into the water, and of her crew of 674 only three men were saved—one by a Japanese torpedo-boat and two by a British merchantman next morning.[2]

---

[1] Communicated to our Attaché at Tokyo by an officer who was present.

[2] Accounts of survivors are given in the *Novoe Vremya*, August 9th, 1905 (*Attaché Reports*, III., 221) and in the *Russ* 5th Jan., 1906; also in the *Japanese Confidential History*, sec. xiv., "Action of the Russian Fleet." But here it is made to appear that she was torpedoed during the main attack when brought to a standstill by a previous hit. In the MS. copy that has been supplied all mention of mines has been suppressed. But in section v., which contains the report of the 4th destroyer division there is an obvious omission. It relates how after making certain the stranger was a Russian battleship " they increased to 15 knots " to get ahead of the enemy, but when they had passed the enemy on " the same course and got 2000 metres ahead " they saw another ship, " this time of the *Sisoi* class," which they attacked with torpedoes. It is clear, then, that what they did to the first ship has been suppressed. Even her name is not mentioned, but she can have been none other than the *Navarin*. The reason given to our Attaché for their not going back to rescue the crew was that they were afraid of fouling their own mines.

The success of the mining division had been complete ; nor did it end here. As they ran on after hearing the explosions, they were aware of another ship of the *Sisoi* class further ahead on the starboard bow. Pressing on at high speed they soon overtook her, fired three torpedoes at her and carried on for Fusan without waiting to see the result. In fact, they had scored another success. It was the *Sisoi* herself and one of the torpedoes had taken her aft and entirely wrecked her rudder. At first no vital injury appeared to have been done, and as she could still steer with her engines Captain Ozerov continued on as he was to the northward. After a time, however, the water began to gain so fast astern that by dawn it was clear she could never make Vladivostok. Seeing, therefore, that his only plan was to beach her, he turned round and made for the coast of Tsushima. It soon became doubtful whether even this could be accomplished, and it was with great relief that at 6 a.m., as the day was breaking, he saw the *Monomakh* making towards him with a destroyer in company. He signalled for assistance but only to find that none was to be had ; she could only reply that she, too, was in imminent danger of sinking, and she steamed off towards the coast.

She was, in fact, in no case to assist anyone. As we have seen, she had been torpedoed early in the general attack, owing, it is said, to the trick of the Japanese destroyer who repeated the *Gromki's* recognition signal. She had, however, managed to plug the hole, and in spite of numberless other attacks that were made upon her was able to struggle on to the northward, with the *Gromki* in company. All went well till about midnight when she encountered a stray Japanese torpedo boat, and in turning too suddenly to avoid her tore out the plug. Her case was then hopeless, and ordering the *Gromki* to go on independently for Vladivostok she too turned back for Tsushima. But not alone, for as the *Gromki* failed to take in the order for independent action she still kept company.

Shortly after leaving the *Sisoi* the *Monomakh* found herself, though her list was continually increasing, near enough to the shore to feel certain of saving her crew, and about 8.0 she ordered the *Gromki* to go back to the *Sisoi's* assistance. By this time, moreover, she could see to the southward the *Nakhimov*, also close inshore, with Japanese vessels standing by her and apparently sinking under the Japanese flag. Unable owing to her low speed to follow Admiral Enkvist, the

Nakhimov had attached herself to the battleship line and
had been the first ship to be torpedoed. The shot, it is
said, as in the *Monomakh's* case, came from a destroyer,
which she mistook for a Russian, and it struck her forward.
Though in all subsequent attacks she was untouched and
managed later to plug the hole in her bows, during the night
she made so much water and settled so deep by the head
that before dawn she too had turned back for Tsushima.
As she neared the shore her Kingston valves were opened
and her boats lowered ; but as the wounded were being
removed and preparation being made to blow her up, there
appeared on the scene the Japanese destroyer *Shiranui*, the
senior officer's boat of the 5th division, which, having lost all
her consorts, was making for Miura for a fresh supply of
torpedoes. In answer to a challenging shot the men in the
Nakhimov's boats began to wave white flags. She therefore
drew near and demanded the surrender of the ship,
adding that if any attempt was made to sink the ship no
quarter would be given to the men in the water ; but as it
was soon evident she could not be saved, the threat was
not carried out. Just then appeared the *Sado Maru*, who,
after escorting the two prize hospital-ships into Miura in
company with the *Manshu Maru*, was coming on to find the
fleet. She at once called up the *Manshu Maru* to bring on
the hospital-ships to receive the Russian wounded and then
in concert with the *Shiranui* proceeded to take possession of
the ship and rescue the men who had taken to the water.
The officer who had been sent on board the prize had hoisted
the Japanese ensign, but seems to have been unable to haul
down the Russian, nor, though force was used, could he
induce Captain Rodionov and his navigating officer to leave
the sinking ship.

While they were thus engaged they were surprised by
the appearance of another Russian ship coming down upon
them. She was, of course, the *Monomakh*, which had been
following on almost in the *Nakhimov's* wake. Faced with the
prospect of a rescue the Japanese immediately recalled their
boats, the men went to quarters and the *Shiranui* steamed
towards the new comer while the *Sado Maru* telegraphed to
her consort to turn back and take the hospital-ships to Sasebo.
Then as soon as she had gathered her scattered parties she
also made for the *Monomakh*. As the Russian ship could now
be seen to be seriously damaged a shot was fired at 10,000 metres

to see if she meant fighting. Thereupon the *Monomakh* turned and began to make to the northward. The *Sado Maru* gave chase and at 6000 metres opened fire in earnest. The chase went on for over an hour, but shortly before 10.0, having been twice hit, the *Monomakh* stopped and hauled down her flag. At that time the *Manshu Maru*, who, not wishing to be deprived of a share in what was going on, had sent the two hospital-ships away to Sasebo unescorted, also came up, and it was decided to take possession of the prize at once. Some of her crew were already making off for the shore in boats, but the bulk of them, reassured by seeing prisoners on board the *Sado Maru*, remained where they were and quietly submitted. Preparations were begun for taking her in tow, but, owing to her being so much down by the head, this was found to be impossible, and eventually it was resolved to abandon her. The Japanese flag was hauled down, the officers and crew removed to the *Manshu Maru*, and at 2.30 p.m. she finally sank.

Meanwhile the abandoned *Nakhimov* with her flag still flying had also sunk, carrying with her her captain and navigating officer, but both these devoted men were eventually picked up by a local fishing boat. Of the rest of her crew, two officers and 99 men reached Tsushima in their own boats, and the remainder, numbering 26 officers and nearly 500 men, were on board the *Sado Maru*. From the *Monomakh* the *Manshu Maru* took off 32 officers (commissioned and warrant) and 374 other ratings and proceeded with them to Sasebo before the ship disappeared.[1]

In the meantime a very similar scene had been enacted with the *Sisoi*, the last of the four crippled ships in the neighbourhood of Tsushima. Having covered with a collision mat the hole which the 4th destroyer division had made she was, as we have seen, holding on north, and at daybreak had been joined by the destroyer *Gromki*, which the *Monomakh* had dismissed. No sooner had they communicated than at 6.30 three Japanese auxiliary cruisers appeared coming up from the southward. These were the *Shinano Maru, Dainan Maru* and *Yawata Maru*. Hoisting battle flags they at once gave chase. Thereupon the *Gromki* made off in a south-westerly direction,

---

[1] The complement of the *Nakhimov* was 637 officers and men, of these she had lost 45 men killed, and one officer and 25 men wounded. The losses of the *Monomakh* were only 8 men killed and 5 wounded out of a complement of 514.

apparently to rejoin the *Monomakh*, which was still in sight. The *Yawata* turned to chase her while the other two held on for the *Sisoi*. By 7.30 they had closed her to 6,000 metres and were about to open fire when she signalled " I am sinking," and then, " I ask for assistance." " Do you surrender ? " was the reply, and in response, being absolutely without fighting power, she hoisted the white flag. She was quickly taken possession of by a prize crew, but, as in the case of the *Monomakh*, all efforts to take her in tow proved unavailing. Moreover, she was obviously settling fast, and there was nothing for it but to abandon her. By 10.50 the Japanese flag had been hauled down, her captain and the last of the officers taken off and " only five minutes later she fell over to starboard and went " down in a tremendous whirlpool." More than a third of her crew had not yet been removed, but the Japanese worked hard to save them, and in the end out of her complement of 660 they took on board 42 commissioned and warrant officers and 571 other ratings.

There now only remained the destroyer *Gromki*, and by this time she was in the midst of an exciting action. After she had left the *Sisoi*, and was about to rejoin the *Monomakh*, the Japanese auxiliary cruiser *Manshu Maru* was just coming up, and the *Monomakh* dismissed her to make the best of her way independently to Vladivostok. She had only coal enough to do the distance by economical steaming, but her commander decided to go at his utmost speed till he was clear of the enemy's torpedo craft, which singly or in couples were making back to Fusan, Ulsan, and other bases. Some of these her officers seem to have thought they drove off, and none of them appear either to have seen or molested her. The *Shiranui* alone was at her heels, but with little hope of overtaking her. Having lost a boiler in the night attack, she could only do 20 knots, while the *Gromki* was making about 24. Before, however, she was out of range the *Shiranui* managed to get a lucky hit with one of her two 12-pounders, which brought down the Russian speed to about the same as her own. A ding-dong chase then proceeded, the two destroyers firing on each other at ranges between 4,000 and 5,000 metres without much effect. This went on till about half-past eleven, when, as they were off Ulsan, a torpedo-boat appeared ahead coming from the eastward. The *Gromki* took her for a destroyer, but she was, in fact, No. 63, the senior officer's boat of the 20th division, which having lost her consorts was making for Ulsan to replenish.[1]   For the last hour she had been making for the smoke, and was now able to head the Russian off.   Mistaking the new comer's force, and seeing it was impossible to elude her, the *Gromki* decided to turn on her first pursuer and endeavour to finish her with torpedoes.   This bold move was skilfully executed.   Running straight at the *Shiranui* she fired both tubes at three cables.   One torpedo, on account of a defective charge, just tumbled into the sea, but the other was so well directed that the *Shiranui* only just avoided it by putting her helm hard over.   The *Gromki's* daring game thus lost her her chance.   Instead of ridding herself of her more dangerous assailant she found herself taken between two fires at short range.   She had . but one 12-pounder and five 6-pounders, and was quite outmatched.   Boiler after boiler and gun after gun were smashed as the *Shiranui* circled round her at her own range.   Still, for three-quarters of an hour the *Gromki* defended herself, till she had only two light guns left and all her ammunition was drowned and inaccessible.   Her last effort was to ram, but she was settling so fast that the attempt came to nothing.   The men then began to take to the boats and the water to abandon her, and as the Japanese closed in they surrendered.   Her captors hurrying on board exhausted every effort to stop her leaks, so as to make a prize of her, but in the heavy swell which still prevailed the water continued to gain and at 12.43 she turned over and went down carrying with her the dead body of her gallant commander, Commander Kern.[2]

So ended the great torpedo attack.   Not counting the four divisions of torpedo-boats that were unable to find the enemy, 53 units had actually taken part in the action, that is, 21 destroyers and 32 torpedo-boats, but of these 14 had failed to get in a shot.   The torpedoes actually expended by the flotilla are returned as 87, that is, 50 by the destroyers and 37 by the

---

[1] The other boats of the division did the same, and as these re-assemblies took place in the case of other scattered divisions, it is to be assumed that each division was allotted a certain torpedo base for replenishing.   The chief rendezvous were at Miura, Fusan, and Ulsan.

[2] This account is taken from the *Japanese Confidential History* compared with the narrative of Sub-Lieutenant Potemkin, published in the *Russkoe Gosudarstvo*, March 26th, 1906.   Potemkin believed they were chased by at least three destroyers, and that they drove off several torpedo-boats, but, in fact, the whole affair was confined to the *Shiranui* and No. 63.

torpedo-boats.[1] The hits known to have been made, exclusive
of those in the daylight attack on the *Suvorov*, were only four,
and in no case was any ship sunk outright. Although this was
very much better than the attack after the battle of August 10th,
when the weather conditions were much more favourable, it
cannot be called satisfactory. It may even be doubted whether
the flotilla attack, heroic and determined as it was, produced any
effect whatever on the final decision. Of the four ships hit, all
except the weak armoured cruiser *Monomakh* had already been
so badly damaged under water by gun-fire during the day that
they were incapable of taking part in another fleet action and
had lost too much speed to have any hope of escaping the
Japanese next day. Yet for these slender results the Japanese
had two torpedo-boats sunk by shell-fire and one by collision,
besides three destroyers entirely disabled by collision and four
put out of action by the enemy's fire, while the casualties
amounted to two officers and 30 men killed and 17 officers and
69 men wounded.

In two ways previous experience of flotilla attack, and
particularly that of the night after the battle of the Yellow
Sea, was confirmed. It was shown, in the first place, that
searchlights were a very doubtful advantage as a means of
defence. The whole brunt of the attack fell on the section
of the Russian fleet in which they were kept burning, while the
leading ships which extinguished theirs were scarcely attacked
at all. The whole affair indeed went to corroborate the lesson
of the earlier Japanese efforts that a night attack on a moving
squadron which does not show lights is not an operation on
which any reliance can be placed for a decisive result.

Even where ships without lights were located it was found
that the attacking boats could easily be thrown out by simple
changes of course. But such changes were necessary, and
here lies the second point to be marked. For it was again
demonstrated that a squadron using these tactics must almost
inevitably lose its formation. This effect of the various attacks
is beyond question. In every case the squadron attacked was
broken into disconnected groups, incapable of standing up to
a concentrated squadron—a fact which points to the conclusion that a flotilla attack is likely to have far greater effect
preparatory to an action than as a means of " completing
the business " of a defeated fleet.

---

[1] This is according to the official return in the *Confidential History*.
It includes those fired at the *Suvorov*, but does not in all cases agree with
the individual flotilla reports.

Still if in this attempt the Japanese did not do better it was certainly not for want of vigour in pushing home the attack. On this occasion, by the testimony of both sides, they came very close and the general range at which torpedoes were fired was between 300 and 400 metres. In rushing on in one mass they were even reckless to a fault, and apart from the fact that the high seas rendered the smaller craft almost unmanageable the comparative failure was undoubtedly due in a great measure to mutual interference. In the delivery of the attack there is no method to be traced. "In the attack that night," says the Flotilla Staff report, "nearly all the divisions ran in at much the same "time. They gathered like bees round the Russian fleet from "all sides, and attacked from starboard when the port side was "on the look-out, both from ahead and from astern, each "division creating a diversion while the other came up, and all "together giving the enemy a very anxious time. But as "they were steaming at full speed through the darkness there "were a good many collisions, while in the endeavour to "avoid accident several boats lost their chance of attacking." It was clearly, then, by admission, a case where divisional initiative was relied on in place of a settled scheme, and a careful study of what happened cannot but raise a doubt whether in the case of so large a flotilla divisional initiative left entirely without guidance is not calculated to defeat its own objects. Even in fleets and in the daylight mutual interference is the danger of initiative, and on a dark and stormy night when 50 flotilla units are thrown in from three different directions in no order or settled succession the danger must be exhibited in its extreme form. The idea on this occasion was obviously to rely on reciprocal diversion for confusing the defence, but so far as our information goes no plan for concerted action had been worked out by the Staff. Commanders of divisions were left free to attack how when and where they could with no regard to the action of other divisions except such as the danger of collision forced upon them. There was, in fact, no reciprocal diversion, at least none that can be traced. The dominating impression is one of constant and disconcerting interference. The effect may have been to produce some confusion in the defence, but it was at the cost of still greater confusion in the attack, a confusion so great as to rob it of the decisive results which might have been expected from so large and spirited a force against a defeated and demoralised enemy.

CHAPTER XX.

ADMIRAL NEBOGATOV'S SURRENDER.

[Chart XIII.]

WHILE the second or flotilla stage of the battle was thus being brought to an end by the destruction or capture of the ships which had sought to save themselves on the shores of Tsushima, the third stage, which was designed to be another fleet action, was being consummated to the northward.

All night long Admiral Togo had held on at 15 knots for the rendezvous which he had given to the fleet on the north side of Matsushima. As he steamed through the darkness a keen look-out was kept for an attack by the Russian destroyers, for, so far as he knew, they were all still capable of dealing him a damaging blow. Nor had he as yet any accurate understanding of the extent of his success against the main body of the Russian fleet. All he knew is revealed by a laconic message which he sent to the Imperial Staff about midnight. " The Combined Fleet," he telegraphed, " has " to-day fought the Russian Fleet near Okinoshima. We have " defeated it; have sunk at least four ships and have greatly " damaged the remainder. The damages to our fleet are slight. " The destroyer and torpedo-boat flotillas attacked after " sunset."

From this it is clear that he underestimated the actual damage he had done. He knew, of course, that a ship of the *Suvorov* class was done for, but he did not know she was the flagship. Two if not three of the ships he stated to be sunk were only auxiliaries, and he certainly was unaware that he had practically wiped out their First Division. It was not indeed till the morning that he even knew the fate of the *Oslyabya* and the *Borodino*.[1] All he could tell for certain was that the Russian speed was less than his own and that everything depended on his bringing them to action again in the morning by getting between them and their base. It was his intention, says the *Confidential History*, " to get ahead of " the enemy and strike them in the morning as they came " north." But at 5 a.m. on the 28th, when day was dawning, he was still 30 miles short of Matsushima with nothing but Admiral Kamimura's division in company.

---

[1] *Attaché Reports*, IV. 21.

During all this time he had issued no further orders to his divisional commanders, except that at 3.15 he had telegraphed to Admiral Yamada, who had been guarding the Western Channel with the Seventh Division, "to go to the "scene of yesterday's action and destroy there what remains "of the enemy." Admiral Yamada therefore set off for Okinoshima with the *Fuso, Takao* and *Tsukushi,* and called up the *Chokai* and *Maya* to follow him if the state of the sea permitted.

The cruiser divisions having no further instructions merely held on after Admiral Togo. Nearest to him at dawn, but still 25 miles on his port quarter, that is about S.W. by S. of him, was the Sixth Division. South-east of this division, about 6 miles and some 30 miles astern of the Commander-in-Chief, was Admiral Uriu with the Fourth Division and half the Third, while 26 miles astern of him was the slow Fifth Division.[1]

Admiral Dewa, after seeing his sinking flagship *Kasagi* into Aburatani Bay, had shifted his flag to the *Chitose* and had started for the rendezvous at 9.30 the previous evening. At daybreak he had fallen in with the Russian destroyer *Bezu-prechni* and had spent over an hour in sinking her, although he was assisted by the *Ariake* of the 1st destroyer division, who having lost her consorts was making for the rendezvous and had steamed to the sound of the guns.[2] Owing to this delay they were still over 100 miles astern of the Commander-in-Chief.

Besides these there were two other ships conforming to the general movement northwards. One was the *America Maru*, which on her own initiative was also making for the Matsushima rendezvous, having apparently been forgotten and being without orders ; the other was the torpedo-parent ship *Kumano Maru*. Her station by the Battle Plan was Miura Bay, and thither she had proceeded early on the 27th. There

---

[1] The actual positions were as follows :—

First and Second Divisions, 30 miles S. by W. of Matsushima
Fourth Division, with half the Third, 60 miles S. by W. of Matsushima.
Fifth Division, 46 miles E. of Cape Clonard.
Sixth Division, 56 miles N.E. by E. of Cape Clonard.

[2] The *Chitose* expended 68 rounds of 12-centimetre and 39 rounds of 12-pounder ; and the *Ariake* added 12 rounds of her 12-pounder. The ranges of the *Chitose* was 5,300 to 2,000 metres, and she only made six hits.

she remained all day supplying and repairing various boats
as they came in, but at nightfall her captain, finding the battle
was shifting northward, made up his mind that Miura Bay
was too far south for him to do any good and decided to
proceed to the northern rendezvous. This he did, proceeding
at 15 knots and calling up the *Mikasa* and his immediate chief
Admiral Kataoka for permission as he went. From Admiral
Kataoka he apparently obtained sanction for his move ; they
were certainly in communication, for about midnight that
officer ordered him to go in to the Oura Signal Station
to telegraph Admiral Togo's report on the battle to the
Imperial Staff. This done he carried on for the general
rendezvous, with the result that part of the arrangements for
preparing the torpedo-boats for another attack broke down. No
steps were taken—perhaps none were possible—to inform the
torpedo-boats where their parent ship had gone. All those,
therefore, which in the morning made for Miura Bay to replenish, had to go on to Takeshiki to seek what they required
at the arsenal there, and were unable to take any part in
the rest of the operations.

The general situation, then, at dawn on the 28th was that
no special arrangements had been made for locating the lost
enemy. All Admiral Togo's cruisers were trailing out more
or less in the wake of the armoured squadron, and even these
ships were not spread. Presumably as a precaution against
being found by the enemy's destroyers, he kept both divisions
i n a single line-ahead with even the two despatch-vessels in
station astern. It is not surprising, therefore, that when day
began to break, and in spite of the morning being brilliantly
fine, there was no sign of the enemy to be seen. Still he held
on as he was, merely altering to N. by W. in order to pass
round the western end of Matsushima and reduced speed to
13 knots.[1] Unable to get any trace of the enemy, he was
about, we are told, " to stretch a search line of cruisers east
" and west so as to cut off the enemy's retreat," when at 5.20
the Fifth Division, now over 60 miles astern, telegraphed,
" Enemy's smoke in several streaks visible to the eastward."
At 5.30 they thought they could make out "four battleships
" and two second or third-class cruisers steaming north-
" eastward." A little later, however, while Admiral Togo still

---

[1] The *Confidential History* gives the change of course at 5.30. Our
Attaché puts it at 5.0, that is, before any message was received from the
cruisers, which seems more likely. (*Attaché Reports*, III., 112.)

held on northward in line-ahead, there came another message saying : " Enemy consists of two battleships, two coast-defence " ships, and one cruiser of the *Izumrud* class, all steaming " N.E." The information was repeated about 5.50 by the Fourth Division, which, however, had not yet seen the enemy ; Admiral Uriu must have been merely passing on the Fifth Division's message. Still it was enough to leave no doubt that the ships seen were the enemy ; and believing him to be in contact Admiral Togo directed him to keep touch. Then shortly before 6.0 he swung round to south and began to steam back, still keeping to 13 knots.[1]

It was, of course, Admiral Nebogatov with the *Nikolai*, *Orel*, *Apraxin*, and *Senyavin* (the *Ushakov* having dropped 15 miles astern and the *Donskoi* still further), together with the only light cruiser he had left, the *Izumrud*. The Fifth Division had seen their smoke a little before 5.0 and had turned N.E. to close, but it was not till 5.30 they were able to make out what they were, and it was at least ten minutes later, and perhaps more, that the *Mikasa* seems to have taken in the message. In any case it was not till 6.0 that Admiral Uriu received the Commander-in-Chief's order that he was to keep touch and ten minutes later he turned to E.S.E., a course which he judged would bring him in contact. As for the Sixth Division they had the warning that smoke had been seen as early as 5.0, but as no position was given they slowed down to wait for further intelligence. Nothing came in, and in about half an hour they turned back S.E. At 6.0 they still had no information as to where the enemy had been seen[2], but by 6.10 they must have been able to see the smoke of the Fourth Division, for they there swung round to the eastward to join them. Indeed, the morning was so extraordinarily clear that at sunrise the top of Matsushima could be clearly made out

---

[1] There is a difficulty about times here, but there can be little doubt the turn was in consequence of the message. The *Confidential History* does not give the time of the turn, but says Admiral Togo was heading south at 6.5. Our Attaché with the First Division says news of the Russians was received at 6.0 a.m. when Matsushima was abeam, and that the fleet then turned. The *Mikasa* reports receiving the message at 5.50.

[2] Their failure to get the position is curious, for the *Chitose* reports having received it from the *Yaeyama*, Admiral Kataoka's despatch-vessel, at 5.30 as " Position 603 steaming north-east." (Ch. III., § iii.) *America Maru* got the same position from *Yaeyama* at 4.50 and explains it as " 40 miles E. by S. of Cape Clonard."

at a distance of 60 miles.[1] Still for some unexplained reason the Russsans were not able to tell whether the Fifth Division were the enemy's or their own ships till nearly an hour after they themselves had been accurately reported to the *Mikasa*.

For some time the situation remained unchanged except that the *America Maru* picked up the *Svyetlana* going north about 35 miles S.S.W. of Matsushima.[2] The Russian cruiser was in a sorry plight from a heavy shell she had received in the action below the water-line forward, which brought her down by the head and gave her so heavy a list that her port 6-inch gun could not be fired. At nightfall, when the torpedo attack had begun, she had tried to follow Admiral Enkvist, but the constant changes of course he made in seeking a way through to the northward had thrown her out and she at last found herself alone. As all her dynamos had been destroyed, her wireless was useless, and at a loss what to do she decided to hold on the fatal course, N. 23° E. Though she saw many torpedo craft none attacked her. With the first glimmer of dawn she found herself in close company with the Japanese Fifth Division and was edging away to escape notice when the *America Maru* got sight of her. The auxiliary cruiser not daring to approach, could only shadow her and telegraph her course and position ; but nobody seems to have paid any attention. Everyone was too busy with the Russian main force. So absorbed, indeed, was the Fifth Division that it did not see the *Svyetlana* at all, but held on, keeping fast hold of the main body.

Admiral Dewa in the *Chitose* was equally bent on getting to the centre of things and nothing would turn him aside. On his way up, after dealing with the destroyer *Bezuprechni*, he had fallen in, about 6.30, with the *Donskoi* on her port beam, and the *Ushakov* on her starboard bow ; " but considering," the *Chitose's* report says, " that it was her most " imperative duty to make for the main fleet she telegraphed " to the *Mikasa* the position of these two ships and still " continued her own course northward." In about half an hour the *Donskoi* dropped out of sight on her port quarter, but the coast-defence ship, ignoring Admiral Dewa and his light cruiser, held on her way and remained in sight

---

[1] From the *Svyetlana* it was visible at sunrise, and at 7.0 she was still 50 miles south of Matsushima. (*Kronstadt Messenger*, Sept. 2 and 6, 1908.)

[2] Position 806. Lat. 36° 50′, Long. 130° 30′.

unmolested till 8.25, when by edging to the eastward she, too, disappeared N. by E.

It was not the *Svyetlana's* fate to come off so easily. The course she took in edging away from the Fifth Division only brought her straight to the Fourth Division as it was coming in to close. The moment she saw her danger she made away to the northward at the highest speed of which she was capable, and about 7.0 Admiral Uriu without changing his own course detached in chase the two Third Division ships that were with him, *Otowa* and *Niitaka*, while the *America Maru* had to turn tail and clear out of the *Svyetlana's* way.

Up to this time Admiral Togo, owing probably to the inadequate Japanese method of indicating positions at sea, had not been able to make out where the main body of the enemy was. At 6.40 they had been reported 40 miles south, but this must have been found to be incorrect; for at 7.30 he turned S.E. by E.,[1] increasing speed again to 15 knots, and for the next hour we are told "the two divisions frequently " altered course, making movements to bar the enemy's progress." During this period the *Asama*, unable to stand the increase of speed, had once more to fall astern in order to attend to the injuries she had received the previous day. The details of the movements which Admiral Togo made in his efforts to get contact are not known. Obviously the difficulty in locating the Russians accurately continued, and this was, no doubt, due in part to the fact that they too made several alterations of course. Soon after Admiral Nebogatov had sighted the Fifth Division he appears to have had some idea of engaging them. For after enquiring the state of his squadron's guns and receiving encouraging replies, he signalled to turn 8 points together to port and to prepare for action. This seems to have been shortly past 8 o'clock when Admiral Uriu, an hour after detaching the *Otowa* and *Niitaka* in chase of the *Svyetlana*, was just coming into sight. He had now only three ships with his flag, for the *Akashi*, like the *Asama*, had had to be left astern to plug her shot holes. Still, with the *Naniwa* and *Takachiho* he placed himself on the enemy's port beam, while to the *Tsushima* he gave liberty of action "in his desire to " maintain complete contact." This precaution may have been due to the fact that, as the Russians turned to close, the

---

[1] The *Confidential History* here agrees with our Attaché with the Second Division who made it E.S.E. (compass).

Fifth Division edged away, so at least Admiral Nebogatov affirms.   He was still holding his new course, but in some uncertainty as to whether the dimly seen Fourth Division was Russian or Japanese.   The *Izumrud* was sent forward to ascertain the truth.   By the time Admiral Nebogatov had been on his new course about ten minutes she returned to say they were Japanese, and with a very exaggerated estimate of their strength.   The Sixth Division was also coming into sight, and the *Izumrud* reported that amongst the new comers, which it had been hoped might be Russian, were five Japanese armoured cruisers.[1]

By this time it appeared to the Russians that the three Japanese divisions in sight had formed the line of battle.   This impression was no doubt due to the fact that the Fifth Division would now have edged away so far as to be more or less in the wake of Admiral Uriu ; we also know that the Sixth Division took station astern of the Fifth.   But whatever was the cause, Admiral Nebogatov on receiving the *Izumrud's* report, signalled for the original course to be resumed.   " I decided," so he said at his court martial, "to proceed to Vladivostok, and " should they touch me to force my way through them.   .   .   . " I prayed to Nikolas, the Wonderworker, that he would assist " us in some way."

Certainly nothing but a miracle could save him, but never-theless his last move seems to have caused Admiral Togo some anxiety.   As yet he had seen nothing of the enemy and was still heading S.E. by E., a course which he now suddenly discovered would not bring him ahead of the Russians. About 8.40, therefore, he turned E. by N. $\frac{1}{4}$ N. and then signalled to the Second Division "to go ahead at full speed and make " contact with the enemy," and away Admiral Kamimura went at 17 knots.   Before, however, he had had time to draw clear the anxiety passed.   By 9.18 the Fifth Division could be seen hull down S.E. by S. ; in another quarter of an hour (9.32) the Fourth Squadron, also hull down, was sighted to the S.E. ; and, very soon after, the Russians could be made out on the same bearing, that is, a little before the *Mikasa's* starboard beam and apparently on a north-easterly course.   It was a position from which Admiral Togo's superior speed would enable him

---

[1] Evidence of Admiral Nebogatov and Commander Vedernikov (of the *Nikolai*) and that of Lieut. Polushkin, senior navigating officer of the *Izumrud*.

" to press the van " without change of course. He therefore hel
on as he was, sounding " Action " and hoisting battle flags.[1]

As soon as Admiral Nebogatov could make out what the
last comers were he seems to have given up all hope. Not
only were the large ships clearly in a position to bar his
way, but astern the three cruiser divisions were now moving
to cut off his retreat. " It was clear," says Admiral Nebogatov,
"they were making a ring round us with a well-defined radius
" which they were able to select owing to their superior
" speed." [2]

By 10.15 the Japanese First Division had closed to 12,000
metres, and the Second Division must have been nearer,
and as the Russians still kept their north-easterly course the
range was fast diminishing. By 10.30, when the Japanese
had reached nearly ahead of the enemy, it was down to 8,000
metres, and as the *Izumrud* was pushing ahead as though to
use her torpedoes Admiral Togo with all his old cautiousness
turned the First Division slightly to port to avoid her.
Admiral Kamimura conformed to this movement at once
(10.33) by leading north-east. The next minute the *Kasuga*
tried a sighting shot, the range was passed at from 7,000 to
8,000 metres, and in a few minutes more all the ships were
firing.[3] The First Division opened on the *Nikolai* at 10.38,
and ten minutes later the Second Division began to lead
more to starboard again to close the enemy more rapidly.
From the Russians there was no reply. According to Admiral
Nebogatov he had ordered his gunnery officer to open fire,
but the answer was that the range was impossible. It was
this, the Admiral asserted, that determined him to surrender.
His own 12-inch guns were of an obsolete pattern. Except in
the *Orel*, there were no others of that calibre in the squadron,
and the *Orel* was little better than "a mass of scrap iron
without ammunition—spent and exhausted."[4] The 10-inch guns

---

[1] *Attaché Reports*, III., 113.

[2] Evidence at court martial.

[3] The range is important here as Admiral Nebogatov justified his
surrender on the ground that the Japanese would not come within range
of his guns. The *Japanese Confidential History* says the range *Kasuga*
to *Nikolai* at 10.33 was 8,000 metres. In the *Adzuma* at 10.36 the
range was passed as 7,000 yards. (*Attaché Reports*, III., 113.)

[4] This is confirmed by the Japanese report in the *Confidential History*,
Ch. III., sec. ii., sub-section 2. They found she had received on the port
side nine 12-inch hits, five 8-inch, and thirteen 6-inch, and the largest of the
holes was 9 ft. 4 in. by 6 ft. 3 in; on the starboard side, three 12-inch

of the *Apraxin* and *Senyavin* were useless at the range the
the Japanese had chosen, and by no possibility could the
Russian Admiral with his inferior speed reduce it against the
Japanese will.   Whether his estimate of his gun capacity was
not too low is very doubtful ; it certainly was not accepted
by the Court Martial which tried him ; but his belief that the
Japanese would not close had much justification in the fact
that Admiral Togo had actually edged away when the *Izumrud*
drew too near, and that the Second Division with the First
in its wake was then inclining more to starboard as though
beginning an encircling movement.   Rightly or wrongly he
judged that resistance was out of his power, and that it was
therefore his duty to surrender without further useless sacrifice
of life.

  There seems little doubt that his decision was in accordance
with the general feeling in the squadron.   The re-appearance
of practically the whole Japanese Fleet, untouched—so far as
they could see—by the terrible struggle of the previous
day, had had an overwhelming moral effect, under which
the spirit of the Russians had simply collapsed.   In the
lower deck the rumour was that the unbroken fleet that was
surrounding them could not be that which had handled them
so severely the day before ; the word, indeed, went that there
must be two, and that one of them was a British fleet which
had come to the Japanese assistance.   A Russian officer has
given a vivid impression of how relaxing the atmosphere was.
" The fierce battle," he wrote, " which had lasted from 2 p.m.
" on the 27th right through the night had not lowered the
" spirit of our men who had been fighting so hard.   All
" expected the battle to begin again at daybreak, and they
" were fully prepared for it, and all orders had been directed
" to that end.   But when at dawn we found ourselves sur-
" rounded by an iron wall of 27 large enemy's ships, none
" showing any trace of damage, both officers and men lost
" hope . . . they fell on their knees and cried that all was
" lost.   That splendid array of ships, the whole Japanese fleet

---

two 8-inch, and seven 6-inch, besides two 6-inch holes in the conning
tower.   " The decks were broken up ; the interior of the ship presented
a sight pitiable to see."   One of her fore 12-inch had been broken off
two metres from the muzzle.   Out of a complement of 30 officers and
825 men, 26 officers and 779 men became prisoners, of whom 14 officers
and a number of men were wounded.   In the action she had lost only
4 officers and 46 men killed.

" with no vessel missing, which was making a ring round
" this poor remnant left to us, who could look at it without
" feeling as if his soul had been torn from his body ? . . .
" That is why at the moment of surrender no man had
" power to show his wit or courage." [1]

However the event may be judged, it is clear from all the
evidence that there was a sudden moral collapse against which
the Admiral himself was not proof. In his eyes all further
effort was worse than useless, and as soon as the Japanese
opened fire he ordered the Russian ensign to be lowered to
half mast and signalled his intention to surrender by the
International Code. For some time the Japanese did not realise
what was being done. The splendid resistance of the Russians
on the previous day had done nothing to prepare them for so
tame a catastrophe. For ten or fifteen minutes, therefore, the
firing continued. At first the practice was not good and hits
were few, but as it improved and the International Code signal
was disregarded Admiral Nebogatov ordered a white flag to be
hoisted. Still the firing continued, and it was not till he
ordered the Japanese ensign to be flown over the Russian
that the astonished and exultant enemy realised the position,
and the " Cease fire " sounded. All four of the battleships
submitted to the Admiral's decision without protest, but for
Captain Ferzen of the *Izumrud* the main reason for surrender
did not exist. He at least had speed, and when he saw the
last degradation of the Japanese flag flying in the flagship he
resolved to shift for himself before it was too late. By this
time the Japanese Second Division had crossed the Russian
course and was already N. by E. of them, threatening to close
the gap which lay between it and the Sixth Division which
had been working up on the Russian starboard quarter to
envelop their rear. But the gap was still open and Captain
Ferzen called his officers to council to tell them he meant to
break through. There was little coal left and steam pipes had
been injured, but it was his intention if he could win through
to make for the nearest land, which was the Oki Islands
about 70 miles away to the S.E. There he would land his

---

[1] Compare also *Last Days*. The author says up till this moment all
had been calmly awaiting a renewal of the action, " joyfully ready to
" die . . . but on the appearance of the enemy's main squadron,
" apparently entirely uninjured, we were disillusioned, and even the
" strongest characters relapsed into a state of utter indifference to what
" was taking place."

crew and blow up the ship if there was no other way of saving her from the Japanese flag. No sooner was this bold resolution taken than he swung round to starboard and went off to the south-eastward at 20 knots. The Sixth Division, which was nearest, at once gave chase, but in point of speed they were quite outclassed, and the Russian was soon lost to view below the horizon.

By this time (11.30) both fleets were stopped at a point 18 miles S.S.W. of the Liancourt Rocks, with the various Japanese divisions disposed in a complete circle round the Russians. It was here the final triumph was carried out, well up in the open waters of the Japan Sea and 180 miles from the spot where the battle had begun. A few minutes before noon, and just 24 hours after the Russians had fired their first random shots at the cruisers that had located them entering the Eastern Channel, Admiral Togo accepted the surrender, and officers were sent off to the *Nikolai* to arrange the details. All took place in decorous silence. "There was no cheering," we are told, "everybody took it quite quietly; they were all happy, but "nobody seemed to want to make a noise."[1]

But the fighting was not yet over. While the painful process of handing over the prizes was proceeding, other ships which had not been dominated by the sight of the "wall of "iron" were displaying a spirit very different from that of the main squadron.

There was first the wounded *Svyetlana*, which we left at sunrise running to the northward at the best speed she could attain with the *Otowa* and *Niitaka* in hot chase and each her superior in strength. By 8.0 o'clock they had recognised her and could see she had been joined by a destroyer (*Buistri*). As the actual speed of the two Japanese cruisers was 18 knots, while the crippled *Svyetlana*, with 400 tons of water in the bow compartment, could do barely 15, it was clear an action was inevitable, and that it could only end one way. At 8.0, therefore, Commodore Shein assembled his officers in the ward room, and asked for their opinions. All were for fighting to the last round and then sinking the ship; this the commodore announced was also his decision, and turned in desperation for the Korean coast.

The whole engine-room staff was already fairly exhausted, but so well did they work that in an hour's time the Japanese

---

[1] *Attaché Reports*, III., 96.

were still 10,000 metres astern. In half an hour the range was down to 9,000, and the *Svyetlana* fired a challenging shot, but the range was too great, and it was not till 9.40 that the *Otowa* replied with her 6-inch. The *Niitaka* followed, but finding her shot fell short she ceased fire. The *Otowa*, however, being ahead kept on, and about 10.0 had the luck to get a 6-inch shell home on the chase's stern. It seemed to have disabled her steering gear for she began to zigzag to starboard and port ; but according to the Russian account she could still steer, and these movements were intentional changes of course to disturb the Japanese aim. Still in spite of all she could do the range diminished rapidly and hits came faster and faster. The Japanese cruisers had also been joined by the destroyer *Murakamo*, of the 5th division, which, having failed to get in her attack the previous night, was making for the rendezvous, and was able by keeping ahead to prevent the *Buistri* from interfering.[1] By 10.20 the *Niitaka* was able to reopen with her 6-inch at 8,000 metres ; a quarter of an hour later she had closed to 6,000 and could use her 12-pounders and the *Svyetlana* was soon a mass of flames and smoke. Her ammunition was fast failing, her port engine was disabled, and it was obvious to them all the end was at hand. " The " cruisers," writes one of her officers, " came closer and poured " in a terrific fire, every shell took effect, the whole hull trembled " from the incessant explosions of bursting shell. . . . Fires " broke out ; all the cartridges were expended, and in com- " pliance with an order given earlier the engineer opened the " after valve and all the watertight doors." [2]

As the cruiser's fire ceased the destroyer *Buistri* made away to the northward. The *Niitaka* and *Murakumo* at once went off in chase, while the *Otowa*, keeping clear of the torpedo-arc of the *Svyetlana*, continued to pour in a destructive fire at ranges as low as 1,000 metres. Under this hail of shell the Russians were busy with preparations to abandon the burning ship. The Japanese History, with admiration, thus describes her end :
" Although there was nothing to be done the crew determined " to die and refused to hoist the signal of surrender. Bathed " in a shower of shell they waited for the ship to sink. The " captain was killed, the commander mortally wounded ; the " ship gradually heeled over ; most of the crew jumped into

---

[1] She also tried to "spot" for the cruisers, but the attempt proved a failure.

[2] *Kronstadt Messenger*, September 2nd and 6th, 1908.

" the sea.   By 10.50 . . . we saw she was on the point of
" sinking, and the *Otowa* ceased fire." It was just the hour
when Admiral Nebogatov was hoisting the Japanese flag.

At this moment a wireless message came in from the
America Maru, who after running from the *Svyetlana* had
turned again to join the *Otowa* and *Niitaka*. It announced
that a Russian gunboat and two other ships were in sight, and
the *Otowa* had to go off to deal with them. As she passed
the *America Maru* she told her to go to the sinking Russian
cruiser and save the crew. The gallant ship had gone down
at last shortly after 11.0 about 20 miles east of Chukupen
Bay, and the *America Maru* arrived in time to save 11 officers
and 279 other ratings.[1] As for the *Buistri*, seeing in a few
minutes that escape from her two pursuers was impossible,
she turned to port straight for the Korean shore, and at 11.50
brought up hard on the rocks about five miles north of
Chukupen Bay. There having partially blown up their
ship, the crew landed, and after an attempt to penetrate the
mountains gave themselves up to the slender guard of the
Chukupen signal station.[2]

The chase of the *Izumrud* was not so successful. Just as
she had run the Sixth Division out of sight, Admiral Dewa in
the *Chitose* appeared hurrying up from the south at high
speed and headed her off her course to the northward. She
was then forced to give up her attempt to reach the Oki Islands,
and her pursuers had still a chance of overhauling her. Seeing
this Rear-Admiral Togo detached the *Akitsushima* of the Sixth
Division to carry on the chase with the *Chitose*, and with
his other three ships turned back to rejoin the Commander-
in-Chief. But though the *Chitose* took up the chase at her
utmost speed—and her legend speed was 23 knots—she gradually lost ground, and by 2.0 o'clock she gave up, leaving the
Izumrud entirely free to make her way to Vladivostok.

By this time all arrangements had been made for taking
over the captured ships. It had been readily agreed that
commissioned officers might retain their swords and personal
effects, and that no injury was to be done to hulls, armament,

---

[1] The Japanese gave the position as approximately lat. 37° 6';
long. 129° 50'. The *Svyetlana's* casualties were 11 officers and 157 men
killed, and 1 officer and 22 men wounded, out of a complement of
20 officers and 439 men.

[2] The prisoners included 5 officers and 77 men, 10 of whom had
been rescued from the *Oslyabya*.

or fittings of the surrendered ships. Of the crews, two-thirds were to remain in the prizes to navigate them in conjunction with the prize crews, and on arriving in Japan they would be permitted to take possession of their private belongings. These terms were formally settled by Admiral Nebogatov, who at Admiral Togo's invitation had come off to the *Mikasa*. About 2.30, after an hour's stay, he left the Japanese flagship to return to his own, and the work of taking possession could begin.

It was a process that must take some time, and till it was complete, Admiral Togo felt he must keep his fleet concentrated, but it was a necessity that presented grave drawbacks. He had at last learnt exactly what damage he had inflicted on his enemy. It was with considerable disappointment that the Russian flagship was not found in the captured squadron. For the first time it became known that Admiral Rozhestvenski's flag had been flown in the *Suvorov*, but what had become of him no one could say. It was further ascertained that the *Borodino*, *Alexandr* and *Oslyabya* had all gone down. So that there could no longer exist any formed body except Admiral Enkvist's cruisers. They, if left unmolested, might do a considerable amount of harm, but nevertheless it was regarded as out of the question to· attempt for the present to operate against them. " So much time," says the *Confidential History*, " was expended in the process of taking possession " of the surrendered ships, that the opportunity of giving " chase to the remnant was lost. As, moreover, Admiral " Togo considered it necessary to have a powerful escort for " the prizes on the voyage, he abandoned the idea of chasing " the others, and decided to proceed with the prizes to " Sasebo."

This self-restraint was the more necessary since, besides the light cruisers which were already in chase in various directions, he had now to detach two of his armoured cruisers. For scarcely had the work of taking possession begun when, about 2.30, the coast-defence ship *Ushakov* was seen coming up from the south. This ship, it will be remembered, had been kept in sight some time by the *Chitose* as she was trying to rejoin, but ignoring the light cruiser the *Ushakov* had held on her way till at noon, finding herself alone with no enemy in sight, she had turned N.W. intending to make the Korean coast and steal up along it to Vladivostok. Finding this course brought her in sight of the enemy's main body, she at once turned back to the southward. Admiral Shimamura, who had first sighted her, begged to be permitted to chase with his flagship *Iwate* and the *Yakumo*. Leave was given and away he went, but as the *Ushakov* was hull down when he started the chase was likely to be a long one.

Though they worked up to 18 knots it was 5.0 o'clock before they overhauled her about 50 miles to the westward of Oki Island. Then at about seven miles distance, Admiral Shimamura, in pursuance of the Commander-in-Chief's instructions, began signalling to her in the International Code. " Your Admiral has surrendered. I advise you to surrender." But he was to find that he had metal to deal with very different from that which his chief had found so pliable, and already a council of the *Ushakov's* officers had resolved to destroy the ship rather than strike the flag. For some time they were unable to read the signal and merely hoisted the answering pennant. But by 5.30 when the Japanese had approached to about 9,000 metres they could make out the advice to surrender, but not the rest, and the *Ushakov's* immediate reply was to open fire.[1]

She was then running to the westward, and the *Iwate* and *Yakumo* turned south-west to cut her off, engaging her hotly with their port batteries. In response the *Ushakov* gradually edged off to port till she was going about south. As her fire, which at first had been good, began to slacken, the two armoured cruisers turned together to port to close the range for five minutes, and then at 5.45 turned back into line ahead.[2] By that time the *Ushakov's* fire had nearly ceased, and she seemed to be stopping, and in fact she had taken so great a list, that the guns she had left could not be used. Still the two cruisers drew in, firing upon her slowly from both sides. They were now some 60 miles due west of Okishima, and at 6.7 out of the cloud of their bursting shells, the Japanese saw a huge explosion. As the smother cleared the *Ushakov* could be seen heeling right over, and in three minutes she was gone, leaving the sea covered with floating men and gear.

What exactly happened has never been made quite clear.

---

[1] These details are from a Russian monograph called, *The Battleship Ushakov : its Voyage and Loss*, by N(ikolai) D(imitriev). The author was the gunnery Lieutenant.

[2] Lieut. Dimitriev says it was ten minutes before the Japanese got the range, and then every shot told.

Some of the prisoners said the catastrophe was caused entirely by the Japanese fire, but there is no doubt that Captain Miklukha had taken measures to destroy his ship, rather than let her fall into the enemy's hands. Some said he merely opened the Kingston valves when he stopped; others, that the bottom was blown out with gun-cotton.[1] In any case, the Japanese paid due honour to the resistance which the stubborn old coast-defence vessel had made. Hurrying up at once, both cruisers lowered their boats, and in the end out of her complement of 422, they saved 339 including 12 officers, but the gallant Miklukha went down with his ship.

By 8.45 all was over, and Admiral Shimamura made back E. N. E. to try to rejoin the Commander-in-Chief who was now almost destitute of cruisers. For in spite of the fact that the detaching of these two ships had seriously weakened the guard of his prizes, the quiet way in which the Russians were submitting to the terms of the surrender at length convinced Admiral Togo that he could spare further strength to re-establish his guard of the Straits. For this purpose, at 3.45, an hour and a half after Admiral Shimamura was well away on his chase, the Fifth and Sixth Divisions were ordered to proceed to Osaki, where they would be in a position to deal with Admiral Enkvist's missing squadron if it was to make to the southward. The captured ships were therefore now guarded only by the First Division, part of the Second, the Fourth, and various stray destroyers and torpedo-boats that had managed to rejoin. And soon there came another call. The Fifth and Sixth Divisions had scarcely been gone an hour when a suspicious ship was reported to the north-west, and the Fourth Division was ordered to chase with three boats of 2nd destroyer division which had just come up.[2] The strange ship proved to be only the torpedo parent ship *Kumano Maru* which, on her self-imposed mis-

---

[1] Lieut. Dimitriev says nothing of any explosion. Her sinking he states was due to the Kingston valves being opened, but he adds that even without this she would have gone down by the enemy's fire alone.

[2] This division, after making its night attack and being severely handled by the Russians, had held on for the rendezvous, less the *Ikadzuchi* entirely disabled. At 8.30 a.m. they had sighted the *Donskoi* and two destroyers 50 miles east of Cape Clonard but they thought it their duty to carry on to attack the enemy's main force. They therefore made for Liancourt Rocks and found the fleet at 3.0 p.m. They thus lost their chance of capturing the Russian Commander-in-Chief. *See post*, p. 328.

sion, had reached the northern rendezvous at 1.0 p.m., and found nothing there. In reply to a telegraphic request for instructions, she was ordered to Liancourt Rocks, and was now on her way there. From her Admiral Uriu obtained some information which seems to have been connected with the movements of the *Otowa* and *Niitaka*, but what it was is not clear ; at all events it caused him to make a cast towards Matsushima to see what he could find.

There was now indeed little chance of any Russian unit escaping detection, so covered was the sea with auxiliaries, and chasing cruisers, besides torpedo craft hurrying up to be ready for another night attack, which according to the general plan was to follow the second action. Amongst these the *Sazanami* of the 1st destroyer division and the *Kagero* of the 3rd had the luck to add the last touch of radiance to the Japanese victory. Both of them after the night attack had put into Ulsan to replenish and make good defects, and they had left in com-pany next morning for the Matsushima rendezvous.[1] By 2.15 in the afternoon, about 40 miles short of the island, they saw smoke lines going from S.E. to N.W. By 4.0 they could make them out to be two Russian destroyers, and, increasing to 23 knots, they gave chase.

They were, in fact, the destroyers *Byedovi* and *Grozni* with Admiral Rozhestvenski and his staff on board. The *Buini*, to which he had been originally transferred from the sinking *Suvorov*, had had a breakdown with her engines in the night and had become isolated. In the morning, however, she picked up the *Donskoi* with the other two destroyers in company. Though urged to board the *Donskoi* the Admiral elected to shift into the *Byedovi* since her engines were still good. As soon as the Admiral was safely on board she and the *Grozni* parted company with the cruiser and headed north. Their course thus cut that of the two Japanese destroyers proceeding from Ulsan. After half-an-hour's chase (4.30) the Japanese had gained so much that it became obvious to the Russian staff that the *Byedovi* could not escape and the *Grozni* was ordered to save herself. A quarter of an hour later with the range down to 4,000 metres the Japanese opened fire. The *Grozni* replied as she made off, but the *Byedovi* was silent. She had, in fact,

---

[1] At Ulsan they found the other parent ship *Kasuga Maru*, but how she came there is not explained. Her original station by the Battle Plan was Fusan.

stopped and was hoisting the white flag. Thereupon, while the *Kagero* held on after the *Grozni*, the *Sazanami* ceased fire and, closing on the *Byedovi*, sent a party to take possession.[1]

There they found Admiral Rozhestvenski still suffering so much from his wounds that the Russian doctor begged he might not be moved. The destroyer, therefore, was disarmed and taken in tow. But what to do with so precious a prize was not easy to decide. The result of the battle was quite unknown to the Japanese and for all they could tell they might at any time be forced to abandon their capture. It was therefore decided to make back to Ulsan as the nearest point at which instructions could be obtained, and for that port they started at 7.20. Firing could be heard to the eastward, but they kept clear of it and nothing was seen. So the night closed down upon the last stage of the ill-starred Admiral's voyage himself in tow of his enemy and nothing but a single crippled destroyer left to him out of the most powerful fleet that had ever appeared in Eastern waters.

The firing they heard to the eastward must have been the last fight of the *Donskoi*. It will be remembered that about 5.0 Admiral Uriu had begun making a sweep in this region with the Fourth Division, and shortly before 6.0 he was rewarded by sighting the *Donskoi* W. by S. of him and running at high speed north-westward. The news was at once telegraphed to Admiral Togo, who thought well to send away the *Asama* in support of the light cruisers. As the speed of the Russian armoured cruiser was about the same as that of the Japanese light cruisers there was little chance of bringing her to decisive action. Admiral Uriu therefore tried to get her to surrender by repeatedly sending by wireless the words *" Donskoi, Donskoi*, Admiral Nebogatov surrendered already ! "* But Captain Lebedev paid no attention and held on his course ; but not for long. In about half an hour he was seen to edge away to the northward straight for Matsushima and Admiral Uriu began to gain fast. The reason was soon evident. Away to the westward the *Otowa* and *Niitaka* appeared, forcing him off his course. After finishing the *Svyetlana* they were making their way E.S.E. to rejoin Admiral Uriu when they, too, had sighted the *Donskoi* and had made for her at 18 knots. Her fate was now sealed and she was making a desperate effort to run herself ashore at Matsushima. Shortly

---

[1] The *Kagero* failed to overhaul the *Grozni*, who escaped into Vladivostok.

after 7.0, about 20 miles south of the island the *Otowa* got within 8,000 metres and opened fire. The *Niitaka* followed in a few minutes, and by 7.40 all the Fourth Division were able to join in at 7,000 metres. The *Donskoi* replied with spirit, but in the storm of fire which was sweeping her from either hand accurate laying was soon impossible. Fires kept breaking out, and as the Japanese closed up her punishment became more and more severe. By 8.0 the Fourth Division's range was down to 4,000 metres and that of the *Otowa* and *Niitaka* to 3,000. The effect of the concentrated fire is said to have been terrible. Besides her own crew the *Donskoi* had on board 270 men from the *Oslyabya* and the destroyer *Buini*, which had sunk, so that the casualties caused on her crowded decks were unusually heavy. Amongst those killed was her gallant captain. Then her steering gear was disabled, her steam pipe damaged, and it became obvious to the Japanese she was in serious difficulties. Her end could not be far away, and as the sun was setting Admiral Uriu decided to finish the business before dark by running athwart her bows and cutting her off from Matsushima. But he had misjudged the heroic resistance of his enemy, and just as he turned the *Naniwa* to lead round to port a 6-inch shell took her aft and did so much injury that in a few minutes she was heeling 7 degrees and had to be withdrawn out of action. So sharp, indeed, was the lesson that the intercepting movement had to be given up and the field left to the destroyers. By 8.30 it was too dark to see the enemy at all and by the time the *Asama* got up she found herself too late to be of any use.

For the Russians it was a fine performance of which they might well be proud—as an example of the resistance a well-handled armoured cruiser of the poorest type can offer to a swarm of light cruisers. She had survived their combined attack for an hour, and they had to leave her still gamely steaming. The *Otowa* and *Niitaka* had been recalled by Admiral Dewa to rejoin the *Chitose*, while Admiral Uriu had to take his division back to Sylvia Basin.

The torpedo attack was no more successful. As soon as the firing ceased the 2nd destroyer division tried to run in between the *Donskoi* and the land to finish her, but found she was already too close to the rocks and had to deliver an unsuccessful attack from seaward. Four other boats of various divisions which had been keeping company with the *Otowa* and *Niitaka* also tried to attack after dark. Three of them could not find the enemy at all under the shadow of the island and even the fourth *Fubuki* which did get in was received with so heavy and accurate a fire that all her shots missed.

Thus the *Donskoi* was left to anchor quietly under the land and to abandon ship without molestation. By 6.0 next morning all her crew were ashore except a small party told off to take her out into deep water and open her Kingston valves. In this plight she was found at daybreak by the destroyers, which in company with the *Asama* had been standing by. Preparations were at once made to take possession but before the Japanese could reach her she turned over and sank.

It is, of course, impossible not to contrast the behaviour of the *Donskoi* and the other ships that did likewise with the course which Admiral Nebogatov felt it right to take. But it must not be forgotten that the cases were not exactly parallel. The Admiral had no possible chance of escape ; he was caught in the early hours of the morning with no land near which he could hope to reach. In the case of all the other ships there was a fair chance of escape, or at least of reaching land, where the ships could be destroyed and the men saved. And it must be remembered that it was on the question of the men's lives that Admiral Nebogatov's decision turned. In his judgment, and on his reading of the articles of war, he had no right to sacrifice thousands of lives on what could be no more than a point of honour. Rightly or wrongly it was on this principle that he surrendered, and as the *Donskoi* was finally beating off her pursuers, he and his four ships with the Japanese flag flying were making their way to Sasebo under escort of the First and Second Divisions.

The voyage was not made without difficulty. Owing to machinery defects and other hindrances it was long after dark before they could start and trouble of all kinds was experienced owing to the state of the prizes and the misbehaviour of the prisoners. In the *Orel* things went so far that she soon broke down altogether. The engines were found to have been tampered with, boiler water failed and the prisoners would not reveal where the reserve was stored. She had therefore to stop engines altogether, the electric light could not be burned and every effort to signal to her escort by wireless and rockets

---

[1] Out of her crew of 24 officers and 496 men the *Donskoi* lost 3 officers, and 50 men killed, and 5 officers and 90 men wounded. Captain Lebedev died of his wounds in Sasebo Hospital.

proved unavailing—a fact which speaks eloquently of the reaction after the long strain of the battle. Admiral Togo went on and the *Orel* soon found herself alone with nothing but the destroyer *Usugumo* in company. So ugly was the demeanour of the prisoners that the officer in command did not dare to detach her for assistance. At dawn, however, there was an improvement, prisoners came up and offered assistance, and the destroyer was sent back to get in touch with the Matsushima signal station and ask for a tug. Meanwhile, by 8. a.m. boiler water was found and at 8.20 the *Orel*, being then 16 miles S. by W. of Liancourt Rocks was able to proceed slowly towards Maizuru, the nearest port. In an hour's time all danger was over, for the *Usugumo* had met the *Asama* returning from her search for the *Donskoi* off Matsushima and the *Asama* at once proceeded to assist. Ten minutes later Admiral Togo appeared. Finding at dawn that the *Orel* was missing he had turned back and now ordered her to carry on to Maizuru, which she reached on the 30th with the *Asahi* and *Asama* for escort. By that time the other three prizes had reached Sasebo in safety, as well as the destroyer *Byedovi*.

As for the crew of the *Donskoi*, who had landed on Matsushima, they were reported to be quietly encamped, apparently believing themselves to be on an uninhabited island. No attempt was made to molest the signal station, of whose existence they were probably unaware. It was therefore able to communicate with Admiral Togo, who on the 29th sent back the *Kasuga* to deal with the situation. To her the Russians quietly surrendered in the afternoon, content with having saved the honour of their flag.

Of all the ships that had been present at the last scene the only one that remained unaccounted for was the *Izumrud*. Of her nothing had been heard since she ran out of sight of the chasing *Chitose*. Once having shaken off her pursuers she found it necessary, owing to machinery damage, to reduce speed, and it then became evident she had little chance of making Vladivostok without being intercepted. Captain Ferzen therefore decided to make for St. Vladimir Bay to the northward. The coast was badly surveyed, and in feeling his way in during the night he ran on the rocks. As all attempts to get her off proved unavailing, and as the Japanese were expected to appear at any moment, her crew were landed and she was blown up to save her from capture.

So was consummated perhaps the most decisive and complete naval victory in history. The Japanese had lost 117 officers and men killed and 583 wounded. Three torpedo-boats had been sunk and two or three other units of the flotilla disabled, but not one ship had been injured seriously enough to prevent her carrying on the campaign. The losses of the Russians were about 5,000 killed or drowned, and the prisoners numbered close on 6,000.[1] Four ships and one destroyer had been captured, twelve ships, four destroyers and three auxiliaries had been sunk either in action and by their own crews in a disabled condition, nearly all the rest had fled, and of the whole 38 units of the Baltic Fleet, only one cruiser, the *Almaz*, and two destroyers, *Grozni* and *Bravi*, got through to tell the tale at Vladivostok.

---

[1] The official figures are :—Killed or drowned, 216 officers, 4,614 men. Prisoners, 278 officers, 5,629 men (many of whom were wounded). Interned in neutral ports, 79 officers, 1,783 men. Escaped in their own ships to Vladivostok and Diego Suarez, 62 officers, 1,165 men. Total (dead, prisoners or interned), 573 officers, 12,036 men.

CHAPTER XXI.

Operations Consequent on the Battle of Tsushima.

[Charts Xb, XIII.]

It was not without anxiety that Admiral Togo had found himself compelled to devote his fleet to securing the four Russian prizes instead of making detachments to pursue the ships that had escaped him. On the morning of the 30th there were still unaccounted for the five cruisers, *Oleg*, *Avrora*, *Almaz*, *Izumrud* and *Zhemchug*, four destroyers, and four auxiliaries, *Anaduir*, *Irtuish*, *Koreya* and *Svir*. Of these the *Almaz* by hugging the Japanese coast had escaped, as we have seen, into Vladivostok. The destroyer *Bravi* had done the same, while the *Grozni* had got away along the Korean coast. The *Izumrud* was a wreck, while the *Irtuish*, having been too badly injured in the battle to make a voyage, ran for the Japanese coast, where off the Iwami Province, five miles east of Yokoda, she was abandoned and left to sink. The rest, including the other two destroyers *Blestyashchi* and *Bodri*, had run off to the southward, but only the *Oleg*, *Avrora* and *Zhemchug* were in company under Admiral Enkvist's flag.

His first idea when he had made up his mind that it would be impossible to break through to Vladivostok was to make for Shanghai, where the fleet colliers had been sent, and after filling up from them to renew the attempt to reach his destination, taking one of the colliers with him.[1] With this design he made back through the Eastern Channel, and although the state of the ships compelled him to reduce to 10 knots, by noon on the 28th he fixed his position as 45 miles west of Torishima (Pallas Rocks).[2] Here, being well clear of the danger zone, he stopped to bury the dead and to transfer his flag to the *Avrora*, whose injuries, though she had lost her captain, were less severe than those of the *Oleg*. While

---

[1] Schubert, *New Material*. Admiral Enkvist was thus reported on by a British Naval Officer who saw him at Jibuti in January 1906 when he was taking the remains of his squadron back to Russia, " A worn " and fragile-looking old gentleman with white hair and long white " beard. . . . I could never imagine him capable of standing the " strain of naval war."

[2] Pallas Rocks are about 30 miles S.W. of the Goto Islands and 120 miles S.S.W. of Tsushima.

thus engaged he had been sighted by the British steamer *Doric*, who was making her way to Nagasaki 170 miles due east of his position. This, however, seems to have been unknown to the Admiral, and having completed his arrangements he held on, but not for Shanghai. Having ascertained that the *Avrora* drew too much water for the Yangtse bar, he announced his intention of taking her to Manila, but at the same time he gave the other two cruisers liberty of action, and they decided to keep to the original programme. About 9 a.m. on the 29th they fell in with the *Svir*, also escaping south, and so carried on together all that day. Towards evening there was a fresh change of plan. The captain of the *Oleg* on reconsideration came to the conclusion that at Shanghai they would be interned and not allowed to coal; he therefore proposed to the *Zhemchug* to keep company with the *Oleg*. But soon a new difficulty arose. After passing the Korean Strait they had nominally coal for 1,300 miles, but it was soon apparent that owing to injuries to funnels the *Oleg* and *Zhemchug* were consuming fuel so fast that it was doubtful whether they could reach the new destination. The Admiral therefore decided to make for Sual, a port in the Gulf of Lingayen on the west coast of Luzon, about 200 miles north of Manila, where for some reason he hoped to find hospital accommodation for his wounded and coal and stores for proceeding with his design.

As he held on thus to the southward all trace of him was lost to the Japanese, but it was not long before an alarm arose which upset the dispositions which Admiral Togo was making. Early on the 29th the *Doric* put into Nagasaki and reported that at 2.45 the previous afternoon she had sighted off Pallas Rocks three Russian men-of-war working their pumps and clearing themselves of water, about 50 miles from Nagasaki. Clearly an error had occurred in transmitting the intelligence, but in this inaccurate form the alarm was telegraphed to all stations, and two destroyers were at once despatched from Sasebo to reconnoitre the supposed position of the Russian ships.

The situation justified the somewhat exaggerated anxiety that appears to have spread in all quarters, for the information looked as if the three cruisers were lying in wait on the direct line of communication with Europe. The fleet was still scattered and out of hand after the battle. Neither Admiral Togo nor Admiral Kamimura had yet reached

Sasebo with the prizes, nor was it till next day that they came in and the *Asahi* and *Asama* reached Maizuru. The light cruisers were making back singly or in small groups to occupy the Straits position, but most of them had only just given up their search and were far to the northward. The only division that was in reach was the Third, and that was still scattered. At 11.30 a.m., however, the *Kasagi* got the signal as she was about to enter Osaki. She passed it with a request to be allowed to chase to Admiral Dewa, who in the *Chitose* was coming down the West Channel and was only a few miles to the northward off Mine Wan. He at once decided to chase with all his division and called up the *Otowa* and *Niitaka* whom Admiral Uriu had ordered to rejoin their proper flag after the action with the *Donskoi*. They got the order at 1.0 and increased to 16 knots. South-west of Tsushima Admiral Dewa was joined by two destroyers and three torpedo-boats which had been proceeding to various destinations after completing repairs. Later on other ships also took up the chase. Shortly before 3.0 p.m. the *America Maru* and *Sado Maru* appeared at Sasebo with Russian prisoners rescued from sunken ships and received an order from the Naval Staff, who knew nothing of what was already being done, to proceed at once and search for the reported ships, but it was 6.30 p.m. before both of them could clear the prisoners and start. Admiral Shimamura, who with the *Iwate* and *Yakumo* was approaching Sasebo with the survivors of the *Ushakov*, was just rounding the south of Hiradoshima when at 4.30 p.m. he intercepted a wireless message from the *Chitose* to the *Mikasa* to inform the Commander-in-Chief what she was doing. Admiral Shimamura at once decided to join the chase without landing his prisoners, and he set off at 15 knots for Osesaki, the southernmost cape of the Goto Islands.

Meanwhile Admiral Dewa was calling up the Takeshiki Port Admiral to ask for definite information as to the position of the Russian ships and when and by whom they had been seen, and he received the reply that at 2.45 p.m. on the previous day they were about 36 miles west of Pallas Rocks, course and speed unknown. Thereupon, "seeing there was no possible chance of overtaking them," he turned back just as the *Otowa* and *Niitaka* were joining and made for Osaki. Admiral Shimamura was more persevering. At 5.50 p.m. he, too, took in the message from Takeshiki giving the enemy's true position. He saw at once that even if the Russians could only steam 10 knots he could not hope to overtake them with a day and a half's start. But he also argued that if they were greatly damaged they would make for the nearest neutral port, which was Shanghai. Furthermore, he calculated that there might be other enemy's ships on the Shanghai route ; he therefore held on for that port, searching as he went. But that night the sea got up so much that the plug by which a shell hole had been filled in the flag-ship was forced out and she was obliged to stop, while the *Yakumo* went on alone. Till the following morning she held on, when, having reached 200 miles short of the Yangtse, she was recalled.

Thus nothing was left in chase of Admiral Enkvist except the two auxiliary cruisers *America Maru* and *Sado Maru*. It was not till 8.0 a.m. on the 30th that they reached the spot where the enemy had been reported on the 28th. Finding nothing there their captains decided to carry on independently and search the waters about Shanghai ; but in the afternoon they were so badly enveloped in fog that the *Sado* stopped, and then finding her wireless would not work she decided to return to Sasebo. The *America*, however, held on, and early next morning (the 31st) began searching the islands off the Yangtse. No enemy being found she tried further south, and finally, on June 1st, ran down to Keelung in the north of Formosa for orders and intelligence. There she learnt that three Russians were reported to have entered Shanghai, and as the need for further search seemed at an end she made back, reaching Osaki on June 4th.

Meanwhile, in view of these alarms and of the fact that the cruisers at Vladivostok were still believed to be in being, Admiral Togo, on May 30th, had ordered Admiral Kamimura to proceed at once with all available ships of his division to Sylvia Basin, there to take command of all ships of the First and Second Divisions and also of the Special Service Squadron of auxiliaries. At the same time Admiral Kataoka, who was then at Takeshiki, was directed to take out the Third Squadron and guard the straits against the remnants of the enemy and seize all ships trying to run contraband into Vladivostok. But in the view of the Naval Staff this was not enough, and Admiral Ijuin in a private note suggested that a squadron ought to be detached to the southward to operate in the Shanghai district.[1] In response to this hint

---

[1] *Japanese Published History*, Book V., Ch. i.

Admiral Togo on June 1st submitted that "it would be well to detach a small squadron in support of diplomatic processes . . . in case there should be need of using armed force." The Imperial Staff approved the idea, and accordingly he issued the following order to Admiral Kamimura : "You are to form " a detached squadron of one first-class cruiser, two second- " or third-class cruisers and two destroyers and send them " under Admiral Uriu's command without delay direct to the " mouth of the Yangtse River. Admiral Uriu is to search " for any remains of the enemy at the Chusan Archipelago " and to threaten the Russian auxiliary cruisers and transports " which are at Shanghai and Wusung, thereby strengthening " our diplomacy.   At a suitable opportunity he is to cruise " as far as the coast of Fukien in South China and threaten " the enemy's transports, which it has been reported are now " assembling at Saigon."[1] The ships detailed for this "Southern " Detached Squadron," as it was officially named, were *Tokiwa*, *Naniwa* and *Takachiho*, and the same day Admiral Uriu sailed with his flag in the *Tokiwa*, his orders being to communicate directly with the Imperial Staff and the Commander-in-Chief. Just as he was raising anchor on the 2nd word came in from Tokyo that six Russian merchant ships had put into Wusung on May 25th and that the auxiliaries *Koreya* and *Svir* had also arrived and were discussing the question of disarmament and internment.   Admiral Uriu therefore had no time to waste if he was effectively to assist "diplomatic processes," parti- cularly as the *Svir*, it will be remembered, was the vessel that Admiral Enkvist had sent to bring on his colliers.

He was still entirely lost ; the report of his being at Shanghai was false.   In fact, as Admiral Uriu was leaving Sylvia Basin he was entering Sual in Luzon and was soon well looked after.   Having reached the port at 6 p.m. on the 2nd he found to his disappointment that there was no hospital there and no telegraph, except that of the American Military Department, which refused to forward private telegrams.   He decided, therefore, as the weather was fine enough for his coal to last, to carry on to Manila.   Next day as he neared the port he was aware of a strange squadron of five ships coming towards him.   He at once cleared for action, but quickly found he was in the presence of the American Squadron, with Admiral Train's flag in the battleship *Ohio*.   After exchanging salutes

---

[1] *Japanese Published History*, Book V., Ch. i.

Admiral Enkvist held on while the Americans turned round and shadowed him. When it became obvious that the Russians intended to enter Manila harbour the Americans increased speed and, entering almost simultaneously, they anchored in a ring round the intruders. The Russians were thus entirely at the mercy of the neutral authority and a diplomatic situation of no little interest was the result.

Admiral Enkvist began by boldly demanding permission to repair his squadron and take in coal sufficient to carry him to the nearest Russian port, which was Vladivostok, his strategical destination. This request the Governor forwarded to Washington asking that it might be granted, while the American Admiral examined the state of the ships. His report to Washington was that the repairs of the *Zhemchug* would take a week, those of the *Oleg* a month, and those of the *Avrora* two months. Upon this, on June 5th, the Governor of the Philippines received the following instructions : " The damages of the Russian men-" of-war which have come to Manila are entirely due to battle. " The policy of our Government being to prohibit absolutely " any work by a belligerent in neutral ports, the President " is unable to allow the said Russian warships to make any " sort of repair unless they are interned in Manila Harbour " until the conclusion of the present war. You must convey " this pronouncement to the Russian Admiral and also inform " Admiral Train that he must secure strict neutrality." [1]

The American Government, in fact, took up the position quite frankly that the principle which allows emergency repairs to belligerents in neutral ports does not apply to the repair of damage received in action. This decision was communicated to the Russian Admiral with a request to know whether he would leave Manila within 24 hours if he was provided with coal and provisions enough to take him to the nearest Russian port. This offer seems to have been made by the Governor on his own authority, for a reference to Washington elicited the reply that the 24-hour rule was to be strictly enforced and no coal or provision was to be embarked beyond what was required for that period. " The principle of this," the orders concluded, " is identical with the principle of our instructions " dated June 5th concerning the refusal of time to repair the " damages received in battle." It is to be deduced, therefore,

---

[1] This quotation and those which follow are from the Japanese translation of the original papers as given in the *Confidential History*, Part II., Bk. ii., chap. 4, sec. 3.

that the principle on which the American Government acted was that the rule of neutral supply of coal and provisions to enable a belligerent to reach his nearest port does not apply when the exhaustion of the stores in question is the direct consequence of an action. In this case at least—seeing what the strategical objects of the two belligerents were—the soundness of this attitude seems beyond question. For Admiral Enkvist there was nothing to do but refer the matter to St. Petersburg for instructions, and on June 8th the reply came that he was to intern the three cruisers at Manila, leaving all arrangements to the United States Government. He accordingly handed over his ships, but as the order from Washington mentioned only detention they were not disarmed.

As these proceedings became known at Tokyo they caused no little anxiety. Admiral Enkvist's presence at Manila was known to the Imperial Staff some time on June 4th, the day that Admiral Uriu with the Southern Detached Squadron reached the Saddle Islands and began to search the surrounding waters. With some difficulty, owing to fog, he proceeded with the flagship to Gutzslaff Island and there found officers from the Japanese consulate awaiting him in a British ship. From them he learnt that three days previously eight Russian auxiliary cruisers and transports had entered Shanghai and Wusung and that they were to be detained, but that no other trace of the enemy had been seen. Next day he had his squadron, including his collier and the two destroyers, concentrated, and was proceeding to allot stations for watching the port when he heard that the Russian destroyer *Bodri* had been found by a British ship disabled and alone—for her consort the *Blestyashchi* had gone down—and had been towed into Wusung. He also learnt that Admiral Enkvist was at Manila. Admiral Uriu, however, made no movement or any alteration of his plans except to prepare to send in his destroyers to deal with the *Bodri;* but as later on he heard she had agreed to disarm, this measure was no longer necessary. Still he made no move, although on the 6th he was informed by the Naval Staff at Tokyo that the Russian auxiliary cruisers had been seen on the 4th about 80 miles north of Hongkong and that on the 3rd the *Rion* had searched a vessel between Shanghai and Moji. He knew that all arrangements for interning the Russian ships in the Yangtse had been completed, yet he decided to maintain his watch till the 9th, when he intended, if nothing occurred, to proceed for Amoy.

Meanwhile, however, reports from the Japanese Consul at Manila gave the Home authorities reason to believe that Admiral Enkvist was about to leave. Precautions at least became necessary, and late on the 7th Admiral Uriu received from the Commander-in-Chief and the Naval Staff an identical telegram informing him of the state of the Manila negotiations; that is to say, that the Russians were not to be allowed to repair unless they disarmed. "Our Manila Consul," the message concluded, "thinks Enkvist . . . will depart without " making repairs, the United States Government being appa- " rently inclined to permit this. You must go at once to " threaten the Enkvist Division. You will proceed first to " Makung and there await orders." In pursuance of these instructions he started the same night, but for the Japanese Staff this was not enough. On the 8th it was understood that the time limit for the Russians to leave had expired, and that though detention had been ordered from Washington the Governor had told the Russian Admiral that there were no orders about disarmament. That same night, therefore, Admiral Shimamura was hurried off in the *Yakumo* to meet Admiral Uriu at Makung and take over the command from him. The meeting took place on the 12th. Admiral Uriu went home in the *Naniwa;* but before the new Admiral could act all was over.

On receiving the final decision from Washington Admiral Enkvist in accordance with his instructions from St. Petersburg had given the American Government a definite promise to take no further part in warlike operations. The only question that now remained was whether or not the Russians were to disarm. The point was referred to Washington; the answer was that disarmament must be carried out; and on June 15th the breach blocks of the guns were handed over and deposited in the arsenal at Cavité. Thereupon the mission of the Southern Detached Squadron came to an end with instructions to Admiral Shimamura to act on the orders of the Commander-in-Chief, and next day he was recalled.

In the wording of the order it was explained that not only were all the ships of the Baltic Fleet which had escaped to the southward now interned or disarmed, but that " the auxiliary cruisers which had been occasionally seen off " the coast of South China were now apparently all to the " westward of Singapore." This referred to the merchant cruisers which Admiral Rozhestvenski had detached on the eve

of his final approach with the intention of confusing his enemy
and making a diversion. In this they had entirely failed.
The *Terek* and *Kuban*, which had been directed to operate
on the east coast of Japan, were not even heard of till a
week after the battle. Their movements are not known.
The first that was heard of them was that on June 5th the
Terek sank the British steamer *Ikona* (3,382 tons) with
Rangoon rice for Japan about 150 miles north of Hongkong.[1] On the 22nd she sank the Danish steamer *Prinsesse
Marie* (3,518 tons) with provisions and hardware from Singapore to Japan,[2] and on the 29th landed her crew at Batavia.
There she demanded coal and provisions, but they were refused
and she was interned. Of the *Kuban's* operations nothing is
reported except that while cruising along the east coast of
Japan she heard of the destruction of the Baltic Fleet and
thereupon returned to Kamranh Bay. Thence on June 14th
she put into Saigon, brought out two transports, and proceeded on her voyage to Russia.

The *Rion* and *Dnyepr*, which had been told off to the
Yellow Sea, did little better. On May 28th, about 60 miles
S.S.E. of Shantung Promontory, the *Rion* captured the German steamer *Tetartos* (2,409 tons) under Japanese charter from
Otaru to Tientsin, and finding she hindered her movements
sank her next day.[3] Then after four days' cruising in the
Yellow Sea without result—for on the 27th all sailings from
Korea had been stopped—on June 2nd being then 80 miles
from Wusung she fell in with the British steamer *Cilurnum*,
from Shanghai to Moji. This vessel she searched, and
after throwing overboard her cargo of beans and cotton-
pods, let her go. She next appeared on the 14th at
Batavia, where she landed the crew of the *Tetartos*, and
a week later sailed for Russia on strict orders from
home. The cause of these orders was the outrageous
conduct of her consort the *Dnyepr*. She seems never to
have entered the Yellow Sea but in spite of her instructions
to have turned southward at once, for on June 1st she
searched a German ship a little north of Luzon, who reported
her presence to Admiral Enkvist as he was approaching the
island. On the 4th she seized the British mail steamer *St.*

---

[1] Lat. 20° 2′ N., long. 134° 1′ E. (*N.I.D. Diary*, 285).

[2] The position was lat. 13° 57′ N., long. 113° 15′ E.

[3] In. lat. 36° N., long. 122° 4′ E., that is about 90 miles due East of
Kyou-chou.

Kilda (3,629 tons) from Hongkong to Japan, and sank her after destroying the Japanese mails. A week later she turned over the native crew and the undestroyed mails to a Dutch steamer north of Sumatra but retained the British officers as prisoners.

These proceedings naturally produced a very bad impression in England. In August the previous year, in the course of the discussions about the *Knight Commander*, destroyed during the raid off Tokyo, the Russian Foreign Minister, while maintaining the right to take extreme measures in exceptional circumstances, had given a verbal undertaking that no more neutrals would be sunk. The British Government, who maintained that under no circumstances could naval officers take the law into their own hands, at once entered an energetic protest against the proceedings of the *Dnyepr*, and the situation was soon made the more serious by news of what the *Terek* had done. A special aggravation was found in the fact that the *Rion* and *Dnyepr* were identical with the *Smolensk* and *Peterburg*, whose piratical action had caused so much trouble before. On the whole the protest was well received by the Russian Foreign Office. They urged, when the truth of this news could no longer be doubted, that they did not know where the offending cruisers were, that they were quite out of control, and they accepted the offer of the British Government to send cruisers to find them and deliver the orders which the Russian Admiralty professed itself unable to convey. In the end orders were sent for the offending cruisers to return to Libau direct " for administrative and strategic reasons," and though Russia did not categorically abandon her contention it was understood that no further destruction of neutrals was to take place and that the question of compensation would be entertained.

Thus every ship of the Baltic Fleet was accounted for except the fleet-transport *Anaduir*. During the night of the battle she had run south, and nothing was heard of her for a whole month; but on June 27th she suddenly appeared at Diego Suarez in Madagascar with over 300 men on board whom she had saved from the auxiliary cruiser *Ural*. Without interruption she sailed again for home, and this was the only ship that had taken part in the battle which found her way back unmolested to the Baltic.

Never in the history of war had a fleet been so completely annihilated. In the theatre of war Russia had nothing left except the *Rossiya* and a few torpedo craft in Vladivostok. Not once in our most successful naval wars had we obtained a command of the sea so nearly absolute as that which Japan now enjoyed, nor is it likely, in view of recent developments of material, that such an uncontrolled sway can ever be won again. That Russia while this condition lasted would ever regain the ground she had lost was out of the question ; that she could drive the Japanese from Korea and Kwangtung with her army alone was a military impossibility, so naked would her communications with those sea-girt territories lie to coastal penetration. It was open to Japan to throw in troops when and where she chose without any chance of the blow being accurately anticipated, and there was nothing afloat to detect and interrupt such operations. In short she had absolutely secured her hold· on the territorial objects of the war and she was free to open the third phase of the operations : that is she was at liberty to bring such pressure to bear as she could in order to force her enemy to recognise the conquest ; and for this purpose she was free to strike wherever the Imperial Staff saw the point best suited to their resources. In Russia the situation was fully realised. The only question was where would the thrust be delivered.

CHAPTER XXII.

The First Sakhalin Expedition.
[Maps IX., XIV., XV., Chart VI.]

It was Vladivostok which in Russian eyes was the most probable objective of the next campaign. Indeed, ever since the fall of Port Arthur—months before the fate of the Baltic Fleet was settled—the northern port had been a source of much anxiety, and it was natural to expect that the first use the Japanese would make of their victory would be to strike a blow at the only remaining base from which naval operations could continue. As early as January 2nd, the day after the capitulation of Port Arthur, General Kuropatkin had ordered plans to be prepared for largely increasing all arms in the Pri-Amur District, "as he was fully convinced," we are told, "that "the district would form the theatre of military operations "from the commencement of the spring."[1]

The reports which he called for declared the place to be open to assault and that the Japanese could land a large force by surprise, as they had done elsewhere, almost at any point they chose. The ice was no bar, for it was held that the enemy could disembark straight upon it. Two more infantry divisions were declared to be indispensable so as to bring the force up to four divisions, while all other arms required a proportional increase. When in the latter half of January the Japanese cruisers appeared in northern waters to blockade the approaches to the port, the apprehensions became graver, and finally, after the defeat at San-de-pu, which made the Russians still more anxious about a flank attack upon their main line of communication, the Tsar signed an order for Vladivostok to be raised to the status of a first-class fortress.

Early in February this appreciation of the Japanese intentions was so strongly confirmed by a secret intelligence agent that on the 12th the purport of his report was issued to all concerned. The communication was as follows: "Extract from a Secret Agent's Letter. (Telegram from "General Dessino, No. 104.) The main strength of the

---

[1] *Russian Military History*, Vol. IX., Ch. xiv.

" Japanese fleet is concentrated at Sasebo which will be its
" chief base for further operations. From many sources it
" appears that further plans are as follows :—Under pro-
" tection of the fleet an army of 100,000 men is to make a
" descent under General Nogi in the neighbourhood of Posiette
" or on the east coast of Korea, at Gensan for example, and
" then to advance to the Nikolsk-Vladivostok road.[1] The major
" portion of this army is to advance on Nikolsk Ussuriski with
" the object of falling on the rear of our army, while the lesser
" fraction is to attack Vladivostok. Such Japanese army will
" consist of troops from Port Arthur and reserve units to which
" will be added siege guns. Oyama's army will not advance
" until the movement of this Nikolsk army has developed.
" Large reinforcements will not be sent to Oyama's army.
" In order to prevent the Baltic fleet interfering with the
" descent of the Japanese the following arrangement is con-
" templated :—Until everything is in train the Japanese fleet
" will remain concentrated at Sasebo, and if our fleet arrives
" in the Sea of Japan then the Japanese fleet will avoid a
" decisive contest, but will endeavour to lead our fleet over
" the minefields of which there are many in the Strait of
" Korea ; if our fleet goes round Japan then the Japanese fleet
" will move northwards. The Tsugaru Strait is thickly mined
" and strongly fortified. A large mining flotilla will be con-
" centrated there. If our fleet manages to reach Vladivostok,
" then the Japanese fleet, basing itself on some place in the
" neighbourhood, will proceed to blockade Vladivostok. Four
" cruisers—the *Asama, Tokiwa, Idzumo,* and *Iwate*—with some
" destroyers, have been detailed to watch the cruisers of the
" Vladivostok Detachment."[2]

Although in the light of the knowledge we now enjoy
this report has all the appearance of having been deliberately
fed to the Russian agent by the Japanese at the time, it
cannot but have been taken seriously by the Russian Staff.
Indeed whether by accident or design it received immediate
corroboration that was not to be denied. The week February
6th to 12th saw Admiral Kamimura's appearance at Gensan to
establish it as an army base, with four cruisers, two of which
were amongst those named by the agent ; and this, ten days

---

[1] Nikolsk of the Ussuri District was the junction where the Khabarovsk
branch of the Trans-Siberian railway joined the main line about 50
miles north of Vladivostok.

[2] *Russian Military History*, Vol. V., App. xiv.

later, was followed by a report that a considerable flotilla of Japanese torpedo-craft had appeared off Vladivostok itself.[1]

By that time the garrison had reached twenty-two battalions of infantry and four of fortress artillery ; but in view of the above intelligence, formidable as this force was, it was not nearly sufficient in the eyes of the Commandant, to secure him from the expected *coup de main*, and he begged the officer commanding the naval squadron to organise a scouting service of fast steamers that he might have timely warning of an attack. But the Admiral could only report that there were no such steamers to be had and that his torpedo craft were unfit for the work. Fresh demands for more men and some modern guns were the result, backed by an urgent appeal that they were indispensable for saving the last hold of the Russians on the Far Eastern seas.

By the middle of March the Japanese landing at Song-chin and their triumphant occupation of Mukden after the ten days' battle accentuated Vladivostok as the vital point in the situation. If the Russians were to retain a footing at all in Manchuria—still more if they were to recover anything they had lost, it was essential that they should feel their rear was absolutely secure. Quite apart therefore from its value as a naval base from which the Japanese oversea communications could be harassed, it now stood out as a position so important for the future of the land operations, that its security was obviously as vital for the Russian Army as it was for the Fleet. At the same time and for the same reasons it became more clearly indicated than ever as the next Japanese objective. So strongly was this felt that one of the first Imperial orders which General Linevich received, after he had superseded General Kuropatkin as Commander-in-Chief, was one fixing his attention on the threatened point. On March 9th he informed the Commandant of the place that the Tsar had been pleased to signify that amongst other important objects of the military operations the first must be the absolute security of Vladivostok and its being placed in a condition to withstand a prolonged siege.[2]

General Linevich at once took the matter in hand, sending his Chief of the Staff to report what was required. Although by

---

[1] *Russian Military History.* Vol. IX., Ch. xiv. It was probably a false alarm ; no such movement is mentioned in the Japanese History. Admiral Kamimura's force was three armoured cruisers, *Idzumo*, *Tokiwa*, *Kasuga* with the *Suma* and two destroyers. *See ante*, p. 160.

[2] *Russian Military History*, Vol. IX., Ch. xiv.

this time the strength of the garrison had been further increased he was obliged to pronounce the defences of the fortress absolutely unfitted for resisting an attack and its garrison so inadequate, that another whole division was wanted. Owing to the confusion of the various authorities within the place, he said, little or nothing had been done on any coherent system to improve its defences, and its armament was still dangerously defective. One result of this report was that General Linevich reorganised the command by placing the Cruiser Squadron under the officer commanding the troops. The words of the order are remarkable. "I place the Cruiser Squadron," he wrote, "entirely under your control. Whenever the Cruiser "Squadron is in Vladivostok the Squadron Commander will "receive instructions of a general nature from the Com- "mandant regarding the joint operations of the fleet and "fortress. He will promote by every means in his power, "the success of the military operations and the defence of "the fortress in every way, provided that it does not interfere "with the special work of the squadron. The Port Com- "mander is the assistant to the Commandant of the Fortress "being under the latter's command in military matters, but "enjoying complete independence in his arrangements of the "port and the ships . . . The initiative and adoption of "measures for the greater security of the port from the sea "will rest with the Port Commander subject to the assent "of the Commandant. In all dealings with the cruisers in "Vladivostok, the officer commanding the detachment will "be subordinate to the Port Commander, as regards matters "of active naval defence. The naval detachments will be "subordinate to all the arrangements of the Commandant. "In cases of special importance or of urgency the Com- "mandant has the right to make arrangements in the sphere "of jurisdiction both of the Port Commander and of the "officer commanding the Cruiser Squadron, but with this "reservation, that the Commandant will inform me of any "such arrangement by telegraph."[1]

If such an order was really calculated to simplify matters they must indeed have been in need of simplification. Occasions for overlapping of authority and surfaces for irritating friction seem to protrude from every clause. There is little or no trace of lessons learnt from the bitter experience of Port Arthur. But, perhaps, nothing better is to be expected

---

[1] *Russian Military History*, Vol. IX., Ch. xiv., April 7th.

where the Continental idea prevails, that the problem of unity of action between the two Services is to be solved by subjecting both to a single Commander-in-Chief selected from one of them. In the earlier part of the war the officer in supreme command had been an Admiral, and the only result of the lamentable breakdown of co-ordination that ensued was that the experiment was to be repeated with a General in the Admiral's place. And this arrangement was clung to in face of the fine results which the Japanese had obtained from adopting the well-tried British system of two co-ordinate Commanders-in-Chief.

Besides this attempt to re-organise the command and various detailed measures for the actual defence of the place, provision had to be made against the expected attempt to sever its communications by a force acting from the coast. Ever since the Japanese landing at Song-chin this had been an ever-present danger. At all costs it was felt that the line of the Tumen River, which formed the frontier between Korea and the Russian Pri-Amur Province, must be held in order to cover the important railway centre at Nikolsk, where some 50 miles north of Vladivostok the lines from Kharbin and Khabarovsk met. Little or no information of what the Japanese Song-chin force was doing could be obtained. On March 31st the advanced Cossack patrols came into collision with it at Kil-tsiou, but could only report that the Japanese were fortifying a screen position which it was impossible to penetrate. It seemed to be occupied by about 5,000 men; but, as the report said, "this number was possibly being increased daily " owing to their holding the command of the sea."[1] This was followed by definite intelligence from the Russian secret agents that 15,000 men had actually left Hiroshima with the object of landing on the coast in order to cut the Nikolsk-Vladivostok railway ; and the Chief of the Staff felt compelled to recall the bulk of the troops that had been deployed in North Korea to the left or Russian bank of the Tumen for fear their retreat should be cut off.[2]

About the middle of April the Commander-in-Chief received another piece of information equally precise and of even graver import. It was that the Japanese were preparing an army of 80,000 men and 200 guns to operate directly

---

[1] *Russian Military History*, Vol. IX., Ch. iii.
[2] *Ibid.*

against Vladivostok itself.[1] During the next month no further change in the situation was reported, but on May 20th intelligence obtained "from foreign sources" reached the Manchurian Headquarters to the effect that a Japanese division about 12,000 strong was "advancing from the new base at Gensan in the direction of the Tumen with the object of isolating the fortress," which, of course, meant seizing the railway. As a consequence the line of the river had to be reinforced, and this anxiety was increased when a week later spies reported that the Japanese advance had actually begun by their occupying Kil-tsiou.[2]

By this time, however, the garrison of the fortress had been brought up to 40 battalions, and the returns showed that as soon as expected drafts arrived the infantry alone would number 50,000 bayonets. Supplies, moreover, had been accumulating for 15 months, and considerable progress had been made with the defences. Still by the middle of June, when the battle of the Yellow Sea had opened the way for an attack in force, Vice-Admiral Birilev, who had been sent to inspect the state of the ships and the place, found there was still much to be desired in both the strength and the character of the garrison no less than in the fixed defences and in the armament. In short the place was still in no case to resist an attack in force, such as the Russian intelligence and appreciations led everyone to expect.

But whether or not the reports which reached the Russian Staff were purposely spread by the Japanese, Vladivostok was not the objective which they had in mind for the new stage of the war. True every possible means was adopted, as will appear directly, to keep the menace alive; in their most intimate communications the Japanese Ministers continued to speak of it as an open question; but when all was over the Russians were satisfied from "private Japanese sources," that all the movements in the direction of Vladivostok had for their primary object not so much the capture of the fortress as the application of pressure upon the Russians with a view of hastening the conclusion of peace.[3] This probably very fairly represents the Japanese attitude. For the present, at any rate, their plans were far less ambitious and more

---

[1] *Russian Military History*, Ch. xiv., April 18.

[2] *Ibid.*, Ch. iii. Kil-tsiou is just south of where the watershed of the Yalu system runs out to the sea at Cape Bruat.

[3] *Ibid.*, Vol. IX., Ch. xiv.

discreetly adjusted to the slender resources which remained available after the needs of their difficult position in Manchuria were satisfied. The objective they had in mind was one as clearly indicated by the material as it was by the moral conditions of the war, and that was Sakhalin. For the past thirty years, ever since in 1875 Russia had finally shouldered them out of the island, its loss had been rankling as an open wound to the national honour that smarted only less painfully than the loss of Port Arthur. Forming, as it did, the last link in the chain of the island empire it was still part of unredeemed Japan, and apart from the material value of its fisheries—so vital to her northern population—she could not rest till it was hers again.

As the main object of the third stage of the war its conquest was undoubtedly wisely chosen, even from a purely strategical point of view. It was clearly of much higher value to Japan than it was to Russia, and was therefore one which would call forth higher efforts from the Japanese than the Russians could afford to spend on it.[1] On the other hand, the alternative, Vladivostok, was of higher value to Russia than it was to Japan. By Russia it was regarded as quite as much a part of the Muscovite Empire as Sakhalin was regarded by the Japanese as part of theirs. Any formal attack upon the adjacent provinces, moreover, would suggest an intention to drive Russia from the Pacific shores altogether. Such a prospect by all natural law would inspire Russia to a further deployment of military force in the Far East beyond anything which it was possible for the other objects of the war to provoke ; and of all strategical principles there is none sounder or more universally applicable than that which warns a belligerent to avoid any operation tending to arouse fresh energy in the enemy.

Beyond all this there was yet a further consideration. From first to last Japan had planned and conducted the war on limited lines, and the well-marked danger of this nature of war is its tendency as the struggle is protracted to be converted to war of an unlimited character. Hitherto Japan had confined her operations to sea-girt objectives lying beyond the confines of her enemy's real territory ; and to attack a continental province which was an integral part of the Russian Empire would inevitably change the nature of the

---

[1] Cf. ante, Vol. I., pp. 66–7.

war. It would become essentially a continental struggle that
must turn on the overthrow of armies, and Japan would
find herself deprived of those natural advantages which she
had so vigorously exploited as an island power in command
of the naval theatre of the war. To confine her operations to
an island in the coming stage of the war was to preserve the
limited lines which had served her so well, in that it aimed
still at a strictly limited and sea-girt objective and at the
same time strengthened her defence against an unlimited
counterstroke. For while the Fleet was operating and securing new bases in northern waters, it was out of her enemy's
power to deliver a blow from Vladivostok or the maritime
Provinces, from which alone such a stroke. could now be
developed.

Although, then, at the time, both in Japan and elsewhere,
something pusillanimous was found in the decision of the
Imperial Staff, and although to many it seemed that the correct
and drastic way of securing a triumphant peace was to strike
direct at Vladivostok, there can be little doubt that the choice
of the lower objective was on all grounds the one most in
accordance with the dictates of the higher strategy and sound
war policy. However bravely the popular voice might cry,
those who sat at the Staff table at Tokyo knew too well that for
continental offensive operations they were at the end of their
tether, that to try for the overthrow of the enemy's forces
was to try beyond their strength and to present to Russia all
the advantages of making war under continental conditions
which so far they had succeeded in denying her.

As to the nature and extent of the resistance with which
their new venture was likely to meet the Imperial Staff appear to
have had but little accurate knowledge. It was decided to
devote to it at first one division, while another, it would seem,
was kept in reserve.[1] Both these divisions were amongst the
four new ones which had been formed since the fall of Port
Arthur. The division which was to open the operations was
known as the XIIIth Independent Army Division. It was to
be divided into two wings—the first to deal with South Sakhalin
and the second to follow for the northern part of the island.
Other troops were to be landed and deployed on the sea-board
of Northern Korea, but these operations were of a purely
diversionary or preventive character, to hold the Ussuri army to

[1] See *post*, p. 376.

the defence of its own district. This abundance of caution—
so characteristic of the Japanese Staff—was no doubt justified
by the uncertainty of their information and the extreme importance of avoiding any reverse at the stage the war had
reached. Be this as it may, the scale upon which the operations
were designed was beyond anything that was needed.

Since the fall of Port Arthur the Russians, pre-occupied
with the prospect of an attack on Vladivostok, had given up
all idea of being able to hold Sakhalin. In January orders had
been issued that in case of a landing of the enemy in force
the troops in the southern districts were to avoid an action
and fall back to join those in the north. While arrangements
to this end were being made it occurred to the Staff that
the Japanese might land not only in the Bay of Aniwa to
seize Korsakovsk, but also at Naibuchi on the east coast. In
that case the retreat of the southern troops would be cut off.
It was decided, therefore, to organise these troops into five
independent columns, which instead of retiring at once were
to commence guerilla operations to harass the progress of the
invaders, and five officers from the Manchurian Army were
appointed to command them. The Korsakovsk column would
number about 500 men (including 60 seamen of the *Novik's*
crew) and the rest an average of about 200, making less than
1,300 men and 8 guns against half a Japanese division. The
northern section was better defended. Including militia and
mounted troops the garrison numbered nearly 6,000 men and
16 guns, the bulk of it being concentrated about Alexandrovsk.[1]

Even more striking than the provision which the Japanese
made to deal with these slender and scattered forces was that
which they made at sea to protect the passage and landing of
their troops. By June 4th the decision had been taken, and on
that day Admiral Togo returned to Sylvia Basin to resume
the command of the fleet from Admiral Kamimura and to
superintend the naval arrangements. The actual situation, as
the Japanese appreciated the results of the late battle, is thus
laid down in their published history :[2] " That victory had
" almost completely swept the enemy's navy from the Far
" Eastern seas, but there still remained a few powerful ships
" in Vladivostok harbour, and at Shanghai some auxiliary

---

[1] *Russian Military History*, Vol. IX., Chapters vii and viii.

[2] Book V., Chap. i. This is the fullest authority we have for these
operations from the Japanese side. No translation has yet been issued.
The references are to the original.

" cruisers which occasionally appeared in that neighbourhood."
Against the latter, measures were already on foot. On June 2nd
the Staff had directed Admiral Kamimura to form a detachment
under Admiral Uriu of one first-class cruiser, two second or
third-class and two destroyers " to operate in the Shanghai
" zone against the Russian volunteer cruisers."   But before
anything further was done a diplomatic step had been taken,
which profoundly influenced the whole situation, nor can the
subsequent operations be rightly appreciated without realising
how from this time diplomacy began to resume the domination.

During the first week in June it began to be whispered that
President Roosevelt was offering the mediation of the United
States. The whispers grew in force and coherence during the
next few days till on the 9th it was known that the matter had
gone so far that both at St. Petersburg and Tokyo the American
Ministers had presented an identical note urging each belligerent
to open direct negotiations with the other.   Next day, the 10th,
it was officially announced that the note had been accepted at
both capitals.   A few days later it was announced that a peace
conference would be arranged in America, but not a word was
said about an armistice and it was understood that unless
Russia proposed a cessation Japan intended to prosecute the
war with vigour.

In view of the new state of affairs Admiral Togo's first care
was to re-organise the Fleet for the work in store for it, and
on June 14th the following organisation in four squadrons
was established for the Combined Fleet :—

First Squadron.

Admiral Togo, Vice-Admiral Misu, Rear-Admiral Ogura.

FIRST DIVISION.—*Mikasa* (flag of Commander-in-Chief), *Shiki-
    shima, Asahi, Fuji* (flag of Vice-Admiral Misu) *(Tatsuta)*.

FOURTH DIVISION.—*Naniwa* (flag of Rear-Admiral Ogura), *Taka-
    chiho, Akashi, Tsushima*.

FLOTILLA.   1st and 3rd destroyer divisions, 14th torpedo-boat
    division.

Second Squadron.

Vice-Admiral Kamimura, Vice-Admiral Uriu, Rear-Admiral
Shimamura.

SECOND DIVISION.—*Idzumo, Tokiwa, Asama, Iwate, (Chihaya)*.
THIRD DIVISION.—*Chitose, Kasagi, Niitaka, Otowa*.

MERCHANT CRUISERS.—*Nippon Maru,*[1] *America Maru.*

FLOTILLA.—2nd and 4th destroyers, 19th torpedo-boats.

THIRD SQUADRON.

Vice-Admiral Kataoka, Rear-Admiral Togo, Rear-Admiral Yamada.

FIFTH DIVISION.—*Yakumo* (flag), *Adzuma, Kasuga* (flag of Admiral Yamada), *Nisshin* (*Yaeyama*).

SIXTH DIVISION.—*Suma, Chiyoda, Idzumi, Akitsushima.*

MERCHANT CRUISERS.—*Yawata Maru, Hongkong Maru.*

FLOTILLA.—5th and 6th[2] destroyers, 9th torpedo-boats.

FOURTH SQUADRON.

Vice-Admiral Dewa, Rear-Admiral Taketomi, Rear-Admiral Nakao.

SEVENTH DIVISION.—*Chinyen, Iki,*[3] *Okinoshima,*[3] *Mishima.*[3]

EIGHTH DIVISION.—*Itsukushima, Hashidate,*[4] *Matsushima.*

NINTH DIVISION.—*Chokai, Maya, Akagi, Uji.*

MERCHANT CRUISERS.—*Manshu Maru, Dainan Maru* (flag of Admiral Nakao).

FLOTILLA.—1st, 10th, 11th, 15th, 20th torpedo-boat divisions.

In addition to the above there was the Special Service Squadron under Rear-Admiral Inoue, which comprised the Fleet auxiliaries and temporary gunboats, including the two flotilla parent ships, *Kumano Maru* and *Kasuga Maru.*

Thus at the end of the war, after annihilating their enemy at sea the Japanese were able to show a fleet of four squadrons and nine divisions; even its flotilla was slightly stronger than that of the original organisation. But, of course, its strength was to some extent illusory; for the Russian prizes which it included were not fit for service, and many Japanese ships were being sent in by turn for repairs and the replacement of damaged guns. Indeed, it seems to have been mainly a parade or administrative organisation; part of the scenery in fact amidst which the Plenipotentiaries were to play their part. In the ensuing operations it was almost entirely disregarded;

---

[1] *Kumano Maru* afterwards substituted from Special Service Squadron.

[2] This additional destroyer division consisted of the two Russian prizes *Byedovi* and *Ryeshitelni*, renamed *Satsuki* and *Akatsuki*.

[3] These were the Russian prizes *Nikolai*, *Apraxin* and *Senyavin*, and were, of course, not available until thoroughly repaired.

[4] Flag of Admiral Taketomi.

but one new feature deserves special notice, and that is that the excellent service which had been rendered by the merchant cruisers is marked by two of them being definitely attached to each of the squadrons.

No sooner was the organisation issued than it began to be broken up. Within a week of the mediation being accepted, the Japanese Imperial Staff had decided the lines on which their vigorous prosecution of the war was to proceed while the negotiations were on foot, and on June 17th, in preparation for what was coming, Admiral Togo ordered Admiral Dewa to take over the guard of the Straits from Admiral Kataoka, and for the latter officer's command he began to form what was known as the Northern Detached Squadron, consisting mainly of the Third and Fourth Squadrons, but with details from other squadrons. At the same time he instructed the *Hongkong Maru* and *Nippon Maru*, which had been allotted to the Second and Third Squadrons, to carry on with their watch of the northern approaches to Vladivostok. The day this was done orders came from the Imperial Staff to provide an escort for the XIIIth Independent Army Division, which was to sail under Lieut.-General Haraguchi from Rikuoku Gulf in the Tsugaru Strait. Thereupon he recalled Admiral Dewa and the Fourth Squadron from the Straits and replaced him by Admiral Kamimura with his own squadron (the Second) and "some portions of other squadrons."[1]

The explanatory instructions which he issued to Admiral Kataoka were as follows :—

"I. The Independent XIIIth Army Division, which has the duty of capturing Sakhalin, will send its first landing party to seize Korsakovsk ; it will then send its second landing party on ahead to seize Alexandrovsk.

"The Transport Squadron containing the first landing party is expected to be ready for sailing from Rikuoku Gulf by the 30th of June.

"Cape Notoro and all the landing places are to be connected with the home country by submarine cables.

"II. You will have the duty of guarding the Tsugaru Strait with the Detached Squadron and of assuming the direction at sea of the transports of the Independent XIIIth Army Division when they are in Rikuoku Gulf and to

---

[1] Fourth Division from the First Squadron, 1st and 10th torpedo divisions from the Fourth, and the 16th, 17th and 18th from Takeshiki.

the north of it. You will protect the XIIIth Division's disembarkation, after consultation with General Haraguchi, who commands that division.

"III. After the date of your arrival in Rikuoku Gulf you will receive orders direct from the Imperial Staff."[1]

The last provision as to the supreme command will be noted as being in accordance with the traditional British practice for combined expeditions.

The naval force allotted for the operation was out of all proportion to the possibilities of interference from the sea. It was composed as follows :—

THIRD SQUADRON (Admiral Kataoka).

FIFTH DIVISION.—*Yakumo* (flag), *Adzuma, Kasuga, Nisshin* (flag of Rear-Admiral Yamada).

SIXTH DIVISION.—*Suma* (flag of Rear-Admiral Togo), *Chiyoda, Idzumi, Akitsushima.*

DESPATCH VESSEL.—*Yaeyama.*

MERCHANT CRUISERS.—*Yawata Maru, Hongkong Maru.*

FOURTH SQUADRON (Admiral Dewa).

SEVENTH DIVISION.—*Chinyen.*

EIGHTH DIVISION.—*Itsukushima* (flag), *Hashidate* (flag of Rear-Admiral Taketomi), *Matsushima.*

NINTH DIVISION.—Gunboats *Chokai, Maya, Akagi, Uji.*

MERCHANT CRUISERS.—*Dainan Maru* (flag of Rear-Admiral Nakao, in charge of the gunboat division) and *Manshu Maru.*

FLOTILLA.

DESTROYERS.—1st, 5th, and 6th Divisions.

TORPEDO-BOATS.—9th, 11th, 15th, and 20th Divisions.

PARENT-SHIPS.—*Kumano Maru, Kasuga Maru.*

He had thus at his disposal four armoured cruisers, the three heavy *Itsukushimas,* four light cruisers, one coast-defence ship and four gunboats, besides auxiliaries and a flotilla numbering 10 destroyers and 16 torpedo-boats. Hoisting his own flag in the *Yakumo,* he ordered Admiral Yamada to proceed in the *Yaeyama* to Kuré and hoist his flag in the *Nisshin,* which had just completed docking there, while Admiral Dewa

---

[1] *Confidential History,* Part III., Ch. I., Sec. 1.

was directed to proceed at once with the bulk of the force to Ominato and from that base to guard the Tsugaru Strait and the Kurile Islands passages.

By the end of the month the whole of the " Northern Detached Squadron," as it was styled, was assembled at Ominato ; the first contingent of the expeditionary force was ready to embark ; and, according to the plan, operations could commence at once. They were conducted with an elaboration which, allowing much for the characteristic care and caution of the Japanese, is eloquent of the anxieties which inevitably beset the moving of large bodies of troops even over well commanded seas. Amongst other precautions for covering the operation we have again four " Guard Lines." The fourth or outermost was off the western entrance of La Pérouse Strait, apparently between Rebun To and Moneron Islands ; and the second was within the strait. The third is not specified, but the first was between Capes Notoro and Siretoko, the two horns of the bay of Aniwa within which Korsakovsk lies.[1] The fourth or outer of these lines was to be occupied and furnished with a look-out station by Admiral Nakao, and the operations began by his moving out on July 2nd with his flagship the *Dainan Maru*, and the rest of the Ninth or Gunboat Division escorting all the torpedo-boats with their two parent ships, and a collier.

Two days later Admiral Kataoka followed with the first wing of the expeditionary force, having for its escort the Fifth, Sixth and Eighth Divisions, besides the *Chinyen*, which was all there was of the Seventh, two merchant cruisers and three divisions of destroyers—in all twelve ships. This meant that he had for a covering squadron four first-class armoured cruisers, with Rear-Admiral Togo's light division for scouting work, besides the merchant cruisers. For his escort squadron there were the *Chinyen* and the three *Itsukushimas*, admirably adapted by their heavy armament for affording tactical support for the troops, while for close inshore work there were the four gunboats of the Ninth Division and his formidable flotilla.

By noon on July 6th the whole force was assembled at Rebun To Island, where Admiral Nakao had already established a look-out station, and the approach could begin. While Admiral Nakao was left with his flagship and another merchant cruiser

---

[1] *Confidential History,* Part III., Bk. I., Sec. 1 (b).

to hold the fourth guard-line, Admiral Dewa was sent forward with the whole of his squadron—that is, the *Chinyen*, the three *Itsukushimas* and the gunboats with all the torpedo-boats and the 5th destroyer division as mine sweepers—to select and sweep the landing-place. This was to be on the north side of Aniwa Bay, as close as convenient to Korsakovsk. Admiral Kataoka himself with the Fifth and Sixth Divisions took over the escort of the troopships, while Admiral Nakao proceeded north to Moneron Island, where on the 9th he hoisted the Japanese flag and set up a signal station "in accordance with the programme of orders."

Since no effort was made to conceal the approach, it was seen at 5 p.m. by the guard of the Cape Notoro lighthouse and telegraphed to all the Russian stations, so that they had as much warning as they could expect. By dawn Admiral Dewa was off the southern edge of the area to be swept and a rapid destroyer reconnaissance revealed that no works had been erected at the desired landing-place, which was at the village of Mereya, about 12 miles east of Korsakovsk. The water was found to be deep and the beach excellent for a disembarkation, and nothing was seen but a few mounted scouts, who galloped off towards Korsakovsk. Sweeping, therefore, began at once, and no mines being found it proceeded so rapidly that by 3.40 a.m. the boats were within 5 miles of Mereya village. The Seventh and Eighth Divisions then advanced into the swept area, while the Sixth followed with the transports. At the edge of the area Admiral Kataoka stopped his armoured cruisers while he sent away steam and pulling boats to act as a landing flotilla and then ordered Admiral Yamada with the *Kasuga* and *Nisshin* to patrol the first guard line between Capes Notoro and Siretoko. Admiral Kataoka with the *Yakumo* and *Adzuma* took station as an inner covering line 15 miles N.N.W. of Cape Siretoko. As this was the seventh of a series of established rendezvous it is to be assumed the operations were proceeding upon a plan which had been previously worked out in detail.

By 11.0 all units were anchored in position, and the landing could begin. It was conducted on the principle which the Japanese had followed in all their descents on an open beach—that is, the footing was seized by a naval brigade drawn from all the divisions. No resistance was met with ; and while covering positions were occupied the sweeping flotilla worked up as far as Point Enduma where begins the inner bay known as Lososei and behind which Korsakovsk lies. The idea was to clear all the water in which the ships would want to operate in supporting the advance on the town, and while this work was in progress the troops at 12.50 began to land. Still no opposition was encountered, but at 2.30, as the sweeping flotilla approached close to Point Enduma, it came under a heavy artillery fire from the shore.

The fact was that as soon as the officer commanding the Korsakovsk column knew in what force the Japanese were approaching, he decided to burn and abandon the town ; and in order to gain time for the work he placed a militia rear-guard with two guns on the Enduma ridge, with orders to begin the burning at the first indication of a bombardment. These men had opened fire on the leading torpedo-boats as they appeared. The gunboat *Akashi*, which was guarding the sweeping flotilla, replied vigorously as well as the torpedo craft, but without ceasing to sweep. As other units came up the duel increased, but with no harm done ; and eventually, after firing their last rounds into the town, the Russians retired to a position which they had prepared to the northward, at a village called Solovevka.

Meanwhile the landing had proceeded without interruption. The troops were organised in four sections, the first two of which only were to be landed at Mereya. By 3.0 the landing of these sections had proceeded so far that the Naval Brigade were able to hand over to the Army what they called "their village" and by 7.0 the whole of the first two sections were ashore. There the disembarkation ended for the time, the rest being intended to land at Korsakovsk itself as soon as the place was occupied. Next morning, therefore, at 3 a.m., Admiral Dewa, in order to support the attack, ordered the *Idzumi* and the rest of the gunboats to Enduma Point, but hearing later that the town had been occupied by the troops without opposition, he pushed on a sweeping flotilla, formed from all the Fleet steamboats, into Lososei Bay under escort of the *Kasuga Maru* and two destroyers. To the northward of the town at 6.30 they found a Russian detachment posted on the hills with two guns, on which they immediately opened fire. This was the Solovevka position to which the retirement had been made, but it was soon found that as the destroyers' guns were enfilading it from a range too great for the Russian guns, the Commandant ordered it to be abandoned and retired further north.

While this was going on Admiral Taketomi, second-in-command of the Dewa Squadron, moved up the rest of the transports to Enduma Point; but as it was found that most of the town was in ashes and the pier burnt, they were put ashore at a village close by. The second disembarkation began at noon and was finished by 6 p.m. Thus by the evening of the 8th—the day the Japanese Plenipotentiaries sailed for America—they had Korsakovsk already in their pockets. The next day was apparently consumed in landing stores, but by the evening of the 10th the whole of the naval work was done and the Admiral could report that the landing had been smartly carried out without the loss of a man. Admiral Nakao was now recalled from the fourth guard line and Rear-Admiral Togo despatched with half his division, one infantry company, and a division of torpedo-boats to seize the Notoro Lighthouse. This he did with the infantry and one company of seamen without resistance by 9 a.m. on the 10th. Leaving the troops behind him, on whom devolved the duty of keeping the light burning,[1] he was back before dark.

Admiral Kataoka was now free to set about the second part of his programme, which was to bring forward the other wing of the expeditionary force intended for North Sakhalin. Accordingly he proceeded at once with the Third Squadron to Hakodate, leaving Admiral Dewa on guard with the Fourth in Lososei Bay.

---

[1] A similar duty was performed by Wellington's troops near San Sebastian at the request of the naval officer commanding the blockading force.

CHAPTER XXIII.

THE SECOND SAKHALIN EXPEDITION.

[Maps IX, XIV to XVIII.   Chart VI.]

FOR reasons that will appear directly there were inherent risks attending the northern operations which were absent from the southern theatre, and it is only what we should expect from the extreme care with which the Japanese Staff habitually sought to abate such risks, if we find that elaborate precautions were already on foot to smooth Admiral Kataoka's path.   The most striking of these arrangements appear to have been aimed at concealing the objective of the new expedition.   In the first place, before leaving Korsakovsk he had been directed by telegraphic orders from the Staff at Tokyo to detach Admiral Yamada with the *Kasuga* and *Nisshin* and the first destroyer division to make a demonstration in St. Vladimir and Olga Bays, which lie some 200 miles up the coast from Vladivostok.   Here, during a three days' reconnaissance of the coast with the destroyers, they discovered the wreck of the *Izumrud*, and, after ascertaining she was unserviceable, returned to Hakodate on July 15th.

But this was by no means the end of the diversionary operations.   Shortly after Admiral Kataoka had started with the Northern Detached Squadron from Tsushima, the Imperial Staff had decided to increase the forces in North Korea, in order to press up along the seaboard to the Russian frontier. Accordingly on July 6th, the day the approach on Korsakovsk began, Admiral Togo had been informed that two transports were coming to Sylvia Basin, bringing troops from Talien-hwan and Yongampo, at the mouth of the Yalu, and that he was to arrange for their safe transit to Song-chin, where they were to be landed.[1]   The escort ordered by the Staff was one first-class cruiser, two of the second or third-class, and a couple of destroyers.   But this Admiral Togo apparently regarded as insufficient, for the detachment he placed under

---

[1] The Japanese North Korean force was at this time 3 brigades of infantry, a squadron of cavalry, 4 batteries of field artillery, and a company of engineers.   The reinforcements, which were 2 squadrons of reserve cavalry and one company of engineers (*Published History*, Book V., Ch. iii., sec. 3), would bring it roughly to the strength of one division.

Admiral Kamimura for the service comprised two armoured cruisers (*Iwate* and *Tokiwa*), two light cruisers (*Chitose* and *Niitaka*), and a complete division of destroyers, and to these a third armoured cruiser (*Idzumo*) and the despatch-vessel *Chihaya* were subsequently added.

With this powerful escort Admiral Kamimura, having Admiral Shimamura as second-in-command, sailed with three transports on the 14th, just as Admiral Kataoka returned to Hakodate with the Third Squadron to prepare for the second part of his operations and while Admiral Yamada was completing his demonstration in Olga Bay. By the 16th the landing of the troops was complete, and that day Admiral Kamimura, leaving the *Niitaka* at Song-chin to assist in landing the stores, moved on to make a reconnaissance in force up the coast. At dawn on the 17th the *Chitose, Chihaya*, and the two destroyers, which had been sent ahead, were off the Tumen, and while the *Chitose* went forward for Askold Island, off Vladivostok, the *Chihaya* and the destroyers proceeded to carry out a close examination of all the inlets in Gashkevich Bay, just south of the Tumen estuary. Here was the village of Ongi, the centre of the Russian coast defence, and in Audacious Bay the destroyers reported they had seen some 200 troops and driven them off. Moving southward as far as Najin Po, in Kornilof Bay, they found a good military road with a newly-erected telegraph line, which was, of course, part of the system connecting Ongi with the Russian advanced line. While, therefore, the *Chihaya* kept at bay troops that could be seen on the hills north of Cape Geka, and the armoured cruisers off Linden Point shelled a similar post north of Anna Bay, a party was landed from the flotilla, who quickly destroyed a mile of the telegraph. This done they continued the coast reconnaissance southward, seeing nothing but Cossack patrols, till by 3.0 they were off Kolokoltsef Point. Here the *Chitose* joined them, having been prevented by fog from showing herself at Askold Island, and Admiral Kamimura, having effectively alarmed the whole coast, led back for Osaki Bay to resume his guard of the Straits.

It was a good day's work, and its effect on the Russian dispositions in North Korea was all that could be desired. A general retrograde movement was promptly ordered to the extreme north corner of Korea, where it narrows down between Kolokoltsef Point and the Tumen, and the Russian efforts were to be restricted to resisting a landing either in Kornilof or

Gashkevich Bay, and to securing the retreat of the whole force
to the Tumen. This movement, of course, cleared the way
for the advance of the Japanese, who, finding nothing but two
or three sotnias of Cossacks on their front, occupied the town
of Pureng on July 22nd with their advance guard.[1]

By this time Admiral Kamimura had resumed his guard of
the Straits, and on the 20th Admiral Togo took the battleship
division for a cruise up the Japanese coast. Its object is not
stated. We are told that he visited various Japanese ports as
high as Maizuru, carried out various combined drills, and
was not back at Sylvia Basin till August 8th—that is, it was a
cruise of nearly three weeks, which coincided with the invasion
of North Sakhalin and the operations ancillary to it : for it
was the day after Admiral Togo sailed that Admiral Kataoka
finally got away with the second expeditionary force.

Whether or not the Commander-in-Chief's cruise was intended as what the Japanese called "indirect support," there is
little doubt that they regarded the second part of the northern
operations as likely to prove more serious than that which had
just been carried through so easily. From prisoners captured
at the Notoro Lighthouse they had learnt that, although Alexandrovsk was believed not to be mined, it had a regular
garrison of 1,400 men, which on mobilisation would be rapidly
expanded to between 4,000 to 5,000. But, apart from the fact
that more real opposition was likely to be met with in the
northern section, the distance which the expedition had to
cover to its objective at Alexandrovsk was little less than 700
miles, through ever-narrowing waters flanked the whole way
by the enemy's coast ; and at any point it was exposed to attack
from the Vladivostok squadron, about which no information
could be procured. The precautions that had to be taken to
ensure its safety were consequently, as we shall see, very carefully studied. On this occasion the transports were to assemble
at a point of departure outside the Tsugaru Strait. The port
chosen was Otaru, on the west coast of Yezo, the northernmost
of the "Defended Areas," which had been declared "Prohibited"
on the first day of the war. The reason for selecting this place
would appear to be that, as the Japanese were by this time in
full occupation of South Sakhalin, the General was bringing
up part of the force he had employed at Korsakovsk in order
to strengthen the new expedition. We know, at any rate, that

---

[1] *Russian Military History*, Vol. IX., Ch. iii.

three transports were to leave Korsakovsk for Otaru on the same day that the bulk of the expedition moved from Rikuoku Gulf.

It was on the 17th, while Admiral Kamimura was making his demonstration on the Korean coast, that the movement began. The transports proceeded by groups, and to ensure their safety Admiral Kataoka, who was at Hakodate, ordered Rear-Admiral Togo with the Sixth Division to move with them, "keeping guard at a suitable distance outside the usual "sea route." Admiral Yamada did the same for the second group, and Admiral Kataoka the third, and by the afternoon of the 18th the whole force was concentrated at the assembly point. Here, however, they were fog-bound for over two days, and it was not till about noon on the 21st that they were able to put to sea.

The plan of operations was laid down in the following general order which Admiral Kataoka had issued to his command on the 12th :—

"I. No further intelligence about the Vladivostok "Squadron has transpired. Korsakovsk is occupied by "our troops and the Russian soldiers who were there "have fled in a northerly direction. There appears to "be no other particular variation in the defences of "the island as described in my previous order.

"II. The Northern Detached Squadron in the course "of the first stage of its operations has escorted the "Southern Landing Force of the Independent XIIIth "Division to Korsakovsk and landed it there ; the Army "and Navy have acted in collaboration ; and the occupa-"tion of South Sakhalin by our Army has been effected. "We shall now escort the Second Transport Squadron "to Alexandrovsk and make a landing there with the "object of quickly completing the occupation of Sakhalin.

"III. The *Suma* and *Chiyoda* of the Sixth Division "will guard the van of the transport squadron. The "*Idzumi, Akitsushima, Yawata Maru* and *Hongkong* "*Maru* (she had relieved the *Manshu Maru* on the 1st "of July) will lead part of the transport squadron.

"The Fifth Division will guard the port side of the "transport squadron, and the *Yaeyama* will steam parallel "with the transport squadron, on its port quarter.

"The 5th destroyer division will be outside the Sixth "Division, and the 1st destroyer division outside the "Fifth Division.

"IV. Admiral Dewa, with the Fourth Squadron, the
"9th torpedo-boat division, the parent ship *Kumano*
"*Maru*, one water ship and two colliers under him,
"will proceed from Korsakovsk one day before these
"operations begin. On the third day from the com-
"mencement of the operations he will reach Cape Tuik
"at the southern entrance of Mamiya Strait[1]; he will
"then send a detachment from his force to reconnoitre
"and threaten Castries Bay, and with the remainder will
"make a selection of the intended landing place. He will
"cause another detachment to make an appearance at
"suitable places in front of Alexandrovsk and Due, and
"will then recall the detachments to the main squadron.

"V. At dawn on the fourth day Admiral Dewa will
"arrive in the offing of the appointed landing place,
"and will order the torpedo-boat flotilla to sweep rapidly
"under the protection of the fleet. He will at a favour-
"able opportunity send ashore a landing party to seize
"the landing place. When the army has disembarked
"it will relieve the naval landing party, which will then
"return to the fleet.

"*Note.*—These operations must be commenced only
"after wireless communication with myself has been
"established. The plan for the sweeping operations and
"the organisation of the landing party will be settled by
"Admiral Dewa.

"VI. I give Admiral Dewa the duty of landing the
"army expeditionary force. The steam and pulling
"boats of the Fifth and Sixth Divisions must be sent to
"such places as the Admiral Commanding the Fourth
"Squadron may require.

"VII. The transport squadron will reach the appointed
"landing place at early morning of the fourth day.
"The guiding ships will lead the transports through
"the swept area in accordance with Admiral Dewa's
"instructions."

That same day Admiral Dewa issued the following
instructions :—

"I. I have selected for the landing place of the
"Northern Landing force, the coast from Alexandrovsk

---

[1] Mamiya Strait is the Japanese name for the narrows where the
Gulf of Tartary ends some 50 miles north of Alexandrovsk.

" northwards up to the parallel of latitude 51° (*i.e.*,
" eight miles).

" II. Since the first area to be swept should be as near
" to Alexandrovsk as possible a direction of S.W. by S.
" towards the landing place must be taken."[1]

The Army transports, including two despatch-vessels and
a hospital-ship, numbered twenty-two sail, and the whole
armament amounted to forty-two.

A striking feature of the programme, it will be observed,
is that Admiral Dewa with the advance guard was not to proceed
directly off Alexandrovsk, but to pass by it to the entrance of
the Mamiya Strait and commence his operations from there.
The motive is not stated, but it points to an attempt to
solve the dilemma which was a constant feature of our own
operations of this kind. We had always found that two
elements of success were almost inevitably in conflict. The
one was the advantage of surprise, the other the advantage of
isolating the objective as soon as possible. The process of
isolation could scarcely fail to indicate the objective, and a
nice adjustment between the two opposing aims was always
a cardinal point in settling the plan of operations. In this
case the choice of Cape Tuik as the final rendezvous points
to a desire to find such an adjustment : for by passing by
Alexandrovsk they were doing their best to leave the objective
in doubt till the last moment, and at the same time were taking
a position which would prevent its receiving supplies and reinforcement from Nikolaievsk at the other end of the Mamiya
Strait. It would also permit of certain demonstrations to the
same ends, which, as we shall see, were the first movements
undertaken.

In accordance with the above programme Admiral Dewa
with the Fourth Squadron had proceeded independently from
Korsakovsk as soon as the fog permitted, and on the morning
of the 22nd, as the main force, hugging the Japanese coast,
had passed up inside Rebun To they got into wireless touch
with one another at 120 miles, and this they succeeded in
maintaining. Next morning at 3 a.m., Admiral Dewa, after
passing Alexandrovsk detached Admiral Taketomi in the *Hashidate* with a division of torpedo-boats to make a demonstration
and reconnaisance in Castries Bay, which lies on the mainland
immediately north-west of Alexandrovsk. A little later two

---

[1] *Confidential History*, Part III., Bk. i., Sec. 2.

other torpedo-boat divisions (11th and 15th) were detached
with their parent ship *Kasuga Maru*, the one to select a landing
place at Arkovo, seven miles north of the town, and the other
to make a diversionary demonstration off Due, a village about
four miles to the south of it, while the Admiral anchored the
squadron at the appointed rendezvous south of Cape Tuik.

The disposition of the Russian troops at the moment was
well designed to meet the Japanese plan of attack. In
Alexandrovsk itself was the main force consisting of two
battalions, four militia companies, four field guns, six machine
guns and a mounted detachment. At Arkovo and Due were
two wing detachments each of four companies, and two militia
units, with four field guns at Arkovo and two machine guns
at Due. All told, including a militia unit of 150 men in reserve at Ruikovsk, where the Alexandrovsk road joins the main
north and south road, the defence force numbered a little short
of 6,000 men, with one field battery and one of machine guns.[1]

Of these arrangements the Japanese reconnoitring detachment could see nothing. In the evening it returned to Admiral
Dewa at Cape Tuik to report that the place seemed to have
no fixed defences and no garrison; they had seen nothing
but a few horsemen at Arkovo, and the villagers there had burnt
their huts, boats, and a lighter laden with ammunition. Though
the place was not favourable for deployment after landing,
there being little level ground behind the beach and the country
beyond thickly wooded, the beach itself was very good, and
large ships could anchor within four cables of it. It had therefore been swept and buoyed. At Due no troops of any kind
had been seen, and a similar report from the Castries Bay
detachment brought assurance that it was equally quiet there.
At midnight, therefore, Admiral Dewa raised anchor in order
to commence his preparatory operations at dawn, and at the
same hour Admiral Kataoka, according to programme, detached
Rear-Admiral Togo with half his division and two destroyers
to make a demonstration at Barracouta Harbour, and then to
establish a signal station on the opposite coast at Stukambis
Point, 135 miles south of Alexandrovsk. By the end of the
third day (the 27th) he was to occupy the First Guard Line
which ran south of Stukambis Point to the Tartary coast.
The other two destroyers of the division were sent to repeat
the demonstration in Castries Bay, after which one was to

---

[1] *Russian Military History*, Vol. IX., Ch. viii.

remain on guard in the bay and one to meet the *Hongkong Maru* and patrol the entrance of the Mamiya Strait—that is, off Cape Tuik, where apparently was the Fifth Guard Line.

The presence of the Japanese on the coast was reported to General Lyapunov about mid-day on the 23rd, and although this with the preliminary reconnaissance left him in no doubt as to what was coming, little or nothing was done to improve the position. No emplacements were constructed to defend the harbour ; the only defence, indeed, seems to have been on the Jonquière Heights just south of the town, where some trenches had been constructed to command the road leading to Ruikovsk. His orders from General Linevich were that, if he found he could not hold his own against superior forces, he was to retire to Cape Lazareva, where steamers would be sent to transport his troops to Nikolaievsk. How this was considered a possible operation in the face of the Japanese squadron is difficult to understand, but it may have been thought they would hesitate to pass the narrow waters of the Mamiya Strait.

The order clearly had a very bad effect. Considering what his troops were it is certain General Lyapunov can have had no illusions as to being able to hold his own, and his posting his reserve at Ruikovsk suggests how much he was pre-occupied with the idea of retreat. Instead, therefore, of employing the short time at his disposal to perfecting his means of resistance he devoted his attention to quite another affair. The previous day a number of boats laden with provisions and ammunition had arrived from Nikolaievsk, and as they had not yet moved from the beach he ordered the whole—boats, ammunition and stores—to be destroyed, the destruction, as we have seen, being witnessed by the Japanese flotilla during their reconnaissance. As their movements had threatened both his flanks no change was made in the disposition of his force, the main body being distributed between the heights on either side of the town.

By 4.30 a.m. Admiral Dewa was at the edge of the area which had been swept the day before, eight miles from shore, but so thick was the mist that he was not seen by the Russians nor could he find the buoys which had been laid down. He therefore had to begin sweeping afresh, but as he had three divisions of torpedo-boats and four picket-boats, and no mines were found, the work caused little delay. By about 7.30 the Russians thought they could make out 70 vessels in all deployed parallel to the coast, and an hour later the 5th destroyer division began searching the landing place at Arkovo with its guns.

As to the precise manner in which the landing was carried
out and the extent to which it was supported by ship fire we
have but meagre detail.   But it seems clear that the Third
Squadron took little part in it, being for the most part employed as a covering force.   Rear-Admiral Togo was still away
engaged with half his division in demonstrating about Barracouta Harbour, and under orders to occupy the First Guard
Line.   His other two light cruisers after sending their steam
and pulling boats to Admiral Taketomi, who in the *Hashidate*
had immediate charge of the landing, went off to join their
flag on the First Guard Line.   Admiral Yamada's sub-division
of the armoured cruisers also dropped their boats at the edge of
the swept area and then proceeded to occupy a position known
as No. 27, which was 25 miles west of Alexandrovsk.   With
the other two cruisers of his division Admiral Kataoka eventually entered the swept area and anchored off Arkovo, and
he may, therefore, have taken part in the bombardment.   Of
the part played by the merchant cruisers nothing is known,
except that the *Hongkong Maru* was stationed on the Fifth
Guard Line, which probably was to the northward, to watch
the route from Castries Bay and Nikolaievsk, but its position
is not specified.   In any case, the bulk of the artillery support
came from the Fourth Squadron, which was the true supporting force.   As the sweeping flotilla advanced towards the beach
it was followed closely and protected by the Ninth or Gunboat Division (*Chokai, Maya, Akagi, Uji*).   Then followed the
Seventh Division represented by the solitary *Chinyen*, and then
the three *Itsukushimas* forming the Eighth.   Besides the flotilla
guns and the minor armament of the ships the troops had
therefore at their back three 1·25 inch, two 8-inch, two 6-inch,
48 4·7 inch, and 42 12-pounders, or close upon 100 guns,
of which considerably more than half could come into action
simultaneously, and this is not counting anything Admiral
Kataoka's own sub-division may have done.   Such an overwhelming battery was, of course, more than sufficient to put
the issue beyond doubt.

So quickly had the sweeping progressed that shortly before
9.0 it was decided to commence the landing.   It was to begin,
as usual, with a naval brigade, which was drawn from all
three divisions of the Fourth Squadron.   It was of considerable strength amounting to one infantry brigade and one
field-gun company, besides the usual attached parties.   It
was 8.55 when, covered by the guns of the supporting

ships, they pushed off. So heavy was the fire developed upon the forest-covered shore that the advanced troops of the Arkovo wing had at once to fall back upon their reserves at Arkovo II., whence if pressed they would be able to retire to the Kamuishevi Pass, the position at which General Lyapunov had been instructed to make his first stand. The seizure of the beach was thus effected practically without opposition. So rapid was the success that by 9.15 Arkovo was occupied by the seamen, and a quarter of an hour later the advanced guard of the troops began to follow. Simultaneously the sweeping was pushed on towards Jonquière Point . under the covering fire of the gunboats, while the transports were conducted in. By 1.0 they were all anchored in position a mile from the beach, and at 1.20 the Naval Brigade was able to hand over to the first section of the troops.

During this time the 5th destroyer division in preparation for the second landing, which, as in the Korsakovsk plan, was to be at Alexandrovsk, were using their guns to prevent the destruction of the pier. Early in the afternoon the *Chokai* and *Akagi* came to their assistance with a company of troops, who were put ashore and seized the pier. So severely, however, were they galled by two machine guns which the Russians had placed to command the town landing place, that the two gunboats had to put in again and devote themselves to their protection. Further to the southward, beyond Jonquière Point, the other two gunboats were busy at Due and the little port at Niomi a mile to the north of it, which served the adjacent coal-mine and was connected with Alexandrovsk by a tramway. Here there was a jetty and large stores of coal ready for transportation, which were being fired, but early in the afternoon the gunboats landed a fire brigade and another infantry company, so that not only was everything saved and a large quantity of coal captured, but a diversion made which materially disturbed the Russian dispositions.

As soon as General Lyapunov heard how the beach defence on his right had collapsed, he began to turn his attention to a further retreat to the Kamuishevi Pass. The reserves at Ruikovsk had been called up to reinforce it, but owing to. the naval demonstration that was going on before Due he did not dare move anything from that wing till nearly noon. Finding, however, that no preparation for a landing developed he ordered the Due reserve battalion and both the machine guns attached to it to move to the Pass, leaving only two militia units on guard. But as by this time the Japanese had begun a second landing south of Arkovo it was considered unsafe for the reinforcement to march by the direct route through Alexandrovsk, and it had to make a long detour inland by way of the hill passes, that is by the line Mikhailovka, Pilenski Pass, Tuimovo, and Armudan.

By 1.0 p.m. when the Japanese transports were all anchored in position the main or Alexandrovsk force was distributed in this way. On the heights north of the town was a battalion of the Nikolaievsk Fortress Infantry, the backbone of the garrison ; on the Jonquière heights to the south were the four militia units, one of them composed of convict volunteers ; and in support of them at Korsakovskaya were the Alexandrovsk reserve battalion, half a field battery (four guns), and six machine guns.

Such was the position when shortly after 3.0 p.m. General Lyapunov was informed of the landing at the coal port beyond Jonquière Point. This meant—assuming it was the prelude to a disembarkation in force—that the Japanese would cut off the two militia units that had been left there, and that then having nothing to oppose them they would seize the Verblyuzhi Pass, which would give them command of the Alexandrovsk Valley, and the Mikhailovka heights and enable them to take the Alexandrovsk position in reverse. The consequence was that the Due reserve battalion had to be promptly withdrawn from the support of the Arkovo wing and devoted to the defence of the Verblyuzhi Pass in order to make head against the new danger. This was the more unfortunate since the Arkovo wing, hard pressed by the Japanese advance, which by this time had fully developed, was retiring on the Kamuishevi Pass, blowing up their reserves of ammunition on the way. So hasty, indeed, was the retreat that they lost touch with a whole militia unit which shortly afterwards was compelled to surrender.

Scarcely had this distracting incident been realised when it was seen that a fresh landing was developing at Alexandrovsk itself. The Jonquière trenches which faced the defiles of the valley were promptly occupied by a company of the Alexandrovsk regiment, and two militia units, while another company and two machine guns were called up from the reserve and posted near the church. By about half-past four a whole Japanese battalion was judged to have landed, which at once proceeded to assault the Jonquière Heights and the town.

They were checked, however, by the church post, the first Russian success, but at the same time it became apparent that the Japanese left was pushing on so rapidly from the direction of the Arkovo valley that the right flank of the Nikolaievsk battalion at Polovinka was threatened. Reinforcements from the Alexandrovsk regiment had to be sent to meet the danger, but at that moment the supporting fire from the ships began to increase alarmingly. The heights on which the threatened right flank was situated were soon, we are told, "enveloped " in a continuous sheet of flame." Under cover of the storm of shell the Japanese infantry pressed on ; the heights became absolutely untenable, and the whole Nikolaievsk wing had to fall back to a position further inland known as Kavkaz.

By this time the Japanese flotilla had completed the sweeping right up to Jonquière Point, and the ships were able to draw in and develop an equally destructive fire on that side under cover of which they were able to push on the second landing in force. As it now became evident to the Russians that this was the real attack and that at Due only a feint, the Due troops, which were holding the Verblyuzhi Pass, were called up to Korsakovskaya, and upon that position the whole Alexandrovsk force retired as darkness fell. The result was that by about 7.0 p.m. the Japanese were in full occupation of the town, and of all the adjacent heights which the Russians had originally occupied for its defence. Still it was not till 9.0 p.m. that the two first sections of the expeditionary force were all ashore. It had taken just 12 hours since the naval brigade pushed off. What units formed the first disembarkation we do not know beyond the fact that the 26th infantry brigade occupied the town, and that towards evening some cavalry were operating with the Arkovo wing. Both columns continued to push on during the night, that operating from Arkovo turning the right flank of the Russians, so that towards morning General Lyapunov had to retire his whole force to the Pilenski Pass.

The landing of the third and last section of the Japanese troops seems to have been commenced the same night, but the work of landing the force went on all next day, most of the transports moving up to the town. Eventually it was not till 7.0 p.m. on the 27th that the whole force with its stores and train was completely disembarked and a general advance could be made.

In spite, therefore, of the large amount of naval assistance and the fact that a pier and wharves were available, the whole

operation consumed four days. In the circumstances it is easy
to understand how scrupulously careful Admiral Kataoka
was to maintain adequate cover upon his guard lines,
and to keep the enemy amused on their own coast. The
second demonstration at Castries Bay was, in fact, pushed
very far. After landing at the lighthouse and finding it deserted
Commander Fujimoto went up the bay to destroy the telegraph
stations. There as his boats were suddenly fired on he bombarded the settlement and laid it in ashes. He then returned
to the squadron, but was again detached to reconnoitre the
southern part of the Mamiya Strait, and destroy the cable at
Pogobi where the strait is narrowest. Here he put a party
ashore, destroyed the land connection, and removed the instru-
ments, and then after further destruction of the telegraph near
Boronina Cape he rejoined the squadron on the 27th.

Rear-Admiral Togo, with his two light cruisers and two
destroyers, had been equally active in the zone of the First
Guard Line. Having landed twice at Barracouta Harbour and
found it deserted, he went across and established his look-out
station at Stukambis Point, and he also rejoined the squadron
on the evening of the 27th.

By that time, as we have seen, the combined operations
were at an end, and the Fleet was free to leave the Army to deal
with the enemy in the interior. The whole affair was one
which deserved the hearty congratulations which the Forces
received from the Court. With apparently little more than
half a division, which would mean normally 7,000 or 8,000
men, they had forced a landing in twelve hours, on an open
beach where an attack had long been expected and in the face of
a warned enemy numbering nearly 5,000. True, the troops at
General Lyapunov's disposal were in a great part of very poor
quality ; but, on the other hand, the Japanese division was one
that had been raised only a few months, the men were quite
raw and had never smelt powder till they were engaged. That
they succeeded as they did must be put down, in a great
measure, to the irresistible support that they had from the ship
guns. The enemy's artillery was absolutely overpowered from
the first, and according to the Russian reports it was the devastating effect of the overwhelming naval fire which put resistance out of the question.

Although from all the evidence we have it is clear that the
tactical support which the squadron gave was the decisive
factor, it cannot detract from the merit of the green troops

in making the most of it.   The initial attack must have been carried through with great skill and spirit, particularly when we remember how unfavourable the back of the beach was for deployment.   The pursuit, at any rate, was a fine performance.   So vigorously was it pressed that owing to their having landed north of the town they were able to cut off part of the Arkovo wing, and force it to abandon the Kamuishevi Pass.   By this means they were able to push on and seize the northern road at Derbinsk.   Thence on the 27th they advanced along the road upon Ruikovsk, upon which place General Lyapunov was also retiring since he knew his position at the Pilenski Pass had been turned owing to the failure of his right wing.   The Japanese right column was in full pursuit and thus, with the bulk of his force, he was driven southward down the Onor Road towards their own troops in the Korsakovsk district.   For five days, amidst woods and morasses, in overpowering heat, the Russians were given no rest, and eventually on the 30th, the General having reached the village of Onor, about 60 miles south of Alexandrovsk with his force entirely exhausted and demoralised, and rapidly melting away, decided to surrender.   A few small parties stole away into the forests.   According to the Russian return, a quarter of his original strength had been lost in killed, wounded, and missing, and more than half his artillery was gone.   The actual numbers which laid down their arms were 60 officers and 3,819 men, with two field guns and four machine guns.

With the news of their success the combined work of the Northern Detached Squadron was at an end.   It will have been observed that the completeness and rapidity of the success is to be traced on this occasion to the fact that the operation had been carried out on true combined principles. Full advantage had been taken of the flexibility of an amphibious force to operate securely on two lines, with the result that the Russians were unable to concentrate so as to prevent their retreat being cut off.   This had been done very much in the manner of Wolfe's final attack at Quebec by holding one wing of the enemy by a feint which allowed their centre to be penetrated by the landing at Alexandrovsk.   In contrast with the cases of the battles of the Yalu and Nan-shan it was a true feint : that is to say—the Japanese did not content themselves with a purely naval menace, but actually landed troops at Due, upon the Russian left.   It was a mere handful, but enough to hold that wing from being used to reinforce either the Russian right or centre and to keep it out of action the whole day. The general plan of operation, in fact, bore a much closer resemblance to our own traditional method of conducting enterprises of this nature than anything they had hitherto done.

It now only remained for Admiral Kataoka to dispose his force so as to cover the conquest and protect the communication of the Army. Before starting on the second expedition he had informed the Imperial Staff and Admiral Togo that on the completion of his programme he intended to employ the Third Squadron for the guard of La Pérouse Strait and the defence of Sakhalin, basing it on Lososei Bay by Korsakovsk. The Fourth Squadron based at Hakodate or Ominato, would guard the Tsugaru Strait and the northern part of the Japan Sea from lat. 42° to lat. 45°, which meant that as Otaru was now the base of the Sakhalin army, its communications would be covered till they entered the sphere of the Third Squadron. These arrangements he now proceeded to carry out, though from time to time they were modified on orders from the Imperial Staff. Rear-Admiral Togo, for instance, with half his division, was sent up to examine Petropavlovsk and the adjacent parts of Kamchatka. Later on a general re-distribution took place, because, we are told, although there was no further information about the Vladivostok squadron it was believed there were two gunboats and seven or eight torpedo boats at Nikolaievsk. Admiral Dewa, with most of the Fourth Squadron, was therefore permanently based at Alexandrovsk. But, generally, it may be said, that for the rest of the war the northern detachment was engaged in protecting the army's line of communication, in stopping contraband running to Nikolaievsk, and in assisting General in dealing with isolated parties of Russian troops who had avoided surrender and from time to time appeared on the Sakhalin coast. In the end, according to the Russian returns, of the 5,500 men in North Sakhalin and 1,500 in the South there were taken prisoners 81 officers and 4,400 men, and all that succeeded in crossing to the mainland were 8 officers and 270 men. The list of killed was under 100, but the missing amounted to 1,660.

The rapidity and cleverness with which the conquest of the island had been effected gave the Japanese, besides the material and diplomatic value of the acquisition, another advantage of the utmost importance. It was that early in August they found themselves able to send the whole of the new XIVth Division to join the Army in Manchuria, and further to reinforce the troops on its right wing in North Korea.[1]   In view of the fact that the formal negotiations were about to begin—August 10 being the day the Plenipotentiaries were to meet—this was a point of great importance.   Since the Russians on their part claimed they had now in Manchuria a stronger army better equipped, better trained, and better organised for offensive operations than they had yet possessed, it meant everything to the Japanese to show that their power of developing fresh force and of carrying on further offensive operations on the continent was not yet exhausted, in spite of their efforts in Sakhalin.   It is natural, therefore, to find that the last work in which the southern half of the fleet was employed was in assisting in the new development.

The moment the conquest of Sakhalin was assured Admiral Togo's co-operation was called for.   As early as August 3rd, while still on his cruise, he had been told that transports carrying an infantry brigade and drafts were going to assemble in Sylvia Basin and that an escort was required for them to Song-chin.[2]   Again the duty was committed to Admiral Kamimura, who after handing over the guard of the Straits to Admiral Uriu formed the escort squadron of his own division (except the *Iwate*) the *Otowa* and *Chihaya* and six destroyers.   At Sylvia Basin he found seven transports awaiting his arrival.   In charge of them was an officer of the General Staff from Headquarters, who met him with a suggestion which placed him in no small difficulty.   For what the General Staff had to propose was a change in the arrangements since the orders received from the Naval Commander-in-Chief did not suit the military situation.

The reason was this.   As a consequence of Admiral Kamimura's last demonstration the Japanese had been able not only to occupy Pureng, but their advance had been pushed still further on, till on July 5th they had captured the advanced position which the Russians had been occupying to the northward of Pureng, at the Paksabong and adjacent passes, with their right flank guard at Tizenko Bay.[3]   By this success the Russian advanced force had been pushed back to a line

---

[1] *Japanese Published History*, Book V., Ch. ii., Sec. 3, Sub-sec. 1.   On August 6th Admiral Ijuin telegraphed to Admiral Kataoka that this division had been sent to the Manchurian Army.

[2] This was apparently the port from which the Japanese advanced base at Kil-tsiou was now being supplied.

[3] In reconnoitring the coast Admiral Kamimura reports that he saw a Japanese communication post in this bay.

extending from the sea near Linden Point to Herien on the
Tumen, where the river turns northward, with the centre slightly
advanced.   This meant that they had been forced back into the
extreme corner of Korea, and in view of the peace negotiations,
which were now in full swing, the situation was causing grave
anxiety at the Russian Headquarters.   For in spite of the
restricted area occupied Admiral Kamimura's demonstration had
kept alive the fear of a landing in rear and all they had to
rely on to prevent it was the force maintained at Ongi, in
Gashkevich Bay, and the patrols which were watching the bays
along the coast as far south as Linden Point. So insecure
was the situation that General Linevich found it necessary to
reinforce the North Korean Army with five more battalions, and
while informing the officer commanding it of his intention he told
him he was expected to offer the strongest possible resistance
to the Japanese.   For the present he assured him they would
not have enough troops to land in Posiette Bay, but in no
case whatsoever were they to be permitted to pass the
Tumen River and seize the district of New Kiev—that is, the
district between the river and Vladivostok. A further telegram
despatched on news of the last retrograde movement reiterated
these orders with a reprimand for having disregarded them.
"For us," said the General, "this evacuation of North Korea
" is extremely unsatisfactory."   But the assurance that the fear
of a landing at Posiette Bay could be eliminated was far from
convincing the officer in command who had the sea at his elbow.
He could only reply that although he knew the importance
of retaining his hold "for political reasons as well as to
" prevent the enemy entering our territory" he could do no
more than act on the defensive since the movements of his
force were tied down by the threatened landing in his rear.

Whether or not the Japanese General Staff realised the
Russian apprehensions, they were not contemplating such a
movement as was feared ; their request to Admiral Kamimura
was much more modest. As in the case of Nan-shan there
seems to have been an inexplicable failure to realise the amphibious possibilities of the situation, although it is evident from
the extreme anxiety of the Russian Commander for his
retreat that a real threat in his rear would have caused a
general retirement to the Tumen.   But no such operation
was contemplated. What the General Staff asked was that
as, in consequence of the recent Japanese advance, Song-
chin was now ten days' march from the front and the roads

very bad, two transports "with men and horses" should be
landed at Kion-sen (Chon-jin) instead, a place which lay a
little south of Kolokoltsef Point and close to Pureng.

Modest as was the change of programme, it was one not
unattended with risk.   Kion-sen was apparently being used as an
advanced supply base, and only the week before—on August 3rd
—a Japanese merchantship had been sunk off the port by two
torpedo-boats from Vladivostok.   It was a significant re-
minder that under modern conditions, even in a more marked
degree than in the old wars, the most decisive fleet actions
cannot ensure absolute immunity for sea communications, so
long as any fragments of the enemy's fleet remain in the
threatre of operations.   It was probably for these reasons that
Admiral Kamimura felt unable to assent to the General Staff's
request without referring to his chief, and as Admiral Togo,
having returned from his cruise on the 8th, had left next
day for Sasebo, a start had to be made before an answer could
be received.

Leaving Sylvia Basin early in the afternoon of the 12th, at
midnight he sent forward the *Chihaya* and a destroyer division
to reconnoitre and sweep in the usual way, and at dawn reached
a point a few miles south of Kil-tsiou Point.   Finding the sweeping was just completed he sent the transports into Plaksin Bay
in charge of the *Otowa* and with his three armoured cruisers
took up a covering position off Cape Bruat.   By 5.30 on
the 15th the Song-chin landing was all but complete, and
meanwhile a reply had been received from Admiral Togo
authorising the proposed landing at the Japanese front, " pro-
"vided it would not take more than one day."   Why he was
so anxious for the return of his second-in-command is not
clear, except that he seems to have been under orders to
proceed to Nagasaki to welcome Prince Arisugawa, who was
just returning from representing the Emperor at the German
Crown Prince's wedding.

Proceeding at once Admiral Kamimura was off Kion-sen
at dawn on the 16th.   There the two transports were dropped
and the disembarkation began immediately without sweeping,
while the Admiral proceeded up the coast to threaten the
enemy's communications between Kion-sen and Najin Po.
As no signs of a Russian advance were seen, two destroyers
went into the latter port and found that the telegraph, which
had been destroyed during the last demonstration, had not
been repaired—a further indication of how easily a landing in

rear of the enemy might have been effected and maintained under cover of ship fire. As it was the landing amounted to nothing but a slight strengthening of the Japanese advanced force, which left it still too weak to deal with the increasing strength of the enemy in its front. The result was that in spite of a good deal of fighting, they had been unable to make any real impression on the Russian position, when on September 5th instructions were received that the Peace Plenipotentiaries had agreed to an armistice.

At first sight, then, it would appear that the Japanese had lost a good opportunity of using their command of the sea to improve their position ; but it may be doubted whether the policy they pursued was not the wisest. In the time available they could scarcely have gained enough to modify materially the balance of the situation, or to warrant a risk of failure at the critical moment. Had there been a prospect of the negotiations failing it might have been well to venture more vigorous action, with a view to the continuation of the war ; but as the Japanese realised that the negotiations could only break down by their insisting on a war indemnity, which they knew they could not demand, there was nothing to be gained by merely crossing the Russian frontier. By no possibility could there have been an occupation of Russian territory extensive enough to warrant a demand for an indemnity, and, on the other hand, the success of the Russian defence of the frontier was a solace to Russian *amour propre*, which made it easy for them to accept the rest of the Japanese terms.

The terms agreed on were those on which Japan had originally insisted before the war, so far as Korea and Manchuria were concerned ; and over and above she secured Port Arthur and South Sakhalin. Peace was, in fact, made on the basis of the *status quo*, and the retention of all conquests with the exception of North Sakhalin. So much the Russians could fairly insist on, since its retention by Japan gave her the power of dominating the entrance to the Amur River ; but in compensation she received the right of fishing along the whole Russian Pacific Coast up to the Behring Sea.

It was undoubtedly a peace cleverly snatched by the Japanese at the most favourable moment, but in Japan it was received with execration. The astute Plenipotentiaries were branded as traitors, particularly for having abandoned the claim for an indemnity. But everyone responsible knew that such a claim cannot be enforced unless the claimant is in possession of a large part of the enemy's country or in a position to crush or cripple his national life. Japan was far from being in such a position. Strictly speaking, her armies had not occupied an inch of Russian territory, and her navy, though completely victorious at sea, could not use its control so as to have any appreciable effect on Russian finance or subsistence. She was far from having crushed her enemy's armed forces or his power of resistance; his real national life was practically unaffected : and yet she had forced her will upon him, and had obtained all, and more than all, she set out to obtain.

CHAPTER XXIV.

CONCLUSION.

[Chart IV.]

IF the results of the Russo-Japanese war were such as are not to be explained at first sight by the principles derived from other great wars, it must be that it has some special characteristic which differentiates it from what has come to be regarded as the normal type. Now, regarding it in its broadest aspect, its most conspicuous feature is admittedly that it was a war in a maritime theatre, where, as with our last two European wars, the Peninsula and Crimea, naval and military operations were so intimately connected as to be inseparable.

That the issue of the war must turn on the just co-ordination of the sea and land arms was recognised from the first by both belligerents. Both of them attempted such a co-ordination, but it was the Japanese alone who attained it with any measure of effectiveness. Here, then, it is to be assumed we must seek for the explanation of their success ; for here alone did they show any marked superiority over their opponents. Indeed, in most other directions they were actually inferior. Their army, numerically, was greatly inferior to that which the Tsar's vast empire could boast ; their resources, material and financial, were greatly inferior ; their fleet, even without reckoning the Black Sea squadron, was also inferior ; and yet their victory was practically complete. Much, no doubt, was due to the moral advantage which the object of the struggle bestowed upon the Japanese ; much, too, was due to their superior training and preparation ; but at the outset of the war these points of superiority were not so great as they became after the back of the Russian resistance was broken. The concentration of their army at the decisive point, Liau-yang, was quite as slow as that of the Russians, their attack on Port Arthur in military skill was not superior to the defence, and at the battle of the Yellow Sea they displayed no marked superiority over their enemy either in tactics, gunnery, or spirit.

When the world began to recover from its astonishment at the result, a facile explanation was found in the assumption that the Japanese from the first onset had the " command of the sea." In whatever sense we interpret that loose expression this view was certainly not that of the Japanese themselves. But, as the point is of vital interest to our inquiry, it will be well at once to ascertain how Admiral Togo saw it all when in the flush of victory he looked back on the struggle in which he had played so great a part.

Towards the end of October, after the peace had been ratified, the whole Navy gathered in Tokyo Bay to celebrate with a grand review the triumphant conclusion. As soon as Admiral Togo arrived at the head of his still powerful fleet and the train of prizes that graced it, he was summoned to the Imperial presence. With him he carried his report of what the Navy had done, and this is what he said [1] :—

" At the opening of the first stage of our operations by sea
" with the Combined Fleet, I, in obedience to your orders,
" carefully considered the nature of the theatre of war, the
" configuration of land and sea, and the line of operations on
" which the land forces would act, and chose as the primary
" object of my strategy that I should confine within the Port
" Arthur zone the main portion of the enemy's fleet and
" prevent its getting away to Vladivostok." Here is the first
point to be marked. It will be seen there is no suggestion
of basing his plan on an effort to obtain command of the
sea in a decisive battle. The plan has no offensive basis, it
is clearly stated to be preventive. His first consideration is
the army's line of operation. With the army lies the offensive
part of the war plan, and his part is to provide the defensive
support by confining the enemy's main fleet to an area from
which it cannot interfere with the army's progress.

The operations by which he sought to carry out his idea
are then summarised. " I began," he proceeds, " by striking
" swift blows on the enemy at Port Arthur and Chemulpho,
" and then followed them up with a succession of further
" attacks, which step by step gradually reduced the enemy's
" strength. At the same time, efforts were made to restrict
" the enemy's movement by adventurous attempts to block the
" port and by laying mines in front of it. Part of my fleet
" I kept permanently in the Korean Straits in order to main-
" tain a firm hold on that naval position, to maintain a watch
" on the Vladivostok squadron, and to form a second line of
" battle against the enemy in Port Arthur. During the early

---

[1] *Published History*, Book VI., ch. iii., sec. 3, p. 424. *See also Confidential History*, Vol. III., p. 464.

" part of these operations the enemy adopted throughout a
" passive attitude, relying upon 'the advantage of their situation.'[1]
" Our forces made repeated attacks, but were unable to achieve
" much result, until in the middle of August the enemy's main
" force attempted to escape from Port Arthur to Vladivostok,
" and the battle of the Yellow Sea and the battle of Ulsan
" took place in which we unexpectedly were able to break
" down completely the enemy's war-plan and to achieve more
" than half the object of our operations."

The last sentence is significant. For if the primary object
of his squadron was to destroy the enemy's fleet he could
scarcely have expressed himself in this way. There had been
no decisive victory, the material strength of the enemy was
merely reduced by two ships, and yet he considered he had
" unexpectedly" achieved more than half his object. Clearly,
then, he considered his object as being primarily preventive ;
and having foiled the Russian attempt to concentrate the whole
of their Pacific Fleet, and having forced the main squadron
back into the area where he wished to confine it, he regarded
himself as more than halfway to the realisation of that object.
He as clearly suggests, by using the word " unexpectedly," that
he did not anticipate that with the force at his disposal he
could realise that object otherwise than defensively. For since
we know that for some time before the battle he had been
anticipating his enemy being forced to sea by land pressure,
it cannot have been the sortie but the victory that was unexpected.[2] The plain inference, then, is that he did not consider his relative strength great enough to warrant the pursuit
of his object by offensive methods—or, in other words, by

---

[1] This is a technical expression derived from Chinese strategical lore,
of which Admiral Togo was a recognised master. It comes from the
philosopher Mencius, who laid down the principle that "advantage of
" situation" (*Chiri*) "is of higher value in war than advantage of time"
(Chamberlain, *Japanese Writing*, p. 382). The idea Admiral Togo is thus
succinctly expressing is that the only advantage the Japanese could gain
was advantage of time, that is the capture of Port Arthur and its squadron
before reinforcements could come from Europe, and that the Russians chose
to oppose to this a prolonged defensive, such as the strength of their
position permitted them to count on, for the exhaustion of their enemy,
who had no reinforcements in sight.

[2] It should be recalled that in Admiral Togo's eyes the object of the
land bombardment was not to make the harbour untenable so much as to
prevent the Russian squadron being repaired so as to be able to come out.
He specially requested General Nogi to use the naval guns with this object
Confidential History, Vol. II., p. 209. *See ante*, p. 44.

seeking a decision in battle—if by any means he could avoid it. So far as there was any seeking out of the enemy's fleet with intent to destroy it, that function, at least after the failure of his early bombardments, was imposed upon the army, and his own function in regard to it was secondary and protective. This view may be read between the lines of his narrative as from this point we continue it.

" After this period," he says, " the land fighting gradually " advanced. Finally, the ceaseless pressure of our besieging " army in rear of Port Arthur and the untiring blockade " maintained at sea brought about the total destruction of the " main part of the enemy's fleet under the protection of the " fortress itself." It is clear, moreover, that he regarded this phase of the war as the real preparation for the offensive return. " During this first period," he adds, "of ten months fighting " we were able by taking advantage of the progress of the " operations to accumulate a series of successes ; and this, I " venture to think was what gave to the spirit of our officers " and men its ultimate temper. It ripened their courage and " ability more than any other part of the war . . . . It " was then that the issue of the war which had hitherto hung " in the balance was definitely settled and the seeds of victory " which afterwards fell to our lot in the Japan Sea were " sown in those months."

Having dealt with what he called the first stage of the operations during which, without fighting a decisive battle, he had paralyzed the action of the Russian main fleet and had finally exposed it to destruction by the Army, he goes on to deal with what he calls the " second stage."

" With the arrival of the spring of that year," the report continues, "our operations advanced to their second stage, and " our Fleet, after renewing its fighting power and working " it up to its keenest edge, made preparation to meet the " enemy's Second Squadron." But these preparations, he hastens to explain, were not permitted to interfere with the duty of supporting the land operations. " We blockaded the coasts of the Russian possessions," he goes on to say, "and cut off all transport of warlike supplies from the " enemy's country. A detachment of the Fleet was sent into " southern waters in the endeavour to threaten the enemy's " sea passage. Meanwhile we seized over 30 vessels near " the Straits of Tsushima, Tsugaru, La Pérouse, and Kunoshiri. " By May the enemy's Second Squadron appeared in our

" home waters. From the beginning the plan was to con-
" centrate our whole Fleet in the Korean Strait, and so ' in
" comfort and well-being to take advantage of the enemy's
" fatigue.[1] . . .' In this way the courageous conduct
" of our officers and men through the help of the gods,
" achieved success after success, and in the battle of the
" Japan Sea we swept the shadow of the enemy completely
" from the sea and brought that part of our operations to a
" conclusion."

So ended the second stage. Then, and not till then, he
considered his country had "command of the sea" and the
third stage could begin. "Thenceforward," he explains, "the
" seas passed, in name and in fact, into the control of our
" fleet. The third stage of our operations then commenced, but
" in these the naval responsibility was light. In co-operation
" with the army we carried through the occupation of Sakhalin,
" and discharged our combined duty almost without losing a
" man. Occasionally we made movements in North Korea to
" threaten the enemy, and all the time maintained without
" relaxation the blockade of the Russian possessions."

Finally, he summarised the whole in these words : "The
" operations of the Combined Fleet were settled by the result
" of the first stage of them ; the second stage decided the
" victory ; and in the third stage we began to reap the fruits
" of that victory."

With regard to the actual influence of the fleet upon the
progress of the war. The first point which this appreciation
brings out is that, in Admiral Togo's opinion, the Japanese did
not secure command of the sea till the battle of the Sea of Japan
brought the second stage of the war to a successful conclusion.
During the first two stages the relative strength of their fleet barely
sufficed to maintain locally in the Yellow Sea and the Straits
of Korea a control which was just strong enough to prevent
the enemy from interfering effectively with the communications
of the Army or using their own communications to Vladivostok.
It was not strong enough to permit the free movement of

---

[1] This is another technical expression of Chinese strategy, taken from
the classical writer on war, Sonshi. The passage in which it occurs is as
follows : "Near your own home await your enemy's coming from afar ;
" in peace and well-being at home await his fatigue ; with your belly full
" await his hunger ; this will husband your strength." Admiral Togo
substitutes "take advantage of " for "await," but the full significance of
his quotation would be understood by all Japanese students of war.

troops to any point that was desired, nor even to place beyond
anxiety the supply lines which passed through the area actually
occupied by the fleet. A real command which would have
given the action of the Japanese army all the flexibility which
the Russians dreaded could only have been won by courting
a decisive battle in the first stage. But, in the opinion of the
Admiral at least, a drastically offensive treatment of the situation was beyond the relative resources at his disposal. For
it was no mere question of the comparative strength of the two
fleets on the spot. Behind the Russian force actually in Far
Eastern waters, there was another fleet in the Baltic, slowly and
painfully coming into being, yet a stern reality to be reckoned
with. From the first its menace cramped and overshadowed
the Japanese strategy—it compelled a husbanding of their fleet,
as the only means of meeting the danger. Admiral Togo was
forced to deny himself the attractions of the offensive and to
support the military offensive by a general preventive attitude.
By minor attacks he made his defence as active as possible,
even to the extreme limits of prudence, and sometimes beyond
what the Admiralty Staff could approve.[1] But defensive his
strategy remained, until that attitude gave him a chance for his
overwhelming offensive return, and, as he said, the enemy's
fleet was swept from the sea.

If any doubt remained that this was the real attitude of
the Japanese Naval Staff to the war, it would scarcely survive
a comparison with their known attitude in the analogous case
of their war with China. Indeed, it is only by taking a
general view of the opening of the previous war that we can
fully appreciate the conceptions which held the field when the
war plan against Russia was framed. Such a view is to be
obtained from a work published in September, 1904, but of
course written earlier, by Captain Ogasawara, I.J.N., who was
lecturer in History and Strategy at the Naval War College, and
responsible for the two official histories of the Russian War.
It was entitled *A History of Japanese Sea Power*, the 12th chapter
being devoted to the war with China.

In dealing with preliminary considerations he points out
that in this war, as in the war with Russia, the Japanese regarded
the enemy's sea forces as superior to their own ; but as the
Chinese fleet was divided into four independent commands,
they hoped to find a way of dealing with it in detail.

---

[1] *See ante*, p. 44.

The Northern Squadron, based on Wei-hai-wei, was the only one immediately dangerous, but the possibility of one or more of the others combining in the theatre of war dominated the whole of their opening strategy.

The period of strained relations that had arisen out of the struggle to control Korea culminated in the Chinese landing troops at Asan, on the invitation of the Korean Court. The Japanese Cabinet, on June 2nd, then determined to act, and within 14 hours a naval brigade had landed to seize the Seoul-Chemulpho road. Japanese troops were then hurried out to occupy Seoul, and the vital position being thus secured the navy took up a purely defensive attitude. Leaving three small ships as a guard at Chemulpho, the rest of the fleet " with Sasebo as its base" barred the seas in the area " Tsushima, Goto, Fusan, Port Hamilton, and Quelpart, so as " to guard the line between Japan and Fusan," that is, of course, to secure a line by which troops could be passed into Korea.

This strictly defensive attitude, adopted by June 21st, was maintained while the Japanese naval mobilisation proceeded, and a state of nominal peace continued. The day after the Japanese moved to their new position, Admiral Ling with the Northern Chinese Squadron appeared at Chemulpho, and general preparations were made in Japan to resist coastal attack. Admiral Ling, however, had also assumed a defensive attitude and confined himself to holding the waters between Chemulpho and Asan, presumably to prevent the direct reinforcement of the Japanese at Seoul. Although war had not yet been declared, by the end of June it was regarded as inevitable, and Admiral Ling was recalled to Wei-hai-wei to organise a "grand fleet"—so at least the Japanese supposed—with the intention of "seizing " the command of the seas."

Thus each side stood waiting its chance, and active operations were confined by both Governments to pushing forward more troops. This went on till the middle of July, when their naval mobilisation being complete the Japanese resolved to endeavour to extend their zone of command to the west coast of Korea ; but this ostensibly was still a measure of peace strategy designed to improve their position for the expected outbreak of war.

On July 20th the Japanese delivered their ultimatum, on the 23rd their garrison at Seoul, which now numbered 5,000 men, seized the Palace and on the 25th advanced to attack the Chinese at Asan. At the same time the Chinese were assembling an army on the Yalu, and for this purpose were sending part of the troops direct by sea. To prevent this the Japanese fleet was moved up, and on the day their troops started from Seoul to attack Asan, it fell in with a weak convoy, captured one of the escort and sunk a large troop transport with all hands.

This action of Poung-do as it was called, though of little more significance materially than Admiral Uriu's affair at Chemulpho, had a pronounced moral effect. In the Japanese fleet, we are told, it stirred up *Teki gai shin*, "the desire to destroy the enemy," or, as we should say, an offensive spirit; while, on the other hand, it paralysed that of the Chinese and led to their giving up their original intention of seizing the control of the Bay of Korea. Their fleet remained at Wei-hai-wei with orders to defend the Gulf of Pe-chi-li.

It was an attitude which caused the Japanese considerable embarrassment, for as long as that fleet remained in the theatre of war undefeated they could not regard their control as established. "The route to Chemulpho," Admiral Ito, the Commander-in-Chief, telegraphed on July 31, "cannot be re-" garded as safe until the enemy's fleet is destroyed. It makes "my blood run cold to think that a great transport full of "troops can be sunk by the smallest cruiser. The safest plan "is to disembark at Fusan."

With a view to bringing about the desired decision Admiral Ito took up a position near Baker Island; that is, he contented himself with defending the sea area that was required to be kept undisturbed for the military communications. This move he could rightly regard as giving him the initiative. China could only obtain the object of the war by passing into Korea and maintaining there an army sufficient to dislodge her enemy, and, owing to the geographical conditions, this could only be done effectively by using the direct line of passage. This line Admiral Ito had now barred, and he was in a position to compel the Chinese to conform. They must either abandon Seoul to their enemy or else make a prompt effort with their fleet to recover the control of the route to Asan. In short, to attack Admiral Ito in the commanding position he had taken up was the only way of reinforcing in time their troops which were isolated at that place. As, however, it was soon known that these troops had evaded the Japanese force from Seoul and had succeeded in withdrawing to Ping-yang, Admiral Ito had to shift his ground to a station off that place as being now the position most likely to lead to contact with the enemy, but at the same time to complete his strategic attitude he kept a continual cruiser watch on the approaches to Asan and Chemulpho.

This sound, if cautious, disposition, however, was not maintained for long. Impatient of inaction and persuaded the Chinese had no mind to meet him, Admiral Ito took his fleet across to Wei-hai-wei and bombarded it, but quite ineffectually, for the enemy's fleet was not there. It would seem that it had actually gone to Ping-yang; the two fleets apparently had crossed, and no action took place. It was an interesting case of an admiral losing his chance of a decisive battle by prematurely seeking out the enemy with no certainty of contact, instead of patiently holding a defensive position which secured him the initiative in the objective area and from which sooner or later the enemy must seek to drive him. Logically, of course, it was a false move, but in this case it must be remembered, as in the Russian war, the time factor was in a high degree confusing, that is to say, the situation was complicated by the extreme importance of the Japanese securing a decision against the Chinese Northern Squadron before the other squadrons could be concentrated in the theatre of war. Still venial as the eccentric movement was, the normal retribution followed. Its moral effect as an offensive movement was indeed considerable, but it worked to reduce the chance of a battle still further. For at Pekin it aroused so great a fear of territorial attack that the Chinese admiral was recalled and condemned to a purely defensive attitude.

The result was something like a deadlock. It had been the Japanese intention to establish an advanced base at Ping-yang from which they could maintain their control of the Bay of Korea and operate offensively against the Chinese fleet as opportunity offered. But this was now seen to be impossible. In spite of "the desire to destroy the enemy" they had to face the fact that that desire is not always to be realised. Though Ping-yang was well placed for covering the offensive operations of their army in Korea and acting offensively against the Chinese at sea, it did not cover the vital point, and that was the Straits of Korea. Behind the Chinese Northern Squadron were the other squadrons, and in the far background was the memory of their last invasion of Korea, when having lost command of the Straits they lost their entire army. "By this time,"

says Captain Ogasawara, "the fact that the control of the
" Western Korean waters was in our hands became obvious
" to the Commander-in-Chief ; but the enemy's main force
" was still in existence, and it would not be safe to establish
" a base in a place geographically unsuitable. The Commander-
" in-Chief, therefore, on August 14, proceeded to Long Reach
" (in the extreme south of Korea), a spot very easy to defend
" and to keep watch from, and that place he established as
" his advanced base.[1] The place was also constituted the
" 'middle rendezvous' for military transports and a depôt for
" stores." "It was like having Sasebo on the south coast of
" Korea," Captain Ogasawara adds, "whereby our radius of con-
" trol at sea was extended right out to the coasts of China."

For the work which the Japanese had in hand Long Reach
was not nearly so well placed as was Hakko in the Russian
War. But as their fleet was too weak to divide, they felt
compelled to regard the command of the Korean Strait as
its primary object. The pressing military necessity was to
pass on to Chemulpho the remainder of the troops which
were required for dislodging the Chinese from Ping-yang, but
it had to be done without the direct cover of the main fleet.
The operation was risked with no better cover than scouts
off Port Arthur and Wei-hai-wei and a patrol system on the
Korean coast similar to that adopted in the Russian war ;
and with these precautions to prevent surprise the whole fleet,
instead of covering the line of passage in the orthodox way,
escorted the transports to their destination.

The analogies between this opening and that of 1904 are
too obvious to need emphasising. In both cases the dominating
idea is the necessity of devoting the fleet to the protection of
the army communications, so long as the enemy has an
undefeated fleet capable of disturbing them. Every opportunity for active minor operations was to be seized for
extending the area of control, but no offensive movement must
be undertaken which risked the permanent control of the vital
zone. This was obviously the lesson of the false but attrac-
tive move to Wei-hai-wei. It was clearly taken to heart, and
we see its lasting influence in Admiral Togo's reluctance to
take his fleet to Port Arthur as the first move of the next war.

---

[1] Long Reach (*Admiralty Plan*, 1560) is entirely landlocked between
three islands in lat. 34° 22", long. 126° 50". It is about 16 miles long
by five broad and lies 30 miles N.W. of Port Hamilton. The Japanese
believed the Chinese had intended to seize it.

It is thus easy to see, when the initial events of the Russian war are read in the light of those of the previous war, why the Japanese in the early stages never regarded themselves as enjoying any kind of command beyond the waters they actually occupied in force ; that is to say, the Yellow Sea and the waters about the Straits of Korea. The Gulf of Pe-chi-li was not regarded as a commanded sea. No thought of passing troops through it to Newchwang or elsewhere was contemplated, although in Russian eyes this was the most deadly move open to their enemy. But so far from the Japanese regarding such an operation as practicable, it was a long time before the gulf was deemed to be available even as a secondary line of military supply.

In this connection it is necessary to clear another aspect of the fleet's action. Because it opened with an apparently offensive movement towards the enemy's coast, it is often said it was " free to go anywhere and do anything." But this was far from the truth. Not only was it strictly tied to positions which covered the army's communications, but it was also tied to positions which would cover the heart of the homeland from a counterstroke. In the nature of the war which the Japanese were waging—a war whose object was to conquer a definite piece of territory without any hope of being able to " overthrow " their enemy—such cover was an essential basis. This security, as well as that of the main army communications, was obtained by the blockade of Port Arthur and the occupation in force of the Korean Strait zone, for in this way the whole strength of the Japanese fleet, disposed in two well-connected divisions, was concentrated on the only line by which such a counterstroke would be carried out. It is true that the disposition left the Northern Island open to an attack from Vladivostok, but this was unavoidable in view of the naval resources available. Still it mattered little, for a raid on the Northern Island was provided for by two Army Divisions, and in any case it would not amount to a counterstroke of the kind required to change the nature of the war, and an invasion in strength even of the Northern Island was out of the question so long as the Japanese fleet remained undefeated.[1]

This policy had also its analogy in the Chinese war. Captain Ogasawara tells us that it was fully realised how the concentration of the fleet and its being based at Long Reach laid the Japanese islands nearest to China open to attack. " This would have been most unpleasant," he says, " but as we had so few ships we could not possibly divide them for

These two functions, then, severely restricted the operations of the fleet, but so favourable were the geographical conditions for the Japanese that the positions they took up served both ends. That is to say, the same positions which protected the lines of their limited offensive operations also barred an offensive counterstroke by the enemy; and in cases where the object in dispute is well adapted to the limited form of war, a successful counterstroke of this nature is the only way in which the superior Power can confidently count on converting the war to the form in which its greater strength can tell. It was, indeed, such a conversion from the limited to the unlimited form by an invasion of Japan that General Kuropatkin's original war plan contemplated as the sole means of bringing the contest to a successful issue.[2] In this case, as has been pointed out earlier in the work, the territorial object was peculiarly well adapted to the limited form. A narrow and sea-girt appendage of the Asiatic continent, mountainous and poorly cultivated, without roads and abounding with defensive positions, Korea was an ideal object for an inferior Power, situated within easy reach of it. It was easy for Japan to develop there the utmost military effort of which she was capable, while for Russia, unless she could win free use of the sea, the case was entirely different. The remote distance and restricted conformation of the objective territory rendered it physically and politically difficult for her to deploy there by land a superiority of force, and they rendered absolutely impossible the deployment of such a superiority as she would require for successful offensive operations against the force which Japan could easily place in line against her. And it was not only that Japan could easily deploy her army as required, but also that she could easily support it, so long as Russia could not develop in the local area a naval force capable of driving her own from the sea.

For both sides, of course, the use of sea communications was essential: for Japan, because she was an island kingdom;

" the defence of our coasts. We had to keep them massed to deal with the " Northern Squadron. Even if the Southern or other Chinese Squadron " arrived and bombarded our coasts, our only course was to let them " have their way, while we destroyed the Northern Squadron. Then " we were free to deal with the others at our leisure." The context seems to show he was thinking only of attacks on the more outlying islands nearest to China. The Russian war, of course, showed that central attacks could not be ignored.

[2] *See ante*, Vol. I., p. 49.

for Russia, because of the length and impracticability of the land lines. But the advantage of Japan was that for her the degree of command that was essential was much less than it was in the case of Russia. In the last resort Japan could maintain and develop her force in Korea, through Fusan and Masampho, by short lines of communication which passed through her zone of highest control; whereas the lines that were necessary to Russia were long, and passed through open seas at a distance from her base where her power of control was weak. They were, therefore, difficult to defend, and lay open to continual raids from the Japanese area of naval concentration. By no means, then, could the Russians solve the situation except by destroying the Japanese fleet. There was no other way of making her own communications secure or depriving Japan of those which she required. But for defeating the Japanese fleet the Russian must have a distinct preponderance of force, and such preponderance was put beyond their reach in the initial stages by the moment the Japanese chose for declaring war and the success of their opening operations. By repeated minor offensive movements, as Admiral Togo explained in his summary of the war, they were able to prevent the Russians from recovering the blow, and were thus able not only to maintain their defensive attitude, but were able gradually to extend their sea control, in accordance with the needs of the army. But this they could not do indefinitely, and their ability to do even what they did was due rather to the absolute inertness of the Russian fleet than to the intrinsic strength of their own.

It was not, then, that the Japanese success in the first two stages of the war was due to their having command of the sea; but that they were able to prevent the Russians from obtaining it. Owing to the nature of the war and its object that was all that was required. By increasing their area of control they were able to rivet more securely their hold on Korea, and more quickly to convince their enemy it was not within his power to break it. But from the first it was a strategic certainty that unless Russia could get so complete a control as to be able to pass troops freely oversea, she could never hope to develop strength enough locally to dislodge the Japanese from the objective territory, which she had been unable to prevent them from seizing.

With these considerations may be compared the Duke of Wellington's final dictum on the Peninsular war. When in

September 1813, after the fall of St. Sebastian, he was preparing to push the French beyond the Pyrenees, he had an interview with Admiral Martin, who had been sent out to him by the Admiralty to know precisely what it was he wanted the Navy to do. At the end of the conference, on taking leave of the Admiral, the Duke used these words, "If anyone wishes to "know the history of this war, I will tell them that it is our "maritime superiority which gives me the power of maintaining "my army while the enemy are unable to do so."[1] Here the principle is the same though the two cases differed materially. In the Peninsular war the French had seized the territorial object and Wellington could not succeed without taking the offensive. On the other hand, owing to the security of his sea base and communications, he could always fall back to the defensive when hard pushed and wait till the difficulties of supply weakened the enemy sufficiently to permit an offensive return. This happened three times, and the third time Wellington succeeded. Had the Russians won the great battles in Manchuria it is clear the same situation would have arisen. The peninsulas of Korea and Kwangtung were far better points of retreat than was Portugal so long as the Japanese retained some domination at sea, and, as Admiral Skruidlov plainly hinted in his original appreciation, it is difficult to see how any amount of military success in Manchuria short of annihilating the Japanese armies would have brought ultimate success to the Russians.[2]

In yet another aspect the position of the Japanese was better than our own in the Peninsula. Wellington spoke of his success being due to our maritime "superiority," and this the Japanese cannot be said to have had in a decisive degree during the initial stages. But for them a marked superiority was not necessary ; for us it was. For whereas the Japanese operations in support of their armies covered the homeland, ours did not. And not only did our operations in the Peninsula tend to weaken the home defence, but they also required relatively more strength since they had to be conducted on lines which were flanked by French naval and privateer bases—a danger which did not exist for the Japanese. For us, then, a decisive superiority was needed, whereas in the Japanese

---

[1] Martin to Lord Keith, 21st September, 1813. *Letters of Byam Martin*, II., 404 (Navy Record Society).

[2] *See ante*, p. 11.

case the geographical conditions were so favourable that equality sufficed.

Is it, then, to be concluded that in no way could the Russians have given a better turn to the war and that the long and painful anxiety of the Japanese was uncalled for ? By no means was that the case, for there was a way by which they might have been deprived of the equality of force which they were permitted to enjoy at all stages in the theatre of war. It could almost certainly have been managed had the Russians done practically anything but keep their fleet inactive. Of this Admiral Makarov was fully aware. Had he lived to realise his policy of prudent but incessant offence with a view of disputing the Japanese control, had he carried out his resolution that at any hazard the landing of the Second Army in Liau-tung should not be permitted without drastic interference from his squadron, the course of the war must surely have been very different. It is inconceivable that in face of any display of naval activity from Port Arthur, the Second Army could have been landed when and where it was. Had that landing been displaced or even materially delayed the whole Japanese war plan would have broken down. That the Japanese Imperial Staff knew this is clear from the fact that in pressing on the landing they were ready to run the risk of Russian naval activity in spite of Admiral Togo's view that he could not guarantee security short of absolutely blocking the enemy in their port. True, Admiral Makarov might have been defeated and his squadron eventually reduced to impotence, but even so the siege of Port Arthur must have been seriously delayed and the Japanese Manchurian concentration still more so. Still more important is the consideration that the Baltic Fleet need not have been so strong ; it could, therefore, have started sooner, been more mobile, and arrived much earlier ; and if the Japanese were to retain anything like equality they must have begun repairing their ships in time to meet it, and the blockade of Port Arthur must have been raised before the squadron it sheltered could have been destroyed.

It is indeed scarcely too much to say that Admiral Makarov's death, since its affect was to condemn the fleet to passive defence, was the turning point of the war. Had he lived it would at least have been impossible for the Japanese to conduct it as they did. The strain which their plan of operations put upon the fleet was as great as that which exhausted our own in the Great War after Trafalgar ; and had the Port

Arthur squadron done anything more enterprising than persist in its passive attitude, the endurance of the Japanese navy might well have proved unequal to the task.

That the Russian Government realised the error of the passive attitude is true. Again and again they urged Admiral Vitgeft to attempt active operations, but that will not excuse the failure. Admiral Vitgeft was no more than an acting Commander-in-Chief, notoriously unfit—as he himself pleaded—to conduct operations which called for the highest qualities of leadership. Why was he not relieved? Three other admirals specially appointed were in the theatre of war—with no squadron to command—and yet not one of them, so far as is known, made any attempt to find his way into Port Arthur and take over the command. The place was not too closely blockaded at least for the first two or three months and their own staff officers were passing to and fro. Surely the omission to make the attempt says little for the spirit which the higher Russian ranks brought to bear upon the war.

And what of the spirit of the rank and file, and what of the spirit of the Russian people? It is needless at this point to dilate on the well-known fact that while for Japan it was a people's war, for Russia it was not. The heart of Russia was never stirred, and such enthusiasm as existed at the outset was only aroused by the governing classes, whose war it was, putting abroad that by striking at Japan they were striking at England. When that goad would no longer sting, soldiers, sailors and people fell into sullen discontent, and from that to mutiny, strikes and revolutionary unrest, all solely because they had no interest in the war. The point is of capital importance. For it has been urged that the inability of the Tsar's Government to deploy sufficient strength in the Far East to overcome their inferior enemy was not due to the limited character of the war, but to the fear of revolution at home. But this amounts to the same thing. Both sides counted on the danger of revolutionary opposition as inherent in the conditions of the war. One of the strongest arguments. of those of the Tsar's councillors who opposed the war was that a war for an object so remote and so much out of touch with the national spirit would only fan the flames of revolution.[1] The Japanese being fully aware of the internal state of Russia, equally recognised the danger as an element of strength which

---

[1] *See ante*, Vol. I., p. 53.

the nature of their object secured for them. It was a very simple matter. For every statesman knows that in counting forces for war the first thing to determine is to what extent the spirit of the people will be enlisted, and what sacrifices they will be induced to make for the object in view. In this case it was obvious that in Japan the end in view would call forth practically unlimited effort, while in Russia the limit of willing sacrifice would be quickly reached. It was, in short, due to the nature of the object that Japan was able to undertake the war, with all the moral elements of strength at her back as well as the physical ; and it was due to her strictly logical method of making the territory in dispute her primary objective that she was able to reap to the full all the advantage which those elements of strength offered her. That is the simple explanation of why the weaker Power was able to force its will upon the stronger : and to account for the Japanese success there is no need to invoke miracles of administration or temper. In organisation and general readiness, in the training and behaviour of the officers, they certainly had an advantage, but in the Russian rank and file the devotion, endurance, and warlike spirit displayed throughout the struggle were no less admirable than their own.

Yet it must not be denied to them that they did display in a conspicuous degree a temper which is perhaps the most creditable that war can show. It was that their long condemnation to a general defensive attitude, the enforced husbanding of their fleet, and shrinking from decisive battle, did not sap their offensive spirit. In the case of the Russians, and in that of the French in the old Franco-British wars, defence did kill the offensive spirit, and if the Japanese were able to preserve it they deserve to be credited with warlike character of the highest kind—a character rising high above mere devotion to a headlong offensive which is kept moving by its own impetus. It is here, then, if anywhere, in this enduring capacity to withstand the demoralising influences of a prolonged defensive, that the Japanese showed upon the sea, at any rate, a distinctly higher genius for war than their enemy.

APPENDIX A.

Russian Preparatory Strategy.

Since the first volume went to press, the *Russian Naval Staff History* has begun to appear. So far as it is at present available it affords little fresh light beyond what was obtained from the *Military Staff History*. But the following extracts are now given as amplifying the conclusions already arrived at in regard to the preparatory strategy of the war.

I.—Far Eastern Staff Plans of Naval Operations, 1901–3.[1]

In 1901 Vice-Admiral Skruidlov, who commanded the Russian Squadron in the Far East, drew up a plan according to which the base of the Fleet was Vladivostok.

Admiral Alexeiev dissented. He laid down that the first duty of the fleet was to bar the route to the Yellow Sea to the enemy's fleet, whose probable object would be to land troops at Chemulpho and at the mouth of the Yalu, for which purpose the main body of the fleet should be based on Port Arthur. The second duty of the fleet was to divert a portion of the enemy's fleet from the Pechili and Korean theatres, for which an independent cruiser squadron based on Vladivostok would be required.

On the arrival of the squadron under Rear-Admiral Shtakelberg in 1903 a conference was held on April 23rd, at which were present:—Admiral Alexeiev, Vice-Admiral Stark, Rear-Admiral Kuzmich, Rear-Admiral Vitgeft, Rear-Admiral Greve and Captain Ebergard (flag-captain).

Captain Ebergard proposed that the whole fleet should be based on Masampho. The rest of the officers opposed this plan.

On April 30th Rear-Admiral Vitgeft formulated a " War-plan for " the naval forces in the Pacific Ocean, 1903," with two appendices : " Distribution of the naval forces" and "Mobilisation arrangements."

War-Plan for the Naval Forces of the Pacific Ocean in 1903.[2]

No. 1.

3rd May 1903.

The continuous growth of our land and sea forces in the Far East, which places us in a strong position as regards the political situation and gives us the predominance in Manchuria, must have induced a state of nervous strain in Japan, which undoubtedly under unfavourable conditions may cause serious complications and even lead to war.

Owing to the necessity of offering a firm and resolute resistance in any circumstances that may arise a definite war-plan for our naval forces in the East is essential.

---

[1] Summarised from the *Russian Naval Staff History*, Vol. I., pp. 62 *et seq.*

[2] Pp. 65-71. On page 101 it is stated that this plan was never communicated to the Headquarter Staff at St. Petersburg.

This plan must be based on the probable operations of our future enemy, and the nature of these operations may be clearly surmised by Japan's aspirations and the measures taken by her during peace.

According to information received from our Naval Attaché in Japan her principal efforts in the event of war will be: (1) the occupation of Korea; (2) to prevent us consolidating ourselves in Manchuria; (3) a disembarkation in the nature of a demonstration near the Maritime Province; (4) a similar disembarkation in Kwangtung; and (5) should these two landings be successful—an attempt to subdue these Provinces.

To put these plans into execution Japan must (a) move her active army into Korea; (b) then move it into Manchuria; and (c) endeavour to land troops near Vladivostok and Kwangtung, or in Kwangtung.

A Japanese army may be transported to Korea and disembarked either on the eastern coast—at Masampho, Fusan, Gensan and perhaps Goshkevich Bay—or on the western coast at Chemulpho, Ping-yang or the Yalu and near the Yalu.

Our naval forces will be unable to prevent a Japanese army from disembarking on the eastern coast of Korea owing to its proximity to Japan and the possession by Japan of a strong and convenient base-screen (Fusan—Tsushima—Sasebo—Kure) since (1) the eastern coast is 600 miles distant from Port Arthur and only 100 miles from Japan, and (2) the initiative will be on the side of Japan. She is seeking war and will assume the offensive, while we are only preparing to prevent the blow or to parry it.

But the landing of a Japanese army on the eastern coast of Korea cannot have any decisive influence on the operations in Manchuria, since the landing-place would be too far removed from the latter, and owing to the mountainous nature of Korea there are no suitable ways of communication for the movement of a large army with artillery and transport.

Such an operation could only be of secondary importance. It might be carried out with the object of compelling us to draw off a portion of our forces from the main army and retaining them in the Maritime Province.

A disembarkation near the frontier of our Maritime Province would be attended with risk for Japan. But since the attempt may be made measures must be taken to oppose it in order to safeguard ourselves and to cause the enemy to refrain from hazarding such an undertaking. These measures will be stated below.

A landing in Kwangtung or the vicinity presents no especial advantages, since it would be necessary to take Port Arthur, which is strongly fortified and defended. The objects of such an operation would be mainly to screen off our troops in Kwangtung from Manchuria and the moral effect that would be produced by the occupation of Port Arthur and the possession of an advanced base for the Japanese Fleet.

Allowing, however, that the advantages outweigh the risks, a disembarkation in Kwangtung could only be possible (a) if our fleet had been first defeated, or (b) if it had been drawn off too far for active operations into the Korean archipelago in order to advance its base and had been closed in there by a more powerful enemy resting on his adjacent well-equipped and fortified ports, from which it would be easy to supplement his squadron of offence with a large defensive flotilla of torpedo craft.

Thus, Japan will strive mainly to become mistress of the Yellow Sea and Bay of Korea, and to transport her army to the western coast of Korea and disembark it at Chemulpho, Ping-yang, or the Yalu.

In considering these probable points of disembarkation, we see that Chemulpho has no other advantage than the moral effect of obtaining possession of the Korean capital, since the occupation of Chemulpho is bound up with the occupation of Seoul.

All the advantages are in favour of Ping-yang and the Yalu, viz.: (1) the proximity of Manchuria; (2) a knowledge of the country which has been studied in the China-Japan war, and (3) this is the most cultivated part of Korea and is capable of supplying the army.

The deductions consequently follow that the main tasks for our naval forces in the Far East must be: (1) the necessity of retaining the mastery of the Yellow Sea and Korean Bay, based on Port Arthur; (2) not to allow a Japanese army to land on the western coast of Korea, and (3) by secondary naval operations from Vladivostok to draw off a portion of the Japanese sea forces from the main theatre of operations, and prevent a Japanese landing near the Maritime Province.

If, however, we assume that Japan will be content with a landing on the eastern coast of Korea, or that a landing on the western coast has perchance succeeded, the above tasks must be modified thus: (1) to seek out the Japanese Fleet in the waters of the Yellow Sea and Strait of Korea; (2) to destroy this fleet, and (3) to stop the sea communications of the Japanese army in Korea with Japan.

To whatever extent our task may be modified, in every case the base for our Fleet must be Port Arthur, and on no account must it be advanced into the Korean archipelago, which with the existing relative strengths of the Japanese and our own naval forces would involve an undesirable risk.

The use of Port Arthur as its base will not prevent our Fleet putting to sea to break the sea communications of the enemy's army or to attempt to strike a decisive blow on his fleet should he have already succeeded in landing or be intending to land on the western coast of Korea.

Should the objects aimed at by the Japanese Fleet be attained, an attempt to paralyse their success justifies even the loss of a portion of our Fleet or its disablement, since this will involve also losses to the fleet of the enemy. But we must not lose sight of the main object. Looking with confidence to the ultimate result of our operations, we must preserve our sea forces as long as possible, so as to retain a control of the Yellow Sea and be a constant threat to a hostile disembarkation. This must be the basis on which all plans must be formulated; on no account must dangerous enterprises be undertaken, however much something daring will be expected by public opinion and by even part of the personnel of the fleet.

The loss of our fleet in the early period of the war, even though it be victorious, may entail serious consequences, unless final results have been obtained.

A modern naval action will put out of action for a long space of time, not to mention the casualties, the vessels both of the vanquished and the victor. This is especially true in the absence of a well-equipped port as a base, as is the case with Port Arthur.

Three cases may arise in the first period of the war which would necessitate our fleet accepting action : (1) the arrival of the Japanese Fleet off Port Arthur ; (2) an attempt to effect a landing at Chemulpho, Port Arthur, or the Yalu, and (3) an actual disembarkation of the enemy's army on the western coast of Korea. In all these circumstances it is obvious that the principal base for our main naval forces and operations can be, and must be, only Port Arthur with all its disadvantages.

Vladivostock may be used for the operations of cruisers. It is unsuitable as a base for the main body of the fleet—it is too far removed from the probable theatre of operations (about 600 miles), while Japan has formed a screen for the defence of the channels Fusan-Tsushima-Sasebo.

In this case the proximity of her well-equipped ports would give the advantage to the Japanese Fleet, whereas, with our base at Port Arthur, the advantage will be on our side, since the enemy will be forced to withdraw from his base.

On the strength of the above considerations, the Japanese fleet in time of war will be divided into three squadrons : (1) a fighting squadron of offence ; (2) a protective squadron for the transports, and (3) a defensive squadron for the ports.

The fighting squadron for active operations will consist of the best modern ships of the following strength :—six battleships, six 1st-class armoured cruisers, five to eight scouting cruisers to proceed for long and short distances, and about 15 destroyers. Of this number, however, it is probable that Japan will be obliged to detach the six 1st-class armoured cruisers to oppose our cruiser squadron of three armoured and two protected cruisers at Vladivostok—for cruiser warfare.

The protective squadron for escorting transports and scouting service off her own shores will consist of the older vessels—seaworthy but of less fighting value—viz., two battleships, ten cruisers of the 2nd and 3rd class, six auxiliary cruisers of 6,000 tons and upwards, and 24 torpedo-boats of more than 120 tons displacement.

The defensive squadron will comprise five armoured coast-defence vessels and two coast-defence dispatch-vessels, 20 gun-boats and old sloops and 40 small torpedo-boats.

To carry out the plan of operations and resistance to the Japanese fleet laid down for our naval forces, our fleet must be divided into (1) a fighting squadron, (2) an independent cruiser squadron, and (3) squadron for the defence of Port Arthur and Vladivostok.

In 1903 our fighting squadron for active operations in the Yellow and Korean Seas comprises : six battleships, five protected cruisers, four scouting cruisers of the 2nd and 3rd class for long and short distances, and nine destroyers.[1] The base of the fighting squadron is Port Arthur.

The independent cruiser squadron will consist of three 1st class armoured cruisers, one protected cruiser and one or two auxiliary cruisers of the Volunteer Fleet, based on Vladivostok. Its duties will be (1) to cruise off the Japanese coasts and make raids on the ports, (2) to attack the communications of the Japanese army landed in Korea on the eastern coast, and (3) to draw off the Japanese cruisers from their fighting

---

[1] *Note in original.*—Three more destroyers may join in the autumn after their boilers have been re-tubed.

squadron in order that the strength of the Japanese and Russian fighting squadrons shall be equalised.

The defensive squadron for Port Arthur will consist of three gunboats, one despatch-vessel, two mining transports, seven destroyers, seven 1st class torpedo-boats and a mine and boom defence. That for Vladivostok will consist of four gunboats, two transports, three 1st class and six 2nd class torpedo-boats, and one mining transport with the mine defence of the port.

There are two reasons against the armoured cruisers joining the fighting squadron. In the first place they are not ships of the line, and have been built specially for cruiser warfare, and secondly, their addition to the fighting squadron would enable Japan to add her own six, and thus increase the preponderance of strength of the Japanese fighting squadron. In view of this, they have been detached into an independent cruiser squadron for special service.

Here follow (pp. 71–9) tables showing the proposed distribution of ships. These tables, with one or two unimportant exceptions, are identical with those already given in Volume I, Appendix A., p. 472–3. Then are given the Mobilisation arrangements, which are of no importance.

II.

STAFF CONFERENCE OF DECEMBER 31, 1903.

Detailed schemes for the disposition and duties of the ships having been drawn up, on December 31st—four weeks after the arrival of the *Tzesarevich* and *Bayan*—a conference was held under the Presidency of the Viceroy, the other members being Vice-Admiral Stark, Rear-Admiral Vitgeft and Captain Ebergard. Its purpose was to discuss (1) the modification of Admiral Vitgeft's plan, (2) the return of the cruisers from Vladivostok, and (3) the best method of keeping a look-out in the Bay of Korea for the appearance of the enemy.[1] The opinion of officers present are given. The Viceroy said it was undesirable to recall the vessels from Vladivostok, but added that, "after the arrival of the reinforcements and transports " he considered it possible to modify the existing plan and to act " aggressively, steaming towards the Japanese shores to defeat the " enemy." He then gave directions to the Commander of the Squadron (Rear-Admiral Stark):—

(1) To calculate the coal expenditure for the passage of the whole squadron to Japan at 12 knots speed and returning at 14 knots.

(2) To draw up a plan for cruiser warfare and raids on Japan and her mercantile fleet with the Vladivostok cruisers.

(3) To draw up a plan for reconnaissances in the Bay of Korea and off the west coast of Korea with the Port Arthur cruisers.

The final decision of the Conference, approved by the Viceroy, was as follows:—

(1) Not to modify the plan of naval operations for the present.

(2) Not to recall the cruisers from Vladivostok, and

(3) To act aggressively in the direction of the Japanese coast, after the junction of the vessels coming out from the Mediterranean, and then to change the plan of operations, our forces being considered equal (*i.e.*, to the Japanese).

---

[1] *Russian Naval History*, pp. 82–4.

III.

INSTRUCTIONS FOR THE VLADIVOSTOK SQUADRON.[1]

On the 9th January 1904 Vice-Admiral Stark sent the necessary instructions to Rear-Admiral Baron Shtakelberg at Vladivostok. These have been summarised in Vol. I., pp. 47-8, from the *Russian Military History*, Vol. I., pp. 329-331 (French translation). But the following paragraph relating to the treatment of commerce is worth quoting verbatim :—

"I must point out that Japan has not subscribed to the Paris
" Declaration of the 16th April 1856; and therefore we shall not
" hesitate to inflict as much damage as possible to the enemy on
" the sea. Being convinced that during war the Japanese merchant
" vessels will not think twice about flying the flags of other
" nationalities, I am forwarding to your Excellency copies of the
" regulations laid down for Japanese merchant vessels, which may
" be of use in establishing the actual nationality of vessels stopped
" by you, of which only valuable prizes captured at no great
" distance from Vladivostok may be sent to that port; all the
" remainder must be sent to the bottom without considerations
" of pity and without hesitation."

Besides these instructions there was a plan for reconnoitring the western coast of Korea, which had been submitted by Admiral Stark to the Viceroy on the 8th February 1904. It was approved with slight limitations, and the service was to commence on the 10th February.

IV.

THE VLADIVOSTOK FLOTILLA.[2]

In the autumn of 1903 Admiral Vitgeft's plan was modified to the extent that torpedo-boats Nos. 203, 204, 205, 206, 208, 210 and 211, which were at first intended for the defence of Port Arthur, were transferred to Vladivostok. The reason for this change was that a number of destroyers had been sent out to Port Arthur by the Nevski works in sections to be put together there and took the place of the torpedo-boats.

V.

COMMAND OF THE YELLOW SEA.[3]

As regards Admiral Vitgeft's appreciation referred to in Vol. I., p. 42, in which he stated that he "did not admit this possibility of the Russian " fleet being defeated by the Japanese in the waters of the Yellow Sea " and Bay of Korea, even with the existing relative strengths," it now appears that at the time he gave the assurance he was reckoning on Admiral Virenius's squadron (*Oslyabya*, etc.) arriving in the Far East, and did not know that Japan was about to purchase the *Nisshin* and *Kasuga*.

VI.

THE QUESTION OF A NEW BASE.

From the date of the occupation of Port Arthur in 1898 to the beginning of the war in 1904, Admiral Tuirtov was at the head of the

---

[1] *Russian Naval History*, pp. 85-9.   [2] P. 92.   [3] P. 97.

Navy Department as Minister of Marine. On his death Admiral Avelan, who had been Chief of the Naval Headquarter Staff, was appointed Minister of Marine, and Rear-Admiral Rozhestvenski was appointed Chief of the Naval Headquarter Staff. This was on the 30th March 1903. "Immediately on taking up my appointment," he has stated, " I, knowing " the negative qualities of Port Arthur, suggested to the Minister of Marine " some other base and pointed out the urgency of properly equipping " it and of exercising the fleet in the new surroundings. The Minister " of Marine at once got into communication with the Naval Commander- " in-Chief in the Far East, who expressed no opinion on essentials, but " was only inclined to accept the proposal to send to him steamships " of the Volunteer Fleet to furnish supplies to the squadron and to " carry out auxiliary operations. When the vessels were obtained, the " Commander-in-Chief refused to take up a strategically advantageous " position and to carry out the necessary exercises, lest he should incur " the wrath of the Japanese, and added that he had another plan in " accordance with which he was deploying the naval forces under his " command."

VII.

ADMIRALTY STAFF PLAN, 17TH OCTOBER 1903.[1]

Meanwhile a war plan was being drawn up independently at the Naval Headquarter Staff, and on October 17th, 1903, Commander Brusilov handed to Admiral Rozhestvenski a memorandum or a plan of operations in the Pacific Ocean and of preparation for the coming war, in which the problem is thus stated. " Only a complete victory over Japan and the " deprivation of her right to possess a fighting fleet will place us in the " Far East in an exceptionally favourable position and give us that " undoubted supremacy for which we are striving. It is impossible at " the present time to attain this object by a war with Japan, owing to " our unreadiness for war, in consequence of which decisive results " could not be obtained. It is therefore advisable to avoid war now " at the cost even of considerable concessions, but at the same time to " make a firm resolve to declare war on Japan in two years and to " prepare strenuously for this war in the broad sense of the word. We " must prepare not only for war but for certain victory."

Brusilov then goes into details, but as these deal with the question of preparation and not the plan of war, the headings only will be given :—

(1) Relative strengths after two years—greatly to Russia's advantage.
(2) Ammunition supply.
(3) Coal stocks.
(4) Docks and shops.
(5) Training of men.
(6) Cruisers always to steam not less than 16 knots instead of existing practice of steaming full speed twice a year for a few hours, which is no training for the engine-room staff.

The memorandum concludes thus :—

"The preparations must include arrangements for a military " expedition to Korea, using Manchuria or the Maritime Province " as a hinterland (sic).

---

[1] P. 102 et seq.

" The section of the Siberian railway round Lake Baikal must
" be completed.

" On the hypothesis that we shall go to war with Japan in two
" years' time, our diplomacy must be directed accordingly.

" Having a considerable advantage in naval strength and
" sufficient troops for a preparatory expedition into Korea, rapid
" and decisive results may be attained, even if now, in order to
" avoid war, we allow Japanese troops to invade Korea, without
" resorting to force of arms, so that in two years' time we shall be
" able to cut off this corps from Japan and at the same time
" advance into Korea from the land side."

The comments of Admiral Rozhestvenski on this memorandum are
of special interest :—

" Thus, our object is not to wipe out Japan, but only to annexe
" Korea to our possessions. Until this is done we require a fleet
" equal to that of Japan in order to simplify the task of our
" Army. When the annexation is an accomplished fact we shall
" require a fleet equal to the Japanese fleet in order to live at
" peace with Japan."

" Victory over Japan can only be in Korea. After driving
" the Japanese out of Korea there will be a period of inactivity."

" There is no necessity to have a crushing preponderance at
" sea over the Japanese. It is sufficient to be equal in strength,
" and not to allow the Japanese to obtain sovereignty at sea, so
" that our Army may the better be able to drive them out of
" Korea."

" The great point is never to have a weaker fleet than the
" Japanese."

Admiral Rozhestvenski has several further comments on the measures
proposed in preparation for war, which show that, like General Kuropatkin, he was opposed to the whole idea of the war with Japan as
bad policy. One comment, for instance, runs : " All the suggested
" measures are quite rational and should be realised in the shortest
" possible space of time, but only so that there shall be no war, for a
" war with Japan can be of no possible advantage to us. We are ready
" now more than we ever have been for war with Japan, but war is
" undesirable," etc.

It was on October 18th, 1903, that the above comments were made
by Admiral Rozhestvenski, yet only a month later, November 18th,
the following appreciation was drawn up at the Naval Headquarter
Staff by Commander Stetzenko :—

" After careful consideration the following conclusions must be
drawn :—

" (1) For every Russian ship of war in the Pacific Ocean the Japanese
" have a corresponding one, but more powerful, and, moreover,
" they have a considerable advantage in numbers, chiefly
" cruisers of small displacement, coast-defence vessels, and
" torpedo craft. Their torpedo flotilla, according to our
" Attaché, is especially efficient.

(2) There is strong reason to believe that in material our naval
" forces in the Pacific are weaker than those of the Japanese.

"(3) As regards disposition of bases, means of communication, &c.,
" the Japanese fleet has a great advantage over our Pacific
" naval forces.

"(4) As regards all manner of resources such as transports (*i.e.*, ships),
" military, and other stores (*i.e.*, ammunition, &c.), means for
" effecting repairs, &c., the Japanese have an enormous
" advantage.

"To sum up :—

"The Japanese Fleet is somewhat more powerful than the
" Russian naval forces in the Pacific Ocean ; it has a considerable
" advantage as regards its disposition in the theatre of naval
" operations, and in the matter of all material resources it is
" crushingly superior."

Such were the diverse points of view of the Naval Headquarter Staff
in the autumn of 1903, and consequently no plan of war was compiled
then. The plan drawn up at Port Arthur was not known to it,
and therefore it could not know what the fleet would do in case war
broke out. In spite of the fact that all proposals for war plans came under
the jurisdiction of the Naval Headquarter Staff, it was only a month
before the opening of hostilities that an "Operations Department" was
formed in the Naval Headquarter Staff, whose duty was to work out plans
of war. From this sprang—but after the war—an independent department which now deals with all questions of the fighting preparation of
the fleet and war plans, and is known as the Naval General Staff (*i.e.*,
as distinct from the Naval Headquarter Staff).

VIII.—NAVAL WAR GAMES.

War Games played at the Nicholas Naval Academy, St. Petersburg,
the idea being a War between Russia and Japan. [1]

The first game was played in 1896, the forces of both sides being as
on December 13th, 1895. The result was the complete defeat of the
Russian Fleet. The conclusions arrived at are of no importance.

The next game was played in 1900, Rear-Admirals Rozhestvenski and
Skruidlov taking part in it. The game was not finished. Owing to the
conditions prevailing at the time the deductions have no importance,
except perhaps to show the ignorance displayed regarding strategy
generally.

In 1902-03, the subject was set by the Minister of Marine. "War
between Russia and Japan in 1905 "—*i.e.*, the year when the 1898 building
programme should have materialised. Admiral Rozhestvenski took a
leading part in the game. Japan was to open operations without a
declaration of war. Reinforcements could not be expected from the
Mediterranean and Baltic.

The distribution of the Russian forces was: at Port Arthur—10
battleships, 13 cruisers, 36 destroyers and 24 torpedo-boats ; at Vladivostok
—4 cruisers.

Owing to war breaking out so suddenly the Russian vessels in
foreign ports were disarmed.

A cruiser and a gunboat were at Chemulpho. The telegram sent
to recall them having to pass partly over a Japanese line was not

---

[1] Pp. 107-121.

received, but destroyers sent off at the same time arrived in time to bring them back.

The Russian main body was concentrated behind the mole in Talien Bay; the approaches to Dalny were mined. The Japanese main fleet approached Port Arthur by night, and sent in destroyers, but they found no ships there and were destroyed by the Russian destroyers in the roadstead.

The next morning a naval action was fought in Talien Bay; the Japanese lost two-thirds of their battleships, and the Russians half of theirs. The Japanese withdrew and the Russians gave chase. Two days later an action took place off Quelpart. All the Japanese ships were put out of action in $2\frac{1}{2}$ hours, while the Russians lost three battleships, three cruisers and seven destroyers.

After this action the Russian fleet divided up. Part proceeded to Port Arthur, while the other part which made for Vladivostok for repairs was destroyed in the Korean Strait by the combined forces of the Japanese Fleet.

Attempts of the Russian cruisers to prevent the Japanese Army landing in Korea resulted in the sinking of a large number of the cruisers, after which the transport of Japanese troops continued without interference.

The umpire's decision was shortly as follows:—Highly important to gain command of the sea early in the war. Consequently must have on the spot forces superior to the Japanese. Such will be the case in 1905. Our Pacific Squadron must be increased. The main body of our fleet must not be confined inside Port Arthur, since the entrance is narrow and could easily be blocked. A still worse position is Dalny, since it has no fortifications. Incomparably the best anchorage for the fleet is Vladivostok. Our squadron ought to be at Vladivostok during peace. The disadvantage of Vladivostok is the ice.

The most convenient position for our fleet would be somewhere in South Korea, such as Alexeiev roadstead, Chikhacher or Vladimir, Monomakh, Masampho. The issue of a general action would then have to be decided before the Japanese could transport any troops. But our fleet could hardly be expected to reach Masampho without an action with the Japanese. Our fleet should, as soon as it is ready, put to sea, and steer for the Korean Strait and engage the enemy, or if possible avoid him and take up a position near Masampho, and remain ready to move out to fight a general action when desired.

The deductions to be drawn from the different war games may be summarised thus:—

(1) The insufficiency of our naval forces in the Pacific.

(2) Insufficient equipment of 'our bases: Port Arthur and Vladivostok.

(3) Necessity of fighting preparation of the squadron instead of its lying in reserve at Port Arthur and Vladivostok.

(4) Probability of a sudden declaration of war.

(5) Warning stationnaires in Korean and Chinese ports of opening of hostilities by telegrams alone not sufficient.

(6) Danger of anchoring vessels in Port Arthur outer anchorage; necessity of preparing booms against torpedo attacks.

(7) Possibility of enemy sinking transports at only entrance of Port Arthur.

(8) Impossibility of leaving Dalny with all its workshops undefended.

(9) Impossibility of Dalny as a base owing to its defencelessness.

(10) Impossibility of Port Arthur as a base owing to its insufficient equipment.

(11) Necessity of an intermediate base at Masampho.

(12) The only possible place for the main base of operations of the Pacific Squadron—Vladivostok.

The last deduction fully accords with a resolution come to by a Special Conference which assembled under the Presidency of the Grand Duke General-Admiral Alexis Alexandrovich in 1886, and approved by the Emperor, "henceforth not to seek for any other bases for the Pacific " Fleet either in the Japan Sea or elsewhere, but to devote all attention " to the thorough equipment of Vladivostok."

None of the above deductions, which the bitter truth of 1904 proved correct, were made use of. They were only filed as interesting material for records.

IX.—ADMIRAL MAKAROV'S APPRECIATION.[1]

The following letter was written by Vice-Admiral Makarov, C.-in-C. of Kronstadt, on February 8th, 1904, to the Minister of Marine :—

"From conversation with men returned from the Far East, I " understand that the fleet is to lie not in the inner basin of Port " Arthur, but in the outer roadstead.

"If this is so all the coal reserves will be used up in a short " time and the fleet will be doomed to complete inactivity.

"The presence of vessels in an open roadstead enables an enemy " to make night attacks. No precautions can prevent an energetic " enemy during the night from attacking a fleet with a large " number of torpedo craft and even with steam picket-boats. The " result of such an attack would be very serious for us, for the " torpedo nets do not protect the whole of the ships' sides, and, " moreover, many of our ships have no nets.

"With our vessels lying in the large roadstead of Port Arthur, " increased vigilance will be required every night. Patrol vessels " must be sent out and, none the less, we must be on the alert in " expectation of a torpedo attack. The appearance of any chance " boat will cause alarm and the nights will be spent in anxiety. " It is common knowledge that the anticipation of a torpedo " attack is fatiguing to the ships' companies and is detrimental to " morale. If the Japanese fleet also had no closed anchorages and " had to lie in full strength off an exposed shore, our tactics " ought to consist on the first possible night after the rupture of " negotiations in carrying out the most energetic night attack on " the fleet. The Japanese will not allow such an unparalleled " opportunity of damaging us to pass. I am even of the opinion " that the hope of weakening our fleet by making night attacks " was one of the courses that influenced them in declaring war. " Had we possessed at Port Arthur a large inner anchorage from " which the squadron could emerge at any minute, the Japanese " would not have declared war so lightly.

"There are apparently three reasons against keeping the fleet " in the inner basin : (1) the small size of the basin itself ; (2) the " impossibility of the whole squadron proceeding out at one and

---

[1] P. 192.

" the same time, and (3) the possibility, by sinking a ship, of
" blocking the entrance.

"However confined may be the space in Port Arthur, by dint
" of practice vessels will be able to steam out rapidly.   I think
" that with practice, when the weather is favourable, large vessels
" will be able to go out at intervals of not more than 20 minutes
" after each other and I see no danger in going out separately.
" I am told that the enemy's fleet may approach the entrance and
" destroy the ships as they come out.   I do not believe it, for the
" enemy will at the time be under the fire of the coast batteries
" and every ship as she comes out will augment the fire of the
" latter.

" As regards the possibility of blocking the entrance by sinking
" a steamship, as was done by the Americans at Santiago, this
" would be no simple matter, and, moreover, Port Arthur is rich
" in dredging appliances, and consequently if we do not quickly
" raise or blow up the vessel we can dig a passage along her.

"I fully appreciate the fact that for the fleet to lie in the inner
" anchorage of Port Arthur is an evil, but not so great an evil as
" lying at anchor in a large roadstead, which will involve an
" enormous expenditure of coal, extreme fatigue to the crews
" and the possibility of great losses from torpedo attacks.

"Of the two evils the lesser should be selected, and I therefore
" think that common sense requires that the ships not employed
" in operations should remain in the inner basin of Port Arthur,
" the coal expenditure being reduced to a minimum by discontinuing
" the electric light and by other measures.

"If we do not now place the fleet in the inner basin we shall
" be forced to do so after the first night attack and have paid
" dearly for our mistake."

Although this letter reached its destination, it did not produce the
effect desired by Admiral Makarov. Whether it was delivered too late
or it was considered undesirable to circulate it, is not known, nor does
it matter, for in any case the suggestions contained in it could not have
been acted upon until high water on the morning of February 9th.
But it is a valuable historical document, and cannot be passed over in
silence in describing the events of the 8th February.

Note.—The following remarks appear on this letter: "Reported to
" His Majesty 27/1 (*i.e.*, February 9th)."   "To be kept strictly secret.   No
" copies to be made.".

The reason this letter was stopped at the Naval Headquarters Staff
is given shortly by Admiral Rozhestvenski. In his report of February
14th, 1906, to the Minister of Marine, he stated that it was "not in
" keeping with the principle of 'full power to the Commander-in-Chief.
" And, besides this, the Chief of the Staff would have laid himself open
" to censure had he by any method obtained consent (*i.e.*, Imperial
" consent) to a request to keep the squadron of the Pacific Ocean in
" harbour."

X.—Progress of Admiral Virenius's Squadron.[1]

There is a great deal about the slow progress of the *Oslyabya*, etc.
Admiral Virenius was anxious to go on without the torpedo-boats

---

[1] Pp. 141-149.

but Head-quarters considered the torpedo craft the most important part of his squadron. On February 1st, 1904, he received the following telegram from Admiral Rozhestvenski :—

> "Your proposals differ entirely from instructions given to you. You are to hasten out to Port Arthur, stopping nowhere without orders. The route to Saigon is clear. You must not deviate from it in the slightest. The torpedo craft can clean boilers when under way. They constitute the main portion of your squadron. You are not to abandon one, however bad a state she is in. Only these vessels inspire awe in the enemy, etc."

The torpedo-boats had to be towed, and owing to the weather and heavy seas Admiral Virenius soon found they could never reach the Far East.

On February 15th, when at Jibuti, he received a direct order from the Emperor to return to Russia.

APPENDIX B.

JAPANESE ORDERS AND INSTRUCTIONS.

I.

ADMIRAL TOGO'S BATTLE INSTRUCTIONS, 14th SEPTEMBER 1904.

Extracted from the *Japanese Confidential History* [Vol. ii., p. 214–6].

On Sept. 14th, Admiral Togo settled his plan of operations against the enemy's fleet as follows :—

> He considered that, as more than a month had passed since the Battle of the Yellow Sea, the damaged ships would have finished their repairs and would make an attempt to get out and escape.

> I. *Order and Disposition in Action.*—The order and disposition in action are to be as follows, unless special orders depending on the circumstances are given. They must be maintained till we are within 10,000 metres of the enemy, after which the separate divisions will adopt suitable movements. The destroyer and torpedo-boat flotillas will come up from the rear of the divisions to which they are attached and will take up position on their disengaged sides.

>> Starboard line : *Tatsuta* ; Third Division, and Blockading flotillas on duty ; Fifth Division (*Hashidate*, &c.), and Flotillas of the Seventh Division.

>> Port line : First Division with *Nisshin* and *Kasuga*, and Blockading flotillas of the next watch ; Sixth Division, and Blockading flotillas of the watch below.

> The Fifth Division's position will be as convenient.

II. *Duties in Action.*—(*a*) The First Division, with the *Nisshin* and *Kasuga* have for their chief object the sinking of the enemy's battleships. If opportunity serves, the *Nisshin* and *Kasuga* will be detached independently to deal with isolated battleships of the enemy.

(*b*) The Third Division's chief object is to sink the *Bayan* and *Pallada*. If these two ships endeavour to utilise their speed to separate and escape, they must be followed up to the end and sunk. If they should be in the battleship line and oppose us, the *Yakumo* and *Asama* should, so long as these cruisers remain there, join up with the First Division and act with the battleships against the enemy.

(*c*) The Sixth Division will act as circumstances dictate either to protect our destroyers, to sink the enemy's destroyers, or when the enemy's formation is broken up to keep touch with them, leading our destroyers and sending them to make night attacks.

(*d*) The Fifth Division (*Hashidate*, &c.) is the reserve squadron and has the duty of dealing with damaged and isolated ships. Its chief work is to destroy ships which are trying to get back to Port Arthur.

(*e*) The chief duty of the *Tatsuta* and *Yaeyama* is the carrying of messages and passing on of signals. If there is an opportunity they will attack the enemy's destroyers.

(*f*) The destroyer flotilla will as much as possible act with the Divisions to which they are attached, and will attack under the orders of the admiral in command of their own Divisions. Before sunset they will, without further orders, keep in touch with the enemy, and at night they will lose no chance of making attacks. Also, even in daytime they must be prepared to attack the enemy's destroyers or injured ships. The objective for their attack will in general be: for the flotillas attached to the First, Fifth, and Sixth Divisions, Russian battleships; and for the flotillas attached to the Third Division, the *Bayan* and *Pallada*. Should they not get orders from the flagships of their own divisions, the senior flotilla commander will indicate the objective for their attack according to his own judgment.

If the flotillas become separated and lose sight of the enemy, any division which discovers the Russian ships will give notice by the same signal used to indicate a night sortie of the enemy's squadron (rockets and guns fired in rapid succession); they will also wave their searchlights vertically up and down to inform the other division of the enemy's position. After they have made their attacks they will still keep touch with the enemy, observe their movements next morning, and if possible warn the battle fleet.

III. *Tactics.*—The tactics of the various Divisions are the same as have been adopted heretofore, and I will not repeat them here.

26th September 1904.

Each boat of all the flotillas will make from suitable materials several dummies in imitation of our spherical mechanical mines; these are to be painted as in the picture below:—

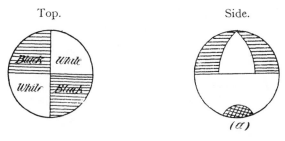

Top.   Side.

(a) The weight may be hung from the bottom.

These dummy mines are to be dropped in daytime in front of the enemy to upset their formation or to retard their escape in a chase. Orders for dropping them will be given by the senior flagship of each Division, and the special signal to be used is fixed as follows:—

Boats "move" flag and Y hoisted together.
Meaning:—"Destroyers to lay dummy mines."

Destroyer divisions which have received this signal will proceed at full speed to a position 10 or 12 thousand metres ahead of the enemy's fleet and cut across their course. They will then rapidly throw overboard the dummy mines as if to surround them. The method of laying the mines will be fixed as convenient by each flotilla commander.

IV. *Movements of the Sections of the Fleet when the Enemy come out at Night, or we are unable to bring a Daytime Action to a Conclusion.* —If the enemy come out at night the flotillas on blockade duty, in accordance with the instructions already given, will make the code signals and attack with all their power. The other destroyer and torpedo-boat divisions will come up as quickly as they can and make attacks till dawn, when they will do their utmost to join their own proper Fleet Divisions.

Each Division will come south on the courses laid down in the attached plan of projected courses. If their are no special orders they will proceed to the first guard line, stop there, lay out search lines on both sides of their track, and wait for the enemy. According with the time of the enemy's emergence, the flagship *Mikasa* may give orders as to the guard line and the time it is to be reached. If the enemy are still north of us when we reach the guard line, it may happen that the course will be reversed, and each Division steam north, spreading out search lines on either side of the appointed track. If there is an indecisive daytime action this procedure will also be adopted.

V.—During the absence of the *Yaeyama* from this district, the *Tatsuta* will follow the track appointed for that ship.

VI.—When the *Matsushima*, now keeping guard at Chemulpho, gets news of the enemy's sortie southward, she will leave port at once, proceed to Position 180, N.W. of the Clifford Islands, and stop there, keeping guard against the enemy's arrival in those waters. She is to keep up communication with our fleet.

VII.—If I recall the Second Squadron from the Straits when the enemy come out and go southward, the first rendezvous is fixed at Position 127, S.E. of Ross Island.

II.

FLOTILLA ATTACK ON THE " SEVASTOPOL."

(a) COMMANDER KASAMA'S INSTRUCTIONS, DECEMBER 14TH, 1904.

[Japanese Confidential History, Vol. ii., pp. 449–51.]

December 14th, Captain Imai of the *Chinyen* gave all the torpedo-boat flotilla orders to attack the *Sevastopol*, and made Commander Kasama of the 15th division drew up a plan of stations for the attack. Commander Kasama called all the officers commanding torpedo-boat divisions to the parent-ship for a meeting, which settled the plan of attack as follows :—

I. Objects of the operations—
    To attack and destroy the *Sevastopol* which has broken out of Port Arthur and is anchored on guard under Jo-to-san; also the gunboat *Otvazani*, and the blockade-running merchant ship.

II. Forces to be employed—
    The 15th torpedo-boat division (*Hibari, Sagi, Udzura, Hashi-taka*), the 9th division (*Aotaka, Kari, Tsubame, Hato*), the 14th division (*Chidori, Kasasagi, Hayabusa, Manadzuru*), the 10th division (Nos. 40, 41, 42, 43), the 2nd division (Nos. 37, 45 and 46), the 21st division (No. 49), the 16th division (No. 39), the 6th division (Nos. 56 and 58), the 12th division (No. 52), and the picket-boat of the *Fuji.*

III. Duties of Flotilla—
    The first attack will be made by the three boats of the 6th and 12th divisions and the *Fuji's* picket-boat.

    The forces for the second attack will consist of the 15th division (which will make a diversion), the four boats of the 2nd and 21st divisions, the five boats of the 10th and 16th divisions, the 14th division and the 9th division.

IV. Time, formation, and speed of attacks—

The two attacks will be made between midnight and dawn, according to the times of moonset and high tide.

Divisions will leave Ping-tu-tau in single line ahead. Those for the first attack will deliver their blow on the enemy's ships about midnight. Those for the second attack will follow in order, and will make their attacks in succession on the flowing tide after 1 a.m. on the 15th. The 15th division after its attacks will go to the situation decided upon for a diversion, and will burn searchlights and fire guns to clear the way for the attacks of the other division. The *Fuji's* picket-boat will run in and make its attack when a chance presents itself, during either the first or second attacks.

The distance apart of boats is to be 500 metres, as usual.

Normal speed 12 knots. Half-speed 8 knots. Slow speed 5 knots.

The speed during the actual attacks is left to the discretion of divisional commanders.

V. Rules—

(*a*) All boats must show tail lights till they come to the position for attack.

(*b*) They will put out the tail lights when they turn to come southward after making their attacks; but will show side lights to avert collisions.

(*c*) Boats which on the way are in danger or lose control of their movements are to inform their consorts by shouting or blowing the whistle. Boats near will give assistance.

(*d*) Attacks are to be carried out inside the line from which Man-tse-ying searchlight bears N.N.E. ¼ E. (that is, within 600 metres of the Russian ships).

(*e*) The 15th division will lead the other divisions as far as the attacking position. After delivering its attack this division will turn to starboard, and will then make a diversion by showing lights and firing guns near the position from which Golden Hill searchlight bears about two miles north.

The other divisions will turn to port after delivering their attacks, and will retire on the track decided upon.

(*f*) In each boat, one torpedo is to be adjusted for a depth of 6 metres and the other for 4 metres, except in the 15th division where each boat will make ready torpedoes adjusted to zero depth to be used for destroying the net defence.

(*g*) If the enemy open fire on us during the attack we shall not reply to it.

(*h*) Boats will return to Ping-tu-tau after firing all their torpedoes.

(*i*) Boats which have sighted the enemy and are in the process of attack will finish their attacks before rendering assistance to any other boat which may have made signals of distress.

(*j*) The group first for attack will go ahead of the rest and make its attack about 1 a.m. The second group, when it sees that the first group has finished, will operate as convenient, delivering its attack before dawn.

(*k*) The senior divisional commander will settle the times and order of departure.

(*l*) At the conclusion of an attack each divisional commander will collect his boats and make for the rendezvous.

(*m*) The rendezvous is Ping-tu-tau East Bay.

VI. Courses—
As shown in attached chart.

(*b*) COMMANDER SEKI'S INSTRUCTIONS:

[*Japanese Confidential History*, Vol. ii., pp. 455–6.]

The 14th division which came next after the 10th division had tried to make an attack on the night of the 12th of December, but were hindered by the searchlights which prevented them from seeing anything of the enemy, and were finally unable to make their attack. Commander Seki of the 14th division accordingly issued the following instructions to the captains of his boats, before leaving for the present attack.

I have been much gratified to find that in the last attack you all carefully observed my instructions and refrained from firing torpedoes, as you were not certain of the enemy. It is the duty of torpedo-boats to think nothing of running up with shell flying all round them; but I have heard of cases where at such moments boats fired at what they thought looked like the enemy, or trusting to luck, at the estimated position in which they had caught a momentary sight of her in a gleam of the searchlight. People who do that sort of thing, think that it is enough to run up and fire a torpedo, behaviour which can hardly be called attacking the enemy's ship. This division in the previous attack, while bravely running up through the searchlight rays and heavy firing of the guns, caught a glimpse of the enemy and then lost sight of her again on account of the glare; but we kept quite calm and did not fire at random, which is most satisfactory. We braved the particularly violent firing and searchlights, and made several rushes until 6 a.m., but failed in our object, and had to abandon our attack on account of the approach of low tide, as is well known to you all. I have heard, however, that some people in authority have given utterance to the criticism that in an attack, torpedoes should always be fired, whether they are likely to be effective or not, and that to withhold fire is wrong; but I do not believe this sneer to have been expressed by our wise staff or by order of the Commander-in-Chief. Since I have received no official orders that my methods are unsuitable, I shall continue to employ the same tactics in the endeavour to secure success for my division. In the attack of to-night I shall lead you in what experience has shown to be the best way for finding the enemy, and I hope that you will carry out the operations with that idea in your minds.

APPENDIX C.

ADDITIONS TO THE JAPANESE NAVY AVAILABLE DURING THE PERIOD OF THIS VOLUME.[1]

Name.	Date of Launch.	Builders' Name or where Built.	Displacement.	I.H.P.	Speed.	Coal Supply.		Armament.			Complement.
						Normal.	Maximum.	Ordnance.	No. of Tubes.	No. of Torpedoes.	
						Tons.	Tons.				
(a) CRUISER.											
Otawa	Nov. 1903	Yokoska -	3,000	10,000	21 Knots.	—	—	2, 6-in.; 6, 4·7-in.; 4, 12-pr.	—	—	312
(b) DESTROYERS.[2]											
Arare	1905	Kure -	375	6,000	29	—	—	2, 12-pr.; 4, 6-pr.	2	—	61
Ariake	1904	Yokosuka	375	6,000	29	—	—	2, 12-pr.; 4, 6-pr.	2	4	61
Fubuki	1905	Yokosuka	375	6,000	29	—	—	2, 12-pr.; 4, 6-pr.	2	—	61
(c) TORPEDO BOATS—FIRST CLASS.											
Kiji -	1905	Kure -	137	4,200	29	—	25	1, 6-pr.; 1, 3-pr.	3	—	—

[1] These are in addition to those in the list in Volume 1, Appendix K., page 526. Of the ships there enumerated they had lost by the end of September—2 battleships (Hatsuse and Yoshino); 2 cruisers (Miyako and Yoshino); 2 destroyers; 2 torpedo-boats; and 3 gunboats (Oshima, Kaimon, and Heiyen). By the time Port Arthur fell they had also lost one more cruiser, Takasago; 2 gunboats, Atago and Saiyen, and 2 more torpedo-boats.

[2] At the beginning of the war the armament of these vessels consisted of one 12-pr. and five 6-pr. guns. It was changed during 1904.

APPENDIX D.

JAPANESE AUXILIARY VESSELS.[1]

Name.	Date of Launch.	Where Built.	Gross Tonnage.	When Armed.	——
I. ARMED MERCHANT CRUISERS.[2]					
Taichu Maru -	1897	Sunderland	3,319	Jan. 1904	
Tainan Maru -	,,	,,	3,311	,, ,,	
Yawata Maru -	1898	Glasgow -	3,816	,, ,,	
America Maru -	,,	Newcastle -	6,307	Feb. 1904	
Hong-kong Maru	,,	Sunderland	6,169	,, ,,	
Nippon Maru -	,,	,,	6,169	,, ,,	
Yobu - - -	—	—	—	Mar. 1904	Ex-Korean gun-vessel.
Bingo Maru -	1897	Glasgow -	6,247	Mar. 1905	
Manshu Maru -	1894	Greenock -	5,248	,, ,,	
Sado Maru -	1897	Belfast -	6,222	,, ,,	
Shinano Maru -	1900	Glasgow -	6,387	,, ,,	
Taihoku Maru -	1891	Newcastle -	2,796	—	Depôt of Fleet Mining Staff.
II. TORPEDO PARENT SHIPS.[3]					
Kasugo Maru -	1897	Glasgow -	3,819	Jan. 1904	
Nikko Maru -	1903	Nagasaki -	5,538	,, ,,	
Kumano Maru -	1901	Glasgow -	5,076	Mar. 1904	
Karasaki Maru -	1896	Newcastle -	5,627	,, 1905	
Toyohashi - -	—	—	—	—	Ex - Russian Volunteer SS. *Ekaterenoslav.* Originally intended for submarine parent ship.
III. REPAIR SHIPS.					
Koto Maru -	1883	Glasgow -	3,182	—	
Miike Maru -	1888	Sunderland	3,364	—	
Kwanto Maru -	1900	Copenhagen	6,193	July 1904	Ex-Russian E. Asiatic SS. *Manchuria.* See *Attaché Reports*, III., 167.
IV. GUNBOATS.[4]					
Kereyo Maru -	1903	Osaka -	745	April 1904	2nd class, converted by repair ships in Hai-ju Bay.
Kohan Maru -	,,	,, -	632	,, ,,	Converted as above. Discharged Jan. 1905.
Uwajuna Maru I.	1895	Kobe -	377	,, ,,	3rd class.
Uwajuna Maru II.	1901	Osaka -	444	,, ,,	2nd ,,

Name.	Date of Launch.	Where Built.	Gross Tonnage.	When Armed.	
IV. Gunboats—*continued.*					
Godaishima Maru	—	—	—	May 1904	
Himikawa Maru	1894	Osaka	420	,, ,,	
Kagawa Maru	1903	Kobe	613	,, ,,	
Kaijo Maru	—	—	—	,, ,,	1st class
Manda Maru	1900	Osaka	248	,, ,,	
Onogawa Maru	1893	Kobe	318	,, ,,	
Sobogawa Maru	1890	Osaka	313	,, ,,	
Shinyu Maru	1903	,,	414	,, ,,	
Ychime or Eshime Maru.	,,	Kobe	613	,, ,,	
Yoshidogawa M.	1890	Osaka	309	,, ,,	
Wakigawa Maru	—	—	—	,, ,,	
Ohito Maru	—	—	—	—	1st class.
Bunryo Maru	—	—	—		
Heijo Maru	1903	Kobe	1,201	Dec. 1904-Mar. 1905.	1st class.
Keijo Maru	—	—	—	,, ,,	1st class
Otagawa Maru	—	—	—		
V. Hospital Ships.					
Kobe Maru	1888	Glasgow	2,877	—	See Attaché Reports, III., 236.
Saikyo Maru	,,	,,	2,904	—	
VI. Miscellaneous.					
Chishima Maru	—	—	—	—	Mine sweeper at Port Arthur.
Hinode Maru	1872	London	1,115	—	,, ,,
Hayata Maru	—	—	—	—	,, ,,
Kocho Maru	1890	Osaka	329	—	,, ,,
Chidori I. Maru	—	—	—	—	,, ,,
Shibata Maru	1886	Sunderland	2,783	—	,, ,,
Ryojan Maru	1897	Osaka	170	—	Mine layer.
Okinawa Maru	1896	Renfrew	2,232	—	Cable ship.
Yamashiro Maru	1890	Sunderland	3,320	—	Ammunition depôt ship.

[1] Exclusive of supply ships.

[2] The normal armament of these ships was two 4·7 and six 6 pounders.

[3] These ships were armed with light guns.

[4] In this category are included some ships of over 1,0co tons, which, though rated by the Japanese as "First-class gunboats," were rather what were formerly called "gun-vessels."

Note.—The above list cannot be regarded as exact or complete. In November 1904, when Admiral Ito objected to Admiral Togo's proposal for using mines for port defence on account of their danger to commerce, he expressed the Staff preference for coastal torpedo-boats. Thereupon Admiral Togo replied that he had a scheme for fitting out 16 auxiliary gunboats with torpedo tubes. He also said he had four ships with mine dropping gear, and that he intended later on to fix six more. (*Confidential History*, II., 227.)

APPENDIX E. 1.

RUSSIAN WAR VESSELS AVAILABLE IN THE FAR EAST DURING THE PERIOD COVERED BY THIS VOLUME.

(a) BATTLESHIPS, CRUISERS, GUNBOATS, MINING TRANSPORTS AND DISPATCH VESSELS.

Name.	Class.	Date of Launch.	Where Built.	Displacement.	I.H.P.	Speed.	Coal Supply Normal.	Coal Supply Maximum.	Armour W.L.	Armour Deck.	Armour Gun Protection.	Armour Conning Tower.	Armament Ordnance.	Torpedo Tubes Submerged.	Torpedo Tubes Above Water.	Complement.
				Tons.		Knots.	Tons.	Tons.	Ins.	Ins.	Ins.	Ins.				
Admiral Nakhimov	Armoured cruiser	Nov., 1885	St. Petersburg (Baltic Works)	8,524	7,768	16·6	—	1,300	10	2	8	6	8 8-in.; 10 6-in.; 2 2½-in.; 12 3-pr.; 10 machine guns.	—	3	572
Admiral Senyavin	Armoured coast defence vessel	Aug.,1894	St. Petersburg (New Dockyard)	4,960	5,337	16·1	260	400	10	2⅜	8	8	4 10-in.; 4 4·7-in.; 2 2½-in.; 6 3-pr.; 18 machine guns.	—	4	404
Admiral Ushakov	Armoured coast defence vessel	Nov., 1893	St. Petersburg (Baltic Works)	4,126	5,769	16·1	260	400	10	2⅜	8	8	4 10-in.; 4 4·7-in.; 2 2½-in.; 6 3-pr.; 18 machine guns.	—	4	404
Aleut ...	Mining transport (Vladivostok)	1886	Christiania	892	730	12·2	—	70	—	—	—	—	4 machine guns; can carry mines.	—	—	104

(a) BATTLESHIPS, CRUISERS, GUNBOATS, MINING TRANSPORTS AND DISPATCH VESSELS—continued.

Name.	Class.	Date of Launch.	Where Built.	Displacement.	I.H.P.	Speed.	Coal Supply. Normal.	Coal Supply. Maximum.	Max. Thickness of Armour. W.L.	Deck.	Gun Protection.	Conning Tower.	Armament. Ordnance.	Torpedo Tubes. Submerged.	Torpedo Tubes. Above Water.	Complement.
				Tons.		Knots.	Tons.	Tons.	Ins.	Ins.	Ins.	Ins.				
Almaz	Dispatch vessel	June, 1903	St. Petersburg (Baltic Works)	3,285	7,500	19	—	560	—	—	—	—	4 12-pr.; 8 3-pr.	—	—	336
Avrora	Cruiser, 1st class protected	May, 1900	St. Petersburg (New Dockyard)	6,731	11,610	20	900	1,430	—	3	—	6	8 6-in.; 2 2½-in.; 24 12-pr.; 8 machine guns.	2	1	570
Bogatwir	Cruiser, 1st class protected	Jan., 1901	Stettin (Vulcan Works)	6,645	19,500	23	900	1,430	—	2¾	5	5½	12 6-in.; 12 12-pr.; 2 3-pr.; 2 2½-pr.; 4 machine guns.	2	4	573
Borodino	Battleship, 1st class (Vladivostok)	Sept., 1901	St. Petersburg (New Dockyard)	13,516	16,300	17·8	—	1,250	7⅞	2 9/16	10	8	4 12-in.; 12 6-in.; 2 2½-in.; 20 12-pr.; 3-pr.; 10 machine guns.	2	2	830
Dmitri Donskoi	Armoured cruiser	1883	St. Petersburg (New Dockyard)	6,200	6,609	17	400	—	6	¼	—	—	6 6-in.; 10 4·7-in.; 2 2½-pr.; 6 3-pr.; 22 machine guns.	—	5	503

General-Admiral Apraxin	Armoured coast defence vessel	May, 1896	St. Petersburg (New Dockyard)	4,126	5,000	16	260	400	10	$2\frac{1}{2}$	8	8	3 10-in.; 4 4·7-in.; 2 $2\frac{1}{2}$-in.; 10 3-pr.; 12 machine guns.	—	4	404
Gromoboi	Armoured cruiser (Vladivostok)	May, 1899	St. Petersburg (Baltic Works)	13,220	15,500	20	800	2,500	6	$2\frac{1}{2}$	$4\frac{3}{4}$	12	4 8-in.; 16 6-in.; 24 12-pr.; 12 3-pr.; 2 $2\frac{1}{2}$-in.; 22 machine guns.	4	—	874
Imperator Alexandr III	Battleship, 1st class	Aug., 1901	St. Petersburg (Baltic Works)	13,516	15,800	17·6	—	1,250	$7\frac{5}{8}$	$2\frac{9}{16}$	10	8	4 12-in.; 12 6-in.; 2 $2\frac{1}{2}$-in; 20 12-pr.; 20 3-pr.; 10 machine guns.	2	2	830
Imperator Nikolai I	Battleship, 2nd class	June, 1889	St. Petersburg (Franco-Russian Works)	9,672	7,842	14	—	1,200	14	$2\frac{3}{8}$	10	8	2 12-in.; 4 9-in; 8 6-in.; 2 $2\frac{1}{2}$-in.; 16 3-pr.; 8 machine guns.	—	6	623
Izumrud ...	Cruiser, 3rd class protected	Oct., 1903	St. Petersburg (Nevski Works)	3,103	17,000	24	400	510	—	2	—	$1\frac{3}{16}$	6 4·7-in.; 1 $2\frac{1}{2}$-in.; 6 3-pr.; 4 machine guns.	—	5	336
Knyaz Suvorov	Battleship, 1st class	Sept., 1902	St. Petersburg (Baltic Works)	13,516	15,800	17·6	—	1,250	$7\frac{5}{8}$	$2\frac{9}{16}$	10	8	4 12-in.; 12 6-in.; 2 $2\frac{1}{2}$-in.; 20 12-pr.; 20 3-pr.; 10 machine guns.	2	2	830
Navarin ...	Battleship, 1st class	Oct., 1891	St. Petersburg (Franco-Russian Works)	10,206	9,144	15·9	400	700	16	3	12	10	4 12-in.; 8 6-in.; 2 $2\frac{1}{2}$-in.; 18 3-pr.; 12 machine guns.	—	6	622
Oleg ...	Cruiser, 1st class protected	Aug., 1903	St. Petersburg (New Dockyard)	6,645	19,500	23	900	—	—	$2\frac{3}{4}$	5	$5\frac{1}{2}$	12 6-in.; 2 $2\frac{1}{2}$-in.; 12 12-pr.; 6 3-pr.; 4 machine guns.	2	—	580
Orel ...	Battleship, 1st class	July, 1902	St. Petersburg (Galerni Island)	13,516	15,800	17·6	—	1,250	$7\frac{5}{8}$	$2\frac{9}{16}$	10	8	4 12-in.; 12 6-in.; 2 $2\frac{1}{2}$-in.; 20 12-pr.; 20 3-pr.; 10 machine guns.	2	2	830
Oslyabya ...	Battleship, 1st class	Nov., 1898	St. Petersburg (New Dockyard)	12,674	15,053	18·3	1,060	2,060	9	$2\frac{3}{4}$	9	6	4 10-in.; 11 6-in.; 2 $2\frac{1}{2}$-in.; 20 12-pr.; 20 3-pr.; 8 machine guns.	2	3	769

(a) BATTLESHIPS, CRUISERS, GUNBOATS, MINING TRANSPORTS AND DISPATCH VESSELS—continued.

Name.	Class.	Date of Launch.	Where Built.	Displacement. (Tons.)	I.H.P.	Speed. (Knots.)	Coal Supply. Normal. (Tons.)	Coal Supply. Maximum. (Tons.)	Maximum Thickness of Armour. W.L. (Ins.)	Deck. (Ins.)	Gun Protection. (Ins.)	Conning Tower. (Ins.)	Armament. Ordnance.	Torpedo Tubes. Sub-merged.	Above Water.	Complement.
Rossiya ...	Armoured cruiser (Vladivostok)	May, 1896	St. Petersburg (B a l t i c Works)	13,675	18,426	19·7	1,000	2,500	8	2	5	12	4 8-in.; 16 6-in.; 12 12-pr.; 30 3-pr.; 2 2½-in.; 6 machine guns.	—	5	839
Sissoi Veliki	Battleship, 1st class	June, 1894	St. Petersburg (New Dock-yard)	10,400	8,494	15·7	500	800	16	3	12	6	4 12-in.; 6 6-in.; 12 3-pr.; 16 machine guns.	—	6	586
Svyetlana...	Cruiser, 2nd class pro-tected	Dec., 1896	Havre (Forges et Chantiers)	3,727	10,100	20·2	400	—	—	2½	—	4	6 6-in.; 10 3-pr.; 2 machine guns.	—	2	402
Vladimir Monomakh	Armoured cruiser	1882	St. Petersburg (B a l t i c Works)	5,593	7,044	17·5	400	—	6	4½	—	—	5 6-in.; 6 4·7-in.; 2 2½-in.; 16 3-pr.; 8 machine guns.	—	3	493
Zhemchug..	Cruiser, 3rd class pro-tected	Aug., 1903	St. Petersburg (N e v s k i Works)	3,103	17,000	24	490	510	—	2	—	1 3⁄16	6 4·7-in.; 1 2½-in.; 6 3-pr.; 4 machine guns.	—	5	336

(b) DESTROYERS.

Name.	Date of Launch.	Where Built.	Displacement.	I.H.P.	Speed.	Coal Supply.	Armament. Ordnance.		Torpedoes. No. of Tubes.	Torpedoes. No. of Torpedoes.	Complement.
			Tons.		Knots.	Tons.					
Bezuprechni ...	1902	St. Petersburg (Nevski Works)	350	5,700	26	80	1 12-pr. ; 5	3-pr....	3	6	62
Blestyashchi ...	1901	St. Petersburg (Nevski Works)	350	5,700	26	80	1 12-pr. ; 5	3-pr....	3	6	62
Bodri	1902	St. Petersburg (Nevski Works)	350	5,700	26	80	1 12-pr. ; 5	3-pr....	3	6	62
Bravi	1901	St. Petersburg (Nevski Works)	350	5,700	26	80	1 12-pr. ; 5	3-pr....	3	6	62
Buini	1901	St. Petersburg (Nevski Works)	350	5,700	26	80	1 12-pr. ; 5	3-pr....	3	6	62
Buistri	1901	St. Petersburg (Nevski Works)	350	5,700	26	80	1 12-pr. ; 5	3-pr....	3	6	62
Byedovi ...	1902	St. Petersburg (Nevski Works)	350	5,700	26	80	1 12-pr. ; 5	3-pr....	3	6	62
Gromki ...	1904	St. Petersburg (Nevski Works)	350	5,700	26	80	1 12-pr. ; 5	3-pr....	3	—	62
Grozni ...	1904	St. Petersburg (Nevski Works)	350	5,700	26	80	1 12-pr. ; 5	3-pr....	3	—	62

(e) TORPEDO BOATS—FIRST CLASS.*

Number.	Date of Launch.	Where Built.	Displacement. Tons.	I.H.P.	Speed. Knots.	Coal Supply. Tons.	Armament. Ordnance.	Armament. Torpedoes. No. of Tubes.	Armament. Torpedoes. No. of Torpedoes.	Complement.
No. 203	1889	Abo (Crighton's Works)	175	1,956	20·4	30	3 machine guns	3	—	21
No. 205	1886	Havre (Normand)	96	737	19·2	29	2 machine guns	2	—	21
No. 206	1886	Havre (Normand)	108	837	19·7	29	2 machine guns	2	—	21
No. 209	1897	St. Petersburg (New Dockyard)	120	1,460	18·5	40	2 machine guns	3	—	21
No. 210	1898	St. Petersburg (Izhora Works)	120	1,460	18·5	40	2 machine guns	3	—	21
No. 211	1898	St. Petersburg (Izhora Works)	120	1,460	18·5	40	2 machine guns	3	—	21

* At Vladivostok.

(d) TORPEDO BOATS—SECOND CLASS.*

Number.	Date of Launch.	Where Built.	Displacement. Tons.	I.H.P.	Speed. Knots.	Coal Supply. Tons.	Armament. Ordnance.	Armament. Torpedoes.	Complement.
No. 91...	1878	St. Petersburg (Baltic Works)	24	220	—	—	—	1 Whitehead... ...	8
No. 92...	1878	St. Petersburg (Baltic Works)	24	220	—	—	—	1 Whitehead... ...	8
No. 93...	1877	St. Petersburg (Baltic Works)	24	220	—	—	—	1 Whitehead... ...	8
No. 94...	1878	St. Petersburg (Baltic Works)	23	220	—	—	—	1 Whitehead... ...	8
No 95...	1878	St. Petersburg (Baltic Works)	23	220	—	—	—	1 Whitehead... ...	8
No. 97...	1878	Abo (Crighton's Works)...	23	220	—	—	—	2 spar... ...	8
No. 98...	1878	Baird	23	220	—	—	—	2 spar... ...	8

* At Vladivostok.

APPENDIX E. 2.

RUSSIAN AUXILIARY VESSELS.

Name.	Class.	Date of Launch.	Where Built.	Displacement.	I.H.P.	Speed.	Coal Supply.	Armament.	Complement.	Remarks.
				Tons.		Knots.	Tons.			
Anadwir	Armed transport (used for carrying coals and provisions)	1903	Barrow ...	12,000	5,000	13	—	Light Q.F. and machine guns	—	Ex-steamship *Franche-Comte* (bought from Vickers, Sons and Maxim).
Argun	Armed transport (Vladivostok)	1902	Middlesbrough	7,000	—	Under 12	—	Not known ...	—	Ex-Renck (Hamburg) steamship *Hafis*.
Bianka	Transport (Vladivostok)	1899	Lubeck ...	2,200	—	—	—	Not known ...	—	Ex-Eimboke (Hamburg) steamship *Bianca*.
Bintang	Transport (Vladivostok)	1901	Leith ...	1,404*	—	—	—	Not known ...	—	Ex-Danish East Asiatic Co. steamship *Bintang*.
Dnyepr	Armed transport	1894	Newcastle	9,460	11,200	19	1,100	7 6-in.; 4 12-pr.; 12 machine guns	—	Ex-Volunteer steamship *Peterburg*.
Don ...	Auxiliary cruiser	1890	Stettin ...	10,500	16,400	19·5	2,750	Light Q.F. and machine guns	—	Ex-Hamburg-Amerika steamship *Furst Bismarck*.
Graf Strogonov	Tank vessel ...	1903	Newcastle ...	7,016*	—	Under 12	—	Under merchant ensign	—	Owned by Northern Steamship Co.
Hermann Lerche	Transport ...	1902	Stockton ...	3,126*	1,350	Under 12	—	Under merchant ensign	—	Owned by Northern Steamship Co.

Name	Type	Year	Where built			Speed		Armament		Remarks
Irtuish	Armed transport	1900	Newcastle	7,500*	4,000	12	—	Light Q.F. and machine guns	—	Ex-Hamburg-Amerika steamship *Belgia*.
Kamchadal	Transport (Vladivostok)	1892	Glasgow	900	—	11·5	—	2 machine guns	—	
Kamchatka	Repair ship	1902	St. Petersburg	7,200	2,800	12	—	6 6-pr.	267	
Kiev	Transport	1896	Clydebank	10,850	3,000	13	1,204	Under merchant ensign	81	Volunteer steamship.
Kitai	Transport	1898	Leith	4,660*	2,200	10	—	Under merchant ensign	52	Owned by Russian East Asiatic Steamship Co.
Knyaz Gorchakov	Transport	1901	West Hartlepool	3,882*	1,400	10	—	Under merchant ensign	—	Owned by Northern Steamship Co.
Kolwima	Armed transport (Vladivostok)	1893	Middlesbrough	3,400	—	—	—	Not known ...	—	Ex-Jebsen (Hamburg) steamship *Emma*.
Koreya	Transport (used for carrying ammunition)	1899	Flensburg	6,163*	2,800	12	—	Under merchant ensign	48	Owned by Russian East Asiatic Steamship Co.
Kostroma	Hospital ship	1888	Newcastle	6,800	2,600	13	541	Under Red Cross	—	Ex-Volunteer steamship.
Kuban	Auxiliary cruiser	1889	Stettin	10,500	12,500	18·5	—	Light Q.F. and machine guns	—	Ex-Hamburg-Amerika steamship *Auguste Victoria*.
Kuronia	Transport	1890	Glasgow	4,572*	2,500	Under 12	—	Under merchant ensign	—	Owned by Russian East Asiatic Steamship Co.
Lili	Transport (Vladivostok)	1890	Sunderland	3,500	—	Under 12	—	Not known ...	—	Ex-Drummond Co. (Liverpool) steamship *Drummond*.
Livonia	Transport	1902	Flensburg	5,782*	—	Under 12	—	Under merchant ensign	—	Owned by Russian East Asiatic Steamship Co.

RUSSIAN AUXILIARY VESSELS—*continued.*

Name.	Class.	Date of Launch.	Where Built.	Displacement.	I.H.P.	Speed.	Coal Supply.	Armament.	Complement.	Remarks.
				Tons.		Knots.	Tons.			
Malaiya	Transport	1898	Glasgow...	4,847*	1,660	Under 12	—	Under merchant ensign	44	Owned by Russian East Asiatic Steamship Co.
Merkuri	Transport	1900	Kiel	4,046*	2,325	11·5	—	Under merchant ensign	42	Owned by Russian Steam Navigation and Trading Co.
Meteor	Tank vessel	1901	Middlesbrough...	4,259*	2,000	Under 10·5 12	—	Under merchant ensign	45	Owned by Russian Steam Navigation and Trading Co.
Mongugai	Patrol duty (Vladivostok)	1891	Flensburg	1,012*	—	Under 12	—	Not known ...	—	Ex-Struve (Germany) steamship *Pronto.*
Nadezhni	Ice-breaker (Vladivostok)	1896	Copenhagen	1,525	2,920	13·8	—	2 machine guns	—	
Okhotsk	Transport (Vladivostok)	1882	Greenock	1,000	—	—	—	Not known ...	—	Ex-China Navigation Co. steamship *Chung-King.*
Orel	Hospital ship	1890	Newcastle	8,175	9,500	19·25	765	Under Red Cross	—	Ex-Volunteer steamship.
Rion	Armed transport	1902	Newcastle	12,050	16,500	20	1,580	8 4·7-in. ; 8 12-pr. ; 6 3-pr. ; 2 machine guns	—	Ex-Volunteer steamship *Smolensk.*
Rus	Ocean tug	1903	Tonning	611*	—	—	—	Under merchant ensign	—	Ex-Verein (Hamburg) steamship *Roland.*

Name	Class	Date	Where built	Tonnage		Speed	H.P.	Armament		Remarks
Selenga	Armed transport (Vladivostok)	1899	West Hartlepool	6,219	—	9	—	Not known ...	—	Ex-Anderson (Hamburg) steamship *Claudius*.
Shilka	Armed transport (Vladivostok)	1896	Newcastle	3,500	—	—	—	Not known ...	—	Ex-Jebsen(Hamburg) steamship *Erica*.
Sungari	Armed transport (Vladivostok)	—	Newcastle	6,970	—	9	—	Not known ...	—	Ex-Anderson (Hamburg) steamship *Tiberius*.
Svir	Ocean tug	1898	Kinderdijk	542*	—	Under 12	—	Under merchant ensign	—	Ex-Smit & Co. (Rotterdam) steamship *Zwartezee*.
Tambov	Transport	1893	Dumbarton	8,950	2,500	12·5	958	Under merchant ensign	82	Volunteer steamship.
Terek	Auxiliary cruiser	1889	Birkenhead	10,000	13,330	19	—	Light Q.F. and machine guns	—	Ex-Hamburg-Amerika steamship *Columbia*.
Tobol	Armed transport (Vladivostok)	—	—	5,500	—	—	—	Not known ...	—	Ex-British steamship *Cheltenham*.
Ural	Auxiliary cruiser	1890	Stettin	13,600	17,300	20	—	Light Q.F. and machine guns (16 guns)	490	Ex-North German Lloyd steamship *Kaiserin Maria Theresia*.
Ussuri	Armed transport (Vladivostok)	1893	Belfast	3,400	—	—	—	Not known ...	—	Ex-Jebsen(Hamburg) steamship *Elsa*.
Vladimir	Transport	1895	Dumbarton	10,750	3,000	13	1,185	Under merchant ensign	80	Volunteer steamship.
Voronezh	Transport	1895	Dumbarton	10,750	3,600	13	1,170	Under merchant ensign	83	Volunteer steamship.
Yakut	Transport (Vladivostok)	1880	Purchased in England in 1892	700	867	12	—	2 3-pr.; 2 machine guns	95	Volunteer steamship.
Xenia	Repair ship	1900	South Shields	3,773*	1,800	10	—	Under merchant ensign	—	Owned by Russo-Baltic Steamship Co.

* Gross tonnage.

APPENDIX F. 1.

MERCHANT VESSELS SEIZED OR SUNK BY THE JAPANESE FROM THE COMMENCEMENT OF HOSTILITIES TO THE END OF THE WAR.

Name.	Nationality.	Gross Tonnage.	Voyage.	Cargo.	Place of Capture.	Date of Capture.	Remarks.
Ekaterinoslav ...	Russian ...	5,627	Vladivostok to Odessa	General ...	Near Fusan ...	6.2.04	Captured by *Saiyen*. Appeal dismissed. Now under Japanese flag; name changed to *Karasaki Maru*.
Mukden ...	Russian ...	1,567	Nagasaki to Vladivostok	General ...	Fusan ...	6.2.04	Cleared at Nagasaki on the 5th February before hostilities commenced. Appeal dismissed. Afterwards owned by Japanese Navy Department and named *Hoten Maru*.
Argun ...	Russian ...	2,458	Dalny to Nagasaki	General ...	South - west coast of Korea	7.2.04	Captured by *Asoma*. Condemned on final appeal.
Rossiya ...	Russian ...	2,312	Dalny to Karatsu	General ...	South - west coast of Korea	7.2.04	Captured by *Tatsuta*. Appeal dismissed. Now owned by Japanese Government. Present name *Saisha Maru*.
Hermes ...	Norwegian ...	1,358	Moji to Port Arthur	Coal	Near Port Arthur	9.2.04	Released 9th March because vessel started before hostilities were known.

Name	Nationality	Tonnage	Voyage / Engaged	Military stores, etc.	Place	Date	Remarks
Manchuria (East Asiatic Co.)	Russian	6,193	Baltic to Port Arthur	Military stores, etc.	Near Port Arthur	9.2.04	Captured by Takasago. Condemned on final appeal. Afterwards owned by Japanese Navy Department and named Kanto Maru.
Nikolai (whaler)	Russian	124	Engaged fishing	None	East coast of Korea	10.2.04	Condemned on final appeal.
Alexandr (whaling transport)	Russian	261	Engaged at fisheries	Provisions	Idzuhara	10.2.04	Condemned on final appeal. Afterwards owned by Japanese Navy Department and renamed Rekisan Maru.
Michail	Russian	3,603	Engaged at fisheries	Iron bars, etc.	East coast of Korea	10.2.04	This vessel was a whale oil factory. Condemned on final appeal.
Kotik	Russian	400	In port	Iron bars, etc.	Yokohama	12.2.04	Condemned on appeal.
Lyesnik (schooner)	Russian	100	In port	Salt	Nagasaki	17.2.04	No appeal against confiscation.
Manchuria (Chinese Eastern Railway)	Russian	2,937	Repairing	Provisions	Nagasaki	17.2.04	Unable to leave as engines dismantled. Condemned on final appeal. Renamed Manshu Maru.
Nadeshda (schooner)	Russian	68	In port	None	Hakodate	17.2.04	Sealing schooner. No appeal made.
Bobrik (schooner)	Russian	125	In port	None	Hakodate	17.2.04	No appeal against confiscation.
Briagravia	German	6,477	Hamburg to Kiao-chao	General	Moji	28.3.04	Seized in consequence of guns on board, but released when shown they were for German Government at Kiao-chao.
Tarria (schooner)	Russian	120	In port	None	Hakodate	13.4.04	Sealing schooner. No appeal against confiscation.
Hsiping	British	1,981	Shanghai to Newchuang	General	Near Chefoo	14.7.04	Captured by Hong Kong Maru. Contraband cargo for Newchuang confiscated. Balance released.
Peiping	Chinese	400	Shanghai to Newchuang	General	Near Chefoo	17.7.04	Contraband cargo for Newchuang confiscated. Balance released.

VESSELS SEIZED OR SUNK BY THE JAPANESE—*continued.*

Name.	Nationality.	Gross Tonnage.	Voyage.	Cargo.	Place of Capture.	Date of Capture.	Remarks.
Georges ...	French ...	179	Shanghai to Port Arthur	Provisions ...	Near Port Arthur	19.8.04	Ship confiscated, cargo having been transferred to a Russian steamship. Appeal dismissed.
Osaka (sailing vessel)	British ...	546	Shanghai to Vladivostok	Ammunition ...	Yetorup Island (Kurile Group)	26.9.04	This vessel was stranded when captured.
Si-shan ...	British ...	1,351	Hong Kong to Newchuang	Live stock and provisions	Newchuang ...	7.10.04	Ship and cargo released as illegal seizure in neutral port.
Fu-ping ...	German ...	1,393	Shanghai to Port Arthur	Arms, ammunition and general	Near Newchuang	12.10.04	Final appeal dismissed. Now owned by Japanese Government and renamed *Chozan Maru.*
Veteran ...	German ...	1,199	Shanghai to Port Arthur	Provisions, clothing and false papers	Near Chefoo...	19.11.04	Ship and cargo confiscated. Final appeal dismissed. Now owned by Japanese Government and renamed *Yaura Maru.*
King Arthur ...	British ...	1,416	Port Arthur to Shanghai.	None ...	12 miles from Chefoo	19.12.04	Final appeal dismissed. Sold by Japanese Government to Kobe owners and renamed *Otowa Maru.*
Nigretia ...	British ...	2,368	Shanghai to Vladivostok	Kerosene ...	Korean Strait	19.12.04	Two Russian naval officers from Port Arthur found on board. Appeal dismissed.
Roseley ...	British ...	4,370	Cardiff to Vladivostok	6,500 tons of coal	Korean Strait	11.1.05	Captured by *Tokiwa.* Appeal dismissed.
Lethington ...	British ...	4,421	Cardiff to Vladivostok	6,500 tons of coal	Korean Strait	12.1.05	Captured by Torpedo Boat No. 72. Appeal dismissed.

Name	Nationality	Tonnage	Route	Cargo	Place	Date	Remarks
Wilhelmina	Dutch	4,295	Shanghai to Vladivostok	6,897 tons of coal	Korean Strait	16.1.05	Captured by *Naniwa* and Torpedo Boat No. 60. Ship and cargo confiscated. Appeal dismissed.
Bawtry	British	2,407	Kiao-chao to Vladivostok	Provisions, machine oil, and shipbuilding material	Korean Strait	17.1.05	Captured by *Tokiwa*. Appeal dismissed.
Oakley	British	3,798	Cardiff to Vladivostok	5,900 tons of coal	Korean Strait	18.1.05	Captured by *Tokiwa*. Cargo condemned. Appeal dismissed.
Burma	Austrian	3,071	Cardiff to Vladivostok	4,100 tons of coal	Tsugaru Strait	25.1.05	Captured by Torpedo Boat No. 30. Appeal dismissed.
M.S. Dollar	British	4,216	San Francisco to Vladivostok	Fodder and provisions	Tsugaru Strait	27.1.05	Captured by *Asama*. Ship and cargo confiscated. Appeal dismissed.
Wyefield	British	3,235	San Francisco to Vladivostok	Fodder ...	Tsugaru Strait	30.1.05	Captured by *Musashi*. Appeal dismissed.
Siam	Austrian	3,160	Cardiff to Vladivostok	4,100 tons of coal	South Coast of Yezo	31.1.05	Captured by *Asama*. Appeal dismissed.
Eastry	British	2,998	Moioran to Hong Kong	4,100 tons of Japanese coal	Tsugaru Strait	7.2.05	Captured by *Matsushima* and taken to Yokosuka. Seizure illegal. Released.
Paros	German	2,398	Hamburg to Vladivostok	Shipbuilding material, provisions	Yetorup Island	10.2.05	Captured by *Hong Kong Maru*. Ship and cargo confiscated. Appeal dismissed.
Apollo	British	3,829	Cardiff to Vladivostok	5,690 tons of coal	Yetorup Strait	14.2.05	Captured by *Hong Kong Maru*. Appeal dismissed.
Scotsman	British	1,677	Saigon to Vladivostok	2,200 tons of rice	Tsugaru Strait	14.2.05	Captured by Torpedo Boat No. 30. Ship and cargo confiscated. Appeal dismissed.
Powderham	British	3,019	Cardiff to Vladivostok	4,000 tons of coal	Korean Strait	19.2.05	Captured by *Nikko Maru*. Ship and cargo confiscated. Appeal dismissed.

VESSELS SEIZED OR SUNK BY THE JAPANESE—*continued.*

Name.	Nationality.	Gross Tonnage.	Voyage.	Cargo.	Place of Capture.	Date of Capture.	Remarks.
Sylvania	British	4,187	Cardiff to Vladivostok	6,534 tons of coal	Korean Strait	19.2.05	Captured by *Nikko Maru.* Ship and cargo condemned. Appeal dismissed.
Severus	German	3,307	Cardiff to Vladivostok	3,845 tons of coal	Near Yetorup Island	23.2.05	Captured by *Hong Kong Maru.*
Romulus	German	2,630	Cardiff to Vladivostok	3,500 tons of coal	Tsugaru Strait	25.2.05	Captured by *Iwate.* Advertised for sale by Japanese.
Easby Abbey	British	2,963	Cardiff to Vladivostok	Coal	Near Yetorup Island	27.2.05	Captured by *Nippon Maru.* Appeal dismissed.
Vegga	Swedish	2,562	Cardiff to Vladivostok	Coal	Korean Strait	3.3.05	Captured by *Nikko Maru.* Condemned; appeal dismissed.
Venus	British	3,558	Cardiff to Vladivostok	5,225 tons of coal	Near Yetorup Island	4.3.05	Captured by *Nippon Maru.* Condemned; appeal dismissed.
Aphrodite	British	3,949	Cardiff to Vladivostok	5,600 tons of coal	Near Yetorup Island	6.3.05	Captured by *Nippon Maru.* Condemned; appeal dismissed.
Saxon Prince	British	3,471	Singapore to Mororan	Railway material, not intended for enemy	Korean Strait	9.3.05	Taken to Sasebo. Released 16th March.
Tacoma	American	2,812	San Francisco to Vladivostok	Provisions, ship-building material, and machinery	Near Kunashiri Channel	14.3.05	Captured by *Takachiho.* Ship and cargo confiscated. Appeal dismissed.
Harbarton	British	3,265	Cardiff to Vladivostok	Coal	Near Yetorup Strait	18.3.05	Captured by *Akitsushima.* Condemned; appeal dismissed.
Industrie (salvage steamer)	Swedish	839	—	None	Near Fusan	28.3.05	Captured by *Kasuga.* Arrested for espionage.

Name	Nationality	Tonnage	Voyage	Cargo	Place	Date	Remarks
Henry Bolchow	Norwegian	1,006	Shanghai to Korsakovsk	18,190 sacks of meal	Yetorup Strait	7.4.05	Captured by *Kumano Maru*. Cargo confiscated.
Lincluden	British	2,746	Nikolaievsk to Kobe	3,600 tons of barley	South Coast of Korea	15.5.05	Taken to Sasebo. Released 23rd May.
Quang Nam	French	1,431	Saigon to Shanghai	General ...	Pescadores ...	18.5.05	Captured by *Bingo Maru* for espionage. Ship confiscated. Appeal dismissed.
Risawa	German	—	—	—	—	24.7.05	—
Australia	American	2,755	(?) to Nikolaievsk	Flour, tea, etc. ...	Petropavlovsk	12.8.05	Captured by *Suma*. Condemned.
Antiope (sailing vessel)	British	1,486	—	Salt ...	East Coast of Sakhalin	13.8.05	Captured by *Tainan Maru*.
Lydia	German	1,059	Hamburg to Nikolaievsk	Tools, salt, and oil	Lu Chu Islands	13.8.05	Ship and cargo confiscated. Appeal dismissed.
Montara	American	2,562	—	Skins from Kamchatka for Russian Government agent	Bering Island	18.8.05	Condemned.
Barracouta	American	2,152	(?) to Nikolaievsk	Provisions ...	South Coast of Sakhalin	16.9.05	Captured by *Fubuki* and taken to Yokosuka.
Hans Wagner	German	1,594	—	Iron, building material, etc.	Korean Strait	10.10.05	Captured by *Otowa* and taken to Sasebo. Released.
M. Struwe	German	1,582	(?) to Vladivostok	Provisions ...	Near Fusan ...	10.10.05	Captured by *Akashi* and taken to Sasebo. Released.

APPENDIX F. 2.

MERCHANT VESSELS SEIZED OR SUNK BY THE RUSSIANS FROM THE COMMENCEMENT OF HOSTILITIES TO THE END OF THE WAR.

Name	Nationality	Tonnage	Voyage	Cargo	Place	Date	Remarks
Argo	Norwegian	1,394	—	—	Port Arthur...	5.2.04	Released 14th March.
Brand	Norwegian	2,003	—	—	Port Arthur...	5.2.04	Released 14th March.
Seirstad	Norwegian	995	—	—	Port Arthur...	5.2.04	Released 14th March.
Ras Bera	British	3,837	—	—	Port Arthur...	5.2.04	Escaped about 13th February.
Foxton Hall	British	4,247	—	Coal ...	Port Arthur...	8.2.04	Released about 12th March.

VESSELS SEIZED OR SUNK BY THE RUSSIANS—*continued.*

Name.	Nationality.	Gross Tonnage.	Voyage.	Cargo.	Place of Capture.	Date of Capture.	Remarks.
Fu-Ping ...	British ...	1,393	—	—	Port Arthur...	Previous	Released 10th February.
Hsiping ...	British ...	1,981	Ching-wang-tao to Shanghai	—	Off Port Arthur	10.2.04	Ordered to Dalny. Released after four days.
Wenchow ...	British ...	898	—	—	Port Arthur...	10.2.04	Released about 18th February.
Naganoura Maru ...	Japanese ...	1,084	—	—	Off Tsugaru ...	Previous 11.2.04	Seized and sunk by Vladivostok cruisers.
Ettrickdale...	British ...	3,775	Barry to Salang ...	Coal	In Red Sea ...	11.2.04	Seized by *Oslyabya.* Released 28th February. Indemnity paid.
Frankby ...	British ...	4,182	Barry to Hong Kong	Coal	In Red Sea ...	19.2.04	Seized by *Oslyabya.* Released 28th February. Indemnity paid.
Matilda ...	Norwegian ...	3,480	Penarth to Sasebo	Coal	In Red Sea ...	19.2.04	Seized by *Oslyabya.* Released 28th February.
Rosalie ...	British ...	4,303	—	—	At or near Vladivostok	Previous	Released 22nd February.
Hamyei Maru ...	Japanese ...	76	—	—	—	22.2.04	Seized and sunk.
Fa-Wan ...	British ...	—	Chemulpo to Newchuang	—	Newchuang ...	26.3.04	Released 3rd April.
Goyo Maru...	Japanese ...	600	—	—	Gensan Harbour	About 2.4.04	Seized and sunk by torpedo boats.
Haginoura Maru ...	Japanese ...	219	—	Fish and vegetables	Japan Sea ...	25.4.04	Seized and sunk by Vladivostok cruisers.

Vessel	Nationality	Tonnage	Bound	Cargo	Place	Date	Remarks
Junks (46 in No.)...	—	—	—	...	Liao River ...	About 10.5.04	Seized.
Allanton	British	4,253	Mororan to Singapore	Coal ...	Japan Sea ...	16.6.04	Captured by cruisers and taken to Vladivostok. Released 9th November. Appeal allowed.
Ansei Maru (sailing vessel)	Japanese	105	—	—	Between Oku and Kojima Islands	16.6.04	Seized and sunk by Vladivostok cruisers.
Yawata Maru (sailing vessel)	Japanese	198	—	—	Between Oku and Kojima Islands	16.6.04	Seized and sunk.
Seiyei Maru (sailing vessel)	Japanese	114	—	—	—	16.6.04	Seized and sunk by Vladivostok cruisers.
Hatsiman Maru (schooner)	Japanese	—	—	—	—	16.6.04	Seized and sunk by Vladivostok cruisers.
Hatsuku Maru	Japanese	200	—	Fish, etc. ...	—	18.6.04	Captured by cruisers and taken to Vladivostok.
Seisho Maru (schooner)	Japanese	122	—	—	Gensan ...	30.6.04	Sunk by torpedo boats.
Koun Maru (schooner)	Japanese	57	—	—	Gensan ...	30.6.04	Sunk by torpedo boats.
Cheltenham...	British	3,741	Otaru to Fusan ...	Chiefly 67,500 sleepers and logs and 375 cases of beer	Off Coast of Japan. (In Japan Sea)	4.7.04	Captured by cruisers and taken to Vladivostok. Ship and cargo confiscated. Appeal dismissed.
Malacca	British	4,045	Antwerp and London to China and Japan	3,000 tons general and 40 tons of explosives for Hong Kong	In Red Sea ...	13.7.04	Seized by *Peterburg*. Released at Algiers 27th July. Claim settled.
Fa-Wan	British	—	—	—	In Japan Sea	Previous 15.7.04	Taken to Port Arthur. Released.
Prinz Heinrich	German	6,263	Hamburg to Yokohama	—	In Red Sea ...	16.7.04	Seized by *Peterburg*. Released after having given up 31 sacks of letters and 24 sacks and boxes of parcels intended for Japan.

(b) VESSELS SEIZED OR SUNK BY THE RUSSIANS—continued.

Name.	Nationality.	Gross Tonnage.	Voyage.	Cargo.	Place of Capture.	Date of Capture.	Remarks.
Hipsang	British ...	1,659	Newchuang to Chefoo	Provisions, etc. ...	Off Pigeon Bay	16.7.04	Torpedoed by *Rastoropni* for refusing to stop when ordered. Sinking justified by Prize Court.
Ardova	British ...	3,533	New York to Manila	Explosives, rails, etc.	In Red Sea ...	17.7.04	Seized by *Smolensk*. Released at Suez 25th July.
Skandia	German ...	—	Hamburg to China	General and Government stores	In Red Sea ...	18.7.04	Seized by *Smolensk*. Released 24th July.
Okassina Maru ...	Japanese ...	—	—	—	Japan Sea ...	20.7.04	Seized and sunk.
Kyodounya Maru ...	Japanese ...	147	—	—	Japan Sea ...	About 20.7.04	Seized by Vladivostok cruisers. Released, since most of her passengers were women.
Takashima Maru ...	Japanese ...	319	—	160 boxes of powder for mining purposes and 589 bales of miscellaneous goods	Tsugaru Strait	20.7.04	Seized and sunk by Vladivostok cruisers.
Kiho Maru ... ... (sailing vessel)	Japanese ...	140	—	—	Pacific Ocean near Tsugaru Strait	20.7.04	Seized and sunk by Vladivostok cruisers.
Hokusei Maru ... (schooner)	Japanese ...	91	—	—	Pacific Ocean near Tsugaru Strait	20.7.04	Seized and sunk by Vladivostok cruisers.

Name	Nationality	Tonnage	Route	Cargo	Locality	Date	Remarks
Arabia	German	4,438	Portland (O.) to Hong Kong	Flour, railway material, etc.	100 miles north of Yokohama	22.7.04	Captured by cruisers and taken to Vladivostok. Ship released. Appeal as to confiscation of flour allowed.
Knight Commander	British	4,306	New York to Chemulpo via Japan	General and railway material	75 miles south-west from Yokohama	24.7.04	Seized and sunk by Vladivostok cruisers. Appeal dismissed.
Jizai Maru (schooner)	Japanese	199	—	—	Near Gulf of Tokio	24.7.04	Seized and sunk by Vladivostok cruisers.
Fukuju Maru (schooner)	Japanese	121	—	—	Near Gulf of Tokio	24.7.04	Seized and sunk by Vladivostok cruisers.
Hokatsu Maru	Japanese	91	—	—	Japan Sea	24.7.04	Seized and sunk.
Tsinan	British	2,269	Australia to Japan	—	Off Gulf of Tokio	24.7.04	Released for the purpose of carrying 21 lascars of the crew of the *Knight Commander* to Yokohama.
Formosa	British	4,045	London to Japan	—	In Red Sea	24.7.04	Seized by *Smolensk* and taken to Suez. Released 27th July.
Holsatia	German	3,349	—	—	In Red Sea	24.7.04	Seized by *Smolensk* and taken to Suez. Released 27th July.
Thea	German	1,613	For Yokohama	Fish manure and fish oil	Off Coast of Japan	25.7.04	Seized and sunk by Vladivostok cruisers. Appeal allowed except as regards cargo.
Calchas	British	6,748	Tacoma to Japan, China and Liverpool	General and flour. 2,411 tons on board at time of seizure	30 miles from entrance to Gulf of Tokio	25.7.04	Captured by cruisers and taken to Vladivostok. Released about 29th October. Supreme Court at St. Petersburg confirmed cargo confiscated except wheat.
Hull Fishing Fleet (*Steam Trawlers*)	British	—	Fishing	—	Near Dogger Bank, in North Sea	21.10.04	Fleet fired on by Russians. Trawler *Crane* sunk, *Moulmein* and *Mino* seriously damaged.

VESSELS SEIZED OR SUNK BY THE RUSSIANS—continued.

Name.	Nationality.	Gross Tonnage.	Voyage.	Cargo.	Place of Capture.	Date of Capture.	Remarks.
Daishen Maru	Japanese ...	—	—	—	—	May, 1905	Seized by torpedo boats, but afterwards recaptured by Japanese and taken to Gensan.
Yawata Maru	Japanese ...	100	—	—	—	5.5.05	Seized and sunk by torpedo boats.
Oldhamia ...	British ...	3,639	New York to Hong Kong	165,000 cases of oil	Japan Sea ... Near Formosa Island	19.5.05	Prize crew on board. Run ashore and burnt Yetorup Island about 8th August. Court found in favour of owners in November, 1906, but final decision postponed for further expert inquiries. Libau Court in June, 1907, found vessel and cargo liable to confiscation. Claim for compensation refused. This judgment was upheld by Admiralty Appeal Court.
Teturtos ...	German ...	2,409	Otaru to Tientsin	Wooden sleepers ...	North China Sea	30.5.05	Sunk by Rion. Three-fifths of claim paid to owners of vessel.
Cilurnum ...	British ...	2,123	Shanghai to Kobe	General	80 miles from Wusung	2.6.05	Stopped by Rion. Released after 411 bags of beans, 125 bales of cotton, and 12 boxes of antimony had been thrown overboard.
Ikhona ...	British ...	5,252	Rangoon to Yokohama	Rice and mails ...	150 miles north of Hong Kong	5.6.05	Sunk by Terek near Hong Kong. Appeal allowed.

St. Kilda ...	...	British ...	3,518	Hong Kong to Yokohama	Rice, sugar, gunnies, etc. Transhipment cargo Ex-*Kum Sang* (s) from Calcutta	Near Hong Kong	5.6.05	Sunk by *Dnyepr*. Appeal allowed except as to a portion of her cargo.
Prinsesse Marie	...	Danish ...	5,416	Copenhagen to Yokohama, etc.	Reported not contraband	South China Sea	22.6.05	Sunk by *Terek* in South China Sea.
Idzumi Maru	...	Japanese ...	Small	—	—	—	24.8.05	Captured and taken to Vladivostok by torpedo boats. Vessel and cargo confiscated.

APPENDIX G. 1.

RUSSIAN LOSSES IN WAR VESSELS.

Name.	Class.	Date.	Remarks.
Varyag ...	Cruiser, 1st class, protected	9.2.04	Sunk by own crew after action near Chemulpo.
Koveetz ...	Gunboat ...	9.2.04	Sunk by own crew after action near Chemulpo.
Yenisei ...	Mining transport ...	11.2.04	Blown up by own mines in Ta-lien Bay.
Boyarin...	Cruiser, 3rd class, protected	14.2.04	Wrecked in Ta-lien Bay after striking a mine.
Vnushitelni ...	T.B. Destroyer ...	25.2.04	Sunk by gun fire in Pigeon Bay.
Mandzhur ...	Gunboat ...	25.2.04	Interned at Shanghai, where she had been lying from the commencement of the war.
Steregushchi ...	T.B. Destroyer ...	10.3.04	Sunk in destroyer action off Port Arthur.
Petropavlovsk ...	Battleship ...	13.4.04	Sunk by Japanese mines off Port Arthur.
Strashni ...	T.B. Destroyer ...	13.4.04	Sunk in destroyer action off Port Arthur.
Vnimatelni ...	T.B. Destroyer ...	26.5.04	Abandoned after striking a rock in Pigeon Bay.
No. 204 ...	Torpedo boat...	30.6.04	Blown up by own crew after running ashore off Gensan.
No. 208 ...	Torpedo boat...	17.7.04	Sunk by mine near Vladivostok.
Lieutenant Burakov ...	T.B. Destroyer ...	24.7.04	Sunk by Japanese torpedo boat near Port Arthur.
Sivuch ...	Gunboat ...	2.8.04	Blown up by own crew in Liao River.
Burni ...	T.B. Destroyer ...	11.8.04	Wrecked off Shan-tung after the battle of Yellow Sea.
Ryeshitelni ...	T.B. Destroyer ...	12.8.04	Captured by the Japanese off Chefoo.
Rurik ...	Armoured cruiser ...	14.8.04	Sunk in battle of Ulsan.
Tzesarevich ...	Battleship ...	16.8.04	Interned at Kiao-chao, where she had taken refuge after battle of Yellow Sea.
Bezposhchadni ...	T.B. Destroyer ...	16.8.04	Interned at Kiao-chao, where she had taken refuge after battle of Yellow Sea.
Bezshumni ...	T.B. Destroyer ...	16.8.04	Interned at Kiao-chao, where she had taken refuge after battle of Yellow Sea.
Bezstrashni ...	T.B. Destroyer ...	16.8.04	Interned at Kiao-chao, where she had taken refuge after battle of Yellow Sea.
Gremyashchi ...	Armoured gunboat...	18.8.04	Sunk by mine near Port Arthur.
Novik ...	Cruiser, 3rd class, protected	20.8.04	Sunk after action with Japanese cruisers off Korsakovsk, when attempting to escape after battle of Yellow Sea.
No. 201 ...	Torpedo boat...	21.8.04	Wrecked near Vladivostok.
Vuinoslivi ...	T.B. Destroyer ...	24.8.04	Sunk by mine near Port Arthur.
Askold ...	Cruiser, 1st class, protected	25.8.04	Interned at Shanghai, where she had taken refuge after battle of Yellow Sea.
Grozovoi ...	T.B. Destroyer ...	25.8.04	Interned at Shanghai, where she had taken refuge after battle of Yellow Sea.

Name.	Class.	Date.	Remarks.
Diana	Cruiser, 1st class, protected	4.9.04	Interned at Saigon, where she had taken refuge after battle of Yellow Sea.
Lena	Armed transport ...	11.9.04	Interned at San Francisco after crossing from Vladivostok.
No. 202	Torpedo boat ...	1.10.04	Sunk in collision near Vladivostok.
Zabiyaka	Gunboat	25.10.04	Sunk by gun fire at Port Arthur.
Stroini	T.B. Destroyer ...	13.11.04	Sunk by mine outside Port Arthur.
Rastoropni	T.B. Destroyer ...	16.11.04	Blown up by own crew at Chefoo, after bringing dispatches from Port Arthur.
Poltava	Battleship	5.12.04	Sunk at Port Arthur from explosion of magazine, caused by gun fire.
Retvizan	Battleship	6.12.04	Sunk by gun fire at Port Arthur.
Pobyeda	Battleship	7.12.04	Sunk by gun fire at Port Arthur.
Pallada	Cruiser, 1st class, protected	7.12.04	Sunk by gun fire at Port Arthur.
Peresvyet	Battleship	7.12.04	Sunk by own crew at Port Arthur after being severely damaged by gun fire.
Gilyak	Gunboat	8.12.04	Sunk by gun fire at Port Arthur.
Bayan	Armoured cruiser ...	9.12.04	Sunk by gun fire at Port Arthur.
Vsadnik	Torpedo gunboat ...	15.12.04	Sunk by gun fire at Port Arthur.
Amur	Mining transport ...	18.12.04	Sunk by gun fire at Port Arthur.
Bobr	Gunboat	26.12.04	Destroyed by gun fire at Port Arthur.
Razboinik	Gunboat	2.1.05	Sunk by own crew in Port Arthur gullet.
Otvazhni	Armoured gunboat...	2.1.05	Sunk by own crew outside Port Arthur.
Sevastopol	Battleship	2.1.05	Sunk by own crew outside Port Arthur.
Gaidamak	Torpedo gunboat ...	2.1.05	Found sunk at Port Arthur.
Dzhigit	Gunboat	2.1.05	Found sunk at Port Arthur.
Bdilelni	T.B. Destroyer ...	2.1.05	Found sunk at Port Arthur.
Boevoi	T.B. Destroyer ...	2.1.05	Found sunk at Port Arthur.
Razyashchi	T.B. Destroyer ...	2.1.05	Found sunk at Port Arthur.
Silni	T.B. Destroyer ...	2.1.05	Found sunk at Port Arthur.
Storozhevoi	T.B. Destroyer ...	2.1.05	Found sunk at Port Arthur.
Serditi	T.B. Destroyer ...	2.1.05	Interned at Chefoo after escaping from Port Arthur.
Skori	T.B. Destroyer ...	2.1.05	Interned at Chefoo after escaping from Port Arthur.
Statni	T.B. Destroyer ...	2.1.05	Interned at Chefoo after escaping from Port Arthur.
Vlastni	T.B. Destroyer ...	2.1.05	Interned at Chefoo after escaping from Port Arthur.'
Boiki	T.B. Destroyer ...	2.1.05	Interned at Kiao-chao after escaping from Port Arthur.
Smyeli	T.B. Destroyer ...	2.1.05	Interned at Kiao-chao after escaping from Port Arthur.

Battle of the Sea of Japan.

Name.	Class.	Date.	Remarks.
Oslyabya	Battleship	27.5.05	Sunk by gun fire.
Ural	Auxiliary cruiser ...	27.5.05	Sunk by gun fire.
Imperator Alexandr III	Battleship	27.5.05	Sunk by gun fire.
Kamchatka	Repair ship	27.5.05	Sunk by gun fire.
Knyaz Suvorov... ...	Battleship	27.5.05	Sunk by torpedoes after being rendered helpless by gun fire.
Borodino	Battleship	27.5.05	Sunk by gun fire.
Navarin	Battleship	28.5.05	Sunk by torpedoes.
Sisoi Veliki	Battleship	28.5.05	Sunk by torpedoes.
Admiral Nakhimov ...	Armoured cruiser ...	28.5.05	Sunk by torpedoes.
Vladimir Monomakh ...	Armoured cruiser ...	28.5.05	Sunk by torpedoes.
Imperator Nikolai I ...	Battleship	28.5.05	Surrendered.
Orel	Battleship	28.5.05	Surrendered.
General-Admiral Apraxin	Armoured coast de-fence vessel	28.5.05	Surrendered.
Admiral Senyavin ...	Armoured coast de-fence vessel	28.5.05	Surrendered.
Svyetlana	Cruiser, 2nd class, protected	28.5.05	Sunk by own crew after engagement with two Japanese cruisers.
Admiral Ushakov ..	Armoured coast de-fence vessel	28.5.05	Sunk by own crew after severe engagement with two Japanese armoured cruisers.
Blestyashchi	T.B. Destroyer ...	28.5.05	Foundered.
Bezuprechni	T.B. Destroyer ...	28 5.05	Sunk by gun fire.
Buini	T.B. Destroyer ...	28.5.05	Sunk by gun fire.
Buistri	T.B. Destroyer ...	28.5.05	Blown up by own crew after running ashore.
Gromki	T.B. Destroyer ...	28.5.05	Sunk by gun fire.
Byedovi	T.B. Destroyer ...	28.5.05	Surrendered.
Dmitri Donskoi ...	Armoured cruiser ...	29.5.05	Sunk by own crew after severe engagement with several Japanese cruisers.
Izumrud...	Cruiser, 3rd class, protected	29.5.05	Destroyed after running ashore in Vladimir Bay.
Irtuish	Armed transport ...	29.5.05	Foundered.
Oleg	Cruiser, 1st class, protected	3.6.05	Interned at Manila.
Avrora	Cruiser, 1st class, protected	3.6.05	Interned at Manila.
Zhemchug	Cruiser, 3rd Class, protected	3.6.05	Interned at Manila.
Bodri	T.B. Destroyer ...	5.6.05	Interned at Shanghai.

APPENDIX G. 2.

JAPANESE LOSSES IN WAR VESSELS.

Name.	Class.	Date.	Remarks.
Kinshu Maru ...	Armed transport ...	26.4.04	Sunk by *Rossiya* near Gensan.
No. 48 ...	Torpedo boat... ...	12.5.04	Sunk by Russian mine in Kerr Bay.
Miyako ...	Cruiser, 3rd class ...	14.5.04	Sunk by Russian mine in Kerr Bay.
Yoshino ...	Cruiser, 2nd class, protected	15.5.04	Sunk in collision near Port Arthur.
Hatsuse ...	Battleship ...	15.5.04	Sunk by Russian mines near Port Arthur.
Yashima ...	Battleship ...	15.5.04	Sunk by Russian mines near Port Arthur.
Oshima ...	Gunboat ...	17.5.04	Sunk in collision in Gulf of Liao-tung.
Akatsuki ...	T.B. Destroyer ...	17.5.04	Sunk by mine near Port Arthur.
Izumi Maru ...	Armed transport ...	15.6.04	Sunk by *Gromoboi* in Japan Sea.
Hitachi Maru ...	Armed transport ...	15.6.04	Sunk by *Gromoboi* in Japan Sea.
No. 51 ...	Torpedo boat... ...	28.6.04	Wrecked on Dangerous Reef off Kerr Bay and sank.
Kaimon ...	Cruiser, 3rd class ...	5.7.04	Sunk by Russian mine off Ta-lien-wan.
Otagawa Maru ...	Improvised gunboat	8.8.04	Sunk by mine near Port Arthur.
Hayatori ...	T.B. Destroyer ...	3.9.04	Sunk by Russian mine near Port Arthur.
Heiyen ...	Armoured gunboat...	18.9.04	Sunk by Russian mine off Iron Island.
Atago ...	Gunboat ...	6.11.04	Wrecked near Port Arthur.
Saiyen ...	Cruiser, 3rd class, protected	30.11.04	Sunk by Russian mine off Pigeon Bay.
Takasago ...	Cruiser, 2nd class, protected	12.12.04	Sunk by mine between Port Arthur and Chefoo.
No. 53 ...	Torpedo boat	14.12.04	Sunk off Port Arthur during attack on *Sevastopol.*
No. 42 ...	Torpedo boat... ...	15.12.04	Sunk off Port Arthur during attack on *Sevastopol.*

Battle of the Sea of Japan.

Name.	Class.	Date.	Remarks.
No. 34 ...	Torpedo boat... ...	27.5.05	Sunk by gun fire.
No. 35 ...	Torpedo boat... ...	27.5.05	Sunk by gun fire.
No. 69 ...	Torpedo boat... ...	27.5.05	Foundered after colliding with the *Akatsuki* (ex-*Ryeshitelni*).

(B 4726)   Wt. w. 2120—526   750   2/16   H & S

APPENDIX H.

Work and Organisation of the Japanese Staff.

In the first volume it was announced that comments on this subject, particularly in relation to the co-ordination of the Naval and Military Staffs, would be reserved till all the relevant facts had been studied. The propriety of this course will now be evident, since it cannot have escaped attention that the concluding volume presents many points at which naval and military needs were in plain opposition, and many situations that could only be solved by harmonious Staff co-operation. With more or less success and promptitude the causes of friction were reduced, but as to how precisely the machine was made to move as smoothly as it did we are still very much in the dark.

With regard to the constitution of the Imperial Headquarter Staff (as the Joint Staff was called) there is nothing to add to what has been already explained. It was formed, so far as is known, simply by moving both the Admiralty and the General Staff into the Imperial Palace and installing them under the same roof with the Emperor as Chief. But as this was not done till after the commencement of hostilities, the combined organisation did not frame the original war plan, but was only concerned with its subsequent developments and the direction of operations. The war plan must have been finally decided by what was known as the "Grand Council of War" which included, besides the "Board of Marshals" the Ministers of Marine and the Army, the Chiefs of the Naval and General Staffs, and such other officers as might be specially appointed.

With regard to the actual procedure, it appears to have been much the same before and after the formation of the Joint Staff. The practice was for each staff to prepare its schemes for the Emperor's consideration, and on his approving them the necessary orders and instructions went out with his authority. This process, of course, applied to the general direction of operations. Minor orders appear to have been issued by the respective Chiefs of the two Staffs, while, on the other hand, there were occasions of high political moment when the Emperor issued commands not as chief of the staff, but as chief of the state. A notable instance was the original order to Admiral Togo to commence hostilities, an order which has been widely taken to have been a command to destroy the enemy's fleet—that is, an operation order. But, in fact, it was not. A naval operation order issuing from the staff was a *Dai-kai-rei*, or " great navy order "[2]; but this was a *Tai-mei*—that is, a personal order of the Sovereign issued in virtue of his power to declare war which rested with him alone as head of the State. It was therefore a political and not a strategical order.

---

[1] *See* Vol. I., pp. 68-9. The Japanese words translated "Imperial Headquarter Staff" are *Dai-hon-ei* (or *Dai-hen-yei*), meaning literally " great principal dwelling."

[2] Literally " great sea order," but *kai* is only short for *kai-gun*, meaning " Sea army "—that is, Navy or Fleet.

Directions issuing from the Headquarter Staff can be traced in two forms. Besides the *Dai-kai-rei*, or "Great Navy Order," there was the *Dai-kai-kun*, meaning "great Navy instruction," *kun*, or more properly *kun-rei*, meaning, according to the best authorities, "an order explaining " a principle only, the method of executing it being left to the receiver." "Instruction," therefore, is the nearest English equivalent, although it is doubtful whether a clear distinction of meaning between "Order " and "Instruction " has ever existed in the British Service.

Examples, unfortunately, are not numerous, for the text of very few of these Orders and Instructions is available. "Order No. 1 " was issued at the outbreak of the war, but all we know about it is that it was apparently addressed to Admiral Kataoka, and that its first paragraph defined the object of the Third or Straits Squadron. At the time, it will be remembered, this squadron was a separate organisation distinct from the "Combined Squadron." It was not under the command of Admiral Togo till the whole Fleet was unified three weeks later. Admiral Kataoka was therefore in the fullest sense a Commander-in-Chief, which explains why he received a *Dai-kai-rei* direct from Headquarters; for, as a rule, and apart from exceptional circumstances, it would seem that these great Orders and Instructions were only issued to Commanders-in-Chief.

The next *Dai-kai-rei* we have is Order "No. 6." It was issued to Admirals Togo and Kataoka by the Chief of the Naval Staff on February 29th, 1904. This was the Order which re-organised the fleet and placed the whole of it under Admiral Togo. It was in two parts. Part I., addressed to Admiral Togo, was as follows :—

1. Vice-Admiral Kataoka, Commander-in-Chief of the Third Squadron, is under your orders.

2. You must as convenient carry out the object expressed in Great Navy Order No. 1, paragraph i.

Part II. directed Admiral Kataoka to place himself under the orders of Admiral Togo.[1]

The four Great Navy Orders Nos. 2 to 5, which are not mentioned, may be accounted for as having related to the landing at Chemulpo, the opening attack on Port Arthur, the decision to send the whole of the XIIth Division, which formed the advance guard of the Expeditionary Force, straight to Chemulpo instead of Fusan, and possibly the first attempt to block Port Arthur—all of these being operations concerned with the main lines of the War Plan.

The next order, No. 7, was issued to Admiral Togo on February 29, after the Headquarters Staff had decided that a naval demonstration must be made off Vladivostok for the purpose of holding as many of the enemy's troops in that district as possible.[2] But although it is called an "order," in form it was more like an instruction. "If possible,"

---

[1] *Confidential History*, I., pp. 153-4. As the function of the Third Squadron had originally been to protect the Straits, it seems fairly certain that "Order No. 1," which Admiral Togo was now to observe, must have referred to the defence of that area. If so, it is additional evidence that the Japanese Plan of Naval operations was built up logically on the defence of the Straits just as our old plans were built up on the defence of the Channel. A further explanation of this being the first great Order issued is that it probably contained directions for what were really the opening moves of the war—the seizure of Fusan and Sylvia Basin.

[2] *See* Vol. I., p. 138. It is there stated the order came from the Naval Staff, but what Admiral Ito actually communicated was a *Dai-kai-rei*.

it began, "you should detach a strong section of your command, &c."
On this Admiral Togo issued "instructions" to Admiral Kamimura, and
Admiral Kamimura issued "Orders" to his detachment.[1]

With regard to "Great Naval Instructions," we have still less to go
upon. The only one whose text we have is that issued on December 23,
1904, directing Admiral Togo to hand over the Port Arthur area and
come home. Its text was as follows:—

> "I. In order to complete the strategical preparation of the
> "combined fleet to meet the enemy's reinforcing squadron you
> "must leave at Port Arthur and in the Korean Strait a sufficient
> "force to guard against the remains of the enemy's fleet, and to
> "stop contraband running. The remainder you will bring back
> "to Japan, and will then make plans for refitting the ships
> "   .   .   ."

> "II. You must depute Admiral Kataoka to carry out the pro-
> "visions of clause 4 of *Dai-kai-kun* No. 4. You and Admiral
> "Kamimura must visit Imperial Headquarters as soon as convenient."

Dai-kai-kun No. 4, it is explained, related to co-operation with the
Third Army.[2]

The only other instances of Great Naval Instructions that can be
traced are those relating to detachments for the northern blockade and
for the reconnaissances into the China Sea in anticipation of the coming
of the Baltic Fleet. These reconnaissances were all specially called for
by the Headquarters Staff, and the officers in command were ordered to
report to and expect orders from Headquarters. This was, of course,
perfectly logical—since Headquarters was the intelligence centre, and it
was essential to its effective working that the Intelligence Section should
have a call on the fleet when essential information was unobtainable
except by means of cruiser reconnaissances. But it seems, further, to
imply that, as in our own traditional practice, Admiral Togo's authority
was confined to a certain station or area, analagous to our own Channel
and North Sea stations and that when squadrons were thrown off from
it they passed under the direct control of Headquarters. Some doubt,
however, must have existed on the point: for when Admiral Kamimura
was detached to make the demonstration at Vladivostok under "Great
Instruction No. 7," he seems to have been in doubt under whose orders
he was; and when he had to decide whether to obey Admiral Togo's
order to rejoin or to stay at Gensan to defend it, he asked for further
instructions, and received from the Headquarters Staff the reply that he
"should act in accordance with Admiral Togo's orders."[3]

It is clear, moreover, that the Headquarters Staff reserved to itself the
power of giving direct orders to divisional and squadron commanders,
who by the organisation were under Admiral Togo's flag. The conspicuous
case is, of course, their order to Admiral Kamimura to proceed to the
East Coast of Japan during Admiral Iessen's raid off Tokyo, and this
order was sent without informing the Commander-in-Chief. Yet Admiral
Kamimura had evidently no doubt it was his duty to obey it, much
against his better judgment.

---

[1] *Confidential History*, II., p. 3. Another great order issued about this time must have
related to the advance of the First Army's base from Chemulpo to Chinampho. *Ibid.*, I.
p. 187, and *see ante*, Vol. I., p. 139.

[2] *Confidential History*, II., 256.

[3] *Ibid.*, III., pp. 19, 20, and *see ante* Vol. I., p. 196.

A similar case of interference where the Army was primarily concerned is even more remarkable. In November 1904, when the situation at Port Arthur was highly strained, Admiral Togo became convinced that greater exertions were necessary ashore "to secure the fall of the place " at the earliest opportunity, and this opinion," we are told, "he sent to " Imperial Headquarters."[1] It is clear that Marshal Oyama endorsed this view, for about the same time "he requested Imperial Headquarters " to send the Eighth Army Division to reinforce the Third Army." But in spite of the strong demand by both the Naval and Military Com-manders-in-Chief the Emperor, we are told, "sent that Division to increase " the armies in the North."[2] Such a proceeding seems quite out of harmony with Japanese principles of war direction, but no explanation of the decision is given.

There were also cases when the Imperial Headquarter Staff assumed control of even single ships within the Combined Fleet station, but this is only known to have occurred when political considerations were involved. Thus when the *Akitsushima*, in January 1905, was sent to Chifu to deal with the destroyers that had escaped from Port Arthur she was ordered "to deal with the matter under the direct orders of " the Imperial Headquarters."[3]

But except in cases when political considerations or the main lines of the war plan, or wide movements beyond the theatre of operations were concerned no orders or instructions from home are to be traced. The Naval Staff, however, continued to exercise some kind of control, but it was only by means of "suggestions" and these suggestions the Admiral generally, if not always, adopted. A conspicuous instance occurred when, in September 1904, they thought it desirable to send a ship to Chemulpo to protect the newly-raised *Varyag*. The Vice-Director of the Naval Staff sent to Admiral Togo's Chief of the Staff a suggestion that a ship should be detached for that purpose if he thought well, and Admiral Togo, in spite of the strain of the blockade and the near expectation of an action, detached the *Matsushima*.[4]

A curious instance of direct dealing with officers under Admiral Togo's command were the "Instructions" which the Chief of the Naval Staff addressed to all flotilla officers reprimanding them for their failure to make any impression on the enemy's fleet, either on June 23rd or August 10th.[5] It is clear, indeed, that the Naval Staff did retain some kind of special control over the flotilla. We are told, for instance, that the opening destroyer attack on Port Arthur was worked out by the Headquarter Staff and not by the Admiral's staff, and when, in September 1904, he wished to reorganise the destroyer flotilla owing to the losses it had sustained he applied to the Naval Staff for permission to do so, and the Staff, while withholding its formal consent for the present, gave him authority to combine crippled divisions.[6]

In matters which involved operations not strictly naval it is natural to find the consent of the Imperial Staff regarded as necessary, although the scope of their authority does not seem to have been accurately determined. On September 5th, 1904, Admiral Togo telegraphed to them that as it was absolutely necessary the next assault on Port Arthur

---

[1] *Confidential History*, II., p.238.   [2] *Ibid.*, p. 239.   [3] *Ibid.*, p. 333.   [4] *See ante*, p. 48.
[5] *Confidential History*, p. 387.
See ante, p. 48 ; *Confidential History*, II., 212.

should succeed he had landed two of the *Fuso's* 6-inch guns. The reply was a request that he would consult Imperial Headquarters before landing guns for the use of the Army.[1] The traditional practice of our own Service was different, for the common form of an Admiral's instructions in a combined expedition not only gave him authority to land guns and men to work them, but as a rule required him to do so at his discretion.

As a general inference it may be taken that although the Admiralty Staff became a section of the Imperial Staff, it did not cease to exercise some control over the naval operations of its own motion, and that its views were conveyed to the Fleet Staff in the form of suggestions, which Admiral Togo seems to have treated with little if any less respect than he did the great orders and instructions of the Imperial Staff.

With regard to the action of the Imperial Staff itself, we may safely deduce the following conclusions :—(1) That the line between " Orders " and " Instructions " was a very fine one and not easy to follow. (2) That these " Great Orders and Instructions " were issued comparatively rarely. For example, the "Combined Fleet Confidential Order," by which Admiral Togo gave effect to *Dai-kai-kun* No. 13, was numbered 1,449. (3) That they were never issued except when the development of the war-plan as a whole called for some special movement or detachment, or for some re-organisation of the Fleet for military reasons. But even here we cannot be sure that the practice was invariable.

In the operations against North Korea and Sakhalin, with which the war concluded, there is no mention of a Great Order or Instruction initiating them. Here, if anywhere, we should have expected the direct action of the Imperial Staff, yet it is merely stated that Admiral Togo received from the Admiralty Staff orders to despatch a suitable force to act in co-operation with the expeditionary army. Its strength and constitution were left entirely to his discretion, which would look as though what the Admiralty Staff communicated was a short general order such as we know a *Dai-kai-rei* to have been.[2] It is also certain that Admiral Kataoka, who commanded the naval force, received orders for the Admiralty Staff during the conduct of the operations, and that he reported directly to the Imperial Staff as well as to Admiral Togo. It is to be assumed, therefore, that while Admiral Togo was responsible for providing an adequate force, the operations so far as they were not left to Admiral Kataoka were directed from head-quarters. In the case of North Korea, on the other hand, which, though a minor affair, was essentially combined in its nature Admiral Kamimura considered himself bound by the instructions of Admiral Togo.[3] Yet in this case we are informed that the operations had been initiated by the Imperial Staff, and that an order to make the necessary naval arrangements " was passed on " to Admiral Togo by the Director of the Admiralty Staff.[4] On the evidence, therefore, we may take it, that both these operations were initiated by a Great Staff order and controlled from the Imperial headquarters.

---

[1] *Confidential History*, II., 213.

[2] *Ibid*, iii., 437. As before Admiral Togo issued "instructions" to Admiral Kataoka, and he in turn issued "orders."

[3] See *ante*, p. 379.

Published History, Bk. V., ch. iii., sec. 3.

Except in such cases as these it is clear that, as a rule, naval operations were not interfered with from Tokyo. Having been once put in possession of the functions of the fleet in each successive stage of the war plan, the Commander-in-Chief was left a free hand except for the suggestions which from time to time were made by the Chief of the Naval Staff. No direct order as to how the fleet was to be handled for the attainment of the naval object was ever given except on that one conspicuous occasion during the time of Admiral Iessen's raid off Tokyo, when the Headquarter Staff deliberately overrode Admiral Togo's strategy and gave a direct order to his second-in-command.

If the practice of the Japanese is compared with that of the British Admiralty in the palmy days of our old maritime wars it will be found that in our case direct orders from Headquarters were much more frequent. But this does not mean any difference of principle; it is to be explained by a cardinal difference in the conditions. Compared with the world-wide theatre in which our wars with France and Spain were waged the theatre of the Russo-Japanese war was very small. By submarine cables and wireless telegraphy it was reduced comparatively still further. Japan had never to provide for sudden calls for detachments to the ends of the earth—calls which could only be dealt with at the centre of intelligence. Japan had no distant colonies open to raiding attacks and no web of trade the protection of which was vital to her power of carrying on the war. Compared with the elaborate and ever-shifting task which the old British Navy had to perform the function of the Japanese fleet was simple and constant; and Admiral Togo, when once the object was settled, could be left free to pursue it in his own way with little fear of extraneous interruption. That the narrowness of the threatre of war was what rendered possible the abstention from interference is fairly beyond doubt, when we recall that in all cases of distant detachments, whether for chase or reconnaissance, trade interruption or political pressure, the force detached was handled directly from the Imperial Headquarters.

Restricted as was the direct action of the Imperial Headquarters Staff the Japanese attribute the smooth co-operation of the Army and Navy mainly to the existence of this body. The impression conveyed by the actual events as recorded in the Confidential History is different. From that record it would seem that, notwithstanding the official unification of the two Staffs, they continued to operate very much as separate departments, and that the smooth working of the joint machine was chiefly due to the tact and consideration of the commanding officers at the front.

Instances of orders being issued by one staff without regard to the other were too frequent. One occurred within a week of the opening of hostilities, when Admiral Togo was surprised by quite unexpected news that the landing place for the whole of the XIIth Division had been changed from Fusan to Chemulpo, and that the troops were already on their way. At the moment the fleet was committed to a widespread operation, and was in a condition of dispersal that had no relation to the protection of the military movement. Yet, apparently without any inquiry as to the precise naval situation, the movement was started independently by the General Staff, and Admiral Uriu, who had charge of the objective area, was not informed at all, until rumours prompted him to make inquiry.[1] Where the blame lay for the faulty Staff work is not clear, but here was certainly an instance where the action of the Headquarter Staff did not make for harmonious co-operation of the two services.

Other cases occurred with irritating frequency from army supply ships persistently disregarding the fleet regulations for approaching the area of the Port Arthur blockade. In the case of the Formosa rice ships, which the General, without informing the Admiral, had ordered to proceed through the blockaded area to Dalny, the friction threatened to lead to serious consequences, and, indeed, went so far that the Port Admiral responsible actually placed an army transport under arrest, and refused to allow it to discharge. The trouble did not cease until Admiral Togo formally referred the matter to the Imperial Staff, and they issued an order on the subject which went considerably beyond what the Admiral had asked.[2]

But the severest test to which the co-ordinating power of the Imperial Staff was put was, of course, the case of 203-Metre Hill. The facts have been already set out so far as they are ascertainable, but, unfortunately, as the part of the Confidential History which deals with the co-operation of the two services has not been communicated, the whole process by which the solution was reached remains to a great extent a matter of inference. It is fairly evident, however, that the final decision was a compromise that was practically unavoidable when Admiral Togo suggested that the objective of the siege army should be changed from General Nogi's chosen front of attack to 203-Metre Hill. The view of the General Staff must have been that the Navy was seeking to dictate to the Army how a siege should be carried on, and that was a pretention they could not possibly admit. This view, as they themselves eventually came to see, was incorrect and superficial. A more just appreciation would have shown them that as the true object of the siege was the destruction of the Port Arthur Squadron the objective was naval, and that Admiral Togo was within his province in pointing out what, in his opinion, was the quickest and easiest way of attaining a naval objective. But, in view of the very plausible attitude of the General Staff, the Imperial Staff evidently did not feel justified in departing from their principle of interfering as little as possible with the conduct of operations. No order was issued. They were content to formulate with the greatest possible precision exactly what the general situation was and what the limitations and necessities of the fleet in relation to it; and, having thus placed Marshal Oyama in full possession of the facts, they left him to judge what orders to give General Nogi.

The actual course of the controversy was this: On November 6, after the failure of the third assault on the front of attack, the chief of Admiral Togo's Staff telegraphed to Admiral Ijuin, the Vice-director of the Naval Staff, begging for information as to the movements of the Baltic Fleet, " as the Combined Fleet must make arrangements in accordance with " their movements, since we cannot forecast the date of the fall of Port " Arthur. . . . At any rate, I beg you will promote a discussion at

---

[1] *Confidential History*, I., pp. 116–17, and *see ante*, Vol. I., pp. 126–7.
[2] *Ante*, pp. 62–64, *Confidential History*, II., 221–2.

" Imperial Headquarters on the means of bringing about the fall of
" Port Arthur more quickly." [1]

In reply next day a telegram was received from Admiral Ijuin, "giving
" the movements of the Baltic Fleet and his ideas concerning the capture
" of Port Arthur," but what these ideas were we are not told. A further
telegram, however, from Admiral Ito, Director of the Naval Staff, gives
a clue. "Since the reduction of Port Arthur," he said, "may still take a
" long time, and it is impossible to fix any date for a successful seizure
" of even the heights and positions in rear of the fortress, and as,
" moreover, the enemy's reinforcing fleet is coming rapidly in this
" direction, how would it be to take this opportunity of preparing our
" fleet for battle by sending your battleships and other vessels one at a
" time for a rapid refit." This proposal which Admiral Togo had rejected
earlier he now accepted.

Still he was not content, and on the 10th, "feeling the necessity of
" securing the fall of Port Arthur at the earliest opportunity, he sent his
" opinion to Imperial Headquarters" and also sent a Staff Officer to
General Nogi "to express the same wish."

A staff conference of the siege army was then held, and on the 13th
its decision was communicated to the Admiral. It was "that they
" would not for the present attack 203 Metre Hill as the engineers had
" not yet finished their work." This message was followed by another
stating that they expected to blow up the counterscarp of the front of
attack at two points within a week.

Meanwhile the tension between the Naval and the General sections
of the Staff at Tokyo appears to have been growing seriously accentuated. On the 13th Admiral Hosoya, the officer who had been most
intimately in touch with the army, was telegraphed for to come home
to Tokyo, and on the 14th a council was held in the presence of
the Emperor "on the subject of naval and military strategy." Its
proceedings we do not know, but the result as communicated to Marshal
Oyama was that it had been decided that if the situation at Port
Arthur had not progressed when the enemy's Second Pacific Squadron
was within a month's steaming of Japan, the Imperial fleet must raise
the blockade and most of it be withdrawn to the home country to
prepare for the enemy, whether Port Arthur had fallen or not. It was
significantly added that this would have very great influence upon
the whole Japanese strategy.[2] It further appears that a memorandum
was drawn up giving "the opinion at Headquarters about the approach
" of the Baltic Fleet and the actual position of the two opposing
" fleets ; also that there was a limit to the capacity of the Dockyards
" and it was impossible to carry out the refitting of the whole fleet at
" once."

This document or its purport Admiral Togo sent by a Staff Officer
to General Nogi, reiterating " that from the fleet point of view he hoped
" that at the next assault 203 Metre Hill would be the first objective
" so as to ensure the destruction of the enemy's fleet as soon as
" possible."

The principle, then, on which the Imperial Staff acted in this highly
difficult situation is fairly evident. While fully recognising the strength

---

[1] *Confidential History*, II., 235.   [2] *Ibid.*, 239.

of the naval contention that unless the Army could more speedily get at the fleet in Port Arthur the whole war plan would be upset, they refrained from pressing upon the Army by a categorical order the method of operation which the Navy desired. They would go no further than to lay before Marshal Oyama a full and precise appreciation of the situation as the Navy saw it, to warn him clearly of what the consequences to himself and Japan would be if he failed to obtain in time what was essential to the Navy being able to perform its main function and then to leave to him the decision as to what operations were best calculated to solve the situation.

Right or wrong such a decision is one which critics free from the overpowering tension of the moment are apt to characterise as showing weakness. Yet it may be doubted whether the decision to leave a matter which depended fundamentally on an intimate knowledge of the local conditions to the man whom they had trusted on the spot did not require a stouter moral courage than would a "strong" and categorical handling of a situation of whose niceties they were in no position to judge.

In the end it was proved that Admiral Togo's view was right, but the restraint which declined to force it upon the Army prematurely was probably more than justified. Apart from all strategical consideration it must have done much to prevent the relations between the Services becoming disastrously embittered. In any case it must always live as a leading precedent wherever in the future the relation between Army and Navy or between the Headquarters Staff and forces at the front call for the same delicate adjustment as that which the Japanese Staff had to handle at the great crisis of the war.

INDEX.

ABOUT THE EDITORS

JOHN B. HATTENDORF is the Ernest J. King Professor and director of the Advanced Research Department at the Naval War College. A former serving officer in the U.S. Navy, he studied history at Kenyon College, Brown University, and the University of Oxford, where he earned his doctorate in modern history. The author and editor of a number of books and articles in the field of naval and maritime history, he is senior editor of the Naval Institute's Classics of Sea Power series. Among his most recent publications are *England in the War of the Spanish Succession* (1987), *Maritime Strategy and the Balance of Power: Britain and America in the Twentieth Century* (coedited with Robert S. Jordan, 1989), *The Limitations of Military Power* (coedited with Malcolm Murfett, 1990), *British Naval Documents, 1204–1960* (coeditor, 1993), *Mahan Is Not Enough: Proceedings of a Conference on the Works of Sir Julian Corbett and Admiral Sir Herbert Richmond* (coedited with James Goldrick, 1993), and *Ubi Sumus: The State of Naval and Maritime History* (1994).

DONALD M. SCHURMAN is emeritus professor of history at the Royal Military College of Canada. He studied history at Acadia University and as a graduate student was a research fellow at Sidney Sussex College, Cambridge. He is a student of the Royal Navy and its historians. In 1965 he wrote *The Education of a Navy: The Development of British Naval Strategic Thought, 1867–1914* and in 1981 *Julian S. Corbett, Historian of British Maritime Policy from Drake to Jellicoe, 1854–1922.* He also contributed to the conference on Corbett and Richmond held at the U.S. Naval War College in 1992.